MEDIEVAL LITERATURE:
THE EUROPEAN INHERITANCE

THE EDITOR

Boris Ford read English at Cambridge before the war. He then spent six years in the Army Education Corps, being finally in command of a residential School of Artistic Studies. On leaving the Army, he joined the staff of the newly formed Bureau of Current Affairs and graduated to be its Chief Editor and in the end its Director. When the Bureau closed down at the end of 1951, he joined the Secretariat of the United Nations in New York and Geneva. On returning to England in the autumn of 1953, he was appointed Secretary of a national inquiry into the problem of providing a humane liberal education for people undergoing technical and professional training.

Boris Ford then became Editor of the *Journal of Education* until it ceased publication in 1958, and also the first Head of School Broadcasting with independent television. From 1958 he was Education Secretary at Cambridge University Press, and then in 1960 he was appointed Professor of Education and Director of the Institute of Education at Sheffield University. He moved to the new University of Sussex in 1963 as Dean of Cultural and Community Studies and later became Chairman of Education. From 1973 until his retirement in 1982 he was Professor of Education, School of Education, at the University of Bristol. Boris Ford has been editor of *Universities Quarterly* since 1955. He has also edited *Young Writers, Young Readers*.

Medieval Literature:
The European Inheritance

VOLUME

I

PART TWO

OF THE NEW PELICAN GUIDE TO
ENGLISH LITERATURE

EDITED BY BORIS FORD

*With an Anthology of Medieval Literature
in the Vernacular*

PENGUIN BOOKS

Penguin Books Ltd, Harmondsworth, Middlesex, England
Penguin Books, 40 West 23rd Street, New York, New York 10010, U.S.A.
Penguin Books Australia Ltd, Ringwood, Victoria, Australia
Penguin Books Canada Ltd, 2801 John Street, Markham, Ontario, Canada L3R 1B4
Penguin Books (N.Z.) Ltd, 182–190 Wairau Road, Auckland 10, New Zealand

First published 1983
Reprinted 1984

The acknowledgements on pp. 608–9 constitute an extension of this copyright page.

Made and printed in Great Britain by
Cox and Wyman Ltd, Reading
Filmset in Monophoto Bembo by
Northumberland Press Ltd, Gateshead, Tyne and Wear

CONTENTS

CONTENTS

PART III

GENERAL INTRODUCTION

The publication of this *New Pelican Guide to English Literature* in many volumes might seem an odd phenomenon at a time when, in the words of the novelist L. H. Myers, a 'deep-seated spiritual vulgarity ... lies at the heart of our civilization', a time more typically characterized by the Headline and the Digest, by the Magazine and the Tabloid, and by Pulp Literature and the Month's Masterpiece. Yet the continuing success of the *Guide* seems to confirm that literature – both yesterday's literature and today's – has a real and not merely a nominal existence among a large number of people; and its main aim has been to help validate as firmly as possible this feeling for a living literature and for the values it embodies.

The *Guide* is partly designed for the committed student of literature. But it has also been written for those many readers who accept with genuine respect what is known as 'our literary heritage', but for whom this often amounts, in memory, to an unattractive amalgam of set texts and school prizes; as a result they may have come to read only today's books – fiction and biography and travel. Though they are probably familiar with such names as Pope, Boccaccio, George Eliot, Yeats, Chrétien de Troyes, Dr Johnson, they might hesitate to describe their work intimately or to fit them into any larger pattern of growth and achievement. If this account is a fair one, it seems probable that very many people would be glad of guidance that would help them respond to what is living and contemporary in literature, for, like the other arts, it has the power to enrich the imagination and to clarify thought and feeling.

Thus the *Guide* does not set out to compete with the standard Histories of Literature, which inevitably tend to have a lofty, take-it-or-leave-it attitude about them. This is not a Bradshaw or a *Whitaker's Almanack* of literature. Nor is it a digest or potted-version,

nor again a portrait gallery of the great. Works such as these already
abound and there is no need to add to the number. What it sets
out to offer, by contrast, is a guide to the history and traditions of
English and Medieval European literature, a contour map of the
literary scene. It attempts, that is, to draw up an ordered account
of literature as a direct encouragement to people to read widely in
an informed way and with enjoyment.

The *New Pelican Guide to English Literature* consists of ten volumes:

The *Guide* as a whole is devoted to English literature. But it has
seemed an attractive and valuable idea to include a new volume on
medieval European literature which would complement the volume
on English medieval literature. For many of these English writers,
while creating their own vernacular literature, were deeply familiar
with and often indebted to their European contemporaries: they
treated common themes and drew on common sources of romance
and epic. The two volumes enrich each other.

Though the *Guide* has been designed as a single work, each separate
volume exists in its own right and sets out to provide the reader
with four kinds of related material:

(i) *A survey of the social context of literature* in each period, providing
an account of contemporary society at its points of contact with
literature.

(ii) *A literary survey* of the period, describing the general characteristics of the period's literature in such a way as to enable the reader to trace its growth and to keep his or her bearings. The aim of this section is to answer such questions as 'What *kind* of literature was written in this period?', 'Which authors matter most?', 'Where does the strength of the period lie?'.

(iii) *Detailed studies* of some of the chief writers and works in the period. Coming after the two general surveys, the aim of this section is to convey a sense of what it means to read closely and with perception; and also to suggest how the literature of a given period or language is most profitably read, i.e. with what assumptions and with what kind of attention.

(iv) *An appendix of essential facts for reference purposes*, such as authors' biographies (in miniature), bibliographies, books for further study, and so on.

In this European volume, and also in the parallel volume on medieval English literature, there is included an anthology. This anthology of medieval European literature in translation is closely linked to the individual chapters and together they may lead many readers to discover and follow up writers and works of great quality. If a single volume on medieval European literature can be no more than a beginning, it can hardly fail to be a compelling one.

Among the many individuals I consulted when planning this volume, I would like to single out two for my special thanks: Peter Dronke, whose suggestions helped to determine the shape of the volume; and Derek Brewer, without whose encouragement, enthusiasm, and constant advice the volume would probably never have come into being.

BORIS FORD

PART I

MEDIEVAL EUROPE

J. C. HOLT

This book is concerned with literature, especially with vernacular literature. It concentrates, therefore, on only part of the intellectual endeavour of Christian Europe in the Middle Ages. It does not seek to examine the Latin tradition of monasteries and schools and all that stemmed therefrom. Its story is of the supplementation and supplanting of that tradition by the different vernaculars. It is not immediately concerned with achievements in philosophy, history, theology, law, music, sculpture, painting and architecture, in some of which medieval Europe can stand comparison with any other age or setting. Yet vernacular literature cannot be divorced from any of these. Moreover, though it supplanted Latin, the influence on it of Rome and of the survival of things Roman was profound.

One way to explore the literary culture of medieval Europe would be to investigate the manner in which these Latin and Roman influences changed. In the beginning men were struggling to preserve something of classical civilization in a barbaric world in which the Christian religion was the main solace and intellectual stimulus; the ruins of Rome were visible as the reminder to the humble of past human glories. At the end of our period men still turned to Rome and increasingly to Greece, and they were often still humble in the presence of the classical achievement, but now they used it and recreated it to illuminate their own consciousness: in politics, law, art and literature.

That would be only one route into the medieval world. Another would be to examine the development of language, of the different European vernaculars and of the local or national cultures, whichever we care to call them. Another would be to examine the development of education and the spread of literacy, and yet another to study the history of the audience, the emergence of a reading public and the varied and changing patterns of its tastes. The student of literature must be concerned with all these matters. The historian has to describe the material conditions which encouraged or constrained writers, listeners and readers. And he will falsify development if he treats literature too much in isolation. Great verse or prose may penetrate to the core of the human condition, but they are a peripheral spin-off social change. It is not only chastening but essential to remember that, for it establishes the proper context for studying the historical background to literary achievement in its widest sense.

The Shifting Christian World

In medieval Europe that background had to be constructed, if not from scratch, then at least from a mixture of tradition and novelty which were now assembled in a novel manner and put to new purposes. At first, it was a matter of establishing an identity, a shared experience of some common culture, a sense of being European. For in the fourth and fifth centuries, Europe as we know it, as the Middle Ages knew it, did not yet exist. It was divided along the Rhine; Britain was an outpost; Scandinavia was an alien world. More important still, those provinces which lay within the Empire were more or less peripheral to a vast, cumbersome organization which was centred on the Mediterranean, politically on Rome and Constantinople, economically on North Africa, Egypt and the Bosphorus. In this Spain and Gaul were of less consequence than Greece and Syria. The most important development in the later Empire, Christianity, came from the eastern Mediterranean. So also did much that was best and most influential in its art and philosophy. Its language became predominantly Greek.

The Christian world of the thirteenth century was very different. Italy was still part of it; the see of Rome was its ecclesiastical centre; Mediterranean trade was still vital to the welfare of Europe as a whole; Italian conquest was one of the recurrent lures attracting European monarchs: German, French, Spanish or English. But the lands north of the Alps which now lay within the bounds of Christian Europe were no longer peripheral. They had been vastly extended to embrace Scandinavia and the north Atlantic as far as the western coast of Greenland, and to include the whole of the German hinterland to the Oder and beyond. The Bay of Biscay, the Channel, the North

Sea, the Baltic and the river systems penetrating the northern and western European coast-line had become the centres of trade and industry, in French wines, English wool, Flemish woollens, Baltic furs. Many of the most typical features of European civilization were now to be found, not in the Mediterranean world or in Italy, but in the lands north of the Alps, in Germany, the Netherlands, England and above all in France. It was northern not southern Europe which gave birth to feudal institutions, to chivalry and to much of the enrichment of the religious life of the Middle Ages.

This shift in the centre of gravity did not come about suddenly or as a result of a single set of circumstances. Some stages in it have been a matter of considerable controversy: the extent to which the unity of the Mediterranean world was shattered by the settlement of Germanic tribes from across the Rhine and the Danube in the western provinces of the Empire in the fifth and sixth centuries; the consequences for Europe of the Arab conquests of the seventh century which extended along the eastern and southern shores of the Mediterranean and then into Spain and southern France; and the significance of the re-establishment of the western Empire, defunct since 476, with the coronation of the Frankish Charles the Great in St Peter's Rome on Christmas Day 800. Later stages in the shift were marked by the schism between the eastern and western churches of 1054, which finally divided Rome from Byzantium, the appeal of the Byzantine Emperor Alexius to Pope Urban II which led to the preaching of the first crusade in 1095, and the sack of Constantinople and establishment of a Latin Empire in the East with the fourth crusade of 1204. That put beyond doubt not only that western Europe had an identity of its own, but that it was no longer an inferior appendage to the imperial tradition of the east.

This long struggle left its mark on the collective consciousness of western Europe. Charles the Great became one of its great figure-heads, a monument to kingship. A petty rearguard action in which his forces were overwhelmed by the Christian Basques of northern Spain was the incidental source of the great dramatic climax of the *Chanson de Roland*. The continuing war against the Saracen in Spain set the scene for *El Cid*. Voyaging was inseparable from the ethos of the Scandinavian saga; the crusade was integral to the ideal of Christian chivalry; it took the conflict between Christian and Saracen to launch the notion of a holy war. The expansion of western Europe, therefore, provided some of the subject-matter of its literature.

But there was more to it than that. How, for example, did it come about that the European tradition came to embody something more than a mishmash made up from the recollection of the classical world, the memory of Teutonic origins and the experience of conflict with neighbouring rival cultures? Why not settle for such a mixture? Why did men want more?

For such a mixture could be potent and alluring. In frontier areas, in regions of racial, linguistic and artistic interpretation, it could become a culture in its own right, worth studying on its own terms. The Norman adventurers who journeyed to southern Italy in the eleventh century, ultimately to establish their rule over a kingdom of brilliant artistic achievement, were conscious enough at first of moving into a strange world and surrendered easily enough to its attractions. The establishment of the Sicilian diocese of Agrigento was the subject of a charter of debatable authenticity attributed to Count Roger of Sicily in 1093. Authentic or not, the author could at one and the same time reflect on the inevitable and just destruction of the Saracens and admit that their palaces were 'of marvellous design' (*studio mirabili compositorum*), as indeed they were beside a Norman keep. So also were the palaces of the new Norman masters of the region, a splendid blend of Arab architecture and Byzantine decoration. So also were the churches, both Greek and Latin, which included some of the greatest masterpieces of Greek mosaic work at Cefalù, Palermo and Monreale. There is room for argument how far northern and Norman influences played a part in the church of St Nicholas of Bari, for example, or at Cefalù. But the argument is itself evidence of the cultural mix. The complexity of that mix is well illustrated by a less famous and imposing church of SS Peter and Paul, in the valley of the Agro in north-eastern Sicily. This, which was begun in 1116 and reconstructed in 1172, belonged to the Greek Order of St Basil. It is topped by two cupolas sustained internally by complex squinch arches; all that is Arab in style and design. Yet an inscription incised in Greek over the west door records that the reconstruction was the work of Girard the Frenchman, and the whole of the exterior of the church is covered with well executed blind arcading more reminiscent of St Botolph, Colchester, or the original west front of Hereford cathedral and other northern churches, than of the Norman south. The result is somewhat discordant, a chimera rather than a fertile hybrid. Elsewhere the different elements, northern and southern, Christian and Saracen, eastern and western, were blended in an amalgam of high artistic achievement: the great church of Cefalù or the cathedral and cloister of Monreale.

These are some of the more obvious features of the civilization of the Norman kingdom in the south. They could be matched, *mutatis mutandis*, with similar features in other frontier zones of western Christendom. But even in the Norman south, the student is brought up short by the appearance of unexpected intrusive nuggets of material which are entirely foreign. The floor of the cathedral of Otranto, a single mosaic which is the work of a Byzantine master of the 1160s, is a tree of life running the whole length of the cathedral. In its upper limbs, near the altar, there is a grotesque figure astride an even more grotesque, cloven-footed mount, labelled *Rex Arturus*, King Arthur. Now it is easy to imagine how the Arthurian legend was carried by the northern crusaders to one of their main ports of embarkation for the Holy Land, but that cannot obscure the fact that in this southern cultural frontier zone Arthur was alien, an intruder from the north, a manifestation of a culture which drew its strength from sources external to the Mediterranean world and much less immediately dependent on the classical tradition. The cumbersome figure of Arthur at Otranto stands for the original contribution of transalpine Christian Europe. It is worth noting that to a Byzantine artist of the twelfth century it still seemed relatively insignificant.

But that was the view from one of many social and geographic viewpoints. To move from Apulia to Brittany, or Wales, or England, would be to raise Arthur from the status of some strange half-barbarous intruder to the very emblem of Celtic independence and then, in England, to a figure so appealing that the Angevin kings would imagine that his was a legend potent enough to constitute a focus of attention which would rival the *Chanson de Roland* and match the paternal superiority which this cast over the house of Charles the Great and its successors. And the Arthurian legend was but one of the cycles which northern Europe was now able to sustain. By the time Arthur was embedded in the mosaic at Otranto some of the main themes of European literature were taking shape and some of the characteristic features of transalpine European society were being formed. How did this come about? How in particular did it come about that this society should be both homogenous and fragmentary, made up of communities which shared in a common culture but yet developed conflicting ambitions, different languages and different literary and artistic traditions?

The Changing Countryside

It was a matter in the first place of economic expansion and social and political stability. The Teutonic settlements of the fifth and sixth centuries did not themselves create a new order. In their political life they were savage and unstable. In their organization many of them were remarkably dependent on Roman and Christian tradition. The more important changes came in the countryside, slowly at first and then at a rapidly accelerating pace from roughly A.D. 1000. Western Europe was born through a vast and extended process of internal colonization which brought new land into cultivation both in the old imperial provinces and in the lands east of the Rhine. Some have argued that technical developments, the use of the stirrup and the heavy plough, played an important part in this; others have linked development with favourable climatic change. This perhaps reflects no more than the desire to discover singular causes for dramatic changes. It may simply be that the steady expansion of population accelerated into a demographic explosion in the eleventh, twelfth and thirteenth centuries. Whatever the causes, the changes themselves were far-reaching. There was an enormous accession of wealth. Those with money expected a better standard of living. Prices were inflated, in the central period from the mid twelfth to the mid thirteenth century as fast, or almost as fast, as in the Price Revolution of the sixteenth century. There was a revolution in social organization. Government and law became markedly more sophisticated. The monastic order was diversified. Universities were founded. Western Europe was able to stand on its own feet by the side of the Byzantine remnant of the old Empire, because, in addition to establishing and expanding its frontiers, it had dragged itself up by its own boot-straps.

The Emergence of Western Europe

An observer of Europe in this formative period between the eleventh and thirteenth centuries would have been struck by the newness of what he saw around him. In the twentieth century the material remains of the Middle Ages are mostly sear and moss-grown. Their physical appearance in the twelfth century must have been more reminiscent of a new-town development: building activity and newly designed buildings everywhere, monasteries, cathedrals, parish churches, castles, town-walls and gatehouses, even for the very wealthy stone-built town-houses. For the first time in transalpine Europe men were surrounded with their own buildings which could match, even outshine, the glories of the ruins of the Roman past; indeed they even plundered the remains for convenient building material. And they sensed their achievement in more than the material sphere. The first man to use the word 'modernity' in something approaching its present sense as an antithesis to antiquity was Suger (d. 1151), abbot of St Denis, minister of Louis VI and Louis VII of France, and men became ever more conscious of their modernity as the twelfth century advanced.

But this did not involve the rejection of the past. Poets used Virgil as their model. Philosophers turned increasingly to Aristotle for both their method and their problems. The new theology was founded on the Bible and the Fathers; its concern was to discover how their truths should be interpreted and applied in the contemporary world. Historical study likewise was concerned with origins; indeed it was fashionable to discover Greek, Trojan or biblical ancestors for the descendants of wild and pagan Teutonic or Scandinavian settlers. Law might develop in new directions revealed in entirely novel procedures but it also looked back to the *Corpus Iuris Civilis* of the Emperor Justinian or to immemorial custom. It was therefore as successors to the classical world that learned men envisaged their achievement: 'Greece was the first to be famed for her chivalry and learning. Then chivalry came to Rome and the heyday of learning. And now it has come to France and God grant that it remain there.'

Thus Chrétien of Troyes. At one and the same time he acknowledged the past and, within his own world, put France on a similar footing to Greece and Rome. Pride and modesty, achievement and dependence went hand in hand.

In the simplest view the structure of western Europe was determined by the initial settlement of the Teutonic tribes in the fifth and sixth centuries: Visigoths in Spain, Salian Franks in the Low Countries and northern France, Ripuarian Franks in the Rhineland, Ostrogoths and Lombards in Italy, Anglo-Saxons in England. Again it is possible to trace the origins of France and Germany and of Franco–German conflict to the Treaty of Verdun of 843 which in reality was little more than a temporary division for dynastic purposes of the empire established by Charles the Great. Such interpretations now seem hackneyed if not blatantly anachronistic. They are based on little more than the fact that the settlements of the fifth and sixth centuries and the division of 843, like the more settled realms of the thirteenth century, were conditioned by the physical geography of western Europe. But the simple political approach which they embodied, which turned on war, dynasties and frontiers, was realistic and illuminating in one respect. The kingdoms and dominions from which the states of western Europe originated were intensely competitive and quarrelsome. War, conquest, dynastic dispute, internecine family contention were at the core of politics. When chronicles recounted political as opposed to ecclesiastical events, this is what they wrote about.

The Juxtaposition of Languages

Political divisions were related in the long run to other, deeper contrasts. Again a simple view would assume that subjects of the Holy Roman Emperors were Germans and spoke German, the subjects of the King of France were French and spoke French, and so on; but linguistic and racial definition were much more complex than that; High and Low German in Germany, northern and southern dialects in France with old Catalan and Old Provençal providing further variety on its southern boundaries; English, northern French, southern 'Italian' all to a greater or less extent infected by a Norse intrusion which marked the path of the Scandinavian settlers and their descendants. Individuals were thrust into situations in which, like British soldiers in Imperial India, they learned to get along with a multifarious but limited polyglot vocabulary. What language was spoken by Queen Emma (d.1052), daughter of Richard I, duke of Normandy, and wife first of Aethelred the Unready and second of Cnut the Great? What did she learn from her cradle – French or Norse? Or was she in a rudimentary fashion bilingual? In any case how much English did she know? Did she manage with a very limited vocabulary and with stilted syntax in all three languages or was she a good linguist? Is it not possible that in the long centuries of tribal settlement and racial shift which were prolonged by the intrusion of Vikings and Normans men were far better linguists within a restricted vocabulary and range of use than we would now imagine possible? In any event how did one linguistic element come to predominate over another? The Danes who invaded England in the ninth and tenth centuries still left powerful traces of their language in the English of the eleventh and twelfth centuries. In contrast the Danes who invaded Normandy at roughly the same time had far less influence on French and indeed took to French very rapidly, perhaps within a generation or so, certainly within a century, of their settlement. They then took their new language with them to England where they effectively murdered Old English. The conquerors' French was a mark of distinction, and if ultimately they surrendered to English in a new hybrid form, that recast language in its turn served as a language of conquest to be imposed on Welsh and Irish. Each of these developments is not difficult to explain in isolation. But why after acquiring French so readily in Normandy did the Normans reject Old English in England? And why, having brought themselves to accept English, did they reject the Celtic languages?

These questions are easier asked than answered; some of the problems involved are perhaps insoluble. But they lead to an important feature of the development of western Europe. Great literature was unlikely to result from a fluid situation in which men were struggling with novel linguistic difficulties in an attempt to communicate in elementary fashion about everyday matters. Vernacular literature predicates a settled, reasonably sophisticated language. This is one reason, although clearly not the only reason, why scholars, historians and poets chose to write in Latin; there was often no alternative. It also suggests reasons why, in areas of less linguistic fluidity, like Anglo-Saxon England, vernacular literature survives from an early date to reveal a strong, well-rooted tradition of writing. Old English, from *Beowulf* to Aelfric, is a consequence of England's relative isolation and insulation from linguistic turmoil. It suffered Scandinavian intrusion, but the linguistic effects of that, though marked, were minor by the side of the sharp juxtaposition of Teutonic and Latin languages which occurred in continental Europe.

The Law and Local Customs

However, in the eleventh century a man would no more have thought of defining his 'nationality' by reference to his language than by claiming to be a citizen of this or that state. Nor could he turn to the simple answer of a passport. But, if pressed, he would have had an answer, best revealed in those areas where races intermingled. To say that one was English or Norman in England, or Lombard, Greek or Norman in southern Italy, was to claim to participate in, and enjoy the customs and protection of a particular law. This notion was of great antiquity. Rooted in the pattern of the original Teutonic settlement, it was greatly reinforced by Old Testament example and by the Roman law of citizenship. It was still the basis of the distinction between English and Welsh, Slav and German, Anglo-Norman and Irish in the thirteenth century. It remained embedded in the law of southern Italy in the *Liber Augustalis* of Frederick II of Hohenstaufen, promulgated at Melfi in 1231, which still retained distinctions between Greek, Lombard and French law especially in matters of succession and inheritance.

Men carried their law with them to the areas they settled. The first Normans to arrive in southern Italy at the beginning of the eleventh century were no more than a bunch of adventurers. Their rule took shape through the imposition of their language and law. William of Apulia, writing in 1095–9, said of the earliest Norman settlements: 'If any neighbouring evil-doer fled to join them, they welcomed him with open arms. They taught all-comers their language and their customs so as to make one race (*gens*).' William was a little optimistic. Southern Italy and Sicily were so polyglot that still in the twelfth century the officials of the Norman kings used three languages of record: Latin, Greek and Arabic. But he had grasped the essence of race, and the pattern he described was repeated over again. The Normans took their law to England; the crusaders called on the customs of their homelands for the law embodied in the Assizes of the kingdom of Jerusalem; in the Statute of Pamiers (1213) the Albigensian crusaders established the custom of the Île de France to regulate their mutual relations in their newly won lands in the county of Toulouse.

By this time the variegated pattern of local custom was overlain and changed by subsequent jurisdictional structures. What originated as the law of the folk became the custom of the local court, and the local court was often a feudal court, the boundaries of its jurisdiction coinciding with the feudal superiority of its lord. What the law books and custumals of the thirteenth century describe, therefore, is the Ancient Custom of Normandy or the Customs of Beauvaisis or the laws of Anjou. And these were the higher levels. Lower in the social order the vast majority of the population of western Europe lived their lives under the custom of the local manor without sight of earl or count, bishop or abbot, still less of king, emperor or pope. This localization of law and of the social relations which were the law's concern remained undisturbed in many parts of western Europe throughout the Middle Ages.

But not everywhere. The pattern was changed wherever kings could exercise a more than nominal superiority. The Carolingian rulers legislated. Their capitularies still influenced local custom long after they had ceased to have any real force as expressions of royal authority. Later kings established the new monarchies which emerged in France, England, Italy and Germany between the eleventh and thirteenth centuries first by advancing the feudal superiority which the crown enjoyed as the ultimate court of appeal to its vassals, then by developing the procedures of the royal courts as the instruments of that superiority, finally by legislating, not simply declaring but making law through the appropriate processess of consultation. This was achieved with varying success by Frederick Barbarossa and Frederick II in Germany and in the latter's case in southern Italy, by the Capetians from Philip Augustus to Philip the Fair in France, and by the Angevins and Plantagenets from Henry

II to Edward I in England. Their work altered men's ideas of nationality and law to something much closer to the territorial state. By 1215 Frenchmen, even Normans might be condemned in England as foreigners (*alienigenae*), and that by men who spoke normally in French and were themselves descended from the motley crowd of Frenchmen who followed Norman William in 1066.

Hardening Divisions and Prejudices

So kings and dynasties played a part in hardening divisions within western Europe. And they did so at a time when the main vernaculars were taking firmer shape and when men, ever more conscious of their different local characteristics, were rubbing up against each other in trade, in war, in pilgrimages, on the Crusade, in ecclesiastical councils or in legal disputes and on other occasions which took men to Rome. Definition and prejudice went hand in hand, and prejudice required little encouragement since it could draw on a strong classical tradition, in which Sallust was probably the most influential writer, which emphasized national characteristics. These were now given a sharp critical edge. If by the early thirteenth century the French ran the risk of being regarded as foreigners in England, they in their turn had come to regard Anglo-Norman as a grotesque distortion of their mother tongue. They were amused by the suggestion that Englishmen had tails. Anglo-Norman aristocrats in their turn regarded the Scots as trash with half-clad backsides. All those who went on the Crusade, whether French, German or English, came to regard the Greeks as treacherous allies, full of guile, ever ready to betray the Crusaders to the Saracens. In Italy the Normans looked down on the Greeks as easy meat – clever but spineless, a bunch of women; only the German soldiers of the western Emperor, fair, tall and handsome, seemed worthy opponents; this respect was not returned by the Germans who derided the lesser stature of the Normans. Thus wrote William of Apulia. The detail, much of which is derivatory, matters little, but the pattern of thinking matters a lot for it became ingrained in men's minds. Later, at the great universities which marked the advance of western Christian thought and stood for the universality of learning, the students were divided into nations.

The world which feudal lords and kings created was turbulent and aggressive. Feudal lordship was subject to challenge. The track from lower to higher jurisdiction was by appeal of default of justice; it was often halfway to rebellion. Feudal jurisdiction was competitive; boundaries were drawn, not as sharp territorial demarcations but as areas where rival lordships were in dispute. The power of the feudal superior was subject to challenge even when he was endowed with all the authority and majesty of a king. Loyalty left room for formal defiance. The punishment for rebellion might be no worse than the temporary deprivation of estate, more easily ordered by a king than put into effect. Still in the twelfth century treason was treachery to a lord. It was only from the thirteenth century that it became a capital crime against the crown.

Rifts in Christian Europe

Much of this energy was turned outwards. The Spanish monarchies were founded on the ruins of the Moorish kingdoms. Much of the development of Germany was determined by its east-ward expansion from the original Rhineland provinces to the Elbe, then over the Oder and to the south down the Danube. But it was above all on the old Mediterranean world that attention was con-centrated. Rome was the centre of Christendom and the old seat of Empire. The north Italian towns canalized the traffic in luxuries from the East. Beyond Italy lay Byzantium and the holy places. There were irresistible attractions which brought south of the Alps Carolingian and German kings seeking the renewal of Empire and real authority in northern Italy, Norman adventurers seeking fortune and power in southern Italy, and men from every province of northern Europe to visit Rome, to travel onwards to the Holy Land, and above all to fight in the Crusade.

Both internal restlessness and external aggression are reflected in the evidence in slanted fashion. Feudal society is pictured from the top downwards, in government instructions, in intervention by higher in lower jurisdictions. As a result we know more about kings than knights and more about knights than peasants. That is only to be expected. More serious is the fact that the evidence leads persis-tently to the impression that the crown stood for order, the noble for anarchy. It is only in rebellion against a tyrannous king that the feudal opponents of royal power acquire moral quality.

In like manner the story of the external aggression is told as a heroic adventure, as the advance of European and Christian ideals against schismatic, infidel, heretic or pagan. Arab historians tell a different story of Christian inroads into Spain and the Holy Land. So also do the Greeks. To Anna Comnena, daughter of the Byzantine Emperor, Alexius I Comnenus, the first Crusade signified, not the holy war launched by Pope Urban II at Clermont, but an invasion by 'all the barbarian tribes from beyond the Adriatic as far as the Pillars of Hercules'. Western Europeans rarely suffered such intrusion as they inflicted on their neighbours. When they did, for example under the sword of the Vikings, they complained just as much as their own victims. 'Never was such a slaughter heard of in these lands': so wrote the annalist of St Wandrille of the Scandinavian raids on northern France in 851–2. Historians are still trying to disentangle the cultural and economic contribution of the Scandinavian people from the confusion of hostile comment which their expansion left embedded in the narrative sources.

These rifts in Christian Europe were striking, the occasion of disorder and rebellion, war and Crusade. There were other differences which, though obvious, drew less comment from contemporaries, and some are still difficult to understand and explain. The division between the Greek east and the Latin west is obvious and comprehensible enough. There were also differences between northern and southern Europe. In southern Europe, for example, Roman Law was still a working system centred as an academic subject on the University of Bologna. In the south the customary law introduced by Lombards and Normans was an intrusion into a long established structure. In the north in contrast Roman Law was superimposed to varying degrees on feudal law in the course of the twelfth and thirteenth centuries. On the whole its influence was relatively slight. It might provide a framework for legal textbooks or support for the authority of kings, but it only established itself as a working system in particularly appropriate branches of the law. So legally France, for example, was divided roughly along the line of the southern bounds of Angoumois, Auvergne and Burgundy: customary law to the north, *droit écrit*, that is Roman Law, to the south. Beside that somewhat arid contrast stands another, concerned with anti-semitism. In 1096 some of the German crusaders prepared for their holy work by massacring the Rhineland Jews. Thereafter virulent anti-semitism spread rapidly in northern Europe, its course marked by the myth of ritual murder which appeared in England in 1144, Germany in 1147 and northern France in 1163. The Jews were protected; they were often the chief source of credit to kings and others in authority. But they lost their importance in the course of the thirteenth century as Italian bankers extended their range of operation northwards. They were expelled from Maine and Anjou in 1288, Gascony in 1289, England in 1290 and the Île de France in 1306. They survived in Germany only to suffer in further extensive pogroms in 1348 at the time of the Black Death. Yet little of this occurred in southern Europe. Attempts to transplant tales of ritual murder failed and there was little official persecution; the hostility of the Angevin kings of Naples was something they brought south with them from their French homeland. The south provided less fertile ground for anti-semitic prejudice. The Jews were often only one element in a mixed population which included Greeks and Arabs as well as Latin Christians. That necessitated greater tolerance.

An International Community

Yet when all the differences within western Europe are allowed and all the sources of internal disturbance and external conflict examined, it still remains possible to see a certain unity: in experience shared, ideas interchanged, social organization replicated, in patterns of ecclesiastical government and monastic order extended far beyond the bounds of single countries and in claims to authority reaching even further to embrace the whole of Christendom. The whole West acknowledged the supremacy of the see of Rome. In peripheral areas, to be sure, papal government was sometimes ineffectual. It took thirty days to travel from southern England to the Holy See. The Curia's judgements might be based on information at best second-hand, at worst falsified, always in times of crisis out of date; and the administrative difficulty was changed rather than overcome by delegation to legates or judges delegate. It is also true that the more extreme statements of papal supremacy were the result of challenge, a consequence very often of conflict between empire and papacy in which each superpower cloaked its practical ineffectiveness by large claims to theoretical sovereignty. None the less, the papacy exercised leadership and moral authority. It launched the crusade, protected the monastic order and constituted the highest court of appeal in the large range of causes which came under ecclesiastical law. A disputed election to the papal throne might produce schism: only the thirteenth century was entirely free from such quarrels and some were serious; but they were always healed.

Medieval Europe was therefore an international community in a very real sense. Beside the papacy, the monastic and mendicant orders, the cathedral schools and the universities all transcended internal divisions and political boundaries. Common bonds were not purely ecclesiastical. Towns and cities, merchant and craft guilds, enjoyed chartered and statutory privileges to a broadly uniform design. Municipal independence originated in the establishment of communes in northern Italy in the eleventh century, then in France, Flanders, the Rhineland and England in the twelfth and thirteenth centuries. Nor did it all have official blessing. Communes smacked of rebellion against feudal and royal lordship. Heresy, like the trade routes it tended to follow, was 'international'.

It was in this wide community that men made their careers. The reform of the Norman church under Duke Richard II at the beginning of the eleventh century was spearheaded by William of Volpiano. The reputation of the great Norman abbey of Bec was established and sustained by Lanfranc of Pavia and Anselm of Aosta, both of whom became archbishops of Canterbury. The strong links running through the Norman world allowed Robert of Selby to act as chancellor of Roger II of Sicily, Simon of Apulia to occupy the see of Exeter and Thomas Brown to serve both Roger II of Sicily and Henry II of England.

Travel and interchange left permanent effects. The appearance of King Arthur in the mosaic floor at Otranto is only one of many such examples. Along the lines on which Arthur travelled south Byzantine influences travelled north to appear in manuscript illumination at Winchester and wall-painting at Canterbury. At Cashel in Ireland Cormac's chapel still stands with its twin-tower transepts as silent evidence to the influence of Ratisbon and other German churches, the link provided by Irish monks who returned to their homeland to collect money for their monastic building in Germany at the very time when the church at Cashel was designed and built. At Kilpeck parishioners to this day worship in a church graced with the unique style of decoration of Herefordshire masons of the twelfth century which owed some of its characteristics to the church of St James of Compostella and to French churches on the route to Compostella whither the local lord, Oliver de Merlimond, founder of the church of Shobdon, where the style was introduced, had gone on pilgrimage. Artistic and architectural 'influences' of this kind were not wind-borne infections. They were brought by men who travelled and saw novel designs in strange lands or by designers and craftsmen who came seeking patrons for stylistic innovation.

Above all this, as in other epochs, the royal families of Europe played an important part. The Hohenstaufen exercised dominion both in Germany and Italy. The rule of Henry II of England extended from Ireland and the Scottish border to the county of Toulouse. That most foreign of all English kings, Richard I, who became an English national hero at the very point at which anti-French sentiment was born in England, saw nothing incongruous in introducing his German cousin, Otto of Brunswick, as count of Poitou or earl of Northumberland. Richard I's nephew, Henry III, sought the realm of Sicily for his younger son. Henry III's brother, Richard of Cornwall, became king of the Romans and claimant to the Empire. And all this had cultural consequences. Richard I was himself a poet. Henry II and his queen, Eleanor of Aquitaine, were patrons of poets; their courts were famed throughout Europe as centres for the learned, the talented and the witty.

The Feudal Order

All these links forged by ruling houses, crusaders, administrators, pilgrims, merchants or craftsmen, were strengthened by experience of a common social order. This was feudal. That term cloaks many local variants in the tenure of land, the possession of rights and the performance of service. But it none the less denotes a social system of considerable uniformity. When the crusading armies came to-gether from Germany, France, Flanders, Norman Italy and England they proved a quarrelsome lot, but they were at least organized in roughly the same way; when they wished they could fight alongside each other without much difficulty. And their common experience extended well beyond military organization. Gentlemen shared similar notions of what constituted nobility. Throughout Europe they would have been in broad agreement about the standing and duties of a knight. Chivalry was a common ethos. Castles and manor houses were characteristic dwelling places.

Some features of this structure – the castle, the manor, tenure of land in return for military service, the pyramidal social hierarchy produced by the enfeoffment of tenants who themselves went on to enfeoff tenants of their own – may safely be left to the textbook. But some features of it are of considerable interest in their contribution to the development of western Europe.

First, the notion of leadership, and lordship, of loyalty to a lord, of the benefits which members of a retinue might expect from a lord, and of the lord's interest in rewarding his followers, are very ancient, not simply Teutonic, but Homeric. The crucial development in medieval Europe was not that these ideas and practices were emphasized, even hallowed, but that they were given a territorial basis. This came about not so much through commendation whereby a freeman seeking protection subjected himself to a lord and became his tenant, although that of course did occur. It arose rather from the delegation of public authority, initially by the Carolingian kings, to men who proceeded to recast local government and convert public authority into private right. The process could take several generations. It was accelerated by the collapse of Carolingian defences under Danish and Magyar attack, and it was accompanied by much conflict and feuding among the men who profited from the break-up of central authority. But its end was a new system of local government. The old local divisions, the Carolingian *pagi* or *pays*, disappeared or lost much of their importance. New divisions were formed, 'castleries' centred on the castles of men whose power depended on the exercise of feudal superiority in their own demesne and over vassals acknowledging their dominion.

These changes varied in their incidence and timing. They occurred first and developed most rapidly in France and Flanders in the eleventh century. They came later east of the Rhine, in certain areas not before the middle of the twelfth century. They were imported by the Normans into England where they coexisted for a time, but failed in the end to compete, with an older pattern of local government based on the English shires. In many areas old and new institutions intermingled, either because both reflected the facts of local geography, or because it paid the new feudal lords to perpetuate the rights which they derived from the old Carolingian system or because superior authority, either of kings, dukes or counts, kept the old Carolingian system alive in order to assert their own feudal authority over lesser lords. Hence the changes also varied in their results. The effect in some areas was to produce 'feudal anarchy', extreme subdivision of local power among petty lords over whom little permanent superior authority could be exercised effectively. This was the situation which confronted both English and French kings in Gascony and in the foothills of the Pyrenees throughout the Middle Ages. In other areas, especially those where economic resources could be readily exploited by centralized government, the new pattern of local government was concentrated and disciplined by central government in the hands of dukes, counts and occasionally kings. Normandy, Anjou and Flanders were the earliest models of these new states followed by Artois, Swabia under the Hohenstaufen, Saxony under the Guelfs, and southern Italy and Sicily where the Norman kings could draw on unique resources.

The Dynastic Family

The establishment of feudal forms of government was accompanied by another change, less obvious but even more important. Between the tenth and the twelfth centuries the structure of the aristocratic family underwent a profound change, in the classic centres of feudalism first and then elsewhere. The noble family of the early Middle Ages was a clan; its essential function was to provide its members with support in legal, political and military conflict. It was organized hierarchically, but the head might be selected to suit the convenience of the moment rather than according to fixed rules. It held land, rights and privileges and expected even more, but these were often dispersed collaterally throughout each generation. By contrast the family of the late Middle Ages was a dynasty, its essential components, husband, wife and children, its organization designed to ensure that its rights and properties descended undispersed from one generation to the next, often by absolute or modified rule of primogeniture. It helped to create an aristocratic society which was concerned above all with lineage, with title and succession, and with heritable right. The leaders of that society left their trail, quite unconsciously, in the use of toponymic family names. Earlier the great families like the Arnulfings identified themselves by their clan names; now many of them came to identify themselves by their chief feudal holdings which they expected would pass down like their names from generation to generation. It was thus that the Montgomerys, Lacys, Beaumonts and Percys were born.

This type of family structure was essential to stable feudal arrangements, both in the delegation of public authority and the provision of service. But if in this respect the dynastic family contributed to the wellbeing of feudal society, in another it was the source of disturbance. It produced the cadet, the younger son excluded from the inheritance or allowed only so insignificant an interest in the family lands that he was driven to adventure, to the tournament, to the crusade, to service in the forces of some commander with whom he might in the end found his own fortunes. This was the real social basis of all knight errantry. It was often the motive power of conquest; the Hauteville conquerors of Italy, although not younger sons, had been excluded from their family inheritance. It provided the tinder for rebellion. The 'bachelors' could find excitement and perhaps profit in any cause.

It is plain that this new family structure contributed powerfully to the ethos which informed much of the vernacular poetry composed for aristocratic audiences. The plight of the deprived, the recovery of just title, the consciousness of lineage were all familiar themes. The heiress came to figure as a crucial figure, an embodiment both of marital bliss and success in the pursuit of fortune. The wicked uncle, making his first appearance in *Cligès*, became one of the stereotypes for villainy, impeding the rightful expectations of nephew or niece. The hero king was no longer the great leader and gift-giver of old. He did justice and gave every man his right, and that included title to inheritance. Some measure of the change is provided by a comparison of the *romans* of resistance, say, *Fouke le*

Fitz Waryn or *Eustache Li Moine*, with *Njal's Saga* in which the older clan structure is still largely preserved. There are common elements: loyalty, courage, justice, but they are set in very different social moulds.

Custom and the Liberties of the Subject

The strengthening of family title was only one manifestation of increasing social security. As social institutions became more settled, as law became more sophisticated, so the concept of rights became both more secure and more complex. Some of the subtleties of this might be traced by pursuing the nuances in the meaning of the word *ius*, which stood for both law and right, but that would lead into Romanist complications. A simpler illustration is to be found in the single word *consuetudo* which in the English word 'custom' still possesses that double sense which so admirably illustrates its history. For the word first denoted those rights and power delegated to feudal lords during the collapse of Carolingian government. Customs were exercised by lords over their men, and it is not surprising therefore to find many references to evil customs in the course of the twelfth century. But by then a new note was sounded. Custom, once defined, limited the exercise of lordship; custom might become not an expression of the power of lords but a protection of the rights of vassals. Hence by the end of the twelfth century custom was no longer necessarily 'evil'. Indeed good and ancient custom was one of the best protections a vassal could enjoy especially if it was expressed and confirmed in a charter of liberties or some other formal concession. Hence the definition of custom gradually substantiated the liberties of subjects. That was perhaps the greatest bequest of the medieval to the modern world.

This notion was still far removed from the natural rights of the individual. Rights were attached to status, to the particular rather than the general human condition, and the individual had his niche in an array of finely graded social distinctions, each grade with its own special role to play. The church was a mystical body of which God was the spirit, the priesthood the soul and all the faithful the body. The structure of the state was examined in splendidly anthropomorphic detail; the servants of religion being the soul of the body politic and therefore exercising dominion over the whole body, the priest being the head, the senate the heart, the court the sides, officers and judges the eyes, ears and tongue, the executive officials the unarmed and the army the armed hand, the exchequer and treasury the belly and intestines, landfolk, handicraftmen and the like the feet, so that the state exceeds the centipede *numerositate pedum*; the protection of the folk the shoeing; the distress of these feet the state's gout. Thus John of Salisbury in the twelfth century. The theme was commonplace. It was still repeated by Nicholas of Cusa in the fifteenth century.

The Written Language

In such a hierarchical world, literature was for a small minority: kings, nobles, knights and few others. It reflected the conventions of the feudal society which moulded their lives. It embodied their Christian faith. The men who listened to the *Chanson de Roland* or the tales of Arthur were the patrons of the new monastic foundations of the eleventh and twelfth centuries. Their younger sons and cousins peopled the higher ranks of the clergy. They themselves looked forward to retirement in the family monastery, or to a final act of devotion on pilgrimage or the crusade. Literature fostered their sense of history. Its characteristic themes concerned the great men of the past, real or imaginary, whose lives were both magnified and distorted so as to fortify the conventions on which the audience's own society turned. Just as in law ancient tenure established right, so in literature fact and fiction were so blended that men were scarcely conscious of where history ended and romance began. And at first, as vernacular tradition was taking shape in the eleventh century, it was aimed at a rough, unlearned audience. It was recited rather than read. It was therefore poetry rather than prose.

That changed after the eleventh century, probably more rapidly than is immediately apparent in the evidence. Government at all levels became very much more sophisticated. It depended on written record. It functioned through written mandates sent from royal chanceries to local officials. It was informed through the record of local investigations and inquests which provided the facts essential to the formation of policy. It necessitated regular, accurate accounting for revenue. It could scarcely function effectively without proper procedures for the authorization of expenditure. The twelfth and thirteenth centuries saw the invention of red tape. By 1200 the king's government in England kept rolls of its annual account, rolls of all outgoing correspondence – charters, letters and writs, rolls recording all proffers made to the king for privilege or as penalties, and rolls of household expenditure. The cases coming before the king's court or before his justices in the county courts were enrolled. Copies of agreements reached before the royal justices were filed. All this survives in England to a remarkable degree and England may have been more record-conscious than other realms. But the trend towards written instruments and records was the same everywhere and it reached across both royal and ecclesiastical government and down to the management of the estates of the great nobles. Its effects were to involve more and more men in the work of government and to encourage, indeed demand, increasing literacy. English royal government depended locally on the sheriff, French royal government on *milites literati* who appear under Philip Augustus, the rule of the Hohenstaufen on *ministeriales* who came to be established as lesser feudal tenantry. In all these cases the operation of government depended on the assumption that such men could understand and obey mandates drafted by clerks in Latin. The gap between Latin text and vernacular understanding of documents to be read in public, warranting the grant of privilege or advertising royal mandates, was often bridged by *lectores* who were skilled in rendering a Latin text in the appropriate vernacular, but that kind of mediation cannot have been available all the time whenever and wherever a lay official, judge, sheriff, bailiff or steward, received a mandate or referred to a recorded judgement or turned to an enrolled account. Laymen had to read. This perhaps is hidden by the pervasiveness of Latin, by the clerical domination of the scribal profession and by the inadequacy of the nascent vernaculars. It stands revealed where government used different official languages when faced with different ethnic and linguistic groups among their subjects, as were the Norman kings of Sicily. It may be that similar developments in other parts of Europe were impeded not by lay ignorance of Latin or clerical monopoly of the art of writing, but by lack of precision and sophistication in the vernacular. Hence it was only slowly in the thirteenth century and more rapidly in the fourteenth century that it intruded into official documents.

Increasing wealth, expanding population, greater sophistication in government, the spread of literacy must all have broadened the potential audience. Many more people were acquainted with Roland or Arthur or Tristram in 1300 than in 1150. Literary taste was broadcast. The minstrel bearing his tales from castle to monastery, episcopal or royal residence was copied by local talent which carried his stories outwards to the market place and down the social scale to townsfolk and peasants at the fair or in the tavern. Romance succeeded to epic and ballad to romance.

Medieval Society

The society established in western Europe by the end of the thirteenth century was remarkably vigorous and resilient. Feudal relations had proved malleable. Commerce, industry and credit, the concentration of wealth in great urban centres where the hierarchical structure of rural society was replicated, had been accommodated. Feudal relations involving service had been commuted into rents. Lordship and vassalage themselves were becoming less permanent as bonds. Even the servile condition of the peasantry had been changed, if not ameliorated, in parts of France, Flanders and England. Some of the far-flung enterprise of the earlier Middle Ages had gone. The Crusade had largely failed. Monastic foundation had diminished. But society was still resilient enough to withstand demographic crisis arising from over-population and the onset of plague in the fourteenth century. Amidst crises many parts of western Europe prospered. The Hanse flourished. Switzerland was born. The importance of the fall of Constantinople in 1453 to western Europe was that by and large it no longer mattered very much. By then a society which had become compounded in part from barbarism had entered upon the Renaissance.

We should not be starry-eyed. Europe was still torn by war. Government, both in church and state was afflicted by corruption. Political strife often developed into internecine family squabbles which ended in ambush or on the scaffold. In the early Middle Ages rebellious opponents might be blinded or emasculated. In the later

Middle Ages they were beheaded, or hanged, drawn and quartered. It was a mixed world, as most are. The hero of *Eustache Li Moine* was the son of a knightly family, tenants of the counts of Boulogne. He entered a monastery but abandoned his vows around 1190 in order to avenge the murder of his father. He subsequently served the count of Boulogne, but then fell foul of him and took to the woods as an outlaw. His *roman* is a tale of stratagem and disguise, ambush and trickery. In real life Eustace became a soldier of fortune serving in turn both King John of England and King Philip Augustus of France. His career reached its zenith in 1205 when he seized the island of Sark which he used as a pirate base to dominate the Channel crossing. In 1217 he sailed with a fleet to bring reinforcements to Prince Louis of France and his baronial allies in England. He was defeated by royalist forces off Sandwich on 24 August and beheaded on the spot. It was an exciting, adventurous, if lawless career, in which Eustace may in the end have received his just desert. But who, in trying to sum up the quality of medieval life, would want to choose between that and Galahad's?

PART II

MEDIEVAL EUROPEAN LITERATURE

DEREK BREWER

Stories and songs in our mother tongue are the essence of literature. An extraordinary variety of them comes from the great range of peoples and times that make up the European Middle Ages, and they still make a direct appeal to us. The medieval world has more intense joys and sorrows, it may seem, than ours; life is shorter, the light is brighter, the dark more sombre. Behaviour is more extravagant, for good and bad. It is a large world, for distances are great when travelled by foot or on horseback, and populations small. Men are dwarfed by nature and nature is harsh. It is a less humanized world than ours, for everywhere we look in the Middle Ages mankind has little control over nature. But medieval man is more obviously a part of nature than we usually feel ourselves to be. Nature reflects his own mind, has a life like that of humanity, expresses human feelings. The world is significant and extends beyond the bounds of the visible, and beyond death. Within the world glory is met with glad praises; wickedness countered with satire, with condemnation, and in the end is expected to be defeated; strange contradictions create laughter. There are carnivals and massacres. Kings and beggars meet in the muddy highways.

As the Middle Ages progress kingdoms and universities are founded; cathedrals, castles and towns are built; a new tenderness of love, new extensions of pity are evolved. Men become more individual in feeling. Christianity in manifold forms justifies authority and love with divine suffering; science advances. A sharper sense of the actual world is felt. Men grasp at the written word to locate, enrich and prolong the new achievements of intellect, feeling and imagination. Out of the ruins of the great Empire of Rome is slowly created that multiple, uneven entity of Europe, the fertile seedbed of modern civilization. If we can in any sense nowadays believe in progress it is in contemplating that great struggle towards a richer, more orderly, morally better society which is presented to us by the development of the Middle Ages, and by what may be regarded as the crown of its achievement, the Renaissance. The Middle Ages are the great success story of Western European civilization.

Civilization may be thought to progress, to improve, though only partially and uncertainly, but art is not subject to the same laws of development. The early songs and stories of Europe are neither worse nor better than the later ones just because they are earlier. They are only different; and their very difference is part of their appeal. They may even recall to us forgotten depths of our own experiences, may even teach us wisdom. Medieval literature can certainly teach us about fortitude, pity, love, nobility and comedy. Nor does it speak only as Europeans to Europeans. Being a traditional literature it has bonds across the whole world both with unlettered peoples in all countries, and with more sophisticated traditional societies. It connects easily with mythology and folklore. Many societies in the world of today still recognize the heroic lay, the fantastic comic tale, the riddle, the proverb, the work-song, which the modern West has forgotten, and needs imaginatively to recreate for its own advantage.

The following pages pick out from the dense tapestry of European culture the bright strands of vernacular, secular story and song. That does not deny the pervading civilizing influence of Christianity but determines our line of approach. There is so much material that a lifetime of study would not be enough to master it, and the present essay does not claim to be a full or authoritative survey nor a work of reference. This introductory impressionistic account must have many omissions and shortcomings, but it will have succeeded if it gives a framework to help the reader and encourage further exploration.

The anthology of selected pieces of translation, only suggestive, as any short collection of translations must be, will give a further incentive. The general bibliography lists the more outstanding studies in English to which a reader will wish to turn, and from which the material presented here is drawn.

The Non-Latin and Latin Elements: Conquerors and Captives

About A.D. 448–9 the Roman Emperor Theodosius II, who lived in the Eastern Empire at Constantinople (modern Istanbul), sent an embassy to the barbarian King of the Huns, Attila, 'the scourge of God'. Attila (d. 453) who combined a savage magnificence with some magnanimity and humour, spent his life ravaging both the eastern and western sections of the Roman Empire. In one embassy to Attila was the Byzantine historian Priscus who, writing in Greek, tells us of a splendid banquet given to the Romans and then,

> when evening came on torches were lighted and two barbarians stepped forth in front of Attila and recited poems which they had composed, recounting his victories and his valiant deeds in war. The Banqueters fixed their eyes upon them, some being charmed with the poems, while others were roused in spirit, as the recollection of their wars came back to them. Others again burst into tears, because their bodies were enfeebled by age and their martial ardour had perforce to remain unsatisfied.[1]

The little scene is emblematic of the remote beginnings of medieval European literature and culture. We may easily imagine the contrast of the barbaric splendour and gold of the rich feast in the tents of an army renowned for its ferocious destructiveness, with the guests of refined culture and education from the most advanced and technologically efficient civilization that the world had seen. The barbarians were in process of knocking that civilization into ruins. Although the Huns were themselves of eastern origin there were plenty of western counterparts pressing from the north and west upon the Roman Empire. Alaric the Goth had sacked Rome in 410, Attila all but repeated the destruction in 452, the Vandal Gaiseric accomplished it again in 455. The German Odoacer captured the emperor's throne in Rome in 476. Byzantium, the eastern section of the Roman Empire, survived until 1453, a civilized power in its own right, but from the fifth century was relatively cut off, with Greek as its official language, from western Europe, where knowledge of Greek soon faded almost to nothing until a thousand years later. The very names of the barbarian tribes, Asiatic Huns, Germanic Goths and Vandals, have become in the western mind synonyms for destructive savagery.

Yet we can no longer regard these fierce peoples as being without culture. They clearly possessed an elaborate court poetry on traditional themes. Cultured Romans of east and west despised the 'barbarian buzzing' of the harp, as refined modern readers may despise ancient literature, and the folktale and folksong to which it is so closely related, but it was artistic enough to move stern men to joy and tears.

Another example may be taken from the other end of the ruined Empire, in the far, cloudy west. Germanic tribes of Angles and Saxons had pressed into the island left by withdrawn Roman legions and made it Engla-land, the land of the English, who were the last of a sequence of conquerors of that fertile ground with its convenient if not genial climate. The English too were barbarians who did not live in the empty Roman cities but camped beside them. Eventually they were converted to Christianity and their great historian, Bede the monk of Jarrow (c.672–735), in his *Ecclesiastical History of the English People*, written in Latin, tells how the first Christian poetry was composed and written in the famous story of the peasant Caedmon of the seventh century, which sums up so much of the past and future of European and English literature and culture. Caedmon was the cow-man of the monastery at Whitby, a shy, illiterate man who had never learned how to take his part in the singing that accompanied any festivity. When all were gathered together at a feast, and it was the custom for the harp to be passed round and for each man to play and sing to it in turn, Caedmon left the feast in shame as the harp came near. One night he did this and went to the cow-shed where it was his duty to spend the night, and fell asleep on his bed. He dreamt that a man came to him and said 'Caedmon, sing me something'. He replied he could not; but the man insisted and said 'Sing to me about Creation'. In his sleep Caedmon sang, in the four-stress unrhymed alliterative verse of Germanic heroic tradition. When he awoke he added more. In the morning he reported to the reeve who took him to the abbess Hilda. When she heard him she arranged for learned men to tell him holy stories, that is Biblical stories, and he turned them into traditional verse, as sung to the harp, which they then wrote down. This is a very early, fascinating instance of recording oral poetry from dictation.

Here we are one stage further than at Attila's court. The humble cow-man took part in the feast, and though there were clearly no learned men or superiors there, the feast was obviously no rowdy bawdy sing-song. Caedmon had absorbed the themes, vocabulary and metre of Germanic tradition. He mingled the two traditions, Germanic and Latin Christian. The great English poem *Beowulf*, probably written in the East Midlands in the eighth century, is another perfect example of such mingling. *Beowulf* is an heroic elegy, written down, yet steeped in traditional oral English metre and vocabulary, with the ancient feeling for the heroic concepts of loyalty, bravery, praise, suffering and death. The hero when young defeats monsters, but in age, defending his people, he at last succumbs to the dragon he himself kills. A noble tragic pagan past is evoked. Yet the poet is also profoundly Christian in his outlook, necessarily looking forward, detached from that past, though depending on Latin for its basis in the Bible.

To sum up: the fall of Rome, the survival of Roman culture and literacy in Latin, the immense power of Christianity, the rich and varied vernacular resources of the destructive barbarians, are the elements of medieval European literature. They may be simplified, though oversimplified, to an inheritance and mingling of Latin and non-Latin elements. When the barbarians captured Rome they also captured some elements of Roman culture, especially the verbal and literate elements, always the most powerful and enduring of any culture. But the conquerors were themselves in the end made willing captives of their victim. In the process both were changed almost out of all recognition; but some recognition of their historical origin is vital for understanding them, and for comprehending the complex medieval European identity.

Why Were the Middle Ages So Called?

When you come to think of it, 'Middle Ages' is a peculiar expression, and it is worth while knowing how it came to be used, because it affects our own attitudes. It originates with the scholars of the fifteenth and sixteenth centuries, especially in Italy, France and much of what is now Germany, who were so conscious of their success in reviving knowledge of classical Latin and in using it as the chief instrument of education and learning. They were called humanists. The immense achievements of Roman civilization and literature had been built upon a firm basis of education and literacy. When the Roman Empire collapsed there was a decline in the educational system. Classical Latin, a highly disciplined, learned and artificial language, fell out of use and 'Low Latin' became general. Latin continued both to be taught and to be the instrument of education and learning, but usually at a much lower level, in many fewer schools. Even the Latin of the educated changed, diversified, became, as some scholars felt, 'corrupt' under the influence of the many different vernacular languages, some themselves descended from Latin. Nevertheless, education and learning throughout the Middle Ages meant essentially the reading and writing of Latin. It does not surprise us, with our modern knowledge of the inevitability of linguistic change, that Latin changed. Some medieval Latin is as fine as classical Latin, though different. But much medieval Latin was inferior to that of the great Roman classics, which acted as a magnet to many of the finer intellects. The humanists finally achieved the age-old attempt to equal the ancients by writing Latin like them, and thus came to despise medieval Latin. As it turned out, it was both a fatal and an irrelevant accomplishment. It was fatal because it paralysed Latin as a living language. Latin was barely usable for the advance of contemporary culture when it had to be in classical form. The accomplishment was irrelevant because vernacular culture, that is, the expression of thought and feeling in the mother tongue, was by the fifteenth century flourishing on a written base in many European languages, and the present and the future lay with them.

Yet it was natural for humanist scholars, who had achieved a 'real', because ancient, Latin to regard themselves as at last the true successors to the glories and grandeurs of Rome. Ancient Rome exercised just the same magical appeal over artists and the patrons of art. Thus humanists, and eventually all educated people, came to regard the whole period from the sixth to the fifteenth or sixteenth centuries in Europe as a gulf in time, in the middle between 'then' and 'now', *medium ævum*, a 'middle age', to be regarded with derision and contempt, or at best pity. An associated notion was of the 'renaissance', i.e. 'rebirth', which the humanists saw as taking place in the fifteenth and sixteenth centuries. These notions of successive periods are essential to our ability to understand the processes of history, but they are very approximate, and successive generations produce their own versions, indulging their own preferences. The humanists despised the 'middle age', much as the early twentieth century despised the Victorians.

The great interest and importance of the Middle Ages began to be rediscovered by the Romantic movement in Europe in the eighteenth and early nineteenth centuries. 'Romanticism' implies an interest in the Middle Ages. It became possible to refer to the first centuries after the fall of Rome as the Dark Age, or Ages, covering the period from the sixth to the eleventh centuries, whence indeed relatively little documentary or literary evidence survives. Those centuries saw the painfully slow beginning of that long recovery and remaking of civilization in Europe which really constitutes the Middle Ages, and of which the Renaissance of the fifteenth and sixteenth centuries may well be regarded, in our view, not as a denial, but as the climax and crown. The fundamental break in our culture now seems to be in the seventeenth century, with the development of the scientific revolution which, once harnessed to industrialization, has so changed the world.

As knowledge of the Middle Ages increased, more variety was perceived within them. It came to be realized that in all the darkness of the eighth century the learning of Northumbria, where Bede was pre-eminent, shone like a beacon; Anglo-Saxon missionaries had helped to Christianize continental Europe. The Vikings had smashed that culture, but in the early ninth century Charles the Great (Charlemagne, 768–814), who made himself emperor of much of Europe, created a new revival of learning in France and Germany, which modern scholars now call the Carolingian Renaissance. We owe to it the preservation of most of our texts of the Latin classics. Charlemagne used as a minister the Englishman Alcuin of York (?735–804), pupil of a pupil of Bede's.

The Carolingian Empire did not survive Charlemagne but we can now recognize that the European countries still struggled towards a higher civilization. In Italy the towns were continuously occupied, and probably at no time in that country was there a complete dearth of intellectual culture in Latin, or even of educated laymen. In England, paradoxically, the absence of Latin learning in Alfred's time (871–99) led to his pragmatic insistence on translation into the vernacular, and from this stems the earliest substantial vernacular literature in Europe. In France there was a much stronger continuous tradition of education, and in consequence the vernacular emerged later. But France became the dominant cultural centre of medieval Europe and the great upsurge of learning and literature, both in Latin and in French, in the twelfth century, has led modern scholars to the concept of 'the twelfth-century renaissance'.

In the present day the terms 'Middle Ages', 'medieval', referring to a period of so much diversity, with several 'renaissances' inset, are seen to have a mainly chronological significance. What period of centuries is included in 'the Middle Ages' now depends to some extent on the scholar who is writing. The essential period, and the period of greatest achievement, is that from the twelfth to some time in the sixteenth, but there is much advantage in including in the idea of the 'medieval' the so-called Dark Ages. Hence in the present book it is right to include some reference, if little more than a token, to Old English literature, just as a finger must, so to speak, be pointed towards the wealth of Byzantium, and at the other extreme, in the West, to the very different riches of Celtic literature. Thus 'the Middle Ages' referred to here include the centuries from the seventh to the sixteenth, and an immense variety of lands. But in order to understand them we must now return to the period just before: to the fourth century, to the collapse of Rome and the salvaging of fragments of Roman civilization which laid the foundations of the Middle Ages.

Founders of the Middle Ages

Theodosius the Great was Augustus (i.e. Emperor) only of the East, 379–95, but supreme in power throughout the Empire. He made Christianity the state religion (381) and paganism a political offence. In his lifetime lived the greatest of the Fathers of the Latin Church, Augustine of Hippo (354–430). After Theodosius the Empire split more clearly into East and West, and, in the West, into kingdoms speaking Germanic and Romance (i.e. Latin) languages. In the fifth and sixth centuries, times of trouble and change, lived some of the great 'founders of the Middle Ages', to take E. K. Rand's phrase. (I hope the reader will forgive a list, since the names are so important.) Jerome (c.348–420) translated the Bible from Hebrew and Greek into Latin, replacing the Old Latin Bible with what came to be known as the Vulgate, the staple book, the fundamental base of reference, for all European culture, for the next thousand years. The first great Christian poet was Prudentius (348–410), and the first Christian general historian was Orosius (*fl. c.*400). Macrobius (*fl. c.*400) produced a serviceable handbook of general information which preserved the knowledge of the roundness of the earth, an elaborate theory of dreams, and much else that even the advanced mind of Chaucer in the fourteenth century still fed upon. Macrobius also furnished, along with Servius, the basis of literary comment on Virgil (70–19 B.C.), who remained, with his much younger and very different contemporary Ovid (43 B.C.–A.D. 17 [?]) the staple poetic reading for schoolboys until the twentieth century. Martianus Capella wrote at some time between Alaric's sack of Rome (410) and the Vandal conquest of North Africa (429) a book about the 'marriage' of Mercury and Philology, an allegory of learning which was fundamental to education for eight centuries, perhaps because it is so dry and encapsulated. There are seven 'bridesmaids' for the wedding; Grammar, Dialectic (i.e. a sort of logic) and Rhetoric are the first three, and they form what was later called the *Trivium*, which constituted the course for Bachelor of Arts in medieval universities, and gave us the modern word 'trivial'. Four 'bridesmaids' follow, Geometry, Arithmetic, Astronomy, Music, forming the *Quadrivium*, for Master of Arts. Sidonius of Apollinaris (*c.*430–*c.*488) was a copious Christian writer of letters and poems in the second half of the fifth century who yet gives us the latest indication, as Auerbach notes, of a genuine Roman literary public. After him it fragments and perishes.

In the sixth century something of an educated circle survived, as witnessed by Boethius (480–524) whose *Consolation of Philosophy*, written in prison in anticipation of death, is a book which has refreshed innumerable minds even down to our own day. His philosophical works, unoriginal in themselves, preserved much of classical philosophy and learning as a basis from which the later Middle Ages could develop. The Emperor Theodoric the Goth was served by Boethius the Roman aristocrat, but eventually put him to death. Theodoric himself wished to preserve Roman culture, but could only properly understand his own German Gothic. Another Roman aristocrat, contemporary with Boethius, was Cassiodorus (487–583). He gave forty years to the public service but had an end more fortunate than that of Boethius. He founded a monastery, Vivarium, and devoted himself to collecting a library and writing theological and encyclopaedic works. Like Boethius he preserved much of the classical heritage, and set an example to monasteries of the value of preserving even pagan Latin literature. The pagan nature of Latin literature which was nevertheless educationally necessary and intellectually, emotionally and sometimes even spiritually so outstanding, was a continuous problem for the Christian Middle Ages, but the contradiction was on the whole successfully lived with, despite the difficulties. In the latter part of the sixth century we also find the delightful character Venantius Fortunatus who not only wrote some fine poems but the great marching hymn *Vexilla regis prodeunt*, 'The royal banners forward go', still sung today. Fond as he was of friends and countryside and food and drink, he too ended as a priest, a surely genial Bishop of Poitiers, and died about 600.

A more serious contemporary, profoundly influential, was Pope Gregory the Great, whose *Moralia*, or *Morals upon Job*, was a treasure-house continually drawn on for later biblical study, and whom the English may congratulate for the famous pun made on seeing a captured fair-haired English boy for sale as a slave in the market in Rome – 'non Angli sed angeli'; 'not English but angels'. Whatever scepticism this sentiment may arouse, Gregory nevertheless despatched another Augustine (d.604 or 605) to England, who, landing in 597 in Kent possibly with the copy of the Gospels still preserved in Corpus Christi College, Cambridge, laid the foundations for the conversion of the English. Another Gregory, of Tours (d.694), wrote a history of the Franks in bad Latin, and Isidore of Seville (*c.*560–636) wrote an encyclopaedia by means of analysing what were thought to be the history and components of Latin words, the *Etymologiae* which served the whole Middle Ages.

The intellectual and emotional developments of the later Middle Ages rested on the work of these men of faith, as they saved fragments from a falling world to make the foundations for a better one. Some of the work looks simple and crude enough now, but it led to such works of towering intellect as the vast theological and philosophical *Summae* of Thomas Aquinas (*c.*1225–74) and many another scholastic philosopher, to historical, scientific and imaginative works which, like their counterparts in stone, the medieval cathedrals, must be regarded as major achievements of the human spirit.

The Development of Latin Language and Literature

The use of Latin was basic to the intellectual life of the Middle Ages. Written Latin was always attached to the sheet-anchor of classical Latin, though it changed considerably. The development of medieval Latin made philosophy and science possible. It was a common European learned language, consciously acquired as a second language, explicitly different from the vernaculars, even though inevitably interacting with them.

A full account of medieval European literary culture would have to give a major place to what was achieved in Latin. We have chosen not to do so in this book because we have judged that the emergence of the vernaculars is of primary importance, and we cannot cover everything. All we can do here is to give a brief sketch of the Latin which is so important a counterpart and background of the vernaculars, in the hope that readers will wish to pursue their own studies further.

First, a word about the development of the actual language itself. Medieval Latin is in general easier than classical Latin because the syntax is closer to the order of words of modern European vernaculars (German partly excepted). The sharp distinctions between cases of the noun and between indicative and subjunctive are broken down in many writers, though the better-educated medieval writers preserve them. In vocabulary most words are derived from classical Latin but there are many new meanings and words. The lower the level of style and learning, the more the vernacular element appears, especially in the later Middle Ages. A nice example from England noted in 1261 is *chopio*, 'chop wood'. Many more general and abstract words were developed, as *qualitas* and *quantitas*.

When we turn to consider the use of Latin, its significance as the universal language of the Church can hardly be over-emphasized. The Church was in a real sense the medieval descendant of the Roman Empire, with the Pope replacing the Emperor. Bible, church services, the whole intellectual and administrative effort of the Church as a body, both needed and reinforced the use of Latin, maintaining and relying on its universality and identity. There was indeed an unexpected and terrible issue of this. In some respects Latin became a sacred language. Churchmen foolishly but understandably tried to preserve the sacred truths which had become identified with the Latin of the Bible, of church services and of theology, from the necessary and legitimate demands of the vernacular. Men and women were burnt for possessing the Scriptures in the vernacular in the late Middle Ages. But that is another story.

Latin was not in every respect sacred because for some men (and it is worth recalling that few women were taught it), Latin became a natural, if second language, fit for the highest – and sometimes the lowest – imaginative purposes of those who learnt it for practical reasons of churchmanship, scholarship and administration. The flowering of vernacular literature in the twelfth and thirteenth centuries was intimately associated with an equally vivid flourishing of Latin literature of all kinds, and they were cross-pollinated in a hundred different ways.

Medieval Latin is thus a rich and varied language which, while it maintains its identity, nevertheless has many different manifestations. It was the language of the world of medieval Europe to an even greater extent than English is nowadays the language of the whole world. Although it was predominantly ecclesiastical, serious and utilitarian in purpose, there was room in it for the gratuitousness and the grace of high art. Nowhere is this clearer than in the long course of superb Latin lyric poetry. This was early turned to Christian use. The 'seven great hymns', including 'Come holy Spirit' and 'Jesu the very thought of thee', are still sung. More relevant to our main interest here in vernacular, secular story and song are the love-songs. Most medieval Latin lyric love-poetry is not so highly strung as the highest strains of some vernacular, especially troubadour poetry, but the bitter-sweet joys of spring and the sight of lovely girls are evoked both plaintively and joyfully. There is a variety of expressive or satiric or parodic song, and the ten poems of the otherwise unknown Archpoet, a German Bohemian scholar, as it would appear, with their passionate defiance of asceticism, are amongst the best of European poetry. Not even Helen Waddell's translations can do more than merely suggest their quality, but a snatch from his *Confession* gives a taste.

> Down the broad way I go
> Young and unregretting,
> Wrap me in my vices up,

> Virtue all forgetting,
> Greedier for all delight
> Than heaven to enter in:
> Since the soul in me is dead,
> Better save the skin.[2]

Latin gives us, besides lyrics, the first real medieval romance, the strange *Ruodlieb* (*c.*1050), again German in origin, and a host of longer poems, serious stories and comic (like the satirical *A Mirror for Fools* (1179–80), the book of Burnel the Ass, by Nigel Longchamp), and other beast fables of various kinds, as well as dramatic comedies in verse. The great modern study by Ernst Robert Curtius, *European Literature and the Latin Middle Ages*, and the work of other scholars, have demonstrated how much the inspiration and the commonplaces, the themes and the forms, of later vernacular literature owe to this continuous medieval Latin tradition. Dante in particular, perhaps the greatest medieval poet, with his special relation to Virgil, illustrates the continuously fructifying influence of Latin even when it naturally leads to the vernacular.

Yet in some ways our views are prejudiced in favour of Latin, because for so long it was virtually identified with literacy. To be literate meant to be literate in Latin. In consequence Latin survives, whereas the rich store of vernacular story and song which we have to posit behind even the earliest surviving fragments of vernacular poetry has been irretrievably lost because it was purely oral. The written word has to carry its own context within it if it is to have an effect equal to the spoken word, though by the same token it will be more long-lasting. Latin therefore carried the power of literacy throughout the medieval centuries. It is for this reason that medieval Latin remains powerful as literature today, and happily less neglected than it has been since the sixteenth century.

The Emergence of Romance Languages

As the Roman Empire broke down into fragmented kingdoms, Latin, where it was naturally a spoken language, changed as language inevitably does. Classical Latin as we know it had even at the height of Roman culture been an elaborate, somewhat artificial language, the product of high literacy. The educated spoke something like it, the less educated something much less like it, referred to as the language of the common people, the *vulgus*. This 'vulgar Latin' was the basis of the later development of spoken Latin, diverging from written Latin, and differently influenced by many outside sources in different parts. Different dialects of Latin developed and progressed to the status of different though closely-related languages. Since they were the spoken, native languages of their respective peoples they are now referred to as 'vernaculars' (paradoxically a *Latin* word meaning domestic, native, from *verna* a home-born, i.e. native, slave, though it is a post-medieval word). Those vernaculars which are descended from Latin are called 'romance' languages, from *romanice*, meaning 'in the Latin way'. Hence French, Italian, Portuguese, Provençal, Romanian, Spanish, and very many others spoken by smaller groups.

From 813 onwards, the vernacular is distinguished in France from Latin by being called *romana lingua*. In France, too, are found the first Romance vernacular texts, the Strassburg Oaths, referring to an occasion in 842 when the significance of an oath between Charles the Bald of France and Louis the German had to be made plain to each side. The explanation is in Latin, but the oaths are given in a form of French and a form of German prose. They are practical, not literary.

The earliest vernacular *literature* anywhere is in verse, no doubt because it derives from the oral literature of the people, high and low. Verse is based on repeated rhythms and repeated sounds (like rhymes) and often on repeated phrases, which are relatively easy to memorize. The practised traditional bard carries a stock of verbal formulae in metrical form in his head, along with some larger formal patterns into which formulae and stories are fitted. Verse is suitable for literature because literature is primarily for entertainment, not necessarily trivial. All human beings need such entertainment, but they are not necessarily literate. Prose, on the other hand, does not depend on repeated rhythms and is much less easy to memorize. It presupposes literacy. Among the peoples who spoke the Romance languages the tradition of prose was preserved in Latin, which retained its literate base. Prose needs the resources of technology required by writing – pens, ink, something to write on, education, schools, etc. Its cost and nature cause it in the first instance to be thought of as primarily utilitarian, like the Strassburg Oaths. Prose therefore appears in constant *literary* use only when a culture has achieved a considerable level of stable organization, where wealth has created a class of people who like reading for its own sake because they are reasonably well fed and housed, safe and comfortable, educated, capable of experiencing in some degree of solitude an indirect relationship with other minds through written symbols, rather than a direct relationship through spoken words in immediately present groups. *Literary* prose therefore implies a relatively advanced and organized civilization, with towns, a system of education, some degree of individualization and personal detachment.

The peoples in those parts of Europe where vulgar Latin was spoken and developed into the Romance vernaculars, were themselves of very mixed origin. The French, for example, were predominantly Franks, in origin a Germanic group of nations. An obscure mixture of tribes populated the Spanish peninsula which the Romans had come to dominate, and after the political collapse of the Roman Empire there were further invasions of Spain by Germanic tribes, Visigoths and Vandals. The situation in Spain was further complicated by its conquest by Moslem Moors, only checked by the victory of Charles Martel as far north as Tours in France (732). Christian recovery began in 1002, and was completed by the conquest of Granada in 1492. For eight centuries in Spain there was considerable mutual influence and alliance, as well as hostility, between Muslims and Christians. No single generalization can cover the varieties of peoples, from nomads to city-dwellers, extending over Europe's vast area even to modern Romania, on the borders of Russia. Yet it is likely that the social structures of these peoples were broadly similar, (except where substantial towns survived as in Provence and Italy). The nations were military aristocracies based on peasant agriculture, slowly and unsteadily but progressively Christianized by the efforts of churchmen and the desires of their own outstanding people.

French Literature

In the case of France, after the early Strassburg Oaths we first find religious texts; the *Sequence* (a rhythmic hymn) of *Saint Eulalia* of about 880, the *Life of Saint Leger* of the tenth century, and the very beautiful *Life of Saint Alexis*, which might be called a religious romance, of the eleventh. Then comes most grandly, without prelude, the great French heroic tale, the *chanson de geste* called *Song of Roland*, which was probably written early in the twelfth century by a Norman. It is a traditional heroic lay, whose subject matter is based on an actual historical event, the battle in the pass of Roncesvaux in the Pyrenees, 15 August 778, between the Frankish forces and the Basques. Mere historical incident remembered over several centuries has been turned into a work of grand imagination, and it is said that William's minstrel Taillefer led the Normans into action at the Battle of Hastings singing of the deeds of Roland. Many other *chansons de geste* were composed out of a complex mixture of the ancient themes of battle and praise of warriors mingled with the literary influence of Latin poets, notably Virgil and Lucan, and the normal fervour of crusading Christianity. But treading fast on the heels of the traditional glorification of war and warriors came newer notes undoubtedly to be associated with the progress of education and of courts. There was a wonderful flowering of vernacular literature in twelfth- and thirteenth-century France, fertilized from Provence in particular, which gave France the unquestioned leadership of literary culture in medieval Europe. The didactic religious literature, important as it is, may be less emphasized here for the sake of noting the development of secular poems in the twelfth century; the *Roman de Thèbes* based on the first century A.D. Latin *Thebaid* of Statius, the *Eneas* based on Virgil's *Aeneid*, and the *Roman de Troie*, whose subject was that great medieval theme, the fall of empire, valued partly because Europeans drew (quite mistakenly) their ancestry from Troy via Rome.

Totally different in scale, much greater in artistic achievement, are the exquisite short *Lais* of Marie de France, who probably wrote in England (before 1181 to after 1216), based on folkloric, probably Celtic, narratives. These short poems, as well as the long Latin-based romances, draw much of their power from their treatment of sexual love, fortunate or tragic in outcome. They mark the beginnings in narrative of the supreme topic of personal and emotional concern in so much western literature. The reason they did so (apart from intrinsic interest) was in part due to the influence of the French love-lyric deriving from Provençal lyric, to which we shall return, itself influenced by the Arabic civilization of Spain.

At the end of the twelfth century, around the 1170s, appears Chrétien de Troyes whose half-dozen romances mark the true beginning of vernacular Arthurian literature and the most absorbing and far-fetched concepts of love. From now on appears a previously unparalleled number of romances of love and physical adventure centred on chivalric customs, hopes and fantasies, on brave knights, beautiful chaste ladies, enchantments dire.

Here come the great sequence of Lancelot romances, in prose in the thirteenth century; the sequence of poems, also later much expanded in prose, about Tristan and Isolde; the narratives of Gawain; their great summation for English readers is in Malory's *Le Morte Darthur* of 1470. But in the thirteenth century in France, by a natural reaction against high-flown romance, and for much the same audience of courtiers, clerics and (in so far as they existed) educated townsmen to whom the romances appealed, were produced the *fabliaux*, comic, realistic, mostly bawdy tales in verse. They are the reverse of romance in that they are robustly and sometimes offensively gross, not refined; cynically realistic, not idealistic, about sex; and quite unadorned by the beauties of rhetoric. Partly out of them arose the secular French farces of the fourteenth century, while Boccaccio's prose *Decameron* is an indirect descendant.

Meanwhile the drama in the vernacular also developed to a remarkable degree. The earliest play is the religious and anonymous *Jeu d'Adam* of about 1150, but secular drama was almost contemporaneous, with Adam de la Halle's satirical *Jeu de la Feuillée* and his pastoral *Jeu de Robin et Marion* some ten years later. These and other literary activities arose from the exceptional advantages provided by the prosperous town of Arras. The subsequent great flourishing of medieval drama, sincerely religious in content and message, was itself the product of lay interest and organization in European towns. This led later to secular drama, which flourished mainly in the fifteenth century in France.

France became the richest and culturally dominant power in Europe from the late twelfth century onwards; her literary achievements influenced all European vernaculars. The rise of the universities in the thirteenth century was both cause and effect of a grand appetite for knowledge that found various literary forms, from versified treatises to learned love-poems. The theme of love at its greatest achieved a literally encyclopaedic capacity. The striking example is the single most influential poem of the Middle Ages, surviving in hundreds of manuscripts, *The Romance of the Rose*. It begins as a fresh and delicate allegory of burgeoning youth and romantic love in the garden of courtly leisure, which still today charms and interests the reader with its sensuous flavour and intriguing narrative. The lover seeks to pluck the rose, profound image of love. The poem was written about 1230 and left unfinished, about 2,000 lines long. Forty years later came Jean de Meung, who 'completed' the poem with another 18,000 lines. He brings a medieval clerical mind to the subject; learned, vigorous, satirical, coarse, worldly, philosophical, with a relish for salacious realism. His poem is vividly redolent of the streets of Paris and its university, contrasting with Guillaume's earlier courtly, more gentle picture of the tentativeness and frustrations of romantic love. Such a mixture of materials and attitudes is very medieval, whether or not produced by several authors. *The Romance of the Rose* influenced *The Divine Comedy* in Italy, *The Book of Good Love* in Spain, *The Canterbury Tales* in England. These works triumph through their variousness and are the most characteristic expressions of medieval literary culture. *The Romance of the Rose* was immensely influential and successful.

In the fourteenth and fifteenth centuries French verse became ever more elaborate and rhetorical. Guillaume Machaut (*c.*1300–77) was the most influential poet, and Chaucer owed much to him. He was also a great musical composer, but his copious verbiage, like that of his successors, though a virtue admired for many generations, makes them tedious reading now for all but the specialist. Yet at the very time of the Great (and largely unreadable) Rhetoricians appears François Villon (1431–*c.*63) whose note of personal plangency fills the medieval commonplaces which are the substance of his lyrics with a haunting power. (We have not, alas, found space for an essay on François Villon, beloved of Ezra Pound and T. S. Eliot, who several times quote him.) He confesses himself a rascal, and writes with both comedy and pathos of the underworld of Paris. He is a true descendant of the Goliardic Archpoet and of Jean de Meung. The Gothic poet, unlike the Neoclassical and Romantic poet, attributes no special superiority to himself. But Villon, with his sympathy for the poor, the outcast, and the immoral, himself living a dismal, turbulent life, has also obvious links with the *poète maudit* of the nineteenth-century French Romantic convention. He gives memorable form to ancient commonplaces (*Ou sont les neiges d'antan*), and evokes them through a lively self-portrait (*Dans l'an trentiesme de mon aage*) in a characteristically late-medieval way which appeals directly to our age, as Chaucer, Henryson and Dunbar do.

French prose develops relatively late. The earliest examples are the lucid chronicles of Villehardouin (*c.*1152–1212) and Joinville (1224–1317) describing crusades, and this tradition continues with the more colourful and imaginative chronicles of Jean Froissart (*c.*1337–*c.*1410), Chaucer's contemporary and acquaintance, which have enormous human interest and imaginative appeal, even if they are deficient in the sterner virtues of analysis more valued by modern historians. Amongst other fifteenth-century prose occurs *Les Cent Nouvelles Nouvelles* (*c.*1456), much influenced by Italian works, but most significant, the amazing work of François Rabelais (*c.*1494–1553). He was a learned, satirical, bawdy, spoiled friar, the counterpart two centuries later of Jean de Meung. Rabelais's *Pantagruel* (printed in 1532) and subsequent parts published over the next twenty years, is a great carnival of secular medieval themes and topics renewed and continued into the sixteenth century. It is one of those great books which makes the distinction between medieval and Renaissance almost meaningless except as a notation of the passage of time.

Italian Literature

When we turn to Italy we find that the first Italian vernacular documents are also oaths, written between 960 and 963, in utilitarian prose. (Similar early documents survive scantily from Sardinia, Portugal, Catalonia, a reminder of the cluster of languages from which we are taking only the outstanding examples.) The first great Italian poem is St Francis's *Canticle of Brother Sun* (1225). The earliest vernacular secular poems in Italian are the *cantilena* or songs by Ciullo d'Alcamo and Folcachiero da Siena – it is remarkable that the names are known – also of the thirteenth century. At this time educated people in Italy seem to have used Latin even for speech, but the vernacular existed side by side with Latin and may well have predominated in domestic speech.

The beginnings of secular literature in Italian are associated with the court of Frederick II, emperor of Germany, king of Sicily (1220–50), to whose brilliant court many poets and storytellers were attracted, and who knew both Latin and the 'vulgar tongue'. Here we have already come to the theme of love, and the archaic world of the heroic lay has been left behind. Ciullo's *cantilena* is a dialogue between a lover and his lady, in which she at last succumbs to his requests after sweet, reluctant, amorous delay. It is in every sense a popular topic, and expressed with verve and feeling, but it is conveyed through an intellectualized, sophisticated dialectic, and once again we are only at a beginning in the sense of finding a first record, not a clumsy new start. The language itself is no rustic local dialect but a sort of vernacular *lingua franca* based on the developed literary language of Italian troubadours, derived from those of Provence. Many other lyrics were written, at a high level of education, like the *Intelligenzia*, an allegorical poem full of rhetorical devices.

After Frederick II the centre of poetic achievement moved to the Tuscan towns of central Italy, such as the great university town Bologna, where Latin learning and literature also flourished, and where one of the great Italian lyric poets, Guido Guinicelli, was in 1270 a teacher of rhetoric. He combined love of learning with the learning of love in the *dolce stil nuovo*, 'the sweet new style', and Dante was pleased to call him 'father' in poetry. There were many other remarkable poets. Iacopone da Todi was the poet of passionate religious love, Cavalcanti of refined secular love. Another of Dante's masters, Brunetto Latini, wrote (*c.*1220–95) an encyclopaedic poem in French which is a marvel of philosophical exposition in verse. These and other poets developed a highly self-conscious vernacular poetic art. The supreme poet among them is of course Dante Alighieri (1265–1321), whose *Vita Nuova* 'New Life', and *Divina Commedia* 'Divine Comedy', mark the climax of medieval European poetry. The *Commedia* is a *summa* of love, theology, science and satire, 'comedy' in the medieval sense of having a happy ending, for it progresses through three great stages, from Hell through Purgatory to the joy of Heaven. Dante also wrote, amongst other treatises, the

De Vulgari Eloquentia about writing in the vernacular, though he used Latin to do so.

Italian prose also began to flourish in the thirteenth century, telling many stories, mostly translated from the French, including a notable set of transmuted Arthurian tales, but the great prose-writer was Giovanni Boccaccio (?1313–75). Boccaccio began very young as a poet of love, both sensuous and down-to-earth, but the series of a hundred prose-tales known as the *Decameron* is his masterpiece. They are traditional anecdotes or at least made up from traditional elements, a Gothic mixture of the comic (usually bawdy), and the pathetic; fantastic in plot, yet told with vivid realism. They are a complete counterpart to the *Divine Comedy*: equally medieval, not nearly so profound, almost as great, and a good deal more amusing. Boccaccio as he grew older rather regretted his masterwork and turned in the last thirty years of his life to the great compilation and analysis of classical mythology written, it is worth noting, in Latin, the *Genealogiae Deorum Gentilium* 'Genealogies of the Pagan Gods'. He became the Claude Lévi-Strauss of the fourteenth century and his book was immensely influential in education until the nineteenth century.

The great surge of verse-romance in Italian came much later, with the fantastic, occasionally comic, always entertaining works of Boiardo (?1441–91), the *Orlando Innamorato*, and Ludovico Ariosto (1474–1533) the *Orlando Furioso*. These are the latest and most remarkable transformations of the story of Roland, changed into Orlando, hero of love-romance. The continuity of medieval with Renaissance could not be better illustrated. Moreover, the *Orlando Furioso* first appeared not as a manuscript but in print, in 1516, though as happens with manuscript poems it was revised by the author who reprinted it in 1521 and again in 1532. The subject-matter was traditional, the war between Christians and Saracens; most of the characters were already known, but the author, learned in Greek and Latin, has a playful wit, a depth of psychological insight, a new realism and a new fantasy, with a wonderful narrative power. It is a remarkably rich poem.

The final achievement of such medieval/Renaissance romance was the *Gerusalemme Liberata*, 'Jerusalem Delivered', by Torquato Tasso (1544–95), a much more serious affair but in the same love-tradition, which brings medieval romance into the full flood of Renaissance humanism. It was accompanied in Italy by a huge amount of other literature, and in particular by the most impressive body of theoretical discourse on the nature of literature (to which Tasso himself contributed) which has ever been produced until the twentieth century. That brings us out of the Middle Ages.

Another great fourteenth-century Italian writer also made a vast contribution to European medieval and particularly renaissance literature. Petrarch (1304–74) wrote an extraordinarily influential set of sonnets to 'Laura', in which love was brought to the greatest refinement and beauty of frustrated desire. He wrote much prose and verse in Latin and was a figure of European fame even in his own day, and for centuries after.

Provençal

The immediate origins of Petrarch's love-poetry, as of that of Northern France, Galicia (i.e. Northern Spain), Portugal, Germany, and ultimately of England, lie in Provence. The general area of the Provençal language was roughly speaking the southern half of what is now France from Bordeaux, but including also in the south-west Catalonia and Valencia. It may be thought of as southern Gaul. The central dialect was called Limousin, but some, including Dante, called the general Provençal cluster of dialects the *lingua d'oc*.

The area maintained a continuity of civilization from Roman times. It was less troubled than the north by barbarian invaders and had a more prosperous climate. Courts which could provide the wealth and leisure necessary for the cultivation of the mind and feelings seem to have flourished early, and among them the court of Poitiers seems to have been pre-eminent. William the Great, the third count of Poitou (993–1030), renowned for his wisdom and for his intellectual and religious interests, kept court in Poitiers (where, as may be remembered, Venantius Fortunatus had ended his days), with his remarkable third wife, the cultivated and well-travelled Agnes of Burgundy. Their splendid court was a focus for many influences. Courtly society was itself part of 'the folk', and consequently part of the general flow of story and song. Some influence must have come from Spain, where the more intellectual and sophisticated

Arabic culture seems to have promoted an interest in love and in the cultivation of sexual feeling that gives us, as will be noted, perhaps the earliest vernacular European love-songs, though in Arabic and Hebraic scripts and contexts. Classical Latin, especially Ovid, medieval Christian Platonist teaching, also in Latin, from Chartres in the north, and presumably also Goliardic Latin love-songs, were known in Poitiers.

The earliest poetical Provençal texts, a fragment of commentary on Boethius, and a saint's life, both of the late tenth century, bear witness to literacy and education but give no hint of what is to come. The first recorded poems are remarkable. They are the eleven poems of William IX (1071–1127) of Poitou, grandson of William the Great. William IX was a riotously violent, bawdy-minded, religiously enthusiastic, jovial sensualist who wrote highly sophisticated verse, most of it now lost. Five of his poems are burlesques and satires, one or two of which challenge comparison in content with coarse army songs of the present day. Five are love-poems. The last, written under the fear of death, reveals a consciousness of serious issues and touches a vein of asceticism hinted at elsewhere. In the delicate art of his love-poems he exalts secular love as the highest good (*summum bonum*) and greatest joy of which man is capable. After him come nearly five hundred known troubadours in the next two and a half centuries, all writing in the Provençal tongue, though a quarter of them came from other countries. It is a body of poetry of great significance in European and indeed human culture.

The love-poems of the troubadours are only part of a great number of debates, satires, serious religious and military songs, and such romances as the famous *Flamenca* (*c.*1240–50), vivid and subtle in its sense of life. But it is in the love-poetry that we find most clearly both the strong sense of the personal 'I' which emerges everywhere in later medieval literature, and also the first potent secular expression of the image of the ideal feminine, as a transforming, ennobling and sweetening influence in human life. It had its parallel (some say its origin) in religious devotion to the Mother of Christ, which was often expressed in Latin prose and verse.

Of this development the handful of William of Poitiers' poems are the portent. There are at times major shifts in the sensibilities of whole peoples, taking long to fulfil, never complete, but affecting the whole tone of a culture, in which the kaleidoscope of fairly constant human potential is given a shake and takes on a new pattern. The original impulse, complex as it must be, can sometimes be partly located in time and place. Such a major shift seems to have originated in the eleventh and early twelfth centuries in Provence, and was expressed as romantic love. For all its bewildering complexity and many self-contradictory elements, it seems that the dominant significance lay in a new recognition of what we may call the feminine aspect of human life. Although based on the bitter-sweetness of men's desire for beautiful women, it implied a recognition of gentleness, pity, and sweetness of temper that transcended the harsh ethics, the fierce untender passions of a warrior code. With the recognition of love went a passionate concept of joy, hard to obtain on earth or in heaven, but available as a reward for arduous and fortunate seeking.

Spanish Literature

Spanish (originally four main dialects and many sub-dialects) was deeply interpenetrated by Arabic and Hebraic culture in the early medieval period because of the conquest of Spain by the Moors. It is said that the earliest medieval European vernacular lyrics are the forty-odd love-poems in Mozarabic Spanish which are written in Arabic and Hebraic characters at the ends of other poems written properly in those languages, and dating from 1040. The themes persisted in later Spanish and Galician poems for many centuries. The large number of later love-lyrics are in Castilian or Galician versions of Spanish (which in its modern form derives mainly from Castilian).

Castilian literature begins with the *chanson de geste*, the *Poema de Mio Cid*, composed about 1140. The narrative of conquest is based on a legendary but actual historical figure, who in the poem is a mature man, a loving husband and father. He is loyal, brave and prudent. His objects are the acquisition of wealth and honour and the poem is both vivid and down to earth. It suggests a less 'primitive' society than that of more northern Europe of the time. Lyric poetry naturally flourished, and the language of Galicia became the language for lyric throughout the peninsula, but the major literary landmark is *The Book of Good Love* by Juan Ruiz, the Archpriest of Hita (*c.*1280–1351). Like a number of medieval authors he seems to have spent some time in prison, which gave him the opportunity to write. The work is a series of narratives and lyrics, mostly about love, written, doubtless, at different periods, not organically unified. It claims to have an autobiographical thread. It is another medieval miscellany which holds together rather better than such a term implies, with a Chaucerian mixture of gaiety and seriousness, of secular and religious interests. It seems a truly 'Gothic' work, Gothic not in the sense of the early destructive barbarians, but as contemporary with the great Gothic cathedrals built throughout Europe in the thirteenth and fourteenth centuries, rich miscellanies of different styles of stone and glass, of types of devotion, of religious and secular concern, of tragedy and comedy.

The development of literary prose is marked in Catalan literature by the chivalric and religious romance *Blanquerna* written by the extraordinary Ramon Llull (?1235–?1316) who was also theologian, mystic and poet, most of whose writing is in Latin. His sense of spiritual love and the mystical value of chivalry gave his writings enormous influence over Europe. The great period of Spanish literature, the Golden Age, the Siglo de Oro, usually dated from *c.*1500 to *c.*1681, can legitimately be regarded as an extension of medieval European literature, but would occupy disproportionate space here. It is extraordinarily rich and reveals many developments of which the most notable perhaps, from the point of view of narrative, is the development of realistic and satirical picaresque novels, the very antithesis in spirit of wildly romantic tales of chivalry which also richly flourished. It was the reading of these romances of chivalry which drove Cervantes' hero Don Quixote mad. The conjunction of satirical realism with romance gave us Cervantes' own book, *Don Quixote* (1604) half-medieval, half-modern, but again, as a succession of narratives loosely connected, a development of the medieval Gothic literary miscellany.

The Emergence of Germanic Vernaculars

Germanic tribes in what are now Germany and Scandinavia pressed southward and westward in the early centuries of the Christian era, battering down the Roman Empire, and sometimes fighting and obliterating each other. The Roman historian Tacitus in his

Germania (A.D. 98) describes the Germanic love of freedom, lack of avarice and luxury, but also notes their laziness, drunkenness, violence, and passion for war. He describes their organization, based on the famous *comitatus*, the band of picked warriors, renowned for courage and loyalty, whose devotion to their king made them ready to die with him – the setting for those stories of heroic endurance, and sometimes of bitter treachery, of loyalty and hatred in endless blood-feud, that make up heroic literature. In the early centuries of the Christian era there was much movement amongst the Germanic tribes, and the period of the fourth to sixth centuries is known as the Age of Migrations, when an intensely complex set of movements by many tribes or confederations of tribes passes through the mists of ancient time, revealed only in glimpses, and by half-understood allusions buried in later history and story. Some of the potent legends of later time derive their origin from this period, particularly as preserved, and greatly changed, in the Icelandic heroic lays of the *Elder Edda*, or *Poetic Edda*. We can deduce an extensive repertoire of heroic lays amongst such peoples, as already noted from the account by Priscus of the Huns, but nothing survives apart from the partial translation of the Bible into the Gothic language in the fourth century. Germanic tribes moved into southern parts of Europe but their kingdoms soon failed. They successfully occupied central Europe, England and Iceland.

In Britain, after the Roman legions withdrew, while the Celtic tribes fought amongst themselves, Angles and Saxons from Schleswig-Holstein, just to the south of Denmark, in the fifth century successfully invaded the island and either subjugated the Celts or drove them into the western parts.

The linguistic situation of Germanic and Celtic tribes in relation to Latin was quite different from that of peoples speaking Romance languages. We are bound to suppose on first principles that Celt and Teuton possessed a substantial body of so-called 'oral literature', and evidence from later writings, and allusions in other records, bear this out. The distinction between Germanic vernaculars and Latin was of a quite different degree from the differences between the various Germanic vernaculars themselves. These various vernaculars developed without record in Europe about the fifth century into the languages which we now know as Old Saxon, Old High German,

Old Norse, Old English, Gothic. They developed their own characteristic structures within the 'family' quite independent of Latin, though as they came into contact with Latin-Christian civilization they took over a number of Latin words and concepts, especially concerning religion.

The Germanic peoples only succeeded in finding a successful written form for their own languages when they were converted to Christianity and thus had to use Latin writing. The Germanic cultures became historically noticeable in a creative way in so far as they were converted to Christianity, the religion of literacy, of the Book. There was in consequence a powerful ecclesiastical influence at work on the independent vernacular, and in a number of cases therefore the first records are religious. There is in all these literatures a most interesting mixture of traditional, Germanic, pagan inheritance and Latin-Christian influence. It must be remembered however that traditional Christianity itself was also an amalgam of elements very different from the modern liberal western conceptions of the late twentieth-century Roman Catholic, Anglican and Reformed churches in advanced industrial societies. Traditional Christianity was in temper and attitude often closer to the paganism it fought than to modern western European and North American Christianity. It was much more absolute in belief, accepted miracles and a supernatural universe, angels, devils, a physical Heaven and Hell.

English Literature

The earliest English records are in ninth- or tenth-century manuscripts but the texts date back in some cases to the seventh century (as with Caedmon) or the eighth century, while the actual material may be even more ancient. Some 30,000 lines of Old English verse remain to us. The verse-line of four stresses, of which three begin with the same letter (alliterating), owes nothing to Latin. Its vocabulary retains characteristic Germanic compounds, although apparently similar phrases may be modelled on the language of Latin hymnology. Old English was an independent literature which eagerly borrowed from Latin. The Englishman Aldhelm, who lived in the second half of the seventh century, and has been called 'the first English man of letters' wrote his considerable body of prose and verse in difficult Latin, but he was enormously influential, and his modern translators remark that 'nearly every facet of his literary output found an English imitator'.[3] Poems in Old English are very varied, albeit nothing light-hearted or improper, such as must have existed, has survived. Probably earliest are the scriptural poems, such as Caedmon and his school composed, both rhetorically skilful and solemnly prophetic. Some, not directly biblical, like *The Dream of the Rood*, have a Romanesque colour and heroic magnificence. The greatest surviving poem is *Beowulf*, both heroic and elegiac, Christian, yet recognizing the supreme virtues of bravery, loyalty and justice in the lost pagan world. It presents an heroic almost entirely masculine, aristocratic, vision of life as a constant combat against evil, in which death must in the end prevail. There is much that is similar in the several effective saints' lives.

Prose emerges in the reign, and under the aegis, of Alfred himself, king of the West Saxons (871–901), great defender of his people, innovator and educator. Perhaps the first prose is the preface Alfred himself added to the translation he commissioned of Pope Gregory's *Dialogues*. Another moving passage is his later preface to the translation of Pope Gregory's *Pastoral Care*, where he meditates on the need for promoting learning in the kingdom. His prose is none the less moving for some uncertainty and lack of polish. Smoother prose-writers followed in the late tenth century, most notably the fluent Aelfric (*fl.*1000) and the menacingly rhythmic Wulfstan (d.1023), whose dire sermon on the state of England, desolated by Viking raids and the vices and feebleness of the English, is worth reading for its sombre eloquence, and to remind us that we have come through plenty of difficult times in the past, and that the country is usually in a mess. Wulfstan's *Sermon to the English* however, and many of Aelfric's sermons, show how pulpit eloquence was attracted to that 'warmth' of oral, rhythmical delivery which brings it at least halfway back in form to alliterative verse. The great specifically *prose* monument in Old English is *The Anglo-Saxon Chronicle* which also owes its origin as we know it to Alfred's inspiration. Beginning as a series of annals, it expands especially for the period of Alfred's wars with the Danes to achieve a remarkable stark simplicity and power. Even the *Chronicle*, compiled by learned and literate men, incorporates a passage of heroic narrative, the miniature saga of Cynewulf and Cyneheard for the year 755, which is possibly an exception to the general rule that prose requires literacy, for it tells a story which must have been handed down orally as a traditional anecdote. The substantial body of Old English prose, written mainly in the tenth and eleventh centuries, witnesses to a powerful effort to create a vernacular culture which was conceived of as leading to Latin, but which has its own value.

After the Norman Conquest of 1066 Old English religious literature continued to be copied, and the *Chronicle* to be maintained, until well into the twelfth century, but English was neglected as the language of high culture. It continued as the language of the English people though under pressure from Latin and French. As the language of literature English slowly recovered until in the fourteenth century it equalled anything written in medieval Europe, of which it was an intimate part.

Old High German and Old Saxon Literature

In Germany the first vernacular literature appears in the eighth century under the influence of Anglo-Saxon. Alliterative verse is used for the *Merseburg Charms*, and the *Hildebrandslied* (a fragment of sixty-eight lines) of about 800, both in Old High German. The latter tells the story of a warrior returning to his home who is forced to fight his own son. The battle between father and son is an ancient, widespread motif, but the names here derive from Gothic legend. Old High German did not retain its independence of Latin for long, and it soon turned to rhyming verse, but Old Saxon, a collateral form, retained alliterative verse for the *Heliand*, a poem celebrating the life of Christ, of about 830. It is a potent mixture, if not compound, of Germanic concepts of loyalty and bravery with Christian commands to love one's enemy.

As with Old English, a number of translations into verse and prose from the Scriptures were made, and from the second half of the eleventh century arises a varied literature in which French influence is progressively apparent. A variant of the Tristan story and a translation of the *Aeneid* appear, but the glory of medieval German literature comes with the romances and lyrics of the late twelfth century, beginning with Hartmann von Aue's versions, about 1200, of Chrétien's poems, and other works. Wolfram von Eschenbach's main work, *Parzival*, is only slightly later. *Parzival* is a long, elaborate, inexhaustibly rich re-handling of the story of Perceval and the Grail which originated in a French poem by Chrétien. It is a fully Christian chivalric poem in which the hero progresses from innocence and some degree of folly through suffering to mature stability and married love. Roughly contemporary, equally great, and very different in tone, is the powerful version by Gottfried von Strassburg of the Tristan story. The essential story is of course of extra-marital love. Gottfried exalts secular sexual love to a state of mystical joy, especially in the episode where the lovers live in a forest grotto in an ecstasy of communion. This passage is a beautiful, sustained allegory of the exclusive secular heaven of romantic love. Yet Gottfried also tells much of the story with rhetorical wit and some degree of flippancy – a mixture of tones, and an inclusiveness of varieties of experience which is characteristic of medieval litera-ture. Equally characteristically, like so many Gothic cathedrals, it is unfinished, though in a sense complete. Different again is the *Nibelungenlied*, which draws on native heroic legend to tell, amongst others, the tragic story of Siegfried and Brunhild, which still echoes through the world in Wagner's music and yet further re-handled version.

The flowering of these romantic and heroic narratives was accom-panied by an equally great achievement in lyrics, especially courtly lyrics of love, *minnesangen*. The greatest of several lyric poets was Walther von der Vogelweide, whose passionate poems make an immediate appeal to the modern reader. Like so many of these poets he praises and longs for his beloved, and expresses both the joy of and also the repentance from love. Like the Goliardic poets he weaves into the expression of feeling his response to the various seasons of the year; and he also writes other poems, sometimes satirical, on the events of his times.

Later medieval German writers do not achieve these heights, but even a brief sketch like this should not omit the late development of down-to-earth comic narratives, *fabliaux* in fact, which appeared with much other writing in German, from the thirteenth to the sixteenth centuries. They were part of the general flotsam of the international comic tale, of which examples appear in all European literatures. The writer known as Der Stricker lived in the thirteenth century, and the latest is perhaps Hans Sachs who wrote in the sixteenth century.

Old Norse Literature

Latest of all, and perhaps greatest, to emerge in the Germanic vernaculars is the literature of Iceland in the Old Norse language. For about thirty years before and after 900, disaffected and enterprising Norwegians, resenting the king Harald Finehair's assertion of authority over the whole of Norway, left the country to colonize the harsh but habitable slopes of Iceland, where other settlers from Norse colonies in Ireland and the Hebrides joined them. They established virtually independent farmsteads, without cities or a king, and managed to combine an insatiable thirst for law with an equally obdurate refusal to abide by it. By 930 they had established a central assembly, the Althing, to which all chief men, with their large retinues, rode across the fissured countryside once a year to make the law, and rode away again to break it. They lived according to an unselfconscious complex code of honour and obligation based on blood-relationship, loyalty and fantastic bravery which had many similarities to equally archaic codes spread throughout Europe, some of them surviving almost to the present day.

Christianity came late to Iceland, and the conversion is dated from A.D. 999. There were few foreign clergy, and the new religion was perhaps more obviously grafted on to current religious views, and less of a new start, than in less marginal countries. Certainly the traditional literature continued to flourish, but was not written down till the early thirteenth century. The *Elder Edda* or *Poetic Edda* is a series of traditional poems on Norse gods and heroes, formulaic in vocabulary, revealing its links with Old English and Old High German poems several centuries and many leagues away.

Beside the *Edda* there was a tradition of more elaborate, enigmatic, perhaps more personal 'skaldic' poetry (*skald* being the Old Norse word for 'bard' or 'poet'), much of which is preserved as fragments in the prose sagas which now began to develop. Some vernacular prose writing is found in Iceland in the early twelfth century, but it is utilitarian and fragmentary. A magnificent prose literature developed in the thirteenth century when Iceland was in the full flow of the European Christian literary tradition. Works on all kinds of subjects, literary and functional, were produced. The learned Snorri Sturluson wrote a prose *Edda* about 1220, which is both a summary of mythology and a manual of poetic instruction. Then follows the great glory of Icelandic literature, fully entitling it to a place not only in European but world literature, the prose sagas. They include the *Laxdaela Saga*, the *Saga of Grettir the Strong*, the *Saga of Eirik the Red*, but the greatest, by general consent, is *Njal's Saga*, written late in the thirteenth century. Part of its greatness arises from the conjunction of Christian and heroic elements. We feel the dark passions and the heroic endurance of a race of men, locked into complex human situations, in which history, accident, goodness and badness of character, work out a deeply moving pattern of fate, freewill, loyalty, love, and suffering. These deeply interesting prose narratives are not novels, though they are vividly realistic, nor romances, though love and adventure are present; nor strictly epics, though they tell of characteristically stoic bravery in the face of hopeless odds fought against till death. Women are present, but as wives and lovers, self-sacrificing or vicious, not as cult-objects. The sagas are based on oral traditions but are essentially written works, deeply considered, unobtrusively learned. Family feuds, historic deeds, piratical expeditions, mythical and mythological episodes, are the subject-matter. The sagas have a tone of plain historical actuality, though they have been created by the highest art. Exact reportage, or analysis, of actual character and event are not part of their aim. But they are also varied; many are short, some are comic. They continued to be written until the seventeenth century but the best are of the thirteenth and fourteenth centuries.

The Emergence of Celtic Vernaculars

The Celtic languages were spoken by the ancient Britons who were in origin Gauls of Iron Age culture who moved from Europe to occupy the British Isles probably early in the third century B.C., killing, or mingling with, or expelling their unknown scanty predecessors. The Celts were in their turn subjugated by the Romans, who imposed new social and administrative structures, but who were content to rule rather than extirpate, much as the modern British, that later amalgam of Celts and English, ruled India from the eighteenth to twentieth centuries. The Romans did not impose their own language on the Celts as they did for example in Spain or France. After the withdrawal of the Romans in the fifth century the English forced the Celts into the further western parts of the island – Galloway, Cumbria, Wales, Cornwall and across the sea to Brittany, where modern Breton remains as a Celtic language. The Celts remained unmolested in Ireland, except in so far as the Vikings occupied Dublin and some other parts. In England the Celts have left such traces as the names of rivers (Thames, Avon) and inhabited places (Winchester, Gloucester) and some large Iron Age hill fortresses. The fifth, sixth and seventh centuries saw a confusion of peoples throughout the island of Britain. North of Hadrian's Wall there were various tribes, now little known, including the Picts, who may themselves have been Celtic.

Welsh Literature

There were certainly 'Welsh' (the name is English and means 'foreign') constituting a small kingdom near Edinburgh, in the seventh century, and the earliest text in the language we now call Welsh is the heroic elegy, the *Goddodin*. It is a lament for the warriors of Edinburgh killed fighting the English at the battle of Catterick in Yorkshire about 600, though the single manuscript in which it survives was written much later. The *Gododdin* derives from the period before the irruption of the North Britons into what is now Wales, which really begins Welsh history, but it seems to be the earliest example of Celtic vernacular that we possess. It again illustrates the problem of the idea of 'emergence', for though it is our first example, and may in some respects look 'primitive', it is the product of a long tradition of oral poetry, displaying a highly-wrought art, perfected probably over centuries, and is far from being an example of tentative beginnings. Other Celtic poems from as early as the ninth century survive, vivid, often poignant, enigmatic. From the seventh century derive the names of famous bards, Taliesin, Aneurin and others, but we cannot for certain attach any work to their names.

Prose as usual comes later, from the beginning of the tenth century; the earlier of the two manuscripts, the *White Book of Rhydderch*, which preserve the great prose masterpiece of Welsh literature (the eleven tales of the *Mabinogion*) was not written until the first quarter of the fourteenth century. There is clear internal evidence in the *Mabinogion* from language, allusions, customs, etc. that the material is traditional, with a long history, though the title is (like *Edda*) relatively modern, and based on a misunderstanding. Much of the subject-matter is wild and strange, mythological and folkloric, probably not always clearly understood by the scribe who wrote it down, and sometimes puzzling to the modern reader. The earliest tale, *Culhwch and Olwen*, is one of the first Arthurian tales, though it is very different from the later Arthurian romances, and is different too from the last three tales of the *Mabinogion*, which are Arthurian romances of a more usual kind, revealing influence from the French or Norman–French versions, and thus of the thirteenth century. This is evidence of the interpenetration of Welsh and European literary culture. The wild and primitive stories, mythological and folkloric, of the first eight tales of the *Mabinogion* draw deep from the past of the race, and from our own minds. We are still ruled by love and death, have intimations of deep movements in nature, see, if only symbolically, that we share our life on this planet with the living creatures that are beast and bird and plant. The writer who gave us the final form of the *Mabinogion* was a great artist, with a feeling for character, and a noble vision of life.

Medieval Celtic poets both Welsh and Irish have a fresh and vivid perception of the natural world, though the earlier poets have little interest in love. They prefer battle, and the strangeness of the otherworld. The poetry is technically very elaborate for bards were trained in bardic schools especially in the skills of praise and satire, and if successful were honoured by kings. But the range of literature was wide, including myth and folklore, and it is no wonder that Welsh stories, especially those connected with Arthur, had a liberating effect on the European imagination when their strangeness and mystery, filtering through interpreters in England and France in the twelfth century, were recognized by the genius of Geoffrey of Monmouth and especially Chrétien de Troyes. The outstanding poet of Wales is the fourteenth-century Dafydd ap Gwilym (*c.*1325–80), a member of a noble family loyal to the king of England. He lived probably in the southern half of Wales. The time of the bardic schools had passed but Dafydd's metrical skill is supreme. He shares the later medieval European interest in love, and maintains the Celtic feeling for nature, but he often treats such themes and religion itself with flippancy. In temperament and in his Gothic mixture of tone he may be compared with Chaucer, Juan Ruiz, and Boccaccio.

Irish Literature

Much that is true of Welsh literature in general applies to Irish. The records of Irish literature begin with pieces on the archaic themes of praise and satire, though the first example to survive is praise for St Columba (c.597) a warrior for God, not for the world. Some poems survive from the eighth century, but prose is remarkably early because the monasteries cherished and recorded, probably from the eighth century onwards, some heroic tales which though primitive in themselves are a tribute to the learning and sense of tradition fostered in the monasteries. The stories are of the heroes of Ireland, belonging to three main groups, of which the most famous is the cycle of Ulster tales, whose hero is Cu Chulainn. They are a combination of fantastic bravery, tragic love, and grotesque fantasy. The chief work is *The Cattle-Raid of Cooley (Tain Bo Cuailnge)* which is the product, as is the way with traditional literature, of many authors and scribes, of which the earliest manuscript is known as the Book of the Dun Cow, written in the monastery of Clonmacnoise in the twelfth century. The work is very mixed in nature, preserving ancient layers of story with more recent styles and interests, very violent and direct, extraordinary and fascinating. The style is at times exceedingly elaborate. Some of the themes of love, revenge and sorrow echo long through Irish literature. From the thirteenth century stories about another hero, Finn, give rise to the Fenian cycle, which became more popular and were developed in thousands of lines of ballad poetry, and other poems and tales continued to be produced until they merge into modern Irish folktale.

The Nature of Traditional Literature

As already noted, one of the characteristics of traditional literature is that certain stories, centred on the same main characters, are told again and again with all sorts of variations. A story 'grows', and is adapted by a sequence of different tellers, or authors, according to their own genius, and the changing tastes of the audience or readers. Usually, therefore, it is assumed that the reader knows something in general about the tale, but the tale can be considerably altered in the telling. The *changes* in stories, whether in prose or verse, are themselves a source of interest, while the 'inner idea' so to speak, of a story, has a certain independence of any teller, has its own nature, sometimes partly in conflict with the way a particular author tells the tale. All traditional narratives therefore may be said to be the product of multiple authorship. Obvious examples outside our period are the Bible and the works of Homer. In this respect they differ from novels: they may well give typical, mythical or symbolic narratives, with varied amounts of realistic detail added, and often incorporating several different points of view. This sometimes puzzles the modern reader who too easily suspects irony where there is a different mixture of elements from those to which he is accustomed, or apparent inconsistency. For example, the heroic Cid (cf. above p. 64) raids defenceless towns and accumulates huge quantities of booty, yet is represented as a devout Christian, and is fanatically faithful to the king who has rejected him. In romances heroes are praised for taking foolhardy risks, and the modern Arthurian scholar, Eugene Vinaver, refers to 'the mad world of Arthur'. Stories that are often retold may develop inconsistencies of characterization. Many stories seem to lack 'organic unity', through their episodic nature. In such cases it is well to remember that traditional cultures are unlike our own. Concepts of bravery for men, chastity for women, being in each case the basis of honour, now outmoded perhaps by modern developments in war and medicine, are rooted deep in traditional literature, but also in many of our own deeper responses. We do not have to scratch very deep into the thin veneer of modern civilization to come upon primitive responses.

Medieval short poems and lyrics are also repeated and varied like the stories. When a great poet comes along, such as Walther von der Vogelweide, Dafydd ap Gwilym or Villon, he sets the stamp of his own genius on familiar material. The balance between the group and the individual is different from that of modern times, where the author reaches his reader through the impersonal regularized medium of print, and has to aim at a high level of originality. Although we cannot recapture oral delivery from the past, we can imagine it to some extent from social occasions in our own lives, and from the study of modern instances of traditional literature in societies where it survives. From such imagination we can partly recreate the sense of the 'warm' oral group, and the joys of social cohesion of an archaic society, which are still partly suggested by traditional literature written in manuscript. For such societies literature is a possession of all, and repetition of story or theme with variation is how the group retains yet develops its possession.

Style

Repetition with variation is also the key to the style of a traditional literature, again seen as easily in the Bible or Homer as in the medieval epic, romance or lyric. Repetition with variation leads to internal patterning rather than careful rendering of the appearances of the outside world. A similar characteristic is the word-play, the puns and verbal patterning which are constantly found in traditional literature, and which though genuine 'play' are not necessarily funny. Translation inevitably destroys puns and much other word-play, which is why we are so unconscious of them as a staple element in the style of the Bible. Anyone who reads a medieval work in the original must be alert to word-play, which until recently was almost universally unrecognized, though now sometimes excessively insisted on, especially in indecent senses.

The sense of literature as a social possession also leads to a fondness in medieval style for the folk-wisdom of proverbs, and of 'wise commonplaces'. It is customary for modern critics to despise this element, or, if it occurs in an admired author, to assume that it is ironical, on the assumption that any writer worth his salt rejects the conventional wisdom of society. Such contempt or expectation of irony is usually mistaken. Traditional literature the world over makes unironic use of proverb and wise commonplace, and the 'sententious style' is to be genuinely appreciated.

Another characteristic of the style and indeed the content of medieval literature, as of all traditional literature, is the use of hyperbole. Knights slaughter thousands of the enemy in a morning's battle, fight up to their ankles in blood, serve ladies for endless years while remaining young. This characteristic also is related to the lack of interest in close plausible representation of ordinary life, of the sequences of ordinary cause and effect. Once again it is sometimes mistaken for irony, or inconsistency, or incompetence. We need to respond to hyperbole rather as to word-play, as an appeal to the play, the sport, of imagination, to the grand 'as if'. It is there for emphasis and colour.

Rhetoric

Much of what has been briefly described as traditional style is also the subject of the rhetorical instruction which was a part of medieval education and literary practice especially in Latin. Rhetoric is nowadays a dirty word, but we would understand it better if we thought of it as it was intended, instruction in 'creative writing'. The great rhetorical treatises of classical Rome were known to medieval men, and in the twelfth century more, and rather inferior, handbooks were produced still in Latin. The details are not important here. They were yet another attempt to civilize men, by enabling them to produce ornate, vigorous, disciplined language, to persuade men to virtuous action or delight them with beauty. The effect, to our taste, is sometimes excess of adornment, of obscurity, of diffuseness in meaning, but the attempt was worthy, and all the great writers show the benefit. The handbooks immensely elaborated what are in fact such qualities of speech as pun, hyperbole, repetition, themselves quite natural. Learned and fussy as medieval rhetoric may sometimes seem to be, it is nevertheless closer to natural speech than the much more disciplined discourse possible in an age of print.

It is salutary to remind ourselves that even nowadays ordinary, popular, unaffected speech, the oral situation, makes plentiful use of repetition with variation, of puns, of the sententious style, of hyperbole. We all, when telling a story, use emphases, recapitulations, word-play, exaggerations. And are not contemporary popular songs still full of such characteristics? These are the essence of rhetoric.

Music

This brings us to a brief consideration of music, so far neglected, but an important element in medieval life and literature. One of the themes of the previous few paragraphs has been the relative lack of interest, in medieval literature, in a naturalistic account of the world (though there are plenty of patches of vivid realistic writing). Even more than popular speech and learned rhetoric, music is necessarily more concerned with its inner logic and patterns than in rendering the contours of ordinary life. And like literature and the visual arts medieval music has a deep difference from the music that developed from the sixteenth century onwards.

Medieval music, like medieval literature, is close to the 'folk', and the folk is everybody, high and low. It is based on what are called 'modes', which correspond to modern keys but have as it were a different shape, different harmonics. The type of early medieval music is Gregorian chant, itself based on folksong. Anyone who has heard traditional Indian or Japanese or other non-European music will be struck with certain resemblances to European medieval music, if only in the usual absence of such features as harmonies and a regular beat. Some modern English folksong, with its irregular timing, slurred notes, and modal structure is close to medieval music.

Music claims our attention partly because of the significant parallel it offers to the development of the other arts but especially because a good deal of early poetry was chanted or sung. Music was often part of the social oral context of literature, and reminds us of an emotional warmth associated with lyric and story that we have inevitably lost. Music stirs the emotions. Taillefer led the Normans into battle singing about Roland. Troubadours wooed their ladies in gentler songs of love. A number of lyrics may have been work-songs, as still in traditional cultures and trades. The music for drinking songs, spinning songs, comic songs, as well as many hymns is known. Although we know nothing of the music to *Beowulf* or *The Song of Roland*, the amount of medieval music that survives in France is particularly large and of good quality. By the fourteenth century we come to such named composers as Guillaume Machaut (above p. 58), a better musician than poet, who produced much secular and sacred music. This is not the place for even a sketch of the history of medieval music, but music as a dimension of the literary imagination is another characteristic of medieval literature. Yet medieval music was not so intimately related to the expression of feeling as later music became. It was more generalized, less 'mimetic'.

The Variety of Medieval Literature

Although we have made an attempt to characterize medieval literature in order chiefly to prevent the disappointments arising from false expectations, the variety of works, attitudes, forms and achievements, over so long a period and so wide a range of countries, is equally striking. Within that period great bodies of stories were created, of Arthur and his knights, of Alexander, of the fall of Troy, of the tricks of Reynard the Fox. Within these constantly re-handled tales there was plenty of scope for different treatments, even for irony, certainly for satire as well as love, tragedy as well as romance. The great body of songs covered a vast range of human expression. In the course of the period a new inwardness of individualism came to be discovered within the encompassing group. Loyalty and honour remained dominant themes, but pity often triumphed both as a secular and a religious emotion. The development of writing deeply changed men's capacity for learning. It will be useful, in a primarily literary survey, to conclude with the words of a French historian of culture.

The long period relevant to our history – for us both as professionals and as men living in the flux of history – seems to me to be the long stretch of the Middle Ages beginning in the second or third century and perishing slowly under the blows of the Industrial Revolution – Revolutions – from the nineteenth century to the present day. The history of this period is the history of pre-industrial society. Prior to these extended Middle Ages, we face a different kind of history; subsequent to them, we confront history – contemporary history – which is yet to be written, whose methods have yet to be invented. For me, this lengthy medieval period is the opposite of the hiatus it was taken to be by the Renaissance humanists and, but for rare exceptions, by the men of the Enlightenment. It was the moment when modern society was created out of a civilization whose traditional peasant forms were moribund but which continued to live by virtue of what it had created which was to become the essential substance of our social and mental structures. Its creations include the city, the nation, the state, the university, the mill and the machine, the hour and the watch, the book, the fork, under-clothing, the individual, the conscience, and finally, revolution. It was a period which, for western societies, at least, was neither a trough in the wave nor a bridge between the neolithic era and the industrial and political revolutions of the last two centuries, but was, rather, a time of great creative growth, punctuated by crises, and differentiated according to the region, social cate-gory, or sector of activity in its evolutionary chronology and processes.[4]

We may finally recall that within the history of this fascinating period, within literary history as a whole, there remain works of art which simply exist in their own right as major examples of the human spirit. They are conditioned in time and space: they can only be approached with some degree of knowledge and sympathetic understanding or they cannot be experienced at all. Some of them, like great mountains, will always be a testing experience. In the end, as art, they transcend history and stand as a continual challenge and solace, a continually renewed source of inspiration to those who seek them.

NOTES

1. H. M. Chadwick, *The Heroic Age* (Cambridge, 1912), 84.
2. Helen Waddell, transl., *Medieval Latin Lyrics* (Penguin Books, 1952), 185.
3. M. Lapidge and M. Herren, transl., *Aldhelm: The Prose Works* (Ipswich, 1979), 1.
4. J. Le Goff, *Time, Work and Culture in the Middle Ages*, transl. A. Gold-hammer (Chicago, 1980), x.

PART III

BEOWULF: AN EPIC FAIRY-TALE

G. T. SHEPHERD

In 1933 Professor J. R. R. Tolkien of Oxford delivered a notable lecture, 'Beowulf: the Monsters and the Critics' (subsequently published in 1936). It has been a key essay in guiding English responses to *Beowulf*. It should be added that it remains a key also to an understanding of the genesis and ethos of Tolkien's *Lord of the Rings*.

Tolkien produced an impression of *Beowulf* as a meditative even elegiac narrative about one of the sweet warmen of old, a hero grandiloquent yet ruminative whose achievement and glory reflect the insubstantiality and mutability of earthly life, who is both a resolute agent and the uncomplaining victim of providence: 'something more significant than a standard hero, a man faced with a foe more evil than any human enemy of house or realm, is before us, and yet incarnate in time, walking in heroic history, and treading the named lands of the North'. This concerns Beowulf not Frodo Baggins, guardian of the Ring. Those readers who do not respond too enthusiastically to the high-hearted gallantry and sacrificial gloom of Frodo in *Lord of the Rings* are less likely to accept Tolkien's presentation of *Beowulf*. In the mid twentieth century some readers have preferred to walk in unheroic history and tread the badlands and the wastelands and discover in this old Beowulf a maudlin militarist or a muscle-and-mind-bound sportsman who much too frequently and tediously proclaims himself the greatest. From this point of view Kingsley Amis in his brief poem *Beowulf* gives a neat and compact critique of the old poem, of its inconsequential story and its muddled hero, and of its inflated reputation among academics.

It is not easy to come to terms with *Beowulf*. The poem on the page is however clear. *Beowulf* is the earliest long secular poem in English. It is preserved in a late tenth century composite manuscript – two different Anglo-Saxon MSS were bound up together in the

seventeenth century when they came into the collection of Sir Robert
Bruce Cotton (1571–1631). *Beowulf*, the fourth item of the second
MS, fills seventy parchment leaves on both sides. The preceding pieces
– a *Life of St Christopher*, *The Wonders of the East*, *The Letter of
Alexander* – are in Anglo-Saxon prose. *Beowulf*, which has no title
in the MS, is written out as if it were in prose. The fifth item is
another verse piece, *Judith*, lacking its beginning, dealing with the
slaying of the tyrant Holofernes. The poem *Beowulf* is not referred
to directly in any Anglo-Saxon record. It can scarcely have been
known at all during the long medieval centuries between the Norman
Conquest and the Reformation. Even then it was not copied out
until an Icelander Thorkelin commissioned a transcript made in 1781.
Later Thorkelin, on the basis of his own transcript, produced the
first edition of the poem at Copenhagen in 1815.

In England during the nineteenth century some interest was shown
but on the whole, certainly up to the time of the Great War, the
study of *Beowulf* was dominated by German scholars. There are still
people who talk about it as if it were a Germanic rather than an
English composition. The best edition of the poem is still *Beowulf
and the Fight at Finnsburg*,[1] a splendid trophy of a century of Germanic
philology. Furnished with Klaeber's *Beowulf*, a castaway knowing
no Anglo-Saxon at all when he landed could make himself a complete
master of the poem and return from his desert isle with strings of
curious questions about northern European literature and society
which only the larger libraries of the world could attempt to answer.
No other text in the whole range of the *Pelican Guide* will be found
to be so expansively and so judiciously edited as our *Beowulf* was
by Klaeber.

Beowulf, as printed, is written in 3,182 long lines of four-stress
alliterating verse, which may be exemplified by its opening:

> Hwæt, we Gárdéna · in géardágum
> *th*éodc*ý*ninga · thr*ý*m gefrúnon
> hu tha *æ*thelíngas · *é*llen fremedon.
> Oft Sc*ý*ld Sc*é*fing · sc*é*athena thr*é*atum
> *m*ónegum *m*ægthum · *m*éodosetla oft*é*ah
> *é*gsode *é*orlas · syththan *æ*rest w*é*arth
> *fé*asceaft *fú*nden; · he thæs *fr*ófre gebád . . .
> (*Beowulf*, 1–7; for translation
> see anthology, p. 352)

As can be seen the alliteration is carried on at least two strong stresses of the line and never on the last. The third main alliterating stress of the long line (the first main stress of the second half-line (e.g. thrým) identifies and prosodically generates the whole long line. As it carries this determining stress, the second half-line is more prominent than the first half-line; it is in the second half-line that thought usually progresses. The first half-line of the next line however often serves to emphasize, modify or qualify thought without taking it much further (as *theodcyninga* varying *Gardena*; *monegum mægthum* repeating *sceathena threatum*). This functional use of stressed alliteration may look strange to us. But ordinary modern speech is still full of these two-stressed phrases often alliterated – kiss and cuddle, humming and hawing, sink or swim etc.; and the rhythms are very familiar to us from childhood: Humpty Dumpty sat on the wall, Humpty Dumpty had a great fall ... ; Little Jack Horner sat in the corner ... ; Mary Mary quite contrary ... The same four-stress beat, as is often remarked nowadays, underlines the verse of many later English poets from Chaucer to T. S. Eliot and beyond. When their lines are read aloud for meaning and rhetorical emphasis, the unstressed syllables fall away and the old measure beats out. In *Beowulf* it is likely that the rhythm was reinforced by harp accompaniment. But any modern English speaker reading *Beowulf* aloud with some attention will soon feel comfortable.

The poem is readily recognized as a product of art and artifice. Only a careless ear and a listless eye will dismiss it as no more than a massive word-hoard. Rhythm, diction, syntax, narrative organization work together; and no translation into modern English can reproduce all the ways in which the resources of the old language were exploited and co-ordinated.

Although *Beowulf* comes to us in written form, it employs many of the verbal habits and conventions of oral composition. That does not mean that the author of *Beowulf* as we have it should be regarded as an illiterate bard: he was not. We can properly assume that he read books and could write. But in composing *Beowulf* he certainly intended it to be heard and to that end he continued in use the diction, syntax and structures adapted to native composition before literacy in the vernacular developed. There is nothing pre-historic about this practice. The work of the Americans Milman Parry and his associate

Albert Lord, undertaken in the first place in the 1920s to illuminate the study of Homer, showed how dependent non-literate Slav narrative poets of the twentieth century still were upon their own trained and capacious memories, upon a stock of formal conventions and particularly upon the use of 'oral formulas'. But through the later medieval centuries, which are indeed often regarded as supported by a manuscript culture, even up to the seventeenth century when public communications are habitually put through printing presses, English poets working in the vernacular – Chaucer, Langland, Lydgate, even Shakespeare as dramatist – still went on composing according to such conventions of oral delivery: they all rely heavily on fixed phrase and proverb-like utterance. They still regarded public recital as the primary method of publication. Manuscripts were *aidesmemoire* rather than a direct medium of communication.

The diction of *Beowulf* is rich as well as formalized. Many words are found nowhere else in Old English poetry nor in prose (all such usages are marked in Klaeber's glossary). Nouns are the most emphatic words in the verse and the most numerous. This dominance of nouns, together with the habit of compounding and variation, in conjunction with the prosody give a characteristic static quality to the poetry. There is weight and force but little flow. Syntax is largely a matter of juxtaposition and aggregation. Subordination of what would now be organized as temporal or concessive clauses seems very indistinct. But the narrative does not proceed in gasps and shudders. Rather it is developed as blocks – in printed texts as paragraphs, often closing with a generality, an essential statement, a proverb or gnome. We like to seek and discuss the ultimate constituents of poetry in shifting but linked imagery with a sharp particularity about it. In *Beowulf* we are not looking for imagery so much as listening for sonorities heavy with undifferentiated meanings. There were aspects of Old English poetry that Gerard Manley Hopkins apprehended, admired and in his fashion imitated.

In *Beowulf* the manner of composition is evolved and developed for narration, but narration understood primarily as the first person utterance of a skilled poet rather than as the detached reporting of events by an objective observer. There is a story in *Beowulf* although it is buried deep in the noise of the narration. Many people have wondered whether the story is adequate for the weight of presentation.

The story when abstracted is simple to follow. When Hrothgar, a successful king of the Danes, builds a splendid hall the malignant humanoid Grendel is aroused to active hostility and for many years the Danes suffer horribly from his assaults and can do nothing to protect themselves.* Far away a young champion, Beowulf the Geat, resolves to help, crosses the sea to Denmark and in single combat in the hall tears an arm off Grendel who flees to his retreat in the wastes to die. The ceremonious rejoicing in the hall turns to grief again when another monster, the mother of Grendel, comes for her revenge and carries off another Dane to devour. Beowulf follows the tracks, dives into an infested mere, finds the she-monster in the underwater cave and slays her with an old sword hanging there which melts down to its hilts in the poison of her blood.* On his triumphant return to the hall, Beowulf is acclaimed, rewarded and exhorted by King Hrothgar to persevere in a life of virtue.* Beowulf leaves Denmark for home and there recounts his adventures to Hygelac King of the Geats. Time passes and Beowulf has himself become King of the Geats and rules for many years, until a dragon slumbering on his treasure-hoard is incensed by the theft of a precious cup to visit the land of the Geats with fire and destruction. In his old age Beowulf prepares to defend his people, and with twelve companions seeks out the dragon's lair. There alone he fights the dragon, is himself mortally wounded but succeeds in slaying the dragon. A young warrior, Wiglaf, who had rallied to Beowulf's assistance in the last fight, rejects the treasure and prophesies doom to the Geat people. Beowulf is splendidly cremated on a headland and his praises sung by his proud and sorrowing people. In this last part dealing with the dragon fight there is much associated material looking backwards and forwards in time, much of it dealing with the cruel dynastic wars among the Swedes.

Nursed on real and varied horrors a modern reader can perhaps understand, in Kingsley Amis's phrase, Beowulf's 'boredom with dragons'. At its simplest the poem is about three fights, and all monsters are very much alike as opponents. *Beowulf* tells much the same story three times over. It is essentially an old fairy-tale. There are all sorts of marvels in it: Grendel, and Grendel's mother, the

* See anthology pp. 352 – 63.

old dragon, the monsters of the mere, memories of the ancient giants, a dreadful cave with supernatural lights and weapons, charms and curses and prodigious feats of strength and endurance. And Beowulf himself falls under suspicion. Is he bee-wulf, the honeyeater, the bear who kills by hugging as Beowulf crushes the ribs of a Frankish champion? What sort of human hero is it who boasts of swimming seven nights on end, who fights underwater a daylong battle with ancient demons, who carries thirty suits of armour in his arms when swimming from Frisia to Skåne? Beowulf is one of the wonders of the North. Seeking analogies for the main story, Friedrich Panzer in 1910 published a collection and study of some hundreds of the 'Bear's Son story' from many parts of the world. In *Beowulf* we have the oldest of the northern versions but not of course the original. Beowulf is as much a part of the fantasy as Grendel, a fairy-tale hero set against a fairy-tale villain. As Kingsley Amis notes, only with Grendel (and his like) is Beowulf really man-to-man: their encounters are remarkably direct and matter-of-fact. Grendel carries an ingenious bag to pop his Danish victims into. Beowulf, once he has caught Grendel, uses the holds of a professional wrestler, technically described. In fighting the dragon Beowulf has a special iron shield made to protect him from fire; and in the final encounter the dragon bites Beowulf in the neck. The poet keeps an eye firmly on un-imaginable objects and all the time the noble braggart verse beats on in a sequence of generalities and idealizations. We cannot think that the poet was trying to be sensational in flashes. But his method does not agree with our notions of literary decorum whereby we expect fact and fiction, realism and idealization to be mutually exclusive. We can recall that *Beowulf* occurs in a manuscript devoted to marvels; the fragments of the legend of Christopher, gigantic, reputedly dog-headed; the reports that Alexander the Great sent back to his master Aristotle of all the wonderful things he had seen in India which if he had not seen for himself he never would have credited. We should be wrong to deny that in these narratives there was no intellectual curiosity and no acquisition of knowledge; but they raise problems of credibility which are familiar to modern readers only in space fiction.

The historicity of the background to *Beowulf* against which the fairy story is set has been closely investigated. The pursuit of historical fact seems to be now in the main a chase of shadows. Nothing in the poem can be plainly related to the known history of the English or of England. Though there is an impressive scatter of names and events relating to Sweden, few Swedish historians nowadays think that an accurate account of Sweden in the sixth or seventh centuries can be constructed from them or round them. There is, however, one event in *Beowulf*, the raid by Hygelac on Frisia, the raid from which in the poem Beowulf carries off his thirty suits of armour, which seems to be corroborated by the Frankish historian Gregory of Tours (*c*.540–94) who would place the raid somewhere about 520, but speaks of Hygelac (Chochilaichus in Gregory) as a king of the Danes not of the Geats. A century later than Gregory an anonymous Latin *Liber Monstrorum* refers to Hygelac, king of the Geats, as a giant whose huge bones were still preserved on an island in the Rhine and gazed on with wonderment. In northern antiquities the Geats, Beowulf's people, are a very elusive tribe, renowned for prodigies, inhabiting mysterious margins, in some ways very like the tribes of which Alexander writes to Aristotle.

Of course there is a lot of historical information in *Beowulf*. It appears to deal directly in the language and thoughts of an historic society – Anglo-Saxon society – with strict court and military etiquette, with kin-structures and family obligations and with personal and social values. It also refers constantly to the material objects of the culture, to halls, arms, ships, equipment and furnishings. There was a time, notably after the discovery of the ship-hoard at Sutton Hoo in Suffolk in 1939, when it was thought that the field archaeology of Anglo-Saxon England would illuminate the study of *Beowulf*. Indeed so it has. It enables us to give a material presence to some of the fittings of which the poet speaks, to the boar-helmets, the swords, the arm-rings, and necklaces, the artefacts of social ritual. To gaze in museums upon material objects stirs the mind. But one is tempted to suspect now that *Beowulf* throws more light on Sutton Hoo than Sutton Hoo does on *Beowulf*.

Questions about the historicity and factuality of *Beowulf* affect opinions about the authorship and date of the poem. The questions are unavoidable no doubt, the attempts to answer them interesting, the conclusions it must be admitted are merely speculative. Obviously the poem was composed before it was written down, shortly before the year 1000, in the language of the West Saxons, the standard literary language of late Anglo-Saxon England. Obviously also it was composed after the Christianization of England in the early seventh century. On a balance of probabilities it has been generally held for some time that the poem comes from the eighth century. The strongest argument for this dating was an assumption that the favourable treatment of the Danish story would have been distinctly unlikely during the centuries when the Vikings were raiding England (and the first raid was in 793 on Lindisfarne). Further, some Mercian traces in the language of *Beowulf* and some faint cultural and historical associations have combined to convince scholars that *Beowulf* should be related to an Anglian court – perhaps to the court of Aldfrith of Northumbria (d.705), more likely to the court of Offa the Great of Mercia (d.796). There is no solid evidence for either or for any similar ascription.

On several counts it is unfortunate that the provenance is so obscure. *Beowulf* has as a poem sufficient scope and genius for it to be regarded as a summation of a culture, as the *Faery Queene* is of Elizabethan culture or Tennyson's *Idylls of the King* of the Victorians. These two later poems give to a national story what at first sight seem timeless treatments, which yet on scrutiny become highly informative and interpretative of very distinctive phases of English life. *Beowulf* seems to be that sort of poem. That it cannot be properly localized or dated produces an effect of telescoping all Anglo-Saxon cultural history – all five long centuries of it – into one mould and temper. In this respect and in other matters relating both to form and content it is facile to ask more of *Beowulf* than it can fairly be expected to provide.

For *Beowulf* responds all too vaguely to over-simple and over-comprehensive inquiries. It alludes to and subsumes schemes of thought and the milieu of a particular society, reminiscences of a social past to all of which we have no real access. We would like things to be much clearer and often pretend that they are. It is a fairy-story wrapped up quite confidently in an unexplicit Christian metaphysic. There may be bits of a more ancient mythology sprinkled through it, but the old myths cannot be reconstructed. It suspends even the normal workings of a fairy-tale. At the very points in monster-killing stories where magic is brought into play – for example, when the gift sword Hrunting should be put to use – the poet substitutes and emphasizes instead the efficacy of human virtue and divine providence. There are marvels in the world of *Beowulf* but no magic. To many readers of fiction this seems irrational, perhaps even disappointing. We would prefer a stronger paganism, we might even be satisfied by a more up-to-date Christianity. As it is we often seek crude tensions in the poem; or we try to remythologize the narrative, or allegorize it and wonder whether Beowulf the dragonslayer with his twelve men is not to be related to Christ and the disciples; or we moralize the story with the help of the Church Fathers and explain it all as an exemplification of the vanity of this world and the cupidity of unregenerate man. Such interpretations abound and most of them assume ingenuity and cryptographic skill on the part of the poet and his audience, ancient and modern, which are scarcely credible.

That early audience took the poem more directly. At the same time it is unlikely that they understood it fully in the way that modern scholars, and indeed modern readers, would wish to understand so challenging a text – that is, to know the meaning and weight of each phrase, to recognize each allusion and every gnomic form, to trace a taut line of argument throughout and bind the whole into a message. *Beowulf* is no genuine oral composition out of one tribe's memory. It draws on many pasts. It recalls the Flood and the curse of Cain, the names of lost tribes, half-forgotten distant dynasties, scraps of stories floating in the dark backward over continents. It looks as if *Beowulf* is the reflective composition of a Christian man, aristocratic and traditionalist in sympathies, well practised in fitting English words together, acquainted with some Latin, pretty certainly with service books, probably a cleric, possibly a layman. It may be remembered that the layman King Alfred of Wessex was primarily responsible for a development of vernacular composition, lay bookishness and literacy and for some of the historical enthusiasms of the late Anglo-Saxon period, as well as for the promotion of the West Saxon dialect as its literary vernacular. In some households of thanes in the tenth century learning, antiquarianism and a traditional vernacular piety flourished. And this milieu would suit the author of *Beowulf* well. By the year 1000 some such households were undoubtedly Anglo-Danish in inheritance.

The poet's interest in the past is not of course well summed up by our word antiquarianism. It is better described as a romanticism. It is this aspect of *Beowulf* which Tolkien exemplifies much more powerfully in *Lord of the Rings* than he did directly in his lecture about *Beowulf*. The poem is charged with evocation of an ancient unrealizable world of which the details may sound precise and solid, but it is their resonance that matters.

A patient reader working through the Old English text will again and again find lines and paragraphs that produce the high romantic shiver. The monsters of the deep

> symbel ymbsæton · sægrunde neah
>
> (sit around the banquet near the bottom of the sea).

The sword melts into battle-icicles as ice does

> thonne forstes bend · Fæder onlæteth
> onwindeth wælrapas · se geweald hafath
> sæla ond mæla
>
> (1609–11)
>
> (when the fetters of frost the Father
> releases, unwinds the ropes on the pools,
> for He has control of times and seasons).

But the poet's power is shown best in longer passages: in battle encounters (and no poetry in English brings out more strongly, without prurience or prudishness, the desperation of hand-to-hand combat); or the barbaric solemnities of cremation, when the smoke rises and the flames roar, heads of the dead melt and old wounds gush with blood; the melancholy of the so-called elegies,★ the laconic stillness of the death of Beowulf when his spirit is heavy, wavering, ready for the dying, the end so very near. Throughout the poem the vigorous formal verse is fully charged with sentiment, carried by verbal choice, nuance and contextual contrast. And often, and perhaps surprisingly within their scope, these fairy-tales open up to reflection the great unanswerable Byronic questions:

> What are we and whence came we? What shall be
> Our ultimate destination?

★ See anthology pp. 362–3.

There is perhaps a touch of theatricality about it all as befits romantic poetry. It is primarily an entertainment dignified by style and by wonders. In the tenth century we may note that there are several Anglo-Saxon works, little read nowadays, which seem to cater for a similar appetite, with stories and lore from Greece and from India, apocryphal scriptures and lives of astonishing saints. In the last century of Anglo-Saxon culture, when *Beowulf* was put into a manuscript, there was a precocious interest in what, when it developed more fully in the twelfth century, is classified as medieval romance.

It may be that *Beowulf* was composed much earlier and that tales of wonder and imagination were always peculiarly attractive to the Anglo-Saxon mind. In a general history of English literature and culture this old inheritance has not been commonly admitted. Matthew Arnold, who it would appear never read *Beowulf*, admired in some areas of learning and scholarship that patience, honesty and earnestness which he saw as the marks of contemporary Germanism. He saw the dominating element of English culture similarly – 'The Englishman as far as he is German – and he is mainly German' in his practicality continued 'the humdrum habit of the creeping Saxon'. According to Arnold it was from the early Celts that later English poetry 'got three things: its turn for style, for melancholy, and for natural magic'. It is in Welsh, in the work of the Welsh storyteller above all, that 'one is struck by the use of material of which he knows not the history, or knows by glimmering tradition merely; – stones "not of this building" but of an older architecture, greater, cunninger, more majestical'. All this may be true. Nevertheless, whenever *Beowulf* was composed its poet was certainly master of these crafts, in style, and in the management of sentiment and memory. Perhaps an 'insular culture', the Anglo-Celtic culture, developed in Britain during the first millennium was more a common culture than we like to admit. The Normans after the Conquest regarded the people of this island as a whole as an odd, rather old-fashioned set, in particular as over-subtle, too dreamy and imaginative. Sometimes when reading *Beowulf* we may think the Normans right.

NOTE

1. Fr. Klaeber, ed., *Beowulf and the Fight at Finnsburg*, with introduction, bibliography, notes, glossary and appendices (New York, 1922).

BYZANTINE LITERATURE

ROBERT BROWNING

By Byzantine literature is meant the Greek literature of the Middle Ages, from the end of the fifth to the middle of the fifteenth century. The Byzantines were aware that their culture had roots both in that of classical and post-classical Greece and in the Judaeo-Christian culture of the early Christians and the age of the Church Fathers, to say nothing of the political ideals and practices which they inherited from the Roman Empire, of which the Byzantine Empire was the continuation. Their literature reflects their complex past; it is Greek in language and expression, Christian in tone and content, and often Roman in the consciousness of superiority which permeates it.

Many of the classical Greek literary genres had become obsolete or transformed by the fifth century A.D. Dramatic performances no longer took place, or if they did it was at a sub-literary level. There were no longer occasions for choral lyric. Political oratory had no place in the Christian Roman Empire, and forensic oratory almost as little. Yet there was perhaps more public speaking than ever before, in the form of panegyrics, funeral orations, addresses of welcome, church homilies and the like. Indeed the art of rhetoric not only formed the basis of the higher education of the upper classes, but came to dominate in greater or less degree all forms of literary expression.

At the same time new literary forms developed to answer new needs, in particular those of the Christian church and a Christian society. The sermon, an address of moral and doctrinal exhortation to a congregation, became an important form of applied rhetoric. The life, virtues, and death of the holy man provided the subject for a new type of biography. Church discipline, theological polemic, and ascetic practice each gave rise to a body of writings placed midway between literature proper and technical instruction. The liturgical needs of a church which no longer maintained the humble profile of a minority group led to the growth of a rich and complex ecclesiastical poetry whose style, metre, and content were very different from those of classical Greek poetry.

The slow process of linguistic change meant that already by the sixth century spoken Greek was in many respects closer to modern Greek than to the language of Sophocles or Demosthenes. Yet such was the prestige of classical literature and such the strength of a teaching tradition based on its study, that almost all Byzantine literature until the last centuries of the empire is written in an archaizing language, command of which called for long study, and which grew more and more distinct from the Greek of everyday intercourse. Yet it was not a language unintelligible to the mass of Byzantines, as Latin was unintelligible to most western Europeans in the Middle Ages. Literacy of an elementary kind was widespread by medieval standards. Schools were often to be found in provincial cities. Though a small minority could compose with assurance in the learned tongue, passive and limited comprehension of it was common. Certain kinds of writing, such as technical manuals and works of popular devotion, were often composed in a language intermediate between the spoken and the learned tongue.

In what follows the main genres of Byzantine literature will be surveyed. Purely technical writing, on such subjects as medicine, law, and mathematics will not be discussed, nor will such educational works as manuals of grammar and rhetoric and commentaries on ancient authors. Much ecclesiastical writing, including homilies, dogmatic, polemical and ascetic treatises, works on canon law and the like, will also be omitted. It must be borne in mind, however, that many such works were widely read and appreciated by the Byzantines, whose criteria of what constitutes literature were not the same as ours.

Secular Poetry

The epic tradition never died out in the ancient world, and in the fifth century it was given new life. Nonnos of Panopolis' immense *Dionysiaca* is epic in form only and is in reality an extended panegyric of the god. Shorter narrative poems in Homeric verse were written by Tryphiodoros (*The Fall of Troy*), Musaios (*Hero and Leander*) and Kolluthos (*The Rape of Helen*), and much occasional poetry in hexameter or elegiac metre was written in the sixth century. Paul the Silentiary's poem on the church of Hagia Sophia in Constantinople, an expansion of the traditional Hellenistic description of a work of art, is an adaptation of an old form to a new theme.

Homeric verse, however, was difficult to write and to appreciate, both because of the metre and because of the peculiar vocabulary and morphology of the traditional epic language. Around A.D. 500 one Marianos 'rewrote' the works of many Hellenistic poets in iambic trimeters, using the language of literary prose. It was in this metre and language that George of Pisidia, in the early seventh century, wrote his long poems on the wars of the emperor Heraclius and on the six days of the Creation. In abandoning Homeric language and metre for his narrative poems he was breaking with a tradition of nearly a millennium and a half. The devices of rhetoric took the place of Homer's surge and thunder. The poem on *The Recapture of Crete* by Theodosius the Deacon (tenth century), and the many historical poems of Theodore Prodromos (twelfth century) are composed in the same metre and style, and display in a higher degree than George of Pisidia the tendency to let panegyric replace narrative.

Occasional poetry too abandoned the traditional metre, language and style, and adopted the iambic metre and the language of prose. From the early ninth century a succession of poets composed short occasional poems. Those of Theodore of Studios (early ninth century) are spare and neat. By the tenth century John Geometres, who also occasionally tried his hand at Homeric metre, writes iambic poems of great clarity, linguistic purity, and imagination, which suggest close study of classical models. Less distinguished epigrammatists of the tenth and eleventh century included Leo Choirosphaktes, Christopher of Mitylene and John Mauropous. By the twelfth century there were few men of letters who did not compose occasional verse, usually in iambic metre. None equalled Theodore Prodromos* in virtuosity and output. Many of these twelfth-century poems are of considerable length. The distinction between the epigram and the panegyrical narrative poem was being effaced, and a

---

* See anthology pp. 372–3.

new poetic genre emerging. The epigram and the expanded epigram remained favourite Byzantine literary forms till the mid-fifteenth century. Most writers do not get beyond elegant versification. Manuel Philes (mid fourteenth century) rises above his contemporaries in fertility of imagination and occasional satiric vigour.

Side by side with the iambic metre and the more recherché Homeric metre we find from the eleventh-century poetry written in a metre and style which had no classical antecedents. This was a fifteen-syllable line with stress rhythm – corresponding to 'the king was in his counting-house, counting out his money' – which lent itself to antithetic and triadic construction. The new metre suited the natural rhythm of the language, soon rivalled the iambic metre, and became and remained the favourite vehicle for popular poetry and folk-song. It was chosen by a notable eleventh-century mystic, Symeon the New Theologian, for most of his remarkable poems. It was much used in compositions addressed to the less learned, such as John Tzetzes' allegorical explanations of Homer and his vast and discursive commentary on his own letters. Constantine Manasses composed in it his romantic world chronicle. In the later Byzantine period it was used in poetry of every kind.

The twelfth century was innovative in content as well as in form. Purely fictitious narrative had been rare in the ancient world and unknown in the earlier Middle Ages. In the mid twelfth century a number of romantic novels were composed, mainly in iambic or fifteen-syllable verse, although one is in prose. They owe much in plot and treatment to the Greek novels of Achilles Tatius, Heliodorus and Xenophon of Ephesus and like these are set in a timeless antique world. Often tedious and repetitive, they nevertheless show on occasion sharp psychological insight. First-person narrative, flashback and other devices contribute to a sophisticated narrative technique. Fictitious narrative of another kind is represented by the poem of *Digenis Akritas*,★ recounting the adventures of a hero in the wild borderland between the Byzantine Empire and the Muslim Caliphate. It survives in several versions, of which the earliest belongs to the twelfth century. It may owe something to lost oral ballads. But it is the work of a literary poet, not unacquainted with classical tradition. The

★ See anthology pp. 373–4.

differences between the surviving versions may indicate subsequent oral transmission. It is thus only partially comparable with the Old French *chansons de geste* and the Spanish *Poema de Mio Cid*. Scenes from the Digenis story are often represented on middle Byzantine painted pottery.

The twelfth century also saw a few occasional attempts at poetry in the spoken tongue – satirical or genre poems to which the imitation of vulgar speech added piquancy. It was not until after the disaster of the Fourth Crusade and the break-up of the Byzantine Empire that vernacular Greek found significant literary use. The late thirteenth and early fourteenth century saw a sudden burst of vernacular poetry. The principal genre represented was the romance of chivalry, of which some half a dozen survive. All are marked by a complex plot, a flowing narrative style, elaborate descriptive passages, and a mixture of realism and folk-tale or fairy-tale motifs. All show the influence of western romances of chivalry, and some are actual adaptations of surviving Old French or Italian poems. At the same time they all embody much that is traditionally Byzantine in theme and treatment. Among other vernacular poems of the period were *The Chronicle of The Morea*, a long account of the foundation and early history of the Frankish principality in the Peloponnese, several treatments of themes from the Trojan cycle, pseudo-historical poems on Alexander the Great and Belisarius, satirical allegories of the beast-fable type, laments for defeats in war, poems of moral edification, and much else. None of these poems is likely to have been composed orally, although certain versions of some of them may have passed through a stage of oral transmission. Though some of this vernacular literature was composed in areas of Frankish occupation, much of it is clearly Constantinopolitan, and there is no reason to suppose that the use of the vernacular originated in regions under western rule. Rather it reflects a certain crisis of confidence in traditional values within Byzantine society. So great, however, was the prestige of the learned language and the tradition which it embodied that the spoken tongue remained limited to what was in medieval terms frivolous literature. There was no breakthrough of the vernacular on all fronts, and no Greek Dante.

Liturgical Poetry

Song formed part of the liturgy of the church from the earliest times. Short rhythmical stanzas of prayer or glorification known as *troparia* developed out of the responses following psalms and lessons. At the same time many Christian writers from Clement of Alexandria (d. *c.*215) to Sophronios, Patriarch of Jerusalem (d.638) composed religious poems in classical metres and style, but these were not found suitable for liturgical use.

In the sixth century a more elaborate poem, the *kontakion*, replaced the simpler *troparia*. In form the *kontakion* was a series of up to twenty stanzas, all constructed according to the same rhythmical pattern, and all concluding with the same short refrain. In content it was a narrative homily recounting an event of biblical history or the life of a saint or martyr, often in dramatic form. In its developed form the *kontakion* was a poetic form of great richness, complexity, and versatility, which challenges comparison with the choral lyric of ancient Greece. Like the latter it was a combination of words and music forming part of a ritual occasion.

The greatest composer of *kontakia*, Romanos the Melode,* was a Syrian, possibly of Jewish origin, who came to Constantinople early in the sixth century. More than 1,000 *kontakia* were attributed to him, of which eighty-five, not all authentic, survive. His lucid and uncomplicated style, simple but striking imagery, psychologically credible dialogue, and endless rhythmical inventiveness guarantee him a place among the greatest of Greek poets. Theological subtleties escape him. But he can combine deep religious feeling with warm human empathy. The music of his *kontakia* is unfortunately lost. A *kontakion* of unusual form and unknown authorship, the Akathistos hymn, is still in liturgical use in the Orthodox church.

By the end of the seventh century a new form of liturgical poem was in use, the *kanon*. In form this is a series of nine odes, each of several stanzas, each ode displaying a different rhythmical pattern – as it were, nine successive *kontakia*. Unlike the *kontakion*, the *kanon* was concerned solely with praise, and each of its odes echoed and alluded to one of the nine biblical canticles. As nine different melodies

---

* See anthology pp. 365–6.

were called for, and as a more ornamental, melismatic style of singing was developing, the music played a more important role than in the *kontakion*. The length of the poem encouraged repetitiousness and inflated style. The first great composer of *kanons* was Andrew of Crete (*c.*660–*c.*740) one of whose *kanons*, of 250 stanzas, is still in liturgical use. Others included John of Damascus (first half of the eighth century), Theodore of Studios (d.826), Joseph the Hymnographer (d.886), Leo XI (d.912) and John Mauropous (d. *c.*1055). After the eleventh century no new hymns were added to the Constantinopolitan liturgy. But *kanons* were still composed as literary exercises or for local use up to the end of the Byzantine period. Many are still unpublished.

History

The Byzantines were proud of the long and continuous literary tradition of Greece, going back to Homer, of the political traditions of the Roman Empire, originating in the conquest of the Hellenistic east by Rome, and of the unbroken current of Christian thought which linked them in the past to the Apostles and in the future to the Second Coming. They therefore valued history, which they sometimes saw as their own private possession.

From the first they found themselves heirs to a historiography which had two roots. The first lay in classical Greek and Roman historians, who, though with many differences of approach, were interested in historical causes and the influence of personalities on events, and in general dealt with their own times or those immediately preceding. They were men of letters, using elevated language, rhetorical speeches, graphic descriptions, and a high, moralizing tone. The other was in the Christian world chronicle, whose purpose was to exhibit the working of providence in history. The chronicler's view of causation was theological, and his characters black and white. As befitted technical writing, he used a plain and unrhetorical style and avoided displays of learning. Since such writing demanded less effort to read and appreciate than did the more literary history, it easily became material for entertainment as well as for edification.

The century between the accession of Justinian in 527 and the Arab conquests of the late 630s saw a notable development of both types of history. Procopius (d. *c*.562) wrote of Justinian's great wars of reconquest, and provided in his *Secret History* a malicious but revealing commentary on his own work. Agathias (d.583) took up the story in 552 where Procopius left off, and continued it to 558. His *History* was continued up to 582 by the lost work of Menander Protector, which in turn was continued to 602 by Theophylact Simocatta. Much as they differ, all four historians share an imperial point of view, a serious interest in causes and characters, a lofty style and a detached literary persona. During the same period world chronicles from the Creation to their own age were composed by John Malalas of Antioch (*c*.565) and by the anonymous author of the *Paschal Chronicle* (*c*.628). Both adopt a strictly annalistic structure, attribute the cause of events to divine favour or wrath, avoid speeches, descriptive set pieces and rhetorical ornament, and use unpretentious language marked by popular traits. Malalas shows great interest in anecdotes, marvels, and local Antiochene affairs and has a naïve narrative talent. The *Paschal Chronicle* is less lively and more narrowly theological in tone. Side by side with these two main historical genres, others were also practised – antiquarian studies by John the Lydian (*c*.490–*c*.560) and others, accounts of particular wars by such as John of Epiphaneia (*c*.600), church history by Zacharias Scholasticus (d.553), Evagrius (early seventh century), and John of Ephesus (*c*.507–*c*.586) (who, though living in Constantinople, wrote in his native Syriac).

The Persian and Arab conquests brought a political, economic and cultural break, which is reflected in literature. Like classicizing poetry, classicizing history ceased to be written and was not revived again until the ninth century. George of Pisidia recounted Heraclius' wars as Procopius had of those of Justinian; but his medium was iambic verse, his tone panegyric, and his language strongly biblical. Thereafter only chronicles seem to have been written. There are indications of lost Greek chronicles in the eighth century and the beginning of the ninth. But the next complete texts to survive are the chronicles of George Syncellus, extending to the age of Diocletian, and its continuation by Theophanes Confessor (d.818). Theophanes draws on a variety of lost sources, and is of great value for the history of the Dark Ages, although his approach is theological and uncritical. Theophanes' chronicle was translated into Latin by the papal librarian Anastasius *c.*875. His contemporary Patriarch Nicephorus (d.829) composed a history of the period 602 to 769, evidently intended as a continuation of the work of Theophylact Simocatta. But his methods and style are worlds apart from Theophylact's, and recall those of Theophanes. The world chronicle of George the Monk, written a little later, was in its earlier portion an uncritical compilation, and in its later a naïvely theological account of events. An early translation into Old Slavonic influenced early Russian historiography.

The later ninth and early tenth centuries saw political and military recovery and an attempt to recreate the classicizing culture of late antiquity. Artists often abandoned the flat and abstract manner of the early Byzantine world and turned to illusionistic classical models for both iconography and style. Ancient Greek historians were eagerly copied and read. This renewed interest was reflected in two histories of the ninth century composed under imperial patronage, those of Genesios and of the so-called Continuators of Theophanes. Both have a political rather than a theological point of view, an interest in character, a versatile narrative style, and classicizing language. They bear witness to what their generation had learned from the classical historians and from Plutarch. Despite their air of objectivity both were partisan, and occasionally dishonest, works; but they mark a return to a tradition of historiography forgotten for three centuries. From then on to the Fourth Crusade there was no generation without its historian, who often took up his narrative where his predecessor had ended. All followed the restored classical tradition. Many had experience of affairs and privileged access to information. Together they provide a continuous and detailed narrative of two and a half centuries of Byzantine history.

Symeon Magister wrote a world chronicle whose last section was a detailed account of the first half of the tenth century. Leo the Deacon recounted events from 959 to 976. The *Chronography* of Michael Psellos★ covers the years from 976 to 1059; in its latter portion the author's own personality and opinions are to the fore. His brilliant descriptions and subtle depiction of character often mask a notable lack of objectivity. Michael Attaleiates recounted events from 1034 to 1080, while John Skylitzes took a longer view of the years 811 to

★ See anthology pp. 367–71.

1057, drawing on many historical works now lost. The life and times of Alexius I Comnenus were treated by his son-in-law Nikephorus Bryennios, whose *Materials for History* deals with the years 1070 to 1079, and at greater length by his daughter Anna Comnena. Her *Alexiad* is both a panegyric of her admired father and an imaginative recollection of her own youth. Anna was a woman of passion and prejudice, incapable of the objectivity for which she sincerely strove. Intelligent, uniquely well informed, and with a natural talent for narrative and description, she is one of the greatest historians of the Middle Ages. Her stilted, classicizing language and her delight in displaying her not inconsiderable learning hinder but do not break the grand sweep of her narrative. The *Alexiad* was continued in more modest and sober tone by John Kinnamos, whose history covers the years 1118 to 1176. The task of narrating the catastrophic decline and collapse of the empire of the Comneni was taken up by Niketas Choniates, writing after the capture of Constantinople by the Fourth Crusade. His history deals with the years from 1118 to 1206, the period after 1180 being treated in greater detail. A man of wide interests and good access to information, Niketas knew that he was living in a period of rapid decline, the causes of which he sought to illuminate. His analysis of the deterioration of relations with the west is lucid and pitiless, his account of the inadequacies of the successors of Manuel I avoids over-simplification. A complex narrative style, which occasionally blurs chronology, and a versatile and creative use of the traditional learned language make him a difficult but reward-ing historian.

World chronicles continued to be written in the twelfth century, but the old naïve theological approach no longer satisfied more sophisticated readers. John Zonaras brought to his chronicle the critical judgement of the historian. Constantine Manasses gave to his chronicle – in fifteen-syllable verse – something of the romantic tone of the twelfth-century novels.

After the Byzantine restoration of 1261 George Akropolites picked up the story of the empire where Niketas Choniates had left it. His history deals with the Nicaean rulers, their gradual ousting of all their rivals, and their return under Michael VIII to Constantinople in 1261. His narrative was continued to 1308 by George Pachymeres. Both historians are lucid, objective, occasionally sceptical, much preoccupied with religious disputes. Pachymeres affects a more inflated and rhetorical style than the spare Akropolites. The mid fourteenth century produced two notable but very different historians. Nikephoros Gregoras, a polymath and all-round man of letters, covered in his history the years from 1204 to 1359, but treated in detail only the last forty years. Serious, critical, well-informed, with an eye for social change as well as for politics and war, he tended to diffuseness and lack of structure. When he came to narrate the religious disputes of the 1340s, in which he played a part, he lost control of his narrative, and even included some of his own speeches and writings verbatim. The emperor John VI Kantakuzenos (1347–54) wrote his history as a monk after his abdication. It covers the years 1320–56, and is essentially an apology for his own failure, behind which he discerns the failure of the Byzantine empire and its society. His clear structure and smooth narrative lend an air of objectivity to a personal and partisan memoir. Both Gregoras and Kantakuzenos were using the traditional form of classical history to respond to unprecedented challenges, and not fully succeeding in their endeavour. For nearly a century after them history remained silent. The times were too disjointed, the problems too disconcerting, and the leisured, urbane society for which historians had written too threatened. Only jejune or derivative chronicles and occasional local histories were produced.

The shock of the capture of Constantinople by the Turks in 1453 and the end of the Byzantine empire offered a new challenge, to which four men responded, each in his own way. The statesman and courtier George Sphrantzes wrote an account of the years 1413 to 1477, which is a kind of expanded diary. He sees events from the standpoint of the imperial court, yet can criticize many of the decisions made there. His style is direct and unpretentious. Dukas spent a lifetime in the service of Genoese rulers in the Aegean. His *Chronicle* treats the period from 1341 to 1462. His Latin connections and sympathies do not blind him to the tragedy of the Byzantines, which he recounts with clarity, objectivity, and occasional passion, in a strange mixture of learned and spoken Greek. The Athenian Laonikos Chalkokondyles covers the years 1298 to 1463. His history of Byzantium gradually becomes a history of Ottoman expansion to fill the vacuum left by Byzantine decline. With a Polybian sweep he surmounts the limits of the traditional Constantinople-centred and providential history. Lastly, Michael Kritoboulos, a trusted vassal of Sultan Mehmed II, writes the history of the years 1451 to 1467 from an Ottoman standpoint, applying all the motifs of imperial panegyric to Mehmed. Yet he wrote in an even more learned and allusive Greek than any of his contemporaries. In these various ways Byzantine historians adapted the traditions of their art to the new circumstances.

Biography

The Byzantines, perhaps because of their theological view of the world, did not retain the classical interest in individual character. There is no secular biography until the thirteenth century and little then. Though some histories, such as those of Psellos and John Kantakuzenos are partly autobiographical, there is little formal auto-biography. One type of character, however, was of absorbing interest – that of the holy man. The pattern of the saint's life was already set in the fourth century by Athanasios' *Life of Antony*. Many thousands of Byzantine saints' lives survive, from every period from the fifth to the fifteenth century. They can be roughly divided into popular lives and high-level lives. The former are often of provincial origin, and celebrate the superhuman virtues and miraculous powers of the man who turns his back on his society in order to become a bridge between heaven and earth. The latter are usually metropolitan and recount the tribulations and triumphs of one high in the church hierarchy; doctrinal orthodoxy and church discipline play a larger part in such lives than miraculous healing powers. But the distinction must not be pressed too hard. Many saints' lives found liturgical use, and were collected in Menologies, Menaea, Synaxaria, Panegyrica and other liturgical compilations. The revived classicism of the tenth century led to a stylistic revision of many of the early saints' lives, in which much of their concrete detail was replaced by elegant rhetoric and pious reflection. By the eleventh century the liturgy had become fixed, and the composition of saints' lives became a purely literary activity, which was pursued with undiminished zeal by men of letters up to and beyond the fall of Constantinople. Lives of saints are important not only for the information they often contain, but for their reflection of the ideals, desires and fantasies of Byzantine society. In some ways they filled the place which in other societies is filled by works of fiction.

Oratory, Essays, etc.

The study and practice of rhetoric were the basis of higher education in the Byzantine world, and its influence permeated every kind
of literature. The practice of preaching sermons lapsed in the early
Middle Ages, but was soon restored.

Thousands of specimens of this ecclesiastical oratory survive, either
separately in liturgical collections, or in collections of homilies by a
single author. The contents vary from doctrinal subtlety to moral
exhortation, from textual exegesis to social criticism. Among the
more noteworthy preachers were Andrew of Crete and Joseph of
Thessalonica (eighth century), Photios and Leo VI (ninth century),
John Mauropous (eleventh century), John Xiphilinus and Eustathios
(twelfth century), Nikephoros Choumnos and Gregory Palamas
(fourteenth century). Secular oratory took the form of panegyrics on
emperors, patriarchs and dignitaries, funeral and memorial speeches,
and miscellaneous ceremonial addresses. From the eleventh century
on there is an immense wealth of this occasional literature, which
often fulfilled a function comparable to that of modern journalism
in disseminating information and forming opinion. Repetitive,
mannered, rich in allusion but poor in content, they nevertheless yield
much information on political and intellectual life; and their technical
virtuosity is often remarkable.

Akin to the speech is the letter,* a literary genre eagerly cultivated
by the Byzantines. Their letters are rarely vehicles for concrete information – that was provided orally by the bearer – but they often
reflect with great subtlety the nuances of personal relationship. Other
letters are in effect literary, moral or philosophical essays. Still others
are state papers or official pronouncements. All have to be read with
alert attention to the rules of the genre, which were well known to
the writer, the addressee, and the audience to which the addressee read
out the letter. Only in the last centuries of the empire did the essay
break away from the formal traditions of the public speech or the
letter, in some of the writings of Nikephoros Choumnos, Theodore
Metochites, Nikephoros Gregoras in the fourteenth century, and
George Gemistos Plethon in the fifteenth. The first three often reflect

* See anthology pp. 375–6.

the dilemma of late Byzantine culture, entrapped in a tradition of classicizing grandeur which bore little relation to the sorry condition of society and state. Plethon tried to make a new beginning, by rejecting both Roman imperial tradition and Christian religion. His dream of a Greek nation-state, worshipping Olympian gods who were really personifications of philosophical categories, was impossible to realize in the harsh world of Ottoman conquest. Though essentially a medieval thinker, Plethon foreshadows some features of the Italian renaissance. The lectures which he gave at the Council of Florence in 1439 inspired Cosimo de' Medici to found his Platonic Academy.

Writers and Readers

Literacy and education were never a clerical monopoly in the Byzantine world, nor did the clergy constitute a separate order in society, with its own status and privileges. Many of the greatest Byzantine writers were laymen. Others, like Photios or John Kantakuzenos, entered the clergy late in life. Nevertheless the leisure and the opportunities for patronage which the clergy often enjoyed meant that many Byzantine writers on secular topics were in fact clergymen. Alternatives to ecclesiastical patronage were the support of members of the imperial house, or the holding of high state office. Yet in the middle and late Byzantine periods some writers contrived to get by without patronage or office, as the first professional men of letters.

Handwritten books were expensive objects. Yet readership extended far beyond the narrow circle of writers. There were libraries in monasteries and churches, in the palace, and in certain schools and other imperial foundations. Private libraries were confined to the rich, but not to men of letters. An eleventh-century government official and landowner in Cappadocia owned seventy-five books. A fifteenth-century general had a considerable library in his house in the Peloponnese. Another soldier in the fourteenth century boasts that no man has so extensive a library. It is probable that books were more accessible and readers more numerous than in western Europe, at any rate until the fifteenth century.

THE SONG OF ROLAND

RICHARD AXTON

Roland is the earliest and greatest of the *chansons de geste*. It is perhaps
the only Old French epic to have been read continuously by non-
specialists and to have been compared seriously, following Matthew
Arnold, with the *Iliad*.[1] The sound of Roland's battle horn rever-
berates through European literature, so that Dante, startled in the
ninth circle of the *Inferno* by a tremendous sound, reflects how, 'After
the dolorous rout when Charlemagne lost the sacred army, Roland
did not sound a blast so terrible' –

> Dopo la dolorosa rotta quando
> Carlo Magno perdè la santa gesta,
> non sonò sì terribilmente Orlando

and a melancholy echo is heard faintly in Alfred de Vigny's 'Dieu!
que le son du cor est triste au fond des bois'. It signals doom and
triumph, the paradigm of tragedy.

The text of the poem was copied out in England, *c.*1125–50, from
a version composed in north-western France in about 1100 and
associated with 'Turoldus'. By chance, the earliest version of the
exploits of Count William of Orange, *La Chanson de Guillaume*, also
survives in an Anglo-Norman copy.[2] From this one might hazard
that the Norman aristocracy who ruled both sides of the English
Channel at about the time of the First Crusade (1096–99) shared a taste
for warfaring 'songs of deeds' in which the legendary exploits of their
Carolingian ancestors were commemorated. Despite the great difference between the characters of the named heroes – Roland, headstrong, simple, pious, and Guillaume, an effervescent, romantic
adventurer of a more comic type – there is a broad similarity of
conception in the two poems: a nephew (Roland, Vivien) suffers a
martyr-like defeat by Saracens and is finally revenged by his uncle
(Charlemagne, Guillaume). Loyalty to the king and to France, and

the defence of Christendom against Islam are the most cherished values. They are the 'modern' face of narratives which must be much older than the first written versions to survive. According to Norman chroniclers, a *cantilena Rollandi* was sung at Hastings in 1066 to urge on William the Conqueror's knights with an example of heroic courage.

Turoldus's tradition is hallowed by long association with church authority. He attributes the number (400) of Saracens slain at Roncesvaux by Archbishop Turpin to *la geste* and to 'him who fought there according to the worthy St Giles who made the charter in the minster of Laon'. And Roland's great ivory horn, the olifant, is said to be a relic upon the altar of St Severin in Bordeaux. According to the 'classical' view of Joseph Bédier, the *chansons de geste* were composed by monks who made use of performers travelling on pilgrim routes to attract visitors to monastic shrines (Roncesvaux lies on the pilgrim route to Santiago de Compostella through the Val Carlos to northern Spain). This view would emphasize the importance of early Latin 'schoolroom epics' – the so-called Hague Fragments of a siege poem about Charlemagne and Guillaume, and the tenth-century *Waltharius*, which tells of hostages escaping from the court of Attila the Hun.[3] A more 'romantic' view sees the *chansons* as traditional, shaped by the communal values of generations of oral composers, reaching back to a common Frankish tradition of war-songs. Such a popular origin is suggested by the grouping of lines by assonance (a device for projecting the voice and aiding memory) into *laisses* (strophes) of uneven length, and by the ballad-like repetition of sections (*laisses similaires*), often in triple patterns at high points in the story.[4]

To say that the *Roland* poet preserves a traditional *geste* by using the traditional techniques of chanted narrative poetry is not to deny that he could also have had a good clerical training and have read some Virgil or Statius in his youth. When he says (perhaps following the words of his author) that the Emir of Babylon 'has outlived Virgil and Homer', he is not making a scientific chronology but establishing the antiquity of the pagan enemy by poetic means. The crucial thing is that he chose to compose his *Roland* in a vernacular poetic tradition and not in Latin, the language of ecclesiastics, of the liturgy and the imperial court. His immediate audience – patrons, perhaps – would probably have been the Norman aristocracy. A few generations earlier, the piratical ancestors of these feudal barons had seized land and sacked churches; once settled in northern France, they became Christians, founded abbeys, and employed clergy as chaplains, secretaries, tutors, and poets. Among the stories devised by one such, Gérold, to educate his patrons at the Norman court of Chester beyond warring and wenching were the exploits of Guillaume d'Orange against the Saxons in Spain and in forsaking the world for a monastery. Vernacular and Latin, popular and clerical cultures were not distinct; a Latin saint's life might be turned into a French strophic poem, as in the case of *La Vie de Saint Alexis* (extant in an Anglo-Norman manuscript of about 1123), and be transformed in the process to reflect the political and religious aspirations of the feudal class who were the new patrons of vernacular literature.[5]

To its contemporary listeners *Roland* told a tale of feudal betrayal and heroic martyrdom, set within the greater conflict of Christianity and Islam. The story is told with rapt seriousness, in the high style, approving without question the values of militant Christianity (including the practice of conversion at the sword's edge) that were orthodox at the time of the First Crusade. The poet is dramatist; he does not pause to explain and his moral reflections are few: 'Christians are right, pagans are wrong', or 'He who has suffered has learned many things'. His meaning inheres in the structure of episodes, in the shaping of the story, rather than in imposed observations. The narrative preserves the meanings that generations of storytellers have found in giving an account of a 'true story'.

Official Carolingian history says little about Roland. Charlemagne's biographer Einhard, writing *c.*830 about the year 778, records a successful campaign in Spain, marred only during the return home by an ambush in which the French army's rearguard was slaughtered and the baggage stolen.[6] According to Einhard, the attackers were *Wascones* (Gascons, or possibly Basques), who chose a steep, wooded ravine for the treacherous attack; their escape with the army's booty was aided by nightfall, so that pursuit and revenge by the main army were not possible. He reports merely: 'In this battle were killed Egginhard, surveyor of the royal table; Anselm, Count of the Palace, and Roland, Praefect of the Breton Marches, along with many others.' Nothing more is heard of Roland before the eleventh century, though two coins bearing *Carlus* on the obverse and *Rōdlan* on the reverse may suggest that the praefect of Brittany was an important man. The omission from a chronicle written in 842 of the names of those who died in the campaign, 'because they are so well known it would be superfluous to relate them', hints at unofficial history, at heroes kept alive by word of mouth.[7]

The story of Roncesvaux emerges suddenly with great precision of detail from a monastic chronicle, written *c.*1065–75 in northern Spain:[8]

In that year [778] King Charles came to Saragossa. In those days he had twelve nephews [*neptis*: possibly 'grandsons'], each of whom had 3,000 knights, together with their armed men; the names of these: Roland, Bertram, Ogier Short-Sword, William Hook-Nose, Oliver, and the Lord Bishop Turpin. And each of them with his men served the King for a month. The King was forced to stay his army for a while in Saragossa. After a while his men gave counsel that he should accept great gifts for fear lest his army perish from hunger, and should return to his own country. Which was agreed. Thereupon it pleased the King for the safety of his men in the army that the mighty warrior Roland with his men should go as rearguard. But when the army passed through the Sizer Gate, Roland was killed in Roncesvaux by the Saracen people.

In contrast to the blandness of Einhard, everything in this terse account is specific: Charlemagne's French army pauses 'ad Caesaraugusta' and returns home through the 'portum de sicera'; Roland is killed 'in Rozaballes gentibus sarrazenorum'. A strong thread of causality runs through the story, marking Roland as the victim of pagan treachery. The revelation that Charlemagne's army was tired and hungry convincingly explains the French agreement in council to be bought off by 'munera multa'. Roland is chosen rearguard because of his prowess and for the army's safety. The wantonly treacherous Gascons of Carolingian history have been transformed into the Saracen enemies of eleventh-century Christendom. The Spanish monk has heard about the apostolic Twelve Peers and he offers a curious, mythic explanation of 'why they were twelve'. Oliver, Ogier the Dane and Bishop Turpin are all figures of heroic stature in the *Song of Roland* (though the last two are not among the Twelve). Bertram and his uncle Guillaume d'Orange, the hero of a cycle of six heroic songs, do not appear in the Oxford manuscript *Roland*, but they must have been important in the southern version known to the monastic chronicler. In his quaint, hopelessly un-grammatical, 'official' Latin can be read the characters of a vernacular Spanish poem, in which each hero had his epic appellation: Roland is *belligator fortis*, Ogier is *spata curta*, and the adjective *alcorbitanas* renders the phrase *al corb nes*, 'with the hook nose'. So the *Nota Emilianense* proves the currency of other songs of Roland earlier than the earliest text. But the ghost Spanish version does not seem to have included the traitor Ganelon, nor Charlemagne's revenge and the counter-offensive of the Emir Baligant.

Archaeological evidence corroborates the widespread popularity of the Roland story in the Romanesque period. The stern warriors Roland and Oliver, who flank the huge doors of Verona Cathedral (1139), had been comrades in arms for more than a century; baptismal registers in southern France during the eleventh century record twin brothers named Roland and Oliver. In the earliest carvings Roland is recognizable by his olifant. A carved stone in a house wall, now in the Cluny museum, shows a disc with a figure bearing a sword and a great horn which breaks through the design at the upper left.[9] In visual testimony the olifant is ubiquitous; it is the essence of the memory of Roland in Roncesvaux; it is the most important object in the *Song of Roland* and may provide a point of entry into the poem's structure.

The story tradition has given Roland the prodigious olifant so that his exploits and the fate of the rearguard trapped in a remote moun-tain valley may be conveyed to the world; Charlemagne can return, discover the dreadful loss, mourn his dead, treasure their bodies and collect visible relics of their heroism. With the olifant Roland has power to summon Charlemagne; therefore it is important that he should not blow until it is too late to expect rescue. The narrative paradox and potential inherent in the horn motif is at the core of Turoldus's poem, for he has two symmetrical horn-blowing scenes. Roland must first refuse to sound the olifant when to do so would be interpreted as a cry for help and thus bring shame; yet he must sound the olifant when all is lost, when all that can be hoped is recognition of total sacrifice, decent burial, and revenge. The possible incon-sistency of this behaviour is minimized by the introduction of Oliver, his 'double' and the friend-in-conflict, to propose an opposite course of action in each case. The importance of this pair of balanced scenes (laisses 82–9 and 128–32) is conveyed by their mirror-symmetry and by the use in each case of the balladic, triple repetition of formulae in separate laisses.

As the rearguard rides into the dark mountain valley, Oliver has climbed to the rim and surveyed the massing enemy ranks. Three times (laisses 83, 84, 85) he urges, 'Cumpaign Rollant, kar sunez vostre corn!' and three times Roland replies, varying only slightly the form of words:

> Melz voeill murir que huntage me venget
> (1091)
> (I would rather die than shame should
> come upon me).

The poet comments here that 'Roland is fierce and Oliver is wise' ('Rollant est proz e Oliver est sage'). His praise is equally bestowed and one must resist the temptation (prompted by a knowledge of the poem's outcome) to translate the connective *e* as 'but'. The values of proud strength and wisdom are complementary, and the poet goes on to say,

> Ambedui unt meveillus vasselage
> (1093)
> (Both of them have amazing
> strength in battle).

Oliver, however appealing he may be to the prudent, middle-aged and scholarly, lacks Roland's deeper wisdom that 'A man must endure much hardship for his liege' ('Pur sun seignur deit hom susfrir granz mals'). The narrative impasse is resolved when Turpin, the great warrior Archbishop, supports Roland by recalling considerations beyond death:

> Se vos murez, esterez seinz martirs
> (1134)
> (If you should die you shall be
> blessed martyrs).

This confrontation is replayed fifty laisses later, when the French are reduced to sixty men.* With no choice but to fight to death, Roland proposes three times to sound his olifant, for 'How shall we

---

* See anthology, p. 385.

send the King news?' The roles are now reversed, and Oliver bitterly voices Roland's earlier arguments against incurring shame. He cannot resist 'I told you so' and accuses Roland of *folie* and *estultie*, of causing French deaths through his recklessness (*legerie*) for, he says: 'Mielz valt mesure que ne fait estultie.' The observation that 'Moderation is worth more than rash folly' is Oliver's voice rather than that of the poet and, as happened previously, the Archbishop resolves the matter and proves Roland right: Charlemagne must be sent news so that he can revenge; the dead warriors must be planted in sacred ground so they may flower into martyrdom. Notice, too, that Oliver's reproaches are undercut by his distraction, contrasted with Roland's serenity; his gasp of pity or admiration as he notices the blood on Roland's arms (1711) is a non sequitur, and in refusing Roland his sister's love he is merely being petulant (the shadowy Alde later in the poem dies at news of Roland's death). Oliver's physical degeneration leads to a miasmic fit in which he mistakenly strikes Roland. By contrast, Roland is still miraculously undiminished by the enemy. When he sets the olifant to his lips and blows with all his strength, the pain is excruciating, for this is his self-inflicted death-wound; the supreme moment of his striving becomes his acceptance of his fate and his own mortality. Blood begins to ooze from his temples, the place of the soul.

The sound of the horn offers also the most economical and natural way of shifting the scene from the massacre in the dark valley to the army on the plain. Throughout the poem such rapid switches of attention back and forth from Christian camp to Saracen camp have served to generate space and to build up conflict. Now the thrilling sound is made to stretch over three tightly patterned laisses similaires in a suspension of temporal sequence – we cannot tell if Roland really blows three times or if a single blast is lingered on by the repetition – to evoke an immensity of distance. The full meaning of the tragic situation is explored in three as it were simultaneous moments in the distinct responses of Charlemagne, Ganelon and Naimon. Ganelon's character is swiftly consolidated in the insolence of his words to the emperor so that his arrest and disgrace will come as no surprise and will not hold up the mainstream of the revenge narrative. The French acknowledge the hopelessness of rescue even as the revenge, which will occupy the second half of the poem, is set in motion.

By doubling the horn-blowing with a feint in which the possibility of escape is raised only to be rejected, the act when it comes has all the force of destiny. The preparatory scene also introduces an element of tragic irony which will only be perceived later: Roland's death is partly the result of his own rashness, his *estultie*. A comparison with the Old English *Battle of Maldon* (*c.* 1000) can be made here, for there is a core of heroic tragedy common to the two poems: in each, a small band of Christian warriors, bound together by personal loyalty, are trapped in a tight place and fight to the last against impossible odds. The Anglo-Saxon poet may actually have been a survivor of the Viking massacre at Maldon; in any case, his story is told sparely, without hyperbole. What raises the narrative of the death of Earl Bryhtnoth and his *fyrd* to tragic intensity is the element of irony. The earl refuses the advantage that his English bowmen have over the Norsemen stranded across the tidal causeway and waits for the water to ebb, allowing the raiders to cross and set up their shield-wall on dry land. He does this, the poet says, '*for his ofermode*', 'from his heart's recklessness'. Bryhtnoth's *ofermod*, his over-confidence, causes his fatal error of judgement. But though the poet grieves, he does not moralize, commemorating rather the moment when

> Courage shall grow keener, clearer the will,
> the heart fiercer, as our force faileth.[10]

Roland's refusal to sound his olifant can be seen as comparable (expressive of what Yeats calls 'character isolated by a deed, To engross the present and dominate memory') and the lack of *mesure* of which Oliver accuses him as corresponding to the Earl's *ofermod*. But I do not think Roland's act can bear such a weight of tragic irony. This is partly because the network of causality is more complex in *Roland* than in *Maldon*, involving particularly Ganelon's plotting with the Saracens. It is also because, as we have seen, Roland is proved right; though he dies, he is unvanquished, and his death has the serenity of spiritual victory. The *Maldon* poet has no notion of martyrdom; he does not profess to know about supernatural matters and describes the Christian death of Bryhtnoth with a quiet grimness:

> He yielded to the ground the yellow-hilted sword,
> strengthless to hold the hard blade longer up
> or wield weapon. One word more,

the hoar-headed warrior, heartening his men:
he bade them go forward, the good companions.
Fast on his feet he might not further stand;
he looked to heaven...

> 'I give Thee thanks, Lord God of hosts,
> for I have known in this world a wealth of gladness,
> but now, mild Maker, I have most need
> that Thou grant my ghost grace for this journey
> so that my soul may unscathed cross
> into Thy keeping, King of angels,
> pass through in peace: my prayer is this,
> that the hates of hell may not harm her.'

Then they hewed him down, the heathen churls,
and with him those warriors, Wulfmaer and Aelfnoth,
who had stood at his side: stretched on the field,
the two followers fellowed in death.

(*The Battle of Maldon*, 165–84)

By contrast, Roland arranges his own death scene with ceremony and with careful attention to its symbolism:[11]

> Now Roland feels death press upon him hard;
> It's creeping down from his head to his heart.
> Under a pine-tree he hastens him apart,
> There stretches him face down on the green grass,
> And lays beneath him his sword and Olifant.
> He's turned his head to where the Paynims are,
> And this he doth for the French and for Charles,
> Since fain is he that they should say, brave heart,
> That he has died a conqueror at the last.
> He beats his breast full many a time and fast,
> Gives, with his glove, his sins into God's charge...

(laisse 174)

> The County Roland lay down beneath a pine;
> To land of Spain he's turned him as he lies,
> And many things begins to call to mind:
> All the broad lands he conquered in his time,
> And fairest France, and the men of his line,
> And Charles his lord, who bred him from a child;
> He cannot help but weep for them and sigh.
> Yet of himself he is mindful betimes;
> He beats his breast and on God's mercy cries:
>   'Father most true, in whom there is no lie,
>   Who didst from death St Lazarus make to rise,
>   And bring out Daniel safe from the lions' might,

> Save Thou my soul from danger and despite
> Of all the sins I did in all my life.'
> His right-hand glove he's tendered unto Christ,
> And from his hand Gabriel accepts the sign.
> Straightway his head upon his arm declines;
> With folded hands he makes an end and dies.
> God sent to him His Angel Cherubine,
> And great St Michael of Peril-by-the-Tide;
> St Gabriel too was with them at his side;
> The County's soul they bear to Paradise.*

(laisse 176)

In death Roland is flanked by his sword and his olifant, the tokens of his self-sufficiency and its limits. Paradoxically he has fractured the precious olifant in using it to dash out the brains of the last Saracen, yet he has been unable to break his sword. Horn and sword identify Roland in the glowing scenes in the ambulatory glass at Chartres: a double image shows Roland back-to-back with himself; on the left he dashes his sword against a rock; on the right he blows the olifant. Below him lie dismembered limbs and entrails. Above, a divine hand reaches down into the blue medallion towards Roland's halo.

The traitor Ganelon is not mentioned either by Einhard or by the *Nota Emilianense*. Yet the growth of the legend indicated by those accounts makes his entry into the story inevitable. The mythic, idealized pattern of King, his doomed favourite 'son' and twelve 'disciples' was incomplete without a Judas. The notion of betrayal from within and the conflict between Roland and Ganelon give logic to historical events which might otherwise seem random or inexplicable. Thus Charlemagne's unwise agreement to compromise with the Saracen enemy is made to follow on Ganelon's self-interested counsel, albeit the French barons concur and Charlemagne himself expresses a tragically naïve faith that the pagan king 'yet may save his soul'. In the second 'scene' of the poem† Ganelon is introduced on the coat tails of the Twelve as the man 'ki la traïsun fist'. He is presented in opposition to Roland; each of them in the council 'leaps to his feet' and speaks with angry animation. Roland's

---

* The final syllables of a laisse have the same vowel sound, regardless of the consonants that follow.

† See anthology, p. 379.

'Ja mar crerez Marsile' is sneeringly echoed in 'Ja mar crerez bricun' ('Never trust a bragging fool'). For Ganelon the enemy is not Marsile, but Roland.

The choice of Ganelon as ambassador is the logical consequence of his counsel, but this choice is dramatically postponed by the emperor's triple request: 'Seignurs baruns, qui i enveieruns?' ('My lords barons, whom shall we send?') in laisses 17, 18, and 20, and by his rejection of all the names proposed. Roland has made clear the physical danger of negotiating, so that when he names Ganelon this is both a dare and an unmasking of the latter's true motives. The nomination cannot be avoided or withdrawn and, because so many worthy men have been passed over, Ganelon now feels insulted. His anger explodes and he throws off his cloak in a formal gesture of defiance before pronouncing his feud against Roland.

Ganelon blames the well-known hostility of stepson to stepfather for Roland's 'madness', though he cannot refuse for shame of cowardice. A suspicion of darker motives, old scores to be settled, resurfaces a moment later when Ganelon speaks of his journey with no return and his sorrow at leaving his son Baldwin, and reminds Charlemagne, 'My wife is your sister'. The emperor, suspicious of such a display of feeling, dismisses him curtly with 'Your heart is too tender'. There is no explicit allusion here to the widely-known story of 'Charlemagne's sin', but nothing in the poem's presentation of Roland and Ganelon is inconsistent with the explanation (included in the Old Norse, *Karlamagnus Saga*) that Roland was the true son of Charlemagne, begotten upon his own sister.[12]

So Roland and Ganelon seal each other's fates. Roland's naming of Ganelon as envoy justifies and determines Ganelon's naming of Roland for the rearguard. Laisses 58–61 mirror laisses 20–25: the emperor asks his barons for a nomination to take the rearguard; Ganelon names 'Rollant, cist miens fillastre', praising his 'vasselage'. 'Vos estes vifs diables!' the king exclaims, explaining Ganelon's diabolic behaviour by the entry of a 'mortal fury' into his body. Roland's acceptance of his role and his denunciation of Ganelon are voiced in three separate laisses and deliberately force a recollection of Ganelon's behaviour:

Ah! coward wretch, foul felon, baseborn carle,
Didst think the glove would fall from out my grasp
As did the wand from thine, before King Charles?

(763–5)

Charlemagne sits, his head bent low, and plucks his long white beard
as his tears overflow, immobilized by grief. His prophetic dreams
(laisses 56, 57) have already shown him Ganelon's treachery both
explicitly and in animal fable. This treason is openly apparent to
Charlemagne only when the sound of Roland's horn is heard and
Ganelon desperately maintains that the horn is not Roland's. Ganelon's structural antagonism towards Roland is sustained to the last
through the judicial combat of champions, and his association with
Judas is confirmed through the number (thirty) of kinsmen who are
hanged for his sake at the end of the poem.

The third great conflict that shapes the poem is that of Charlemagne and Baligant, of Christianity and Islam. This opposition of
West and East is almost certainly the most modern feature of the
poem's historical genesis. It encloses the feudal conflict of Roland
and Ganelon as that in turn encloses the private, ethical conflict of
Roland and Oliver. A perpetual war of faith spans the whole structure and provides a climax in the second half of the poem (which
some readers have found anticlimactic, following Roland's death)
with the solo combat of the Emperor of Rome and the Emir of
Babylon. Even before Charlemagne has recovered Roland's body
in Roncesvaux, forces are massing: from Alexandria a fleet of
Persians, Armenians and Africans sets sail and the Mediterranean
night sparkles with torchlight upon gem-studded rigging; to the
north, columns of German and Friesian Franks rally to the emperor's
call. With the whole of Christendom in the field the outcome of
this battle must be a victory for Christ. Charlemagne's power is not
personal; it comes to him via the angel Gabriel from God. When
the emperor wakens before battle it is Gabriel who lifts his hand in
the sign of the cross (laisse 203), and when the emir pares his scalp
to the bone, it is Gabriel who intervenes:

King Carlon reels and well nigh falls with it.
But God wills not he be o'ercome or killed;

> Saint Gabriel comes hastening down to him,
> 'And what', saith he, 'art thou about, great king?'
>
> (3608–11)

In twelve lines the pagans have been routed.

The balance of two great battles, Roncesvaux and Saragossa, on either side of Roland's death scene contrasts two images of the Christian warrior: the youthful Roland, delighting in his own strength and self-confidence; Charlemagne, ancient and deliberate, burdened by grief, deeply pious, physically weak but trusting in God. The archangel Michael is associated with Roland and presides over the army at Roncesvaux; God's warfaring angel of the book of *Daniel* and the *Apocalypse*, he is protector in death and guide of souls into paradise. Gabriel, angel of the New Testament, attends Charlemagne with visions and counsel, his name – according to St Bernard – implying 'the strength of God'.[13]

Although the poem's structure insists on Charlemagne as revenger, the image of the emperor conveyed is curious and paradoxical, suggesting authority and helplessness. He is monumentally dignified and archaic – his more-than-200-years a source of wonder and frustration to his enemies – yet he is passive and uncommanding. He images suffering rather than action. His grief and anger consume themselves in fainting and plucking his long white beard as he weeps resignedly each fresh misfortune. This vulnerability is the worldly aspect of his saint-like humility. He inhabits a lonely world of suffering, of prayer and visions. While the narrative insists on his victorious power, the poem seems to linger on Charlemagne's grief and sense of loss. One such moment comes at the centre of the poem when, after the dreadful noise of battle and lamentation, the emperor is described finally falling asleep. A vast panorama of mountains and corpses shrinks in the moonlight down to the solitary figure lying on the field, and in the unaccustomed silence nothing can be heard but the sound of horses' teeth pulling at the grass:

> Clere est la noit e la lune luisant.
> Carles se gist, mais doel ad de Rollant
> E d'Oliver li peiset mult forment,
> Des .xii. pers e de la franceise gent.
> En Rencesvals ad laisét morz e sanglenz;
> Ne poet muër n'en plurt e ne.s dement,

E priet Deu qu'as anmes seit guarent.
Las est li reis, kar la peine est mult grant.
Endormiz est, ne pout mais en avant;
Par tuz les prez or se dorment li Franc.
N'i ad cheval ki puisset ester en estant;
Ki herbe voelt, il la prent en gisant.
Mult ad apris ki bien conuist ahan.

(laisse 184, 2512–24)

(The night is clear and the moon shining bright;
Charles lies awake and weeps for Roland's plight,
For Oliver he weeps with all his might,
Weeps his Twelve Peers, his French folk left behind
In Roncesvaux, slain bloodily in fight.
He cannot help but mourn for them and sigh,
And pray God bring their souls to Paradise.
The King is weary, for grief weighs on his eyes;
He can no more, he sleeps after a while,
And all the French sleep in the field likewise.
There's not a horse has strength to stand upright;
If they want grass they crop it as they lie.
He that has suffered learns many things in life.)

The exhaustion and grief known to all men is described with the utmost simplicity.

This note returns at the poem's close. The emir has been defeated, Ganelon tried and executed, the alarming Spanish Queen Bramimonde christened Juliana in the baths at Aix; but there is no rest for Charlemagne. No sooner has night fallen than Gabriel appears at his bedside, urging him, 'Carles, sumun les oz de tun emperie', to ride to relieve King Vivien, besieged in Elbira by pagans:

'Deus,' dist li reis, 'si penuse est ma vie!'
Pluret des oilz, sa barbe blanche tiret.
('God,' says the king, 'how weary is my life!'
He weeps, he plucks his flowing beard and white.)

During the second half of the 4,000-line poem focus has shifted from Roland to Charlemagne, from exultation in martyrdom to the weariness of life seen apocalyptically as endless warring with evil. We may feel, as at the end of *King Lear*, that

The oldest hath borne most; we that are young
Shall never see so much, nor live so long.

Yet the mood is not one of humanist despair; *Roland* is too deeply Christian for that. Rather, in the figure of the grand old emperor we can glimpse the shadow of the supreme sacrifice, God the father mourning his only son.

NOTES

1. Matthew Arnold, 'The Study of Poetry' (1888). Dorothy Sayers, in the introduction to her translation (Penguin Classics, 1957), 27n., argues that although *SR* is not a greater poem, 'as a whole, it has a much greater theme than that of the *Iliad*'.

2. *La Chanson de Roland*, ed. F. Whitehead (Oxford, 1957), v. Quotations from the French are from this edition, checked against that of Gerard J. Brault (2 vols, Pennsylvania State University Press, 1978). La Chanson de Guillaume is conveniently translated by Lynette Muir in *William, Count of Orange*, ed. Glanville Price (London, 1975).

3. See J. Bédier, *Les Légendes Epiques* (4 vols, Paris, 1914–21), especially III, 291–385; and Jessie Crosland, *The Old French Epic* (Oxford, 1951), ch. 1.

4. Major contributions to the controversy are discussed by J. J. Duggan in *A Guide to Studies of the Chanson de Roland* (London, 1976), section VI.

5. See R. R. Bezzola, *Les origines et la formation de la littérature courtoise en occident*, 500–1200, part II, t. 2 (Paris, 1960), 237ff., 391ff., 485–95.

6. Einhard the Frank, *The Life of Charlemagne*, translated by Lewis Thorpe (London, 1970), 40–41. cf. Brault, I, 2–3.

7. Duggan, *A Guide*, 97–8.

8. The *Nota Emilianense* is printed by D. Alonso, in *Revista de Filologia Española*, 37 (1953), 1–94.

9. Rita Lejeune and Jacques Stiennon, *The Legend of Roland in the Middle Ages*, (2 vols, New York and London, 1971), especially II, pls 38, 57.

10. *The Battle of Maldon*, lines 312–13, quoted from *The Earliest English Poems* translated by Michael Alexander (Penguin Classics, 1966), 114–23.

11. Complete laisses in the text and Appendix are cited from D. Sayers's translation.

12. See Duggan, 84 and nos 102–4.

13. Penn R. Szittya, 'The angels and fortitude in the *Chanson de Roland*', *Neuphilologische Mitteilungen*, 72 (1971), 193.

CHRÉTIEN DE TROYES' ARTHURIAN ROMANCE, *YVAIN*

TONY HUNT

Of Chrétien (or Chrestien) de Troyes' five Arthurian romances *Yvain* or, to give it its medieval title, *Le Chevalier au Lion* is generally regarded as the most satisfying. The satisfaction it affords, however, is that of meeting a profound critical challenge rather than of assimilating a convenient paradigm of medieval chivalric romance. Nothing useful can be said about *Yvain* that does not involve paradoxes and questions – like Chrétien's style. On the one hand it may be viewed as the model of its genre, for it was the most popular of Chrétien's romances in medieval Europe, being widely translated (into German, Old Norse, Welsh, Swedish and English) and no less commonly plagiarized as a result of its unusual clarity of structure, rich combination of realism and fantasy, vivid dramatic force and, of course, its memorable inclusion of the eponymous beast. Further, it appears to combine all the salient features of Chrétien's art with that inimitable *vis comica* which is so important an element of his appeal. Yet recent criticism rightly sees this as only half the story. Once we learn to distinguish the mere presence of familiar motifs in *Yvain* from the specific function which they are made to perform, we are led to a crucial recognition, namely that in the hands of its creator, Chrétien de Troyes, medieval romance may be critical of the very values which it mediates, that it may be far from endorsing what it presents and that it may treat ironically what imitators are content to take at face value. In this perspective *Yvain* appears as the most suspicious and the most provocative of Chrétien's works, offering unequalled opportunities for scepticism of conventional courtly values and expectations. Hence the paradox that *Yvain*'s apparent typicality may be the measure of its subversiveness, its ostensible conformity to conventions of the genre an index of its thoroughgoing radicalness, its commonplaces the symptoms of its challenge.

Very little is known about the poet from the Champagne called Chrétien de Troyes. Wolfram von Eschenbach, in his *Parzival* (finished *c.*1210), gives him the appellation 'master' (*von Troys meister Cristjân*) which certainly implies the intellectual formation of a cleric and may also be intended to indicate his supremacy as a literary writer. Much of Chrétien's learning (*clergie*) is apparent from his romances (he also wrote a number of lyrics). He was an active participant in the twelfth-century 'Renaissance', reworking classical themes and disseminating in the vernacular motifs from contemporary Latin literature. From the prologue to his *Cliges* it seems that he began by translating Ovid – the *Ars amatoria*, a number of stories from the *Metamorphoses*, and the tale of Philomela (his version has come to light in Book 6 of the much later *Ovide moralizé*). He is certainly well versed in Ovid and Virgil from whom he drew much of his imagery, has an interesting reference in his *Erec* to the neo-platonist philosopher Macrobius, and everywhere betrays the influence of Ciceronian rhetoric and Aristotelian dialectic which were staple ingredients of the Liberal Arts courses in the twelfth-century schools. On one level, therefore, his work seems to be aimed at the *litterati* of the court. On the other hand, Chrétien was also familiar with more popular literature. He wrote his own version, now lost, of the Tristan and Isolde story and shows knowledge of the *Chanson de Roland*, Wace's *Brut*, some of the troubadour lyrics and a stock of proverbial wisdom. The evidence of his imitators suggests that he was appreciated by simple lovers of good stories. Finally, Chrétien displays wide knowledge of the Bible from which he draws many of his similes. His intellectual pretensions did not, therefore, preclude popular appeal. But in the nature of things we can never know who his audiences were. His romance of the adulterous love of Lancelot and Guinevere (*The Knight of the Cart*) was apparently composed at the instigation of Marie de Champagne, daughter of the celebrated Eleanor of Aquitaine; for reasons unknown he failed to complete the romance, handing the work over to one Godefroi de Leigni. And his last unfinished romance of Perceval (*The Story of the Grail*) was written for Philip of Alsace, Count of Flanders. Chrétien kept good company, but where he was domiciled and how far he travelled we do not know.

The diversity of Chrétien's literary appeal is manifested in his style. His handling of eight-syllable lines rhymed in pairs is notable for its fluency and the pioneering use of *enjambement* (whereby the sense phrases flow over the break marked by the rhyme). The unrestrained forward movement of the lines is complemented by a fondness for ternary rhythm, apparent in threefold repetition of nouns, adjectival qualifiers, prepositional phrases, which confers a leisurely elegance which was no doubt appreciated by Chrétien's listeners. As well as a striking limpidity of style we also find passages of dazzling preciosity, where brilliant linguistic virtuosity, exploiting all manner of wordplay, seems to count for more than the underlying sense. Chrétien is nothing if not versatile: popular, recherché, allusive, insistent, arch, naïve, racy and demure. The constantly changing tonality of his narrative is a significant part of the interpretative problems posed by his works. He has a dramatist's flair for the handling of dialogue, a deft and economic way with characterization, the sharp confidence of the logician in his handling of rhetorical figures and the self-assurance of the entertainer in the deployment of humour (he is master of the verbal nudge). It is his essential vivacity that one misses most in his imitators. The structure of his romances is exceptionally cohesive and his preoccupation with motif-duplication is a sign of his concern to establish signposts to the course of his argument and the elaboration of his theme. The *Yvain* displays Chrétien's style at its most polished and urbane whilst making no concessions to the complexity of his thought. The *curiosa felicitas* of the writing belies the speed with which Chrétien was able to bring the new genre of the romance to perfection, a process which may have taken a mere decade, for it is now thought likely that all his romances were written in the 1180s.

Whilst the epic is an essentially affirmative mode, providing with almost liturgical solemnity and repetition a celebration of the known and familiar values of a collectivity, the romance represents an inquiring mode, a critical investigation in the course of which more individualistic values are gradually disengaged. The didacticism of the epic (its origins may reside in popular hagiography) contrasts with the interrogation of romance, which has intellectual origins in the more learned milieu of the schools of northern France in the twelfth century. The demonstrative manner of the more popular genre is far removed from the argumentative style of the relatively learned romance. If the epic is based on dogmatic principles, the romance proceeds along inductive lines. In the epic all is clear and direct, in the romance much is ambiguous and oblique. The epic hero is rarely alone and separable from his community, whilst the romance hero becomes a voluntary exile. The theme of romance is the discovery of identity within a world of adventitious happenings, the process of self-realization through 'adventure' (from *ad-venire*, 'to happen'). The hero pursues a solitary quest in which the presuppositions of the courtly world may act as beacons or decoys. His task, just like that of the reader, is thus one of orientation and discrimination, the search for pertinent and durable criteria (the epic hero simply tours an arena of familiar feudal loyalties). It is this search which makes the interpretation of *Yvain* such an invigorating critical experience.

The belief that *Yvain* is a quite special production which exploits indirection and irony as its *modus agendi* receives prompt confirmation from the fact that, alone of Chrétien's romances, it has no formal or explicit prologue. Instead, it opens with a type of indirect preamble,★ termed *insinuatio* in Ciceronian rhetoric, which is egregious on three counts. First, it provides an idealistic sketch of the Arthurian court which has struck recent generations of readers as somewhat discrepant with the more critical presentation of the court in the body of the romance. Secondly, it concludes with an epigrammatic statement to the effect that a courtly man dead is worth more than a boor who is alive. This seems to be an ironic inversion of a line from Ecclesiastes (IX.4) 'Melior est canis vivus leone mortuo' ('A living dog is better than a dead lion') and has serious implications for the moral status of the hero Yvain, who rather boorishly kills the knight Esclados, acknowledged to be a paragon of courtliness. Thirdly, the introduction praises a Golden Age of love which is contrasted with the superficiality, sham and vain pretences of lovers in the author's own day. This is truly paradoxical, when we recall that Chrétien composed his romance at some time in the last quarter of the twelfth century, the period *par excellence* of courtly love-song, Ovidian verse and meditations on the Song of Songs. Why he should describe the amatory preoccupations of his contemporaries as a

---

★ See anthology, p. 390.

travesty (*fable*) is thus unclear and alerts us already to the problem of discovering correct criteria of judgement. Moreover, the praise of love in King Arthur's day is belied by Chrétien's subsequent treatment of Arthurian figures, whose amatory conduct in this romance seems anything but exemplary.

Now, the attitudes which we adopt to this eccentric introduction could be seen as programmatic for our interpretation of the whole romance. For example, the study of rhetoric might lead us to see in the introduction the simple rehearsal of a convention without any necessary link with the contents that follow. There are many rhetorical 'set pieces' in *Yvain* which are to be appreciated *in situ* for their immediate local function and need not be regarded as variations on a single, consistent theme. Chrétien can be seen, not as an *écrivain engagé* whose writing is harnessed to an ideology or morality, but as a rhetorician who employs his verbal skills for purely local effects and does not seek to harmonize all the details of his romance (perhaps written and recited in instalments) in an homogeneous structure which would satisfy the synoptic or comprehensive observation of the modern literary critic. This view emphasizes the storytelling qualities of Chrétien's art at the expense of a consistent 'message'.

But it is possible to take another view. The introduction is perhaps polemical rather than rhetorical. Chrétien may have been out of sympathy with the Courtly Love vogue,[1] critical of its non-conjugal, antisocial nature and possibly, also, resentful of contemporaries who had hitherto been unappreciative of his own literary treatment of love. Critical remarks about love are found at several points in the romance and on one occasion he interrupts his description of a maiden's beauty on the grounds that the present generation is not interested in hearing such things.* It has to be said, however, that Chrétien nowhere in this romance portrays an exemplary love relationship. The reconciliation of the hero and his lady in the *sicut ante* ending of the work is notoriously unconvincing and against the background of their *faux ménage* it is the theme of friendship (*amicitia*), notably between Lunete and Yvain and between Yvain and Gawain, which seems to be accorded the greater moral value. Yet, Chrétien

* See anthology, p. 396.

does seem to have a more than merely factitious interest in love. Should we then see him as a man with a serious interest in conjugal love (and its coordination with chivalric duties), who was opposed to the literary fictions of troubadour love poetry and the frivolity of much 'luf talk', an apologist of love who mocked the fashionable novelties of his day?

Another view of the introduction to the romance yields a third picture. According to this reading Chrétien is being ironic, deliberately pointing up the discrepancy between Arthurian myth and chivalric reality.[2] He may be regarded as essentially a dialectician, a critical mind delighting in its own virtuosity and less concerned with commitment than with exposure, anxious to demonstrate that things are seldom what they seem. The dialectical strain is ever present in *Yvain*. It may involve humorous logic-chopping on the part of the characters (see especially the winning of Laudine), it may function as a serious diagnostic tool (as in the analysis of the combat between Yvain and Gawain*), or it may constitute a structural principle, as we shall see when considering the opening adventure. Rhetorician, apologist, dialectician – there is an appreciable element of truth in all three views of Chrétien and the difficulties arise when critics argue the exclusive adoption of a single one of them.

Not the least idiosyncratic feature of this intriguing romance is that the principal adventure undertaken by the hero before the crisis occurs first of all falls to a young, somewhat ineffectual knight called Calogrenant, who is described as Yvain's cousin-german. It is with his account of his search for adventure which, many years previously, led him to a magic fountain in the forest of Broceliande that the romance begins and it surely upsets received notions of chivalric confidence and pride by its self-deprecating and rueful tone: 'That's how I set out and that's how I came back,' concludes Calogrenant, 'and on my return I considered myself a fool.' Yet, to this dispiriting tale, 'not about his honour, but his shame', Calogrenant prefixes a somewhat grandiose address to the assembled listeners which has all the characteristics of a literary prologue, emphasizing, through a number of traditional metaphors and exegetic commonplaces, that what is heard through the ears must be understood in the heart.

---

* See anthology, pp. 396–8.

It is difficult to avoid the impression that Chrétien here obtains compensation for his renunciation of a formal prologue to his romance and that he is, in an ingeniously oblique manner, alerting his audience to the complexities of his own narrative. At the same time he is able to poke fun at the figure of the courtly narrator by contrasting Calogrenant's narrative pretensions with his incomprehension of his actual experiences, for there is no serious way in which his own unsuccessful adventure can be subjected to the interpretative process the need for which Calogrenant impresses on his listeners. The chivalric failure of a kinsman, however, provides Yvain with just the excuse he desires for engaging his own prowess. His strong need to demonstrate his chivalry is clearly shown by the fact that he leaves Arthur's court clandestinely, unwilling to wait for Arthur's promised expedition to the fountain, in which, significantly, Yvain would not secure the first option to do battle with the fountain-defender. Yvain now repeats Calogrenant's journey to the fountain, whereupon he is confronted by its defender, Esclados, lord of the surrounding country. It is at this point that we reach the first crux for the interpretation of the romance.

The question can be put in this form: what is the moral value of Yvain's undertaking and his conduct of the adventure? A simple answer might be that we have to deal with the avenging of a kinsman by a man who shows an impatient, indeed pre-emptive, desire to undertake the task alone. But the striking repetition of the fountain adventure is, perhaps, to be explained by something more than just the motif of revenge, for it adds a significantly new moral ingredient to the hero's comportment since, unlike his predecessor, he possesses foreknowledge of what confronts him and thereby incurs a greater responsibility for his conduct. In fact, Calogrenant's action in pouring water on the slab beside the fountain produced both unforeseen consequences (a tempest) and fierce criticism from the defender, rapidly leading *a verbis ad verbera*, for Esclados complained that Calogrenant wronged him by provoking a violent, destructive tempest (he calls it making war) without having issued a formal challenge or declaration of hostilities (*défi*). To a twelfth-century audience such grounds for complaint were unimpeachable, but in reality Calogrenant's total innocence and ignorance save him from the charge. Not so in the case of Yvain, from whom the elements of innocence and ignorance have been expelled. He attacks Esclados in full knowledge of the latter's grievance and without offering any remedy for the absence of an official challenge or alert. As if to underscore this omission, Chrétien tells us that in contrast King Arthur sends a messenger (a certain 'dameisele sauvage') to Esclados announcing his coming expedition to the fountain which is planned for St John's Eve.

Chrétien the dialectician here skilfully juxtaposes two chivalric adventures and allows his audience to infer the consequences of the contrasts. Is Yvain already at fault? Certainly his treatment of the fountain-knight increases rather than diminishes the listener's unease. Having dealt his opponent a mortal blow, Yvain insists on pursuing him with the intention of taking him 'dead or alive' and his reason for so doing appears to be that unless he can secure some visible tokens (*enseignes veraies*) of his victory, Kay, to whose taunts he is ostensibly indifferent but actually highly sensitive, will mock him and shame him. Some would therefore argue that there is in the character of the hero an insecurity and immaturity which initially lead to the ruthless and savage exercise of chivalry and present us, to recall the terms of the introduction, with a *cortois morz* (the dead Esclados) and a *vilains vis* (the living, but morally primitive Yvain). According to this view it will be the purpose of Yvain's subsequent adventures to transmute his knightly *vilainie* (the disordered, self-interested violence of contemporary knighthood is a constant theme of twelfth-century churchmen) into a chivalric ideal of service to the community, the *publica utilitas* of which John of Salisbury speaks.

But this is only one way of looking at the hero's development. Many would argue that it is premature to impugn his chivalry in the first adventure and that the manifestation of a deficiency in Yvain is to be located later in the work. Even so, we cannot overlook the problematic nature of his unauthorized departure from Arthur's court (thereby subverting the point of Arthur's formal message to Esclados), the distinct possibility that the time of his attack on the fountain-knight falls within the period covered by the Truce of God, which prohibited fighting on certain days of the liturgical year, the certainty that the omission of a formal challenge is reprehensible, and the likelihood that to pursue a mortally wounded knight who has fled the battle area is a breach of chivalric convention. However this may be, a group of attentive readers prefers to situate the hero's fault, seen as a moral flaw rather than as an Aristotelian *hamartia* or error, in his proposal of marriage to the widow of Esclados. In all but two of the manuscripts of the romance the lady is called simply *la dame de Landuc*, but she is generally referred to as Laudine, on the evidence of a single manuscript which may simply offer us a misreading of *la dame*, a situation which emphasizes the precariousness of much of our understanding of Chrétien!

Nothing could be more ambiguous than the apparent marriage of convenience which takes place between Yvain and Laudine. In an atmosphere of *Machtpolitik* Laudine is enjoined to find a defender for her fountain, since Arthur's arrival is imminent. Pressure on her is maintained by a daring *entremetteuse* called Lunete (following a procedure typical of Chrétien, the naming of her is deferred), who wishes to repay an old debt to the hero and who at first upsets, but later wins over, her lady with a bold display of casuistical arguments. A strong comic element, whilst falling short of cynicism, raises the question of how seriously Chrétien takes the love of Yvain and Laudine. The hero falls in love with the woman he has just widowed at precisely the moment when she appears most grief-stricken (she is described as 'so beautiful in her grief'), after having devastated her lands by raising the storm at the fountain with the same impetuosity that he now displays in the choice of bride. Chrétien's assurance that all Laudine's arguments concerning military necessity are merely *pro forma* and that she loves Yvain and would have married him anyway dispels little of the ambivalence of this episode. As we shall see, in the portrayal of Laudine there is more than a hint of the adage *aut amat aut odit mulier, nihil est tertium*. Exploiting a tradition which stretches from Virgil to Verdi, Chrétien tells us that a woman has many moods (*plus de mil corages*) and is forever changing – an ironic affirmation in view of the fact that Laudine changes from hate of her husband's slayer to love, but later back to hate again! The marriage duly takes place and the episode is concluded with an ironic reminiscence of the opening *sententia* concerning the *cortois morz* and the *vilains vis*: 'Now Sir Yvain is lord, the dead man [Esclados] is entirely forgotten. The man who killed him is married to his wife and they sleep together. The people love and esteem the living knight more than they ever did the one who is now dead.' This denial of the implications of the *sententia* is deliberately problematic and raises the question of how far Yvain's good fortune is deserved. Can we believe in its durability? Is Laudine's craven court (none of her barons would defend the fountain) a reliable touchstone for judging the hero's chivalric status?

Arthur's visit to the fountain gives Yvain the opportunity to settle his score with Kay and defeat him in combat. Having fulfilled his role of provoking Yvain, Kay now disappears from the romance. In his place Gawain steps forward and, following the Arthurian court's unsuccessful attempts to get Yvain to depart with it, he sets about persuading his friend to take leave of his new bride and to consolidate his chivalric reputation at the tournaments. A close examination of his arguments reveals them as specious and entirely self-interested. Yvain's ready acceptance of them is a sign of his immaturity and lack of discrimination. Paradoxically, Yvain's dearest friend here behaves inimically towards him (foreshadowing the similar paradox of their later combat★) and the hero capitulates in what is a clear testing of his responsibility and reliability. Laudine grants him a year's leave of absence and warns him that failure to return on time will result in her love turning to hate. The peripeteia is such an obvious narrative necessity that Chrétien makes not the slightest attempt to surprise his audience. On the contrary, the narrator unambiguously predicts that Gawain will detain his friend beyond the duration of his leave and thereafter no further explanation of the hero's lapse is given. Whatever we may think of earlier locations of Yvain's fault – in the clandestine departure from court, the unheralded attack on Esclados, the pitiless conduct of the combat, the precipitate marriage to the dead man's wife (the Widow of Ephesus provided a clear model), the ready capitulation to Gawain's demands – two things are clear: with Yvain's forgetfulness of the date for his return to his wife we have the structural turning point of the story and just as the romance lacks a prologue, so it lacks a conventional exposition, for the opening adventure is far from exemplary,

★ See anthology, pp. 396–8.

the initial quest punctuated with question marks. There are no certainties in *Yvain*.

The consequences of Yvain's forgetfulness are dramatic. He retreats from the Arthurian company and flees to the woods, the victim of a brainstorm which obliterates his former self and hence prepares for the reconstruction of a new identity. Whilst in the forest he is succoured by a hermit, a recurrent figure in Arthurian romance who may suggest the hero's need of grace. What drives Yvain mad? The gravamen of the speech delivered by Laudine's messenger★ is the outstaying of the period of leave. But is not Yvain in trouble before this symptomatic lapse?

The rest of the romance of *Yvain* is made up of a series of adventures, six in all, which display a compassionate, discriminating prowess placed in the service of the oppressed. Although exemplary, these adventures provoke many important questions. How does Yvain come to embrace such a new conception of chivalric prowess? Are the adventures the gratuitous consequences of pure charity or do they incorporate a residue of self-interest still? Are they graded according to a significant moral pattern? How, if at all, are they related to the theme of the hero's rewinning of his wife? Are they presented as the necessary stages in an inner process of individual self-rehabilitation, as in a psychological novel, or as the public exemplification of a new ideology of knighthood, as in a didactic work? Above all, how are the roles of Laudine and the lion distributed among the adventures? The answers to these questions are no more assured than that to the problem of Yvain's moral condition as he embarks on marriage. It is precisely in the search for clarification that we most effectively experience the restless energy, the intellectual curiosity and the imaginative intensity of that age of sophistication of which Chrétien was the product. The task is a double one: to coordinate the internal elements of the text in a coherent structure and 'meaning', and to examine the mediation of that 'meaning' by a narrator who may successively stand in a detached, sympathetic or ironic relationship to his material and thus modify the signals in the act of transmission. The dexterity with which Chrétien manipulates the resources of the dia-

★ See anthology, pp. 393–4.

lectician imposes this creative obligation on his listeners. Whatever weaknesses critics may have attributed to him, oversimplification is not one of them!

Yvain's first adventure when he emerges from the forest, a transition which is effected with notable touches of humour, is to defend the Lady of Noroison against the invading Count Alier. The contrast with the fountain adventure is unmistakably significant, Yvain's pitiless hounding of Esclados amidst scenes of destruction being replaced by a merciful treatment of Alier and his promise of reparation. The tokens of victory (*enseignes veraies*) formerly desired by the hero give way to the sureties of peace (*ploiges*) which he receives from the defeated count. This technique of using duplicated motifs with contrasting significance is highly characteristic of Chrétien's dialectical manner. Whilst Yvain insisted to the point of arrogance on avenging Calogrenant, his entry into the new adventure is marked by his meek inquiry of the Lady of Noroison's damsel, 'Maiden, tell me, do you need my help?' The new Yvain is thus already formed when his madness is lifted, but his new identity needs to be reaffirmed in such a way as to clarify the nature of his changed chivalric ambitions and to transcend the purely personal quest in favour of a more general, objectively viable ethos. It is at this important juncture that Chrétien introduces the lion.

The lion episode perfectly illustrates how dangerous it can be to jump to conclusions regarding Chrétien's meaning. Just as he may be obliquely critical of the conventions he presents, so he may be sceptical of the symbolism which permeated the mentality of his age. The lion is certainly one of the favourite symbols of the Middle Ages, embracing multiple meanings which range from Christ, justice and charity to the Devil or ferocity. However familiar such symbolism may have been to Chrétien's audience, it evidently has no claims on his hero. Yvain discovers the lion in combat with a fire-breathing dragon.* A number of details in Chrétien's account appear to 'block' the familiar symbolic associations. First, the *rex omnium animalium* is in undignified distress, apparently getting the worst of the encounter. Then, Yvain does not act on any positive recognition of its status, but on the negative grounds that so obviously an evil creature as the

---

* See anthology, pp. 395–6.

dragon deserves nothing but harm and, indeed, he considers it likely that he will later have to deal with an attack from the lion. Further, in order to release the lion he finds it necessary to cut off a small piece of its tail, precisely that part of the beast which is frequently given symbolic significance in the medieval bestiaries and encyclopaedias (*leonum animi index cauda*). A fourth point is that, when it is released, the lion's reaction is described in humorously anthropomorphic terms. Finally, when night falls the lion is described as remaining wakeful to protect, not its master, but the horse which was finding the grass it was chewing rather deficient in nourishment! These details may all be seen as ironic counter-indications designed to forestall too 'heavy' an allegorical interpretation of the lion. The same technique is used elsewhere. For example, the magical connotations of the salve provided by Morgan le Fay to the Lady of Noroison in the previous adventure are neutralized by the Lady's assurance that she will cure Yvain 'with the help of God'. With the same ironic inversion of expectations Chrétien tells us in *Cliges* that Fenice is so called after the bird which is 'unique as the most beautiful of all birds' – there is no reference whatever to the resurrection motif which is to occur later and has an obvious relationship to Fenice's name.

We must conclude that Chrétien did not wish his audience to overload the lion with allegorical significance and thereby substitute for its role in the narrative a meaning drawn from outside the text. Its role in the narrative is, in fact, entirely consonant with a common tag encountered throughout the Middle Ages: *Parcere prostratis scit nobilis ira leonis* – the anger of the noble lion spares the humble(d). This idea, most influentially propagated by Isidore of Seville's *Etymologies*, essentially indicates the legitimate power of moral goodness to humble the proud and succour the humble. It may be said to have obvious relevance to Yvain whose treatment of the courtly paragon Esclados was in clear contradiction of the maxim, whether we take *prostratus* in its original sense of 'defeated' or its moral extension (current in the Middle Ages) of 'humble'. And so, in Yvain's subsequent combats against the proud the lion displays terrifying savagery, whilst in the company of its master it lies down 'like a lamb'. Might is now in the service of Right (Yvain henceforward places his trust in 'God and Justice'), the hero's chivalric acts are now instigated by pity and directed towards the re-establishment of justice.

There are, of course, endless interpretative problems connected with the coherence, gradation and function of Yvain's six major adventures. They are all undertaken in the service of defenceless women, for example. Does this constitute a projection of Yvain's conscience for having left Laudine defenceless? It is anything but clear how the adventures relate to the rewinning of Laudine. Having undertaken the rescue of Lunete, who has been arraigned for treason, Yvain confronts incognito his lady and in a situation of intense dramatic irony speaks with her, whilst carefully avoiding any attempt at reunion. He is greatly affected by both the memory and, now, the sight of her and yet postpones reconciliation. What, then, does he achieve? His interview affords Laudine firsthand knowledge of the Knight of the Lion as Yvain now pseudonymously (as a sign of humility?) styles himself and this is later of crucial importance, yet it is difficult to divine the hero's intentions and even more difficult to see anything more than a technical link between the chivalric adventures and the rewinning of Laudine. For one thing, Yvain never reveals any consciousness of such a connection. There is, admittedly, one crux. He tells Laudine that he must continue on his chosen path until his lady shall forgive him: 'Lors finera mes travauz toz.' Everything hinges on our interpretation of *travauz*. Does Yvain say 'Then my trouble (distress) will be at an end' or 'Then my labour (chivalric exertions) shall cease'? The first sense would be commonplace, the second unprecedently revealing. Chrétien leaves the choice to his audience. Just as important, when Yvain finally returns to the fountain to raise the storm once again, thus producing the need for a defender, he does so not in hope, but in despair, not in the belief that his lady will forgive him on account of his good deeds (which she doesn't), but in the bleak realization that he cannot go on any more. Finally, it has to be noted that Yvain's two most important adventures, his liberation of three hundred captive maidens at Pesme Aventure and the settling of an inheritance dispute in which he has to fight Gawain (who defends the unjust cause),* never come to Laudine's attention and consequently cannot influence her attitude to the Knight of the Lion.

The fact is that the hero and his wife are reunited by means of a *pia*

---

* See anthology, pp. 396–8.

fraus worked by Lunete, who persuades Laudine that only the Knight of the Lion can defend the fountain against the man who now raises the storm and that in return for his services Laudine must promise to do all in her power to reconcile him with his lady. The romance ends as it began – with a trick. Laudine, *semper eadem*, agrees to accept the Knight of the Lion about whom she has heard such good things (as she had earlier on about Yvain). Her reaction to the discovery that she has been tricked and that this knight is none other than her husband is entirely legalistic: 'I'd rather put up with tempests and storms for the rest of my life and were it not perjury, which is a wicked and evil thing, I should never grant him reconciliation at any price.' Once more Yvain adopts the tone of the meek and subservient lover: 'Lady, mercy should be shown to a sinner. I have paid for my folly and it was right that I should. Folly caused my absence and I acknowledge that I am guilty and in the wrong.' To this Laudine gracelessly replies: 'Very well then. I agree, since I should commit perjury if I did not do everything in my power to secure reconciliation between us.'

This leaves every major issue open. Does Laudine still love Yvain, or even forgive him? What does Yvain mean by 'I have paid for my folly'? Does he mean that he has paid for it in suffering – *vincit qui patitur* – or that he has in some sense atoned for it by performing important chivalric services which contrast with the adventure by which he first won his wife? The contrived circularity of this ending is striking and its ambiguity scarcely dispelled by Chrétien's weak assurance that 'Yvain is now loved and cherished by his lady and she by him', an assertion so unconvincing in the circumstances that Chrétien playfully adds a colophon in which he declares 'This is how Chrétien concludes his romance of the Knight of the Lion. I heard tell nothing further and nor shall you, unless someone fabricates additions.' This authorial anticipation of scribal interference with such an unsatisfactory ending is entirely justified by some of the manuscripts of Hartmann von Aue's German version (early thirteenth century) which contain additions, of a naïvely domestic nature, to bolster up belief in the couple's happiness.

We are thus returned to our initial observation that the romance may be used to subvert the same courtly values which it apparently transmits and promotes. The common theme of the romance is what has been termed the 'chivalry topos', namely an ideal co-ordination of chivalric and amatory pursuits. Love of a lady inspires the knight to displays of chivalric prowess which in turn intensify the lady's love. The question is whether Chrétien in the *Yvain* has not systematically dismantled this courtly theme *par excellence*. The winning of Laudine rests on three highly ambiguous manoeuvres: the ambivalent chivalry of Yvain, who kills her first husband, the stage-managing of the wily *entremetteuse*, Lunete, and the political coercion exercised by the urgent need to find a defender of the fountain. These elements undercut the traditional bride-winning motif. Laudine's love for Yvain is never demonstrated and only once affirmed (when she in turn deceives her barons). Laudine is won and rewon through trickery and duress and there is never any explicit connection between Yvain's accomplishment of exemplary chivalric feats and Laudine's attitude to him. Laudine remains mysterious – she cannot be explained by the psychology of *odi et amo* – and the fact that the romance ends in her court, rather than at the court of Arthur, emphasizes Chrétien's independence of mind. His *Yvain* is a puzzle with more than a trace of scepticism concerning romance conventions. The treatment of chivalry offers much food for serious thought and in the constant touches of humour which accompany it we may see the *sprezzatura* of a consummate literary virtuoso at the height of his powers.

NOTES

1. On the major aspects of this theme see the balanced survey by Roger Boase, *The Origin and Meaning of Courtly Love. A Critical Study of European Scholarship* (Manchester, 1977).

2. For the most recent historical work on the problems surrounding the evolution of chivalry see Tony Hunt in *Knighthood in Medieval Literature*, ed. W. H. Jackson (D. S. Brewer, Woodbridge, Mass., 1982), 1–22.

THE *POEM OF MY CID*

IAN MICHAEL

Modern readers who are in any way familiar with the Homeric poems, or with the medieval French *chansons de geste*, will at once perceive in the *Poema de Mio Cid* certain techniques of structure and formulaic features of style which are commonly found in all known examples of primitive epic, and they will discover most of the themes and motifs associated with the genre. These themes are presented by opposites, as the shining obverse and tarnished reverse of antique coins, and they include honour and disgrace, vassalic allegiance and outlawry, valour and cowardice, loyalty and treachery, feuds and alliances, propriety and impropriety. The narrative motifs consist principally of journeys, with stylized departures and arrivals; battles, described in a number of stages: council-of-war, eve-of-battle speech, drawing-up of battle-lines, attack, rout, pursuit, and collection and division of the spoils; court scenes and law-suits, heralded by messengers, preceded by donning of armour and raiment, and religious vigil, followed by formal challenges, considered judgements, and hard-fought trials by combat.

Those readers coming fresh to the Spanish poem will be surprised, perhaps, by its joyous optimism, its insistence on the motivation of personal gain, its relative lack of interest in a holy war against the infidel, and its warm portrayal of the family unit within a turbulent and expanding society. Although the first part of the poem deals mainly with military and vassalic matters, the second part, as in the later *chansons de geste*, brings to the fore elements associated more with romance than with epic: physical outrages committed upon two noblewomen by their cowardly husbands, and the vengeance coldly wreaked upon them by the ladies' father.

For almost a century the *Poema de Mio Cid* has been regarded as highly unusual among extant examples of medieval epic in having been composed very close (*c.*1140) to the events it describes (1092–9), and in its faithful narration of those events. These views were propagated by Menéndez Pidal and his neo-traditionalist school and have been widely accepted in Spain and the rest of Europe and in the Americas. In recent years British scholarship has cast much doubt on these propositions, and has preferred to attribute the poem to the early thirteenth century, perhaps *c.*1201–7, and has pointed to a great deal of fictitious material, not only in the latter part of the poem which had always been recognized, but throughout the text, while explaining the allusions to historical but very minor personages, unimportant to the action, as evidence of documentary research on the poet's part. One British scholar has even proposed classical sources (Sallust and Frontinus) for two episodes (the Cid's attacks on Castejón and Alcocer, respectively). This has naturally brought conflict with those American and Continental scholars who have approached the poem from the 'oralist' standpoint, attempting to show that it was composed of oral formulae by illiterate *jongleurs*, in the manner of the modern Yugoslav heroic poems. It must be recognized, however, that these attempts have not been able to show that much more than a quarter of the extant poem consists of formulae, so that at best, if one accepts the oralist thesis, it can be regarded only as a 'transitional' product between primitive oral versions now lost and learned written texts.

That the poem was intended to be chanted, perhaps sung, in public cannot be doubted, and there is some evidence in the unique extant MS. of fourteenth-century date[1] that it was used for this purpose. But the MS. clearly had monastic connections too, and it may well have played a part in the Cid's tomb cult that sprang up at the Benedictine monastery of San Pedro de Cardeña (Burgos), which is not far from his birthplace at Vivar, where the MS. was found in 1596.

The poem sings of the Spanish national hero, Rodrigo Díaz de Vivar, son of a Castilian baronet and descendant of one of the Judges of the County of Castile. The political tension in the second half of the eleventh century between the young and ambitious Castilian landowners and lesser nobles and the high and old Leonese aristocrats came to a head in 1072 with the assassination of Sancho II of Castile, and the accession to the thrones of León and Castile of his wily brother, Alfonso VI. Rodrigo Díaz, born *c.*1043 and knighted by Fernando III the Great, had been Sancho's standard-bearer, and after his demise suffered ever more difficult relations with Alfonso, who exiled him from 1081 to 1087 and again from 1089 to 1092. During his first period of banishment, Rodrigo served for a time the Muslim emir of Saragossa, but in the second branched out on his own account, attacking Moorish towns in the emirates of Saragossa, Lérida and Valencia, and his military successes were crowned by his besieging and capture of the rich Moorish city of Valencia in 1094, where he remained in great wealth and power until his death in 1099. The early Latin chronicles bestowed the title of *Campidoctor* on him, while the Moors called him *sayyidī* ('my lord'), which was partially Castilianized as *Mio Çid*.

The first account of his exploits was given in a Latin prose chronicle, perhaps written by an eye-witness of the Levante campaigns, the *Historia Roderici* (c.1110), with which the author of the *Poema de Mio Cid* appears to have been quite familiar, although there had already existed a panegyric Latin poem, *Carmen Campidoctoris* (c.1093–4), perhaps composed in the Catalonian monastery of Ripoll. There were also two Arabic histories written by Ibn Alcama (d.1116) and Ibn Bassam (fl.1109) which presented the Cid in a less favourable light, but the poet reveals no knowledge of them. He saw his task, it seems, as a re-shaping of the historical accounts available to him into a poetic coherence, eschewing as much unfavourable material as possible. Thus he telescopes the two banishments of his hero into one, presumably because it would have been structurally inconvenient to have a rise into renewed favour followed by a further fall and rise, though this is exactly the macro-structure he achieves by the arrangement: vassalic dishonour – royal pardon – family dishonour – vengeance. To have retained the double banishment would have caused immense structural difficulties, though the poet himself (or some lost earlier source) introduced the marriages of the Cid's daughters to the Infantes of Carrión (little-known nephews of a Leonese count) and the disastrous outcome, which are historically quite unattested. The poet suppresses quite as much as he invents: the Cid's alliance with the emir of Saragossa is not mentioned, though he is shown to have one faithful Moorish ally in Avengalvón (Ibn Ghalbûn of Molina); his two imprisonments of the Christian Count of Barcelona are reduced to one, and the Cid's churlish treatment of the count is transformed into a childish hunger-strike on the count's part, overcome ultimately by the Cid's magnanimity; in the battle scenes, only the knights' exploits are described, while the foot-soldiers are mentioned only *en passant* and the bowmen not at all (perhaps out of clerical disapproval); the Cid's rather haphazard movements are re-ordered into a journey from Vivar to Valencia, made up of campaigns along the principal rivers, and the order of conquests in the Levante is changed to make Valencia the climax. Yet, when this comes, it is passed over quickly, with much less detail than the siege of Alcocer, which is both geographically and historically dubious; San Pedro de Cardeña is given full prominence, while the other monasteries favoured by the historical Cid are passed over in silence.

The essential bipartite macro-structure of the poem is cut across by indications in the text that it is to be broken into three *cantares* or songs consisting (in the extant text) of 1,084, 1,193 and 1,453 lines, respectively. This tripartite division appears to correspond to the exigencies of length for a single performance and not to any natural breaks in the poetic structure. There is, however, some evidence that the poet was numerologically obsessed, especially with three and its multiples: the First Cantar contains three campaigns along the rivers Henares, Jalón and Jiloca respectively; the Cid sends three gifts to King Alfonso before he is pardoned; three judicial duels are fought in the Third Cantar. As well as an overt reference to the Mass of the Holy Trinity, more of the numerals of detail are multiples of three than of any other number.

It is impossible for the modern reader to assess the literary quality of the *Poema de Mio Cid* by comparison with other medieval Spanish epic poems, since it is the only survivor of them in nearly complete form. The late and decadent *Mocedades de Rodrigo* which contains much fantastic material concerning the Cid's youthful exploits is a much shoddier production, and any quality to be found in the 104-line *Roncesvalles* Fragment, a thirteenth-century Navarrese version of the *Chanson de Roland*, derives from the French original. The various attempted reconstructions of lost Spanish heroic poems found embedded in the prose of thirteenth- and fourteenth-century chronicles are too uncertain to be judged with any confidence, but they seem pedestrian in comparison with their august survivor. In contrast to the paucity of extant Spanish epic material – some 5,000 lines in all – the French corpus of over seventy *chansons de geste*, providing over a quarter of a million lines for study, is enormously impressive. We cannot easily adduce reasons for a greater rate of loss of MSS in Spain, but it is clear that south of the Pyrenees there were far fewer lay patrons willing or able to employ the minstrels or to have their efforts recorded in writing. The poorer economic conditions, the lower level and narrower spread of learning and the greater and more prolonged involvement in military affairs must have played their part.

In many respects the Spanish epic appears to be closely modelled on the French (a number of verbal similarities have been noted), but it employs longer lines of a wildly varying syllable-count, faultier assonance in each laisse or stanza, and there is no sign of the newer system of laisses monorrimes with full rhyme that took hold in France by the middle of the twelfth century. Strikingly similar are the compositional unit of the half-line or full line, with repeated or slightly modified formulae, the frequent use of epic epithets for personages, towns, horses and swords,* the roll-call of warriors in the hero's battle-lines,* the listing of toponyms, the incantatory, almost magical, exploitation of language, and the direct appeals to the listening public. On the one hand the style is spare and terse, lacking descriptive adjectives or precise details of time, season, place, weather and physical appearance of the characters, while on the other it is superabundant in verbs, both directly and periphrastically used to recount the action, reaction and interaction of the participants.

Each laisse has a micro-structure which does not necessarily assemble the events in straightforward linear progression, but often turns back to give a different focus on to something that has already been narrated in briefer form, or it fills out with more or different detail, and it may even give a partially contradictory account of the same event. When this technique is found within a laisse it constitutes a kind of 'double narration' or insistent allusion,* and when it occurs between two or more laisses it is a form of parallelistic repetition. Sometimes there is an even more ambitious effort to break out of the confines of linear progression to which literature, whether aural or read, is condemned, when laisses similaires are employed to recount

---

* See anthology, p. 412; p. 412, laisse 37; p. 415.

simultaneous and similar, but separate, events in successive stanzas.★ These tricks of composite, similar or parallel laisses have been explained in terms of the entirely oral performance for which the medieval epic was intended; but more than this, these complex micro-structures form the very texture of this poetry of action and are the high point of the *jongleur*'s art. Over that texture, he applies the linguistically archaic patina of the style-surface, which is a deliberately sought effect, a *Kunstsprache*, rather than a mere cultural accident.[2]

All these *jongleuresque* techniques are put to the service of establishing Rodrigo Díaz's pre-eminence in contemporary society, and well beyond the grave – hence the proud cry at the end 'Today the Kings of Spain are related to him and all gain lustre from the fame of the fortunate Campeador' (lines 3724–5). The contrast with the poem's bleak opening could not be greater: there the Cid is presented as the unjustly banished vassal, grief-stricken at King Alfonso's treatment of him, but loyally refusing to lay the blame on the monarch; rather he inculpates his enemies at court, who are unspecified at this stage (line 9); they will later be shown to be responsible not only for his banishment but also for urging the king to arrange the marriage of the Infantes de Carrión with Rodrigo's daughters, which brings further dishonour on the Cid. As he leaves Vivar, he weeps openly at the sight of his abandoned estates, now forfeit to the king, yet he demonstrates his unbowed spirit by thanking God for the test imposed on him. On the bitter road to exile, the Cid sees two birds, one of good and one of ill omen, and, Aeneas-like, he shrugs off the latter, urging his right-hand man Alvar Fáñez to rejoice in the midst of vicissitude.★ This scene of rejection is reinforced by his being shut out by the townsfolk of Burgos, afraid of the *ira regis*. Their cry 'What a good vassal. If only he had a good lord!' (or 'Would that he had a good lord!', line 20) deliberately plays on a Castilian audience's ancient antagonism to the Leonese faction at court who have the king in their thrall. Not until the formal reconciliation between king and vassal in the Second Cantar is Alfonso VI presented in a more favourable moral stance, though

★ See anthology, pp. 414–15, laisse 128, and cf. laisses 129–30; p. 410.

there is no overt, or even implied, attack on the institution of monarchy itself.

The desolate opening presentation of the Cid in late middle age, at the nadir of his fortunes, becomes the yardstick by which we judge his later military conquests, culminating in the capture of Valencia, and the ultimate vindication of his family, at the court held in Toledo, which leads to the trial by combat of his disgraced sons-in-law and the second marriages of his daughters to princes of Navarre and Aragon. The concept of honour in the poem is complex: it involves one's position in society, one's estates and possessions, one's prowess in battle, one's social conduct and the *nuevas* or reputation one has in the eyes of others. The double dishonour suffered by Rodrigo, first vassalic, then family, though it cannot be restored to its former state (since the dishonourable deeds cannot be undone), can be redressed with increase, *pagado con creces*, as Spaniards still say. Thus the poet never shows us the Cid returning to Old Castile to his estates at Vivar (though we are given to understand that they are restored to him), nor is he seen to enter Burgos or the abbey of San Pedro de Cardeña again. Instead we see him in grander state, installed as lord of Valencia, in reality posing a potential political and military threat to King Alfonso, though the Cid explicitly rejects any suggestion of disloyalty. He appears at the King's court in Toledo, which he has demanded, with all the trappings of a visiting rival monarch,★ yet he is careful to make exaggerated obeisance to his liege, and emerges as morally superior to the king, who is upstaged in every respect.★ Likewise, when the Infantes of Carrión abandon his daughters after ill-treating them in most ignoble fashion, the dishonour to the Cid's family cannot be undone, but it is redressed with a vengeance by the Infantes' moral and physical defeat in the duels and by the daughters' second marriages to royal princes.

The double structure of the poem can be likened to two parallel rising spirals: no one and nothing ever return to the exact point of departure nor to the *status quo ante*. It is this rising structure that gives the work its triumphant thrust and distinguishes it so sharply from the pessimistic falling cadence of the *Chanson de Roland*. Just

★ See anthology, p. 416; p. 417.

as the opening of the poem appears to be missing (though it is difficult to imagine a more effective start), so its ending seems to be truncated, possibly because it conflicted with certain details of the tomb-cult that had grown up at San Pedro de Cardeña by the third or fourth decade of the thirteenth century. The very faulty metre and pious banality of lines 2726–30, alleging that the Cid died on Whit Sunday, are the final example of clerical retouching which the poem betrays throughout. The great sweep of the original conception remains, however, and still has the power to grip the modern reader. Reflection of, and propaganda for, the warrior class it doubtless was, yet it sings of universal human qualities, expressed in action, with a power that can surprise us.

NOTES

1. Biblioteca Nacional, Madrid, MS. V^a 7–17.
2. These verbal archaisms are similar, though not identical, to those employed in the Spanish ballads of the fifteenth and sixteenth centuries. In the *Poema* they include: apocope of object pronouns, syntactic phonology, appositional use of the copula *e(t)*, archaic verb tense-forms, intensive pleonisms, Latinized and legalistic lexical forms.

CHURCH DRAMA AND POPULAR
DRAMA

RICHARD AXTON

Within a year or two of 969, when King Edgar published a letter
to 'those of monastic status', complaining that 'a house of clergy
is known as a meeting place for actors (*histriones*) ... where mimes
(*mimi*) sing and dance', Bishop Ethelwold's *Regularis Concordia*
recommended that English Benedictine houses adopt an Easter 'play'
of the *Visit to the Sepulchre*.[1] There is not a real paradox here in
the Church's attitude towards drama, because the references are to
different kinds of performance: the subjects of the 'plays', the modes
of performance, the status and intentions of the actors are all distinct.
Professional performers offered a variety of entertainment: music,
dance, tumbling and juggling, impersonations, puppetry, tricks with
animals. Their shows – to judge from the condemnations of them
– were often satirical and indecent; their favourite targets, women
and clergy; their purpose, food, drink and money. From the
thirteenth century there survive English and French texts of such
'mimic' plays: a Flemish farce of a blind man and his boy, and two
versions of an English wooing play in which the clerk is aided by
an old bawd who performs a trick with a dog. Collection of money
from bystanders is part of both performances.

In contrast, the Benedictine monks who made and acted what we
think of as the first Christian 'plays', worked within the confines
of the church service, embellishing the service at the great festivals
of the year (principally Easter and Christmas) with new compositions;
these were sung in Latin to melodies generated from the Gregorian
chant of the liturgy itself. In the case of the *Visitatio Sepulchri*
approved by the Bishop of Winchester, the performers are 'four
brethren' dressed in ecclesiastical garb and 'carrying thuribles with
incense'. They process gravely through church space, nave and choir,
to a church monument (the Easter sepulchre) where sacred objects
are stored and displayed. These things, done 'in imitation of the angel

seated on the sepulchre and the women coming with spices to anoint the body of Jesus', are performed 'for the strengthening of faith'.

The two traditions are distinct because they are antagonistic. There were other kinds of drama at this period too: the knowledge of Latin drama (Terence and Plautus) was not lost and from time to time scholarly Latin 'comedies' were composed for reading and perform-ance, in cathedral schools and cloisters. Elements of drama are found in many social pastimes – in popular dances and court entertainments, in tournaments and battle-drill; these, too, had some importance for the development of dramatic forms in the Middle Ages. But the evidence favours the Church, whose play texts adorned the Word of scripture and were written as carefully as were the service books. The survival of the Middle English *Interlude of the Clerk and the Girl* on a little parchment roll with the speakers' names noted merely by letters in the margin is something of a freak, whereas liturgical play texts were given careful rubrics and often musical notation; the so-called Fleury Playbook (also from the thirteenth century) contains texts and music for plays on sacred subjects appropriate to feasts of the liturgical calendar.

In comparison with the great Latin sung plays from the monasteries of France and Germany in the twelfth century, the two earliest vernacular plays are much more popular, in two respects: in their use of spoken Anglo-Norman French and in their outdoor perform-ance. Staging the *Play of Adam* (*c.*1150) and the *Holy Resurrection* (*c.*1180) would have required the resources of a monastery or cathe-dral school, but these are plays intended for lay audiences. The dialogue is the language of the courts and nobles, and of many town-dwellers in southern England. The rhymed prologue to *La Seinte Resureccion* speaks of performance 'devant le puple' and of preparing 'asez large place' to contain the 'houses' and fixed places for more than forty-two actors.[2] Meticulous Latin stage directions for *Adam* direct the devils during the temptation scene to run about 'through the crowd' (*per populum*) and 'through the acting place(s)'. The great care and fullness of these rubrics make *Adam* an ideal focus for the study of medieval acting.[3]

In its manuscript, *Adam* is entitled *Ordo representacionis Ade*, as if it were an 'order of service' in church worship. A Latin lesson (*lectio*) is intoned to signal the beginning of each of the two formal sections of the play (Adam and Cain; the Prophets) and in the course of performance eight Gregorian responsories are sung by a choir. Performance is outdoors, but against the church door, possibly using the porch and steps at the west end (traditionally known as paradise) to advantage. The actor playing God ('*Figura*', the 'figure' or 'the Saviour', as he is called) comes from and retires to the church. He is robed in a priest's dalmatic and wears a stole when, to the accompaniment of choral singing, 'By the sweat of thy brow', he must expel Adam and Eve from paradise in a manner reminiscent of an Ash Wednesday ceremony for 'expulsion of sinners'. The playwright's indebtedness to the ceremonial drama of the church liturgy is plain. He need not specify what the choir shall wear, nor where they shall stand, nor give the musical notation for responsories, because all these matters would be known. To this extent the 'play' overlaps with familiar worship.

However, in representing the fall of Adam and murder of Abel in action animated by vernacular dialogue, the playwright seems conscious of breaking new ground:

And let Adam be well trained not to answer too quickly nor too slowly, when he has to answer. Not only Adam but all the actors (*omnes personae*) shall be instructed to control their speech and to make their actions appropriate to the matter they speak of; and, in speaking the verse, not to add a syllable, nor to take one away, but to enunciate everything distinctly, and to say everything in the order laid down.

By such scrupulous control episodes which might appear ludicrous when acted are stylized – for example, nakedness and violence, both objects of condemnation in popular entertainments. Even if nakedness had not been thought actually indecent and had been simulated, it would hardly have been possible for male actors playing Adam and Eve to show discovery of their shameful state. So they are clothed in 'ceremonial robes', red and white respectively, (betokening, perhaps, St Paul's 'robes of righteousness') and placed behind the curtain wall in paradise. When they taste the apple, then Adam 'shall strip off his fine clothes and shall put on paupers' clothes of fig leaves sewn together'. The couple's shame and grief are inscribed by their bodies, 'bent forward', no longer fully upright. Similarly, in the killing of Abel, though it is brutally life-like (Cain 'shall strike as if he were really killing Abel'), having Abel 'kneel towards the east' stylizes the murder. The inner meaning of Abel's sacrifice as a 'figure' of Christ's death is conveyed in a familiar icon.

Details of costume (robes, crowns, beards) are given for sixteen of the speaking characters, for all, that is, except two: these are both diabolic. Diabolus himself, who tempts Adam and Eve (and is recognized by them as Satan); and 'the Jew' who interrupts the prophet Isaiah, mocking his prophecy of the Virgin birth.[4] Why is this? It seems the playwright can safely rely on a knowledge of convention in such matters. The Jew 'thrusts forth his "hand"', pretending that Isaiah is a palm-reader and quack doctor, since by his 'devinaille' he can diagnose a miraculous pregnancy. (See below for the occurrence of this motif in folk-play.) We do not know how Satan and the *demones* were costumed: certainly grotesquely, perhaps with the beast-heads or masks so persistently condemned in popular dramatics and associated with pagan rites of the dead.[5] The *demones* are stagehands whose job is to remove all dead bodies (Adam, Eve, their children, the eleven prophets) when their scenes are played and to take them to hell. Satan cannot wear a full-face mask because he must change expressions; leaving Adam 'sad and with downcast face' he greets Eve 'fawningly, with a smiling face'; and his appearance does not alarm either of them.

Satan shares with the non-speaking devils freedom to rush energetically through the acting place and audience. While Adam and Eve 'walk about, decently enjoying themselves in paradise', the devils 'meanwhile *run to and fro* through the place, making appropriate gestures'. They have no set speech and must mime when 'they show Eve the forbidden fruit as if tempting her to eat it'. When Adam and Eve are dragged in chains to hell, the devils 'make a great dance and jubilation' in their diabolic kitchen, 'shouting to one another', making an uproar of kettles and cauldrons and a stench of smoke. In their mimicry and hilarity, their wild dancing, their freedom to improvise and be intimate with the audience, one may see 'the subliterary survival of the tradition of the antique mime'.[6] The devils embody the forms of play-behaviour condemned by the church in other auspices.

The mixing of church and popular styles which is apparent in the acting is found also in the words of the play. As I have mentioned, the 'authority' for the story is given in the Latin readings and responsories sung by the choir; the vernacular French dialogue expands and animates their textual message. The verse — mostly short-lined octosyllabic couplets — is easy to memorize and enunciate in the open air; it is compact, rhythmic, and dignified, as in God's injunction to Adam:

> Je t'ai duné bon cumpainun:
> Ce est ta femme, Eve a noun.
> Ce est ta femme e tun pareil:
> Tu le devez estre ben fiël.
> Tu aime lui, e el ame tei,
> Si serez ben ambedui de moi.
> Ele soit a tun comandement,
> E vus ambe deus a mun talent.
>
> (9–16)

> (I've given you a good companion:
> She is your wife, her name is Eve,
> She is your wife and partner; you
> Must stay faithful to her and true.
> May you love her and in turn she
> Love you; both will be loved by me.
> She must answer to your command,
> The two of you be in my hand.)

or more contrivedly rhetorical, in the anguished repetitions of Adam's remorse:

> Ai, mort, por quoi me laisses vivre?
> Que n'est li monde de moi delivre?
> Por quoi faz encombrer al mond?
> D'emfer m'estoet tempter le fond.
> En emfer serra ma demure,
> Tant que vienge qui me sucure.
>
> (329–34)

> (O death, why don't you seize on me?
> Why cannot the earth be rid of me?
> Why do I encumber the world?
> I should be plunged in deepest hell.
> In hell shall be my dwelling place
> Till One shall come to rescue me.)

The Devil introduces a more casual and colloquial speech, with a greater variety of tones of voice to match his mobile face:

DIABOLUS: Creras me tu? Guste del fruit.
ADAM: Noel frai pas.
DIABOLUS: Or oëz deduit!
          Nel feras?
ADAM: Non!
DIABOLUS: Kar tu es soz!
          Encore to membrera des moz.

and, after a parley with his crew and a foray through the place:

> Adam, que fais? Changeras tun sens?
> Es tu encore en fol porpens?
> Jol te quidai dire l'autrier,
> Deus t'a fait ci sun provender,
> Ci t'ad mis por mangier cest fruit.
> As tu donch altre deduit?
>
> (169–78)

> (Will you believe me? Taste the fruit.
> I will not.
>   That's fun to hear!
> Why won't you?
>   No!
>   You're a fool.
> One day you'll say, 'He told me so!'

> Well, Adam? – will you change your mind?
> Are you still set in your stupid ways?
> I meant to say the other day,
> God has made you a mere dependant,
> And put you here to eat his fruit.
> Do you have any other fun?)

The voice modulates from wheedling, through an ironic 'aside', to outright scorn. After the 'interlude' in which Satan presumably attempts to get the audience on his side, the casualness with which he resumes his conversation and the sarcasm of *deduit* (he has debased the notion of innocent pleasure – '*honeste delectantes*' – in his use of the word six lines earlier) are masterly.

In rendering the story of Genesis in human terms, the poet concentrates on the relationships between the characters. Adam and Eve are any married couple set at odds by the attentions of a smooth-tongued stranger. Their obligations are conceived in contemporary feudal terms: God is the ultimate overlord and protector; Adam,

Eve, Cain and Abel are his vassals, holding land in fief from him and offering dues and service in return for protection. God's first injunction to Adam is that he must never make war (*mover guere*) against him. Eve is Adam's *bon cumpainum* and *pareil* to whom he must be *ben fiel*. She swears obedience to Adam as her *seignor*; she will offer him *bon conseil*, the duty of a good vassal to his lord. The vows of mutual comfort and love in marriage are made outside paradise, probably at the church door, where marriages were contracted; God then installs the couple in paradise as if it were a fief to be held from him on certain conditions. If Adam eats the fruit, he will betray a lord and 'should be judged by traitor's law'. In his despair Adam sees his trespass in legal terms; he has 'no friend or neighbour who might get me out of his pleading'.

The story of Cain and Abel is similarly shown as feudal treachery of older brother against younger. But this feudal quarrel of brother farmers is also touched with philosophical arguments. Cain mocks Abel's *doctrine*, pronouncing like Edmund his own more modern, atheistic creed: 'De nus amer Nature nus enseigne.' Equivocally this seems to mean that Nature teaches us to love ourselves rather than to love one another (*s'entramer* is not used; nor does the word *ambedui* ('both'), notable in the vows of Adam and Eve, appear here). After the failure of his sacrifice, Cain claims that Abel is a 'proven traitor' and raising his right arm in menace, vowing to prove the charge by force (surely a damning view of judicial combat, which the Normans had introduced into England). He scorns Abel's appeal to his faith and his lord (*fiance*) and pronounces formally his defiance: 'Jo toi defi.'

Viewed within this network of hierarchical values, the relationship of Adam and Eve with its paradoxical emphasis on mutuality and equality (Eve is to love Adam 'as my equal and the stronger') is vulnerable. In his temptation of Eve* Satan reformulates the relationships and obligations in his own cynical terms. To Eve, Adam is 'very noble' (*mult francs*) but to Satan he is 'very servile' (*mult serf*). God's ideal marriage is debased in Satan's speech to a 'mal cuple'; she is 'trop tendre', Adam 'trop dur'. The Devil's picture of Eve as a fragile rose, pure as driven snow, in need of protection, contains also – by courtly logic – the assertion that her wisdom is superior.

* See anthology, p. 418.

Granted her fair body and face, the 'chance' (*aventure*) Satan offers will make her 'lady of the world'. There is delicious irony in bestowing on Eve, beginner of man's woes, the title of Mary, queen of heaven and mother of the redeemer. The vocabulary throughout this exchange assumes an audience familiar with 'new ideas' of the psychology of love. The world of Eleanor of Aquitaine, patroness of troubadours and arbiter of courts of love, Queen of England from 1154 to Henry II's death in 1189, is a world that the *Adam* poet regards suspiciously. In his interpretation of the fall, courtly ideas pose a direct threat to the Christian ideal of marriage; overthrowing a husband's *discipline* leads to *traison* and, in the next generation, to murder.

The construction of *Adam* is as innovatory as its dramatic technique; it consists of a series of discrete scenes of Old Testament history, chosen for their theological significance rather than their part in a continuous narrative. Adam and Eve do not overlap with their children, Cain and Abel; and each of the eleven prophets in turn is similarly removed to hell. Through the discrete episodes the main theme emerges: the necessity for man's salvation, hinted first in Adam's hopeless knowledge that

> None will ever give me aid
> Except the son who shall be born of Mary
> (381–2)

and spelled out triumphantly in the words of the prophets, seven of whom specifically predict Adam's deliverance. Jeremiah speaks to the audience as God's household (*sa maisnee*), inviting them by word and gesture to enter by the church door 'to adore the Saviour', who 'shall rescue Adam from prison, giving his own body for a ransom'. The fearful sense that Christ's coming as saviour is also his coming as judge is fully exploited in the verse sermon on 'Fifteen Signs of Judgement' with which the play text concludes. This cyclic construction – Adam, Cain, Prophets, Doom – is a model to be followed by religious drama until the sixteenth century.

It is impossible to place *Adam* in the calendar of the liturgical year, because its subjects belong to different seasons: Adam and Cain to pre-Lent, the Prophets to pre-Christmas. Neither time is very suitable for outdoor production and it may be that the 'sweet smelling flowers

and foliage' planted in paradise indicate a spring or summer performance. Once the church playwrights looked outside the confines of
church building and church services towards popular audiences, the
summer time was obviously more suitable, as well as being traditionally a time for outdoor entertainments.[7] The great majority of Latin
liturgical plays belonged to the Christmas or Easter seasons, leaving
the summer/autumn half of the year free from major feasts of
doctrinal importance. Corpus Christi (established 1264 and generally
adopted by the early fourteenth century) filled this vacuum by providing a church feast to rival popular observance of May and Midsummer. Corpus Christi became the time for outdoor processions
of civic and religious guilds, of pageants both sacred and profane,
and of cyclic plays showing the plan of man's salvation, from
Creation to Doomsday, centring on the Passion.

A 'mixed style' of presentation is used for dramatizing the Passion
narrative in a late twelfth-century play from Bavaria. The text is
found in the celebrated *Carmina Burana* manuscript, together with
dancing-songs in Latin and German which show that the monks of
Benediktbeuern did not shun contact with the world. The Passion
play and an accompanying Christmas play are ambitious in scope
and spectacle, whether for indoor or outdoor performance one
cannot be sure. This is the most ambitious of the few known Latin
Passion plays; it shows Jesus's entry into Jerusalem, Judas's bargain,
Jesus's agony and arrest, his trial and crucifixion, Judas's suicide, the
sorrow of Mary, the miracle of Longinus, restored to sight by pierc-
ing Christ's side, and Joseph of Arimathea's request to take down
the body. A framework of narrative is provided by choral singing
of Latin responsories, antiphons and hymns, together with passages
from the various gospel narratives. Meanwhile, much of the action
is shown in dumbshow, rather scantily described (e.g. 'Let the lord
advance alone to the shore to call Peter and Andrew, and let him
find them fishing'). Simultaneous presentation of all the places necessary for the whole action (as in *La Sainte Resureccion*) requires the use
of a very large acting area and allows for some exciting, filmic effects.
The crowd of Jews, 'following Judas, with swords and clubs and
lanterns', circle the acting place while the Last Supper is mimed, and
Jesus ascends and descends the Mount of Olives three times,
rebuking the sleeping disciples. Finally, the two parties confront one

another for the dramatic arrest of Jesus. In a later sequence Judas hangs himself while the crucifixion is being prepared:[8]

Then let Jesus be led to crucifixion. Then let Judas go singing to the chief priests and, having thrown down the pence, say weeping:
Paenitet me graviter quod isti argenteis Christum vendiderim.
(I urgently repent me that for this silver I sold Christ)

The priests reply in the words of St Matthew's gospel: 'What is that to us, Judas Iscariot? See you to it.' Then,

Immediately let the devil come, and lead Judas to hanging, and let him be hanged. Then let lamenting women come from afar off, to weep for Jesus, to whom let Jesus say:
Filiae Jerusalem, nolite flere super me, sed super vos ipsas.
(Daughters of Jerusalem, do not weep for me but for yourselves.)
Then let Jesus be hanged on the cross.

The devil has appeared earlier, attending to the affairs of Mary Magdalene and her lover. This surprising scene, designed as a little morality play of sin and repentance, is the playwright's invention. It is linked in by the motif of ointment: before she anoints Christ's feet and goes to embalm his body, Mary Magdalene is shown buying cosmetics and flaunting her body before the men in the audience. She sings of the delights of the world, first in Latin:

> Mundi delectatio · dulcis est et grate,
> Eius conversatio · suavis et ornata.
> Mundi sunt deliciae, · quibus aestuare
> Volo, nec lasciviam · eius devitare.

> (The delight of the world is sweet and gratifying,
> Its commerce pleasing and lavish.
> There are pleasures of the world for which I long
> Passionately to burn, rather than shunning its
> wantonness).

then in vernacular German; the frank sensuality and the jaunty melody with its provocative refrain –

> Seht mich an,
> iungen man,
>   lat mich eu gevallen!

> (Look at me,
> you young men,
>   let me give you pleasure).

seem to demand that Magdalene dance bewitchingly before her audience. Before withdrawing, freshly perfumed and adorned, to the bed, to which the devil will escort her lover, she instructs the audience in the art of courtly love:

> Love, you worthy men,
>   love women capable of love.
> Love makes you full of highest joy
>   and lets you appear in high honour.

taking up the theme a second time –

> That man must be free from cares
>   who is to enjoy my love.

This courtly teaching comes – as it does in *Adam* – from the devil. Later, after the promptings of the good angel, Mary 'shall put aside her worldly attire and put on a black mantle; and the lover shall withdraw, and the devil'.

The stylized presentation of Mary's sinful life avoids the indecency of a mimic performance (such as is appropriate at the end of the Middle English *Dame Sirith* or the Latin *Pamphilus*)[9] by showing her as the soloist of a popular dancing-game. When Magdalene enters the action she comes 'cum puellis', that is, attended by a chorus of girls who dance round her as their 'queen'. The self-adornment and amorous exploits of 'bele Aelis' and her sisters-in-May-games are well documented in German, French and Provençal dancing-songs and had been condemned from the pulpit as seductions of the devil.

The mixture of ecclesiastical and popular styles is not confined to plays with a liturgical 'skeleton', but is one of the most delightful aspects of much medieval vernacular drama. A fine example is Jean Bodel's *Play of Saint Nicholas* (c.1200), composed for a guild of clerks employed by the city of Arras, to be performed on the eve of their patron saint's day (6 December). The story, of a king's treasure guarded by St Nicholas's image and stolen, but recovered by the saint, is similar to a miracle dramatized simply in a Latin version. Bodel's French runs to over 1,500 lines. It was written at the time of fervent preparations for the Fourth Crusade and puts on stage the epic pretensions of Christendom, martyred and finally triumphant in the battle of faith against Mahomet. Interwoven with this high plot are the antics of the drinkers and gamblers in an Arras tavern who steal the

Saracen king's treasure. Staging this ingenious action requires thirty-odd actors and, at least, a 'palace' with a shrine for the treacherous pagan idol Tervagan, a 'prison', and a 'tavern'. There are several distinct styles of speech, ranging from the heroic Alexandrines, deliberately reminiscent of the *chansons de geste*, in the rallying cry of the Christians:[10]

> Sains Sepulcres, aïe! Segneur, or du bien faire!
> Sarrasin et paien vienent pour nous fourfaire:
> Ves les armes reluire: tous li cuers m'en esclaire.
> Or le faisons si bien que no proueche i paire;
> Contre chascun des nos sont bien cent, par devise.
>
> (396–400)

> (The Holy Sepulchre aid us! Now for great deeds.
> Pagans and Saracens come to destroy us;
> Look, how their weapons shine! My heart lights up.
> We'll do such deeds, our prowess shall be seen;
> Each one of us, it seems, must fight a hundred.)

through the grave song-with-refrain of the comforting angel:

> Tous jours li prie ensi, et Diex te secourra,
>   Qui son home ja ne faurra.
>
> (1269–70)

> (God will deliver you; pray ceaselessly to the saint.
>   God will never fail his servant.)

to the wine crier's professional *Spiel*:

> Le vin aforé de nouvel,
> A plain lot et a plain tonnel,
> Sade, bevant, et plain et gros,
> Rampant comme escuireus en bos,
> Sans nul mors de pourri ne d'aigre;
> Seur lie court et sec et maigre,
> Cler con larme de pecheour,
> Croupant seur langue a lecheour;
> Autre gent n'en doivent gouster.
>
> (645–53)

> (New wine, just freshly broached,
> Wine in gallons, wine in barrels,
> Smooth and tasty, pure, full-bodied,
> Leaps to the head like a squirrel up a tree.
> No tang of must in it, or mould –

161

Fresh and strong, full, rich-flavoured,
As limpid as a sinner's tears;
It lingers on a gourmet's tongue –
Other folk ought not to touch it!)

and the nonsense-language uttered by the idol Tervagan (1517–20) before his destruction. There is much here that is playful, exuberant, comic; the language is rich in slang, puns and proverbs. Most remarkable, perhaps, in contrast to the controlled 'figural' realism of *Adam* (where the colloquial dialogue exists only to give moral meaning to relationships between the characters) is the sheer delight in minutely recreating the trivia of a corrupt, physical world. Tavern reckonings for each drinker are kept up throughout the play, the price of candles is reckoned, and interest is charged on loans. Each throw of the dice is greeted with exclamations of delight or dismay and just enough explicitness to enable the audience to calculate the scores in a complex game of *hazard*.

Transitions in style and in physical space are made by skilful use of messengers. In the opening sequence★ the pagan king sends Connart to summon an army 'from the land of Prester John to Caramania' and Auberon to call up 'giants and Canaanites'. Promising to outstrip a camel in speed, Auberon passes the tavern, piously observing in its hoop-sign the emblem of St Benet and allowing himself to be persuaded inside for a pint. When the landlord refuses to make change, one of the regulars suggests a game of dice and Auberon escapes scot-free – to the orient, where he salutes the emirs in the name of the king and Mahomet. By such exhilarating shifts of tone, the 'high' and 'low' images of ungodliness are juxtaposed and the plot sprung into motion.

The purely secular theatre of the Middle Ages is more scantily represented among surviving play texts, but here, too, the most notable work is both traditional and experimental. The bawdy neo-Roman verse-comedies produced in the cathedral schools of the Loire valley and in England in the twelfth century and the popular thirteenth-century farces in English and French fit comfortably into well-defined traditions; this shows in the consistency of their styles. But this is not the case with the much more ambitious and interesting

★ See anthology, p. 424.

plays of Adam de la Halle. His *Robin and Marion*, composed it is thought for the expatriate Artois court in Naples some time before 1288, weaves a slender comic plot of knightly wooing and rustic innocence around twenty-one songs. The tunes were traditional in Picardy, many of them dances. Singing, dance-display, flute- and bagpipe-playing are interspersed with formal wooing, a country 'feast', quizzing games, flirting and clowning. The charm and freshness that *Robin and Marion* still has for modern audiences springs, I think, from the intermingling of modes. 'Drama' is not yet tied to generic categories; it is fluid, experimental.

The same observations apply in a greater degree to Adam's *Jeu de la Feuillée*, composed *c.*1276 for performance in his native Arras to mark his imminent departure (real or pretended) to Paris in order to study. The *Feuillée* has been described as a transcript of a carnival, a folk-play, a satirical review, an Aristophanic comedy, a sophisticated autobiographical allegory. It is all of these, for it is *sui generis*. Its mixed nature is evident in the cast-list, a medley of real people and stock figures with supernatural creatures: Adam and his father and friends; a quack doctor, expert in urinalysis to diagnose pregnancy (cf. the sceptical Jew in *Adam*); a monk, bearer of the relics of saint Acaire, patron of lunatics; an obscene fool and his father who pretend to be man and wife, bull and cow; a messenger to Hellekin, king of fairies; Morgan le Fay and two sister fairies; Fortune, a mute person or effigy bearing a wheel with life-like effigies or dolls on it; an Arras innkeeper.

Generically the play appears to be a particular, well-known poet's version of a traditional summer festival show; play-time is a night watch (appropriate to Midsummer) during which formal set-pieces are linked by the satirical chat of the author and his friends. The centre-piece of the show is the appearance of the fairy trio to sup at a table which has been prepared in a bower of greenery (the *feuillée* of the play's title) and to bestow luck or harm upon the main characters, redirecting the hero's love-life. In this version of a Midsummer night's dream the king of fairies does not appear in person and cannot bring his Titania to heel. Rather, the fairies and women of Arras are triumphant and set about physical revenge on men who have offended their sex. All the elements of popular theatre condemned by ecclesiastics are found here: superstitious practices, violent and foolish behaviour, obscene antics, drunkenness. The satire is topical, ranging from the naming of 'shrewish' wives to denunciation of trade practices and the corruption of the papacy. The territory claimed for comedy by Aristophanes and shunned by church drama with its textual and historical basis and refined modes of presentation is here used as a platform from which to flout and subvert all forms of constraint: marital, civic, ecclesiastical.

The dramatic styles are as various as the cast list would suggest: solo 'turn', satirical dialogue, masque-like tableau, pure buffoonery; and the language veers from refined rhetorical courtliness, as in Adam's 'biographical' top-to-toe description of the sweetheart who has become the 'fat and shapeless hag' to whom he is married, to the Fool's attempt at epic recitation of the 'deeds of Anseis and Marsile', to the Innkeeper's parody of the Monk, exhorting the company to worship the relics of the patron of lunatics.

The profanity of Le Jeu de la Feuillée is that of a tradition of popular drama that has preserved an aggressive independence of the Church. Indeed, through its bizarre motley of masks the vox populi can be heard grousing against the injustices of rulers, neighbours, and wives. Yet on closer inspection the play shows curious signs of indebtedness to the church traditions. As dawn breaks, the sexes separate, the women to follow the fairies and the men to light votary candles at the shrine of the Blessed Virgin, exhibited, as was usual in summer between Pentecost and the Assumption, in a nearby public square. And in the last words of the dialogue, the Monk relates the ringing of St Nicholas's church bell (or, possibly, directs his acolyte to ring a portable hand-bell to mark the end of performance).[11] The manuscript title Li jus Adans, 'Adam's play', hints at a playful biographic allegory. The play contrasts Adam's lover's paradise and the hell of domesticity, showing his attempt to reform, the help and harm given by the fairies, his temptation into the tavern and, finally, while the Monk snores, his fall again into the ribald pandemonium of the tavern.

Just as the religious plays carry the impress of popular drama, particularly in the representation of evil (the courtly Satan and antic devils in Adam, the dance-play seductress in the Carmina Burana Passion, the tavern 'hell' in Saint Nicholas) so, in reverse, the profane drama pays a tribute – if a parodic one – to that 'official' world of Church values.

Church drama and popular drama flourished in Europe for a further two hundred years before the suppression of religious plays by the forces of Reformation. The building of 'theatres' in the sixteenth century, which gave a new respectability to drama, also marked an increased professionalization of acting and a retreat from the large areas of people's lives that had been in various ways sacred. A new humanistic consensus about what plays are and how they should be constructed and written certainly stimulated the development of secular drama. But the ambivalence found in the best medieval plays by virtue of their twin allegiance – to the Church and to the world – disappeared for ever from the drama.

NOTES

1. The *Visitatio Sepulchri* from the *Regularis Concordia* of Winchester is printed with an English translation by David Bevington, *Medieval Drama* (Boston, 1975), 27. King Edgar's letter is quoted by J. D. A. Ogilvy, '*Mimi, Scurrae, Histriones*: entertainers in the Middle Ages', *Speculum*, XXXVIII (1973), 608.

2. *La Seinte Resureccion* is printed by Bevington (p. 123) and translated by him and by R. Axton and J. Stevens, *Medieval French Plays* (Oxford, 1971).

3. *Adam* is printed by Bevington (p. 80). My quotations are from the Axton and Stevens translation.

4. In the Benediktbeuern Christmas Play (Bevington, p. 183) a Jew called Archisynagogus leads a chorus of Jews in protest against St Augustine's prophecies, 'shoving forward his fellow, shaking his head and whole body, striking the ground with his foot, imitating with his staff the behaviour of a Jew in all ways'.

5. See Meg Twycross and Sarah Carpenter, 'Masks in Medieval English Theatre', *Medieval English Theatre*, III:1 (University of Lancaster, 1981), 24–7.

6. Erich Auerbach, *Mimesis* trans. W. Trask (Princeton, 1953), 159.

7. In Beverley *c*.1220 there was a play of the Resurrection in summer in the churchyard 'on the north side' (the traditional side for folk practices). Performance was 'by masked actors as is usual'. See my 'Popular modes in the earliest plays', in *Medieval Drama*, ed. N. Denny (Stratford-upon-Avon Studies, 16, London, 1973), 27.

8. The *Carmina Burana Passio* is quoted from K. Young, *Drama of the Medieval Church*, I, 518; my translation. I have regularized spelling of the German text. See also Bevington, p. 202.

9. The argument that *Pamphilus* was meant for performance is well put by P. Dronke in *Journal of the Warburg and Courtauld Institutes*, XLII (1979), 225–30.

10. *Le Jeu de Saint Nicolas*, ed. F. J. Warne (Oxford, 1951). Translation from Axton and Stevens, *Medieval French Plays*, 77.

11. *Le Jeu de la Feuillée*, ed. J. Dufournet (Ghent, 1977). Translation by Axton and Stevens, p. 213. For discussion of these closing lines see my review of Dufournet's edition in *Medium Aevum*, XLIX (1980), 157.

TROUBADOURS AND MINNESANG

INGEBORG GLIER

Vernacular love-poetry was relatively late in arriving on the literary scene of the Middle Ages. A lively, documented tradition of writing and composing love-songs did not begin until the end of the eleventh century in southern France, and not until the middle of the twelfth century in southern Germany. It is indeed noteworthy and curious that a theme we have come to regard as such a fundamental one in poetry of many different ages and in many different languages should have taken so long in establishing itself. What about it then in the preceding centuries?

There are a few love-lyrics and poems in praise of women in Latin (by Marbod of Rennes, Baudri of Bourgueil and in the 'Cambridge Songs', for instance),[1] but fascinating as some of them are, they are scattered, remain *Gelegenheitsgedichte* (or occasional poems) rather than form a coherent tradition. As a matter of fact, an outpouring of Latin love-songs did occur at roughly the same time that their vernacular counterparts were beginning to flourish. A rich collection of these Goliardic songs is contained in the famous *Carmina Burana* manuscript (formerly in Benediktbeuren, now in Munich) which was assembled in Styria around 1220/30 (definitely before 1250) and also includes religious plays and satirical poems. Its Latin love-poetry mostly originated in the twelfth century and differs markedly in tone and literary genres from contemporary Provençal and German love-songs. It resounds with a more carefree and sensuous kind of love, favours narrative more (especially pastourellas) and fairly frequently delights in the mixture of languages (Latin and German). It is also earthier and less given to reflection and suffering. The authors of these songs, who remain mostly anonymous, were presumably *clerici vagantes*, wandering scholars, who composed them for and recited them to educated, i.e. clerical audiences. The spheres of the Latin and the vernacular poetry do not seem to have touched too often. There is little evidence that they stimulated each other decisively. Both are rather like two different strong plants growing from the same rich soil.

Of vernacular love-poetry, there are even fewer traces before the twelfth century. In the Carolingian period, for instance, we find a somewhat puzzling reference in one of the capitularies of Charles the Great. There nuns are forbidden *winileodas uel scribere uel mittere*, i.e. to write or send songs of or to a friend/lover.[2] None of these songs, of course, survived, but it seems safe to assume that the activities mentioned must have been fairly widespread to warrant an imperial prohibition.

Traces of a different kind are poems in mixed languages. We know, for example, a Latin dawn song (preserved in a late tenth-century manuscript) that contains a refrain in Provençal.[3] And the Latin epic *Ruodlieb* (late eleventh century; Bavaria) includes a charming short 'salute of love' that is sprinkled with German words: *loubes*, *liebes*, *vvunna*, *minna* (leaves, pleasure, joys, love), all pertaining, as later German songs will abundantly show, to the basic vocabulary of love. These are significant, but certainly isolated examples. A whole body of texts, however, is preserved from Moslem Spain. It was written during the eleventh and twelfth centuries and consists of poems in classical Arabic or Hebrew in which the last stanza was followed by a refrain in the regional vernacular, a *kharja*. These lyrics preceded those of the first troubadour, Guilhem IX of Aquitaine, by at least half a century, and they continued to be written while troubadour poetry and Minnesang were on the rise. Their mixture of languages resembles to a certain extent that of the tenth-century dawn song, and since most of the *kharjas* are women's love-songs, it is tempting to at least associate them with the *winileodas*. Thus, finally, the ominous question of the origins of troubadour poetry and Minnesang arises.

The arduous and at times heated debate about these 'origins' cannot possibly be related here in detail. Yet an indication of feasible backgrounds might be helpful. Both, the first troubadour and the first minnesinger we know by name, seem to come out of nowhere, and each was in his own way not a beginner but a master. It is therefore not surprising that the question where they got it from should have been so dominant in scholars' minds. But so far, we do not have a theory or an explanation that is generally accepted.

Each of the following theories or a combination thereof covers certain important features of troubadour or minnesinger art, yet leaves others unexplained. It has, for instance, been suggested that classical and/or medieval Latin love-poetry had a decisive impact on vernacular love-songs. Yet while Ovid and Cicero (especially *De amicitia*) certainly played a role here and there and while clerical Latin love-letters offer striking parallels in sentiment, they clearly did not trigger vernacular love-songs. Others have maintained that the cult of the Virgin Mary or the feudal system were influential models, especially for the concept of courtly love (*fin'amors, hohe minne*). Indeed, the idea of a lover loyally serving his most worthy and beautiful lady or even worshipping her reflects in some ways the relations of vassal and lord, and when the lady appears as an almost divine being there are clear analogies between religious and amorous service. But neither can courtly love be explained as a secularized religion nor does it mirror the social system of the time on an individual level. As Peter Dronke has shown,[4] the phenomenon of courtly love is not a prerogative of twelfth-century central European literatures, but is to be found in many literatures and different ages.

Much discussed also was the question of possible Arabic influence from Moslem Spain. Yet while this issue might be legitimately raised concerning the first troubadours from the south of France, it would be irrelevant in the case of the first minnesingers in Austria or south Germany. There is no denying an often overlooked fact: Minnesang, though starting about half a century later than troubadour poetry, is in its earliest stages quite independent of it. At a later stage, however, there is noticeable Provençal influence on Minnesang. Vernacular love-poetry of the twelfth century, therefore, has not just one origin but at least two. That, among other things, leads to the assumption of a preceding anonymous Romance and Germanic tradition which remained mostly oral. Although that sounds plausible enough, the problem persists that almost nothing of that tradition was transmitted and that we get a few glimpses of it here and there at best. Moreover, this assumption, while tentatively answering the question of origins or beginnings, would raise other problems. We would then have to ask why all of a sudden names were attached to texts and why this poetry was preserved in manuscripts (even if this did not happen until roughly a century after it was composed in some cases, more or less than that in others). Though the various theories about 'origins' contributed in many ways to our understanding of vernacular love-poetry in the twelfth century, a mystery remains. But we should also not forget that it is one of several literary mysteries of the period. Similar questions arise for King Arthur and Arthurian romance entering the literary scene, or the rediscovery of Charlemagne and his peers, of the *matière de Rome* (Aneas) and the *Nibelungensaga*. Each poses, of course, rather different questions about tradition and background, but no matter how many explanations have been suggested for them, unresolved problems remain in each case. This is not to say we should stop worrying about them, but rather a reminder that vernacular love-poetry is one fascinating 'new' phenomenon in a century that was particularly active in breaking new grounds.

Before we, however, enter into the discussion of individual troubadours and minnesingers, a few remarks on how their art fundamentally differs from modern love-poetry. A troubadour or minnesinger was not only a poet but also a composer. Text and melody were created by the same person simultaneously. Yet whereas a relatively large number of troubadour melodies was preserved, transmission of Minnesang melodies was scarce. There are, however, quite a few German texts the metrical patterns of which either are identical with or so closely resemble those of Provençal songs, of which the tunes survived, that it is safe to assume they were sung to the same melodies, i.e. were contrafacts. A poet was not only a composer, he apparently was also expected to create a new metrical stanzaic pattern for each song; repetitions and borrowings were relatively seldom except in the case of German borrowings from Provençal songs mentioned above. But even though formal creativeness was emphasized, it turned into an art of variation. A dominant stanzaic pattern in Provençal as well as in German songs was the *Kanzone*, a tripartite form in which the first two parts are metrically identical, the third is different and longer, yet could occasionally repeat elements of the first two. Stanzaic variation was mostly a matter of rhyme schemes, of number and length of lines (also of melody), and it is amazing to see what number of different forms the basic patterns yielded. Besides, there were other less dominant stanzaic forms as well, especially in the early stages of Minnesang and in troubadour poetry throughout.

Another aspect in which these medieval love-songs differ considerably from modern love-poetry is that they were meant to be recited publicly, not read in the privacy of one's room. Only at later stages, from the thirteenth century on, do we find references to singing *and* reading. We are not too well informed about the details of performance, but it seems safe to assume from manuscript illuminations that the singers accompanied their songs on an instrument, usually a fiddle. The poet–composer was presumably in most cases also a singer, but there were also *joglars/spilman*, minstrels who performed the works of others. Like other vernacular literature of the period, love-songs served as a fascinating combination of courtly entertainment and education. They were created for the social elite and their followers. A remarkable number of poet–composers even ranked rather high in the social hierarchy, as for instance the first troubadour, Guilhem IX, Duke of Aquitaine and Count of Poitou, who was one of the French kings' most powerful vassals. About a century later, the Emperor Henry VI seems to have at least briefly joined the ranks of the minnesingers. Love-poetry became a prime medium for the courtly minded to develop and probe a new secular identity.

The Troubadours

The term *trobador* is related to the verb *trobar* which means 'to find, invent, write poetry and compose melodies'. It is quite often used in the songs themselves, later on also consistently in the *Lives of the Troubadours*[5] which were written in Provençal prose from the thirteenth century on, i.e. long after the poets had died. These *Lives* are a Provençal speciality and document a lasting interest in the poets as individuals, even if they mix fact and fiction at times rather dramatically or even amusingly.

Although the songs of the troubadours were predominantly love-songs, we find other literary genres or types developed as well. Next to the *canso*, as the love-song proper came to be known since about the mid twelfth century, the *sirventes* became rather popular, a panegyric or satirical type of song which also could relate martial events. *Tenso* and *partimen* (or *joc parti*) were forms of debate; typical for the latter one is that the challenger offers his opponent a choice of argument. The *planh* laments the death of an important person. Narrative elements finally characterize the *alba* or dawn song, which centres on the lovers' parting at dawn, and the *pastorela*, in which a shepherdess is either seduced by a knight or prevents it wittily. It will be important to keep this list of genres in mind because – as will be apparent later – the poets of Minnesang made some interesting selections.

Guilhem IX of Aquitaine is the first troubadour whose name has come down to us. Many scholars, however, deem it likely that he had anonymous predecessors. Since he was very actively involved in political affairs – governing and extending his large territories, once (in 1101) even leading a crusade and loosing an army in Asia Minor, yet also successfully fighting in Moslem Spain (in 1120) – medieval historiographers were more eloquent on him than on most other troubadours. The portrait they offer is vivacious, full of contrasts and at times even vitriolic; anecdotes about Guilhem abound. He is projected as hot-tempered, aggressive, a *macho* and philanderer, a splendid entertainer, a loyal and brave lord. The *vida* sums up some of these tendencies rather nicely:

> The count of Poitou was one of the most courtly men in the world and one of the greatest deceivers of ladies, and a fine knight in deeds of arms, and generous in wooing; and he knew well how to compose and sing. And he travelled for a long time throughout the world in order to deceive ladies . . .[6]

Under Guilhem's name, eleven songs are preserved which are usually divided into two groups (of five each), namely one of jesting, bawdy poems and one of more serious love-lyrics, and a poem which is a farewell and a testament. In its diversity this oeuvre presents a dire warning to all those who tend to enshrine troubadours – or for that matter, minnesingers – neatly into pigeon holes. Guilhem's songs encompass the full range from lewdness to courtly love. He composed on the one hand a song in the manner of a popular *fabliau*. Here the first-person narrator is a traveller who pretends to be deaf-mute, thus suggesting to two ladies – Agnes and Ermessen – that he will keep any secret. They test him painfully by dragging a huge cat, clawing his flesh, over him, yet he manfully survives the test as well as the next eight exhausting days of frolicking à trois. On the other hand and in another poem, the singer does exult in the supreme happiness which his lady is and might bestow, yet he is content to keep it a secret and would be ready to serve her by conforming to every courtly demand.

Guilhem's famous song 'In the sweetness of new spring'★ strikes a magnificent balance by celebrating shared love. Delicate and powerful images of nature provide a strong counterpoint for human longing and uncertainties as well as for exuberant memories of happiness. The painfulness of present separation gives way to the glory of past closeness which again leads to the bold and confident challenge of the last lines. Guilhem creates a rich variety of *personae*, and Love has many faces in his small oeuvre. It is hard to imagine that he created them completely *ex nihilo*.

Marcabru (*fl.*1135–50) belongs to the next generation of troubadours and is quite a different figure. He apparently was of low social rank; the *vidas* claim, based on one of his songs, that he was an illegitimate child or a foundling. Guilhem's son patronized him until his own sudden death, and then Marcabru roamed the courts of Spain and Portugal. His oeuvre is considerably larger than Guilhem's, about forty songs are attributed to him. He was very likely one of those troubadours who had to live from their artistic skills.

Marcabru is a fierce, aggressive poet and the early master of the *sirventes*. Only rarely is he given to such translucent lyricism as in the beginning of 'By the fountain in the orchard'.★ But even this song is full of unexpected twists and turns. It begins like a *pastorela* (Marcabru also wrote a witty and elegant genuine pastourelle), but as soon as the appropriate situation is delicately established, it turns into a lady's lament and her polemic against the crusade (Marcabru also wrote a rousing and passionate crusade song). The poet, a would-be lover, finds himself concerned with her looks and confined to the role of spiritual adviser. Yet to no avail; the grief of the young woman is not that easily alleviated, and she asserts her right to lament the loss of her joy. Many poets, Provençal and German, wrote

★ See anthology, p. 436; p. 431.

straightforward crusade songs during the twelfth century, yet when this service of the lord and the service of the lady were discussed within the same context judgements differ widely. No poet defended seriously staying at home, at least not until the thirteenth century (Neidhart, Tannhäuser), and only a few ranked the crusade clearly higher. The majority wrestled earnestly with the problem and tried to achieve some kind of harmony between these duties or challenges, another indication that the dividing line between the courtly and religious spheres did not run deep.

Marcabru's 'I say he's a wise man'* indicates that in a different way and is in many respects more representative for his art than 'By the fountain'. It is an unflinching, skilful attack on *fals' amors* and all those who proclaim and commit it. Since part of it is a literary feud (against troubadours, l.7) it seems likely that Marcabru polemicizes against some of Guilhem's songs or similar ones. He angrily decries mere sexual desire (calling it *Amars*, i.e. bitterness) and falsity in love. *Fin'amors*, or true/perfect love, for Marcabru means *Jois, Sofrirs e Mesura* (l.24): joy and happiness – patience, humility and endurance – restraint and balance. This creed is aggressively and colourfully couched, yet it subtly merges courtly and religious codes and turned into a theme with many variations for troubadour generations to come.

Jaufré Rudel (*fl.* mid-twelfth century) was a younger contemporary of Marcabru. He may have personally known Guilhem, and Marcabru very likely addressed a song to him and sent it to the Holy Land where Jaufré presumably took part in the crusade of 1147. Jaufré's fame rests mainly on a legend and a concept, both of which are loosely related to his songs. According to the legend, transmitted in his *vida*, Jaufré fell in love with the countess of Tripoli, without even seeing her, only by hearing of her excellence. He composed songs about her; and compelled by the desire to see her, he took the cross and travelled to the Holy Land. On the way he became very sick, was brought to Tripoli, could finally and briefly enjoy her presence and died in her arms. She had him honourably buried and took the veil for grief over his death. It is little wonder that this legend has inspired poets throughout the ages!

* See anthology, p. 433.

The legend in turn was clearly inspired by Jaufré's song 'When days are long in May'*. That song, however, was even more noted for its concept of *amor de lonh*, a 'distant' love. This love for a lady far away added a few important aspects to the spreading ideas of *fin'amors*, namely trust, loyalty and suffering. To overcome the vast physical distance, the bond has to be all the stronger, and although the poet imagines pleasures of closeness to his beloved that are quite real, they remain wishes and dreams. He is at the end of the song even more desolate than at the beginning. In a way, the legend has been kinder to Jaufré, even if so rather in Hollywood style.

By the decades after 1150, troubadour art was growing and spreading in southern France. From that period on, we do not only know increasingly more poets by name, but individual oeuvres also tend to be more sizeable, like those of Bernart de Ventadorn, Raimbaut d'Aurenga or Peire Vidal. As we have seen, there were contacts between early troubadours, as for example Marcabru and Jaufré Rudel. After the mid twelfth century, however, individual troubadours engaged more frequently in debates, i.e. *tensos* and *partimens*. Though rivalries for the attention of patrons and audiences must have been strong, they are acted out playfully and wittily enough. During the later part of the twelfth century, we also witness that troubadours were much more aware of themselves as a group or professional 'class'. This is all the more remarkable since nothing comparable to that is visible in Minnesang. Such awareness manifests itself in among other things two *sirventes*, one by Peire d'Alvernhe (*fl.*1150–80), the other by the Monk of Montaudon (*fl.*1180–1200). Both review jestingly a series of contemporary troubadours, one in each stanza, and the Monk even refers explicitly to the poem of his predecessor, thereby also establishing a kind of continuity.

It is comparatively easy to discern individual approaches and styles in the works of the early troubadours. There seems still to have been much room for experiment and change. Once the courtly concepts began to more or less dominate, however, it becomes more difficult to outline the individual features of a troubadour's oeuvre. This is not to say that most of them did not develop a 'handwriting' of their own, quite a few as a matter of fact did. But it takes more

* See anthology, p. 437.

probing into and more familiarity with their works to discover it. Incidentally, we shall observe similar features in Minnesang once it came under Provençal influence, or when many minnesingers, especially in the thirteenth century, did not go very much beyond imitating their predecessors. It seems also no coincidence that troubadour poetry in its more courtly phase had its broadest European impact. In the decades after 1160/70, it was not only echoed in northern France, it also turned the development of Minnesang in a decisive new direction. The courts of Europe increasingly proved to be receptive audiences.

The poet who perhaps represents this phase best is by common consent Bernart de Ventadorn (*fl.c.*1150–80). According to his *vida*, he was of low social origin, the son of a servant at the castle of Ventadorn. From the few facts we can reasonably ascertain about his life, he had an impressive career. He was well known as a poet throughout the south of France and also became quite influential in the north. Count Raimon V of Toulouse, whose court grew into an important centre of troubadour art, was one of his last patrons. Bernart wrote quite a few songs about Eleanor of Aquitaine, the granddaughter of Guilhem IX. She was first married to the French King Louis VII and then, after her divorce, to Henry of Anjou who became King Henry II of England in 1154. Eleanor and her second husband, as well as her daughters, were famous as generous patrons of poets and writers. Bernart may even have attended their coronation in London.

Bernart's songs celebrate courtly love fervently and eloquently, though not singlemindedly. It is true, the beloved woman now has become the exalted lady whose unwillingness to yield may and does cause the singer/poet much suffering, just as the smallest gesture or token of love induces great joy in him. Yet even only serving someone that excellent can be considered a reward in itself and a source of happiness. There are visions of mutual love in Bernart's songs, but they remain mostly imaginary. Occasionally, the poet even uses his very submissiveness and timidity as a temptation for the lady and also shows a sense of humour.

Bernart's famous song 'When I see the lark moving'* is an im-

* See anthology, p. 439.

pressive example for the ease and force with which he expresses his
inner turmoil. He uses images rarely but whenever he does they are
precise and highly suggestive, as in this case the rising and falling
of the lark which so sharply contrasts with the poet's state of mind.
Rather unusual for Bernart is, however, the change from utter des-
pondency to rebellion and the poet's awareness that in all his submissiveness he also has the power to 'answer her with death' by not
singing of the beloved anymore. And yet, even the final desperate
lines of this song manifest – albeit in the negative – that singing,
joy and love spring from the same powerful root.

One of Bernart's younger contemporaries was perhaps the
Comtessa de Dia. Unfortunately, we know almost nothing about
her, neither whether her first name was really Beatriz nor if she was
the wife or the daughter of the count of Poitiers, Guilhem I de
Valentinois (1158–89). Her oeuvre is tiny compared to that of Bernart
and others: four songs and presumably one *tenso* with Raimbaut
d'Aurenga (who probably for that reason was rumoured to have
been her lover). However, she was one of the very few poetesses
among the troubadours.[7] She shows herself well versed in the various
poetic conventions, and she also knew how to adapt and break them.
She could have either imitated the submissive *persona* of her male
fellow troubadours or explored in depth the *persona* of the unyielding
lady. In her song 'I have been in great distress',⋆ however, she did
neither. Instead she chose the role of a woman in distress, but remarkably straightforward in expressing even her physical desires. There
are the (courtly) elements of suffering and separation, yet there are
also the memories of past real happiness and the projection of future
closeness and fulfilment. In a highly sophisticated way, the Comtessa
here echoes themes and emotions which resound in the archaic genre
of the woman's song in many European languages and beyond.

With Peire Vidal (*fl.c.*1180–*c.*1205) we turn to a still younger
generation of troubadours which is also the last one before the
Albigensian Crusade (against the Cathar heresy, 1209–29) disrupted
the society and culture of southern France mercilessly. Peire's *vida*
mentions that he was born in Toulouse and the son of a furrier.
The *vida* and several *razos* also relate many anecdotes about his life.

⋆ See anthology, p. 441.

From facts we can ascertain more safely, it appears that he travelled widely, not only in southern France and Spain but also to northern Italy, Hungary and the Holy Land. Towards the end of his life, he seems to have spent some time on Malta. He excelled in many forms: *canso*, *sirventes*, *tenso*[8] of which about forty are transmitted in all.

In his songs, Peire can be boastful, aggressive, even chauvinistic, yet he is still very much a courtly poet. He does not question the courtly ideals fundamentally, but occasionally presents them with touches of humour and even self-irony. For Peire's gentle side, the well-known song 'With my breath I draw toward me the air'* is a good example. It begins – and probably was – a song composed abroad. Since it praises Provence so warmly and glowingly, one could imagine it was also well received there. Deftly balanced, the praise of the beloved almost grows out of the praise for the country. Although there seems to be a touch of sadness here and there in the poem, it becomes elusive as soon as one tries to point it out. The poet praises his beloved in a lucid and entirely courtly fashion. Suffering and distress do not seem to exist in the realms of this song. Being utterly dependent upon the lady here becomes for the poet a reason for gentle pride, and the images of *Proensa* (Provence) and the beloved imperceptibly merge into or mirror one another.

By the time the Albigensian Crusade had run its deadly course, troubadour art was not quite destroyed, but it never reached again the richness and variety it had developed in the preceding century. Large oeuvres still originated, as for example that of Peire Cardenal (*c*.1180–*c*.1278) or that of Guiraut Riquier (*c*.1233–92). They are in fact very large indeed since they consist both of around ninety songs. Both poets, however, turned away from the love-song and almost exclusively or increasingly towards religious and other themes.

Nevertheless the thirteenth century was crucial for troubadour art in other respects. It was of prime importance for the harvesting of the crop, because troubadour songs and oeuvres were only then collected on a large scale and assembled in comprehensive manuscripts, some of which were beautifully illuminated.[9] Without them (and the activities of those collectors) our knowledge of troubadour art would be seriously impaired. As we shall see, similar activi-

---

* See anthology, p. 442.

ties preserved a little later most of the Minnesang we know today.

Just as the troubadours had a strong impact upon Minnesang for some time after 1170, they became of vital importance in the beginnings of vernacular Italian poetry over a century later. The troubadour Arnaut Daniel (*fl.c.*1200), for instance, was admired by many poets in later ages, but especially by Dante and Petrarch who also knew and esteemed works of other troubadours. Thus transformed into another vernacular language and a new style, the heritage of the troubadours stimulated European poetry for centuries.

Minnesang

The German poets used the terms 'minnesanc' and 'minnesinger' far less frequently than their Provençal counterparts referred to 'trobador' and 'trovar'. They seem also not to have been quite as aware of themselves as a community of artists. Yet their works demonstrate unmistakably that they, too, developed and adhered to certain common patterns and traditions. Most of Minnesang can be grouped into three basic genres: *Lied*, *Spruch* and *Leich*. The *Lied* is the love-song proper but occasionally also opened up to other themes (crusade, palinody, praise of food and wine). Differing from the *Lied*, the *Spruch* normally consists of one stanza only, but several of such stanzas can also combine to form a loose larger unit. *Sprüche* are highly flexible, concerning subject matter as well as approaches (praise, lament, satire, didactics, etc.). The *Leich*, finally, is a complicated metrical (and musical) form which instead of stanzas employs irregular groups of verses (*Versikel*), following each other in complex patterns and variations. Its main themes are love and/or dance, yet in the thirteenth century religion played an increasing role as a topic. As for the Provençal genres, *sirventes*, *tenso*, *partimen* and *pastorela* never really caught on in Minnesang. The *canso* had a decisive influence for a while, and the *alba* or dawn song was – from 1200 on – considerably more popular in Germany than in the Romance countries.[10]

The first extant love-songs in German can be dated roughly to the mid twelfth century. As in France, they originated in the south of the country. There are a few anonymous stanzas either transmitted in a Latin context or ascribed to later minnesingers on the one hand

and on the other small oeuvres attributed to specific names. The much quoted stanza 'You are mine, I am yours'* is a good example of the former group. It is preserved at the end of a love-letter in Latin prose, written by a young woman to a *clericus*, a learned friend, and copied in a Bavarian manuscript of around 1160. We do not know if she herself composed the stanza or if she quoted a popular song. It has much in common with others of the earliest German songs. They tend to be utterly and sophisticatedly simple, to consist of one or at the utmost two stanzas and to display a rich variety of *personae*, quite a few of them women. A typical form for this earliest stage is the so-called *Wechsel*, a combination of two stanzas, one usually spoken by a woman, the other by a man. These *personae*, however, do not engage in a dialogue. They speak 'past' each other, yet about the same feelings, problems or events.

The first minnesinger known by name is Kürenberc (*fl.* mid twelfth century). He may have been a nobleman and very likely lived in Bavaria or Austria, but otherwise nothing of his life is known. Some fifteen stanzas are transmitted under his name. Their metrical patterns are almost alike and closely resemble that of the later *Nibelungenlied*, the powerful heroic epic which originated in the same geographical area. Kürenberc composed a few *Wechsel* but also a number of songs consisting of a single stanza. No matter if they are male or female monologues or whether one of each are combined in a *Wechsel*, they express a remarkable variety of emotions, speak of sorrow, desire and tenderness, answer challenge with counter-challenge or even delight in frivolity.

The best known and most debated of Kürenberc's songs is the so-called *Falkenlied* 'I nurtured a falcon for more than a year'.* Its enig-matic simplicity has raised many questions: Is it a monologue or a *Wechsel*? Does a woman speak or a man? Is the falcon a pet, a messenger or a symbol for the beloved? Do the silken fetters and the gold in the second stanza point to a rival of the speaker? Nearly every possibility mentioned in these questions has been argued for or refuted at some point. That this could be so is primarily a tribute to the utterly condensed and highly suggestive style of the poem, a style that is typical for these early songs in general and culminates

---

* See anthology, p. 447.

in Kürenberc's *Falkenlied*. The sophistication manifest in these songs certainly differs from that we observe in Guilhem IX of Aquitaine's poems. As in Guilhem's case, however, it is difficult to maintain that Kürenberc and his younger contemporaries, like Meinloh von Sevelingen, Dietmar von Eist and others, created a tradition that was entirely without predecessors.

Around 1170 Minnesang entered a new phase. Its centre moved further west to the Rhine, and for about two decades it came strongly under Provençal influence. That proved to be a gain as well as a loss. Following Provençal models, Minnesang gained on the one hand a greater formal and musical variety, songs extended beyond two stanzas, and they also reflected more intensely the concepts of courtly love. On the other hand that precisely meant a loss since the *persona* of the poet/lover, submissively serving his exalted lady, came to dominate the scene. The emotional directness of the earliest songs and their richly different voices of men *and* women were almost submerged for a while. But it did not take long until the minnesingers began to grapple individually and independently with *fin'amors*.

Friedrich von Hausen (*c.*1150–90) perhaps best represents the generation of minnesingers that looked south-west for inspiration. In Germany, he is the first minnesinger who is well documented historically. He came from a Rheno-Franconian family, was a *ministerialis*, not a nobleman, but served no less a lord than the Emperor Frederick I, Barbarossa and went on several diplomatic missions throughout Europe. He also took part in the Third Crusade and was killed, like Barbarossa, in Asia Minor. The Latin chroniclers unanimously praise Hausen's energy and honesty as a knight, but characteristically remain silent on his poetry. Seventeen love-songs are transmitted under his name.

Hausen quite often borrowed metrical patterns of troubadour songs (presumably also their melodies) and was thoroughly familiar with their topical conventions, yet he was also prepared to meet the challenges of their art. He adopted their plaintive attitude caused by the separation from the beloved lady. But underneath he developed precise, well-structured and at times playful arguments. Moreover, separation in his songs frequently means real physical distance as the poet is travelling in faraway countries, a similar, yet reverse situation to the one we found in some of Jaufré Rudel's songs.

Hausen's song 'I think sometimes'* for instance, subtly plays on the contrasts of closeness and distance, in reality as well as figuratively. Despite the poet's mounting distress he can end on a note of hope since he can persuade himself that he is closest to his beloved when he is farthest from home. An imaginary response to the paradoxes of *hohe minne* ('lofty love', l.11). Hausen basically accepted them, but they were later to come under relentless attack.

The generation of minnesingers following the Hausen group depended less on Provençal models. Rather, by that time, the forms and concepts of the troubadours were already so well integrated into the German tradition that individual minnesingers felt free to define themselves within that heritage. But quite a few minnesingers seem to have also been aware of the fact that they were part of a European literary venture. As in the case of the troubadours after 1150, it becomes more difficult to outline specific literary personalities after and when Minnesang more or less conformed to established concepts of courtly love.

One who essentially conformed to these ideas and yet developed an impressive style of his own is Heinrich von Morungen (d.1222?). About his life we almost know nothing. Morungen presumably was a *ministerialis* of the margraves of Meissen and may have died as a *miles emeritus* in the St Thomas monastery in Leipzig. At any rate, he must have lived in the then eastern part of the middle region of Germany, and that indicates that Minnesang at that stage did not have one definable centre any longer (as in the earlier stages) but originated in many regions except the far north. Morungen's oeuvre consists of thirty-three songs.

Morungen rarely deviated very far from the by now familiar pattern of the submissive, suffering poet and the nearly unattainable lady. But he approached it again and again – unlike others – as a visionary. Thus the beloved may appear as an almost demonic being who has the power to work magic. Or he projects the relation into an existence after death, thus subtly changing it into a spiritual, almost mystical union. In his song 'On the heath I heard'* on the other hand, Morungen envisions three encounters of the poet and his beloved. The song moves in finely etched scenes abruptly, yet com-

---

* See anthology, p. 448; p. 444.

pellingly from a carefree rendezvous at a dance to a secret tryst, overshadowed by the woman's grief over her lover's supposed death, and finally to a glorious meeting high up on the battlements where his desires figuratively seem to set the world ablaze. Yet the end of the song remains suggestively elusive.

In another famous song 'Alas, shall her body never again'* Morungen skilfully blended the subgenre of the *alba* or dawn song with the archaic *Wechsel*[11] and created the most beautiful and haunting song of this kind. A man and a woman speak past each other, but of deeply shared happiness and sorrow. Their memories, feelings and images mingle and complement each other perfectly, and unlike in other *Wechsel*, they even share verbally what separated them: the refrain 'Then the day came' (*do taget ez*). There is no lament in all of Minnesang that is phrased in such utter and lucid simplicity and that suggests as strongly the *unio* in and despite the separation.

Morungen was not the only one in his generation to explore within and beyond the limits of courtly love. Hartmann von Aue (*fl.c.*1180–1205), who is perhaps better known as an author of Arthurian romance (*Erec*, *Iwein*), composed quite a few songs more or less in the traditional vein. But in others he rather bluntly attacked the idea of serving a lady without ever attaining some kind of reward. Occasionally Hartmann ranked serving God by going on a crusade definitely higher than the service for a lady, but he also pleaded persuasively for combining both. He even composed a song in which the poet is actually taking leave before going on a crusade, and here he invokes a personified *Minne* who strangely hovers between the courtly and spiritual sphere.

Compared to Morungen's and some of Hartmann's songs, the oeuvre of Reinmar (von Hagenau, *fl.c.*1180–*c.*1205) might impress one as rather conventional at first sight. But then the early on narrowly and hastily conceived image of Reinmar as the 'Scholastiker der unglücklichen Liebe',[12] an Aquinas of unhappy love so to speak, is now finally about to be revised. Although Reinmar composed many songs in which the poet proudly submits to and even seems to enjoy the distresses of courtly love, he also revived in others the old Bavarian–Austrian tradition of the woman's song and developed

* See anthology, p. 446.

some startling insights into the emotions of the only seemingly so exalted lady. And if one is not as overly rigorous in not attributing songs to Reinmar (which in the manuscripts actually appear under his name) as some former editors were, Reinmar even celebrated shared love. Some of the negative aspects in his image also derive from the fact that scholars have been so inexorably drawn not only to compare him to Walther von der Vogelweide but also to use him as a negative foil against which Walther's greatness was shining all the brighter.

Walther von der Vogelweide (*fl.c.*1190–*c.*1225) never actually needed that. He has no equal in medieval German lyric poetry and perhaps not even in European lyric poetry of the Middle Ages. We know more about his life than about those of other minnesingers or troubadours, not because Walther is historically better documented (there is exactly one historical document)[13] but because he wrote about a hundred *Sprüche*, many of which refer directly – or obliquely – to historical figures and/or events. For decades of his life, Walther seems to have depended mostly on his artistic skills for a living. He was affiliated intermittently with many German courts and their princes. The early years of his poetic career were spent in Vienna. Later we find him with King Philipp, King and then Emperor Otto IV, at the courts of Thuringia and again Vienna as well as several others until he obtained a fief of his own from Emperor Frederick II in 1220. Walther's life as a wandering poet as well as many of his affiliations are reflected vividly and at times dramatically in his *Sprüche*, and he was never shy to voice his opinions or convictions even in political matters concerning the Empire (which was in much turmoil at the time). Walther mastered the whole scale of expression from gentleness to vitriolic aggressiveness, including humour and self-irony, but above all he was a supremely self-confident poet.

Besides one *Leich* and about one hundred *Sprüche*, Walther's oeuvre contains about seventy songs. A number of them follow the courtly fashion fairly closely. In others he engaged in an extended literary feud with Reinmar. Walther and Reinmar never addressed each other by name – as the troubadours quite openly did in their *tensos* and *partimens* – rather they 'quoted' one another in phrases, rhyme schemes and stanzaic forms. Not until after Reinmar's death did Walther mention his opponent by name (in two *Sprüche* lamenting his demise), and then he did so with high praise for Reinmar's art but explicitly with little regard for him as a person. The song 'To be long silent was my thought'★ was part of that feud and shows Walther's more aggressive side. The end of l.24: 'if I perish, she is dead' is clearly aimed at Reinmar's statement: 'if she perishes, I am dead'. Beyond that, this song is the most devastating barrage Walther ever fired at the courtly ideals. It relentlessly exposes not only that courtly joy and the praise of the lady depends entirely on the poet (reversing the traditional courtly power structure), but it also shatters the image of the unattainable, eternally beautiful lady by switching to farce in the last stanza. Furthermore, this song is a good example for how deftly Walther can play with and engage his audience in both topic and presentation of his songs.

Walther takes a similar, yet quite different approach in the song 'Lady, accept this garland'.★ Its end reveals that the poet is searching for the lady/girl of his dream here and now where the song is performed. This is one of the so-called *Mädchenlieder* in which Walther strives for and celebrates shared love between a man and a woman instead of presenting one-sided courtly submission. The poem is by no means devoid of courtly elements since both *personae* seem to hover between the courtly and a pastoral/rural sphere. The dream of gentle wooing and exuberant fulfilment in an idyllic setting, however, proves so powerful that it has to be pursued in 'real' life. That is a subtler and more poetic way of challenging courtly conventions than in 'To be long silent'. Both poems are but two examples for the many ingenious ways in which Walther stamped his unmistakable and indelible marks on Minnesang. Even his late poems, in which he takes leave of his art and audience or laments the misery of old age, radiate a unique, quiet dignity and hope.

Minnesang was alive and thriving until the early fourteenth century. Although the thirteenth century was full of political upheavals for Germany, none of them had a similar disruptive effect as the Albigensian Crusade had in Provence. Much of thirteenth-century Minnesang is highly and monotonously conventional. This repetitive prettiness, however, is but one aspect, there were also strong tendencies to move into new directions. One of the most

★ See anthology, p. 451; p. 450 f.

productive efforts along these lines was that of Neidhart von Reuental (*fl.c.*1210–*c.*1240). He introduced a rambunctious peasant milieu into Minnesang and fleshed out the *persona* of the poet as either an attractive singer given to seducing village maidens (*Sommerlieder*) or as a downtrodden, petty knight, continuously threatened by upstart peasants (*Winterlieder*). A streak of antagonism runs through most of his songs,★ and it is still an open question whether Neidhart tried to uphold or demolish the ideals of Minnesang. Like Morungen, Neifen and Tannhäuser, Neidhart was soon turned into a literary figure and legend that became the most colourful and productive of all minnesingers throughout the late Middle Ages.

Neidhart was not alone in his attempts to introduce a new 'concreteness' into Minnesang. Others like Ulrich von Lichtenstein, Tannhäuser, Steinmar and Johannes Hadloub tried to do the same, partly influenced by Neidhart, partly quite on their own. No minnesinger, however, turned as strongly to religion as some of the late troubadours. A partly religious song, like Der Wilde Alexander's 'Long ago when we were children',★ is a noticeable exception not only in its startling blend of childhood memories and biblical allegory but also in its haunting, subdued tone.

Soon after 1300 Minnesang as a genre disappeared almost as rapidly and mysteriously from the literary scene as it had emerged about one and a half centuries before. Yet fortunately, that was also a time when it was collected systematically and preserved in precious manuscripts, some of which are beautifully illumined, none of which, however, contains any melodies.[14] There were a few rather isolated and impressive singers of love around 1400, i.e. Hugo von Montfort and especially Oswald von Wolkenstein. But in general the heritage of Minnesang was taken up and transformed by other literary genres, like Meistersang and Minnereden (discourses of love)[15] which carried it to the end of the Middle Ages. Then Minnesang was lost for several centuries. Its final rediscovery remains a lasting achievement of both the Age of Enlightenment and Romanticism.

★ See anthology, p. 453; p. 455.

NOTES

1. F. J. E. Raby, *A History of Secular Latin Poetry in the Middle Ages* (2nd edn, Oxford, 1957), vol. I, 329ff., 337ff., 291ff. P. Dronke, *Medieval Latin and the Rise of European Love-Lyric* (Cambridge 1965/66), vol. I, 209ff., 271ff.

2. What *winileodas* exactly means is still debated, but in content they were probably similar to the much later Portuguese *cantigas de amigo*, women's songs in the vernacular.

3. P. Dronke, *The Medieval Lyric* (London, 1968), 170–72.

4. See note 1.

5. J. Boutière and A. H. Schultz, *Biographies des troubadours* (2nd revised edn, Paris, 1964). There are two kinds: *razos* and *vidas*. The *razo* ('theme of a song') was based on a particular song and 'reconstructed' the situation that had lead to its composition. The *vidas* seem to give somewhat more reliable information, especially concerning the place of birth and death and the social rank of the poet.

6. Provençal text: Boutière, Schultz, ibid. 7. Translation: L. Topsfield, *Troubadours and Love* (Cambridge, 1975), 11. The rest of the *vida* is devoted to offspring: Guilhem's son, his granddaughter (Eleanor of Aquitaine) and two of her sons, Richard (Lionheart) and Jaufre of Bretagne.

7. We know only of about twenty among more than four hundred troubadours.

8. Peire also skilfully combined *canso* and *sirventes* quite often.

9. The oldest of these collections was assembled in Italy around 1254, more followed around the turn of the century, and collecting as well as copying extended far into the fourteenth century.

10. The dawnsong may have had a native tradition before it came for a while under Provençal influence.

11. For a more typical representative of the *alba* see the enchanting anonymous Provençal song 'Deep in an orchard, under hawthorn leaves' (p. 443).

12. Scholars attributed the phrase for a long time to Ludwig Uhland, which seems, however, unwarranted; see M. Stange, *Reinmars Lyrik* (Amsterdam, 1977), 23f.

13. It was found in a record of travel expenses, kept for the Bishop of Passau, Wolfger von Erla, and states that Walther was given money for a fur coat in Zeiselmauer (close to Vienna) on 12 November 1203.

14. The main collections are: MS. A = Kleine Heidelberger Liederhandschrift (late thirteenth century, Strassburg?), B = Weingartener Liederhandschrift (around 1300, Konstanz) and C = Grosse Heidelberger or Manessische Liederhandschrift (early fourteenth century, Zurich?).

15. See I. Glier, *Artes amandi*, Untersuchung zu Geschichte, Überlieferung und Typologie der deutschen Minnereden (München, 1971).

WOLFRAM VON ESCHENBACH: *PARZIVAL*

PETER JOHNSON

The claim that Wolfram von Eschenbach is the greatest poet of the German Middle Ages would be challenged by some, but by fewer than if it were made on behalf of any other. That the claim would have received support in the Middle Ages, too, is demonstrated by the existence of more than twice as many manuscripts of Wolfram's two major poems *Parzival* (over eighty complete manuscripts and fragments) and *Willehalm* (over seventy) as of any other important German literary work of the time. The cost of producing a manuscript of such long works (*Parzival* 24,710 lines; *Willehalm*, although unfinished, all but 14,000 lines) in terms of parchment and labour was such that ordering one represented a considerable commitment to the work in question, always assuming one could obtain an existing manuscript to copy. The commissioning of a *new* work, with the lengthy support of the poet which it involved, was an enormous investment for any but the richest.

The literary impact of Wolfram is shown also by his reputation amongst subsequent poets of the thirteenth century and later. It is as well that it is so, for apart from what Wolfram has to say about himself and his personal circumstances we have no evidence about the poet, his life and his fame beyond these mentions by later writers who admired him. Wolfram tells us that he is a knight, he prides himself on this, and although he revels in being a composer and singer of love lyrics (Minnesang), he doubts the sanity of any woman who would love him on that account rather than for knightly deeds:

I am Wolfram von Eschenbach and something of a minne-singer ... My hereditary Office is the Shield! I should think any lady weak of understanding who loved me for mere songs unbacked by manly deeds. If I desire a good woman's love and fail to win love's reward from her with shield and lance, let her favour me accordingly. A man who aims at love through chivalric exploits gambles for high stakes.

(114,12ff., transl. p. 68[1])

So Wolfram was a knight, but the term is a very unclear one and, like other medieval poets, Hartmann von Aue, Gottfried von Strassburg and even Chrétien de Troyes, Wolfram does not receive mention in any contemporary record, historical document or deed. The name of the lyric poet Friedrich von Hausen (†1190) appears as a witness of important political documents, but it is clear that he was a man of consequence in the service of the Hohenstaufen dynasty. Indeed, he is also mentioned in chronicles, for he died on the same crusade as the Hohenstaufen Emperor Frederick Barbarossa. It is clear that in the case of Friedrich von Hausen 'knight' meant something very different from Wolfram's. For the medieval German poets around 1200 to be named in an historical document was the exception rather than the rule. Wolfram's own modest status is indicated in one of his personal asides. When Parzival arrives at the fortified town of Pelrapeire where he is to win his wife Condwiramurs, he finds it under siege; Wolfram comments on the emaciated appearance of the citizens and says that his lord, the Count of Wertheim, would not have liked to have been a combatant there, given the short rations (184,4ff.); then Wolfram checks himself as he apparently makes fun of the lack of food among the besieged:

I should be a stupid man if I were to blame them for that. For where I have often dismounted and am called 'Master', at home in my own house, no mouse is ever cheered. It would have to steal its food, which by rights none might hide from me, but of which I find not a scrap above board. All too often do I, Wolfram von Eschenbach, have to make do with such comfort.

(184,27ff.; transl. p. 102)

On the whole Wolfram is more free with information about himself (within his works) than either his rather earlier contemporary Hartmann von Aue, who by translating Chrétien de Troyes' *Erec* introduced the Arthurian romance to Germany, or than his rival, Gottfried von Strassburg (see p. 207 ff.). Asides and interpolations, frequently of a humorous nature, point to certain localities or certain allusions (not always completely comprehensible) to places, people and customs which are clearly assumed to be familiar to his audience.

The courtly romance of Wolfram's time was intended principally for performance, originally by the poet, we assume, later by anyone who was capable of it and possessed a manuscript. The bulk of the aristocratic audience would in any case be illiterate. More than any other writer of courtly romances in Middle High German, Wolfram allows for the circumstances of performance and actually incorporates the performance situation into his work. Like other narrative poets he builds the role of a narrator into his work, a procedure which is the equivalent of including powerful and precise stage-directions in the play itself, but in Wolfram the narrator's is a more ebullient and independent one than is usual. And it is precisely this independence of the narrator's role which, by adopting attitudes to the story proper, robs subsequent reciters of much of *their* independence and ensures that they cannot adopt their own attitudes and be, say, ironic when the narrator is not, or ignore irony when Wolfram would have it. Even a Wolfram cannot legislate totally in such matters, but it is hard to see how anyone could go further than Wolfram to ensure that his work is performed as he wanted it. Wolfram's own personal intrusions – the poet now, not the narrator, though it is mistaken and illusory to believe that we can, need, or want to distinguish rigorously between the two – flow over into the role of the narrator, adding to the humane personal touch and providing often the warmth of sympathetic humour.

Can we learn anything concrete about Wolfram from these intrusions? Local allusions concentrate more strongly on Franconia/ North Bavaria than on any other region and when on encountering knights for the first time the untutored young Parzival betrays his ignorance by mistaking them for God, one of them says, 'This stupid Waleis is slowing us down', and Wolfram adds in parenthesis, 'The Waleis, I must tell you, share the same distinction as we Bavarians, but are even denser than Bavarian folk, though stout men with their weapons. Whoever is born in either land will blossom into a prodigy of tact and courtesy.' So North Bavaria/Upper Franconia looks like the area with which Wolfram was associated.

No greater degree of certainty may be reached in trying to date Wolfram. In effect we can date only his works (and these only approximately) and then drape his life around his works, basing our conclusions broadly on such probabilities as that the poems were written neither by a ten-year-old nor by an octogenarian. Wolfram's works consist of *Parzival* and *Willehalm*, both written in the usual rhyming couplets with four stresses per line; *Titurel*, of which only two fragments amounting to 164 stanzas exist; and nine lyric poems – *Minnelieder* – of which one *is* and another *may be* spurious, and which are curious in that no fewer than four are dawnsongs or aubades while yet another takes the form of an (apparent) leave-taking from the dawnsong. What is curious about this is the high proportion of dawnsongs, when before Wolfram the type is hardly represented at all in German.

Although it may have been composed in stages, and not necessarily in the order which the plot would suggest, it seems likely from references to contemporary events, etc. that *Parzival* was written in the first decade of the thirteenth century, while *Willehalm* dates probably from the second. *Titurel*, written in an unusual stanza form consisting of four long lines, rhyming in couplets but with only feminine rhymes, could claim to be the most original work of the Middle Ages. Not only do we have the unusual 'elegiac' form, but the material, too, is derived from a very unusual source. Wolfram seizes on one of the few tragic episodes in *Parzival*, the unhappy love of Schionatulander for Sigune and the killing of the former and turns this background of *Parzival* into the foreground of the new work, and vice versa. Arranging Wolfram's life around these works we must envisage a period from, say, 1175 to perhaps 1225.

Wolfram's main work is his adaptation and completion of the un-finished Old French *Perceval* or *Li contes del graal* (*The story of the Grail*) of Chrétien de Troyes which dates from *c*.1180. If the courtly romance as a genre, particularly in its Arthurian form, owes its re-sounding success to a combination of ingredients of form and of content, which proved *the* appealing recipe for the twelfth and fol-lowing centuries, matching needs and tastes but also shaping and developing them, then this appeal is found raised to a higher power in Chrétien's *Perceval* which both adds the Grail and 'supplies' an open end by being unfinished. This source of the mysterious and the mystic and the invitation to develop the mystery and complete the work constituted a means by which the spiritual could be intro-duced into the Arthurian romance and, going on the number of con-tinuations and adaptations of *Perceval*, a temptation which it was hard to resist. But of all the adaptations of Chrétien, none has the rounded completeness or intensity of Wolfram's *Parzival*, for none found a poet to equal him.

Chrétien's work contains the puzzle of what he intended to make of the Grail, but also a further one, namely the introduction of Gauvain as a second hero to whom sections of the work are devoted to the exclusion of Perceval. This is such a novel departure in Chrétien's works that it has even been contemplated that scribes have mistakenly combined two separate Chrétien stories through a misunderstanding. It is perhaps more likely that Chrétien, having produced a number of courtly romances with a fundamentally similar structure underlying them, decided to experiment with a new structure for variety – one which admittedly comes close to merely doubling the earlier structure, but then interlaces the two plots.

Though it is impossible here to delve into all the explanations that have been given of the origin of the Grail – Celtic ritual and magic, oriental sources and so on – or into all the subsequent forms it takes and the interpretations placed on it, enough must be said to make clear, as far as this is possible, its nature in Chrétien and Wolfram, more particularly since readers may have a conception of the Grail based on Malory and Tennyson which has little to do with our two poets.

A summary of the involved Grail strand of Wolfram's story may help. Since her husband, Gahmuret, has been killed in knightly combat, Queen Herzeloyde decides to raise her son, Parzival, in a lonely forest so that he will remain ignorant of chivalry. Unfortunately he encounters knights and determines to ride to Arthur's court to become one. His mother dresses him as a fool, hoping he will be mocked and will return. When he leaves, she dies of grief. At Arthur's court Parzival demands to be made a knight and to be given the armour of Ither, the Red Knight, whom he has met outside, defying the Round Table. Cynically Keie sends him out to his death, but he kills Ither and despoils the corpse of its red armour. He comes to the castle of Gurnemanz who instructs him in knightly combat and manners and advises him not to ask too many questions. After two weeks he leaves and succeeds in relieving a city of a siege, sending the defeated oppressors to Arthur and marrying Condwiramurs, the Queen of the country.

A year or so later Parzival rides off to seek adventure and see how his mother is faring. Led by his horse to a trackless region he sees a nobleman fishing in a boat on a lake and by him he is directed to a lonely but splendid castle nearby. During the evening he is enter-tained in inconceivable luxury by Anfortas, the (Fisher) King who had directed him there and who is sick and lame. A page runs in bearing a lance dripping with blood; he meets with general lamenta-tion as he runs round all four walls and vanishes. An elaborate pro-cession enters followed by Repanse de Schoye bearing 'a thing, called the Grail', which provides food and drink of the most costly kind. Remembering Gurnemanz's advice Parzival asks no questions. His host presents him with a jewelled sword of immense value and adds *he* used it until God wounded him; the narrator laments that Parzival asked no question for the gift was to encourage him to. Parzival retires and awakes the next morning to find the castle deserted. He rides out and a hidden page raises the drawbridge and curses him for not speaking. He comes across his cousin, Sigune and she rejoices that he has been to the Grail Castle – which one cannot find inten-tionally – for Anfortas will have been healed by his question and Parzival will be lord of the Grail. When Parzival says he has not asked any question, she curses him and sends him away. After success-ful jousts Parzival is led by Gawan into Arthur's court and is made a member of the Round Table. The hideous maiden, Cundrie, appears, cursing Parzival publicly for not putting the question and curing Anfortas. A knight arrives and accuses Gawan of treacherously killing his lord. Parzival renounces his service of God, defying him, and rides off to seek the Grail. Gawan rides off to clear himself of his accusation and for some time the story follows his adventures.

It returns to Parzival at a much later point as riding through a wild region he finds Sigune immured in an anchoress's cell. A recon-ciliation takes place and Sigune tries to direct him to the Grail Castle but he loses the tracks. Eventually he meets a grey knight and his family who reproach him for riding in armour, for it is Good Friday. He begins to soften in his attitude to God and the grey knight sends him to the cell of a hermit nearby, a spot which Parzival recognizes. To him (Trevrizent) Parzival confesses he has sinned by not setting foot near a church. Trevrizent is able to show Parzival that it is over four and a half years that he has been riding around, estranged from God and man. Parzival says he is seeking the Grail and Trevrizent says this is foolish for none but those called by heaven may find it. (Some details had been given to Parzival by Sigune and others to us by the narrator, who has just revealed at this late point that Parzival's mother, Herzeloyde, was the sister of the Grail King – as yet Parzival does not know that he is a member of the Grail dynasty.) Trevrizent explains about the Grail (it is possible to mention only a few of the main points): it is guarded by warriors called *templeise* (not identical with, but reminiscent of 'templars'); the Grail is a (precious) stone and they live from it; anyone seeing it may not die during the following seven days; it receives its power from a consecrated wafer which is placed on it each Good Friday by a dove descending from heaven; on it inscriptions come and go, usually summoning new people to the Grail community; originally it was guarded by the neutral angels who sided with neither God nor Lucifer, but later it was handed over to the human guardians who are summoned.

Trevrizent says that Parzival is like the father of Anfortas and asks who he is. Parzival answers that his father was Gahmuret and that he slew Ither. Trevrizent recognizes Parzival as his nephew (so now Parzival learns that he belongs to the Grail family) and tells him that Ither was his kinsman. He also tells Parzival that he has caused his mother's death. Anfortas had been wounded by an envenomed spear in the groin, a punishment for pursuing love outside the rules of the Grail community. To gain a cure every means had been tried and Trevrizent had become a hermit. Nothing was any use until an inscription appeared on the Grail saying that a knight would come to the Grail and that if he were to put a question Anfortas's suffering would end, but he must not be prompted and he must ask on the first night; since then a foolish man had come to the Grail and had heaped great sin upon himself by not asking, 'Lord, what is the nature of your distress?' Only after a considerable time can Parzival bring himself to confess that it was he who had not cured Anfortas. Trevrizent is shocked but forgives Parzival and gives him absolution; he leaves his uncle and the story returns once more for a considerable period to Gawan.

Parzival reappears, meets Gawan and they fight incognito. It is only Gawan's pages who, by naming him, save Gawan from being killed by his friend and kinsman. After mutual recognition they go together to Arthur's court and Parzival is readmitted to the Round Table. Parzival rides out and after a tremendous joust with an unknown opponent is prevented from killing him when God intervenes and causes the sword which Parzival had taken on slaying his kinsmen, Ither, to shatter; the stranger reveals himself as Feirefiz, Parzival's half-brother, being the son of Gahmuret and a Moorish Queen. Thus God saves Parzival from further parricide. Cundrie appears once again and announces that a new inscription has appeared on the Grail and that Parzival is to cure Anfortas and become the Grail King in his stead. He and Feirefiz ride to the Grail Castle and after prayer Parzival asks 'Uncle, what ails you?' whereupon Anfortas is cured. Condwiramurs is summoned to the Grail and Feirefiz marries Repanse de Schoye, returning with her to the Orient where she gives birth to Prester John who establishes Christianity in India. Of Parzival's twin sons Kardeiz inherits his lands, while the other Loherangrin is to be Parzival's heir at the Grail.

It will be noticed at once that Wolfram's conception of the Grail and his version of its story is very different from others and from what became of it later. He follows his source, Chrétien de Troyes, with a tantalizing mixture of similarity and dissimilarity – at every turn and not merely in respect of the Grail. But, of course, Chrétien's work breaks off at a point which is only some three-quarters of the way through Wolfram's story (9,234 lines in Chrétien and *c.* 19,320 in Wolfram up to that point), so that Wolfram *had* to seek inspiration elsewhere for the last part. Wolfram claims to have used as his source a certain Kyot, a Provençal, who found the story of the Grail in Arabic in Toledo. Chrétien is mentioned only at the very end of Wolfram's poem (827,1ff.) and then only to say:

If Master Chrestien of Troyes has done wrong by this story, Kyot, who sent us the authentic tale, has good cause to be angry. The Provençal narrates definitively how the son of Herzeloyde achieved the Gral as had been ordained for him after Anfortas had forfeited it. The authentic tale with the conclusion to the romance has been sent to the German lands for us from Provence. I, Wolfram of Eschenbach, intend to speak no more of it than what the Master uttered over there.

(transl. p. 410)

This is all very well, but there are problems, the main one being that no Provençal poet of this name who could fit has ever been discovered and 'Kyot' (more properly 'Guiot') is a northern French not a Provençal form. Not only does Kyot appear suspiciously late on the scene in Wolfram – more than halfway through the work – but two of his first three mentions which are clustered closely together are hardly very auspicious:

> ... one of the King's men stood forward that went by the name of Liddamus. Kyot names him so. Now Kyot laschantiure was the name of one of those whose art compelled him to tell what shall gladden no few. Kyot is that noted Provençal who saw this Tale of Parzival written in the heathenish tongue, and what he retold in French I shall not be too dull to recount in German.
>
> (transl. p. 213)

> When Gawan had breakfasted – I am telling you just as Kyot told it – deep attachment found vent in bitter sorrow.
>
> (transl. p. 220)

In each case a rather prodigious effort has been made merely to verify that a character was called 'Liddamus', and that Gawan had had his breakfast. Much weightier matters have gone without such vehement attestations.

One is tempted to see here a leg-pull, a mockery of a general attitude among medieval poets and particularly of such learned ones as Gottfried von Strassburg who set great store by their source and their fidelity to it. This possibility is supported by a rather different ploy, also adopting an anti-scholarly, anti-learned approach, carried to the point of Wolfram's claiming to be illiterate:

> Unless the ladies thought it flattery, I should go on offering you things as yet unheard of in this story, I would continue this tale of adventure for you. But let whoever wishes me to do so, not take it as a book. I haven't a letter to my name! No few poets make their start from them: But this story goes its way without the guidance of books. Rather than that it be taken for a book, I should prefer to sit naked [perhaps rather 'to be found naked'] in my tub without a towel – provided I had my scrubber!
>
> (transl. p. 68f.)

Of course everything down to the bath-whisk, a minimal guarantee of decency to be worn à la figleaf, is meant humorously and the same may be true of the claim to be illiterate, though some take it as literally true. But whatever the truth of it, the cool attitude which it betrays to 'bookish' learned poets is unmistakable.

Naturally, doubt as to the literal truth of Kyot does not mean that if Kyot did not exist, then Wolfram had no source beyond

Chrétien and his own fertile imagination. It is eminently possible that Wolfram knew other, conceivably, oral, versions of the Grail story and that he used one or more of them. But despite the (nominal) embargo on inventing your own stories in the Middle Ages, Wolfram shows repeatedly that he is quite capable of having invented such parts of his story as suited his purpose. Capable of it in two ways: first in being willing to flout any such convention; secondly, in possessing the necessary powers of imagination and invention. We can see this on a large scale in his development of the story of Sigune and Schionatulander, both within *Parzival* and in the 'inverted' *Titurel*. We can see this inventiveness also in a matter as minor as a probable misunderstanding of a single Old French word.

When Parzival is first at the Grail two radiant young noblewomen in the Grail procession carry 'a pair of knives keen as fish-spines, on napkins, one apiece, most remarkable objects. They were of hard white silver, ingeniously fashioned, and whetted to an edge that would have cut through steel!' (transl. p. 125). Much later Trevrizent explains their purpose: under the influence of Saturn Anfortas's wound would become intolerably cold; the only relief that could be obtained was to apply heat by plunging the envenomed spear which had caused the wound into it again; when withdrawn the spear would remove the cold which would harden on it like glass; nothing could remove it except these special silver knives which the almost magical smith, Trebuchet, had fashioned for the purpose. Chrétien knows nothing of these silver knives but in his procession there is a silver *tailleoir*, 'carving dish', which has no counterpart in Wolfram: the French word is related to the verb *taillier*, 'to cut through, to carve', and it is likely that Wolfram has misunderstood the noun as something *with* which one cuts and thus invented, not only the knives, but the whole story of Saturn, plunging the spear into the wound, the glass-like coating, etc. to explain them! (The relation between planets and wounds is not pure Wolfram but part of medieval lore.)

Wolfram's version of the Grail is different in various respects from Chrétien's. The latter's Grail is introduced as *un graal* (with the indefinite article!) i.e. 'a large fairly deep dish', whereas in Wolfram it is first of all merely 'a thing, called the Grail' and later it is described more precisely as a 'stone'. A far remove from that other tradition which saw in it a chalice, often *the* chalice of the Last Supper in which later Christ's blood was caught, when he was on the cross, by Joseph of Arimathea. In Chrétien there were to have been two healing questions: 'Why does the lance bleed?', and 'Whom do they serve with the Grail?'. These twin requests for information contrast with Wolfram's single question expressing sympathy, for 'Uncle, what ails you?', is either an expression of sympathy plus a request for information, or simply an expression of sympathy. An answer like 'Rheumatoid arthritis' would strike us as not being in the spirit of the question. In Chrétien the motif of the Waste Land, infertility and so on which in future centuries was to prove so powerfully evocative, is merely touched on in the reproaches of the Hideous Maiden, while in Wolfram it does not appear at all, except perhaps for the situation of the Grail Castle in a lonely desolate area. Likewise neither in Chrétien nor in Wolfram is there any talk of a general quest for the Grail, another motif which proved so attractive for those desirous of expanding and extending the Grail myth. Only Perceval (Parzival) seeks the Grail, though in Wolfram Parzival compels another knight to seek it, too, for a year and this compulsion is then laid by him vicariously upon Gawan. Lastly, neither in Chrétien nor in Wolfram are people vouchsafed those mystically vaporous, and often vapid, visions of the Grail which appear in later works at frequent but irregular intervals.

In Wolfram the Grail has a religious aura and that, of its nature, remains inexplicable, but everything else about it and the Grail community is explained at the appropriate point. Waiting for the appropriate point, while having provided glimpses enough to invoke the sense of mystery and partial information enough to appreciate the explanation when it comes, is the essence of Wolfram's art as a narrator, but that point we will return to. For the moment I should like to dwell a little on the importance of the Grail as an element in the Arthurian romance and on the use Wolfram makes of it.

Wolfram's *Parzival* contains no fewer jousts and adventures than the usual Arthurian romance. It also has all the other features which made the genre so popular and such an astounding success for centuries to come. The Grail is, however, not only a new element but also a new type of element, certainly as Wolfram used it, and from now on it would be as well to disregard Chrétien, since without the ending we cannot tell what he had in mind. The action of the Arthurian romance had always been supplemented in its more successful representatives by a moral, ethical element which ranged from the level of courtly manners and etiquette to genuine moral dilemmas involving duty and the knightly, feudal code, and reaching to the level of religion, often of an optimistic, unproblematic nature. Such tends to be the plane of the Gawan strand in *Parzival*, though Gawan is admittedly the supreme and radiant exponent of this, what we might call, Arthurian level. Wolfgang Mohr has described the way in which knotty problems of courtly and chivalrous life are untied, or untie themselves, at the appearance of Gawan whom he calls the 'catalyser of humanity'.[2]

Wolfram makes of the Grail a bridge to higher and deeper levels of spirituality. He is a profoundly religious man but no theologian. He even plays down the role of the church in favour of a kind of lay piety: for instance Perceval's mother advises him inter alia to enter churches and cathedrals to pray to God, but Parzival is given no such advice; similarly in the Good Friday scene in Chrétien, Perceval finds his hermit uncle together with a priest and an acolyte celebrating Mass in a small chapel, but Parzival's uncle, though a hermit, appears not to be in holy orders and to live entirely alone in a cave. There is no reference to institutionalized religion such as acolytes, Mass or a chapel.

The hallmarks of the members of the Grail dynasty are *caritas* (the key-word is *triuwe*: loving loyalty) and a capacity for suffering, displayed by Herzeloyde in leaving her courtly life to protect Parzival while mourning his father; by Anfortas in his agony; by Trevrizent in the extreme hardship of his hermit's life which he has taken up to try to win redemption for his brother, Anfortas; by Sigune mourning for years over the corpse of the lover for whose death she blames herself; and by Parzival who, against all predictions, against all hope, and against all advice, undertakes any physical hardship and suffers separation from his adored wife in order to defy his way to the Grail and make good his failure to heal the Grail King, his uncle. These hallmarks extend, *mutatis mutandis*, to the Grail community whose chaste regimen combined with their courtly way of life raises them above and contrasts them with the Arthurian court. Indeed, so tell-

ingly and compellingly does Wolfram portray the life of the Grail
fellowship that it requires an occasional conscious effort on our part
to remind ourselves that it is simply a poetic fiction and not a real
Christian community blessed with the approval of orthodoxy.

The relation between the Round Table and the Grail is one of
intensified spirituality and seriousness symbolized by the figures of
Gawan and Parzival respectively. Seriousness, that is, of narrative
intent, not necessarily of tone. Although I have spoken of 'seriousness', I would agree with Mohr who sees the relation between Parzival and Gawan and indeed the work as a whole as based on a
'polarity of humour'. Seen from the point of view of Parzival's
world, Gawan 'swims along on the surface and is entertainingly
uncomplicated'. Seen from Gawan's secure world, Parzival seems
'touchingly foolish and clumsy' and we are amused 'how hard he
finds it to get on with man and God and how hard he makes it
for God to help him'.[3] Each complements the other and each shows
the other in a relative light. Parzival alone is able and worthy to
go on from the Round Table to the Grail, but this step which
Wolfram apprehends as progress and a raising does not invalidate
or belittle the Arthurian world.

Humour is indeed the dominating note of Wolfram's work; he
is prepared to treat any topic with humour – himself not excluded,
as we have seen – not because nothing is sacred to him, but because
everything is, if it is intact in itself, and humour can no more damage
things which are intact than can frost a smooth round pebble. We
find comedy of situation and action, we find humour of language,
ranging from attacks on worn clichés to outrageous word-plays and
neologisms. Addressing the probable patron of his second work,
Willehalm, apropos of the useful role of the roughneck Sir Kay in
keeping rowdies in place at Arthur's court, Wolfram says 'Prince
Hermann of Thuringia, I have weighed certain inmates of your court
who would go better by the name of "outmates"'; or speaking of
a high-born lady whose clothes are villainously torn to shreds, he
says 'If anyone were to call her "villein", he would be doing her
an injustice [we imagine that Wolfram will go on to say 'because
she was aristocratic despite her "villein-ous" clothes', but he goes
on to say] for she had little on' (playing on Middle High German
vilan which could also be heard as *vil an* 'much on'). The suggestive

erotic tone here is also one which we find often in Wolfram, frequently with humorous effect.

As apparently contradictory as it may seem, it is this combination of humour with the increased spiritual seriousness which the Grail introduces which accounts in part for the great attraction of Wolfram's *Parzival*, but there are other factors, too, which are of the upmost importance. Among these I would see the chief as his style and mastery of language; his consummate skill as a storyteller, as a far-sighted narrator capable of cunningly building up effects which burgeon over a long space of time and then blossom in scenes of dramatic force and urgency; his – for his time – totally unique ability to create a coherent time-plan and geography which stand up to close examination and which are even made to bring the Parzival and Gawan strands into a chronological and spatial relationship with each other; lastly, his ability to create characters and to people his work with a host of people, very many of whom – even the slightest – will be individualized by means of a name, an origin, or some distinguishing personal feature and whose actions may be motivated by such features.

Wolfram's style is very varied, ranging from highly idiosyncratic syntax and wilful, almost baroque, combinations of words to lines of stark and intense simplicity. On the one hand we have the dense concentration of *er brach durch blates stimme en zwîc*, literally 'he broke a twig for the sake of the leaf's voice', meaning 'he broke a twig in order to use the leaf to produce a sound (to decoy the deer)'. On the other hand, when Parzival eventually after prayer and due ceremony puts the healing question, asking 'Uncle, what ails you?', the breathless, urgent description of similar miracles which follows upon the healing of Anfortas and the rapid enumeration of those figures of legendary beauty from the Bible and Wolfram's own work whose beauty Anfortas now exceeds are summed up in a single line of measured tempo, deliberate weight, colossal understatement and monumental simplicity: *got noch künste kan genuoc*, 'Even nowadays, God has art enough' (i.e. to perform miracles of this magnitude).

That even the more tortured side of Wolfram's style is something of which he is aware, is revealed by his remark in *Willehalm*, *mîn tiutsch ist etswâ doch sô krump*, 'my German is a bit crooked in places'.

As an example, for instance, of Wolfram's occasional wilful

preference for asymmetric style we could look at the narrator's importunate questioning of Lady Adventure, his personified source, about the fate of Parzival when the story returns to him after following Gawan for several books:

> den selben maeren grîfet zuo
> ober an freuden sî verzagt
> oder hât er hôhen prîs bejagt?
> oder ob sîn ganziu werdekeit
> sî beidiu lang unde breit,
> oder ist si kurz oder smal?
>
> (433, 16ff.)

> (Take up the tale,
> whether he be despairing of joy,
> or has he won high fame?
> or whether his unblemished reputation
> be both far and wide
> or is it near or narrow?)

In an idiosyncratic way Wolfram switches from indirect question to direct, to indirect and back to direct. This is syntactically disturbing, but in case even indirect, direct, indirect, direct should congeal into a symmetrical pattern Wolfram disrupts it by having the first and second questions occupy one line each, the third two lines, and the fourth one line again. Wolfram is still not done, for where we would expect 'far and wide' to be balanced by 'near and narrow', he writes 'near *or* narrow'.

Yet this knotted style can be twisted or straightened at will and is an instrument which moves us to tears as swiftly as to laughter. Perhaps for the first time, in the hands of Wolfram and Gottfried von Strassburg, does the emergent Middle High German literary language arrive at that level of mastery where we feel that the poet possesses the detachment and distance to employ language as an instrument rather than being wholly or partly engulfed in and carried along by it. Changes of tone, attitude or pace become not merely possible but effortlessly so, so that the mechanics remain invisible.

The coherency of time structure and the (relative) realism of geography – it is possible to draw maps, though not completely definitive ones – are unique in the courtly romance of Wolfram's time, and perhaps in general. Yet even more remarkable is the way in which Wolfram has his work teem with major and minor characters, so that even the latter are recognizable and individualized and are supplied with names. Wolfram equips even background characters with a background and he is fond of creating between them intricate links springing from kinship, common interest, or earlier encounters of which the characters inform us, directly or indirectly, although these events never feature in the foreground. More than any other writer of romances in German Wolfram supplies his characters with a psychology and with motivation and these spring frequently from the cameo background and history with which the character is provided, or at least they become comprehensible against the background.

People are wont to compare the course of the chivalric romance with a highway of life and the hero's adventurous journeys with the journey through life. Such a comparison is justified for, as in *The Pilgrim's Progress*, it seems often in the romance that the hero on his adventures is moving not only through space but also time, as if he is riding towards his own future, so that his ride represents a foreshortening or acceleration of time, and so that his path through the world makes possible a development or maturing in a more compressed space of time than would be feasible if the hero, like us others, so to speak, merely passively allowed time to flow towards him.

Yet if the course of the normal courtly romance is a highway of life, then the course of Wolfram's *Parzival* is a railway, or even a rail-network. I mean by this that it is at once busier and more planned; there is a timetable; there are connections; there are branch-lines; there are signals, if you know how to read them. When Wolfram's characters leave our compartment we do not feel, as with other courtly romances, that they cease to exist until they are needed again for narrative purposes, but rather that they are active elsewhere, leading their own existence and going about their business. By the time even minor figures leave our compartment we know their names, either because they have introduced themselves or because we have been reading their suitcases. Often we know where they are going, either because they have told us or because we notice which platform they go to and the announcer (narrator) says, 'The train at platform 3 is the stopping train to Nantes, calling at Graharz, Pelrapeire, and Bearosche.' In short, in comparison with Chrétien and other writers of romances we are furnished with a very large number of concrete details which extend to the limits of our vision and provide the foreground with a background, and the background with a background, and this background with a background, and so on.

Lack of space prevents me from giving larger, more central examples, but perhaps the slighter peripheral ones are more uniquely characteristic of Wolfram. Here I must have recourse to telling the plot a little. Parzival in winning his wife defeats Clamide's seneschal, Kingrun, and packs him off under oath to Arthur's court. A page rides to Clamide and tells him of Kingrun's defeat, saying (mistakenly) that his conqueror is Ither, the Red Knight, because Parzival is wearing Ither's red armour. It is reasonable to assume that, like his page, Kingrun does not know Parzival has slain Ither. Kingrun finds Arthur at Karminal and he is greeted by Keie as an honoured colleague, since they are both seneschals. Three days later Parzival defeats Clamide and sends him after his seneschal to Arthur, whom he finds at Dianazdrun. We see there has been a 'meanwhile' in the background, too, and further evidence of this is met when Kingrun greets his lord, telling him that they had been defeated by the unknown man who had slain Ither, something new which he must have learnt from Arthur's knights. Much later Orilus, a formidable fighter, whose sister Keie had thrashed, comes to court. As seneschal Keie should find him quarters, but he dare not go near him. Keie remembers that Kingrun is a seneschal and sends him in his stead. Only Wolfram takes the normally empty title seriously and makes it part of Kingrun's and Keie's lives, part of their past, a job, and he takes it seriously even when it is there only for a joke, to show up the cowardly Keie.

A few further brief examples of the motivation of minor characters by means of their past and of the way in which this is used to give depth and warmth to the foreground. Epic poets are compelled to relate as a chronological succession things which happen simultaneously and which a painter could show as such. Wolfram and others describe, for instance, battle scenes in this way: first, the general charge, then individual combats are singled out and described in succession. The technique is used when the news comes to Arthur's camp that against all expectation Parzival is to have a second chance to cure Anfortas: first, the general reaction as the news spreads like wildfire; then the individual reaction, for Orgeluse, Gawan's newly won bride, 'wept for joy that Parzival's question was to put an end to Anfortas's torment'. Wolfram leaves it at that and we may be inclined to see this merely as the mixed reaction of a tender womanly heart, set alongside the general reaction. But if we reflect we *may* recall having been told long before that Orgeluse had been Anfortas's mistress and that it was precisely because of his relationship with her, which broke the rules of the Grail kingship, that God had caused Anfortas to be wounded in the groin. Hence Orgeluse's joy and tears! Sometimes Wolfram gives us a nudge, as when Sigune is found dead on the coffin of her lover, and Condwiramurs's tears are mentioned, Wolfram reminding us that they had been raised together after Sigune's mother had died. On other occasions – as with Orgeluse's tears – Wolfram leaves us to think things out for ourselves, but it is characteristic of him that he is always challenging us to ask, 'How many children had Lady Macbeth?', usually having provided the necessary information, tucked away somewhere or other, for us to answer the question, or at least speculate upon it, ourselves.

The father of Sigune is Duke Kyot of Katelangen whose late beloved wife Schoysiane was a member of the Grail family, being sister to Anfortas; she had died giving birth to Sigune. Kyot (*not* Wolfram's pretended source!), a very minor figure, is given a role at two points, the second being to fetch Condwiramurs to the Grail to be rejoined with Parzival after their five-year separation. Encamped on the journey, in the grey light of dawn, Kyot sees a party of Grail knights riding towards them and recognizes the turtle-dove escutcheon of the Grail. This reaches back into his past and 'the old man fetched a sigh when he saw it, since his chaste Schoysiane had won him great joy at Munsalvaesche [the Grail Castle] and then died giving birth to Sigune'. Kyot's response to the turtle-doves has no role to play in the action of the story. It is there because Kyot is a human being and this is how human beings react. Wolfram is still not finished with this ageing widower: when Sigune is found dead, Wolfram says Kyot did not know as yet of the death of his only child.

Such psychological insights are one of the reasons why Wolfram's *Parzival*, as well as being one of the most humorous of courtly romances, is also one of the most moving and serious. The effort which Wolfram expends on tying up and getting right details of plot, of time and place, of family-trees, of the provenance of concrete objects, and on the working out of convincing psychology has a powerful role to play in the impact his work produces. Using the Grail as a focus and a symbol he presents a humane, ethical and, though lay, profoundly religious view of life which in its seriousness is surprising in the courtly romance. But not even the Grail could have produced this impact without Wolfram's mastery as a story-teller in weaving a world-web of such cunning veracity that it compels us now, as it must have astounded his contemporaries.

NOTES

1. The edition referred to is: *Wolfram von Eschenbach*, ed. Karl Lachmann (6th edn, Berlin, 1926); the translation is Wolfram von Eschenbach, *Parzival*, transl. A. T. Hatto (Penguin Classics 1980), whose version is used in the anthology in this volume (pp. 457–65).

2. Wolfgang Mohr, *Parzival und Gawan*, in H. Rupp, *Wolfram von Eschenbach* (Darmstadt, 1966), 305.

3. As note 2, 306f.

GOTTFRIED VON STRASSBURG: *TRISTAN*

PETER JOHNSON

If asked to name great tragic lovers of the past, it is as likely that we would include Tristan and Isolde as it is unlikely that most of us would ever have heard of Gottfried von Strassburg. Yet his telling in Middle High German of the radiantly tormented lives of these ill-starred lovers is – *pace* Wagnerians – the beacon which stands over and outshines all other versions of the story.

The first point to make is that in a very literal sense we are within a hair's breadth of no one having 'heard of' Gottfried at all; in no historical document is he mentioned and nowhere in his work does he name himself in full. His unfinished poem of 19,548 lines[1] (rhyming couplets of four stresses per line) contains an elaborate continuing acrostic in which we have the first letter of *Gotevrit* (the medieval form of Gottfried) followed in order by the letters of the lovers' names, but repeated and arranged chiastically so that Tristan's letters always embrace Isolde's: G TIIT O RSSR, etc. By the point where the work breaks off we have reached only GOTE[VRIT], TRIS[TAN], ISOL[T]. And this 'GOTE' is all we know of Gottfried's name from his own work, though it is probable that like many medieval poets, including Thomas of Britain his model, on whose Old French version Gottfried's translation/adaptation is based, he would have named himself in an epilogue.

We are not, however, quite so bereft of information, since the unfinished state of Gottfried's work provoked two continuations in the thirteenth century which brought his work (somehow or other) to a conclusion. The earlier by Ulrich von Türheim (*c.*1230) tells us that meister Gotfrit is dead and so Ulrich must complete the work; the later by Heinrich von Freiberg (*c.*1290) also speaks of Gottfried's death and names him 'Meister Gottfried von Strassburg'. Thus 'Gote-' is completed and not only do we learn that he is of Strassburg, but the term *meister* is revealing, suggesting that he may have been a 'cleric' or 'clerk', that is someone who has enjoyed a higher education and functions either in a spiritual or administrative role, perhaps in the city chancery or at the episcopal court. Attitudes and interests appearing in *Tristan* would also seem to point in that direction rather than to his having been a knight. Gottfried is very reticent about himself, so that his work yields little, except by implication, to flesh out the meagre 'biography' above. But on internal evidence we can date Gottfried's work on relative grounds around 1205–15.

The nature of the continuations may be another reason why Gottfried is rarely heard of outside German-speaking lands or circles with special interest in medieval literature. The Middle Ages did not have that taste for fragments and ruins which later centuries have cultivated, so Gottfried's work was not valued by itself. Both continuations represent a considerable fall in level from the heights which Gottfried reaches. They continue and complete the plot, but Gottfried's pyschological and spiritual aims, and the rapturous and intoxicating élan of his language trickle away into the sand. Gottfried's work was completed but not his masterpiece.

One last reason for Gottfried's relative obscurity outside Germany is the general obscurity of German literature outside the country. For largely political and economic reasons Germany in the High Middle Ages was an area which received cultural influence – largely from France – but which did not transmit it on any large scale. Cultural contact means linguistic contact and here, too, Germany remained an importer. Few outside those lands where German was the native tongue knew German, so that the, by any standards, astonishing blossoming of German literature between, say, 1180 and 1230 never had the international impact or won the recognition which its quality deserved. It was left to Wagner to win it for Gottfried, Wolfram von Eschenbach, and the *Nibelungenlied*, by arousing interest in the stories and causing people to look back to the originals.

It is not possible in this brief essay to go into the origins of the Tristan story. It must suffice to say that our earliest extant literary versions – as opposed to rumblings about lost or oral versions – appear in France in the second half of the twelfth century. It is customary to distinguish two main types of Tristan narrative: the first is more earthy and robust after the style of the *jongleur*; the second, a more aristocratically modulated and restrained version, with greater

interest in emotions and states of mind. But both types are intended
for the entertainment of a court. Each type has two representatives
in France and two in Germany. In France of the popular type we
have fragments, considerable ones capable of being read with enjoyment (roughly 4,400 lines) by a poet called Béroul about whom we
know virtually nothing.[2] The same line is represented in Germany,
though less worthily, by the *Tristrant* of Eilhart von Oberg whose
version goes back to the same, or a similar source to Béroul's. The
more sophisticated tradition is represented by Gottfried, and in France
by *Thomas von Britanje* as Gottfried calls him. About Thomas we
know no more than the name and what the poem allows us to gather.
He is more concerned than the popular line to make the parts of
his romance harmonize, to motivate, and to explain how things came
about. Gottfried, who polemicizes against other versions of the
Tristan story, usually on the grounds of a lack of *vraisemblance*,
praises Thomas for his correctness. His version is dated variously
between 1160 and 1190 and it is possible, even probable, that it was
composed at, or for, the Angevin court of Henry II of England and
Queen Eleanor.

Like Gottfried's poem, Thomas's is incomplete, though in a different sense, since whereas Gottfried's was unfinished, Thomas's was
completed but has fallen victim to the loss and damage of manuscripts, so that all we have is a number of fragments, one of them
a substantial one of around 1,800 lines. But the crucial point is that
the bulk of what survives corresponds, if that be the word for so
negative an idea, to the part of Gottfried's romance which was never
written. (Gottfried's continuators turned not to Thomas, but to the
popular tradition.) Above all we 'have' the missing end, and there
is reason to suppose that Thomas represents the lines along which
Gottfried would have completed his work.[3]

A brief summary of the plot may help readers who are not familiar
with Gottfried's version. Tristan, orphaned at birth, is raised by
vassals of his father as their own child. He grows to be supreme
in music, languages, all courtly pursuits and in handsomeness. These
are his passport wherever he goes. He is abducted by merchants who
are, however, compelled by a storm caused by God to land him
in Cornwall where his dead mother's brother, Mark, is king. Tristan's
skills win him a place at court and when his true identity is revealed

he becomes Mark's heir. Tristan alone dares to fight the formidable Morold who comes regularly to claim Cornish children as tribute for Ireland. He kills Morold but receives a poisoned wound which only Morold's sister, Queen Isolde of Ireland, could heal. Posing as a minstrel Tristan wins the heart of the Irish court by his skill and Isolde cures him, provided that he will tutor her daughter Isolde, the acme of all beauty. Tristan does this and then returns to Cornwall. Courtiers envious of Tristan press Mark to marry. He agrees provided Isolde is his bride, imagining that enmity between the lands will prevent it. In his former guise Tristan returns to Ireland, kills a dragon which has been causing havoc and wins Isolde – for Mark. Noticing a notch in Tristan's sword into which a splinter removed from her uncle Morold's skull fits, Isolde recognizes Tristan's identity and tries, hindered by her 'sweet womanhood', to stab Tristan as he lies naked in his bath. Queen Isolde intervenes, reconciliation takes place, and Tristan is entrusted with bringing Isolde to Mark. Queen Isolde prepares a love-potion which Brangane is to give to Mark and Isolde on their wedding-night; it binds those who drink it together in eternal love. On the voyage Tristan and Isolde drink it in error, all Isolde's hostility vanishes and they become lovers. To maintain their reputation in society they sail on to Cornwall. Mark and Isolde are married and Brangane substituted on the wedding-night to conceal Isolde's lost virginity. The lovers are reduced to repeated stratagems to consummate their love. Eventually the intimacy which their glances betray, but which cannot be proved, since the lovers' cunning enables them to counter every trap, leads Mark to banish them. They lead an idyllic life in the semi-mythological Grotto of Lovers, but when a further subterfuge enables them to return to court, they do so 'for the sake of their honour' (i.e. 'reputation in society, surface propriety', which is what had made them continue to Cornwall rather than flee after drinking the potion). Finally Mark discovers them sleeping together in an orchard. They entrust their hearts to each other. Tristan flees overseas and meets a duke's daughter, Isolde of the White Hands. Partly mesmerized by the beloved name and under considerable social pressure, Tristan tormentedly contemplates marrying her. Here the work breaks off.

Only the fifty-two lines of the Cambridge Fragment of Thomas and the first 182 lines of the Sneyd Fragment may be compared

directly with Gottfried (18,195–358, transl. pp. 280–82; and 19,411 to
the end, transl. p. 296f. respectively) to show us what Gottfried has
made of his main source and model. Going on this sparse direct
evidence, Gottfried rationalizes the actions and motivates even more
carefully than Thomas, dwelling on psychological and emotional
states more deeply and penetratingly. In the climactic scene, fortunately surviving in both versions, where the two lovers are discovered
in the orchard, we can see both these tendencies at work together,
though they are not always totally compatible (transl. p. 28off. and
p. 364). In Gottfried's version* the episode tells how Queen Isolde,
having long been unable to be intimate with Tristan, imprudently has
a rich bed made outside in the orchard; retaining only Brangane, she
has Tristan summoned; 'Now Tristan did just as Adam did; he took
the fruit which his Eve offered him and with her ate his death. He
came ...'; unexpectedly, and before Brangane can alert the sleeping
lovers King Mark enters, asking for the Queen; told she is sleeping,
he demands 'Where?';

> Mark repaired there at once – and found his mortal pain there! He found
> his wife and his nephew tightly enlaced in each other's arms, her cheek against
> his cheek, her mouth on his mouth. All that the coverlet permitted him to
> see – all that emerged to view from the sheets at the upper end – their arms
> and hands, their shoulders and breasts – was so closely locked together that,
> had they been a piece cast in bronze or in gold, it could not have been joined
> more perfectly. Tristan and Isolde were sleeping very peacefully after some
> exertion or other.

Mark possesses now the certainty that he had always wanted and
always dreaded, ever sought and ever fled; he goes off to fetch his
vassals as witnesses, but Tristan awakes and sees him go; he wakes
Isolde and with due form commending his heart to her and she hers
to him, they part and he flees the country.

Gottfried's scene is over three times longer than Thomas's. The
first reason for expansion is at once highly characteristic of Gottfried;
however dubious the morality, we have an aesthetically idealized
picture of the slumbering lovers which has no counterpart in Thomas.
Without slipping into triteness, Gottfried's portrayal may be described as 'artistic': in the overt sense of being a beautifully fashioned

* See anthology, pp. 472–4.

scene, but also in the sense that it actually sees the entwined lovers as a work of art, as a thing of beauty. They *are* a sculpture, yet one that transcends any that was ever 'cast in bronze or gold', for not only are they more beautiful, but their 'perfect joining' stands also for their spiritual oneness in love. The narrative perspective is such that this viewpoint is Mark's, though we share it. What we cannot share is the mixture of joy and grief which assails Mark on seeing this artistic vision. His eyes arouse in him the aesthetic pleasure of his nephew's handsomeness, his wife's beauty and their indivisible oneness as a harmonious work of art. But now he has the grief of certainty: he sees the beauty of his wife which since the day that Tristan brought her to him has always ravished his heart, though in it he knows he has never possessed hers. Easing the narrative viewpoint away from Mark again, Gottfried allows himself the wry comment, born of diplomatic ignorance, that 'Tristan and Isolde were sleeping very peacefully after some exertion or other'; at the very moment that Mark achieves certainty, the narrator ironically feigns uncertainty for himself and us of the nature of the lovers' wearying exertions. A revealing example of Gottfried's sophisticated detachment.

The following account of Mark's mental state and Gottfried's reflection on it have no equivalent in Thomas. His Mark was accompanied by the hateful dwarf and he leaves him behind while he goes to fetch witnesses: 'They shall see how we found them. When the fact is proved I shall have them burnt!' Gottfried's scene has perhaps gained a little in credibility, for with the dwarf in tow Mark already has a witness, of sorts! Nor does Thomas tell us what the dwarf does when Tristan awakes. Yet, if one dare embark on such dangerous speculation, we may suspect that Gottfried's motive in removing the dwarf was not so much credibility as emotive and artistic *bienséance*. When, in an earlier scene, Tristan and Isolde are discovered in potentially compromising circumstances in the Grotto of Lovers, as a deliberate subterfuge they are lying apart and it is only the sword between them that is naked. They may, therefore, be discovered thus by a third party, the huntsman who summons Mark. In the orchard, however, this sight of physical beauty and moral shame – in the view of the everyday world! – is not on either count for a gaping public or a spiteful dwarf, but only for Mark, because it is his fate, and for us, because we are of that group of noble hearts (see p. 214f, below). The introduction of the description requires the exclusion of the dwarf, and this is a gain for propriety, with which there goes another reduction in barbarity in favour of a more courtly approach: in Gottfried there is no talk by Mark of having the lovers 'burnt'. He does not even tell his courtiers that he has discovered the lovers, merely that he has heard they are together and his courtiers are to come 'and take note of the pair, so that if they were found there as stated he should be given summary judgement against them in accordance with the law of the land'. Only Tristan speaks of 'killing'. Of burning there is no mention on either side.

The final cause for expansion vis-à-vis Thomas is the extended leave-taking in which greater weight is given to Isolde's loving devotion and spirituality than to Tristan's. (This *may* have been Thomas's intention, too. The fragment breaks off at this crucial point, but it sounds as if Thomas's scene is coming to an end with the handing over of the ring.)

This brief comparison has led us precipitately and prematurely to the heart of Gottfried's poem and materially almost to its end. It would be as well to step back and take a more general view. The emergence within, at the most, one hundred and fifty years of the six versions of the Tristan story, together with the lost Tristan poem of Chrétien de Troyes, and in the thirteenth century three prose versions, two in French and one in Italian, not to mention various shorter offshoots and appendages, attest an intense and widespread interest in Tristan and Isolde in the Middle Ages. It is not surprising that this tale of resplendent and gifted, aristocratic young lovers, the wife and nephew of a king, driven by fatal error and the love-potion to an illicit passion, the consummation of which leads ultimately to their deaths, should have gripped the imagination of men and women in the Middle Ages and since. Yet the immoral nature of its subject-matter, doubtless one reason for its success, did not escape adverse criticism at the time and among literary critics. Particularly in Germany in the nineteenth century and later, voices have been raised against the lasciviousness of a story whose main goal is the consummation of adulterous love. Whatever our views on the power of the medieval church, people at the time could be, and were, generous about such matters, if it suited them, though the *telling* of such a story was something different from merely condoning it. This could present difficulties, particularly for a self-conscious poet like Gottfried.

In German literature around Gottfried's time no case springs to mind of a 'hero' like Macbeth, that is a villain with better qualities and a certain noble grandeur, as *the* central figure of a work. (Without this last condition heroic literature does offer examples.) Nor do medieval poets adopt a neutral, take-it-or-leave-it attitude to their heroes. Heroes require the praise and support of their creators. Béroul's solution is at once eminently simple and eminently successful: he joins Tristan's and Isolde's retinue, he adopts the personal loyalty – based on affection not righteousness – of a Brangane or Curvenal and roundly and unproblematically curses the dogs who seek to trap the lovers. Though this may do for a poet who describes a Mark willing to hand Isolde over to lepers as a punishment – and one to fit the crime, since in the Middle Ages lepers were reputed to be lecherous – it is not a solution open to a more cultured and self-critical poet like Gottfried.

How does Gottfried solve it? Not by a defensive action. Though the love potion is there as an exonerating device, that is not how Gottfried uses it, a topic to which we will return. Far from excusing the lovers 'because they couldn't help it', Gottfried goes on to the offensive and, incredibly, idealizes, one might say idolizes, them and holds them up as models for others, for us, to follow. If more of its original religious force were restored to 'propagandist', then Gottfried is the arch-propagandist of medieval German literature, devoted to an ideal of unreserved and absolute love, physical and spiritual, a creed which possesses religious overtones and which has as its exemplary saints and martyrs, the contemplation of whose persons and story will improve us and inspire us to emulate their perfection, the adulterers Tristan and Isolde.

In his prologue Gottfried pleads for a fair hearing for anything that is well-intended and he tells us that *his* work is intended for a select group of noble hearts who are willing to bear the sorrow which inevitably accompanies the joys of true love and who do not merely seek shallow joy like the world in general (45–130, transl. p. 42f.). They are also those who possess the sensitivity to appreciate Gottfried's story as it is meant. Such an audience of noble hearts desires stories of yearning and Gottfried will 'bestory' them well:

> ich wil in wol bemaeren
> von edelen senedaeren,
> die reiner sene wol taten schin:
> ein senedaer unde ein senedaerin,
> ein man ein wip, ein wip ein man,
> Tristan Isolt, Isolt Tristan.
>
> (125ff.)

> (I will story him well
> with noble lovers
> who gave proof of perfect love:
> [a lover and his mistress,]
> a man a woman, a woman a man,
> Tristan Isolde, Isolde Tristan.)

Gradually logical and syntactical relations break down and Gottfried, and later Wagner in Act II of his opera, can do nothing other than place them and their names in incantatory fashion nakedly side by side. Much ink has been spilt trying to identify the 'noble hearts'. One might also ask, 'Who doesn't belong to them?' The answer is probably, 'No one!', or at least only such as choose to exclude themselves.

Towards the end of the prologue Gottfried places his lovers and their story more and more in a religious light, seeing their lives and deaths with unmistakable eucharistic overtones as the bread of all noble hearts, so that their lives and deaths live on and they live on in their deaths as the bread of the living (230–40, transl. p. 44). Gottfried is endeavouring to exploit the aura of such language, gaining perhaps an extra frisson from its use for such a purpose. These parallel and chiastic — chiasmus is probably Gottfried's favourite form — arrangements of synonyms and antonyms, the balancing and combining of opposites, have often been compared with the language of mystics, seeking to express in paltry words the ineffable of their soul's union with its maker. Such use of language leads us in two directions: on the one hand to religion and theology; on the other to music and art. Both aspects are part of Gottfried's attempt to win us for his lovers.

I stressed earlier that Gottfried had enjoyed a formal education; we can see this in his classical allusions to Apollo, etc., and in his practical knowledge of classical rhetoric. We can see it also in his 'theological' view of his source as something sacrosanct (theoretically at least) and in his method of modification through interpretation, akin to exegesis. Like the prologue, the numerous excursuses scattered through the work serve to show, via interpreting the action, the lovers in a favourable light and to win our sympathy for them. (Incidentally, they are also convenient in 'feigning' the passage of time, for instance the 'sermon of love' (12,183–391, transl. p. 202ff.) after the lovers have drunk the potion and consummated their love and the allegorical interpretations of the Grotto of Lovers serve to give the impression of a period of uninterrupted joy spent together, where Gottfried could hardly present a picture of repeated love-making.)[4]

A further technique which Gottfried employs to gain sympathy belongs rather to the line of Béroul. With the possible exception of Mark, a very ambivalent figure and one hard to assess, the opponents of the lovers are shown as a cowardly, pitiful lot, ready to act as *agents provocateurs* and almost too keen on *trapping* the lovers. The tendency is observable early, for in the whole of Mark's court there is not one who dare meet Morold's challenge – except Tristan. After he has freed them from this shameful tribute and has got himself healed of the wound incurred on their behalf, jealousy begins to show itself and they claim that Tristan achieves his ends through necromancy. At the court we hear almost exclusively only of the reactions of those who are against Tristan and Isolde, and these include a dwarf skilled in black arts, a 'friend' who secretly lusts for Isolde, and so on. Never does Gottfried show us the reaction of a decent ordinary courtier who says, 'Really this is getting to be a bit too much!'

There is also the love-potion.* A rationalist approach might suggest that a sceptical, sharp-minded poet like Gottfried would not believe in a love-potion and would wish to be rid of it or reduce its status to a symbol, except that its fame and the widespread knowledge of it preclude this. There is nothing of this in Gottfried. However we are to interpret it, the potion causes the love between Tristan and Isolde. Attempts to find indications of love before they

* See anthology, pp. 467–70.

drink it fail, though it should be remarked that given a poet of the cunning and sophistication of Gottfried, that love is not *mentioned* before the potion causes it is *not* evidence that it did not exist. Gottfried is skilled enough to keep a subconscious love implicit until the lovers themselves are aware of it; in a lesser poet the silence would have been more conclusive. If there is any hint of attraction on either side, it *could* lie oddly enough in Isolde's violent outbreak *against* Tristan when, with him naked in the bath, she discovers through the notch in his sword that the Tantris they have been harbouring is the Tristan who slew her uncle. She has already dwelt on Tantris's handsomeness and accomplishments, and on the disparity between these and his (supposed) status in life as a merchant. Has she thought that the latter puts any thought of alliance out of the question and dismissed it, only to learn that it is in question and yet is out of it for different reasons? It is the sheer violence of Isolde's rage and lack of tenderness which makes one wonder whether Gottfried intends to hint that maidenly musings have been cheated here.

The potion *is* the effective cause of love between Tristan and Isolde. So does this mean that it has no general or symbolic significance? If its sole suggestive force is, 'Be careful what you drink!', then we are entitled to be disappointed. But it does stand for more: the allegorical figure of Love who by military force occupies the hearts of the lovers after they have drunk the potion (11,707ff., transl. p. 195ff.), stands for a dark, elemental, demonic love which exists in the world and which, unexpectedly and irrationally, seizes the hearts of men and women so that they must cleave to each other blindly, as if they had drunk a love-potion. Tristan and Isolde have. In their case, the elemental force is underlined by the way in which the dregs of the potion, hurled into the hitherto calm sea, cause it to boil up suddenly.

The factual force of the potion does not, however, prevent Gottfried from hedging it round, before and after it is drunk. Any possible reluctance on the part of his audience (figuratively) to swallow a love-potion is undermined in advance by Gottfried, but only with retrospective force. Tristan and Isolde are the acme of manly and womanly beauty; each dresses with superb elegance; no one is more gifted at languages and music than Tristan and never could he have had a more skilled and willing pupil than Isolde; Tristan slays the dragon and it is a well-known fact that dragon-slayers get the princess and half the kingdom, so that it seems like an outlandish perversion when the slayer reports that he has done it only on commission on behalf of Mark; the right to Isolde won by slaying the dragon is confirmed when Mark, through irresponsibility and cowardice, loses Isolde to Gandin (13,104ff., transl. p. 214ff.) and it is Tristan who wins her back and hands her over (once more!) to Mark. Looking *back* from the potion, Tristan and Isolde were predestined for each other.

A potion which is convenient for exonerating the lovers runs the risk of turning them into puppets and diminishing their stature. Gottfried solves this problem in two ways. First, when Tristan learns of the nature of the potion they have drunk, instead of wringing his hands he uses them both to seize the responsibility, accepting willingly and gladly the fate that has befallen them; Brangane says it will mean the lovers' deaths; Tristan replies:

> Whether it be life or death, it has poisoned me most sweetly! I have no idea what the other will be like, but this death suits me well! If my adorable Isolde were to go on being the death of me in this fashion I would woo death everlasting!

> (12,495ff., transl. p. 206)

Gottfried's second method for playing down the potion is that, except in the following scene when Brangane is substituted for Isolde on her wedding-night with Mark, the potion is never mentioned again.

Inevitably the nature of *Tristan* places considerable stress on cunning and successful ruses, elements not normally favoured in the chivalric romance. This is, therefore, a feature which tends to set it apart, a tendency which is reinforced by Gottfried's rather dismissive attitude to knightly combats. (This has encouraged the view that he may be of middle-class patrician origin, or a cleric, or both.) Whereas in earlier versions Tristan's cunning would seem to have gone hand in hand with various crafts such as hunting (for food), wood-carving, etc., in the more courtly versions of Thomas and Gottfried the crafts become arts – singing, instrumental skills, chess, knowledge of foreign languages.[5] In the education of Gottfried's Tristan, unlike that of any other young hero of courtly romance, martial training takes second place to such social accomplishments. Hunting has become an art not a necessity and Tristan gains entry to Mark's court not by a successful joust, the usual passport to the Round Table, but by his expert knowledge of the latest fashion in dressing a stag. Unless one can simply enjoy with gusto the ingenuity of the stratagems adopted – to effect a cure, to prove the true dragon-slayer, etc. and not merely to commit adultery undetected – the cunning, like the adultery, *could* cast a shadow on the work, were it not for Gottfried's ecstatic championing of the lovers and of the rightness of their love. For Gottfried love must be whole-hearted, selfless with regard to one's partner, single-minded, and consummated.

To convince his audience of this, and for every other purpose which he has, Gottfried possesses the perfect instrument, his virtuoso language, rightly so called, since he has every register at his fingertips, reaching from one extreme where language goes unnoticed to the other where it threatens to become an end in itself. Rhyme and metre present no problems; sentences vary enormously in length and structure, now falling in with the verse pattern, now reacting against it; words are combined adventurously or new ones are invented, e.g. *gêvet* from the proper name 'Eve', meaning 'having taken after Eve'; or *gisôtet* from 'Isolde' meaning 'ensnared by Isolde'.

The above neglects an important aspect of Gottfried's language, namely the irrational. Despite the conceptual precision and sharp-witted logic or even casuistry of which Gottfried is capable, he handles language also like music. Acoustic effects such as rhyme (internal and final), alliteration, assonance, and rhythm intertwine with features which merge into meaning, such as enjambement, syntax, parallelism, and antithesis, to weave an acoustic–semantic counterpoint. Let us look at the following lines from the prologue:

> ir süeze sur, ir liebez leit,
> ir herzeliep, ir senede not,
> ir liebez leben, ir leiden tot,
> ir lieben tot, ir leidez leben:
> dem lebene si min leben ergeben.
> (60ff., transl. p. 42)

> [I have another world in mind
> which together in one heart bears]
> its bitter-sweet, its dear sorrow,
> its heart's joy, its [yearning] pain,
> its dear life, its sorrowful death,

its dear death, its sorrowful life.
To this let my life be given.

We see that links and breaks effected by the three principles of rhyme, alliteration, and sense-patterns (the parallel or antithetical arrangement of synonyms and antonyms) interweave with mind-robbing complexity. Breaks in the rhyme are contradicted by links in the alliteration, e.g. 60 and 61 are separated by rhyme but linked by the s-s l-l l s alliteration, while 61 and 62 are linked by rhyme but separated by the new alliteration which links with 63 and is, like the previous alliteration, arranged chiastically, l-l l-t l-t l-l. In 60 'synonyms' alternate (the German order is 'sweet-bitter'), in 61 and 62 they are arranged in tandem (linking these lines which are joined by rhyme, but divided by alliteration), and in 63 their order is chiastic. The cross relations interchange continually, our senses and minds are mesmerized. Only music itself could go much further in this direction and, despite changes of plot and a fundamentally different attitude to love and death – 'love and, if possible, live', is Gottfried's watchword – it may well be that Gottfried would have envied Wagner the opportunity of using music without words at times.

In the last resort, if Gottfried does everything he can to hold up Tristan and Isolde as ideal lovers and as models we should emulate, does this mean that Gottfried is advocating in blasphemous manner compulsory adultery? Through the potion he tells us that love can seek out humans as their fate. Those whom such a love afflicts and enraptures have no higher duty than to live for it and for each other, to be faithful to it and each other, to be emotionally, spiritually, and physically one, and to overcome any obstacles to fulfil these goals. For Tristan and Isolde the latter's marriage is the obstacle, but it is a contingent not an essential one. It, too, must be overcome, if possible in a manner which preserves the propriety of the court, that centre for which Tristan and Isolde and all their elegance and talents were created. To convey this inexpressible and paradoxical love is Gottfried's aim, as it is also the achievement of this supreme attempt, taking a leaf from Gottfried's book, to enword the wordless and unwordable.

NOTES

1. In the edition of Friedrich Ranke, *Tristan und Isold* (14th edn, Dublin, Zürich, 1969); references throughout the text are to this edition. To these are added the relevant page numbers in the excellent translation by Hatto (Penguin Classics 1960), whose version is used in the anthology in this volume (pp. 465–74).

2. Béroul may be read in the lively translation by Alan S. Fedrick in the Penguin Classics.

3. Hatto (see note 1) provides, 301–53, a translation of Thomas in order to round off Gottfried's poem; he also offers as an appendix a translation of the Cambridge Fragment which allows some comparison with Gottfried.

4. In general Gottfried is better at compelling descriptions, for instance the May festival at Tintagel (536ff., transl. 48ff.) or the entry of the two Isoldes, mother and daughter, to the Irish court (10,885ff., transl. 185ff.), or at taut and dramatically effective shaping of individual scenes such as the discomforting of the Irish Steward (11,021ff., transl. 186ff.), or the Ordeal of the Red-hot Iron (15,534ff., transl. 246ff.) than at larger scale linking and disposition of scenes. In all fairness to Gottfried, this may be a consequence of the nature of the Tristan story *per se*.

5. Naturally there is a close association between crafts and cunning, and arts and cunning; we need think only of 'crafty' and 'artful'.

THE *ROMAN DE LA ROSE*

L. T. TOPSFIELD

When, around 1230, Guillaume de Lorris retold his dream of five years before, he could have had no idea that his poem of exquisite romantic love would provide the framework for a continuation which would become a celebrated treatise on the condition of man and the importance of human love within the cosmic order. Yet such was to be the case, and this transformation was effected when Jean de Meung began to compose his 'continuation' of the romance, some forty years after Guillaume had written.

The two parts of the romance have quite separate intentions. The first part, some four thousand lines long, gives us the quintessence of the twelfth-century aspiration to the type of love which the Provençal troubadours called *Fin'Amors*. This love, whether in its philosophical form in the poetry of Marcabru (*fl.c.*1130–60) or in its practical application in the courtly songs which Bernart de Ventadorn (*fl.c.*1150–80) addressed to Eleanor of Aquitaine, had the quality of uniting all desire and aspiration, sexual, mental and spiritual, in one complete and perfect love for the lady. The second part of the romance conveys to us in strong and rugged verse, as it did to the French humanists of the sixteenth century, the philosophical brilliance of twelfth-century France, which was itself a true age of Renaissance, and, in addition, the thirteenth-century conflict, especially in the schools of Paris, between faith and reason, between Christian belief and Aristotelian and Averroist rationalism buttressed by new ideas about experimental science. The importance of the *Roman de la Rose* becomes clearer when we remember that France in the twelfth and thirteenth centuries was the creative dynamo of European culture. Drawing inspiration from ancient Greece and Rome, and from Celtic and Hispano-Arabic traditions, it generated and transmitted to western Europe its ideas on life, love, political and scientific thought, its theories of government and of man's destiny in the world of nature and the cosmos. When the fires lit by these ideas had been dowsed by Church and Inquisition in the late thirteenth century and finally extinguished in the disasters of the Hundred Years' War, it was in great measure the *Roman de la Rose* which, for the educated layman and the writer in French, helped to span the cultural void between this early Renaissance and the later one of the sixteenth century which was fuelled initially by the art and civilization of Italy.

Jean de Meung's encyclopaedic work undoubtedly ensured the success of the *Roman de la Rose* as a whole, and made it into a medieval 'bestseller'. It still exists in nearly three hundred manuscripts, and with the discovery of printing it was produced almost immediately in no less than fourteen editions. It is frequently listed in the catalogues of private libraries in sixteenth-century France. In that century it was updated by Clement Marot, was praised by Ronsard among other writers, and influenced Rabelais. It was also successful outside France, in two early Dutch translations, in two thirteenth-century Italian adaptations and in the middle English version attributed to Chaucer. It also achieved a particular notoriety through the 'Querelle de la Rose', a controversy which lasted in France for nearly one hundred and fifty years, from 1401 to the *Tiers Livre* of Rabelais in 1546. This dispute was sparked off by Christine de Pisan, a twenty-five-year old widow, who, in need of money to support her two children, took up writing as a career. With great vigour she condemned what she considered to be Jean de Meung's anti-feminist attitudes, and in so doing attacked a tradition of clerical misogyny as old as the early Church fathers. Her main ally in the dispute, though for reasons different from hers, was the great theologian Gerson. Yet nowadays it is also the first part of the romance which particularly engages our attention, as it did that of Chaucer. It absorbed and distilled the ideas on love and courtliness of the Provençal troubadours, and in unison with the great Arthurian romances of northern France, it influenced the literary traditions of western Europe and especially of England, to a degree which can scarcely be estimated.

Guillaume's work is a fine poem in a simple and compelling style which defies translation. It has the lightness of touch, the *simplece* of all great courtly poetry, an immediacy of feeling, of joy and sorrow observed in innocence, a sense of virtue immune to the vice and tribulations of the world. With psychological allegory of rare delicacy, Guillaume tells how in a dream he awoke to the idea of love, then fell in love with the Rose, was encouraged, rebuffed, dismissed and left desolate, yet not entirely without hope. Guillaume's longing and sufferings in this sequence of love, close love and love from afar, are not unlike those of the troubadour Jaufre Rudel (c.1147) by whom he was clearly influenced. But unlike Jaufre Rudel and most other troubadours, Guillaume shifts the focus of his attention from his own afflictions to the predicament of his lady, the Rose, as she endures her conflict in heart and mind between the desire for love and her courtly reticence.

Once we appreciate this point, we see that the poem, despite its lyric air, its innocent delights and sorrows, has an intricate structure and a complex intention. Guillaume describes it as an Art of Love: 'And if anyone asks what I wish the romance to be called, which I here begin, it is the Romance of the Rose in which the whole art of love is enclosed.'[1] As an Art of Love, it draws its setting and narrative techniques from Arts of Love going back to classical antiquity. But Guillaume's work is also a love story and as such it is a *summa* or summing-up of the topics, themes, expressions, stylistic methods and psychological allegory of the courtly troubadours of southern France and the *trouvères* of the north. And yet this work is more than an Art of Love and a love story told from within the hearts and minds of lady and lover for the entertainment and instruction of other ladies and their lovers. It is also, and in this it is unique, an extended love lyric of unrequited love, and it is primarily this quality which gives the work its intense immediacy.

Guillaume offers us the first indication of this personal plea in the opening lines: 'Not a single thing which appeared to me in my dream, in the twentieth year of my life, has failed to come to pass, just as the dream related it to me.' Guillaume could scarcely be more covertly explicit. The dream has happened in reality:

> mes en ce songe onques riens n'ot
> qui tretot avenu ne soit
> si con le songes recensoit.
>
> (28–30)

Guillaume connects the Rose of his dream-love five years before with his present lady, who is, as he says, herself worthy to be loved and called Rose. Whether the two loves, the dream and the real, are identical, and they probably are, Guillaume's Art of Love is not solely, or even mainly contained in the rules of behaviour in love which *Amors* dictates to the lover (1,879–2,748). It is much more to be found in the sequence of desire, doubt and fear which he feels as he falls in love, and in the generous response of the lady which then conflicts with her doubts and alarm. In describing the interplay of feeling between himself and his lady, Guillaume's purpose is twofold. He is offering the experience as an *exemplum* to all lovers and their ladies. In addition, and this is the true purpose of the work, Guillaume, by revealing his own love and suffering, and especially his awareness of the feelings of his lady and her dilemma, is asking for her trust and her interest and is entreating her mercy. It is in this concealed plea to the lady that the true meaning (*senefiance*) of the work consists, the closed truth (*verité coverte*) which will be opened (*aperte*), as the dream 'free from lying words' unfolds.

The possibility that Guillaume's work is not only a romance and an Art of Love but also a personal plea greatly enriches our appreciation of his use of allegory. The Rose is the lady of his dream, the lady to whom he offers his work and with whom he hopes to find happiness. The Rose is his love past, present and future. The Rose represents the lady and at the same time the sum of her qualities and feelings, such as her growing awareness of herself in love as the rosebud begins to unfold.[2] The Rose is the pivot on which the planes of reality and illusion, of time past, present and future, are balanced. In a wider sense, the Rose is the symbol of any lady faced with the same situation of *Fin' Amors* in which desire is in conflict with *mesure*, a proper sense of proportion in courtly behaviour and the rational control needed to implement this. We see this wider meaning of the Rose when *Jalosie* builds her wall around the whole rose garden and all the roses in it.

Two teams of allegorical figures are matched in this conflict between reason and desire. Each of these figures represents a psychological motivation or attitude of mind on the part of the lady and the lover, and as the narrative progresses, they are interwoven in a network of human relationships such as one might find in courtly society. *Franchise*, the lady's generous and noble spirit, *Pitié* and their minion *Bel Acueil* or Fair Welcome, all manifest the lady's impulse to accept the lover's advances, and Venus hovers omnipresent behind this avant-garde of sympathy for the lover. Opposition to these outgoing qualities is offered by *Honte*, shame, *Peur*, timidity and fear, *Chastée*, the impulse towards chaste living, and their henchmen, the gruff gardener *Dangier*. The leader of the forces of repression is *Jalosie*. This almost certainly does not represent the friends and relations of the lady, as has been suggested by C. S. Lewis. *Jalosie* is rather the lady's innate desire to preserve her integrity and sense of identity, and the word *jalosie* can have exactly this meaning in Old French.[3]

Jalosie is the dominant quality in the psychological defence of the lady. It is *Jalosie* which pulls back the exposed pawn *Bel Acueil*, castles him within the tower, and encloses the whole rose garden within her new wall. The role of *Jalosie* is most important, for it is with this figure that Guillaume pinpoints his lady's present dilemma. Were *Jalosie* to relent enough to allow *Franchise* and *Pitié* to release *Bel Acueil*, Guillaume's despair would be transformed into perfect joy.

Guillaume is brilliantly original in the skill with which he fashions his allegorical figures into individual characters, each with its distinctive quality, role and style of speech in the drama which he unfolds. The 'humanizing' of these psychological personifications is made easier by the fluidity of Guillaume's attitude to allegory and his lack of a rigid distinction between the allegorical and the existing world of courtly convention. This becomes apparent when he introduces the young men who are the lovers of the courtly virtues. *Richece* pairs off with her materialistic lover; *Largece* with her brave knight from Arthur's court; and *Cortoisie* with the knight who charms her with his eloquence. For Guillaume, the humans who live at court are synonymous with their courtly, psychological motivations. The true courtly knight is the personification of *cortoisie*, the sum of all the courtly virtues and of their expression in society, and *Bel Acueil* is the living manifestation of fair welcome in the lady, both as a principle of courtly behaviour and its expression in courtly society. *Malebouche*, the slanderer, is not out of place among personified aspects of the mind such as *Peur*, *Honte* and *Chastée*. *Malebouche* is the human figure of the courtly slanderer, the *losengeor*, as well as the general allegory of scandal-mongering and the fear of such scandal in the mind of the lady.

Allegory for both poet and audience in France in the twelfth and early thirteenth centuries was a natural, swift and vital device by which a plethora of meanings could be indicated by a single word. Allegory, in the sense of latin *allegoria*,[4] was still free from the restrictive bands of literary convention, and from the erudition and moralizing which would soon begin to drain its life force, even in the works of the great *trouvère* Thibaut de Champagne (1201–53). Allegory for the troubadours and their audience in the twelfth and early thirteenth centuries was an integral part of poetry, endowing it in a single word with rich lyrical feelings or with abstract moral and universal truths open to the perceptive but closed to the ignorant and the *flacs-endurzitz*, the shallow people hardened against feeling. As a simple example of this, let us look for a moment at the word *Jois* or Joy in troubadour poetry. This could be used indiscriminately on the literal or allegorical level. It had many meanings: the exaltation of momentary bliss; the elusive ideal of a serene, rational and lasting happiness; the quest for such happiness and the innate force that inspires the search; the pleasure in the search; the person who can induce either of these forms of joy. It is very probable that Guillaume, who was well acquainted with the works of the leading troubadours, was also using allegory in an equally allusive and evocative way.

Though Guillaume's *Roman de la Rose* is set in its garden within a self-contained system of worldly behaviour, it is enriched by the morality of its courtly values. These derive from its conception of a love, like the *Fin'Amors* of the troubadours, which is true, perfect, and complete, and which, enhanced by touches of light irony, conveys to the reader a sense of the *bien*, the positive and optimistic belief in the goodness and happiness which is to be found in a love inspired by the courtly virtues. On the level of the narrative, this search for true love oscillates, in the manner of Jaufré Rudel, between idealized love from afar and the desire for 'close' love which impels the lover to approach, entreat and kiss the Rose, and then once again to retreat to love from afar and the anguish of desire without reward.

One glorious morning in May, the poet wakes, in his dream, and sewing on bright sleeves, sets out on the path to adventure. Blithely hopeful, he finds beside a river a walled garden in which joy abounds, and birdsong, trees and flowers. He enters through a small gate, opened to him by *Oiseuse* 'Idleness', no lethargic sloth but a damsel with 'lights in her eyes bright-changing like any falcon's', alive and eager for joy's pursuit. Before him he sees the garden of delight (*Déduit*), from which are excluded all the vices that impede the quest for courtly joy: Hatred, Treachery, Envy, Sorrow, Avarice, Covetousness, Churlishness and old and crabbed Age. All, in their hideous reality, are portrayed on the outer wall of the garden.

On the plane of general allegory, this garden represents the Joy of the Court, a communal rejoicing to which each individual contributes his or her own joyfulness. On the personal plane, the garden is the allegory of the poet's state of mind when, as a young man ready for love, he sees that joy, which is now for him the quest and inspiration of life, is attainable through the courtly virtues, *Largece*, *Franchise*, *Cortoisie*, *Jonece* (Largess, Nobility of mind, Courtesy, Youth), whom he sees dancing and dallying in love's delight beneath the trees. The poet's mind is fired:

God what a wondrous life they were leading. A man without such sweet desires is indeed a fool. To have such a life would be the height of happiness, for there is no greater paradise than to woo the beloved whom one most desires. (1,293–8)

The Lover is now ready for love. Gazing into the pool of Narcissus, he sees two crystals in which the whole being of the garden is revealed. Thought yields to sensual desire (*vouloir*) and is then transformed into *desir*, physical and mental desire for one person, when the Lover, glimpsing the rose trees encircled by their defensive hedge, falls in love with one particular rose.

Amors, lord of the garden, reinforces desire by firing five arrows which pierce the Lover's eyes and heart. *Amors* is not only the quickening force of love. He is the guardian of its moral and social values which the Lover must now accept. Were he now to reject them, he would trample the rose garden in lust and pluck the rose. On the individual plane, *Amors* is also the Lover's own psyche, his awareness of love's desires and restraints.

The five arrows of *Amors* which smite the Lover are the virtues which the Lover wishes to see and so sees in his lady, as the idealized vision of her is crystallized on the physical reality of the Rose. In their sequence, these arrows also impel the narrative onwards. The arrow which is *Biauté* robs the Lover of his senses. He moves towards the Rose. *Simplece* enters his eye. Despite himself, he moves nearer.

Cortoisie, the quintessence and sum total of all the courtly virtues, wounds him next. He draws closer but stays outside the hedge. Rejoicing in such nearness to the Rose, he is assailed by *Compaignie*, the being with the beloved which inclines her to mercy. The final arrow *Biau Semblant*, Fair Seeming, the lady's kindly look, afflicts him, bitter-sweet, sharper than a razor, soothed with a balm prepared by Love to console true lovers. This healing balm spreads through his five wounds.

With hands joined in supplication, the Lover makes his feudal and courtly submission to *Amors*: 'My liege, willingly will I yield myself to you and never seek to defend myself against you.' The Lover receives the kiss of feudal and courtly acceptance. A courtly audience and Guillaume's present lady could scarcely fail to believe that the Lover in addressing Love is also addressing her as well as the Rose of his dream, and that he is also entreating her to accept his service, as *Amors* has done in the dream.

The action quickens. The Lover, in obedience to the rules of *Amors*, woos the Rose. *Bel Acueil*, Fair Welcome, gives him leave to approach. The defences of the Rose begin to stir. The Lover, pressed by desire, seeks to assuage his pain by plucking the rose. 'This is my death, my life. I desire no other thing.'

> Ce est ma mort, ce est ma vie,
> de nule rien n'ai plus envie.
> (2,889–90)

He receives short shrift. *Dangier*, hairy, black and large, his face most horrible, throws him out and puts *Bel Acueil* to flight. Behind this ballet of dancing figures lies the lady's conflict of feeling. The Lover tries again. Humble and docile, he placates *Dangier*, and *Bel Acueil*, prompted by Venus, allows him to kiss the Rose. The full defences of the Rose are alerted. *Jalosie*, the lady's fear for her integrity, imprisons *Bel Acueil* within her tower and surrounds the whole rose garden with a wall. The defensive forces of *Jalosie*, *Honte*, *Peur* and their servant *Dangier* possess the lady's mind. The Lover's rebuff is complete. Personal reserve, social sense (*sen*) and *mesure*, the awareness of what is appropriate, have overcome the lady's impulse to be friendly and generous to the aspirant suitor. In his solitude outside the wall, the Lover longs like Jaufre Rudel for the distant idealized

Lady. He rejoices in the thought that he has come close to her beauty
and perfection. His only comfort for disconsolate longing lies in the
thought that he has kissed the Rose.

After the kiss and before the final rebuff, Guillaume had moved
out of the plane of the dream in order to address his present lady:

> Now is it right for me to tell you how I struggled with Shame (*Honte*),
> how I was sorely hurt and how the wall was built and how the rich and
> powerful castle rose up that Love seized later through his efforts. (3,481–6)

This is the poet's plea, stated as clearly as the form of the work will
allow. Once *Amors* has possessed his lady's mind, the wall of *Jalosie*
must vanish and *Bel Acueil* find freedom once again.

Back in the dream sequence, the Lover in desolation outside the
wall, addresses his lady:

> I know not how things are with me, but I am frightened and grieved,
> forlorn and pained by the thought that you have forgotten me. No one,
> nothing will ever console me, should I lose your affection, for nowhere else
> can I place my trust. (4,022–8)

These final words provide a perfect ending to the work, a moment
of impasse, not usual in a romance but customary in the love lyrics
of the Provençal troubadours, and especially in the songs of Bernart
de Ventadorn and the genre of the love-letter, the *salut d'amour* or
domneiaire. Guillaume has transposed his declaration of love from
the Rose of the dream sequence, the Rose of *Temps Perdu*, to the
Rose, his present lady of *Temps Retrouvé*, and the hope of future
happiness.

The poem by Guillaume de Lorris is a thing of delicacy and delight.
Within the walled garden of courtly values, beneath the complex
of psychological allegory, of desire and restraint, dream and reality,
time past and present, it breathes an air of *simplece*, the goodness
and joyous innocence which is the hallmark of the best contemporary
courtly poetry in France. Such *simplece* illumines the songs of Bernart
de Ventadorn, the lays of Marie de France and the Arthurian
romances of Chrétien de Troyes. It is most certainly not to be found
in the eighteen thousand lines with which Jean de Meung concluded
Guillaume's work.

For Jean de Meung, Guillaume's poem was unfinished because the
impasse of love remained unresolved. For Jean, courtly love was an

illusion, its happiness a pretence, its frustration no more than self-deception. Jean, who tells us that death 'went before' Guillaume, was born shortly after Guillaume died, and took up the romance at the age of forty, probably around 1270, in order to 'complete' it. Known as *maître* Jean Chopinel de Meung, Jean was a schoolman who lived in the university quarter of Paris. A scholar and a translator, he was a man of learning, widely read in Plato and Aristotle, and in the works of the Arab philosopher Ibn Roschid, a judge in twelfth-century Cordova who was known to western Europe as Averroes, the 'Commentator' (of Aristotle), as Dante called him.

For Averroes, the only reality was the world soul, the common reason of humanity. Humanity is eternal and the individual perishes without hope of personal immortality. The world was not created by God. The material universe has always existed and always will, however kaleidoscopic its transformations. On these issues academic battle raged in the University of Paris around Jean's ears in the thirteenth century, until the 1270s when Averroist doctrine was branded as heresy and repressed by the Inquisition.

Jean was well acquainted with French literature of the previous century and of his own day, and particularly with the bourgeois—realist tradition, satirical and anti-feminist, found in the *fabliaux*, the *Roman de Renart* and the later *Quinze Joyes de Mariage*. But the positive side of Jean's argument derives from the natural philosophers of the twelfth century, the Chartrian Bernardus Silvestris and his exposition of the Great Chain of Being and the concept of the goddess *Natura* who labours unceasingly to create man, alike human and divine, and able through procreation to combat death, restore the balance of *Natura* and prevent the return of chaos. Alanus de Insulis (1114–1202), who enlarges on these ideas of *Natura*, and contemporary thinkers concerned with Averroist and Aristotelian doctrine also influenced Jean de Meung.

Jean's ideas are by no means new. Yet he shows originality in his ability to synthesize theories. He accepts the Christian view that God created the world, but he also believes that the goddess *Natura* keeps the world functioning. This conjunction of God and Nature may also be discerned, however, in the works of the early twelfth-century troubadour, the great Marcabru, also under Christian influence. But what was implicit in Marcabru is made explicit by

Jean de Meung in mammoth digressions from the bare narrative line of the romance. As a good schoolman he marshals for review the many aspects of love, courtly, idealist, conjugal, corrupt, bawdy, wanton, venal, and demonstrates their futility in comparison with the procreative law imposed on the human race by *Natura*, working in her forge to repair the wastage caused by death. Men and women share the obligation to love fruitfully. Personal morality is to be judged only against this law of *Natura*. Immorality lies in the vow of chastity and in the misuse of sex for purposes other than pro-creation.

For Jean de Meung, the lover must be schooled in Love, in all its shapes, disguises and usages. Once equipped with this learning and cognizant of Love's natural law, the lover will be ready to pick the rose, a duty which he must perform. Jean's narrative line is based on that of Guillaume but his thematic structure is new. The narrative for Jean is of trivial importance, for his attention is focused on the line of argument which threads its way through the great digressive speeches of his main characters. Reason, Nature and Genius discourse on Love as a universal concept, an irresistible cosmic force. Jean's allegorical figures have little to do with Guillaume's personifications of delicate psychological motivations. They are fully fledged orators from the schools, replete with rhetoric and learning, fluent in arguments, *exempla* and classical quotations. Their role is to advocate their own importance in the complex workings of Love as the fierce teacher who turns in scholarly fury on the lover, her wayward pupil: 'Indeed you lie. I do not seek to flatter you. You have not perused the ancient books sufficiently well to put me in checkmate. You are weak in logic'. (5,722–6)

Jean's fundamental purpose is to define the reason for man's existence on earth, his role in the cosmos. Given the immense concept of the universe and of God's intention in fashioning it, what, he asks, is the purpose of human love? What is man's role as an individual, as a member of the human race? If it is to propagate the species, as he believes, what deviant forms of love, contrary to this purpose, must man, must the lover avoid? Jean falls back on the *Timaeus* of Plato and the *Physics* and *Metaphysics* of Aristotle. In his 'baggy monster of a work' he digresses on the phases of the moon, the harmony of the spheres, the aims of alchemy. But his scientific theorizing is in no way irrelevant. It belongs to the basic theme of the balance of creation, of nature ceaselessly recreating itself. It is in the vast context of the dynamic cosmos that Jean considers man and his vital importance in life. In a Rousseauesque discussion he praises the innate goodness of man born free and choosing his own system of government. He advocates gentility of heart as the only criterion of nobility, asserts a Renaissance belief in the dignity of man as an individual and part of God's purpose in creating the world. As Nature says in her confession, nobility in itself is a spurious quality. All men are born alike and equal. The caprice of Fortune creates the difference between men. True nobility comes from the heart and from virtue. Nature's great final speech is matched by that of her henchman, Genius, the essence of man's fecundity and creativity. Genius urges all lovers to fulfil Nature's purpose,

to plough with vigour, to seize the handles of the plough, to sink the blade deep in the straight furrow and couple the horned oxen to the yoke.
(19,671–93)

... Should fatigue incline you to rest, do not weaken in your purpose. Consider how Cadmus sowed serpent's teeth and saw a harvest of knights come forth to help him in the founding of Thebes.
(19,706–22)

... In this way you will enter the Shepherd's Park, abounding in natural life, a verdant paradise in which you will rejoice in days without evening or morning, without past or future. You will enjoy an eternal present, an eternal spring where the sun never sets, a season finer and purer than any in the golden age.
(19,901–20,006)

Inspired by such thoughts, Venus and her cohorts assault the tower where *Bel Acueil* is still imprisoned. *Honte* and *Peur* refuse to submit. Venus delivers her ultimatum: 'If *Bel Acueil* fails to surrender, all the roses in the garden will be ravished by all men, both lay and cleric, religious and unholy.' Venus wields her flame-thrower and sets the castle alight. *Dangier* flees, together with *Peur* and *Honte*, *Cortoisie*, abetted by *Pitié* and *Franchise*, persuades *Bel Acueil* to grant the rose to the lover. 'And I', says the poet, finally taking up his, or rather the lover's story, 'directed myself to the loophole, to accomplish my pilgrimage.' With bawdy, ironical humour the poet describes how the lover deflowers the rose, who rejoices in the process. The wanton brutality of this conclusion mocks the frustrated lamentations of Guillaume's lover outside the tower of *Jalosie*. To Lady Nature the rational restraints of *Fin' Amors* are anathema.

Within Guillaume's garden, the courtly limitations of natural lust offered the lover and lady the hope of joy in body, mind and spirit as well as the fears, pain and sorrow of hope delayed. Their desires and doubts were set within an implicit, universal belief in the courtly way of life and the goodness and joy which it could provide. For Jean de Meung, the true action of the romance proceeds in the opposite direction, from the universal precept, the belief in the rule of Nature and Reason within the divine order, to the case of the individual who must act in obedience to their laws, even against his own inclination. Yet, though Jean casts a cool eye on human frailty, especially in the Duenna, and on existing conventions of morality, he never fails to affirm the dignity of thinking man within the natural order.

The *Roman de la Rose*, in its two divergent and complementary parts, exemplifies the medieval pleasure in wholeness achieved through juxtaposed opposites. With Guillaume, we have what has been called 'the magical view of life', a view of love illumined by human feeling, imagination and ideals of beauty, virtue and restraint. With Jean de Meung, we have a view of man within the macrocosm, of the universal power of love which moves the stars and the planets, the life-giving force of Nature within God's creation. Two major streams of thought in twelfth- and thirteenth-century France have been united in the one work. The courtly humanistic interest in man as an individual capable of rising to the heights of imaginative and spiritual aspiration, has been joined and contrasted with a brilliant 'reader's digest' in the French language of philosophical speculation about the origins and workings of the natural world and of man's function, social, political and amorous, within it. It is essentially to the transmission of these traditions to later ages, and especially to the writers of the sixteenth century in France, that the *Roman de la Rose* owes its pre-eminence in the civilization of western Europe.

NOTES

1. Line references and textual quotations from F. Lecoy (ed.), *Le Roman de la Rose* (Paris, C.F.M.A., 1965, 1966, 1970), 3 vols. Translations of quotations in the text of the chapter are by the author of this chapter. Translations of

the passages in the anthology on pp. 475–8 are taken from H. W. Robbins, *The Romance of the Rose* (New York, 1962).

2. cf. C. S. Lewis, *The Allegory of Love* (London, 1936–8), 129, who speaks of 'the very disastrous confusion which would identify the Rose with the Lady. The Rose, in Guillaume, is clearly the Lady's Love.'

3. In *langue d'oil*, *jalousie* has the meaning 'to preserve integrity', for example, *punir les maux por l'amour et por la jalousie de la justice*.

4. cf. J. C. Payen, 'Genèse et finalité de la poésie allégorique au Moyen Age', in *Revue de metaphysique et de morale*, 78 (1973), 466–79: 'L'allégorisme médiéval n'est pas seulement un procédé d'écriture: il correspond à toute une représentation du réel et, à ce titre, il est fondamentalement idéologique . . . ce mode d'expression etait pour eux [les auteurs médiévaux] non seulement un outil intellectuel, mais bien un élément constitutif de leurs structures mentales.' (Medieval allegory is not only a method of writing: it corresponds to a whole representation of reality and, in this respect, it is fundamentally ideological . . . this mode of expression was for them [the medieval authors] not just an intellectual tool, but rather a constituent element of their mental structures.)

THE ICELANDIC *NJAL'S SAGA*

JACQUELINE SIMPSON

Sagas are prose works written in Iceland during the twelfth, thirteenth and fourteenth centuries; almost all are anonymous and undated, but a relative chronology has been established from internal evidence. They blend in varying proportions the qualities of history, biography, epic, historical novel and adventure story; they are, or claim to be, accounts of actual persons and events. Many factors influenced the genesis and development of this unique genre: the oral culture flourishing in Iceland from its Settlement (*c.*870) to its Christianization (999), which included much poetry, as well as traditions about memorable events in Iceland and Norway; Latin literary models, especially saints' lives, introduced by the Church; the cultivation of storytelling as entertainment and as art form. Sub-genres include: 'Kings' sagas', which are biographies of Norwegian kings, culminating in Snorri Sturluson's great compilation *Heimskringla* (1223–5)[1]; 'Sagas of Ancient Times', based on heroic legends from mainland Scandinavia, of which *The Saga of Hrolf Kraki* and *The Saga of the Volsungs* are famous examples; 'Contemporary Sagas', about thirteenth-century events; 'Lying Sagas', stories of fantastic adventures; and the 'Family Sagas' or 'Sagas of the Icelanders', chiefly concerned with the deeds of Icelanders from the Settlement till about 1030. This last is the genre to which *Njal's Saga* belongs. There has long been controversy as to whether Family Sagas are primarily 'truthful' records or 'novelistic' recreations of the past, and what part oral traditions played in their formation; current scholarship stresses the selective and interpretative artistry of their authors.

This rich literature was hardly known outside Scandinavia before the nineteenth century, but once discovered it aroused enthusiasm, especially in Germany and England. At first it was accepted as a faithful record of Viking Age history, social organization and ethical values; its supernatural and folkloric elements were particularly prized as glimpses into pre-Christian mentality. Above all, it was the heroic themes – honour, vengeance, valiant deaths – which attracted readers, who saw there a Nordic counterpart to the Homeric world. Scholars are now more sceptical, knowing that the image which a community forms of its ancestral heroes and pioneers will be distorted by nostalgia and pride. Nevertheless, the earlier critics expressed many valid insights; W. P. Ker's *Epic and Romance* (1896, reprinted 1957) is still an excellent general introduction to the style and ethos of sagas. The modern reader will share his response to many of their qualities – their heroism, naturally, but also their maturity of vision, their respect for human dignity, laconic humour, their refusal to preach or oversimplify or indulge emotion, their broad social range and rootedness in everyday realities. Sagas, one sometimes feels, are the least 'medieval' of medieval works.

In translating them, unfortunately, most Victorians instinctively adopted archaisms and semi-poetic diction which do not exist in the original texts, but which they thought appropriate. William Morris went further in his passionate love for the Icelandic language, copying its idioms literally and inventing new words from Germanic roots rather than use any from Latin or French ('word-sending', not 'message'; 'corpse-fare', not 'funeral'). His effects are eccentric, but can be powerful; he has had imitators even in this century, e.g. E. R. Eddison's rendering of *Egil's Saga* (1930). But most modern translators agree in admiring the naturalness of saga prose, and seeking its equivalent in contemporary English. Yet even so there are still pitfalls. Obvious slang jars, and so too does 'committee English' ('conflict was avoided' instead of 'no battle took place'); running sentences together loses dramatic force ('Helgi was lying there dead' is weaker than the literal 'Helgi lay there; he was dead'); replacing the ubiquitous Icelandic 'said' by 'retorted', 'warned', 'cried', 'remarked', etc., unnecessarily duplicates the contents of the utterance. As George Johnston has shown in his perceptive analyses of these problems,[2] fidelity to Icelandic idiom, even in such details as its sudden tense-changes, will usually produce vivid, sinewy English narrative.

The classical saga style is quickly recognizable. Sentences are short, limited in vocabulary, simple in syntax, bare of verbal ornament; the story moves fast; dialogue is pithy, idiomatic, and strictly confined to what will advance the action. It is a style well suited for reading aloud (long the chief medium of transmission for sagas), but it demands an alert audience, for there is hardly a moment in which necessary information is not being communicated. The narrative proceeds chronologically, without flashbacks or inset narrations, yet its normal purpose is to trace chains of events – sometimes complex ones – leading gradually to some violent climax. The resulting structure may seem confusing at first; characters are introduced, play a part in some episode, and are then temporarily (or permanently) dropped in favour of an unconnected group, who may also soon be 'out of the saga'. The threads linking them to the central action will become clear at a second reading; the original audience, knowing at least in outline the historical or traditional climax towards which everything was leading, would have grasped the connections more easily. In sagas nothing is irrelevant, there is no mere background. Small details of everyday life, which are plentiful, will turn out to have some bearing on the plot; but months or even years in which 'nothing happened worth telling' are dismissed in a phrase. Certain aspects of the heroes' personalities are vividly described, others left wholly unexplored because they would supply no motivation for the story.

Techniques of characterization are equally distinctive. When someone is first mentioned, the author curtly summarizes his characteristics, physical and mental; one sentence, or perhaps two, is generally enough, for every word carries weight. His genealogy is also given, as an important indicator of social standing and of family links with other persons in the saga. From then on, there will be no more explicit analysis; the man's character will be displayed solely through his words and actions, and through what others say of him. This, as many critics have noted, is the technique of drama. In some respects sagas are even more like the cinema than the stage, as when the writer 'cuts' from one group of enemies to another in a crescendo of pace and tension; or when he shows a distant group of figures before gradually revealing their identities; or when he focuses attention on to a single gesture or significant silence. Visual selectivity replaces explicit comment, enabling him to preserve his assumed role of a coolly detached impartial eyewitness, while still controlling the reactions of his audience.

This reticence and apparent objectivity, so different from other types of medieval writing, is accepted by some critics at face value. Thus Andersson writes, 'There is no guiding principle laid down by the author in order to give his material a specific import ... The saga comes very close to pure narrative without ulterior aims of any kind.'[3] Others do not agree; speaking of *Laxdaela Saga*, Magnusson and Pálsson say that saga-writers' 'history' is 'a stylized image of the past that is being held up as a guiding light for later generations'. Sagas naturally vary in the depth and subtlety of their implications, but at least for the major Family Sagas and Kings' Sagas the latter assessment is the truer. The reader's moral judgements are constantly being guided by the author, who selects material not merely for entertainment value but because it can be made to display examples of conduct, whether praiseworthy or the reverse. In this way, stern ethical values are revealed; a whole 'art of living and art of dying' is taught through concrete instances, not precepts. What relevance this had for the original audience can be deduced. Thirteenth-century Iceland was split by bloody power-struggles until in 1264 it lost political independence; by turning back to earlier centuries, the authors of the Family Sagas could offer examples and warnings, evoke the proud independence of their ancestors, and uphold the endangered values of honour, justice, moderation, magnanimity, and respect for law. They idealized and oversimplified their country's past, but their reasons for doing so command sympathy.

In the world of sagas, tragedy is never far away. Honour and the ethics of the blood-feud may force men to kill against their will, or enmesh them in conflicting loyalties. Men of high worth fall victim to unworthy enemies. The heroes almost always die, usually fighting against odds, or treachery, or occult forces; once they have been avenged the survivors can reach an honourable settlement, but though these endings re-establish justice they are not 'happy'. The tragic atmosphere is reinforced by the frequent evocation of a sense of fate; when approaching major climaxes, the authors make use of prophecies, curses, portents, forebodings and ominous dreams. In doing so, they are not departing from realism (the objective reality of such phenomena was taken for granted); like Shakespeare, they are interested in how destiny and freely made decisions can combine to precipitate a man's doom. Shakespearean, too, is the close interweaving of humour and tragedy, increasing the effectiveness of both; the most memorable jokes in sagas are spoken by men confronting death with stoic defiance.

Beyond these shared features lie many differences. Some sagas are designed as family chronicles or chronicles of a district, others as one man's biography, others as the history of one important event – usually a feud, but occasionally something more peaceful, such as the colonization of Greenland and the discovery of America. There are also sharp contrasts in tone, as a few examples will show.

We may begin with *Egil's Saga*, written *c.*1230, probably by Snorri Sturluson (1179–1241), whose intimate knowledge of history and of tenth-century poetry might well have made him interested in Egil, a poet and Viking warrior whose life brought him into contact with Norwegian and English kings. The dour personality of Egil is interestingly drawn – brutal, miserly, subject to outbursts of fury and moods of sullen gloom, but also capable of love and grief, and a powerful poet. This saga is also a study of a family through four generations, set against a broad panorama of Scandinavian and English history, and a celebration of the stubborn opposition of Icelanders to the power of Norwegian kings.

Turning to *Laxdaela Saga* (*c.*1245), we find a colourful romantic work, whose author seems fascinated by luxurious clothes and weapons, fine houses and great feasts, and whose heroes and heroines are glamorous figures rather larger than life. Here too there are kings of Norway, but they are favourably presented, and their relationship with the Icelandic characters is one of flattering mutual admiration. The climax of the saga is a tragedy of love frustrated and friendship broken, treated with more open warmth of feeling than is usual in the classical sagas.

Again, one can contrast two studies of the bleak life and harsh death of a luckless outlaw. *The Saga of Gisli* (*c.*1225) is tense, sombre, tightly constructed; the conflicts enmeshing its hero involve friendships, rivalries and family bonds intricately woven into a tragic pattern, and realistically described. *Grettir's Saga* (written soon after 1300) has a looser, picaresque structure, some episodes being only linked by the outlawed hero's presence. It incorporates obvious folk-tale motifs, such as the rough jokes Grettir as a boy plays on his father, and the 'hidden valley' where he briefly finds refuge. He is presented simply and sympathetically, a victim of undeserved bad luck; the two most memorable episodes concern curses laid on him, one by a ghost and one by a witch, which eventually cause his grimly heroic death. The tale ends with some romantic adventures of his brother; most readers find them a jarring anticlimax, a decline from the golden age of saga writing.

The longest and most powerful of these works is *The Saga of the Burning of Njal*, or, more briefly, *Njal's Saga*.[4] It was written about 1280 by an unknown author, and centres on two events which had occurred almost 300 years earlier: the killing of Gunnar of Hlidarend, about 990, and the burning of Njal and his family in the year 1011. Two events of more general historical significance, the Conversion of Iceland in 999 and the battle of Clontarf near Dublin in 1014, also form important episodes. It is an account of feuds, their causes and consequences; it is also a work of intricate and superbly structured design, containing impressive characters and many dramatic scenes. At the deepest level, it elicits complex moral judgements, and presents a stern yet ultimately hopeful analysis of the interaction of good and evil within individuals and in society.

At one time, critics accused it of lack of unity, and suggested that it merely juxtaposed two pre-existing sagas, one about Gunnar and one about Njal, together with sundry interpolations of historical and legal material. More recent scholars have thoroughly demolished this view,[5] demonstrating how the author welded his story together by multiple cross-references, parallel incidents, and verbal echoes. Here one example of plot linkage must suffice. Throughout chapters 35–45 the friendship of Gunnar and Njal is threatened by a series of retaliatory killings between members of their households, initiated by Gunnar's vindictive wife Hallgerd. Despite mounting tension, the expected catastrophe of a breach between the two friends never occurs, since both are wise enough to avoid violence; nevertheless, the episode creates evil side-effects which, after Gunnar's death, contribute to the destruction of Njal and his sons. Hallgerd's hatred of Njal's family remains active, and her son, her son-in-law and her lover become in various ways its agents; her insulting joke about Njal's lack of a beard is repeated by others, and at a dramatic crisis its repetition destroys all chance of settling the feud which dooms Njal.

The author's power of characterization is as firm and subtle as his marshalling of the plot, and deploys a considerable variety of techniques. His detailed portrait of Hallgerd is a classic model of how analysis and moral judgement can be conveyed within the convention of 'objectivity' by various oblique devices – the contrast between her honourable birth and the sinister, ruffianly men she so often prefers as her associates and tools; the uniformly unfavourable comments about her from characters whose wisdom commands attention; the ominous references to her long hair and 'thief's eyes', in the first chapter, whose explosive force only erupts later at the crises of her marriage, in chapters 48 and 77. As her personality unfolds, from the arrogant, vindictive girl to the coarsened, ageing woman whom Skarp-Hedin taunts as 'outcast hag and harlot', we may be shocked, but we are not puzzled or surprised, since each development has been realistically prepared. So too with Flosi; each step along the path that leads him to the Burning and then beyond it to eventual reconciliation with Njal's heirs is plainly traced, and his mental conflicts clearly motivated.

Elsewhere, characters are differently presented. Mord's villainy is an irreducible datum, like that of Iago; we are told, twice, that he has a 'malicious, cunning nature' and hates Gunnar, and this minimal information has to suffice. Mord's lies, slanders, and multiple double-crossings can safely be left to make their own impact. For Skarp-Hedin, Njal's eldest son, the author draws a powerful impressionistic portrait, conveyed mainly in two ways: through Skarp-Hedin's ferocious wit, and through recurrent symbolic details, notably his sinister pallor and even more sinister grin. Occasionally, characters supply their own self-analysis, as when Gunnar says, 'I wish I knew whether I am less manly than other men, for being so much more reluctant to kill than other men are', or when Flosi sets out the dilemma which makes him resort to burning.* When the author ascribes such explicit statements to his characters, they invariably have a bearing on one of his moral themes.

Certain fateful turning-points of the plot are, in terms of characterization, shattering surprises. Nothing previously said about Gunnar has prepared one for his sudden decision to remain in Iceland although sentenced to exile, or for the strange motive he gives: an over-

* See anthology, p. 493.

powering yearning for the beauty of his farm. Critics have argued whether this should be taken at face value, or as a mask for a hero's inner need to face death, not evade it, or as the workings of Fate, or a symptom of hubris, or even (less plausibly) as a symbol of Hallgerd's fascinating beauty. The author offers no elucidation; instead, he follows with an immediate second shock. Hitherto, Gunnar had been an almost irreproachable hero (as indeed he will shortly be again, when facing death), but at this juncture his loyal brother Kolskegg utters a stinging rebuke: to refuse exile, he declares, is to dishonour one's pledge. Where a modern novelist would explore motivation but possibly avoid moral judgement, the saga-writer respects the mysteriousness of human behaviour, as exemplified in Gunnar's fatal decision centuries before, but he has no doubt what moral verdict must be passed on it.

At the core of the saga lie philosophical and religious issues. Njal's tragedy, as is often said, is a tragedy of Fate – the story of a man who, by his very efforts to avert the calamity he foresees, precipitates it. The many prophecies and portents drive this point home, and when Njal gives the fatal order to go indoors,* it does indeed seem the irrational act of a doomed and perhaps despairing man. It seems that the saga's message is that no one can escape an evil fate. Yet a few sentences later, as Njal speaks of God's mercy, another interpretation becomes possible; what seemed suicidal folly is revealed as Purgatorial acceptance of suffering, a sacrifice whose value is confirmed by the miracles which follow it. Even Skarp-Hedin, the embodiment of heroic pride, proves by the crosses he brands into his flesh that he too accepts the Burning as a form of expiation.

Christianity is central to *Njal's Saga*; hence the space given to the Conversion and to the Clontarf episode, where the spiritual conflicts implied elsewhere become explicit, and where the aged, wise and non-violent King Brian resembles Njal in passively accepting a painful but sanctified death. But Christian ethics, as this author interprets them, have complexities which may perplex modern readers. First, there is no glib equation whereby heathens are 'bad' and Christians 'good'; the author has no scruples about using heathen allusions to Odin and Valhalla to honour Gunnar in death, nor does

---

* See anthology, p. 492.

he ignore the fact that villains like Hrapp and Mord accepted Christianity, though he does show Mord as a less willing convert than Njal and the major chieftains. This tolerance and realism is admirable in modern eyes; more disconcerting is the author's view of the relationship between Christianity and the code of the blood-feud.

Christianity, non-violence, and the forgiveness of enemies are inextricably linked in modern thought, so it is no surprise to us when the saintly Hoskuld Hvitaness-Priest[6] dies unresisting, exclaiming 'May God help me, and forgive you all!'. Similarly, one admires the nobility of Hall's sacrifice in renouncing any compensation for his son's slaying, risking loss of honour for the sake of peace. His renunciation forms a turning-point, after which enmity gradually yields to reconciliation; appropriately, he had chosen St Michael, the merciful weigher of souls, as his patron saint. But what of Hildigunn urging Flosi to avenge Hoskuld 'in the name of all the powers of your Christ'? Or Flosi and his men attending a church service before the Burning?* And what of the strange miracle enabling the blind Amundi to kill a man for denying him compensation for his father's death? Do these passages show that the author cannot resolve the contradiction between religious values and the dictates of honour?

In medieval theology, death sentences legally imposed in the king's name were no sin, nor was war, if waged by a lawful king for a just cause; only private, personal revenge was sinful. But this neat distinction could not apply in Iceland, where there was no king, and no means of enforcing legal judgements except through the actions of private citizens. The author's purpose in describing Amundi's miracle must have been to show that God did sometimes favour vengeance, but only if and when all other avenues towards justice were blocked. Similarly, warfare can be a way of serving God; Kolskegg, the first convert in the saga, is called in a dream to become 'Christ's knight', and responds by joining the Byzantine army. This author's moral assessment of Hildigunn and Flosi would not depend simply on their desire for vengeance, but on whether bloodshed was their only way of obtaining justice for Hoskuld's death – which,

* See anthology, p. 490.

obviously, it was not. The confusion is in Flosi's mind, not the author's.

Yet, though Flosi's moral perceptions are flawed, he is presented with sympathy, and eventually with admiration.[7] As the saga draws to a close, his generosity of mind, reinforced by the efforts of many men of good will, brings Njal's surviving kinsmen into reconciliation with him. First, however, both Flosi and his chief opponent Kari must make pilgrimages to Rome for the Pope's pardon, since the deaths in this long feud, so the author implies, were not only injuries of man against man or of man against society, but of man against God. So tangled are the rights and wrongs on both sides that justice cannot resolve the issues, but penance and mercy can. And so 'they made a full reconciliation, and Flosi gave to Kari in marriage his niece Hildigunn, the widow of Hoskuld Hvitaness-Priest'. It is an ending worthy of this author: brief, surprising, weighty with implications, and profoundly moving, a fitting resolution for the conflicts in a tragic but ultimately consoling tale.

NOTES

1. Transl. Samuel Lairg (1844), 3 vols, introductions by Peter G. Foote and J. Simpson (London, 1961, 1964). Also transl. by Lee M. Hollander (Austin, 1964).

2. George Johnston, 'On Translation: II', in *Saga-Book*, XV:4 (1961), 394–402; and 'Translating the Sagas into English', in *Bibliography of Old Norse/Icelandic Studies* (1972).

3. Theodore M. Andersson, *The Icelandic Family Saga: An Analytic Reading* (Cambridge, Mass., 1967), 32.

4. Quotations in the present article are from *Njal's Saga* transl. Magnus Magnusson and Herman Pálsson (Penguin Classics, 1966).

5. See I. R. Maxwell, 'Pattern in *Njal's Saga*', in *Saga-Book*, XV (1957–9), 17–47; Denton Fox, '*Njál's Saga* and the Western Literary Tradition', in *Comparative Literature*, XV (1963), 289–310; Richard F. Allen, *Fire and Iron: Critical Approaches to Njál's Saga* (Pittsburgh, 1971); Einar Ól. Sveinsson, *Njál's Saga: A Literary Masterpiece* (Nebraska, 1971); Lars Lönnroth, *Njal's Saga: A Critical Introduction* (Berkeley, Los Angeles and London, 1976).

6. This translation of Hoskuld's nickname *Hvítanessgothi* is misleading, though used by both Dasent and Magnusson and Pálsson. *Gothi* does not mean 'priest' in the Christian sense but refers to the joint function of 'chieftain and heathen priest', of which the latter aspect became obsolete at the Conversion. Hoskuld was simply a chieftain.

7. Internal evidence shows that the saga was written in the district where Flosi had lived, not in Njal's district. One of the author's aims was to explain and excuse Flosi's deed, probably at the request of his descendants; see Lönnroth, as note 5, 137–87.

DANTE ALIGHIERI: *THE DIVINE COMEDY*

JOHN A. SCOTT

> Dante, who loved well because he hated,
> Hated wickedness that hinders loving . . .

Browning's words contain at least part of the answer to the question why present day readers find Dante's poetry fascinating, often over-whelming, as they discover a world which is in so many ways alien to their own. Why do students who prize 'relevance' above all else succumb to his spell? That spell must certainly be due in no small measure to Dante's greatness as a poet, an image-maker and a magician with words and rhythms. And yet his message is based on an affirmation of truths held by the poet to be eternal and essential to human experience and survival – truths which most of us reject. This must be a problem especially for the foreign reader. It is far easier for Italians to appreciate the extraordinary range of Dante's linguistic pyrotechnics and verbal poetry, while most non-Italians must be content with the interplay of images and ideas. The latter form the whetstone on which we may sharpen and test our own beliefs or lack of them. It may be an attraction of opposites; it may be a glimpse of perfection caught in the wasteland of modern times; but an atheist cannot but be moved by the medieval poet's description of beatitude as the experience of:

> luce intellettüal, piena d'amore;
> amor di vero ben, pien di letizia;
> letizia che trascende ogne dolzore.
> (C, X X X, 40–42)★

> ★ Intellectual light, full of love;
> Love of true good, full of joy;
> Joy which transcends all sweetness.

Quotations have been translated as literally as possible for this chapter. Their source is indicated as follows: A = *Inferno*; B = *Purgatorio*; C = *Paradiso*. For diagrams of the detailed ordering of Dante's other world, the reader is advised to turn to those found in any good translation or edition of the *Comedy*.

This example may be taken to illustrate an effect of Dante's poetry. The euphony based on a subtle interplay between liquids and plosives (l, r, m, n; t, p, d, b), the 'vowel music' are immediately accessible; so are the repetitions, leading to a crescendo 'full of love; Love ... full of joy; Joy which transcends all sweetness'. Other points may only reveal themselves to readers familiar with Provençal poetry, who will realize that the Italian poet has used a technique similar to that which created the *coblas capfinidas*, whereby the first word of a stanza echoed or repeated the last of its predecessor. So here the unit of three lines is interlaced and bound together by the repetition of the words 'love' and 'joy', while the echoes of courtly love and its earthly beatitude are evoked by the word for 'sweetness' chosen by the poet (directly reflecting the Provençal *doussor*, instead of the normal Italian form *dolcezza*), which is used only once in the *Comedy* in order to underpin the transcending of all sensual happiness. Again, the repetition of the pause after the sixth syllable in the first two lines finds its fulfilment in the broad unit of the third line, which sets its seal on the ascent from human joy to celestial beatitude.

Such are some of the means used by the poet to convey his message. But let us make no bones about it: Dante, in the *Comedy*, was above all concerned with his message. The modern reader may well reject it in his own life, but in the act of reading he must practise what Coleridge called 'that willing suspension of disbelief for the moment, which constitutes poetic faith'. And in so doing he will discover a faith based on Browning's triad: love, hatred, and the evil that prevents men from attaining their beatitude. Dante's great poetry is an amalgam of sound and meaning. It was intended to convert men and women who had gone astray. It has in greater measure than most poetry the power to make us suspend our disbelief. It possesses bewitching realism. What we must set out to do, while enjoying its beauty, is to discover the emotions and convictions that inspired its message, as well as the message itself and the way it was moulded by the conventions and beliefs of the age in which it was created.

The *Comedy* opens abruptly: the poet finds himself in a dark wood, threatened by three beasts which prevent him from climbing a hill towards the sun. We are not told where this scene takes place or how the poet came to this spot: it is outside the precise topography

DANTE ALIGHIERI: *THE DIVINE COMEDY*

of the rest of the poem. But the first two lines are typical of the mixture of individual and universal in Dante's masterpiece. In *Convivio*, the poet accepted the rule that authors should avoid mention of self unless exceptional reasons justify a departure from this literary convention; and, even in the poem, based as it is on the astounding journey undertaken by Dante, he apologizes for mentioning his own name. Yet few authors have been inspired by such an intensely personal view and experience of life; few have been so autobiographical while seeking and attaining universal significance. The resulting tension creates a synthesis where the claims of the individual and society, of body and spirit, of earth and Heaven, combine to form a unique world picture. So, on a small scale, the first two lines tell us 'In the middle of the journey of our life, I found myself in a dark wood': it is Dante the individual who speaks in the first person, who is the actor in the drama; but at all times his actions and words reflect the human condition, '*our* life'. However, he is not Everyman, as the cliché would have it: over and over again, he insists on the unique nature of his journey, only made possible by God's grace. That journey will reveal truths and dangers that concern all mankind while reflecting the medieval view of man as a pilgrim in this world.

The literal meaning of the first line is that Dante was thirty-five years old when he found himself lost. Born in 1265 in Florence, he accepted the psalmist's reckoning that man's natural lifespan was seventy years. The year 1300 therefore marked the halfway mark in his life. As an individual, Dante reached the zenith of his political career in this year, when he was elected one of the six priors of the city of Florence (15 June, for the usual period of two months). Later, if we are to believe Leonardo Bruni's quotation from a letter by Dante (unfortunately lost), the poet was to claim that the cause of his later misfortunes lay in this election to high political office. Certainly, his exile and the death sentence passed on him (January/March 1302) were a direct result of his opposition to Pope Boniface VIII's attempts to gain political control of Florence. We may be sure that the poet was innocent of the charges of corruption levelled against him, and in letters he referred to his unjust exile. Nevertheless, it may be that he later judged this moment of political involvement to have been unworthy of his sense of universal justice and the need for the political unity of mankind; it is also true that a poem written during his exile, *Tre donne*, hints at some fault he had committed.

However, the personal element, whatever Dante's sins, is finely interwoven with the universal. The year 1300 was not merely a crucial stage in the poet's own life, it was a historical landmark as the beginning of a new century and the first Holy Year declared by Christ's vicar in Rome. It seemed to proclaim the supremacy of the latter in both the spiritual and the temporal spheres. In fact, it led to disaster as surely as the path taken by the pilgrim lost in the dark wood: Boniface was to die in October 1303, his claims to political hegemony punctured by Philip the Fair, king of France. Papal policy during the whole of the thirteenth century was proved disastrously wrong: the popes had done everything in their power to destroy the authority of the empire, but having virtually succeeded, they discovered a far more powerful threat in their former ally, the king of France. As a result, most of the new century was to see the head of Christendom installed in Avignon. For Dante, the year 1300 was a time when humanity was deprived of its two indispensable leaders, the pope and the emperor. Humanity, too, was lost in the terrible wood of perdition.

The abrupt opening echoing the biblical drama of *Isaiah*, 'I said: in the noontide of my days I shall go to the gates of the underworld', would have helped to condition the medieval reader's response to the poet's tragic message. Similarly, the three beasts – the leopard or panther, the lion and wolf – who stop the pilgrim's progress up the hill of salvation are taken from *Jeremiah*. They stand for the sins of lust, pride and greed. The identification with greed/avarice is made in *Purgatory* (XX, 7–12), where this sin is called 'the evil that occupies the whole world'. To understand Dante's purpose in identifying it as the worst threat to mankind, we must realize that the exiled poet bitterly rejected the gradual acceptance of nascent capitalism which characterized the age of Aquinas and the rise of Florentine economic supremacy. Lust is the abuse of the body, pride is the abuse of man's intellect; but it is the wolf that makes the pilgrim lose all hope of reaching salvation.

Typical in this first canto is the marriage of biblical and Virgilian elements. The former are commonplace in medieval literature, where human actions tended to be seen as reflecting the two greatest moments in history: the Fall and the Redemption. In the poem, the dark wood prefigures the 'divine forest' of Eden which the pilgrim reaches at the end of *Purgatory* (B, XXVIII, 1–2). The whole pattern of his journey is modelled on the events of *Exodus* (Psalm CXIII, quoted by Dante in *Epistle* X,7). Egypt is replaced by the wood of sin, and the arrival in the Promised Land after a perilous crossing of the desert and the revelation of the Law on Mount Sinai are reflected in the pilgrim's traversal of Hell, his arrival in Eden (on the crest of the Mountain of Purgatory) and his entrance into Paradise. Death is signified by the waters reminiscent of the Flood (A, I, 22–7). But alongside this biblical framework, there is the other great influence on Dante's poem: Graeco-Roman culture and in particular Virgil's great epic, the *Aeneid*.

It was almost certainly as a result of re-reading Virgil (*c.*1307–8) that Dante discovered the providential mission of Rome and chose the Roman poet as his guide through Hell and Purgatory. It is the shade of the Roman poet that comes to the pilgrim's rescue in *Inferno* I. In II, 70–75, he introduces himself as a pagan, the poet who had sung 'of that just son of Anchises who came from Troy, after proud Ilion was burned to ashes'. Here we discover a miraculous compression of the reasons why Dante selected the great Roman writer. Not so much because the latter stands for Reason, as is often stated: Aristotle (known to the Italian poet in Latin translations) was the supreme philosopher, the 'master of those who know', Homer the greatest poet. Virgil, however, was the unique poetic voice that had divined and proclaimed God's blueprint for the world: the providential voyage of Aeneas to Italy and the divine mission entrusted to Rome, destined to be the political and spiritual capital of the world. The *Aeneid* was the noblest poem known to Dante, who reserved for it the sacred word 'volume', otherwise used to describe God's books. Aeneas's troubled journey made possible the later foundation of Rome; his descent to the underworld was one of the two great precedents for Dante's journey (the other being St Paul's ascent to heaven; A, II, 13–30); his love of justice, his *pietas* and sense of duty were qualities destined to redeem the great sin of Trojan pride and to exalt 'humble Italy' as mistress of the world, first pagan and then Christian.

We thus have a unique creation: an Aristotelianized Virgil who created what may well be described as Dante's 'Bible of the Empire'. Virgil's account is in fact ironed out to leave only unanimity in Heaven and divine assistance for Aeneas on earth. Despite the damnation of contemporary popes, the poet is careful to consign only one emperor to Hell. The universal pattern is clear and woven into the poem's structure: Virgil leads Dante to Beatrice, even as the Roman people had prepared the way for Christ's coming and as the emperor was intended to guide mankind to terrestrial happiness. Dante's guide is truly a poet – but here we have the beginning of a great tradition in European culture, which came to look upon poets as repositories of wisdom and essential knowledge. So, Dante calls him 'master', 'doctor', 'sage', 'teacher' (terms used well over 100 times, besides the fundamental twenty-five occurrences of 'poet'). The guardians of the first five circles of Dante's Hell, the rivers of the underworld, Geryon monster of fraud – all this and so much else are taken from Virgil.

Such an inspiration is unique in medieval literature. But it does not place Dante among the humanists. The latter were concerned with rediscovering the original form and meaning of classical texts, whereas Dante felt no scruples in distorting Virgil's text in thoroughly medieval fashion in *Purgatorio* (B, XXII, 31–45). On the other hand, it is precisely the liberties taken by Dante that create the wonderful bond between the pilgrim and his guide. At first, Virgil plays the taskmaster not without irony and Dante is afraid to speak out of turn; but gradually Virgil becomes a trusted friend, who congratulates his pupil (VIII, 44–5; XIV, 133; XIX, 121–3); finally, the pilgrim weeps for his 'sweetest father' who has to return to eternal exile (B, XXX, 49–54). The reader too feels the wrench, the attraction of ancient culture and the pathos of the absence of Grace in the Christian scheme of things.

Virgilian elements are clearly present in the first canto of the poem.* The image of death by drowning (11, 22–7) recalls the fate of Aeneas and his companions who survive the storm at sea in *Aeneid* I. Aeneas, too, tries to find the way to safety on high; three beasts make their appearance; the Trojan hero is saved by Venus's intervention (cf. Beatrice's appeal to Virgil); while Jupiter forecasts the

---

* See anthology, pp. 503–7.

coming of a great temporal leader (Virgil's prophecy of the Hound who shall save the world by driving the She-Wolf of Greed back to Hell). The rest of the tapestry must be left to the reader to discover. But the Virgilian vision and message, which had long been lost, should help us to glimpse a further dimension in Dante's allegory. The wolf was an age-old symbol for Rome: she had suckled its founder, Romulus. Here she appears as an infernal caricature of Roman justice, driving humanity to perdition; and in her dual role representing both greed and a corrupt image of Rome, she illustrates the polysemy of medieval allegory. The poet of the *Comedy* was no puritan: lust (the leopard) and pride (the lion) are barriers that may be overcome. Greed, on the other hand, was diametrically opposed to Justice. It becomes synonymous with avarice, denounced by St Augustine as the sin most opposed to charity (St Paul's 'the love of money is the root of all evil'), with a semantic field as great as that of the Freudian libido. It is, for example, the popes' mad desire for temporal power, their *libido dominandi*, which has led to the corruption of the whole world. So, the image of the wolf returns in *Paradiso*, IX, where the 'accursed flower' depicted on Florentine coinage is the sole object of papal greed; it has 'turned the shepherd into a wolf'.

The number of the beasts is also significant, for the number three is at the core of the *Comedy*'s poetic structure. A reader of the Italian text is immediately struck by the verse form, the *terza rima* invented by Dante for this poem. The pattern is *aba*, followed by a second group or *terzina*, *bcb*, a third, *cdc*, and so on throughout the canto, with a concatenation of rhymes requiring the richness of Italian endings, impossible to achieve in English. This basic triad, woven into the verse structure, reflects the triune godhead, the imprint of the Creator in the universe. A few examples are the three great sections or *cantiche* (*Inferno*, *Purgatorio*, *Paradiso*); the three major subdivisions to each *cantica*; and the symmetry that introduces a political theme into the sixth canto of each section, rising from the municipal level of *Inferno* VI, through the national level of *Purgatorio* VI, to the universal level of the empire's providential history in *Paradiso* VI. The *Comedy* also contains the sacred number 100 in its cantos (1 + 33; 33; 33). Such details are far from being mere ornamentation; like many of the quasi-invisible details of medieval churches, they were pointers to a hidden reality. Belief in the mystical power of numbers and their arrangement went back to remote antiquity. Among authors known to Dante, Boethius asserts that numbers reflect the very framework of the universe, while Augustine defines beauty (imprinted by God in His works) as a symmetrical proportion based on numbers. So, in what Dante came to call his 'sacred poem', the smallest detail could become a microcosm or an arrow directed at the heart of God's universe. Far from the Romantics' vision of a writer too concerned with the urgency of his message to worry about poetic form, the *Comedy* reveals one of the world's supreme poetic craftsmen: perhaps no other literary work has such a structure, whose complexity finds its closest parallel in the counterpoint of Bach's *Art of Fugue*.

In creating this structure, the poet was imitating God's way of writing. The Creator alone could write with objects and creatures; the Book of Creation was seen as complementary to the Bible. Both were given to man so that he should discover the mark of God in all things. Now for most of us the image of a book appears as mere metaphor. It is hard to realize how literally metaphor could be taken by the medieval mind. It is even more difficult to gauge the force this particular image held before the invention of printing and the introduction of mass education. A book was then a jungle of unintelligible symbols that could be deciphered only by an elite. Its message was there, but it remained hidden from the vast majority, just as God's message was present but concealed amid a forest of signs in the visible universe. In constructing his poem Dante was careful to imitate God's Book and to provide a code for the deciphering of his poetic universe – until at the very climax, he brings back the same image, claiming that in the depths of the godhead he had for one brief moment seen 'bound together by love into one volume the pages that are scattered throughout the universe'. In this vision of the unity of creation the poet shared with a very few saints (such as the Christ-like Francis) the total acceptance of life in all its manifestations.

This totality is reflected in the way the poet refers to his work: his 'comedy'. This stands in obvious contrast with the reference to Virgil's *Aeneid* as the latter's 'high ... tragedy'. It must be remembered that classical drama was only revived some two hundred years later, during the Renaissance, and that in his *De Vulgari Eloquentia*

Dante had defined comedy solely in terms of a stylistic hierarchy, of which the noblest level was 'tragic', the humblest 'elegiac', while 'comedy' was a blend of both. The creation of a new artistic ideal characterizes Dante's great poem, ranging as it does over the whole extent of human language and experience. Based on the Bible's 'humble style', it is capable of embracing the whole of reality from the obscenities of hell and this world to the supreme beauty of paradise.

To return to the three beasts, the Republic of Florence displayed lions on its banner. Heraldic conventions, biblical reminiscences and the moralizing element in medieval bestiaries all helped the poet to depict the corruption of his twin cities, Florence and Rome, as well as the universal degradation of mankind. But they do not necessarily help the modern reader to appreciate Dante's poem. We are not accustomed to fitting together the pieces in the medieval jigsaw puzzle; it is therefore fortunate that allegorical trappings are exceptional in the *Comedy*. In his masterpiece, Dante came to discard most of the abstract signs of the medieval allegorical code, providing us instead with living symbols in the men and women that animate his poem. The revolutionary effects of his method can clearly be seen in the two symbols of lust, the leopard and Francesca da Rimini. The leopard of the first canto has no existence in itself, no meaning beyond its symbolic significance. In canto V,* on the other hand, we encounter a real woman who brings home to us the nature and the force of lust. Once we have discovered the probable significance of the symbolic beast, our interest focuses exclusively on the message enclosed; but with Francesca we can never ignore the totality of the portrayal, the complex power of an artistic creation in which everything speaks to the reader. It is no longer a question of this *for* that (where the first term is quickly eliminated), but of this *and* that with mutual interaction. Human reality is seized upon by the poet and projected against a backcloth of God's eternity, giving a multi-dimensional vision similar to the figural interpretation of the Bible, whereby events and persons in the Old Testament were seen as a prefiguration of the Christian dispensation, without being deprived of their individual historical reality.

* See anthology, pp. 507–9.

The wolf proves to be the insuperable obstacle that drives the pilgrim back 'to where the sun is silent' – where the image of the silent sun has nothing to do with poetic licence but is intended to bring home to the reader the fact that the sun, throughout the *Comedy*, is a symbol of God and His Grace.

Virgil, we know, comes to save Dante. But first the pilgrim has to overcome his doubts: why should he have been chosen after the great examples of Aeneas and Paul? Virgil assures him that his journey is willed by God and desired by the Virgin Mary, Saint Lucy, and Beatrice (the young Florentine woman who died in 1290 and inspired poems of sublime love in the man who placed her among the greatest saints in Paradise).

The two poets set forth and, without any explanation, the 'arduous, woody path' leads to the Gate of Hell with its inscription (reminiscent of a Roman triumphal arch and medieval gateways) proclaiming Christ's victory and God's inexorable Justice, with the terrible finality of 'Abandon all hope, you who enter' (A, III, 9).

As they enter and are surrounded by the sounds of infernal suffering, Virgil explains that the sufferers here are the sitters-on-the-fence who mingle with those angels 'who neither rebelled against nor were faithful to God' – a conception of angelic neutrality quite opposed to Aquinas's angelology, but typical of the poet's rejection of such a lack of *energeia* in all creatures. Life, for him, consisted above all in making a choice. These wretched souls 'were never alive', ignored by Fame. Their torment illustrates the way the poet wished to make the punishment fit the crime in his so-called *contrapasso* (A, XXVIII, 142). Here, the cowards are forced to run behind a banner, something they had refused to do in their selfish lives. So, too, they are stung by insects and made to shed their blood and tears, which they had carefully spared on earth. Among them the poet recognizes the soul of Celestine V, who had abdicated seven months after his election to the papacy in 1294. His successor was Dante's great enemy, Boniface VIII, whose mad ambition and persecution of the Spiritual Franciscans formed a terrible contrast to the hopes aroused by his saintly predecessor. Celestine, on the other hand, by refusing to take up the burden God had placed on him was for Dante truly guilty of 'the great denial'.

The second half of the canto is taken up with the crossing of the black marshy waters of the Acheron. Dante's realistic underworld owes little to its unimaginative Christian predecessors. Instead it looks persistently to Virgil; and nowhere is this more evident than in the second half of canto III. Dante's imitation is quite free of inhibitions about twisting the meaning of a text or image for his own purposes. Such imitation, far from servile copying, could become a free-for-all contest, where the prize went to the strongest. Here, then, far from hiding his sources, Dante is at pains to emphasize his debts to his great predecessors – until he eventually proclaims (A, XXV, 94–102) the superiority of his Christian vision over the poetry of Lucan and Ovid.

One of the great innovations in medieval poetry is the art of the Virgilian simile as practised by Dante. Our first example is the description of the souls crossing the Acheron in the infernal ferry (A, III. 112–17), modelled on the image of the dead leaves of autumn in *Aeneid* VI. The Italian poet adapts every detail to his purpose – and in some ways outstrips his master. In Virgil's poem, the images are only evoked to stress the vast number of souls waiting to cross the Acheron: they are cumulative. In the *Comedy*, they have been separated into two parts, each with its precise function. First, the leaves: it is not just their number (Virgil's *multa ... folia*) but the inexorable baring of the branches and fluttering down of the leaves that struck Virgil's 'disciple' and produced what was for Ruskin 'the most perfect image possible' of the damned souls' 'utter lightness, feebleness, passiveness, and scattering agony of despair'. The idea of the bare branch contemplating the ground strewn with its dead leaves is Dante's own, adding a note of pathos absent from the original scene – while the passage from the Latin plural to the singular 'one by one' reflects and stresses the Christian concept of individuality. Finally the Virgilian symmetry is discarded by Dante, who uses the leaves to indicate movement and fragility, while the image of the birds is transformed by the medieval art of falconry into an extraordinarily effective evocation of the souls' total obedience to Charon. The latter, based on the Virgilian figure, is last seen in an attitude worthy of Michelangelo's Last Judgement, laying about him with his oar to goad the damned souls whose 'fear is turned into desire'.

Charon is the first 'demon' encountered. Such by-words for

wickedness as Nero and Pontius Pilate appear as devils in medieval texts; but not in Dante. It is instead the demons from classical mythology that steal the limelight in the first part of this Christian Hell: Minos, the judge, the guardians of the various circles, the Furies and the Giants. Their importance is another tribute to Virgil's supremacy and veracity, while their picturesque qualities make them far more interesting than their medieval counterparts; for instance, the most medieval of Dante's devils are outwitted in a scene that breaks all theological rules.

The description of Limbo in canto IV is even more important for an understanding of Dante's attitude towards the ancient world and his admiration for the great achievements of non-Christian humanity. This led him to go against Catholic tradition which denied the possibility that there could have been 'virtuous pagans' not saved by God's Grace. Faith is essential for man's actions to be virtuous and pleasing to God: those who lived before Christ were saved by a special dispensation of Grace – but they were saved, not relegated to Limbo, the 'edge' of Hell. Dante ignores this tradition and devotes the whole canto to 'the heroes and heroines' of history. Early Italian commentators are obviously embarrassed by the presence of adult pagans in Limbo; but their embarrassment turns to near-panic when they come to the noble castle (106ff.), with its seven walls and gates, shady lawns and sunny open spaces devoted to intellectual conversation. Whatever the allegorical significance of the details, there is no doubt that the presence of light reflects God, the truth glimpsed during the souls' lives on earth, and a clear violation of the law that governs the darkness of Hell, the 'blind world' as it is defined. Even worse is the presence of the two most influential Arab philosophers, Avicenna and Averroes, notorious for their dangerous teachings (based on Aristotelian doctrine), and Saladin, founder of the Ayubite dynasty, who recaptured Jerusalem from the crusaders in 1187. Readers nowadays may be delighted to find such 'modern' broad-mindedness. As always, however, we must remember that Dante was a Christian poet for whom Hell was a terrible reality; and the inhabitants of Limbo are in Hell.

The preferential treatment accorded to these pagans is a result of two essential aspects of Dante's thought. The first is his fascination with magnanimity, the hallmark of the elite in Aristotle's *Ethics*.

Their memory still thrills the Christian poet, although the idea that pagans deprived of grace did not commit mortal sin had been denounced as the height of folly by St Augustine. The other reason is to be found in the poet's desire to exalt the founders of the empire and the wisdom of antiquity on which its authority rested in the purely human sphere. The two Arabs, Avicenna and Averroes, re-inforced the point that philosophy was independent of theology, just as the empire was independent of the papacy – a point the poet decided to stress even more forcefully by placing Siger of Brabant in Paradise.

Another extraordinary privilege is the one the poet accords him-self. In Purgatory Dante confesses to the sin of Pride. Here, in Limbo, we can measure the extent of his faith in his own genius. No other vernacular poet had profited so much from the lesson of Latin poetry; no other could equal its achievements in poetic technique or wisdom. While accepting the primacy of Homer, Dante (who knew no Greek) concentrated on the authors accessible to him: Virgil, his supreme authority and guide, Horace, Ovid, Lucan – the quartet already found in the *New Life*, which will be expanded in *Purgatory* with Statius and the erudite lists of other writers. From the very beginning of the *Comedy*, however, Dante felt himself the equal of the greatest poets known to the Latin west, one destined to write a Christian *Aeneid*: 'sixth among such wisdom'.

Few better examples of Dante's originality could be found than the fifth canto. The pilgrim passes before Minos, the connoisseur of sins who indicates the circle to which a soul is condemned by the number of times he twists his tail about his body (so different from the grave authority of the Virgilian judge in *Aeneid* VI). Here is a 'place mute of all light', where an infernal tempest tosses the spirits in all directions – an example of the *contrapasso* applied to the carnal sinners, who had allowed their reason to be overcome by the desires of the flesh. Two bird similes are used to illustrate the multitude of souls (starlings against the dark winter sky) and their cries of anguish (cranes who 'chant their laments'). A third simile then introduces a pair of lovers who come at Dante's request 'like doves called by desire' (the dove, bird of Venus, was a symbol of lust).

Two points may be noted. First, Dante's guide behaves in a quite un-Virgilian manner: he virtually ignores his great heroine

Dido* in order to allow the poetic spotlight to be turned on a pair of contemporary lovers who would be unknown if the *Comedy* had not immortalized them. Second, this celebrated episode which has inspired countless readers and artists only begins some two-thirds of the way through the canto (l.88). Before, Dante's list of names is brief and very different from the tedious catalogues often found in medieval texts. It introduces the theme of pity which strikes the pilgrim as he hears the names of 'the ladies and knights of old', exactly halfway through the 142 lines of the canto. Then, in less than sixty lines, Dante creates one of the outstanding heroines of world literature – Francesca, instead of Dido. This shows us that the poet's examples are taken above all from the contemporary world (most of whom, especially in *Inferno* and *Purgatorio*, died between 1275 and 1300). It is the fact that Francesca and her lover Paolo were contemporaries that helped the poet to make them his own and use their example for his audience as he might not have done with the great figures of history or literature. We need only recall the fact that Paolo Malatesta had been in Florence in Dante's youth (1282–3); Francesca's father was there in 1285; and by an irony of fate the poet spent the last days of his life an exile at the court of Francesca's nephew, the Lord of Ravenna. The *Comedy* was nothing if not topical when it appeared. The miracle lies in the fact that Dante's genius was able to confer universality on so many provincial figures and episodes.

Francesca describes her tragedy in three *terzine* (100–107), each of which begins with the word 'Love'. Anaphora thus reveals three cardinal points: her first reference is to Dante's own youthful love-credo; the second calls into play the 'laws' of Courtly Love; the third evokes the medieval theme of the *Liebestod*, of a love that leads to death instead of God. We note that Francesca refers to Love as an absolute external force, and that the pilgrim uses the same personification in his crucial question (118–20) when he asks her to tell him how Love had brought them to 'know the fearful desires'. In the *New Life* (XXV) the commentator–poet had clearly set out to alienate his readers from the convention of courtly literature which required love to be an actor in the drama, the irresistible force of Virgil's *Amor vincit omnia*.

* See anthology, p. 507.

Now, in the pilgrim's voyage of self-discovery, his first great lesson is gradually revealed until it is proclaimed loud and clear at the very centre of the poem: man is utterly responsible for the choices he makes, especially in the vast realm of love (B, XVI–XVIII).

Instead, Francesca is fixed for all eternity in her self-delusion, whereas Dante's Virgil had provided a clue in his advice to entreat Paolo and Francesca 'by that Love which drives them, and they will come'. As the word 'Another' makes clear, this is the supreme power whose Primal Love stands in opposition to the sinners' lust and whose justice condemns these souls to Hell. The pilgrim is dismayed: how were the 'sweet sighs' of two noble souls transformed into the 'fearful desires' of incest and adultery? Francesca's answer is a literary mosaic with references to Boethius, Virgil, the story of Lancelot and St Augustine all contained within the course of eighteen lines (121–38). The more important is the second group. The literary merits and fascination of the Arthurian romances had been admired by Dante about the year 1305; now, the poet of the *Comedy* chose one of the most celebrated to act as a catalyst between the lovers. They had read 'for pleasure' the story of Lancelot's adulterous love for Queen Guinevere; their act is made to stand in exemplary contrast with Augustine's reading of the Bible. In the *Confessions* the saint describes the way he had opened God's book at random and had lighted on St Paul's admonition to the Romans to abandon 'lust and wantonness'. The parallel with the lovers' behaviour is almost too obvious, followed as it is by the phrase 'And I refused to read any further', echoed in Francesca's closing words. We may now be aware of the ideal message contained in lines 127–38, which insists so much on the act of reading. Paolo and Francesca, unaware of their true feelings, read a book for entertainment. That book had been banned by Pope Innocent III. A saint of old had read God's Book with a very different purpose, seeking a message from the God of Love. So we come to understand why Dante replaces the god of love of Francesca's first speech by the book which had become her 'pander': both led to sin and damnation. The allurements of courtly literature and the illusions of Dante's youth are rent. In the process, the poet brought about a literary revolution. His audience would doubtless have been satisfied with a blonde siren, transformed into an old hag (cf. B, XIX, 7–33) to signify the ugliness and transitory pleasures of lust. The poet, however, accomplished a miracle by creating a woman with all the complexities of human nature and real life, one whose story so moves the pilgrim that he faints from pity. Here in the distorting mirror of Hell he has caught a glimpse of his own image. And it is at this point that we must leave the pilgrim to make his own progress.

Our own journey will in some ways be more tortuous. The first stop will be in the third 'pouch' (*bolgia*) of the third great division of Hell. Already the number will tell us that it concerns a sin particularly directed against God: simony, the bartering of ecclesiastical goods, named after Simon Magus (*Acts* VIII, 18). The reader must keep this well in mind to appreciate the full force of Dante's condemnation of a corrupt papacy. The exemplary sinner is Nicholas III (1277–80), who is made to forecast the damnation of Boniface VIII (1294–1303) and Clement V (1305–13) – the latter guilty of the heinous crime of abandoning Rome as the seat of the papacy and the centre of world government. The simoniacs are placed upside down in a hole of the rock of Hell: their position reflects their inversion of God's moral order, their adoration of gold and silver extracted from the bowels of the earth. The flames flickering over their feet are a caricature of the descent of the Holy Spirit on the heads of the apostles. Lastly, they are followers not of the apostles but of the wrong Simon. Dante believed that names should reflect the nature and purpose of things: so Beatrice was the true bringer of blessedness in his life. In the whole history of mankind the most famous example of this truth was the renaming of Simon as 'Rock' (Peter) by Christ. Here, the popes of Dante's times are buried in the infernal rock of greed which stands in diametrical contrast with the rock of the true Church and has made them turn God 'into gold and silver'. Utterly opposed to the holy poverty of Christ and the early Church, their 'avarice corrupts the whole world'.

This is a turning-point in the *Comedy*. The idea of evangelical poverty (declared heretical in 1323) is not present before *Inferno* XIX, least of all in the circle of avarice (VII). In this canto, it inspires the passionate denunciation of papal corruption and the effects of the terrible Donation of Constantine – the gift supposedly made by the Emperor in the year 330, when he 'turned Greek' and moved the capital of the empire from Rome to his own city, Constantinople, thus perverting the divinely inspired order followed by Aeneas from east to west. According to a forged document, Constantine had given the western part of the empire to Pope Sylvester and his successors. This Dante held to be not only illegal but tantamount to a second Fall, when the poison of corruption was infused into Christ's Church (B, XXXII, 124–60). Nothing could be worse than the confusion of God's ideal order, His assignment of spiritual supremacy to the pope and of political power and guidance to the emperor: 'Rome, which made the world good, used to have two suns, which lit up both paths, the world's and God's. The one has extinguished the other' (B, XVI, 106–9). At the centre of the poem, the whole tradition of medieval political imagery is subverted. In the *Monarchy*, Dante reluctantly used the image of the sun and moon to signify papacy and empire. Here, in the face of all the laws of astronomy and medieval thought, the poet claims that the ideal state in the world was reached under the influence of two suns, two powers whose role and authority remained complementary but independent, each stemming directly from God. The message is repeated throughout the poem. Although the poet's hopes were dashed after Henry VII's death in 1313, in true medieval fashion he remained faithful to the theory elaborated about 1307–8: Rome seen as the centre of universal government, with Christ's two vicars, pope and emperor, guiding man to temporal happiness and eternal salvation. The tragedy of 1300 is due to the 'bad example' on high: men see their spiritual leader devoured by greed for riches and worldly power, usurping the emperor's place as dispenser of Justice. From the heights of Paradise, Beatrice repeats the diagnosis of mankind's ills: 'Do not be surprised, but think instead that there is no one who governs on earth: that is why the human family has gone astray' (C, XXVII, 139–41).

This twenty-seventh canto of *Paradiso* is a fearful indictment of the Church's leader. Dante was clearly no proto-Protestant. He accepted the supremacy of the popes as St Peter's successors; but the higher his estimate of their responsibilities, the fiercer his condemnation of their failure to live up to this ideal. Even in his archenemy, the individual most responsible for his exile from Florence, the poet could see Christ crucified and mocked at Anagni, when the emissaries of the king of France took Boniface VIII and subjected him to such humiliation that the old man lost his reason and died soon after (B, XX, 85–96). Nevertheless, in Paradise St Peter himself is made to assert that, in the eyes of Heaven, his seat is vacant on earth – with the most obvious example of anaphora in the poem ('my place, My place, my place, which is empty in the presence of the Son of God'), followed by language which has offended the taste of readers incapable of accepting the poet's 'comic' style in Paradise, describing the effects of Boniface's corruption: 'he has turned my burial-place into a sewer of blood and stench.' The whole of Heaven turns a dark red, to signify both the present shame and the blood of Peter and the martyrs that had once sanctified Rome. That blood is being sucked by the popes from Cahors (John XXII) and Gascony (Clement V). Providence must intervene, that same providence that had helped Rome to universal dominion with Scipio. Nothing could be more striking than this reference to the hero of pagan Rome placed in the mouth of the archetypal pope; no better proof could be found that Dante's vision of universal history had remained the same, despite all setbacks. The Romans had paralleled the Jews as a people chosen by God for His dual purpose: the ancestors of Augustus Caesar had been entrusted with a mission as essential as that given to the ancestors of Christ and Peter, so that even Paradise may be described as 'that Rome of which Christ is a Roman'.

The whole of *Paradiso* is a dialectical movement from good to evil and back to a higher stage. The poet is obviously intent on describing the ideal order of man's true country. Inevitably, however, the perfection for which Dante yearned brought him back to earth and its corruption. The first canto contains an essential hymn to the divine order that rules the universe (103–41), stressing that man's instinct should drive him home to God. It is from canto IX onwards that the movement described characterizes the poet's imagination: mention of the Holy Land leads to a bitter attack on the popes and churchmen who study only the Decretals for gain; praise of St Francis's espousal of Lady Poverty by the Dominican Thomas Aquinas is accompanied by denunciation of the decadence in his own Order (canto XI), while this is paralleled in canto XII by the Franciscan Bonaventure's eulogy of St Dominic and his condemnation of the unworthy followers in both the Spiritual and the Conventual camps. The crusading ideal is celebrated and its loss bewailed

(XV, 139–44). Florence's ideal state in the twelfth century is emphasized by the description of a town 'at peace, sober and chaste' (C, XV, 99), followed by the negative sequence in the next four *terzine*, in utter contrast with her divided condition in 1300, now a prey to Pride, Envy and Avarice (A, VI, 74; XV, 68). But the universal cause of evil is the corruption of the Church, denounced by Peter Damian (C, XXI, 118–35), by St Benedict the founder of western monasticism, by St Peter (C, XXVII), and by the poet himself in his hymn to Eternal Justice, which is mocked by the reality on earth, mankind wholly 'led astray by the evil example' on high, its spiritual leader so intent on adoring the image of John the Baptist on Florentine coinage that he ignores the 'fisherman and old Paul' (C, XVIII, 124–36).

The kinetic art of *Paradiso* is most obvious in the tremendous vision of the thirtieth canto. Here, at the end of the poem, the very moment when one would expect the poet to concentrate his powers on the description of heavenly perfection, his preparation for the Beatific Vision, we find only one seat specifically reserved. It awaits the coming of Henry VII in 1313, after his betrayal by the pope in his attempt to bring peace and unity to Italy. This illustrates Dante's purpose in writing the *Comedy*, as expressed in the Epistle to Cangrande: the *Comedy* was written 'for action, not speculation'. It is no saint or mystic, but an emperor that Heaven awaits. And this proclamation is followed by a terrible vision downwards through the heart of the universe to the corrupt rock of the papacy in Hell, where Boniface and Simon Magus wait for Clement to join them in the shaft. In the limitless world of Paradise we are reminded of the infernal prison that entraps man's soul forever. A similar flashback is glimpsed after the Heaven of the Fixed Stars, where at Beatrice's bidding the pilgrim gazes down from high heaven to the 'threshing-floor' of earth. He sees the centre of the world, from Europa's bestial lust to the 'mad path' of Ulysses: from east to west, the whole cycle of humanity's folly from the sins of the flesh to the sins of pride and the intellect.

The reference to Ulysses opens up once more the theme of the Voyage or Journey, basic to the whole poem. Man's duty on earth is to return to his creator; he must not linger anywhere in this life but strive to reach his spiritual home. The pilgrim of the *Comedy* therefore reflects man's true mission. He plays out the whole drama of Exodus once more on its three spiritual levels: allegorically signifying 'our redemption through Christ'; tropologically, 'the soul's conversion from the wretchedness of sin to a state of grace'; and anagogically, 'the departure of the sanctified soul from the bondage of corruption to the freedom of eternal glory'. This scheme, adapted from the interpretation of Holy Scripture for the purpose of a fuller understanding of a poem now called 'Divine', is set out in the Epistle to Cangrande. It may be fruitfully applied to the structure and pattern of the poem as a whole.

The encounter with Ulysses takes place in the eighth 'pouch' of the circle of Fraud (A, XXVI). Its interpretation is controversial, but I would suggest certain structural correspondences and oppositions. The first is with Aeneas. Ulysses and Aeneas were enemies engaged in a providential struggle at Troy. Ulysses was renowned for his guile and eloquence, typical of the Greeks and opposed to the sense of duty and justice that characterized the Roman people. Virgil's poem is a paean to Aeneas's *pietas*, the way he overcomes all personal desires in order to obey the will of heaven and reach Italy, his predestined goal. Dante's Ulysses, on the other hand, does not return to Ithaca but sacrifices his family and kingdom to his insatiable curiosity and intellectual pride. He rejects the limitations placed on human experience and exploration since the Fall. His voyage ends in disaster within sight of the Mountain of Eden, the archetypal symbol of man's inordinate pride and rebellion. In medieval times, illustrations of Aeneas leading his aged father and young son to safety would have underlined the contrast with Ulysses' desertion of Laertes and Telemachus in Dante's account, which refers to the Roman hero's *pietas* even in the naming of Gaeta.

Another opposition is with Dante's own journey, willed by Heaven. At first, Dante is overcome by pusillanimity (A, II, 45–8). Here we have a good example of the Aristotelian concept of virtue as the mean between two extremes: the other pole to the pilgrim's cowardice is Ulysses' 'mad flight', while true virtue is found in Aeneas's magnanimity which allowed him to descend to the underworld (A, II, 13–27). Dante's own journey, guided by Virgil, is modelled on this ancient precedent, just as this same voyage to God recalls the ancient quest of the Argonauts some twenty-five centuries earlier (with Christ's birth as the mid-way point). So, too, Dante's 'lofty flight' reflects the neo-platonic flight of the winged soul towards its home, in contrast with Ulysses' attempt to turn his ship's oars into 'wings' for his 'mad flight'.

As we can see, the poem only yields up its full range of inter-relationships as we read on and begin to form a total picture in retrospect. Certainly, Dante expected his readers to arrive quickly from Ulysses, the only great sinner taken from antiquity in Hell, to the even more surprising exception made for Cato, the guardian of Christian Purgatory (B, I–II). Cato had committed suicide and opposed Caesar, whereas we have just come across Caesar's assassins in the mouths of Lucifer. How could the poet select Cato for eventual salvation? The religious question is faced in the salvation of Trajan and Ripheus (C, XX, 100–129). The rest of the answer lies in Dante's admiration for the stoic courage and sense of justice displayed by Cato in Lucan's *Pharsalia*, where the ninth book describes the Roman hero's refusal to go beyond the limits placed by providence. Cato's face in the *Comedy* is lit up by the four cardinal virtues, supreme among them Prudence, the most necessary quality in a leader and the one most opposed to guile (Aquinas's *astutia*). Dante glimpsed a prefiguration of Christ in Cato's supreme sacrifice for that true freedom of the spirit which came with the New Law. The contrast between Cato's sacrifice and Ulysses' rebellion is finally emphasized in the scene where the pilgrim is girt with the reed of humility and submission to God's will, on the shores of that same desert ocean which had witnessed the destruction of the pagan's mad enterprise 'as pleased Another' – a phrase repeated as a sign to the reader to link the two episodes together in a fuller understanding of the poet's purpose (A, XXVI, 141; B, I, 133). And once again in Paradise the request for 'royal prudence' made by Solomon, the greatest of kings (C, XIII, 88–108), may remind the reader of Ulysses' failure to carry out his primary duty as a leader of men and king of Ithaca.

Some of the complex web will be apparent. It is for each reader to unravel the whole. So far, little has been said about Purgatory – topographically, the poet's most original creation departing from the traditional idea of purgatorial suffering as basically a part of Hell, though limited in duration and helped by intercession. In

Dante's imagination, its creation as a huge mountain (about 3,000 miles high) occurred when Lucifer was cast out of Heaven. God's enemy was impaled in the centre of the earth, at the end of an immense funnel. The land in the southern hemisphere was driven under the ocean to the northern hemisphere, while the Mountain of Eden (and, later Purgatory) was formed in an attempt to avoid all contact with the arch-rebel (A, XXXIV, 121–6).

The opening of the second *cantica* is in utter contrast with the pit of Hell. Dawn is the symbol of resurrection, of the soul's renewal, Lucifer has been replaced by Venus, the planet of love which lights up the whole eastern sky (B, I, 13–27). The eye delights once more in the beauties of God's creation – pointing to the joy and perfection of Eden at the top of the mountain. Four stars represent the cardinal virtues as originally given to the human race, which must now be reconquered by the individual, a reminder that *Purgatorio* is an allegory of the active life. The pilgrim and the other souls can only ascend during daylight, a detail illustrating the process of purification as co-operation between the soul's free will and God's grace, while the theological virtues take over at nightfall (B, VIII, 89–93). It is all too often forgotten that in the *Monarchia* Dante, writing of the two goals set for man by Divine Providence, equates the first with 'the happiness attainable in this life, which consists in the fulfilment of all man's faculties and is represented by the earthly paradise'. It must be sought under the guidance of the emperor, who must in turn be guided by the teachings of philosophy. This is surely the reason why Virgil is chosen to lead Dante to Beatrice, just as in history the Roman Empire was founded before Christ's birth as a preparation for the coming of the Redeemer. The emperor's role is to safeguard man's freedom; so the purpose of Dante's climb is the quest of liberty and it is Virgil who announces to him at the top of the mountain that his will is 'free, true and whole': the ordering of the words is crucial to the poet's message, that man is driven to good or evil by the type of government that rules him. Good political order, under the emperor, will enable him to make a free and true choice.

Purgatorio has been described as the realm of artists and friends. The encounters with Casella, Belacqua, Sordello, in Ante-Purgatory are memorable; just as mention of Giotto and Cimabue (B, XI, 94–6) reminds us that Dante was an amateur of the arts. Nino Visconti and Forese Donati are friends whom the pilgrim is overjoyed to find in safety. But even more important are those episodes where Dante emphasizes the total originality of his 'sweet new style', which a contemporary poet is made to date from the composition of Dante's first great ode or *canzone*. Dante himself stresses the link between his poetic inspiration and his discovery of the gratuitous nature of love; the poet must love as the Christian loves his God, not for any hope of reward but as an expression of that 'new song' which reveals the rebirth of the individual: 'I am one, who when Love moves me, note down, and what he dictates within I signify' (B, XXIV, 52–4).

The earlier meeting with Sordello had given rise to the most remarkable proof that great poetic genius may turn even a political theme into poetic gold. And those who seek only harmony and sweetness in Dante's verse would do well to read the violent outburst sparked off by Virgil's and Sordello's embrace*: they will find the passionate invective of one who searched for the harshest rhymes to describe the reality of evil (A, XXXII, 1–12), the sword of his anger turned against all those who have transformed Italy, 'garden of the Empire', into a desert – and the sarcasm of the exile who describes his beloved native city as a sick woman incapable of finding a moment's rest: 'tu ricca, tu con pace, e tu con senno!' – 'You, with your riches, peace and wisdom!' – No English translation can render the lash of the Italian double consonants.

Since the Reformation, Purgatory has been seen as a peculiarly religious state. It is therefore difficult for the modern reader to discover the practical application and meaning of Dante's second realm. This is, however, well illustrated in the very middle of the poem, *Purgatorio* XVI,* where a certain Mark the Lombard gives Dante a lecture on the creation of the human soul. In lines that inspired Eliot's *Animula*, the Italian poet tells us that the soul, created directly by God, knows nothing, except that, having come from the source of all happiness, it is naturally attracted by any promise of pleasure. This it encounters first in various lures, which ensnare it, unless it is subject to 'bridle and guide'. It must then amaze us

* See anthology, p. 510; pp. 512–13.

to see the way we are suddenly brought back to Dante's political reality in the verses that follow (94ff.): the bridle, Marco explains, is to be found in the law, even as man's guide is the emperor, who is bound to apply the law and dispense justice while keeping his eye on 'the tower of the true city'. This episode occurs in the *Comedy*'s fiftieth canto. It is exemplary in its brusque jump from theology to politics, the way in which the creation of the human soul leads to an assertion of the need for a universal emperor and the terrible responsibility borne by Christ's spiritual vicar who, by interfering in the emperor's political sphere, leads the whole world astray. The poet of the *New Life* had asserted that vernacular poets should restrict themselves to the theme of love. Some ten years later (*c.*1305) he had opened up the field of vernacular poetry to include the triad arms, love, and rectitude. In 'the sacred poem to which both heaven and earth have contributed' he set out to describe the whole range of human experience. The poet of youthful love, of rectitude and justice denounced the evils in contemporary society and pointed the way to salvation. His meetings with the Christ-bearing figures of Statius and Beatrice in *Purgatorio* are exemplary: a Christianized Latin poet accompanies him to the Earthly Paradise, where a beloved woman hears his confession and prepares him for the ascent to Heaven which begins at midday, the hour of the sun god, and in the spring, season of creation and resurrection.

In his journey through Hell and Purgatory, the 'poet of rectitude' displays an idiosyncratic assessment of evil in its various forms. *Purgatorio* is safely structured on a traditional ordering of the seven cardinal sins; but even here, the pilgrim is appalled to think that Statius was apparently guilty of avarice and is relieved to discover that he had sinned through prodigality – a sin far more becoming to a poet (B, XXII, 19–54). *Inferno* is a complex moral structure, based on a broadly Aristotelian–Ciceronian scheme, divided into three major areas of Incontinence, Violence and Fraud. We have already seen Dante's violent rejection of the 'neutral' souls rejected by both Heaven and Hell; his pity for Francesca and Paolo. We find anger once more in his encounter with Filippo Argenti (A, VIII, 31–63) and with Mosca dei Lamberti (A, XXVIII, 103–11). The latter had in fact been judged by the pilgrim to be among those who had 'turned their minds to good action' (A, VI, 80–81); his condemnation of Mosca as a sower of discord and the cause of Tuscany's civil wars shows us the distance he had travelled towards a discovery of the truth. Admiration is shown for the great souls of sinners such as Farinata and Ulysses. Pity for the suicide, Pier della Vigna, unjustly accused of political treachery; pity for the sodomite, Brunetto Latini who had shown Dante the links between virtue and nobility, the good government of the city. Contempt for the bestiality of a cunning thief, Vanni Fucci, or the usurers who mock the arms of true nobility. Such human reactions create a bond between reader and pilgrim and, unlike the *exempla* of the preachers and theologians, Dante's sinners show us life in the round where very few are totally evil; rather than being black and white, most of reality consists of various tones of grey. The 'comic' interlude, which stretches through cantos XXI–XXIII, is not an example of Dante's sense of humour; it is designed both to highlight the vulgarity of the sin of which Dante had been accused and to provide dramatic relief before the intensity of absolute evil.

The poet discards the authoritative judgement of Aquinas in placing sins of fraud after those of violence. The poet insists that fraud is an evil monopolized by man, as it implies misuse of his God-given intellect, intended to distinguish him from the beasts and lead him towards eternal truths. The Ciceronian fox is therefore replaced by the trinity of traitors against their lord: Judas, Brutus and Cassius. The shock administered to readers of Shakespeare is a salutary one, if it helps them to realize that the Italian poet was no theological computer, programmed by medieval catechism. His overwhelming dislike of treachery was so strong that it led him to assert the quasi-heretical idea that certain sins of treachery are so utterly evil that they send man's soul down to Hell, even before death (B, XXXIII, 124–35). This dramatically effective but theologically perverse concept was echoed by Chaucer in *The Man of Law's Tale* and censored by the Inquisition in Spain.

The reason for this insistence is clear. Dante's hatred of treachery is part of his general view of life, where the political element is predominant. For the exiled poet, the most important thing was for man to be able to live at peace, in a universal community where justice reigned supreme. Treachery not only made this impossible, but it shattered the very foundations of the *polis*, the fabric of society, by destroying the natural bonds of love and trust that should unite mankind. Heaven means union with God, charity linking both creator and creatures; the city of the devil is its antithesis, based as it is on sin and treachery.

And so, at the bottom of Hell, we find the traitors and Lucifer himself imprisoned in ice. After the ingenuity displayed by the poet's imagination in inventing weird and terrible punishments, the reader may perhaps be struck with a sense of anticlimax by the poet's use of ice to punish the worst sinners in the universe. The effort needed to understand Dante's purpose is typical of the difficulties we encounter when we try to understand the *Comedy* without prejudice or anachronism. Of course, we can never achieve this ambitious goal, but we must strive towards it. And in this case we must try to think of what ice meant for a medieval Italian: in the world of nature, something essentially sterile and utterly opposed to life-giving heat. The sun, we remember, is a symbol of God in the *Comedy*: like its creator, it warms the earth and makes life possible. Its warmth helped to make traditional hell-fire a somewhat ambiguous metaphor, while there is very little ambiguity in Dante's portrayal of absolute evil. The Italian poet – unlike Milton, in Blake's phrase – was not on the devil's side without knowing it. The reader will find no heroic representation of rebellion or Satan in the depths of the *Inferno*. The accent is on the essentially negative quality of evil, and this negation is represented by the total sterility of ice, on the one hand, which paralyses the earth and symbolizes the winter of man's soul, and by the enormous mass of matter, unredeemed by spirit, on the other.

There is no hesitation or reservation in Dante's condemnation of evil. Yet he admires Farinata for his strong-minded and heroic defence of Florence, which saved the city from destruction in 1260 at the Council of Empoli. Farinata is condemned as a heretic, and scholars have tended to suppose that his sin is divorced from the poet's portrayal of one of the heroes of the recent past. They have also pointed to the difficulties supposedly encountered by Dante in placing this pre-eminently religious sin in an ethical framework derived from Aristotle and Cicero. But this is to miss the whole point of the *Comedy*'s structure, which is based on the contrasting triad of cities, that of man, that of the devil, and the City of God.

Aristotle's assertion that man was born to be a member of a community had been assimilated into the Christian system, to such an extent that in Dante's Florence a Dominican preacher, Remigio de' Girolami, asserted that no one could be a good Christian unless he were also a good citizen. This extraordinary statement serves to highlight the only pause in the question-and-answer game in *Paradiso*, when Dante replies with an abrupt 'yes' to the question whether it would be worse for man if he were not a citizen on earth (C, VIII, 115–17).

We may now see why Dante placed the heretics at the very entrance to the City of the Devil. Heresy was interpreted as signifying 'division'; its greatest threat was that it undermined the unity of God's city, and Christ himself had warned that 'any city . . . divided against itself shall fall'. Division and destruction provide the fundamental link between heresy and political faction. Farinata and Cavalcante had fought each other throughout their lives on earth, though inhabitants of the same city: their eternal punishment is to be united in the same tomb, thus symbolizing the state to which they had reduced their divided city on earth (tropology) and the fate to which they had condemned their souls by denying their immortality and refusing to accept the existence of life beyond the grave (anagogy). Farinata, a supporter of the imperial cause, and Cavalcante, supporter of the papal party, are made to lie in this desolate cemetery of the soul with the great emperor, Frederick II, and Cardinal Ottaviano degli Ubaldini. Dante had sung the praises of Frederick in *De Vulgari Eloquentia*. But the 'illustrious hero' of the earlier work has been subjected to the *Comedy*'s religious spotlight: the emperor is damned. Even as heresy leads to expulsion from God's church and the life-giving sacraments, so political faction leads to exile and destruction, as the poet himself had learned so soon after 1300. From his position above all parties, the author of the *Comedy* contrasts his former illusions with the universal truths that now revitalized his art. A heretical prince of the Church and a heretical emperor – followed by a heretical pope – add a piquant touch to the message illustrating the havoc wrought by heresy and faction in both church and state.

The exiled poet was obsessed with the need for peace and unity. He sought them in his ascent with Beatrice to the utmost confines of the physical universe and beyond, an anabasis marked by ever-increasing resplendence until he reached that 'intellectual light, full of love' with which we began this chapter. Throughout the journey, the poet's political thought is inseparable from his religious or moral beliefs: in this too he can reflect our ideals. His later pessimism as events refused to bring the longed-for solution was tempered by an abundance of hope in his *Paradiso* (XXV, 52–3). Lucifer's bat, the beast of darkness and ignorance, may never overcome the divine eagle, capable of looking directly into the rays of God's justice. The gloom of Hell's prison must be shunned for the light of God's grace. It is this belief in a better order, in man's ability to change the world about him, that sounds its challenge to us. It is the glimpse of a higher beauty in *Paradiso* (XXXIII)★ that quickens our hearts in 'the devotion to something afar from the sphere of our sorrow'. It is the recognition that the fault lies not in heaven but in ourselves (B, XVI, 82–3) that still makes Dante a positive force for the modern reader.

★ See anthology, pp. 513–17.

JUAN RUIZ: *THE BOOK OF GOOD LOVE*

COLIN SMITH

The poet tells us within his text, twice, that his name is Juan Ruiz and that he is Archpriest of Hita, and includes a further reference to himself as 'of Hita'. Hita is a small town now, of greater importance in the Middle Ages, some 55 kilometres to the north-east of Madrid. The poet may have been born in Alcalá de Henares, close to Madrid on the eastern side, to judge from allusions in the text. Beyond this, we know nothing for sure, and given the nature of ecclesiastical office at the time, we cannot be certain that the poet resided in, or ever went to, Hita. From the little we do know, from poetic itineraries and allusions, it is best to assume merely that he was active in New Castile and in the diocese of Toledo. Something is added by the man who copied the Salamanca MS. in about 1420, Alfonso de Paradinas (1395–1485, later bishop of Ciudad Rodrigo and a noted canon lawyer), probably while a student at Salamanca. He added, or inherited from his model, a series of headings to the sections into which he divides the poem, repeatedly referring to the author as 'Archpriest', and stating in a colophon that 'This is the book of the Archpriest of Hita, which he composed while imprisoned on the orders of Cardinal Don Gil [de Albornoz], Archbishop of Toledo'; Don Gil was archbishop from 1337 to 1350, and cardinal from 1350 until his death in 1367. Paradinas's detail could be correct or at least reflect a sound tradition. The point is important, for on a number of occasions the poet refers to 'this prison' and his wish to be freed from it; some critics take this in a spiritual sense, the prison being that of sin and the flesh, while others, supported by such references as that to the 'slanderers' who have caused the imprisonment and the fact that it is 'undeserved', believe that a real prison was in question. In any case, the nature of the imputed offence cannot be guessed, but if the poem were indeed written in prison, its at times scurrilous nature cannot itself have been the cause.

To the above may be added, as hypothesis only, the wealth of detail adduced in 1972 by Sáez and Trenchs. Juan Rodríguez (= Ruiz) de Cisneros was the illegitimate son of a Palencian lord, born (in 1295 or 1296) with other children from the union of this man with a Christian girl during long captivity in the Moorish Kingdom of Granada. On release, the parents married and, with dispensations, Juan Rodríguez was able to enter upon a moderately distinguished career in the church, and his progress in terms of canonries and other benefices in a variety of places is documented in the papal archives. He achieved a papal chaplaincy and a place in the household of D. Gil de Albornoz, after studies in France (probably at Montpellier) and a visit to Avignon, perhaps also to Italy in the train of his protector Albornoz. The last mention of Juan Rodríguez is in 1353. The one piece of evidence missing, and the only one we have from the poem, concerns the post of Archpriest of Hita; but the silence of the papal documentation on this is natural, for the post was in the gift of the Archbishop of Toledo and did not concern the Pope. Opinion differs about the relevance of all this to the Juan Ruiz known as a poet, for the name was common enough; but Sáez's discovery shows us a man of very much the right kind – in education and cultural ambience – to have been our author, and the dates fit perfectly. The discovery of the birth and early years in Granada adds support to the thesis of Castro (1948) about the influence of Moslem modes of thought and feeling upon the poet, and explains the presence of a few Arabic phrases in the text; but for both there are alternative explanations. The public for which the work was written can be supposed ecclesiastical in part, strongly learned, sophisticated, rather worldly and even merrily cynical; it could have included a bourgeois element, and certainly included women, perhaps nuns; a natural public would have existed in Toledo, and one of the MSS was long in the Cathedral Library there.

Three MSS survive, none complete: 'S' (Salamanca, copied by Paradinas), representing according to stanza 1634 a work of 1343; 'G' (Gayoso, of the late fourteenth century); and 'T' (Toledo, also of the late fourteenth century), representing according to stanza 1634 a work of 1330. Other fragments survive, and there are two folios of what must have been a complete Portuguese translation made in the late fourteenth century. It is known that other MSS existed in the fifteenth and sixteenth centuries, while references to incidents and personages of the poem in the fifteenth century demonstrate its wide circulation. Lack of a complete MS. poses problems for editors of the kind not found, for example, in Chaucerian studies; it has been customary to produce some kind of conflated text based on the three MSS and the fragments, and there are recent critical editions and attempts to restore the original. The numeration of stanzas is virtually unified, giving a total of 1709.

The nature of the composition and its date are controversial. For long, critics believed that there was a first redaction in 1330 (MSS 'G' and 'T') and a revision, with the addition of numerous episodes and stanzas, in 1343 (MS. 'S'). Others, including the recent editors Chiarini and Joset, believe there was a single redaction, in 1343 (the date of 1330 in the 'T' MS. then being mistaken), and that all three MSS derive from a common archetype.

Even with the conflation of MSS and fragments, we do not have Ruiz's complete text. It is recognized that thirty-two stanzas are missing between those numbered 877 and 878, in which the seduction (or surrender) of Doña Endrina was narrated; perhaps some prudish reader of the archetype removed the folios. On a number of occasions within his narrative Ruiz announces that, as part of the progress of a love-affair, he sent a lyric or song to the lady, but this is now missing in our texts; it cannot be determined whether the announcement is formulaic or playfully deceptive or whether the lyrics, once included in the archetype, were for some reason suppressed. However, the poet's statement that he composed, within his *Book*, a variety of songs, rhymes, and lyrics, 'according as this craft (*çiença*) requires', is to be taken literally as a claim to have written a wide range of compositions extending well beyond the contents of the extant MSS.

The title of the poem, *The Book of Good Love*, has long been established on the basis of line 13c in the introductory material. This adequately represents the theme, though the precise sense of 'Good Love' has been intensely debated. In earlier times the poem was known simply as 'The Book of the Archpriest' or 'The Treatise of the Archpriest'. An alternative title, doubtless involving the modesty topos, is indicated in line 12c: 'Little Book of Poems'; to return to this today would be, by implication, to insist on the anthological nature of the *Book*, against the tendency of most modern critics to view it as a reasonably unified whole.

Most of the *Book* is composed in the four-line monorhymed stanzas known as *cuaderna vía*, in use for narrative and doctrinal verse from its invention by Berceo in about 1220 until its demise soon after 1400. The line is the Spanish alexandrine, constructed in strict usage as 7 + 7 syllables. A large number of Ruiz's lines are of this type, but there is much irregularity; sometimes within the stanza a line of 7 + 7 syllables may appear among others of 8 + 8, and lines of 7 + 8 or 8 + 7 are found also. Editors disagree about the extent to which copyists' errors and adjustments have affected the original, but it seems safe to assume that the poet allowed himself liberty and echoed at times the rhythms of speech or the structure of the widely-used octosyllable (to him, a half-line) of lyric and perhaps early ballad. No purpose is served by the rigid regularization, with numerous textual adjustments, imposed by one recent editor. The poet's handling of *cuaderna vía*, generally a very staid and, to the modern ear, rather dull metre, is masterly. He often makes it vivid, even sprightly, a good vehicle for both narrative and direct speech, and he achieves fine effects of balance and contrast. Since large portions of the work were designed for recitation to a listening audience, no doubt with some dramatization, we can appreciate that general liveliness and aural qualities were much in the poet's mind as he wrote. .

Even after the probable loss of poems and songs mentioned above, enough remains for us to appreciate the wide variety of lyric measures which Ruiz commanded. For example, two lyrics to the Virgin near the start show in their light, tripping, and almost immediately *cantabile* quality, all the charm, warmth of sentiment, and technical elegance that one could expect of the best lyric poets of the Middle Ages. These opening lyrics, 'Joys of St Mary' (20–43), occupy their rightful place and are announced in an introductory stanza. Sometimes the link between narrative and lyric is even closer, since each of the four encounters with the mountain-girls is first narrated in *cuaderna vía* and then expressed in lyric form (950–1042), in a double vision of each episode.

The *Book* has a structure that can be described as agreeably meandering rather than strictly linear. A synopsis by sections, even though arbitrary, may be helpful:

1–70: preliminaries: prefatory prayers, prose sermon, purpose of the poem, lyrics to the Virgin, story of the Greeks and Romans (44–70 in anthology in this volume).

71–180: first love-affair, a burlesque song (105–21 in anthology); fables; discussion of astrology, with the tale of King Alcaraz.

181–891: art of Love: instruction for the apprentice lover, followed by a dramatized example of theory put into practice. The allegorical figure of Sir Love (Don Amor) appears and is attacked by the poet for the evil he does (fables, the Seven Sins, a parody of the Canonical Hours); Sir Love replies, instructing the poet (429–48 in anthology); his teaching is reinforced when Lady Venus – wife of Sir Love – visits the poet; finally, the story of Doña Endrina (Lady Sloe) shows the poet applying what he has learned, with the aid of the go-between Trotaconventos (653–9 in anthology).

892–949: mock-serious lecture to the ladies.

950–1042: adventures with the mountain-girls.

1043–66: in an interlude of repentance, the poet composes lyrics to the Virgin and to Christ.

1067–1314: the progress of the Christian year is followed through Lent to Easter. Doña Cuaresma (Lady Lent) with her army of fishes defeats Don Carnal (Fleshly) with his army of meats; Carnal does penance, and the poet inserts a brief treatise on confession; Carnal returns in triumph at Easter, accompanied by Sir Love, their entry into Toledo being greeted by a dancing procession of musical instruments (1225–34 in anthology) and by all the orders of society, among whom the clergy figure prominently; Sir Love sets up his tent, adorned with representations of the seasons.

1315–1519: spring demands new love; the poet, advised by his go-between, begins an affair with the nun Doña Garoça (whose name means 'bride' in Arabic); after a long exchange of fables between the nun and the go-between, the nun accepts the love of the poet but the affair is cut short by her early death (1332–42, 1499–1506 in anthology).

1520–78: the poet's go-between dies, the lament for her involving a general attack on the cruelties of Death.

1579–1605: in repentance, the poet emphasizes Christian virtues and writes a short allegory on the Arms of the Christian.

1606–25: yet the poet draws his work towards a conclusion with two light-hearted episodes, one in praise of Little Women, the other the tale of his errand-boy Don Furón (Ferret).

1626–34: conclusion, on the senses in which the Book is to be taken.

1635–89: lyrics to the Virgin, begging-songs for students and blind men.

1690–1709: the Clergy of Talavera.

It can be seen that the *Book* contains a great variety of materials and tones. Critics have debated the degree of unity which the poet sought to impose upon his disparate elements, and his success in achieving it; but they have often considered the matter improperly, from a modern viewpoint in which logicality of linear structure is valued, rather than from a medieval one in which rich diversity of incident, not wholly subservient to the main theme, was often to be expected, and in which description for its own sake and digression were enjoined as valued rhetorical features. Ingenuous critics have been unaware of the great tradition of 'medieval laughter', and have not reckoned with Ruiz's sudden shifts of tone and sly, subversive ambivalence. What disconcerts the modern reader would not have surprised the medieval one, and what we read on the page has to be assessed in terms of the impact it would have made when offered by a talented presenter to a listening public.

Several features do, however, argue against the *Book* as a fully coherent whole. Poets are usually such all their adult lives, but the *Book* is all we have of Ruiz's work. It may be assumed that, when given leisure (in prison?), he sent for his papers, devised a theme and a structure, and fitted into these much of what he had available, adding a good deal. It is not hard to imagine that he had, perhaps in very early days, composed lyrics to the Virgin, fables adapted from the Aesopic tradition, and perhaps versions of the Art of Love drawn from the Latin *Pamphilus*. That the style of the whole *Book* is unified, assured and mature is certain but may show that earlier materials were rewritten or adjusted at the moment when the *Book* was composed. A second, indisputable feature is that try as he might, Ruiz could not fit into his structure the lyrics of Stanzas 1635–89 nor the episode of the Clergy of Talavera, but since these were too good to waste, he copied them after his formal Conclusion; while the section on Little Women, and that on Don Furón, sit uneasily in their place before the Conclusion. A third factor is that, whereas a central portion of the *Book* follows the rhythm of a year that is both Christian and biological, this structural plan is not extended backwards and forwards to the limits of the *Book*, as may at one moment have been the intention.

Other factors do, however, impose all the unity one can demand. The first is the poet's personality which, although we know so little about the man (in contrast to Chaucer or Boccaccio or, in Spain, Ruiz's contemporary Don Juan Manuel), emerges as a powerful and pervasive one. One must not be misled by the poet's use of 'I' in so many episodes and comments; on the whole there is no genuinely autobiographical or confessional aspect here, and in any case, much of the *Book* is based on literary sources. (There is one episode having no known source, but possessing a fierce dramatic intensity, in which one may guess that the poet appears in a truly autobiographical role: the final stanzas about Doña Garoça, 1498–1506.) The poet's technique is at times like that of the modern comedian who recounts age-old stories as though he were the protagonist, 'A funny thing happened to me ...'; or it involves a process defined by Lecoy – 'The poet has given himself a role in his comedy, and naturally, the most attractive one.' This role involves by turns the narrative poet, active protagonist, and moral commentator, in a complementary rather than contrasting way. Another factor is Ruiz's plainly-stated artistic aim: to give a lesson in the craft of literature, in the widest possible sense: conception, language, range of metrical techniques, rhetoric, handling of received material, and so on. The one thing about which Ruiz is entirely serious is his craft or art.

The *Book* is a tapestry of threads drawn from many traditions, mostly learned, and its basic materials are typical of the Europe of the day rather than idiosyncratic; but the poet has a powerfully original way of handling them. Within Spain, his work is a deep breath of fresh air, for he seems to have brought a revolutionary new sensibility and tone after a long period of earnest didacticism. The poet imaginatively re-creates his received materials, adding to them notes of local colour and personal observation and expressing them all in his vivid, racy Spanish rich in concrete details. Thus the *fabliau* of Pitas Payas (474–89) acquires new life and conveys unexpected lessons, even though the story had been current for perhaps two centuries, and Doña Endrina, metamorphosed from the delicate Galatea of the *Pamphilus*, steps as a wholly Spanish woman into the glaring light of the square of a small Castilian town (653). The Aesopic fables and similar tales and *exempla* are presented in lively fashion and placed within the progress of the arguments. Ruiz modelled his allegorical battle of Lent on a French text, but surpassed this in detail and in verve. The Clergy of Talavera partially echo the English clergy of the *Consultatio sacerdotum* attributed to Walter Map, but in the poet's vernacular acquire special tones of pained indignation and oily hypocrisy. The poet has a devastating way with respected *auctoritates*: he begins stanza 71 in mock-pompous lecturing style, 'As Aristotle says – and it is true ...', but goes on to subvert whatever sound biological doctrine he had found in the Sage, while in 105–6 the words of Solomon about Vanity are amusingly distorted by semantic sleight-of-hand. There are parodies of epic style, of legal pomposity, etc. In moments of devotion Ruiz composes his charming lyrics to the Virgin, and pens his entirely serious reflections on the Seven Sins (twice) and the Arms of the Christian, and in his treatise on confession even takes up a question then exercising the Sorbonne. But he places himself within the Goliardic tradition when applying phrases from the Canonical Hours not only amusingly but also obscenely to the conduct of a love-affair, and cheerfully adapts liturgical Latin (*Te, Amorem, laudamus* ...) to celebrate the explosion of amorous feelings in springtime. The sources and traditions are explored by Lecoy (1938); others have added details since.

Parts of the poet's text may have meant more in the context of the mid fourteenth century than they do to us, in the sense that much has doubtless been lost from the literary record of the time. The *serranillas* (poems about the *serranas*, mountain-girls) are inversions or parodies, and concern amusingly 'sick' sex instead of idyllic rustic encounters. One may assume that serious *serranillas* existed in Castilian (or it would hardly have occurred to Ruiz to pervert the genre), but we have no record of them at the time.

At times it has been held that the *Book* is a devout, even devotional work, rich in spiritual values; that beneath its amusing exterior is a solid doctrinal core, even that it is a general allegory to be read in Christian terms. On this view, the attacks on church abuses and descriptions of the loose-living of clergy and nuns, indeed the attack by the poet on Love as a dangerous delusion and the source of all the sins, are to be seen as the work of a severe moralist. The amusing exterior is merely a means of initially attracting a public so that the underlying serious message may be conveyed, and 'Good Love' is 'spiritual Christian love, the love of God'. It is true that Ruiz explains his purpose in terms of that 'deceptive exterior which conceals a message within', in a series of lively images, but it should be noted that this is an amplification of a standard medieval theme, the images being not devoid of humour and irony, and that Ruiz's protestations are perhaps excessive. The point may be that, once the exterior is removed, the interior is hollow and the doctrinal core missing. Since so much of Ruiz's material and comment concerns the deceptive or paradoxical nature of people and the world, and since some of his best moments involve semantic juggling and dextrous transforma-tions, the absence of a doctrinal core can almost be said to be the poet's final, ruefully sincere, offering to the reader.

This is not to deny, of course, that the poet has a serious side to him. He has it in the proportion that most of us have, whether viewed in terms of the psychological and ideological make-up of each individual, or in terms of alternation over a time-scale, be that by the day or following the rhythms of the year. The poet could not be other than a well-informed practising Catholic, and as an archpriest he had special educational advantages and, on occasion, the manner befitting the rank, as when he discusses confession or cites Gratian on canon law. He is not (as was suggested in the last century) any kind of heretic or free-thinker or reformer. What he says about abuses in the Church is direct but only occasionally bitter, as when he condemns the power of money, greedy friars, etc.; but this was common Goliardic form. For the rest, his witty and some-times obscene adaptation of sacred Latin phrases has an air of sophis-ticated, merry intramural joking, and again, had been done all over Europe for two centuries. The same applies to such passages as that on the nuns' rich living, skilled making of electuaries (in part aphro-disiac) and amorous propensities, and that in which the Clergy of

Talavera are lampooned. He moralizes often, but without much conviction, and at times seems to subvert his own messages. At the centre of the poet's faith, untouchable by any humour, utterly human and humane and radiant with light as well, is the figure of the Virgin, to whom Ruiz repeatedly turns in humble repentance when sated and jaded with earthly things. She is the one certainty when so much else is shifting and deceptive.

The opening prose sermon has as its theme *Intellectum tibi dabo*, 'I will give thee understanding', that is, to know right from wrong. Yet this theme is hardly followed through (and the sermon itself is part-parodic and ambivalent). More relevant for what follows is the tale of the Greeks and Romans, in which the sign-language used in the debate leads to hilarious misunderstanding. Much of the *Book* does, indeed, turn on practical illustrations of the difficulty of interpreting what we experience, especially when an element of deceit has been used. The Ovidian Art of Love, supported by illustrations in fables and tales, is precisely of that kind; yet Doña Endrina, deceived in one sense and seduced (the practical outcome of the course of instruction) protests only briefly, for form's sake, and settles down in a permanent union with her lover. Doña Garoça, won over with difficulty and the aid of a procuress, eventually enjoys to the full the affair with the archpriest, who carefully does not allow us to see whether it was platonic or carnal. Deceit in a 'good' cause ('good love'?) is perhaps hardly reprehensible. In any case, can the Church's teaching about woman, the evil temptress, be all that sound? In stanza 109 – insufficiently stressed by critics – the poet states a logical dilemma: 'If God, when he created Man, had thought that Woman was evil, he would not have given her to Man as a companion, nor would He have made her out of him; and if she were not made for good, she would not have emerged so noble.' One recalls the fighting talk from the Wife of Bath on this subject. In this way, the *Book* is a major contribution to the debate on the Woman Question which so occupied literary, legal and theological people in the later Middle Ages. Beyond the general aspect, the poet is a particular case: fascinated by astrology, he concludes a discussion of it by insisting in orthodox fashion on God's ultimate power to alter astrological prediction or predisposition, but remarks of his own case, more ruefully than proudly, that since he was born in the sign of Venus he has been ever inclined to the love of women, which is sufficient reason for the nature of his *Book*. If the poet is not being truly autobiographical here (or anywhere), we can recognize that such a type exists and that love is of central concern to mankind. One's clear impression is that Ruiz was not merely book-learned about women and love; he knew it and them, profoundly, and he let the women have their say while showing a genuine sympathy for them. 'Good love' (*buen amor*) has a considerable semantic range, and critics who have defined it narrowly have not, in the very nature of the matter, succeeded; as noted earlier, there is no indication that Ruiz or his early copyists and readers used it as a title.

The one thing that brooked no ambivalence or joking was Death. On the one hand, the deaths of Garoça and then of Trotaconventos are natural within the narration; they also remind the poet of the inevitability of his own death, and lead to the reflections of 1520–67. On the other hand, Death for the poet seems to have little to do with Judgement or the Grace of God, or with Heaven and Hell, so far as he personally is concerned. As he expresses it, it is simply an ending, a destruction, a stilling of the music and the dance which he has so much enjoyed. When so much of his poem has been a torrent of words and energy and good cheer, Death makes a final bleak paradox which he cannot resolve, and which he cannot wholly palliate by his wry notion that the devoted go-between must be seated in Heaven with the martyrs, or by his brilliant mock-epitaph for her tomb.

In sense and intention, the *Book* is open-ended, addressed differently to each. In the last introductory stanza, the manuscript raises its voice to say precisely this: 'I, this book, am kin to all instruments; well or ill, according as you the reader play me, so will I speak to you.'

EDITIONS

The poem was first printed by T. A. Sánchez in 1790. Modern editions include those of J. Ducamin (1901), J. Cejador (1913), G. Chiarini (1964), M. Criado de Val and E. W. Naylor (1965), J. Corominas (1967). The most accessible to readers is probably that of J. Joset in the Clásicos Castellanos series, Nos 14 and 17, with excellent introduction and full notes. There is a version in modern Spanish verse by M. Brey Mariño (1965). There are three English versions, the best being that of R. S. Willis (1972), with seventy-five pages of introduction and the Spanish text with the English prose paraphrase on facing pages.

GIOVANNI BOCCACCIO: THE *DECAMERON*

ROBIN KIRKPATRICK

Seven years before the outbreak of the Black Death in Florence, described in the prologue to the *Decameron*, Boccaccio (?1313–75) returned to his native Tuscany from Naples where he had spent fourteen years of his adolescence and early manhood. He arrived in Naples at the age of thirteen to join his father, who was a representative of the great Florentine banking house of Bardi. It was intended that Boccaccio should follow his father's profession, and he was also put to the study of canon law. He left Naples in 1341 during a period of crisis in the affairs of the Bardi bank.

Boccaccio never subsequently engaged in business; his career was that of a man of letters and occasional emissary of the Florentine Republic. Yet there is hardly a story in the *Decameron* (1349–51) which does not in some way mirror the highly-developed commercial culture of fourteenth-century Europe. The work has been described as the 'epic of the mercantile life'; and it contains much both in theme and style to justify this designation.[1] Indeed, the most characteristic theme of the *Decameron* is probably that of the conflict between the actions of Fortuna and the resourceful energies of the merchant. For example, the merchant Landolfo (Day II, tale 4) is ruined when the market is suddenly glutted with the goods in which he specializes. He repairs his fortunes by becoming a pirate. And after a time, here, too, ill-luck comes his way; he is shipwrecked. Floating to safety, however, on a piece of wreckage, he discovers that he has in fact been clutching a chest full of precious stones. He sells these shrewdly and retires both from business and piracy upon the proceeds.

The image of Landolfo, tossed by the waves and 'clinging grimly with both hands' to the box of treasure, powerfully expresses the voracious and often amoral instinct for survival which Boccaccio pictures in many other forms in the course of the *Decameron*. Indeed an 'attachment to things' is manifest in the very details of Boccaccio's style, which, in one aspect, is sharply realistic. Even at moments of pathos or high drama, Boccaccio can speak with relish of the qualities of a fabric or golden vessel.

Important, however, as such features are, they do not by any means represent the sum of Boccaccio's achievement and do little to illustrate how sophisticated and diverse an artist Boccaccio was. From first to last, Boccaccio's writings are characterized by an acute, at times even anxious, awareness of literary problems and of the author's own standing in relation to literary and intellectual tradition. It was Naples that first instilled this consciousness.

The Naples in which Boccaccio grew up was under the dominion of the French Angevins, and during the reign of King Robert (d.1343) had become an international centre of learning. The substance of the education which Boccaccio received there would have been medieval in character; Naples under King Robert was well situated in time and place to offer a comprehensive assessment of late medieval thinking. Yet in some respects the intellectual interests of the Neapolitan court foreshadowed those of Renaissance humanism. Thus Boccaccio himself developed, through his studies in the royal library, an interest in pagan myth which led him, while he was writing the *Decameron*, to begin a lengthy commentary on the subject. This is the *Genealogia Deorum* (1350–75), a work which was to enjoy a considerable reputation among Renaissance thinkers influencing even English writers, among them Spenser, Jonson and Milton. At Naples, too, Boccaccio probably came to know the writings of Petrarch. His acquaintance with Petrarch, in the years after the *Decameron*, was a close and personal one. And between them, Petrarch and Boccaccio did much to prepare the way for Italian humanism.

In literary as in intellectual matters, Naples provided an important stimulus. Not only were the classics highly valued, but the city was also open to the influences of Arabic and Near Eastern culture. A number of stories in the *Decameron* are set in the Orient; and, for some, it is possible to discover oriental analogues. However, it is clear that Boccaccio was affected most directly by the remarkable achievements of French and Italian literature in the generations preceding his own. The French tradition of chivalric romance –

though diffused throughout Europe – would naturally have received particular attention at the court of the Angevins, while the native Italian tradition of love-literature – which, in the Tuscan 'dolce stil novo' and supremely in Dante's *Commedia*, had surpassed its French and Provençal progenitors – was a source of pride to the expatriate Florentine community of Naples.[2]

Boccaccio's early writings represent an ambitious response to both the French and the Italian traditions. Three works in particular deserve attention, the *Filostrato* (1335?), the *Filocolo* (?1336–8), and the *Teseida* (?1339–41). All of these are lengthy compositions, and Chaucer was sufficiently impressed by them to use the *Filostrato* as a source for *Troilus and Criseyde*, and the *Teseida* as a source for *The Knight's Tale*. All three, moreover, look forward in some way to the *Decameron*.

The *Filostrato* explores the conventions of courtly love, and in its portrayal of Troilus expresses an interest in the extremes of experience which are generated by a devotion to the code. The same interest appears, in a serious light, in *Dec.* V 9; III 7; X 5 and 6, and comically in IX 1 and 5. Cressida, on the other hand, though described in terms of the 'dolce stil novo' as 'angelic', displays the consequences of a rejection of the code; her motives become ambiguous, but are guided by the pragmatic and self-interested intelligence which characterizes almost all the women in the *Decameron* as, for instance, Ghismonda (IV 1) or the wife of Ricciardo da Chinzica (II 10).

The *Filocolo* – a highly elaborate version of the French *Floire et Blancheflor* – introduces some of the themes essential to the *Decameron*. Love is shown, in the adventures of hero and heroine, to be a form of education in which nature is led to triumph over the obstacles of misfortune and social conventions. If there is any central philosophy in the *Decameron* it is this. In the important Prologue to the Fourth Day Boccaccio justifies his own interest in the 'strength and pleasure of natural affection', while he forcefully illustrates the educative power of love in the V 1.

A significant feature of these early writings is the instinct they show for literary experiment. The *Decameron* itself is remarkable for the great variety of narrative forms and styles which Boccaccio employs, ranging from the romance of Madonna Beritola (II 6), to parables of heroic virtue (X 10), and finally to *fabliaux*, farce, and anecdote. Indeed one of the difficulties in translating Boccaccio is the rendering of the variety of linguistic forms which he employs. His technique involves a sharp ear for vernacular speech as well as a sensitivity, expressed sometimes in the form of parody, for literary convention.

In this regard, Boccaccio's early writings constitute an important apprenticeship. The *Teseida* is a sustained attempt to write an epic on the theme of love and arms, while the *Filostrato* and *Filocolo* – which investigate the narrative possibilities, respectively, of verse and prose – are structurally of considerable interest, showing Boccaccio to be aware of questions concerning authorial attitude and the relation of narrative example to moral discussion. On this last count, the *Filocolo* accurately foreshadows at one point the plan of the *Decameron*, where two love stories which are later retold in the *Decameron* (X 4 and 5) are presented for discussion to an assembled band of young people.

On his return to Florence, Boccaccio's experiments entered a new phase. One remarkable work of this period is the *Elegia di madonna Fiammetta* (?1343–4), which is justifiably described as a 'psychological novel' but which also analyses the functions of literary sensibility and of the imagination. At this time, too, Boccaccio begins to pursue the interest in Dante which was to lead at the end of his life to the *Trattatello in laude di Dante* (?1351–5) and the *Esposizioni sopra la Comedìa* (1373–4). The *Comedia delle Ninfe* (1341–2) and the *Amorosa Visione* (1342), are shot through with verbal reminiscences of Dante's work; both are allegorical in structure, and both speak of visionary love and education. Neither, however, is a slavish imitation. And it is in these works that Boccaccio's language develops, along with a highly lyrical and idealistic mode, a capacity for the representation of urban life and sensuous detail which is one aspect of the prose of the *Decameron*.

When Boccaccio came to write the *Decameron*, he was already a writer of considerable maturity, acutely conscious of intellectual tradition, yet an innovator both in theme and narrative style. The *Decameron* is not a naïve work but the product of this preparation; it is Boccaccio's most striking and most complex literary experiment. For the only time in his career Boccaccio wrote a work which was comic in inspiration and concerned primarily with human beings in their social relationships. And the fact that it is a comic work should not be supposed to detract from its literary standing. To be sure, Boccaccio himself contemplates the suggestion that the *Decameron* was a less than dignified enterprise 'a frittering away of time ... on little tales in the most homely and unassuming style' (Prologue IV). Yet he acknowledged this criticism only to rebut it, adducing the name of Dante – not to mention the lesser lights of the Tuscan school, Guido Cavalcanti and Cino da Pistoia – to justify his labours.

Boccaccio does not pretend in the *Decameron* to the high seriousness of the *Teseida* or of the *De Casibus* (1355–60) – which is an account of the changefulness of the human condition from Adam onwards. Yet his comedy, like all great comedy, is still a highly effective instrument of perception and understanding. One thinks of how, say, in Shakespeare's work, the themes of tragedy can be translated with undiminished if altered force into the modes of comedy and romance; it is worth remembering that Shakespeare drew extensively in the comedies and romances upon the Italian *novella* tradition which derives from Boccaccio.[3] But the very plan of the *Decameron*, beginning as it does with Boccaccio's representation of the plague, makes it clear that the work is by no means an evasion of the issues that Boccaccio treats elsewhere under a more solemn aspect.

Both realistically and symbolically, the image of the plague expresses a profound apprehension of disorder. The symptoms of actual disease are described with a fascinated accuracy: some of the swellings 'in the groin or arm-pit ... were egg-shaped whilst others were roughly the size of the common apple'. Boccaccio can also speak, in the manner of a social historian, of how the plague disrupted the normal processes of Florentine life: the decencies of family life and Christian were omitted; both townspeople and peasants were distracted from their usual economic activities; women were forced to allow men to nurse them and 'this explains why those women who recovered were possibly less chaste in the period that followed'.

At the same time the treatment of the plague is highly literary and rich in symbolic suggestion. The whole piece is written in a grave rhythmic prose – displaying Boccaccio's training in the use of the Latin *cursus* – and its climax is reached with a fine rendering of the elegiac topos 'ubi sunt':

Ah, how great a number of splendid palaces, fine houses, and noble dwellings, once filled with retainers, with lords and with ladies, were bereft of all who had lived there down to the tiniest child.

The sense, in such a passage, is of civilization in peril and of history rent by apparently irreparable divisions.

Yet the plan of *Decameron* also provides a balance to the evocation of disorder. The ten young people of the *brigata* (company, party), who withdraw from the stricken city to the healthy countryside, illustrate the possibilities of renewal and continuity; their pursuits are marked by a ceremonious appetite for order and a happy expression of natural instinct in song and dance, while the stories they tell witness to their continuing fascination with the variety of urban life, and many, too, are concerned to celebrate the great culture of the generations preceding the Black Death, as in the case of those which deal with Giotto, Guido Cavalcanti and Can Grande della Scala (VI 5 and 9; I 7).

In the *brigata* – who are to return to Florence when danger is past – the essential life of society is maintained and enhanced. And one may reasonably see in the sequence of stories they tell an educative or moral progression preparing for their return. In the Proem, Boccaccio himself echoing both the *Inferno* and the *Purgatorio*, speaks of how the 'grim beginning of the work' is like a 'steep and rugged hill' which has to be faced if one is finally to arrive at 'the beautiful and delectable plain'. The stories, too, begin with a picture of absolute wickedness in the form of Cepperello and, progressing through as many tales as there are cantos in the *Commedia*, end with the story of Griselda, whose perfect virtue sufficiently impressed Petrarch for him to turn the account into Latin. There is, however, at least one feature of Boccaccio's scheme which appears at first view to undermine any claim one might make for its moral force. This is the youngest member of the *brigata*, Dioneo, a name which Boccaccio elsewhere aptly derives from 'Dionysus', who operates throughout the work as a principle of licensed disorder or anarchy. Nine of the stories which Dioneo tells are designedly ribald (as for instance IX 10).* Yet it is Dioneo who tells the story of Griselda. Nor could one say that he has recanted or been stricken by remorse for his earlier offerings.

---

* See anthology, p. 536.

The presence of Dioneo, then, casts a certain ambiguity over Boccaccio's moral purpose, but equally suggests that there is a complexity in his view of the human being which cannot be contained by rigid and authoritative principle. And in fact from the more obviously dignified of Boccaccio's characters there issues a pragmatic intelligence which can be tuned to an extremely delicate regulation of need and motive. Pampinea, for instance – who initiates the flight from Florence – does so in a speech which is casuistical but nonetheless grave in tone and implication. She is concerned that the *brigata* should leave Florence with honour 'shunning at all costs the lewd practices of our fellow citizens ... merrymaking as best we may without in any way overstepping the bounds of what is reasonable'. It would indeed be a 'gross error to remain', even an impiety, for it would suggest that their lives 'unlike those of others, are bound to our bodies by such strong chains that we may ignore all those things which have the power to harm them'. It is natural and therefore right 'to sustain, preserve and defend one's own life'.

Comedy is the natural mode in which to register the shifts of a philosophy as labile as this. Narrative, too, may be seen as a resource more appropriate than logic or precept for the assessment and organization of complex experience. And in fact the choice of storytelling as a pastime for the *brigata* is a significant one. Thus Emilia argues that games will be a necessary part of daily life in their retreat. But these games should not be contentious as, for instance, chess would be. The virtue of storytelling is that the activity may 'afford some amusement both to the narrator and to the company at large'.

Few writers have understood more fully than Boccaccio the value of 'ludic' activity. The *brigata* exercise their intelligence in the stories they tell. But many of the characters in the stories themselves are also storytellers, creating fictions for their own advancement or preservation. This is to say that in many cases, too, Boccaccio's characters are liars.[4] But the fictions that even the liars devise often prove to be a source of harmony and order.

A particularly good example of the effects of fiction is the famous story of the Three Rings (I 3). Saladin needs to borrow money from the Jew Melchisidech, who is unwilling to oblige him. To embarrass the moneylender, Saladin invites him to declare whether Christianity, Islam, or Judaism is the true religion, and Melchisidech evades him with a story of three precious rings – one of which is a true heirloom, the other two indistinguishable copies. The story itself is important in suggesting a certain relativity in Boccaccio's view of truth: the three great religions correspond to the three rings; one of them is true, but *which* one remains unknown. The result, however, of the act of storytelling is no less important; Saladin is impressed by the wit and skill of the Jew and refuses to press his claim, while the Jew, moved by Saladin's magnanimity, lends him the sum required. The two become fast friends; storytelling has fostered a bond which annihilates a rooted enmity.

It follows from this that, as we read the *Decameron*, we should not expect the progress of thought or the statement of theme to point to definite conclusions. The members of the *brigata* choose their tales often on grounds of aesthetic variety, and their reactions are marked not only by good sense and moral judgement, but also by irony, sophisticated complaisance, compassion, delight, and above all by a willingness to discuss the contradictory implications of each tale, as they do in the case of the Griselda story, 'some taking one side and some another, some finding fault with one of its details and some commending another'. Nor does Boccaccio maintain a constant attitude even to his major themes. Love is variously a physical matter, an agent of spiritual refinement, and a source equally of pleasure and confusion. Here, too, however, in response to the extremity and increasing complexity of experience which the *Decameron* presents, a poised intelligence and healthiness of response is ensured from point to point by the almost unfailing humour that the stories generate.

In this light, the first story of the first day provides a fitting introduction both thematically and stylistically to the whole *Decameron*. The story is that of the Florentine notary Cepperello, described by the narrator, Panfilo, as 'perhaps the worst man ever born'. Though this judgement might be supposed to mark the 'inferno' from which a moral education proceeds, it is by no means unequivocal. To be sure, Panfilo speaks with considerable gravity of how his story is 'a celebration of the marvellous works of God'. But the weight of his words falls equally upon the details of Cepperello's sinfulness, inviting one to enjoy – some would say aesthetically – the vigour of his acts. The apparently secure judgement which Panfilo passes upon Cepperello is in fact the exuberant climax of a catalogue of sins that registers the conscious and anarchic inventiveness of Cepperello's criminal career; he would have considered it 'a slight upon his honour if one of his legal deeds were discovered to be other than false', and took pleasure in 'stirring up enmity . . . the more calamities that ensued the greater would be his rapture'.

The main action of the narrative concerns the death of Cepperello. The notary has been called to Burgundy, where his character is unknown, to assist his fellow-Florentines in their business affairs. But he falls sick and his associates are terrified that when he makes his last confession the revelation of his nature will ruin their credit. Cepperello, however, undertakes to prevent this, and there follows the great scene between Cepperello and his saintly confessor. In a brilliant parody of holy dying, Cepperello presents himself as a paragon of virtue, confessing with assumed bitterness to sins which only a saint would grieve over; though described by Panfilo as 'a prize glutton and heavy drinker', he admits to drinking water as gluttonously 'as any great bibber of wine', and to craving 'dainty little wild herb salads'. The upshot is that the Burgundians on his death proclaim him a saint.

Even *in extremis* and confronted by the sacramental authority of the Church, Cepperello maintains a perverse integrity, dying as mendaciously as he has lived. And in this respect he is the first of a series of characters who will present an exhilarating challenge to ordinarily accepted norms of behaviour (cf. II 4 and 10; III 1). He is also one of a number of linguistic *virtuosi*, whose stories demonstrate Boccaccio's unformulated but persistent interest in the nature of language. Not only does Cepperello stand against the authority of fact by wholly reinventing his own life, but he does so against a background of authorial emphasis upon such binding forms of language as oaths, promises and confessional statements. Other cases, where other aspects of language are considered, include the story of Cecco, the poet, and Cecco, the liar (IX 4), and that of the great natural orator Cipolla (IX 10).★

The representation of Cepperello, however, is not the only important feature of the first tale. The narrator insists that the story does concern God's providence; and weighed against the character-

★ See anthology, pp. 532–5.

istic picture of Cepperello's unfettered intelligence, there is a sense – no less characteristic of the *Decameron* – of the mysteries that govern men's actions and ends. The God of whom Panfilo speaks is a 'hidden God', who may have saved Cepperello at the eleventh hour, and in any case can ensure that honest prayers, even to a false saint, are efficacious. But in Cepperello, too, clear-headed as he seems to be, there are contradictions. For all his devotion to evil, he is impelled to do good, according to his lights, for his fellow-Florentines, and where he has devoted his life to the stirring up of strife, he ends it in such a way as to strengthen the order of religious belief. Nor is it unimportant that the story of Cepperello – for which the *brigata* 'are full of praise' and 'parts of which they had found highly amusing' – should contribute to the well-being of its audience.

The mystery of God is hardly a common theme in the *Decameron*. Yet the second tale of the First Day closely follows from Panfilo's tale, depicting the conversion of Abraham the Jew, who seeing the corruption of the Christian clergy argues that the Church must be supported by the Spirit of God since its own adherents seem determined to destroy it. A more usual expression, however, of Boccaccio's sense of mystery occurs in his depiction of the shifts of Fortune, in his references to the power of magic (VIII 7; IX 10; X 5 and 9), and in his occasional but strong treatment of dreams and visions (IV 5 and 6; V 8; IX 7). Above all, Boccaccio is aware of the mysterious complexity of human motive. This often appears, as in the Cepperello story, in a concern for the levels of intention that hypocrisy can hide. But a whole-hearted devotion to virtue is sometimes shown to produce deeply contradictory consequences, as in the case of Mitridanes (X 3), who while wishing to be thought magnanimous is prepared to murder a man who is more magnanimous than he.

The finest examples of Boccaccio's art are those tales in which the central characters are able to accommodate, as Cepperello largely does, the mysteries that encompass and impel them, and where the author provides, as his comedy is well able to do, a full appreciation of the range of ambiguities which have been brought into play. Two further examples must suffice, the first is the story of Alibech (III 10), the second one of the Calandrino stories.

The young Muslim girl Alibech is eager to become a Christian and 'prompted by nothing more logical than a strong adolescent impulse', seeks out a young hermit 'devout and kindly', who over-whelmed by her beauty, leads her to believe that sexual pleasure is a religious exercise – his own unruly 'devil' must continually be put back into her willing 'hell'. The story is at first view typical of its narrator, the licentious Dioneo, and displays a remarkable anticipa-tion of the notion that religious feelings are a sublimation of sexual impulses. For all that, it is in no way cynical or reductive. The innocence of Alibech remains unimpaired; yet she satisfies the secret and hitherto unawakened demands of her sexual nature while at the same time fulfilling her urgent desire for religion. The reader, of course, does not enjoy a similar innocence; indeed the tale – which is described as 'aptly and cleverly worded' – insists upon his under-standing to the full the comedy of the situation. Yet the comedy promotes a response which will be intelligent, poised and lively.

Calandrino is different both from Cepperello and Alibech, being neither boldly intelligent nor benignly ingenuous. His stupidity is crass and almost totally unsympathetic. Yet his function in the *Decameron* is a subtle one. No other figure appears in as many tales as Calandrino does (VIII 3 and 6; IX 3 and 5). And in part he offers a recurrent contrast to the wit and refined emotion of the *brigata* themselves. Thus the *brigata* recognize that 'anything we may say about him is bound to enhance the gaiety of our proceedings', and it becomes something of a ritual to speak of him. Yet the humour is not in essence mocking. For Calandrino, stupid as undoubtedly he is, offers to the intelligent eye a comprehensive image of the human predicament; he is the victim of continual ruses, initiated generally by his companions Bruno and Buffalmacco, and he is the victim, too, of his own nature, which is blindly alive to all the worst and best impulses of the human psyche, being dominated, in turn, by greed and love, by violence and ambition.

In this regard, the story of Calandrino's quest for the heliotrope (VIII 3) is a particularly important one. Calandrino is led to believe that the magical heliotrope, which will make men invisible, is to be found in the Mugnone. He sees at once the possibility of becoming rich; 'all we have to do is to put it in our purses and go to the moneychangers ... and help ourselves to as much as we want.' Setting out in search, he loads his pockets with stones, while his companions, pretending that he has chanced upon the heliotrope, begin to act as if he were invisible, pelting him with stones and buffets while Calandrino remains resolutely silent. The scene, and the scenes which follow, are farcical. Yet they also carry a strong imaginative charge; the nature of man in both his materiality, weighed down with valueless rocks, yet desiring the freedom of immaterial existence, is fully expressed in the comedy. The antics of Calandrino, as Boccaccio vividly puts it, can be so strikingly bizarre that 'even a blind man' would take notice of them. And this is the function both of Calandrino and of Boccacio's comedy; to sharpen and enliven the perceptions of the onlooker.

Not all the stories in the *Decameron* are comic in character; and it is a further indication of the richness of the work that they are not. Some have a disturbing, if not tragic cast, as, for instance, the tale of Tancred and Ghismonda (IV 1). Others, though treating of guile and adultery, can maintain an epic dignity of tone, as in the great story of Agilulf and his groom (III 2). There are also instances, comparable to the so-called problem plays of Shakespeare, where the issues that Boccaccio raises seem to evade his power to control them. Such a case, the nadir, indeed, of the *Decameron*, is the profoundly discomforting story of the Scholar and the Lady (VIII 7).* The themes of the tale are among the most characteristic of Boccaccio's minor work and of the tradition to which he belongs, touching, in particular, upon notions of love and education which recall the *Filocolo*, and, by contrast, the central themes of the *stil novo* and the *Commedia*. The tale is also one of the most deliberately organized in the *Decameron*, so that the scholar's revenge for the pains he has suffered on a winter's night is executed in the heat of a summer's day. Yet the pattern here produces no harmony, nor does love sharpen and educate the natural man. On the contrary, the scholar is shown to be the prey of his own inexplicable impulses; having set aside 'all philosophical meditations' he at first 'filled his mind exclusively with thoughts of the lady'. But with equal suddenness his love turns to hate and to an obsession with 'elaborate schemes of revenge'. The freedom of intelligence which characterizes the sanest of Boccaccio's heroes is here shackled and self-confined.

* See anthology, p. 535.

Thus at a crucial moment, seeing the Lady naked, he is prompted to compassion by his natural sexual feelings but 'clinging firmly to his resolve' represses 'all his pity and fleshly desires'. From this point forward the story is concerned with the chilling justification of a revenge which is perverse and which the scholar himself knows to be excessive. This sequence, in which the author himself seems to revel, is marked by constant allusion to the commonplaces of misogynistic literature and foreshadows Boccaccio's later exercise in this form, the *Corbaccio* (c.1355). In the context of the *Decameron*, the tale serves to demonstrate what pressures were contained within Boccaccio's prevailing vision of the free and healthy women to whom he dedicates the collection.

The *Decameron* reflects a period of cultural transition. The dominant themes of the work – Fortune, Love, Nature and Intelligence – had been defined in preceding generations, and Boccaccio's systematic understanding of such notions is illustrated, for instance, in his *Esposizioni sopra la Comedia*. Yet in the *Decameron* his view, say, of Fortune clearly points forward to the Renaissance and especially to Machiavelli. The changes of Fortune call upon the 'virtù' of men – which is to say the active engagement of human potentialities as the occasion demands and regardless of preconception.

Nor is it surprising that Machiavelli's debt to Boccaccio should be most apparent in his comedy *Mandragola*. For while the *Decameron* inspired a whole line of *novella* collections, it also contributed greatly to the development of Renaissance comedy in Italy; and the view of human behaviour which emerges from the work is one which drama is well qualified to deal with. The *Decameron* is not primarily concerned with the inward psychology or the exact differentiation of individuals; there is little here which is comparable to the prologues or epilogues of *The Canterbury Tales*. Boccaccio's pre-eminent interest is in the moment of action, when, by word or deed, the mind and the outer world come to coincide. Thus when Madonna Filippa (VI 7)* is charged with adultery, she is able, in court, to save her own life and to effect an alteration in legal statutes by a pungent and well-timed witticism. It is not difficult to see in her a forebear of Shakespeare's Portia.

* See anthology, p. 531.

NOTES

1. The phrase is Vittore Branca's. His *Boccaccio medievale* (Florence, 1956) and *Giovanni Boccaccio: profilo biografico* (Florence, 1977) provide the best introduction to Boccaccio's life and work.

2. For the Neapolitan period of Boccaccio's career, and in general, see G. Padoan 'Mondo aristocratico e mondo comunale nell'ideologia e nell'arte di Giovanni Boccaccio' in *Il Boccaccio: Le Muse, Il Parnaso e L'Arno* (Florence, 1978).

3. See L. Salingar *Shakespeare and the Traditions of Comedy* (Cambridge, 1974).

4. See G. Almansi *The Writer as Liar: Narrative Technique in the Decameron* (London, 1975).

DAFYDD AP GWILYM AND
CELTIC LITERATURE

PATRICK SIMS-WILLIAMS

The title of this chapter is a challenge. A short essay can hardly begin to do justice to one of the most extensive medieval literatures as well as to one of its most gifted poets. I can do no more than indicate some of the qualities in Dafydd ap Gwilym's poetry that attract me, and mention a few facets of the rest of medieval Celtic literature so as to show his place in literary history.

Dafydd ap Gwilym flourished in the mid fourteenth century. (His dates are not known.) He has sometimes been regarded as the father of later Welsh poetry and the first major exponent of the Modern Welsh language, but these are over-simplifications, even more so than the similar claims that have been made for his younger English contemporary, Chaucer. Dafydd's language, style and subject matter had many links with the past, and that past was a long one; there was no obvious break in the literary tradition in Wales, unlike England, where Anglo-Saxon literature was a closed book to Chaucer, and the external influences on Welsh language and literature, though present, were less far reaching. On the other hand, just as few English poets escaped Chaucer's influence, so few Welsh poets escaped Dafydd's: the *cywydd* metre which was particularly associated with him was almost universally adopted, and his chosen themes were worked and re-worked, often effectively, by fifteenth- and sixteenth-century poets.[1]

Chaucer is celebrated for his narrative poems, not for the 'many a song and many a leccherous lay' mentioned in his *Retraction*. Dafydd's *cywyddau*, on the other hand, are lyric poems to be sung to the harp and never tell a story, unless it be a true or fictitious personal anecdote. In this Dafydd reflects a very different literary tradition: in the Celtic-speaking lands the normal medium for narrative literature was prose, and verse was the medium for personal expression and the public arts of panegyric, elegy and satire.

Dafydd shows an attractive Chaucerian gift for self-mockery in many of his best-known anecdotal poems – his debates with the friar and with the magpie, his account of the girls in Llanbadarn church (near Aberystwyth) who laughed at him ('the pasty-faced flirty boy/with his sister's hair on his head'), his *fabliau*-like tale of a disastrous tryst in a tavern, and a whole series of stories about his amorous exploits being thwarted by briars, mists, peat-bogs, guard-dogs, and so on.[2] Yet Dafydd's humour does not obscure, any more than Chaucer's does, the underlying seriousness of his poetry. Behind his poems of requited and unrequited love, whether idyllic or idealizing, whether streaked by savage jealousy or a profound feeling of betrayal reminiscent of *Troilus and Criseyde*, there runs a sense of the cruel impermanence of the world. This sense, deeply felt and rarely expressed in the obvious medieval transience-commonplaces, also underlies and enriches Dafydd's poems on nature and the seasons. The fame brought by panegyric was the traditional bulwark against the ravages of time in Celtic thought, from the Welsh poem in praise of the northern British Gododdin of the sixth century –

> Three hundred gold-torqued warriors set out;
> defending the land there was slaughter.
> Though they were slain they slew,
> and till the end of the world they will be praised

– to Tadhg the Blind's advice to his sixteenth-century Irish patron –

> If the wealth of the world were assessed
> – this is the sum of what you have heard –
> nothing in the world except praise
> is other than futile.

Dafydd certainly subscribed to the values of eulogy, and to the consolations of Christian belief; but neither informed his sensibility much, nor assuaged his unease.

Dafydd does not show the range of human sympathy that makes Chaucer's literary personality so appealing, at times seeming alienated from the human world. His unforced sympathy with the natural world was a compensation, and perhaps a cause. He was indeed a truly remarkable observer of nature, and I know of no poets to match him in the rest of medieval Europe, except perhaps for ninth-to twelfth-century Ireland. His skill in conjuring up the characteristic sights and sounds of a season through a blend of impressionist generality –

> white mist after the wind
> shielding the middle of a valley

and vivid detail –

> a thrush on fresh treetops
> singing loudly before the rain
> golden-voiced notes on tapestry-green,
> and the cheerful-voiced lark,
> dear grey-cowled bird of clever voice,
> taking harmony to the height of heaven
> in utter exhaustion
> (backwards he climbs
> from the bare field, a trailing prince)[3]

remind one of nothing in English poetry so much as the Keats of the *Ode to Autumn*.

For Dafydd, as for other medieval poets, spring, summer, and winter were the seasons par excellence, and autumn attracted little attention. No one had, so to speak, invented the romantic bitter-sweetness of autumn, 'that season of peculiar and inexhaustible influence on the mind of taste and tenderness, that season which has drawn from every poet, worthy of being read, some attempt at description, or some lines of feeling' (to quote Jane Austen). But there may be a deeper reason: Dafydd portrayed the changing year more or less explicitly as an almost mythic conflict between summer and winter, and while he dwells with loving care on the gradual return of summer through the spring, any similar attention to autumn would lessen the starkness of the contrast between the fullness of summer and the onset of winter, battering and plundering the woods of their leaves, enfeebling or destroying living creatures. (Some of Dafydd's seasonal poetry is translated in the anthology.)

Dafydd's technical skill makes his poetry the delight of the reader and the despair of the translator. His *cywyddau* are in lines of seven syllables, rhyming in couplets, with the rhyming syllables alternately stressed and unstressed. A single rhyme is sometimes extended over a long series of lines, as is the alliteration of the first consonant in each line. (In the virtuoso poems *May* and *Summer*,* *Mai* ('May')

* See anthology, p. 541.

and *haf* ('summer') are the stressed rhyming syllables in all twenty-six couplets of the respective poems.) Every line is decorated by *cynghanedd* (internal alliteration and/or rhyme), which often reinforces the sense. In this couplet of *Summer*, for instance,

> Cnwd da iawn, cnawd dianaf,
> O'r ddaear hen a ddaw'r haf

the alliteration strengthens the almost mythopoeic comparison of the (vegetable) crop (*cnwd*) and (animal or human) flesh (*cnawd*) and association between the old (*hen*) earth (*ddaear*) and the coming (*ddaw*) of summer (*haf*):

> A very good crop, unblemished flesh,
> comes from the old earth in summer.

Dafydd's liking for parenthetical asides to pursue several different trains of thought in tandem, and his use of syntactical and lexical ambiguity, make any single translation of his poems inadequate. An instance of lexical ambiguity occurs in the couplet of *The Mist*,

> Tyrau uchel eu helynt,
> Tylwyth Gwyn, talaith y gwynt

which I translate

> Towers progressing on high,
> Gwyn's folk, the wind's crown.

The first of these metaphors for mist also means 'towers of great turmoil', and the third also means 'the wind's province', or perhaps 'of the wind's province' or '[in] the wind's province'. The multiplicity of meanings adds to the effectiveness of the long string of disparate metaphors for mist that make up the major part of the poem (see anthology). Dafydd uses this technique of spinning out long sequences of comparisons (called *dyfalu*) to great effect, sometimes to praise or dispraise his subject, sometimes in a mere *jeu d'esprit* of the imagination, sometimes to personify the inanimate and anthropomorphize living creatures, sometimes to make us perceive likenesses where none might be expected: a star is 'a consecrated wafer ... the saints' dish', icicles are 'the ice's brittle harrow's teeth, candles ... cold tears, daggers of ice', snow is a 'chaff heap' on high, the wind a 'marvellous man' who comes 'from the sky's pantry without a foot or wing', leaves are 'twigs' 'florins' or 'hair', and the stag is a 'fine tall baron'; while a running metaphor throughout Dafydd's work describes birds as poets, preachers, anchorites, or nuns, and their woods as houses or castles. There is more than whimsy in all this. Dafydd is striving to make us look at the world with fresh eyes, to see unexpected relationships, to see analogies between one relationship and another; the moon is 'the ghosts' sun' because it is to them what the sun is to living things, and they are to living things as the moon is to the sun. Dafydd's *dyfalu* is a kaleidoscope in which fragments of the natural world transform themselves into a myriad of alternative world-views and unborn mythologies.

The fully-developed technique of *dyfalu* which emerged in fourteenth-century Wales was indebted to a variety of influences. These probably included native traditions of flyting, satire and name-calling. (These had counterparts outside Wales; Dafydd's vituperation against the magpie and other birds which decline to help his love-suit, and against the hare, may be compared with the earlier Middle English *Owl and the Nightingale* and with a poem on how to revile the hare in a thirteenth-century Shropshire manuscript.) Yet I think its roots lay in the folk-riddle, in the traditional metaphors of early Celtic poetry (answering to the kennings of the Anglo-Saxons and Norse), such as 'whales' plain' for 'sea', 'ocean's white hair' for 'waves', and in that 'natural magic' of the medieval Celtic storytellers, so admired by Renan and Arnold – the sea as a flowery plain to the sea-god, the woman created from flowers, and so on.[4]

Dafydd travelled widely through Wales, to judge by his poems, but his home was in Cardiganshire and he was probably buried at the Cistercian monastery at Strata Florida. His ancestors, some of whom were also poets, were among the landed upper class (*uchelwyr*) of Dyfed. Several of the family held offices under the English crown, and it is reasonable to suppose that Dafydd, living in the uneasy peace between the fall of the last native prince in 1282 and the Glyn Dŵr rebellion of 1400, found his political loyalties somewhat divided. His uncle was constable of the borough of Newcastle Emlyn, and seems to have been an important influence on Dafydd, who calls him 'a poet and a linguist'. Another relative of the poet was one of the most prominent *uchelwyr*, Sir Rhys ap Gruffudd (d.1342), a strong supporter of Edward III, yet also a patron of Welsh literati such as Einion the Priest (to whom a treatise on Welsh poetry and grammar is attributed) and the poet Iolo Goch. Dafydd must have been well aware of the cultural contrasts of fourteenth-century Wales as he travelled between the traditional rural houses of his *uchelwyr* friends, in what was becoming the hinterland of Aberystwyth, such as Ieuan Llwyd of Glyn Aeron and his son Rhydderch of Parc Rhydderch (near Strata Florida), and the busy borough of Aberystwyth (granted its charter in 1277), with its cosmopolitan Monday market, its port, fairs, and taverns, and its English and Welsh burgesses living under the protection of the castle. Dafydd alludes to this bourgeois world from time to time: the Englishwoman who gave him many-coloured woollen stockings, but not her love, was the wife of an identifiable Aberystwyth burgess, 'Robert le Northern' (probably a wool merchant); and 'Ebowa baghan' ('the little hunchback'), mentioned in the same legal document of 1344 as Robert, was the hated husband of Dafydd's mistress Morfudd, to whom most of his love poems are addressed. Dafydd's poems were doubtless intended more for the rural *uchelwyr*'s ears than the burgesses', and they probably relished his racy use of French and English loan-words and imagery drawn from town life, as when he calls leaves 'florins', or the mist a 'broad web of de luxe cambric / coiled abroad like rope, / a spider's web, French booth's produce'.

As we know from the fictitious elegies which they composed in each other's honour, Dafydd numbered among his friends and rivals many of the poets of Gwynedd and Powys whose *cywyddau* have come down to us. All these poets, Dafydd included, received rewards in the traditional way by composing praise poems for patrons; but it is impossible to tell from their surviving works how important for their livelihood these rewards were, as opposed to the poets' private means or the support that they might gain for aiding their patrons in other ways and for composing non-panegyric poetry. Llywelyn Goch ap Meurig Hen, for example, an *uchelwr* himself, describes his 'office' at the houses of his two patrons (his own nephews) as including reading the Welsh law-books and chronicles with them, satirizing the lower minstrels, and 'likening' his mistress, Lleucu Llwyd,

> to a fair garden's beautiful roses,
> to generous Mary, or to the bright sun.[5]

As this quotation suggests, these poets were far from unselfconscious about their status and craft; and this is borne out by the assurance with which they handled language and metre. The production of Einion the Priest's treatise on poetry and grammar (mentioned above) reflects the self-confidence of the poets, which is in some ways comparable with that of the English Elizabethan poets. The treatise included a large number of examples of metre from modern poetry (including Einion's own), especially from love-poetry. The following anonymous example of an *englyn*[a] metre is probably to be attributed to Llywelyn Goch, in view of the passage quoted above:

> Neither the sun leaping across the air,
> nor the moon is better coloured
> (resplendently shining in dazzling-fair
> fashion) than Lleucu Llwyd.

Dafydd himself probably knew this treatise, for Einion the Priest held land in Cardiganshire and shared some of the same patrons as Dafydd – Angharad, probably the wife of Ieuan Llwyd of Glyn Aeron (see above), is frequently mentioned in the metrical examples; moreover, Dafydd's own poetry shows several echoes of poems quoted in the treatise. Clearly, Dafydd moved in a vigorous and varied literary world, in which the traditional distinction between aristocratic patron and professional poet had been partly broken down by *uchelwyr* who were both patrons and amateur poets themselves. The same was true of fourteenth-century Ireland, where Gerald, third earl of Desmond and Lord Chief Justice, was composing love poetry in Irish. In the Welsh courts amateurs had been composing poetry at least since the twelfth century, when Hywel, prince of Gwynedd, made his poems to girls (*rhieingerddi*) and Cuhelyn Fardd of Dyfed, one of Dafydd's ancestors, was both a patron of poets and a poet (*bardd*).[6]

Dafydd was not so preoccupied with innovation as to be uninterested in earlier Welsh literature. Various allusions in his poems show his knowledge of earlier Welsh prose literature. For instance,

---

a A stanza of four lines, earlier also of three lines.

his description of his native Dyfed as 'Pryderi's land' and 'the country of enchantment', and his references to Gwawl son of Clud and 'Math king of Arfon by the seas of Anglesey' recall the eleventh- or twelfth-century *Four Branches of the Mabinogi*; his description of the lark ascending 'with Cai's peculiar gift' recalls this Arthurian hero's gift in the eleventh-century *Culhwch and Olwen* that 'when he wished he would be as tall as the highest tree in the forest'; and he likens his girl's red cheeks and white forehead to 'the bird's blood after the snowfall' in the tale of the 'warrior of yore', Peredur – a reference to an episode in the twelfth- or thirteenth-century Welsh tale *Peredur* (which is related, in a way still uncertain, to Chrétien de Troyes' *Perceval*):

At the end of the day Peredur came to a valley, and at the end of the valley he came to a hermit's cell. And the hermit welcomed him, and he was there that night. The next morning he arose, and when he came outside a fall of snow had settled during the night, and a wild hawk had killed a duck at the end of the cell. And at the noise of the horse, the hawk flew up and a raven settled on the bird's flesh. What Peredur did was to stand and liken the raven's blackness and the snow's whiteness and the blood's redness to the hair of the woman whom he most loved, which was as black as jet, and her flesh to the whiteness of the snow, and the redness of the blood in the snow to the two red patches in the cheeks of the woman whom he most loved.[7]

More generally, the atmosphere of tales such as *Macsen's Dream* is captured in Dafydd's own dream poem:

> As I was sleeping, lying low,
> in a secret place,
> I saw at the first streak of dawn
> a dream on the brow of morning.
> I could see myself striding
> with my pack of hounds in my hand,
> and descending to a forest
> – a fine estate, no surly peasant's place.
> I was, I thought, loosing
> the hounds to the woods at once.
> I could hear shouts and violent voices
> and many horns and hounds pursuing.
> A white hind above the glades
> I saw, liking the hunt,
> and a pack of hounds tracking
> after her, right on course,

> making for the height over the dense summit,
> and over two ridges and hills,
> and back over the ridgebacks
> on the same course as the hind
> – and she, tamed, coming to me
> for refuge, and I empassioned;
> I awoke, my nostrils bare
> – son of a bed, I was in the hut![8]

Dafydd may have known all these so-called 'Mabinogion' prose tales in manuscript form, since they had all been written down before the fourteenth century, and the White Book of Rhydderch, the earliest extant manuscript to contain them all (along with translations of foreign stories of Charlemagne, Bevis of Hampton, etc.) was copied about 1350 and takes its name from the son of Dafydd's patrons Ieuan Llwyd and Angharad. On the other hand, Dafydd may have known variant versions of the tales which have not come down to us, perhaps oral ones. One notes, for instance, that there is only one bird in his allusion to the *Peredur* story, and that a blackbird (but is this just poetic licence? A blackbird was a standard comparison for a girl's eyebrows in Irish and Welsh); and his reference to Math with two other enchanters shows that he was thinking in the first instance of some version of the Welsh *Triads of the Isle of Britain* (but not that in the White Book of Rhydderch), a compilation listing traditional story material in mnemonic threes for the convenience of poets and others. Again, Cai's 'peculiarities' were probably widely famous: a document of *c*.1200 mentions a mountain-pass called 'Cai's fathom', presumably because he was supposed to have been able to span it with his outstretched arms!

It is in any case clear that Dafydd knew a large number of Welsh stories which do not survive in manuscript at all, or only in fragments, such as the tale of Melwas's abduction of Arthur's wife Gwenhwyfar (the ultimate source of Chrétien's *Lancelot*), and stories which cast the reputedly sixth-century bards Myrddin (Merlin) and Taliesin in the unlikely role of philanderers. Dafydd is also more obviously aware of the nature of Annwfn, the Welsh other-world, than the surviving prose tales. Thither leads the fox's burrow, says Dafydd; 'to escape Winter's wind / I go deep down to Annwfn' says his personified Summer; and mist is produced by its witches. In the *Four Branches of the Mabinogi* Annwfn was ostensibly another land bordering on

Dyfed, but for Dafydd, then, it was a Welsh Hades. Another early Welsh view, in the ninth- or tenth-century *Spoils of Annwfn* in the fourteenth-century Book of Taliesin, sets Annwfn on a magic island far out to sea. (In that poem it is attacked by Arthur, accompanied by Taliesin and others.) We see here the Welsh remains of an ancient Celtic mythology, reflected independently in Irish literature, where the other-world across the sea or within the *síd* (tumulus) often appears. 'Wonderful is that land', says a (ninth-century?) Old Irish text:

> Three trees in fruit are always there, and a pig everlastingly alive, and a roasted pig, and a vessel of marvellous liquor, and never do any of them decrease.[9]

Dafydd is unlikely to have had any direct knowledge of Celtic literatures other than Welsh, because of the linguistic barriers. The dialects of the British branch of the Celtic languages – Welsh, Cornish, and Breton – had been diverging since the sixth century, and one of them – Cumbric, the old language of the Britons of southern Scotland and northern England – was extinct; while the Irish branch, with its Manx and Scottish Gaelic offshoots, had gone its own way since before the beginning of the Christian era, so that there was no notion of a common Celtic linguistic community embracing Britain and Ireland. There was, however, some exchange of literature between the British Celtic languages, mostly before Dafydd's time (notably the Arthurian legend, whose land of origin is still uncertain). Thus the story of Trystan and Esyllt (Tristan and Isolde), to which Dafydd refers, had probably come into Wales from Cornwall by the twelfth century; while the Welsh story of Ysgolan, which Dafydd also knew, must have passed to Brittany at some stage, for modern ballad versions of it have been collected there and help to elucidate the obscure Welsh fragment of the legend which survives in the thirteenth-century Black Book of Carmarthen.[10]

Dafydd has only one allusion to an Irish story, that of Deirdre, and it is a vague one, which shows merely that he knew that she was a tragic heroine. His unawareness of Irish literature was shared by his contemporaries and predecessors. There are, nevertheless, many interesting similarities between Irish and Welsh literature, but they are probably due to remote common Celtic origins, to Latin intermediaries, and to independent use of floating international folktale motifs. The last is the probable explanation of the similarity between the passage of *Peredur* quoted above and the following episode in the ninth-century Irish Deirdre story:

> Once Deirdre's foster-father was skinning a calf on snow outside to cook it for her. She saw a raven drinking the blood on the snow. Then she said: 'Beloved would be the one man on whom those three colours might be – hair like the raven, and a cheek like the blood, and a body like the snow.'[11]

It was indeed a great loss, not only to medieval Welsh literature, but to European literature in general, that Ireland's extensive prose literature of the seventh-century onwards was virtually unknown outside Ireland and Gaelic Scotland. Had the early sagas been known, they would surely have made a lasting impression with their archaic mythology, primitive heroic ethos, savage humour, and their richness of style ranging from the fantastic descriptions of Cú Chulainn in the *Cattle Raid of Cooley* (the *Táin*) –

> He was filled with rage as he wielded the shields and urged on the charioteer and cast sling-stones at the host. As high, as thick, as strong, as powerful and as long as the mast of a great ship was the straight stream of dark blood which rose up from the very top of his head and dissolved into a dark magical mist like the smoke of a palace when a king comes to be waited on in the evening of a winter's day[12]

– to the stark simplicity of the end of the Deirdre story, after her lover's death:

> 'What do you dislike most of what you can see?', said Conchobor [king of Ulster]. 'Why, yourself', she said, 'and Eogan mac Durthacht.' 'You shall spend a year with Eogan then,' said Conchobor. Then he brought her to Eogan. Next day they went to Macha fair. She was behind Eogan in a chariot. She had sworn that she would never see her two men together. 'Well, Deirdre,' said Conchobor, 'you're making a "sheep's eye between two rams" between me and Eogan!' There was a great stone boulder in front of her. She dashed her head against the stone and made fragments of her head so that she died.

The real and acknowledged external influences on Welsh literature were not Irish but Latin and French. In Dafydd's case the affinity of his love poetry with that of the mainstream of western literature – endorsed by his own aside, 'I am an Ovid' – is obvious, though evidence of his direct knowledge of Latin and French poetry is hard to find. He doubtless drew to some extent on popular, sub-literary love poetry, while some of the conventions of his poetry derived from the *rhieingerddi* of the twelfth-century Welsh court poets: for instance, the animal which is sent as a love-messenger, or that imagery of white waves and dawn with which poet after poet had conjured up the insubstantial 'form' or 'image' of their idealized, soft-spoken mistresses.

The root of Dafydd's poetic tradition, however, was the native Welsh tradition of panegyric addressed to patrons. (Even the *rhieingerdd* was an offshoot of this apparently; 'she used to pay gold in return for her praising' says Einion ap Gwalchmai in an early thirteenth-century elegy.) The Celtic custom of bardic praise poetry, attested already by classical authorities, flourished throughout the Middle Ages and beyond in Ireland, Scotland and Wales, often with very similar results. Here, for comparison, is the sixth-century Irish poet Colmán mac Lénéni's praise of his patron Domnall's gift of a sword, and part of Dafydd's praise of *his* patron Ifor:

> Blackbirds beside swans,
>   ounces beside pounds,
> shapes of peasant women
>   beside noble queens,
> kings beside Domnall,
>   humming beside song,
> taper beside candle:
>   any sword beside my sword![13]

> As far as man travels,
> as far the summer sun wheels boldly round,
> as far as wheat is sown,
> and as far as the fair dew falls;
> as far as unclouded eye sees,
> (he is brave), and as far as ear hears,
> as far as Welsh survives,
> and as far as fine seeds grow,
> handsome Ifor of courteous custom
> (long your sword), your praise will be sown.[14]

In Dafydd's day the bards were still resolutely conservative. The great Irish poet Gofraidh Fionn Ó Dálaigh (d.1387) cynically admitted to the Earl of Desmond that 'A sovereignty they never get we promise to the Gaels in our odes; you need not take any notice of this, it is our custom.' The Welsh poets saw themselves as the successors of the sixth-century Cumbric bards Taliesin and Aneirin, whose panegyrics survived in Welsh form both orally and in manuscripts such as the Book of Taliesin and the thirteenth-century Book of Aneirin (which contains the *Gododdin*, quoted above), and earlier ones now lost. Such was the grip of this old northern tradition that Dafydd and his contemporaries still described their (law-abiding) patrons as the scourges of the Northumbrians (the enemies of the Gododdin)!

The strengths and weaknesses of the bardic tradition as Dafydd knew it may be seen by perusing the Hendregadredd Manuscript, which contains bardic panegyrics and elegies (and some *rhieingerddi*) from the twelfth century down to the death of the last Welsh prince in 1282 (about the date of writing), for it was apparently owned by Dafydd's patron Ieuan Llwyd. It is interesting to note in passing that it gives especial prominence to the works of the twelfth-century bard Cynddelw, for that poet's poetry (*berw*) is particularly praised by Dafydd. (The basic meaning of *berw* was 'boiling', 'ferment', a word that well expresses the force of Cynddelw's battle-poetry.)

Reading through the Hendregadredd Manuscript one finds prince after prince described in the conventional imagery of Taliesin and Aneirin, for instance as 'lion' or 'boar'. This can be monotonous; for some lesser poets every patron is a falcon (*gwalch*) and every falcon, for the sake of the rhyme, is 'proud' (*balch*). By the thirteenth century the poets scarcely seem to visualize the old imagery, unless in a purely heraldic manner, as, for instance, on folio 27r where Bleddyn Fardd commemorates the son of the last native prince as 'a tall very valiant brave lion brandishing a shield'. Yet at its best this court poetry has a stately and impressive decorum. A good example is Daniel ab y Llosgwrn Mew's elegy on Owain of Gwynedd (d.1170) on folio 21r:

> Alas for me, God, that the rudder of
> Gwynedd and her people's hope has come to death.
> Alas for me, God, that he will not come again
> into the world, into the world's way of life.
> Dispensing with Owain is a hard task
> for Gwynedd's chieftains and their mead-fed followers.
> He was not a man of double speech;

his law was broken by no one.
A man who used to take full booty from England
and lead off her men captive,
seven warbands falling before him —
   he could not be avoided.
He was a generous man to the poor, to the poets,
he was mighty, he was Wales' doorbolt,
he was stubborn, his shield-boss was battered,
   he was rough-browed in battle.
Bloody of hand, he was a lord,
to hosts an open companion.
Neither friend nor comrade delights me;
it does not please me to remain stateless;
because of one like an anchor in a desolate deep sea
my heart burns in deep thought
as straw is burned by fire.

In the original the measured utterance is reinforced by internal rhyme and alliteration. There is no striking image until the third line from the end, and there was nothing new in that; ten years before, Cynddelw had commemorated Madog of Powys as 'a strong anchor in a desolate deep sea' (folio 46v). The 'desolate sea' (*môr diffeith*) recurs in Cynddelw's *rhieingerdd* for Madog's daughter (folio 49r), 'of the hue of dawn on a desolate sea', and it survived to the time of the last prince, who is praised (folio 86v) as 'the rush of a mighty wind over a desolate sea'. It was, then, a stereotyped expression. (This is confirmed by its occurrence in Old Cornish translating Latin *pelagus*, 'ocean'.) But that is not to say that it was stale or sterile; the traditional nature of the expression helped, as C. S. Lewis has remarked of the Homeric 'wine-dark sea' and 'rosy-fingered dawn', to 'emphasize the unchanging human environment'. As well as emphasizing the unchanging environment, the Celtic bards' conservative diction enabled them to purvey the illusion of a static aristocratic social order with unquestioned heroic values.

Such official panegyric poetry was given pride of place in the secular poetic manuscripts of Dafydd's time, both in Ireland and in Wales, reflecting their patrons' interests. Yet an old, non-eulogistic Irish and Welsh poetry also survived to the late Middle Ages, often rather fortuitously in obscurer parts of the great codices, or as examples in metrical treatises, or in isolated marginalia (this habit is attested from the ninth and tenth centuries onwards in both countries), or (to us) invisibly, emerging in post-medieval paper copies. While some of this poetry (especially the nature poems) appears to be spoken *in propria persona* by anonymous poet-scribes, other poems have an actual or implied prose narrative context and are put into the mouths of characters, typically princes who have fallen from power and lead an exiled, destitute, or deranged existence against an outdoor background.[15] The connection between this 'elegiac' poetry in Ireland and in Wales, and between the latter and Dafydd's poetry, is difficult to trace, owing to the fragmentary way in which it has been preserved. Nevertheless, its affinity with Dafydd's poetry is obvious. (The position is rather as if Chaucer or Gower was able to read the *Ruin* or the *Seafarer*.) A clear example is Dafydd's poem on the ruined house, a well-established elegiac theme in early Welsh.[16] Needless to say, however, Dafydd transforms the old theme by introducing a new image – the girl whom he had embraced in the house, 'and my arm, by simple tricks, under the pretty one's left ear'; this detail was more typical of the boasting-poem genre (for instance, 'I love the coast of Merioneth / where a white arm was my pillow' in a boasting-poem by the prince-poet Hywel, son of Owain of Gwynedd).[17]

The early Celtic poets had a wonderfully unforced sympathy with nature:

> The skilful lark calls.
> One goes out to watch it,
> to see its gaping beak
> above against the cloudy, *ninach*[a] sky.

This early Irish quatrain was preserved in the early fifteenth-century *Leabhar Breac* ('Speckled Book') merely to exemplify the obscure adjective *ninach* in a religious text. One may recall Dafydd's close observation of the lark (above, p. 303). Another quatrain, which survives in a margin of the *Leabhar Breac*, flirts cleverly with anthropomorphism:

> Ah, blackbird, it's fine for you
> wherever your nest is in the thicket;

a A word (adj.) of uncertain meaning.

hermit who does not ring a bell,
    sweet, soft, and peaceful[a] is your note.

Compare, on the one hand, Dafydd's

He would not go, bright sweet-voiced lad,
silver-voiced bird, from the one coppice
with its slender branches (bright and clear
his thoughtful song) any more than an anchorite would[18]

and, on the other hand, for the slightly envious note, his

The wise, unembittered blackbird chortles
in the green grove, a house of polished song.
No marled soil is ploughed for her
(but the seed is fertile), nor does she plough.

In the latter case one can actually pinpoint Dafydd's inspiration in the extant early Welsh poetry, in a stanza quoted as an example of an old *englyn* metre in Einion the Priest's metrical treatise:

The blackbird chortles in a grove.
She does not plough, no one ploughs for her.
No one is happier than she.[19]

Dafydd's deliberate verbal reminiscence of the old *englyn* (which includes the archaic verbal ending of 'chortles') is an interesting acknowledgement of his debt to the early 'unofficial' poetry. Interesting too, in the context of his whole poem (translated in the anthology), is the way in which he uses the half-quotation as a foil to an impersonal account of the human condition, 'like ebbing on the edges of a shore', and to a personal statement about his own deception in love. Like all his most characteristic poems, the poem reflects Dafydd's acute sensitivity to literature and life.

NOTES

  I wish to acknowledge my debt at various places in this chapter to research by Rachel Bromwich, D. J. Bowen, and Daniel Huws.

  The Welsh text of the poems translated in the anthology may be found in *Gwaith Dafydd ap Gwilym*, nos 23, 24, 68 and 76.

  a The adjective *sídamail* is probably used with deliberate ambiguity; it also means 'pertaining to the *síd* (see above, p. 310), other-worldly, fairylike'.

1. See e.g. *A Celtic Miscellany*, transl. K. H. Jackson (Penguin Classics, 1971), nos 26–30, 42.

2. For some of the poems mentioned see *A Celtic Miscellany*, nos 175–8.

3. For translations of the poems from which I quote (in my own translations) see *A Celtic Miscellany*, nos 25 and 177.

4. See my discussion in *Studia Celtica*, 12/13 (1977–8), 83–117. For examples of 'Celtic magic' see *A Celtic Miscellany*, nos 127–40.

5. For a translation of the whole poem see Joseph P. Clancy, *Medieval Welsh Lyrics* (London and New York, 1965), 119–21.

6. For translations of Hywel's poems see Gwyn Williams, *Welsh Poems, Sixth Century to 1600* (London, 1973), nos 11–18. On Cuhelyn see the articles by R. Geraint Gruffydd in *Studia Celtica*, 10/11 (1975–6) and 14/15 (1979–1980).

7. Translations of all the Welsh prose tales mentioned here may be found in the various modern versions of the so-called *Mabinogion*. As elsewhere in this chapter, I make my own translation.

8. For a translation of the whole poem see *Medieval Welsh Lyrics*, 43–4.

9. For this text, in the twelfth-century Book of Leinster, and the *Spoils of Annwfn* see P. Sims-Williams, 'The Evidence for Vernacular Irish Influence on Early Mediaeval Welsh Literature', in *Ireland in Early Mediaeval Europe*, ed. D. Whitelock *et al.* (Cambridge, 1982), 235–57.

10. See respectively: O. J. Padel, 'The Cornish Background of the Tristan Stories', *Cambridge Medieval Celtic Studies*, I (1981), 53–81, and D. Laurent, 'La gwerz de Skolan et la légende de Merlin', *Éthnologie française*, I, parts iii/iv (1971), 19–54.

11. For the whole tale see *A Celtic Miscellany*, no. 7.

12. I quote the translation of Cecile O'Rahilly, *Táin Bó Cúailnge: Recension I* (Dublin, 1976), 187.

13. Ed. R. Thurneysen, *Zeitschrift für celtische Philologie*, 19 (1933), 198.

14. cf. *Medieval Welsh Lyrics*, 27–8. A problem of translation is that the repeated *hyd* means both 'as far as' and 'as long as' (of time); Dafydd plays on this.

15. For examples see *A Celtic Miscellany*, nos 14–15, 22–4, 203, 205–7 and 210.

16. *Medieval Welsh Lyrics*, 104–5. cf. the early Welsh poem on Cynddylan's hall, *A Celtic Miscellany*, no. 203.

17. Hendregadredd MS., folio 120r; Gwyn Williams, no. 11.

18. *Gwaith Dafydd ap Gwilym*, ed. T. Parry, 2nd edn (Cardiff, 1963), no. 120.

19. cf. Matthew 6:26; Luke 12, also St Francis's Sermon to the Birds.

FRANCESCO PETRARCH AND THE
POETRY OF LOVE

PHILIP M. J. McNAIR

Most historians of literature agree that Petrarch has had more influence on the vernacular lyric tradition than any other poet of
the western world; whether this is a good or bad thing is open to
question, but the fact itself is part and parcel of Europe's poetic
heritage. Through his Latin writings in prose and verse – on which
he pinned his hope of lasting fame – he also exerted a paramount
influence on his own and succeeding centuries as a pioneer of
humanism and midwife to the Renaissance; and indeed it was
through his Virgilian epic *Africa* that he first won public acclaim.
But although his Latin works far outweigh his Italian lyrics in bulk
and pretension, it is with his vernacular poetry that we are concerned
in this chapter, for in this realm Petrarch reigns supreme. Who was
he, what did he write in his native tongue, and why did he become
the most imitated of all vernacular poets?

Francesco Petrarca (Petrarchus in Latin, in English Petrarch) was
born at Arezzo in Tuscany in 1304, the son of a notary who, together
with Dante, had been banished from Florence two years before; he
died at Arquà in the Euganean hills near Padua in 1374, two days
short of his God-allotted span of threescore years and ten. Within
that vital framework, three dates stand out with special significance
for the poet and his readers: all three in or around Passion week
and intimately linked with one another. The first is 6 April 1327,
when he saw a girl whom he calls Laura in a church at Avignon
and fell in love with her; the second is 8 April 1341, when he was
crowned poet laureate on the Capitoline Hill in Rome; and the third
is 6 April 1348, when Laura died of the Black Death at Avignon
on the twenty-first anniversary of the day on which she first held
him in thrall. In life and in death, Laura became the dominant theme
of his vernacular verse.

Although by accident of birth an Aretine, the poet owed no

narrow allegiance to any one town, but lived in a dozen different centres of civilization and felt himself to be a citizen of Christendom. His was a life of comparative ease and more than average mobility, in which literature loomed larger than action; indeed it might be said that much of his life was lived vicariously through the written word. The mobility began early: from Incisa in Valdarno his family moved to Pisa in 1311, and to Provence the following year, settling in Carpentras. This was a small town about fifteen miles north-east of Avignon, the city that became the seat of the papacy for practically the whole of Petrarch's lifetime.

The young Francesco's education was about as thorough and liberal as anyone of his generation could enjoy. It was the Tuscan schoolmaster Convenevole da Prato who gave him his first grounding in grammar and rhetoric and so equipped him to take his place in the republic of letters; but his lawyer father intended him for the legal profession, and therefore he read civil law at the University of Montpellier from 1316 to 1320, and for the next six years at the University of Bologna. He would have made a reluctant jurist, however, and when his father died in 1326 the twenty-two-year-old poet (whose Latin elegy on the death of his mother seven years before is his first surviving poem) gave up his legal studies with some relief and returned to Provence to live a carefree life at Avignon. And here it was in the Church of St Claire on Good Friday of the following year that he first set eyes on the object of his love and the inspiration of his most enduring art.

Did Laura really live in flesh and blood? There is no good reason to deny her existence or doubt that Laura was her actual name. Quite who she was in the prosaic world of genealogy we cannot tell for certain, although she is often (and plausibly) identified with Laureta de Noves, wife of Hugues de Sade; but what she became in the realm of poetic imagination is the prime subject of a volume of vernacular verse that is Petrarch's chief title to immortality. For most of the poems in this collection are inspired by her qualities of mind and body, and nearly all of them reflect his perennial love for her in life and death. Like the vernacular poets of Provence and Italy before him, he idealized his love after the manner of *l'amour courtois* until Laura assumed the role and character of an intermediary between earth and heaven, a little more than woman and a little less than the Madonna, yet thoroughly human in her heart. So idealized indeed is the portrait Petrarch paints in words of this daughter of Avignon that, although he describes every feature of her face except her nose, she loses all individuality in the process and becomes to all practical purposes indistinguishable from every other woman loved by every other poet of *fino amore*: a bewitchingly beautiful blonde who remains for ever beyond her lover's embrace.

This volume of verse is known to posterity by a variety of titles. Perhaps the commonest of them is *Canzoniere* (meaning song-book or anthology of odes), but almost equally popular is *Rime*, a word reserved for compositions in the vernacular as distinct from Latin. Less frequently heard, but still current, is *Le rime sparse*, taken from the opening line of the first poem in the book, and sometimes used to distinguish this collection from *le rime disperse*, or *estravaganti*, that comprise the poet's other vernacular lyrics not included here. Petrarch himself referred to it as *Rerum vulgarium fragmenta*, or (to spell the title out in full) *Francisci Petrarche laureati poete rerum vulgarium fragmenta*. In this chapter we shall use the first of these titles and call it *Canzoniere*.

The volume contains 366 poems, one for every day of the leap year; 317 are sonnets (displaying ten different rhyme schemes), 29 *canzoni* or odes, 9 *sestine*, 7 *ballate* and 4 madrigals. The collection is divided into two unequal parts: the first 263 poems are written 'in vita di Madonna Laura', and the remaining 103 'in morte di Madonna Laura', but some editors make the division after poem number 266. Petrarch composed these lyrics over a period of many years, and although he belittled them as *nugellae* (or bagatelles), we know that he went on revising and polishing them until the day before he died. It is thought that the earliest nucleus of this anthology goes back to 1336 or 1337, and that the poet added to it year by year for more than three decades.

At the same time, from about 1340 to the last year of his life, Petrarch was composing and furbishing another sequence of vernacular poems called *Trionfi* which in the century after his death proved more popular than the *Canzoniere* itself. Written in *terza rima* in patent emulation of Dante's *Commedia*, this sequence consists of six imagined triumphal processions – of Love, Chastity, Death, Fame, Time, and Eternity – in the manner of ancient Rome. Laura figures in the Triumph of Chastity, and (as we shall see) her mortality is immortalized in the Triumph of Death. But despite some memorable moments, the sequence has not worn well; it is more erudite than the *Canzoniere*, and suffers from its erudition.

Petrarch began to write poetry in the vernacular about one hundred years after the earliest known lyrics had been written in Italian. During that century, the phases of poetical development had been well marked in four recognizably distinct generations. First came the *scuola poetica siciliana* at the court of Frederick II of Hohenstaufen (1194–1250) where the sonnet made its debut; here also re-appeared the moral tension between the service of God and the quasi-feudal service of the lover's lady that had characterized much of the poetry of Provence and the troubadours, a tug-of-love that had often led the poet to renounce all earthly passion and enter a monastery. Secondly, the love-experience (and the God-experience) had been treated by Guittone d'Arezzo (c.1230–94), who wrote more sophisticated and 'conceited' verse than the Sicilians and who was converted to Christ in middle life. The poet who addressed Guittone as his 'father' was Guido Guinizzelli of Bologna (c.1240–76), the author of an influential programmatic *canzone* which suggested a resolution of that old moral tension: when God will tax him on Judgement Day with having used a blasphemous analogy between his lady and the Almighty, he will justify himself by declaring that his lady bore an angelic semblance as though she had come out from His presence. This resolution opened the way for the poetry of the young Dante and the *dolce stil novo*, that harmonious new style of versifying about love which claimed to excel in immediacy of inspiration: for the creator of *Vita Nuova*, Beatrice was indeed a 'donna angelicata', a Christ-figure who had come down from heaven to earth to lead her lover up from earth to heaven. The surviving member of the stilnovistic brotherhood, and the link-man in the literary lineage between Petrarch and the Sicilians, was Cino da Pistoia (c.1270–1336/7), a friend of Dante's and a mentor to the poet of the *Canzoniere*, who calls him 'l'amoroso messer Cino'.

The three levels of loving described by Andreas Cappellanus in his enigmatic *Tractatus de Amore* are all exemplified in these pre-Petrarchan poets, whose love-experience is varied and in whom no one level necessarily excludes the others. For instance, Guido Caval-canti (*c.*1260–1300) – apart from Dante the most powerful lyric poet before Petrarch in Italy – wrote philosophical poems about *fino amore*, poems about particular love-affairs duly consummated, and pastoral poems about chance encounters with peasant girls in woods that owed more to animal appetite than passion. Petrarch, too, loved on different levels in private life (he fathered natural children by women other than Laura), but in his poetry in general he wrote about love only on the highest of the three levels, *amor purus*. Just once in his *Canzoniere* does a lustful note of *amor mixtus* betray the frustration he felt in the face of Laura's virtue (XXII), but it is the exception that proves the rule.

The *Canzoniere* is the culmination of one poetic tradition and the inspiration of another. By no means all the poems in Part I are directly concerned with Laura, however; it has been calculated that more than a seventh of them owe their inspiration to other subjects, such as contemporary politics or the death of Cino da Pistoia; but Part II is almost entirely devoted to her memory. In a special way the first and last poems of the whole collection stand outside Petrarch's love for Laura and pass judgement on it. The opening sonnet (but certainly not the earliest to be composed) is the poet's preface to his anthology and is addressed to its readers: 'You who in scattered rhymes listen to the sound of those sighs on which I nourished my heart during my first youthful wandering [into sin] when I was in part another man from what I am [now].' It is written from the vantage-point of an ageing man who has learned to see the great love of his life in the context of eternity, and to condemn it: the backward look, all passion spent. His absorbing devotion to Laura was his *primo giovenile errore* that led him astray from the path of God's will and soiled his sensitive conscience. He hopes not only for pardon but also pity from those who know by experience what love is. He has shame and repentance for his past, and has come to the clear acknowledgement that whatever pleases the world is a brief dream – 'che quanto piace al mondo è breve sogno'. (This is a typical Petrarchan sonnet, with well-defined octave and sextet, rhyming ABBA ABBA CDE CDE.)

The final poem of the *Canzoniere* is a confessional ode addressed to the Virgin Mary in which the poet repents once more of his *errore*:

but at last his love for Laura is transcended and sublimated in his love for the Madonna, who is the *vera beatrice*.

Have pity on a lowly contrite heart, for if I am wont to love a frail little mortal clod [i.e. Laura] with such marvellous loyalty, what should I not do for such a noble thing as you? If through the help of your hands, Virgin, I rise again from my very wretched and mean state, I shall purify and consecrate to your name both thoughts and wit and style, my tongue and heart, my tears and sighs. Escort me to the best ford [of a holy death], and graciously accept my changed desires.

(CCCLXVI)

Between these two extreme poems of renunciation range the length and breadth of Petrarch's poetic experience as man and lover. In his third sonnet he remembers how the beautiful eyes of his Donna bound him on the anniversary of Christ's Passion, and few of his readers doubt that he is recalling an actual experience – that on a given day and in a given place he fell in love with a particular woman. But life is mediated through literature, and his teeming mind is formed on Ovid no less than on Augustine: just as the context of his enamourment is Christian, so the content of his passion is predominantly pagan, and early in the *Canzoniere* it comes over to us filtered through myth. The process probably begins with one super-significant word, for like every imaginative lover before and since the poet toys with the name of his Beloved and finds it pregnant with infinite meaning. Laureta–Laura: those suggestive syllables lend themselves to fancy's artifice from the fifth sonnet onwards. Laureta is compounded of reverent praise, Laura is the breeze (*l'aura*), but above all Laura is derived from the laurel (*lauro*) and evokes the Daphne myth as Petrarch knew it from the first book of Ovid's *Metamorphoses*.

The daughter of the river-god Peneus is pursued down the vale of Tempe in Thessaly by Apollo, smitten by her beauty, but at the moment of capture she prays for help to her father, who turns her into a laurel-tree (in Greek, *daphne*) which the frustrated god of poetry claims as his consolation prize with the words: 'Quoniam coniunx mea non potes esse, arbor eris certe ... mea' (Since now you cannot be my spouse, you will assuredly be my tree').

Daphne is Laura: Petrarch pursues her, smitten by her beauty, and she flees before him; but in his heart the love of glory vies with

323

the love of woman, and on being denied the consummation of the one he achieves the fulfilment of the other, and of his hopeless passion forms the victorious poet's wreath. The nymph that will not quench his thirst for love shall quench his thirst for glory; the Laura who will not crown his pursuit with surrender is turned into the laurel that will crown his art with universal recognition in Campidoglio on that triumphant Easter Sunday in 1341.

Laura is Daphne – the fugitive love of woman ever pursued and never won; but because that pursuit is vain it becomes the spur to perennial poetry, and the hand outstretched to seize the lover's prize grasps instead the poet's laurel. Twin passions blaze in Petrarch's breast: love and glory. His love for Laura is his means of glory, for in refusing him herself she is awarding him his crown. Laura is lost, the laurel won.

Laura–Daphne is a recurring motive in Petrarch's imaginative writing, intimately bound up with his artistic consciousness; it is not confined to the *Canzoniere*, but may be found in the first books of his *Africa* composed in 1338. It properly belongs to an early phase of his love for the 'giovene donna sotto un verde lauro' (XXX), and in the poems written after his coronation it sounds a less insistent note: indeed, he came to confess as madness this youthful identification of his lady's name with the 'Parnasia Laurus'.

Although myth furnishes one evocative dimension of meaning to Petrarch's presentation of his passion, in the last analysis Laura is Laura, the charming creature of fourteenth-century Avignon who captured his heart and ravished his senses. It is natural, therefore, that a more fruitful and enduring theme of his *Canzoniere* should be her physical beauty. Here he is tireless in her praise. From her hair of fine gold (*de rigueur* in the poetry of Courtly Love, and modelled on Tristan's Isolde) down to her candid foot she is most lovely and alluring. Her eyes alone inspire three odes, and lyric upon lyric describes her face of hot snow (a typical Petrarchan antithesis), her ebony eyebrows, rose-red lips and pearly teeth, her graceful neck and angelic bosom, her agile arms and slender white hands, her musical voice and enchanting smile, her fervent sighs and crystal tears. It is a beauty human yet divine: 'For certain she was born in Paradise!' he declares, and concludes that 'a celestial spirit, a living sun was what I saw'.

But her beauty is purely conventional, described in generic terms that were already traditional by the time these poems were written and would become hackneyed and commonplace when rehearsed *ad nauseam* by later Petrarchists. Unlike Tasso's Armida on the one hand, her attractions are not sultry and exotic, nor on the other hand do her features rivet the eye of the reader in arresting focus. From the word-picture Petrarch paints of her physical appearance it would be impossible to distinguish his Laura from Dante's Beatrice, Cavalcanti's Giovanna or Cino's Selvaggia. There is no quirk of Nature to brand her individuality upon our sight. A later song-writer could confess to his girl-friend that 'the laugh that wrinkles your nose / touches my foolish heart', but no such idiosyncratic trait emerges from the classical perfection of the lady loved by Petrarch. What he has created in his *Canzoniere* is an identikit portrait of the Beloved to which generations of readers can relate in all times and climes. Whether it is Laura, the Blessed Virgin Mary, or a personified Italy in *Italia mia* that he is hymning, the subject of his praise tends towards the Universal Woman, the Eternal Feminine.

In those poems that describe Laura *in vita* she is seldom seen outside the context of Nature. Apart from that Good Friday when Petrarch first saw her in church, she is usually pictured against an outdoor background of meadows, woods and water. Here the charm of her person enhances the delights of her environment, and the poet blends the two together with consummate skill. In that mini-masterpiece of art and artistry, the *canzone* which begins 'Chiare, fresche e dolci acque', Petrarch savours the occasion when he surprised her bathing – probably in the river Sorgue that flows through Vaucluse, the secluded valley in Provence where he had come to live in 1337:

> Da' be' rami scendea
> (dolce ne la memoria)
> una pioggia di fior' sovra 'l suo grembo;
>   ed ella si sedea
> umile in tanta gloria,
> coverta già de l'amoroso nembo.
>   Qual fior cadea sul lembo,
> qual su le treccie bionde,
> ch'oro forbito e perle
> eran quel dí a vederle;

qual si posava in terra, e qual su l'onde;
qual con un vago errore
girando parea dir: 'Qui regna Amore'.
(CXXVI, 40–52)

(A rain of flowers – sweet in my memory – was coming down from the lovely branches on to her lap, and she was sitting humble in so much glory, already covered by the loving cloud. Some flowers were falling on the hem [of her skirt], some on her blonde tresses, which were burnished gold and pearls to look upon that day; some were coming to rest upon the ground and some upon the water; some turning [in the air] with a charming waywardness were seeming to say: 'Here reigns Love'.)

When absent from the poet, Laura is poignantly recalled by the places her presence had hallowed:

Here she sang sweetly, and here she sat down; here she turned, and here she stayed her step; here with her beautiful eyes she pierced my heart; here she said a word, and here she smiled; here she changed the expression of her face.

(CXII)

Vaucluse is haunted by her memory: 'Wherever I turn my eyes, I find a sweet calm of mind in thinking: "Here struck [the lightning of] her lovely eye"' (CXXV). Such recollection is a commonplace with desolate lovers with which most readers can identify – an age-old balm to aching hearts, and all the more appealing for that. Not only do familiar sights remind Petrarch of his love, but familiar sounds as well:

I seem to hear her when I hear the branches and the breezes and the leaves, and the birds making moan, and the murmuring waters slipping away through the green grass.

(CLXXVI)

And when Laura is absent in the long absence of death, he perceives her everywhere and nowhere, as all Nature conspires to conjure up her presence yet conceal her:

If from a fresh and flowering bank – wherever I may sit and write, thinking of love – there is heard the lamenting of birds, or the green foliage rustling softly in the summer breeze, or the hoarse murmuring of sparkling water, I see and hear and listen to her whom heaven showed to us and earth hides from us . . .

(CCLXXIX)

But whether she is absent or present, Petrarch's longing for Laura is unrequited, his passion unconsummated; therefore one of the constant themes of his *Canzoniere* is the travail of love. To be in love is to be in trouble. Love hurts, yet it is a welcome hurt, a pleasurable pain, and the lover welters in *dolendi voluptas*. This paradoxical state is described with telling antithesis in the sonnet 'Pace non trovo e non ho da far guerra':

Peace I do not find, and have no means to make war; I both fear and hope, I both burn and am a lump of ice; I both fly above the sky and lie upon the ground; I both clasp nothing and embrace all the world. Such a one has me in prison who neither opens to me nor locks [me in], neither keeps me for his own nor looses my fetter; Love both does not kill me and does not free me from my irons; he neither wants me alive nor drags me out of the impasse. I see without eyes, I both have no tongue and cry out, I both desire to perish and ask for help, I both hate myself and love another. I feed on pain, weeping I laugh; death and life I equally dislike. I am in this state, Lady, because of you.

(CXXXIV)

The travail of love is fuelled by the Beloved, but not by her appearance alone; indeed, Petrarch hints that Laura's physical beauty was fading even before her untimely death (which in itself is a cogent argument for her historicity), and the praise of that *bella sembianza* yields in time to an appraisal of her moral worth, for she is lovely not only in what she *seems* but also in what she *does* and what she *is*. Her features are flawless not only in their form but in their function; her exquisite mouth, for instance, is not only an object of fragrance in itself but also an agent of fragrant actions, and 'he who does not know how sweetly she sighs and how sweetly speaks and sweetly laughs does not know how Love heals and how he kills' (CLIX). The least movement of her mortal body wakes celestial echoes and is enshrined in Petrarch's memory, for whether she sits, stands, walks, reclines, or bathes her peerless limbs in water, Laura is the paragon of human perfection, the acme of divine creation. Even when she performs the domestic chore of washing her veil she makes her lover tremble, and the supreme act of dying – not witnessed by the poet but imagined – she accomplishes with transcending grace:

> Pallida no ma piú che neve bianca
> che senza venti in un bel colle fiocchi,
> parea posar come persona stanca:
>   quasi un dolce dormir ne' suo' belli occhi,

sendo lo spirto già da lei diviso,
era quel che morir chiaman gli sciocchi:
morte bella parea nel suo bel viso.
(*Triumphus Mortis*, I, 166–72)

(Not pale, but whiter than snow that downward drifts on a lovely hill when no winds blow, she seemed to repose like someone who is weary; what fools call death was like a sweet sleeping in her beautiful eyes, her spirit being already parted from her. Death appeared beautiful in her beautiful face.)

Petrarch was in Parma when he heard of Laura's death, and the news wrung from him that sublimely tormented *canzone* which begins:

What should I do? What do you advise me, Love? It is high time to die, and I have tarried longer than I would. Madonna is dead, and has with her my heart, and if I wish to follow it I must cut short these guilty years, because I have no hope of ever seeing her here [on earth], and waiting is irksome to me, since through her departure my every joy is turned to weeping, every sweetness of my life is taken away.

(CCLXVIII)

Laura is dead; that beautiful body which so entranced the poet's senses lies mouldering in the grave, yet her spirit is radiant in heaven:

Alas! her fair face that was wont to be a surety among us of heaven and well-being there above is turned to clay; her invisible form is in Paradise, loosed from that veil [of flesh] which here cast shadow on the flower of her years . . .

(CCLXVIII)

She is absent in body but present in spirit – indeed the poet is more conscious of her presence dead than ever he had been when she was living. And so begin the 'rime in morte di Madonna Laura', which contain some of the most deeply satisfying poems in the *Canzoniere*.

Laura is beautiful in life and death, yet her true value is not measured in terms of motion or emotion, let alone fair hair or fairer face, but by the essential integrity of her will. It is natural that to her ardent young suitor she should have appeared cruel, but with advancing age and wisdom he acknowledges that she was only cruel to be kind, and after her death he comes to admire the constant virtue that had resisted the importunity of his advances and feel gratitude for it:

Now I begin to wake up, and I see that she resisted me for my good, and tempered with a sweet and severe look those enflamed youthful desires [of mine]. I thank her for it, and for her lofty counsel, which with her beautiful face and soft disdain made me think of my salvation, though I was burning with love.

(CCLXXXIX)

The poet adds cryptically that he won glory for Laura with his tongue, and she made him virtuous with her forbidding brow – meaning perhaps that when he pleaded for her favours and she rebuffed him, *she* increased in moral stature and *he* learned chastity by that rebuff.

Laura's virtue made Petrarch think of his salvation, though he was burning with love, and in one sense the *Canzoniere* that chronicles a passion born on Good Friday is written in the context of the Cross. But her death on that same calendar day in 1348, and three months later the death of his protector, Cardinal Giovanni Colonna ('Rotta è l'alta colonna e 'l verde lauro', CCLXIX), and the wholesale mortality of those years of pestilence that was believed to have carried away one third of the population of Christendom, turned his thoughts darkly inward on himself and the transitory nature of all creation:

Life flees and does not stay one hour, and death follows behind in great leaps and bounds, and present and past things make war on me, and future things as well . . .

(CCLXXII)

His heart is a battlefield of conflicting remorse, desires and aspirations. Laura comes to comfort him in dreams; she brings him sprigs of palm and laurel, and sits on the edge of his bed; but his grief is inconsolable, and he counters her heavenly compassion with the words:

I do not weep for anything but myself, who have been left in darkness and torment . . .

(CCCLIX)

He is his own source of conflict and despair.

The *Canzoniere* shows Petrarch's powers of self-analysis to be acute and developed with practice. He is a very introspective poet, a love-sick patient for ever taking his own temperature and charting the course of his disease: but that course is circular, like the whirlpool, and there is no progress in its cure. Unlike Dante, who with set purpose strides towards his goal, Laura's lover vacillates in inconclusive eddies, always coming back to the same point of uncertainty and inaction. And the root cause of his disease, the basic reason for his dilemma, can be found in his troubled conscience.

For the chief *dramatis personae* of the *Canzoniere* are three: the Lover, the Beloved, and Conscience – and it is the presence of this third protagonist that suffuses the poetry with such pathos and illuminates it with such psychological insight. To love a fellow-creature to distraction with so desperate a passion is to commit mortal sin; the more the poet loves the lovely thing that is not God the deeper festers his sense of guilt. Conscience ensures that even the Lover's image of the Beloved is in double focus, for there is a fundamental contradiction in Petrarch's cult of Laura that in some measure reflects the ambivalence in the medieval view of woman as a temple built on a cesspit. She is for him both a Beatrice who blazes the trail to heaven and a Medusa who turns his heart to stone. With her comes knowledge of both good and evil, for in the *Canzoniere* that old moral tension between the service of God and the service of the earthly lover returns to haunt the Italian love lyric.

This tension is teased out to exhaustion with merciless self-critical candour in a little prose work that Petrarch wrote in Latin after some crisis of conscience in 1342–3. He called it *Secretum meum* (or *De secreto conflictu curarum mearum*), and it takes the form of a dialogue in three books between Franciscus (who represents Petrarch as poet and lover) and Augustinus (St Augustine of Hippo, who personifies Petrarch's implacable conscience) in the silent presence of Veritas (Truth), who appears as a beautiful woman. Some critics have claimed that the *Secretum* holds the key to the *Canzoniere*, and certainly both these works describe the same moral conflict between duty and desire.

In a nutshell, Augustinus accuses Franciscus of being hindered from serving God by two adamantine chains – his passion for Laura and his desire for glory. If he would return to the path of true virtue (abandoned when he fell in love) he must break off both these damning encumbrances; he must renounce the creature for the Creator. Where has the pursuit of Laura–Daphne led him? Conscience is uncompromising: 'Te in splendidum impulit barathrum' ('It has driven you into a glittering abyss').

From that abyss the poet of the *Canzoniere* cries out in one of his profoundest and most moving odes, which echoes the *Secretum* in its clash between desire and conscience: 'I' vo pensando, e nel penser m'assale' (CCLXIV). It begins on a note of self-pity: hitherto he has wept for love, but now he sheds unaccustomed tears because he senses the approach of death and is fearful for his soul's salvation. Those merciful arms of Jesus (in which he trusts) are still outstretched upon the Cross, but fear grips his heart and he trembles for his moral state. Two thoughts speak within his mind; one is the voice of conscience, and it says: 'Wretch, do you not understand with how much dishonour for you time is passing?' He must renounce his earthly passion while he has yet time, and pluck up every root of the pleasure that can never make him happy. It would be better for his peace of mind if Laura (in whom he so delights) were not yet born. She set his heart ablaze, and if that false heat has lasted many years in waiting for the day of her surrender to his desires (and for his salvation's sake may it never come), now let him look up to a more blessed hope in heaven ...

The other thought is 'dolce et agro' and speaks for worldly glory; it oppresses his heart with desire and feeds it on hope; for fame's sake – *per fama gloriosa et alma* – it is insensitive to whether he freezes or burns, is pale or thin, and if he kills it, it is reborn stronger than before ... But 'that other desire' (his love for Laura) of which he is full seems to overshadow all others born beside it, and the light of those beautiful eyes that gently melts him in its clear heat holds him back with a bridle against which no wit or force avails him. What good is it then to have tarred his little boat all over, since it is held among the rocks by two such knots as desire for glory and love of Laura? And so Petrarch touches the quick of his predicament in the lines:

> Ché mortal cosa amar con tanta fede
> quanto a Dio sol per debito convensi
> piú si disdice a chi piú pregio brama.
> E questo ad alta voce anco richiama
> la ragione sviata dietro ai sensi:
> ma perch' ell' oda e pensi
> tornare, il mal costume oltre la spigne

et agli occhi depigne
quella che sol per farmi morir nacque,
perch' a me troppo et a se stessa piacque.

(99–108)

(For to love a mortal thing with that faith which rightly belongs to God alone is more denied to him who most desires merit. And this [disdain which I feel in my heart] still with a loud voice calls back my reason, which has strayed after my senses; but although it hears and thinks it will return, its bad habit drives it further away, and for my eyes it depicts her who was only born to make me die, because she pleased me and herself too much.)

This searching *canzone* ends with an Ovidian line that sums up the whole conflict of Petrarch's irresolute will, poised between the glory of God and the vanity of this world: *e veggio 'l meglio et al peggior m'appiglio* ('And I see the better and I cling to the worse'). And we may take this as the poet's verdict on himself.

FRANÇOIS RABELAIS:
GARGANTUA AND PANTAGRUEL

PETER BURKE

Rabelais is impossible to summarize, but it may be useful all the same to begin with a brief description of the books associated with his name. In 1532 there appeared for sale at the fair at Lyons a little book entitled *The Terrible Deeds and Acts of Prowess of Pantagruel King of the Dipsodes*, written – so the title-page informs us – by 'the late Master Alcofribas, abstractor of the quintessence'. The book took the form of a biography of the royal giant, narrating his birth, childhood, education at the University of Paris and friendship with an amiable rogue called Panurge. *Pantagruel* apparently sold well and it was soon followed by a sequel dealing with *The Most Fearsome Life of the Great Gargantua* (*c*.1535), attributed to the same Master Alcofribas and dealing in a similar manner with the education of Pantagruel's father Gargantua, again at the University of Paris, before switching to his departure to save his country from invasion by the impetuous King Picrochole, a task in which he finds himself assisted by a character somewhat reminiscent of Friar Tuck, the fighting monk Brother John of the Hashes. More than a decade passed before the publication of a *Third Book of the Heroic Deeds and Sayings of the Good Pantagruel* (1546), attributed this time to 'François Rabelais Doctor of Medicine'. This third book centres on Panurge, his difficulty in making up his mind whether or not to marry, and the experts he consults for advice: a sibyl, a poet, a theologian, a physician, a lawyer, a philosopher, a fool, and so on. By the last chapter he is still undecided, and the *Fourth Book* (1552) deals with the voyage of Pantagruel and Panurge to consult the Oracle of the Holy Bacbuc. The *Fifth Book* (posthumously published, 1564), continues and concludes the voyage. Although this fifth book is ascribed to Rabelais on the title-page, many scholars reject this attribution. Rabelais also published a few minor works, including some almanacs and *La Sciomachie*, a description of a mock-battle and other festivities held in Rome in 1549. However, his reputation rests on the first four books of his 'chronicle'.

Rabelais is generally considered to be a robust, coarse, comic writer; in short, rabelaisian. Like many literary reputations, this one is based on a half-truth. Of course there is a rabelaisian side to Rabelais. A great deal of his humour is vigorously oral, anal or genital. Eating and drinking are among the principal activities of the principal characters in his chronicle, and these activities are described in minute, loving, concrete detail. Gargantua and Pantagruel have the appetites of giants, and Panurge and Friar John, though built to merely human proportions, eat and drink on a heroic scale. They are discriminating, of course; after all, they are Frenchmen. If other sources were lost, a Good Food Guide to sixteenth-century France could be assembled from allusions in Rabelais. Mountains of tripe, ham, smoked ox-tongues, dumplings, cakes and many other good things are consumed in the course of the five books, while rivers of wine flow down the parched throats of the various heroes. Drink is a recurrent motif in the chronicle. Pantagruel derives his name from a comic devil in the mystery plays, who personified thirst and poured salt down the throats of drunkards. His kingdom is that of the 'Dipsodes', the book itself is said to have been composed with the aid of wine (rather than midnight oil), and the audience are addressed as 'most illustrious boozers'. The Oracle of the Holy Bacbuc, like Friar John's breviary, takes the form of a bottle.

After eating and drinking, excretion. Gargantua, pestered by the Parisians, 'pissed on them so fiercely that he drowned 260,418 persons, not counting the women and small children'. His father first recognized Gargantua's 'marvellous intelligence' when, after many experiments, he discovered the perfect arse-wiper (a live goose). The genital theme focuses on Panurge, his magnificent embroidered cod-piece, his exploits with the fine ladies of Paris, and his obsessive fear of being cuckolded himself, a fear which is central to the *Third Book*. After sex, aggression. There is a great deal of literally knockabout humour in Rabelais, as in the description of Friar John's defence of his abbey close against the invading army of King Picrochole:

He beat out the brains of some, broke the arms and legs of others, disjointed the neck-bones, demolished the kidneys, slit the noses, blackened the eyes, smashed the jaws, knocked the teeth down the throats, shattered the shoulder-blades, crushed the shins, dislocated the thigh-bones, and cracked the forearms of yet others ... If one of them climbed into a tree, thinking he would be safe there, Friar John impaled him up the arse with his staff.

(*Gargantua*, 27)

All in good fun, of course.

It will be clear even from a summary as brief as this one has been that Rabelais is indeed rabelaisian. However, he is much else besides. The traditional verdict on Rabelais is misleading only in what it leaves out, but it leaves out a great deal. Among other things, it omits the author's concern with language and with society; his parody and his satire.

Right from the start, Rabelais shows his fascination with words and other forms of communication. On his way to Paris, Pantagruel meets a young scholar who speaks French as if it were Latin. For 'visit the brothels' he says 'invisitate the lupanars', and so on. When the giant, irritated by this 'latinicome redundance', takes him by the throat, the frightened student cries out in broad Limousin.* Some chapters later, when Pantagruel first encounters Panurge, they fail to communicate, although Panurge addresses the giant in twelve different languages, and in any case his ragged and starving appearance speaks his needs louder than any words. Some chapters further on, Pantagruel is asked to judge a lawsuit in which the speeches of both plaintiff and defendant, reproduced verbatim, are fluent nonsense, functioning as a parody of legal argument:

My Lords, do not believe that at the time when the said good woman caught the spoon-bill with birdlime, the better to make the younger son's portion for the record of the sergeant, and when the sheep's pudding took detours round the usurer's purses, there was nothing better to preserve us from the cannibals than to take a rope of onions ...

(*Pantagruel*, 12)

Later still in the same book, Panurge defeats a visiting Englishman in a debate conducted entirely by signs, an episode which mocks the disputations of the philosophers and theologians of Paris by

---

* See anthology, p. 558.

de-familiarizing them, a technique not unlike Brecht's *V-Effekt* or watching television with the sound switched off. Rabelais may also be inviting his readers to reflect on the nature of communication.

Language remains a central theme in later books. In *Gargantua*, the sound is switched on again, and we are treated to another parody of the arguments of the scholastics in 'The harangue delivered by Master Janotus de Bragmardo to Gargantua', to persuade him to return the bells which the giant has removed from Notre Dame. In the third book, there is another mock-oration, an encomium this time, Panurge's praise of borrowing, variations on the theme that it is debt (rather than love, as the neo-platonists asserted), which makes the world go round.* In the next book the problem of communication is raised again in the episode of the frozen words, which Pantagruel and his companions hear thawing out (*Fourth Book*, 55).[1]

Rabelais clearly loves to play with words. His writing is a constant flow – indeed, a torrent – of puns, lists, enigmas, spoonerisms (invented long before Spooner), and so on, an exhibition of verbal fireworks which is enough to make translators despair, though one of them, the seventeenth-century Scot Sir Thomas Urquhart, tried to outdo him in this respect. Rabelais is fascinated by the problem of interpretation, an activity in which his characters are constantly engaged, with greater or less success. An obvious example is Panurge's attempt to 'read' dreams and the fall of the dice in order to discover whether his future wife will make him a cuckold. The reader is forced to share these problems of interpretation, for the prologue to *Gargantua* raises the question of the meaning of the comic chronicle itself. 'The author' declares that his books are not only 'mockery, fooling, and pleasant fictions', but have a deeper meaning, like the marrow in the bone (a traditional image for the hidden spiritual meaning of scripture), or the 'divine wisdom' concealed by the fooling of Socrates, or the precious medicines which were in the sixteenth century sometimes contained in gaily painted boxes covered with grotesques. However, the author of the prologue goes on to undermine his previous point by adding that the commentators have found hidden meanings in Homer and Ovid

---

* See anthology, p. 561.

which are not there at all. So what is he trying to tell us? And is the 'author', Master Alcofribas, speaking for Rabelais anyway? Nothing could be more dangerous than to take the 'I' (or any other character in Rabelais for that matter) as anything other than a mask, a persona. The function of the prologue is surely to make things harder for readers, not easier, to tease them, to make them aware that there are no short cuts, no skeleton keys, and that they will have to take each episode on its own terms.[2]

In some cases the allegory is transparent enough, or at any rate would have been transparent in the early sixteenth century. Around 1535, when *Gargantua* was first published, few readers would have missed the parallel between the arrogant, aggressive, ambitious, tyrannical King Picrochole and the Emperor Charles V, then at war with Francis I of France. Picrochole's rash advisers list the many conquests he will be able to make after defeating Gargantua's father King Grandgousier: 'You will cross the Straits of Seville, and there you will erect two columns, grander than the Columns of Hercules, as a perpetual memorial to your name. This strait shall be called the Picrocholine Sea.' Charles V had taken the Pillars of Hercules as his personal device, together with the motto 'Further' (*Plus Oultre*), and he was believed to be bent on ruling the world.[3]

King Grandgousier, by contrast, and his son Gargantua, and Gargantua's son Pantagruel, who fought and defeated King Anarch, are all ideal princes, as reluctant to make war as Erasmus wished princes to be, though brave and resourceful in battle when forced to fight in self-defence, generous to their defeated enemies, and at all times mindful of God. Before his successful combat with Werewolf and his three hundred giants, Pantagruel prays as follows:

if it should please thee at this hour to come to my aid, since in thee alone is my whole trust and hope, I vow unto thee that in every land where I may have power and authority ... I will cause thy Holy Gospel to be preached purely, simply, and in its entirety.

(*Pantagruel*, 29)

This prayer and a number of other passages raise the problem of the religious attitudes of Rabelais and of the theological message which he may have intended to convey. Different scholars have seen him as an atheist, a deist, and a Protestant, as well as some sort of more or less Erasmian Catholic. He was at various times a Franciscan friar, a Benedictine monk and a secular priest, and he certainly knew his theology, but as in the case of his political views, he preferred to proceed by allusion and implication rather than by explicit statement. He had to think of the censors of the Sorbonne. All the same, Pantagruel sounds like a Lutheran at one point in his career, when he tells a prisoner, 'Place all your hope in God and He will not abandon you.' Panurge is not only a rogue and a man who fears to be cuckolded, he also represents the type of superstitious man mocked by Erasmus, Luther and Calvin. The famous description of the storm at sea shows a terrified Panurge praying vigorously and vowing to make pilgrimages by proxy (a common late medieval custom), but doing nothing practical to help himself or others, in contrast to Pantagruel and Friar John.★ Erasmus had made a similar point, in a dialogue called *The Shipwreck*, about the foolishness of appealing to the saints in emergencies. There is strong antipapal and anticlerical satire in the description of two islands which Pantagruel and Panurge discover on their travels: the Isle of Papimania, where papal decrees are literally worshipped as divine, and the Ringing Isle, with its colourful bird population, 'clerijays, monajays, priest-jays, abbeyjays, bishojays, cardinjays, and the popinjay'.★

If we want to infer the religious attitudes of Rabelais from these and other passages, we must heed at least three warnings. The first is biographical. We must not assume that Rabelais had the same attitudes in the early 1550s, when he was working on the *Fourth Book* (and the *Fifth Book*, if it is his), as in 1532, when Pantagruel made his appearance in public. The second caveat is historical: we must not forget that Rabelais belongs to the period before the Council of Trent (which held its final sessions in 1563) made the split between Catholics and Protestants more definite than it had been earlier. Rabelais knew that this hardening of attitudes was taking place, and slipped an uncomplimentary reference to the Council into his *Fourth Book*. But in his day – he died around 1553 – it had not yet been decreed that the doctrine of justification by faith ('place all your hope in God ...') was incompatible with Catholicism, and the pope's authority had not yet been enlarged. The antipapal satire of the *Fourth Book* is satire from a position which

★ See anthology, p. 562; p. 564.

could as well be 'Gallican' as Protestant; the French or 'Gallican' church claimed to be independent of Rome.

The third caveat to interpreters of the religion of Rabelais is a literary one. We must not assume that because Rabelais is playing with ideas such as justification by faith, or attributes them to some of his characters, he necessarily shares these ideas himself. Nor should we assume that Rabelais is merely playing with ideas; he may be making serious points in a playful manner. It is always dangerous to assume that a text has one clear meaning, but especially so in the case of a writer who was, as we have seen, so acutely conscious of the problematic nature of interpretation. The criticisms of the traditional Church and the interest in new ideas are clear enough, but the rest is doubtful. In outwitting the censor, Rabelais also outwitted posterity. Fortunately, our enjoyment of the book does not depend on having a window into the soul of the author.

This question of the relation of Rabelais to the Reformation has provoked a long and sometimes bitter controversy among scholars. By contrast, his relation to the Renaissance has not often been viewed as problematic, though it should be. The traditional interpretation of Rabelais makes him into an unqualified supporter of Renaissance humanism and an opponent of 'scholasticism', the culture of the medieval universities. He does indeed mock this culture, and in terms which allude to a famous humanist satire on scholastic obscurantism, *The Letters of Obscure Men* (1517). There is no doubt of his admiration for Erasmus, to whom he wrote in 1532 addressing him as his intellectual father and mother. There is no doubt either of his interest in the humanist approach to the studies of law and medicine, with its slogan 'back to the sources'; we know that at the University of Montpellier, Rabelais lectured on the Greek texts of the classical physicians Hippocrates and Galen, physicians who had previously been studied in the west only in inadequate Latin translations. We also know that Rabelais visited Italy three times in the 1530s and 1540s, and that he was acquainted with leading humanists in Ferrara and elsewhere.

However, his text is ambiguous, as usual, as a pair of examples will show. The description of the Abbey of Thélème, which Gargantua built for Friar John, has often been interpreted as a humanist Utopia. However, Thélème is an anti-abbey, a playful turning upside down, or inside out, of the ideals of the medieval monastery. Monks live according to rule, but in Thélème the only rule is the anti-rule, 'Do as you please'. A traditional monastery has to be purified if a woman sets foot in it; Thélème, on the other hand, admits women, but has to be purified if a traditional monk sets foot in it.

Again, Gargantua's letter to his student son Pantagruel has often been taken as one of the classic statements of awareness of the Renaissance in sixteenth-century France. When he was a boy, the giant tells his son,

> the times were not as fit and favourable for learning as they are today ... the times were still dark ... But, thanks be to God, learning has been restored in my age to its former dignity and enlightenment ... I find robbers, hangmen, freebooters, and grooms nowadays more learned than the doctors and preachers were in my time.
>
> (*Pantagruel*, 8)

Like his father, Pantagruel has an enormous appetite for learning. At the University of Paris, he posted up 9,764 propositions (or theses), 'on all subjects, touching in them the most debated points in every science', and he defended them with success against all comers.

Perhaps this is simply the playful expression of an ideal which Rabelais shared wholeheartedly, but the question should at least be raised, whether he is not exercising his remarkable gifts for parody at the expense of the humanists as well as their opponents. Pantagruel's challenge to the University of Paris and his 9,764 theses looks very much like a joke at the expense of the most celebrated of humanists, Giovanni Pico della Mirandola, who had offered to debate 900 theses on a wide variety of topics at Rome in 1487. The reference to the culture of 'robbers, hangmen, freebooters and grooms' surely pokes gentle fun at exaggerated humanist claims for the revival of learning in their own time. Rabelais was sympathetic to humanist ideals, but in the Renaissance Battle of the Books he was not so much a participant as an observer, or at the very least a participant well aware of the weaknesses of his own side.

The reader may well be asking what Rabelais is doing in this volume, given his involvement in the debates over Renaissance and Reformation. A possible answer is to suggest that Rabelais could be a Renaissance man and a supporter of the reform of the Church without ceasing to belong to the Middle Ages, just as the château of Chambord, constructed for Francis I, could be at once a medieval fortress and a Renaissance palace. Born in the early 1490s, Rabelais was still a child when Erasmus began to publish, and he was in his twenties when the controversy over Luther broke out. For Luther's supporters and opponents alike, the world could never be the same again. However, it goes without saying that they were all steeped in late medieval culture. In the case of Rabelais, this is particularly clear. More exactly, he belonged to – or was at least well acquainted with – a number of medieval cultures, or subcultures; notably chivalric culture, clerical culture, and popular culture.

Of these he was least involved with chivalric culture, but he was clearly familiar with the romances in which its values were expressed, romances which, to judge by the number of editions published in the sixteenth century, were still very much in favour with the reading public. Rabelais refers to twenty-five romances of chivalry, including such favourites as *The Four Sons of Aymon, Fierabras, Ogier the Dane*, and *Lancelot of the Lake*. His book is, among other things, an affectionate parody of these romances, which makes giants heroes instead of villains, narrates feats of arms performed by a friar, instead of a knight, and describes the quest for the Bottle, instead of the Grail.

The clerical culture of Rabelais is much more than an acquaintance with matins and choirs, habits and chapters. It is essentially the culture of the late medieval university. Rabelais knows his scholastic philosophy and theology, and expects his readers to share this knowledge, critical as they may be of this approach to truth. To appreciate the speech of Janotus de Bragmardo, for example, one needs to be able to recognize technical terms of philosophy like 'quidditive nature' and 'substantific quality', to regard them as useless, and to recognize that they are being misused by Janotus, a foolish man who does not know his own foolish business. Again, the reader is expected to recognize the names of fifteenth-century Paris university teachers such as Bricot, Major and Tartaret, to whom Rabelais pretends to ascribe books 'On the Art of making Puddings', 'On the Varieties of Soups', and so on, in his mock-catalogue of the books in the library of the monks of St Victor. Given the conservatism of the university, even in the 1530s, these texts would still have needed no gloss.

So far I have given examples of medieval texts which Rabelais knew but which he used simply as material to be parodied. However, medieval culture, especially the culture of students, clerks in minor orders, and junior lawyers, secreted its own parodies, the Gospel according to the Mark of Silver, the mock-genealogy of the pope, the burlesque of the Mass enacted at the Feast of Fools, the mock-lawsuits staged at Carnival, and so on. So the account of 'How the Lords Kissmyarse and Suckfizzle pleaded before Pantagruel without Advocates', and of 'The Genealogy and Antiquity of Gargantua', stand squarely in a medieval comic tradition.

Rabelais is also indebted to the culture of the medieval friars, and notably to that of his old order, the Franciscans. St Francis had told his disciples to be 'jesters of the Lord', and in the fifteenth and early sixteenth centuries, before the Council of Trent put an end to it, some French Franciscans kept up this tradition, notably Maillard and Menot. Olivier Maillard (c.1430–1502), was well known for his dramatic delivery and the crowds he attracted to his sermons. When Rabelais tells us that on one occasion Panurge 'preached as eloquently as the little friar Olivier Maillard', that is praise indeed. As for Michel Menot (c.1450–1518), his sermons were full of animal fables and dramatic elaborations of incidents from the Bible. He was careful to contrast the buffoon, concerned merely to entertain, with the preacher, who made his audience laugh the better to point a moral. However, Rabelais may also have been concerned to point a moral, as we have seen.

The students made their jokes in Latin, but the friars employed the vernacular. Their culture merged into medieval popular culture, on which Rabelais also drew abundantly, as has been shown by the brilliant Russian critic Mikhail Bakhtin.[4] On the comic theatre, for example, such as the celebrated fifteenth-century farce *Maistre Pierre Pathelin*. Pathelin's nonsense-language is echoed by Panurge on his first appearance; indeed, one of the bystanders accuses him of speaking *patelinoys*. Pantagruel derives his name from a devil in a medieval mystery play, while Panurge behaves like one. He was

a mischievous rogue, a cheat, a boozer, a roysterer, and a vagabond, if ever there was one in Paris, but otherwise the best fellow in the world; and he was always perpetrating some trick against the sergeants and the watch.

(*Pantagruel*, 16)

Like his German cousin, Till Eulenspiegel, Panurge is a good example of that ubiquitous figure in oral tradition, the trickster. He is fluent in the language of the professional tricksters of his day, the street-doctors or 'charlatans', who clowned to attract attention before selling their medicines. The eloquence of the 'praise of debts'* is an example of Panurge's spiel. He is also a master of what Bakhtin calls 'the language of the marketplace', abuse.

Rabelais also draws on the medieval popular tradition of the *sermon joyeux*, a mock-sermon which often recommends the audience to drink well and addresses them, as he does in his prologues, as 'most noble boozers'. He refers to the medieval popular tradition of the Land of Cockaigne, where men are hired to sleep, as well as to other forms of the world turned upside down. The *Fourth Book* describes personifications of Lent and Carnival, and much of the 'rabelaisian' Rabelais might equally well be described as 'carnivalesque'.

However, Rabelais does not belong to popular culture. He simply draws inspiration from it and draws on it, rather like a predecessor of his, another university man, 'the Parisian poet Villon', whom Panurge quotes on occasion. In a similar manner he draws on classical and medieval traditions as the fancy takes him, and on occasion plays them off against one another. For this reason it is probably a mistake to try to assign his book to a genre, even a genre as flexible as the late classical 'Menippean Satire'.[5] It is better to regard it as *sui generis*.

It is therefore scarcely surprising to find that posterity (more exactly, a succession of very different posterities) has found Rabelais difficult to assess. He was rejected by the theologians of the Sorbonne, by Calvin and by Voltaire – strange bedfellows. Voltaire found him at once filthy, boring, 'extravagant', and unintelligible. On the other hand, his book was much appreciated by Montaigne and La Fontaine, and in Britain by Nashe, Swift and Sterne, who shared his taste for irony and informality and for combining, or at least juxtaposing, learned and colloquial styles. *Tristram Shandy* could hardly be the book it is if Rabelais had not lived and written. The same is surely true of *Ulysses*. It follows that a generation which relishes the allusive-

---

* See anthology, p. 561.

ness, word-play and parody of Joyce is on the right track for licking
out the 'substantial marrow' of these 'fine and most juicy books' of
Rabelais.

NOTES

1. M. A. Screech, *Rabelais* (London, 1979), is at once the most recent and
the most thorough discussion of this concern with the problem of communication.

2. The ambiguities of the text and the self-consciousness of the author
have been stressed in recent criticism, such as T. Cave, *The Cornucopian Text*
(Oxford, 1979), 99f.

3. It was the second edition of *Gargantua* which introduced these allusions,
at a time when Rabelais was in the service of the French diplomats the Du
Bellays. See Screech, note 1.

4. M. Bakhtin, *Rabelais and his World*, Eng. trans. (Cambridge, Mass.,
1968).

5. The argument that the book is a Menippean satire in the style of the
late classical writer Lucian is presented in D. Coleman, *Rabelais* (Cambridge,
1971), ch. 5.

PART IV

AN ANTHOLOGY
OF MEDIEVAL LITERATURE
IN THE VERNACULAR

The Troubadours

Minnesang

INTRODUCTION

Like its companion volume, this volume on medieval European
literature in the vernacular includes an anthology. The range of
literatures with which this volume deals is very great, and few readers
are likely to have first-hand knowledge of them all or to possess the
texts of more than a selection of the writers and works. This
anthology has been selected by the authors of the earlier chapters,
so that people can read immediately some of the poetry and prose
which their essays have been discussing. In this way the volume
may succeed in its main purpose, which is to reveal something of
the fabulous richness and variety of medieval European literature.

The anthology is, of course, in translation, though some twenty
lines are given in the original for each main entry. The quality of
these translations is mixed: some have been newly made, where
existing translations were inadequate. In many instances the most
faithful and sensitive translations of poems prove to be in prose: but
of course the loss is inevitably enormous. Indeed, it is not possible
to read *Dante* in translation: one can only read Dante-in-translation
(whether verse or prose), with all the crucial loss that that implies.
Nonetheless, this anthology does succeed in conveying a good impression, and a measure of the distinctive feeling, of these great and
living works of literature. And it may send many readers to some,
at least, of the originals.

BORIS FORD

BEOWULF
(Eighth century)

Hwæt, wē gār-dena   in gēardagum,
thēodcyninga   thrym gefrūnon,
hū thā æthelingas   ellen fremedon!
  Oft Scyld Scēfing   sceathena thrēatum,
monegum mǣgthum   meodosetla oftēah,
egsode eorl[as],   syththan ǣrest wearth
fēasceaft funden;   hē thæs frōfre gebād,
wēox under wolcnum   weorthmyndum thah,
oth thæt him æghwylc   ymbsittendra
ofer hronrāde   hȳran scolde,
gomban gyldan;   thæt wæs gōd cyning!
Dǣm eafera wæs   æfter cenned
geong in geardum,   thone God sende
folce tō frōfre;   fyrenthearfe ongeat,
the hīe ǣr drugon   aldor(lē)ase
lange hwīle;   him thæs Līffréa,
Wuldres Wealdend   woroldāre forgeaf,
Bēowulf wæs brēme   – blǣd wīde sprang –
Scyldes eafera   Scedelandum in. (*ll* 1–19)

(The miraculous arrival and departure of Scyld, founder of the dynasty. Grendel, part man, part monster, invades Hrothgar's great house, Heorot. *ll* 1–125)

Attend!
We have heard of the thriving of the throne of Denmark,
how the folk-kings flourished in former days,
how those royal athelings earned that glory.

Was it not Scyld Shefing that shook the halls,
took mead-benches, taught encroaching
foes to fear him – who, found in childhood,
lacked clothing? Yet he lived and prospered,
grew in strength and stature under the heavens

until the clans settled in the sea-coasts neighbouring
over the whale-road all must obey him
and give tribute. He was a good king!

A boy child was afterwards born to Scyld,
a young child in hall-yard, a hope for the people,
sent them by God; the griefs long endured
were not unknown to Him, the harshness of years
without a lord. Therefore the Life-bestowing
Wielder of Glory granted them this blessing.
Through the northern lands the name of Beow,
the son of Scyld, sprang widely.
For in youth an atheling should so use his virtue,
give with a free hand while in his father's house,
that in old age, when enemies gather,
established friends shall stand by him
and serve him gladly. It is by glorious action
that a man comes by honour in any people.

At the hour shaped for him Scyld departed,
the hero crossed into the keeping of his Lord.
They carried him out to the edge of the sea,
his sworn arms-fellows, as he had himself desired them
while he wielded his words, Warden of the Scyldings,
beloved folk-founder; long had he ruled.

A boat with a ringed neck rode in the haven,
icy, out-eager, the atheling's vessel,
and there they laid out their lord and master,
dealer of wound gold, in the waist of the ship,
in majesty by the mast. A mound of treasures
from far countries was fetched aboard her,
and it is said that no boat was ever more bravely fitted out
with the weapons of a warrior, war accoutrement,
swords and body-armour; on his breast were set
treasures and trappings to travel with him
on his far faring into the flood's sway.

This hoard was not less great than the gifts he had had
from those who at the outset had adventured him
over seas, alone, a small child.

High over head they hoisted and fixed
a gold *signum*; gave him to the flood,
let the seas take him, with sour hearts
and mourning mood. Men under heaven's
shifting skies, though skilled in counsel,
cannot say surely who unshipped that cargo.

Then for a long space there lodged in the stronghold
Beowulf the Dane,[a] dear king of his people,
famed among nations – his father had taken
leave of the land – when late was born to him
the lord Healfdene, lifelong the ruler
and war-feared patriarch of the proud Scyldings.
He next fathered four children
that leaped into the world, this leader of armies,
Heorogar and Hrothgar and Halga the Good;
and Ursula, I have heard, who was Onela's queen,
knew the bed's embrace of the Battle-Scylfing.

Then to Hrothgar was granted glory in battle,
mastery of the field; so friends and kinsmen
gladly obeyed him, and his band increased
to a great company. It came into his mind
that he would command the construction
of a huge mead-hall, a house greater
than men on earth ever had heard of,
and share the gifts God had bestowed on him
upon its floor with folk young and old –
apart from public land and the persons of slaves.
Far and wide (as I heard) the work was given out
in many a tribe over middle earth,

---

a Not to be confused with Beowulf the Geat, hero of the poem.

the making of the mead-hall. And, as men reckon,
the day of readiness dawned very soon
for this greatest of houses. Heorot he named it
whose word ruled a wide empire.
He made good his boast, gave out rings,
arm-bands at the banquet. Boldly the hall reared
its arched gables; unkindled the torch-flame
that turned it to ashes. The time was not yet
when the blood-feud should bring out again
sword-hatred in sworn kindred.

It was with pain that the powerful spirit
dwelling in darkness endured that time,
hearing daily the hall filled
with loud amusement; there was the music of the harp,
the clear song of the poet, perfect in his telling
of the remote first making of man's race.
He told how, long ago, the Lord formed Earth,
a plain bright to look on, locked in ocean,
exulting established the sun and the moon
as lights to illumine the land-dwellers
and furnished forth the face of Earth
with limbs and leaves. Life He then granted
to each kind of creature that creeps and moves.

So the company of men led a careless life,
all was well with them: until One began
to encompass evil, an enemy from hell.
Grendel they called this cruel spirit,
the fell and fen his fastness was,
the march his haunt. This unhappy being
had long lived in the land of monsters
since the Creator cast them out
as kindred of Cain. For that killing of Abel
the eternal Lord took vengeance.
There was no joy of that feud: far from mankind
God drove him out for his deed of shame!
From Cain came down all kinds misbegotten

355

– ogres and elves and evil shades –
as also the Giants, who joined in long
wars with God. He gave them their reward.

With the coming of night came Grendel also,
sought the great house and how the Ring-Danes
held their hall when the horn had gone round.
He found in Heorot the force of nobles
slept after supper, sorrow forgotten,
the condition of men. Maddening with rage,
he struck quickly, creature of evil:
grim and greedy, he grasped on their pallets
thirty warriors, and away he was out of there,
thrilled with his catch: he carried off homeward
his glut of slaughter, sought his own halls.

(Having killed Grendel, Beowulf dives to the underwater hall and
fights Grendel's mother. *ll* 1492–520)

After these words the Weather-Geat prince
dived into the Mere – he did not care
to wait for an answer – and the waves closed over
the daring man. It was a day's space almost
before he could glimpse ground at the bottom.

The grim and greedy guardian of the flood,
keeping her hungry hundred-season watch,
discovered at once that one from above,
a human, had sounded the home of the monsters.
She felt for the man and fastened upon him
her terrible hooks; but no harm came thereby
to the hale body within – the harness so ringed him
that she could not drive her dire fingers
through the mesh of the mail-shirt masking his limbs.

When she came to the bottom she bore him to her lair,
the mere-wolf, pinioning the mail-clad prince.

Not all his courage could enable him
to draw his sword; but swarming through the water,
throngs of sea-beasts threw themselves upon him
with ripping tusks to tear his battle-coat,
tormenting monsters. Then the man found
that he was in some enemy hall
where there was no water to weigh upon him
and the power of the flood could not pluck him away,
sheltered by its roof: a shining light he saw,
a bright fire blazing clearly.

It was then that he saw the size of this water-hag,
damned thing of the deep. He dashed out his weapon,
not stinting the stroke, and with such strength and violence
that the circled sword screamed on her head
a strident battle-song. But the stranger saw
his battle-flame refuse to bite
or hurt her at all; the edge failed
its lord in his need. It had lived through many
hand-to-hand conflicts, and carved through the helmets
of fated men. This was the first time
that this rare treasure had betrayed its name.
Determined still, intent on fame,
the nephew of Hygelac renewed his courage.
Furious, the warrior flung it to the ground,
spiral-patterned, precious in its clasps,
stiff and steel-edged; his own strength would suffice him,
the might of his hands. A man must act so
when he means in a fight to frame himself
a long-lasting glory; it is not life he thinks of.

The Geat prince went for Grendel's mother,
seized her by the shoulder – he was not sorry to be fighting –
his mortal foe, and with mounting anger
the man hard in battle hurled her to the ground.
She promptly repaid this present of his
as her ruthless hands reached out for him;
and the strongest of fighting-men stumbled in his weariness,

the firmest of foot-warriors fell to the earth.
She was down on this guest of hers and had drawn her knife,
broad, burnished of edge; for her boy was to be avenged,
her only son. Overspreading his back,
the shirt of mail shielded his life then,
barred the entry to edge and point.
Edgetheow's son would have ended his venture
deep under ground there, the Geat fighter,
had not the battle-shirt then brought him aid,
his war-shirt of steel. And the wise Lord,
the holy God, gave out the victory;
the Ruler of the Heavens rightly settled it
as soon as the Geat regained his feet.

He saw among the armour there the sword to bring him victory,
a Giant-sword from former days: formidable were its edges,
a warrior's admiration. This wonder of its kind
was yet so enormous that no other man
would be equal to bearing it in battle-play
– it was a Giant's forge that had fashioned it so well.
The Scylding champion, shaking with war-rage,
caught it by its rich hilt, and, careless of his life,
brandished its circles, and brought it down in fury
to take her full and fairly across the neck,
breaking the bones; the blade sheared
through the death-doomed flesh. She fell to the ground;
the sword was gory; he was glad at the deed.

Light glowed out and illumined the chamber
with a clearness such as the candle of heaven
sheds in the sky. He scoured the dwelling
in single-minded anger, the servant of Hygelac;
with his weapon high, and, holding to it firmly,
he stalked by the wall. Nor was the steel useless yet
to that man of battle, for he meant soon enough
to settle with Grendel for those stealthy raids
– there had been many of them – he had made on the West-Danes;
far more often than on that first occasion

when he had killed Hrothgar's hearth-companions,
slew them as they slept, and in their sleep ate up
of the folk of Denmark fifteen good men,
carrying off another of them
in foul robbery. The fierce champion
now settled this up with him: he saw where Grendel
lay at rest, limp from the fight;
his life had wasted through the wound he had got
in the battle at Heorot. The body gaped open
as it now suffered the stroke after death
from the hard-swung sword; he had severed the neck.

(Hrothgar congratulates Beowulf on his return to Heorot, but warns
him against too much enjoyment of worldly prosperity. *ll* 1724–84)

                    'It is wonderful to recount
how in his magnanimity the Almighty God
deals out wisdom, dominion and lordship
among mankind. The Master of all things
will sometimes allow to the soul of a man
of well-known kindred to wander in delight:
He will grant him earth's bliss in his own homeland,
the sway of the fortress-city of his people,
and will give him to rule regions of the world,
wide kingdoms: he cannot imagine,
in his unwisdom, that an end will come.

His life of bounty is not blighted by hint
of age or ailment; no evil care
darkens his mind, malice nowhere
bares the sword-edge, but sweetly the world
swings to his will; worse is not looked for.
At last his part of pride within him
waxes and climbs, the watchman of the soul
slumbering the while. That sleep is too deep,
tangled in its cares! Too close is the slayer
who shoots the wicked shaft from his bow!

For all his armour he is unable to protect himself:
the insidious bolt buries in his chest,
the crooked counsels of the accursed one.
What he has so long enjoyed he rejects as too little;
in niggardly anger renounces his lordly
gifts of gilt torques, forgets and misprises
his fore-ordained part, endowed thus by God,
the Master of Glory, with these great bounties.
And ultimately the end must come,
the frail house of flesh must crumble
and fall at its hour. Another then takes
the earl's inheritance; open-handedly
he gives out its treasure, regardless of fear.

    Beloved Beowulf, best of warriors,
resist this deadly taint, take what is better,
your lasting profit. Put away arrogance,
noble fighter! The noon of your strength
shall last for a while now, but in a little time
sickness or a sword will strip it from you:
either enfolding flame or a flood's billow
or a knife-stab or the stoop of a spear
or the ugliness of age; or your eyes' brightness
lessens and grows dim. Death shall soon
have beaten you then, O brave warrior!

    So it is with myself. I swayed the Ring-Danes
for fifty years here, defending them in war
with ash and with edge over the earth's breadth
against many nations; until I numbered at last
not a single adversary beneath the skies' expanse.
But what change of fortune befell me at my hearth
with the coming of Grendel; grief sprang from joy
when the old enemy entered our hall!
Great was the pain that persecution
thrust upon me. Thanks be to God,
the Lord everlasting, that I have lived until this day,
seen out this age of ancient strife

and set my gaze upon this gory head!
But join those who are seated, and rejoice in the feast,
O man clad in victory! We shall divide between us
many treasures when morning comes.'

(Beowulf tells how his grandfather Hrethel died of grief after his
eldest son was accidently killed by his second son. *ll* 2444–71)

    Grief such as this a grey-headed man
might feel if he saw his son in youth
riding the gallows. Let him raise the lament then,
a song of sorrow, while his son hangs there,
a sport for the raven. Remedy is there none
that an age-stricken man may afford him then.
Every morning reminds him again
that his son has gone elsewhere; another son,
an heir in his courts, he cares not to wait for,
now that the first has found his deeds
have come to an end in the constriction of death.
He sorrows to see among his son's dwellings
the wasted wine-hall, the wind's home now,
bereft of all joy. The riders are sleeping,
the heroes in the grave. The harp does not sound,
there is no laughter in the yard as there used to be of old.
He goes then to his couch, keens the lament
for his one son alone there; too large now seem to him
his houses and fields.
                  The Helm of the Geats
sustained a like sorrow for Herebeald
surging in his heart. Hardly could he settle
the feud by imposing a price on the slayer;
no more could he offer actions to that warrior
manifesting hatred; though he held him not dear.

    Hard did this affliction fall upon him:
he renounced man's cheer, chose God's light.
But he left to sons his land and stronghold
at his life's faring-forth — as the fortunate man does.

(Beowulf has died, and the dearly won gold is buried with him in his barrow-tomb. *ll* 3137 *to end*)

The Geat race then reared up for him
a funeral pyre. It was not a petty mound,
but shining mail-coats and shields of war
and helmets hung upon it, as he had desired.
Then the heroes, lamenting, laid out in the middle
their great chief, their cherished lord.
On top of the mound the men then kindled
the biggest of funeral-fires. Black wood-smoke
arose from the blaze, and the roaring of flames
mingled with weeping. The winds lay still
as the heat at the fire's heart consumed
the house of bone. And in heavy mood
they uttered their sorrow at the slaughter of their lord.

A woman of the Geats in grief sang out
the lament for his death. Loudly she sang,
her hair bound up, the burden of her fear
that evil days were destined her
– troops cut down, terror of armies,
bondage, humiliation. Heaven swallowed the smoke.

Then the Storm-Geat nation constructed for him
a stronghold on the headland, so high and broad
that seafarers might see it from afar.
The beacon to that battle-reckless man
they made in ten days. What remained from the fire
they cast a wall around, of workmanship
as fine as their wisest men could frame for it.
They placed in the tomb both the torques and the jewels,
all the magnificence that the men had earlier
taken from the hoard in hostile mood.
They left the earls' wealth in the earth's keeping,
the gold in the dirt. It dwells there yet,
of no more use to men than in ages before.

Then the warriors rode around the barrow,
twelve of them in all, athelings' sons.
They recited a dirge to declare their grief,
spoke of the man, mourned their King.
They praised his manhood and the prowess of his hands,
they raised his name; it is right a man
should be lavish in honouring his lord and friend,
should love him in his heart when the leading-forth
from the house of flesh befalls him at last.

This was the manner of the mourning of the men of the Geats,
sharers in the feast, at the fall of their lord:
they said that he was of all the world's kings
the gentlest of men, and the most gracious,
the kindest to his people, the keenest for fame.

(*Trans.* MICHAEL ALEXANDER)

Τὸν δι' ἡμᾶς σταυρωθέντα   δεῦτε πάντες ὑμνήσωμεν·
  αὐτὸν γὰρ κατεῖδε Μαρία   ἐπὶ ξύλου καὶ ἔλεγεν·
  ⟨Εἰ καὶ σταυρὸν ὑπομένεις,   σὺ ὑπάρχεις
|: ὁ υἱὸς καὶ θεός μου.⟩ :|

Τὸν ἴδιον ἄρνα   ἀμνὰς θεωροῦσα
  πρὸς σφαγὴν ἑλκόμενον   ἠκολούθει ἡ Μαρία   τρυχομένη
  μεθ' ἑτέρων γυναικῶν   ταῦτα βοῶσα·
⟨Ποῦ πορεύῃ, τέκνον;   τίνος χάριν τόν ταχὺν   δρόμον
    τελέεις;
  μὴ ἕτερος γάμος   πάλιν ἔστιν ἐν Κανᾷ,
  κἀκεῖ νυνὶ σπεύδεις,   ἵν' ἐξ ὕδατος αὐτοῖς οἶνον ποιήσῃς;
συνέλθω σοι, τέκνον,   ἢ μείνω σε μᾶλλον;
  δός μοι λόγον, Λόγε,   μή σιγῶν παρέλθῃς με,
  ὁ ἁγνὴν τηρήσας με,
|: ὁ υἱὸς καὶ θεός μου. :|

⟨Οὐκ ἤλπιζον, τέκνον,   ἐν τούτοις ἰδεῖν σε,
  οὐδ' ἐπίστευον ποτέ,   ἕως τούτου τους ἀνόμους   ἐκμανῆναι
  καὶ ἐκτεῖναι ἐπὶ σέ   χεῖρας ἀδίκως·
ἔτι γὰρ τὰ βρέφη   τούτων κράζουσί σοι τὸ   »εὐλογημένος«·
  ἀκμὴν δὲ βαΐων   πεπλησμένη ἡ ὁδὸς
  μηνύει τοῖς πᾶσι   τῶν ἀθέσμων τὰς πρὸς σὲ πανευφημίας.
καὶ νῦν, τίνος χάριν   ἐπράχθη τό χεῖρον;
  γνῶναι θέλω, οἴμοι,   πῶς τὸ φῶς μου σβέννυται,
  πῶς σταυρῷ προσπήγνυται
|: ὁ υἱὸς καὶ θεός μου. :|

ROMANOS THE MELODE
(First half of sixth century)

MARY AT THE CROSS

(The complete *kontakion* has seventeen stanzas. The prose translation
cannot do justice to the elaborate rhythmical structure of the poem,
which is based upon variations on the theme --´----´-.)

Come, let us all celebrate him who was crucified for us: for Mary
looked on him upon the cross and said: 'Though you endure crucifixion, yet you are my son, my God.'

Worn out with grief, Mary, the ewe, seeing her own lamb taken
to the slaughter, followed with the other women and cried: 'Where
are you going, my child? For whose sake are you finishing this swift
race? Is there yet another marriage in Cana, and are you hastening
there now to change the water into wine for them? Shall I go with
you, child, or shall I rather wait for you? Speak to me, O Word;
do not pass me by in silence: for you kept me in my purity, my
son, my God.

'I never thought that I would see you, my child, in such necessity
nor did I ever believe that the lawless would rage so, and unjustly
stretch out their hands against you; for still their infants cry "Hosanna"
to you; still the road is strewn with palm-branches proclaiming to
all how the lawless had sung your praises. And now a worse deed
is done, and for whose sake? Alas; how is my light snuffed out, how
to a cross is nailed my son, my God.

'You are going to unjust slaughter, my child, and no one is suffering
with you. Peter does not go with you, Peter who said to you: "Never
shall I deny you even though I die." Thomas deserted you, Thomas
who cried: "Let us all die with him." The others too, the friends and
companions who were to judge the tribes of Israel, where are they
now? None of them is here; but one, alone, for the sake of them all,
you are dying, my child; because instead of them you have saved all,
because instead of them you have loved all, my son, my God.'

Mary cried thus, from her heavy grief; and as she wailed and wept
in her very deep sorrow, her son turned to her and said: 'Why, mother,
do you weep? Why do you grieve with the other women? Lest I

suffer? Lest I die? How then should I save Adam? Lest I dwell in the tomb? How then should I draw to life those in Hades? And yet, as you know, I am crucified most unjustly. Why do you weep, my mother? Rather cry out thus, that willingly I suffered, your son, your God.

'Put aside your grief, mother, put it aside; mourning is not right for you who have been called the All-favoured. Do not conceal the title in weeping; do not liken yourself, wise maid, to those with no understanding. You are in the centre of my bridal chamber; do not consume your soul as though you were standing outside. Address those within the bridal chamber as your servants; for all, when they rush in terror, will hear you, holy one, when you say: "Where is my son, my God?"

'Do not make the day of my suffering a bitter day; it is for this day that I, the compassionate, (now) descended from heaven as manna, not upon Mount Sinai but in your womb; for within it I was conceived, as David once foretold. Recognize, holy one, the "mountain God delighted to dwell in"; I now exist, I, the Word, who in you became flesh. This day I suffer and this day I save; do not therefore weep, mother. Rather cry out in joy: "Willingly he suffered, my son, my God."'

'See, my child,' she said, 'I wipe the tears from my eyes, though my heart I wear down still more; but my thoughts cannot be silent. Why, offspring, do you say to me: "If I do not die, Adam will not be healed"? And yet, without suffering yourself, you have healed many. You made the leper clean and have felt no pain, for so you willed it. You bound the paralytic together, yet you yourself were not undone. Again, when by your word you gave sight to the blind, you yourself, good one, remained unharmed, my son, my God.

'You raised the dead but did not yourself die, nor, my son and my life, were you laid within the grave. How then can you say: "Unless I suffer Adam will not be healed"? Command, my saviour, and he will rise at once and take up his bed. And even if Adam is covered by a tomb, call him forth, as you called Lazarus from the grave; for all things serve you; you are the creator of all. Why then do you hasten, my child? Do not rush to the slaughter, do not embrace death, my son, my God.'

(*Trans.* C. A. TRYPANIS)

MICHAEL PSELLOS
(1018–96/7)

THEODORA 1042 (Book Five)

(The year is 1042. The emperor Michael V Calaphates has banished his adoptive mother, the ex-empress Zoe, daughter of Constantine VIII, to a monastery in the provinces. The leaders of aristocracy and Church resolve to get rid of the pretentious upstart, and in this they are supported by the dynastic loyalty of the people of Constantinople, who rally in defence of Zoe and her sister Theodora, the last descendants of the Macedonian dynasty. On 20 April there is a popular uprising in the city, Theodora is proclaimed empress, the crowd storms the palace, and Michael flees to the church of Hagia Sophia, accompanied by his only remaining friend, his uncle Constantine the Nobilissimus. Psellos is an eyewitness of what follows.)

... Now the mob that had entered the church gathered in a circle round the two men, like wild beasts longing to devour them, while I was standing by the latticed gate on the right of the altar, lamenting. Both of them saw that I was greatly distressed and not entirely hostile to themselves. They detected in me some signs of moderation. Both therefore converged on me. Changing my manner somewhat, I began with gentle censure of the Nobilissimus. Among other faults I charged him with voluntarily supporting the emperor in his persecution of Zoe. Then I turned to him who had formerly been all-powerful, asking him what possible hurt he could have suffered at the hands of his adopted mother and mistress, that he should add such wrongs to her tragic story. Both answered me. The Nobilissimus denied that he was privy to his nephew's plot against Zoe. He had encouraged him in no other designs. 'If I had wished to restrain him,' he said, 'my reward would have been some calamity. The fellow was so headstrong' – and here he turned to the emperor – 'so headstrong in all his desires and ambitions. Had I been able to check his enthusiasms, the whole of my family would not have been mutilated, a prey to fire and sword.'

I would like to interrupt the history for a moment and explain what he meant by this 'mutilated'. When the emperor exiled the

Orphanotrophus, thereby bringing down, as he thought, the pillar of the family, he hastened to the destruction of the rest. All his relatives, most of whom had already reached their full stature and were bearded men, who had become fathers and been entrusted with offices of great dignity in the State, he compelled to undergo castration, making of their life a semi-death. The truth is, he was ashamed to kill them openly: he preferred to compass their destruction by mutilation, a punishment apparently less severe.

Such was the reply of the uncle. The tyrant, however, slowly shaking his head and forcing a tear from his eyes (not without some difficulty) said, 'Truly, God is not unjust' – those were his very words – 'and I am rightly paying the penalty for what I have done.' With these words he again laid hold of the Holy Table. Then he prayed that his change of garment might receive legal sanction, and the ceremony of reception into the Church was performed in respect of them both. Nevertheless, they were utterly dejected, filled with apprehension and dread lest the mob should attack them . . .

Day was already drawing to a close when suddenly there arrived one of the newly-appointed officials, saying that he had received an order from Theodora to remove the refugees to some other place. He was accompanied by a crowd of citizens and soldiers. Approaching the altar at which they had sought sanctuary, he invited them, in a somewhat peremptory manner, to leave the church. Despite this, when they saw the mob talking of public execution and when with their own eyes they perceived the mob leader signalling that the moment was at hand, and when they observed the change in the man – he was more insolent than usual – they refused to come forth and clung even more resolutely to the pillars that support the altar. The other thereupon laid aside his arrogance and addressed them with greater respect. He swore by the Holy Relics and used all manner of persuasion, saying that they would neither suffer any evil nor would he, the empress's envoy, treat them with any more severity than the occasion demanded. Even so, they remained deaf to his arguments, filled with terror and expecting all kinds of disaster to follow their present distress. It was better, they thought, to be slain in the sanctuary than meet with any and every outrage in the open.

So the official abandoned all hope of reasoned persuasion and resorted to violence. At his command the mob laid hands on them and without more ado proceeded to break the law, hounding them out of the church like wild beasts. The victims emitted cries of anguish unrestrained. They lifted their eyes to the Holy Lamb, praying fervently that they might not be disappointed of their hopes, that they might not be cruelly driven away after seeking refuge in the house of God. And most of those who were there with us were indeed put to shame by their sufferings . . .

Theodora's adherents were aware of Zoe's jealousy. They knew that she would be quite willing to see a stable-lad on the imperial throne rather than let her sister share power with herself. They drew the natural conclusion that she would in all probability scorn Theodora completely and promote Michael to the throne a second time, by underhand means. Their unanimous decision, therefore, was to do away with the fugitive emperor. The moderate element, however, was not disposed to favour sentence of death; the ambitions of Michael and his uncle would have to be extinguished by some other device, and, after careful consideration, they determined their course of action. Bold, resolute men were dispatched with all speed. Their instructions were to burn out the fugitives' eyes, as soon as they saw them outside the sacred building.

Actually they had already left the church, and a shameful reception awaited them outside, where the rabble made fun of them, naturally enough under the circumstances. Sometimes the insults were tempered with laughter, but malice inspired others. Anyhow, they brought them out, intending to drive them through the centre of the city, but they had not gone far on the journey when they were encountered by the man who had been commanded to blind the two criminals. His party showed their instructions to the mob and they began preparing for the execution; the iron was sharpened for the branding. Meanwhile the victims heard what wretched fate was in store for them. There was no longer any hope of escape, for while some applauded the sentence, the others did nothing to oppose it, and the two were instantly struck dumb with fright. In fact, they would have nearly died, had not one of the senators stood by them to help. He offered consolation in their misery and little by little restored some courage in their hearts.

In spite of this encouragement the emperor, overwhelmed by the situation and his dreadful misfortunes, showed the same weakness of character throughout the whole time of his tribulation. He moaned and wailed aloud, and whenever anyone approached him, he begged for help. He humbly called on God, raised hands in supplication to Heaven, to the Church, to anything he could think of. His uncle, on the other hand, although at first he followed his companion's example, once he was convinced that safety really was out of the question, braced himself for the trial and, having armed himself, as it were, against the shock of catastrophe, faced suffering bravely. The fact is, he was a man of more dignified and steadfast character than his nephew, a man who would not willingly surrender to adversity. Seeing the executioners all ready for their work, he at once offered himself as the first victim and calmly approached them. They waited with hands athirst for his blood. As there was no clear space between himself and the mob – for everyone there present wished to be the first witness of their punishment – the Nobilissimus quietly looked round for the man to whom the miserable job had been entrusted. 'You there,' he said, 'please make the people stand back. Then you will see how bravely I bear my calamity!'

When the executioner tried to tie him down, to prevent movement at the time of blinding, he said, 'Look here. If you see me budge, *nail* me down!' With these words he lay flat on his back on the ground. There was no change of colour in his face, no crying out, no groaning. It was hard to believe that the man was still alive. His eyes were then gouged, one after the other. Meanwhile the emperor, seeing in the other's torment the fate that was about to overtake him, too, lived through Constantine's anguish in himself, beating his hands together, smiting his face, and bellowing in agony.

The Nobilissimus, his eyes gouged out, stood up from the ground and leaned for support on one of his most intimate friends. He addressed those who came up to him with great courage – a man who rose superior to the trials that beset him, to whom death was as nothing. With Michael it was different for when the executioner saw him flinch away and lower himself to base entreaty, he bound him securely. He held him down with considerable force, to stop the violent twitching, when he was undergoing his punishment. After his eyes, too, had been blinded, the insolence of the mob, so marked before, died away, and with it their fury against these men. They left them to rest there, while they themselves hurried back to Theodora. One of the two empresses was in fact in the palace, the other in the great cathedral of St Sophia.

The Senate was unable to decide between them. Zoe, who was in the palace, they respected because she was the elder; Theodora, who was in the church, because it was through her that the revolt had been brought to an end and to her they owed their preservation. Each, therefore, had a claim on the Empire. However, the problem was settled for them by Zoe. For the first time, she greeted her sister and embraced her with affection. What is more, she shared with her the Empire they both inherited.

(*Trans.* E. R. A. SEWTER)

(?) THEODORE PRODROMOS
(d. c.1166)

THE POOR SCHOLAR'S COMPLAINT

(These are the opening lines of a poem, which is one of four composed in a pastiche of the spoken Greek of the Middle Ages. It is dramatic in form and satirical in intention, and characters such as the hen-pecked husband and the downtrodden monk lament their lot. They may be by Theodore Prodromos, but their authorship is uncertain.)

From the time when I was little my old father used to say to me: 'My lad, learn letters, for your own sake(?). You see so-and-so, my child, he used to go about on foot, and now he has harness with a double breast-plate and rides a well-fed mule. When he was studying, he had not a pair of shoes for his feet, and now you see he wears long pointed shoes. When he was studying, his hair was never combed, and now he is well-groomed and wears his hair in a stylish coiffure. When he was studying, he never saw the bath-house door, and now he has three baths a week. The fold of his tunic used to be full of lice as big as almonds. Now it is full of gold coins of Emperor Manuel. Listen to the words of your old father. Learn letters, for your own sake(?).' And I learned my grammar with great pains. And now that I have become a master of letters, I long for bread and what goes to make it. I curse education, and say with tears: 'Cursed be learning, Christ, and all who desire it. Cursed be the season and the day when they sent me off to school, to learn my letters and to live by them. If only then they had made me a gold-embroiderer, one of those who make gold embroideries and live by their craft, and I had learnt the despised art of embroidery in gold, would not I have opened my cupboard and found it full of bread, with wine in abundance and cooked tunny and slices of fish and sardines and mackerel? But now when I open it, I look at all the shelves, and I see paper bags filled with paper. I open my bread-box to find a piece of bread, and I find another tiny paper bag. I reach into my pocket, to find my purse, I feel for small change, and my purse too is full of paper. When I have searched through every corner I stand dejected and careworn, weak and fainting

because I am so hungry. And because of my great hunger and my
many worries I declare that the craft of silk-embroidery is preferable
to that of learning and grammar.'

(*Trans.* C. A. TRYPANIS, *modified*)

DIGENIS AKRITAS
(Twelfth century)
(*ll 1176–1225*)

(The young Digenis has taken part in his first hunt, in the company
of his father the Emir. He has killed two bears and a deer with his
bare hands, to their admiration. In Greek legend, stories of the hero
precociously killing wild beasts in childhood were told of Heracles,
Achilles, and Alexander the Great among others.)

Indeed the young man had a comely stature,
And fair hair, curling a little, and large eyes,
A white and rosy face, a brow all black,
His breast like crystal was a fathom broad.
Looking on him his father was most glad,
Spoke joyfully to him with great delight,
How that 'The heat is great, it is midday,
Now the beasts hide themselves within the marsh;
Come let us go aside to the cool water,
and you wash the much sweating from your face;
And you shall change your clothes, for they are soiled
With the beasts' foaming and the lion's blood.
Thrice blessed am I that I have such a son,
And I will wash your feet with my own hands.
Now will I cast all care from off my soul,
That I be heedless where I send you out,
To many raids and posted enemies.'
Forthwith they both went off towards the spring;
There was the water wondrous, cold as snow.
Sitting round, some began to wash his hands,
Others his face, likewise also his feet.
The spring ran over, thirstily they drank,

So that they too might become brave therefrom.
And afterwards the boy changed his clothing;
Thin singlets he put on to cool himself,
The upper one was red with golden hems,
And all the hems of it were fused with pearls,
The neck was filled with southernwood and musk,
And distinct pearls it had instead of buttons,
The buttonholes were twisted with pure gold;
He wore fine leggings with griffins embellished,
His spurs were plaited round with precious stones,
And on the gold work there were carbuncles.
But passing eager was the well-born child
To go to his mother lest she grieve for him,
Began constraining everyone to horse;
Changed saddle to a horse white as a dove,
His forelock was plaited with precious stones,
And little golden bells among the stones;
So many little bells a noise was made
Delightful, wondrous, and amazing all.
A green and rosy silk was on his croup
Covered the saddle to keep the dust away;
Saddle and bridle plaited with gold tags
And all the handicraft studded with pearls.
The horse was spirited and bold in play
And so the boy was quick in riding it.
Whoever saw him wondered at the youth,
How that the horse played at the youngster's will,
And he sat like an apple on a tree.

(*Trans.* J. MAVROGORDATO)

THEODORE DAPHNOPATES
(Tenth century)

LETTER TO THE EMPEROR CONSTANTINE BORN IN THE PURPLE

(This letter, written by a statesman and man of letters to the emperor, is a rhetorical showpiece, thanking him for a gift. The writer elaborates on stock topics with a notable absence of concreteness, but with a richness of literary allusion which cannot be brought out in the translation and with a studied elegance of expression.)

When I left for the country at your bidding, beloved and noble Sire, I became at once like the sunless Cimmerians, since I was far from your radiant presence. This is what perforce must happen to all who are distant from your imperial radiance. The others were gathering the grapes busily, eager to tread them in the vats, joyfully singing seasonable songs, impatient to pour their libations over the casks, while the juice that poured forth in streams made the wine-pressers more songful than cicadas. For myself, I at once turned with what speed and reflection I could to literary composition, writing and meditating upon what my mind engendered, what my anxiety for the common good permitted, what my scrupulous loyalty demanded, all of which I have the temerity to send to your generous Majesty.

Observe the character of my reflections. I placed my couch beneath a fair and shady oak, by which there flowed, in the words of the poet, 'bright water', and began to write. With its leaves and boughs the tree provided dense, overhanging cover of great charm and delight. Beneath its very roots flowers had sprung up, not ordinary flowers such as everyone gathers, but such as they say the earth brought forth for Zeus when he lay with Hera. The breezes which wafted over my head shook the leaves and produced a melodious and pleasing sound. The birds that twittered and fluttered above me, each piping its own song, rained down with their diverse harmony such ravishing music that I almost drifted into sweet sleep and beheld in my dreams as in a mirror delight insatiable, and desired never to leave such a spectacle.

I pray, great marvel of the world and ornament of monarchs, that you may long live and enjoy health, and reign for the happiness of all men, and especially of those who have maintained unimpaired the sincerity of their service and will so maintain it for ever.

The rich gifts of your munificent Majesty, delivered to me by my fellow-servant, were a token of your universal providence, and have inspired me to pray with even greater devotion for your God-granted Majesty.

(*Trans.* R. BROWNING)

THE SONG OF ROLAND
(*c*.1100)

(*La Chanson de Roland* was composed for recitation aloud. As in all the earliest *chansons de geste*, the lines have ten syllables and are bound together in *laisses* (stanzas) of varying length by assonance. The final syllables of a laisse have the same vowel sound (e.g. *chers, paien, chef*) regardless of the consonants that follow. This aids the chanting voice of the performer. Lines are end-stopped and divided by a vocal pause, usually after the fourth syllable. Grammatical sense is normally confined to a single line and with little subordination, so that the effect is of sustained and elevated assertion; all action is foregrounded without explanation or digression. Dorothy Sayers's classic translation copies these formal features very successfully, despite the more strongly consonantal endings of modern English, and produces an appropriate stiffness in the line, though she tends to archaize the vocabulary. Readers should consult her section on 'The verse and the translation', pp. 38–44.)

LA CHANSON DE ROLAND

LAISSE 8

Li empereres   se fait e balz e liez:
Cordres ad prise   e les murs peceiez,
Od ses cadables   les turs en abatiéd.
Mult grant eschech   en unt si chevaler,
D'or e d'argent   e de guarnemenz chers.
En la citét   nen ad remés paien
Ne seit ocis   u devient chrestïen.
Li empereres   est en un grant verger.
Ensembl'od lui   Rollant e Oliver,
Sansun li dux   e Anseïs li fiers,
Gefreid d'Anjou,   le rei gunfanuner,
E si i furent   e Gerin e Gerers.
La u cist furent,   des altres i out bien,
De dulce France   i ad quinze milliers.
Sur palies blancs   siedent cil cevaler,
As tables juent   pur els esbaneier,

E as eschecs   li plus saive e li veill,
E escremissent   cil bacheler leger.
Desuz un pin,   delez un eglenter,
Un faldestoed   i unt, fait tut d'or mer:
La siet li reis   ki dulce France tient.
Blanche ad la barbe   e tut flurit le chef,
Gent ad le cors   e le cuntenant fier:
S'est k.il demandet,   ne l'estoet enseigner.
E li message   descendirent a pied,
Si.l saluerent   par amur e par bien.

THE SARACENS OFFER PEACE TO CHARLEMAGNE

LAISSE 8

The Emperor Charles is glad and full of cheer.
Cordova's taken, the outer walls are pierced,
His catapults have cast the towers down sheer;
Rich booty's gone to all his chevaliers,
Silver and gold and goodly battle-gear.
In all the city no paynim now appears
Who is not slain or turned to Christian fear.
The Emperor sits in a great orchard near,
Having about him Roland and Olivere,
Samson the duke, and Anseis the fierce,
Geoffrey d'Anjou the King's gonfalonier,
And Gerin too, and with him too Gerier;
And where these were was many another fere[a]
Full fifteen thousand of France the fair and dear.
Upon white carpets they sit, those noble peers,
For draughts and chess the chequer-boards are reared;
To entertain the elder lords revered;
Young bachelors disport with sword and spear.
Beneath a pine beside an eglantier[b]
A faldstool stands all of the red gold clear;
Of fairest France there sits the king austere.

a companion, *b* wild-rose bush.

White are his locks, and silver is his beard,
His body noble, his countenance severe:
If any seek him, no need to say, 'Lo, here!'
From off their steeds lit down the messengers,
Well did they greet him with shows of love sincere.

9

Before them all Blancandrin forward stood;
And hailed the King: 'God gave His grace to you,
The glorious God to whom worship is due.
Thus speaks the king, Marsilion, great in rule:
Much hath he studied the saving faith and true.
Now of his wealth he would send you in sooth
Lions and bears, leashed greyhounds not a few,
Sev'n hundred camels, a thousand falcons mewed,
And gold and silver borne on four hundred mules;
A wagon-train of fifty carts to boot,
And store enough of golden bezants good
Wherewith to pay your soldiers as you should.
Too long you've stayed in this land to our rue:
To Aix in France return you at our suit.
Thither my liege will surely follow you,
[And will become your man in faith and truth,
And at your hand hold all his realm in feu!']
With lifted hands to God the Emperor sues;
Then bows his head and so begins to brood.

10

The Emperor bode long time with downcast eyes;
He was a man not hasty in reply,
But wont to speak only when well advised.
When he looked up, his glance was stern and high.
He told the envoys: 'Fair is your speech and fine;
Yet King Marsile is foe to me and mine.
In all these words and offers you recite
I find no warrant wherein I may confide.'
'Sureties for this', the Saracen replies,
'Ten or fifteen or twenty we'll provide.

One of my sons I'll send, on pain to die;
Others, yet nobler, you'll have, as I divine.
When in your palace high feast you solemnize
To great St Michael of Peril-by-the-Tide[a],
He'll follow you, on that you may rely,
And in those baths[b] God made you by His might
He would turn Christian and there would be baptized.'
Quoth Charles: 'He yet may save his soul alive.'

II

Fair was the ev'ning and clearly the sun shone;
The ten white mules Charles sends to stall anon;
In the great orchard he bids men spread aloft
For the ten envoys a tent where they may lodge,
With sergeants[c] twelve to wait on all their wants.
They pass the night there till the bright day draws on.
Early from bed the Emperor now is got;
At mass and matins he makes his orison.
Beneath a pine straightway the King is gone,
And calls his barons to council thereupon;
By French advice whate'er he does is done.

12

The Emperor goes beneath a tall pine-tree,
And to his council he calls his barony:
There Duke Ogier, Archbishop Turpin meet,
Richard the Old and his nephew Henri,
Count Acelin the brave of Gascony,
Miles, and his cousin the Lord Tibbald of Rheims,
Gerin likewise and Gerier are convened;
And County Roland, there with the rest came he,

---

a The monastery built on the great island rock called Mont St Michel, off the coast of Normandy. Later it came to be applied to the Archangel himself, '*St Michel del Peril*'.
b The curative mineral springs for which Aix is still celebrated.
c The word 'sergeant', meaning primarily 'servant', was applied generally to almost any man, under the rank of knight, who exercised any kind of office in a lord's household or on his estate.

And Oliver, noble and good at need;
All French of France, thousand and more, maybe;
And Ganelon that wrought the treachery.
So starts that council which came to such sore grief.

13

'Barons, my lords', began the Emperor Carlon,
'From King Marsile come envoys, seeking parley.
He makes me offers of treasure overpassing:
Of lions and bears and hounds to the leash mastered,
Sev'n hundred camels, and falcons mewed and hearty,
Four hundred mules with Arab gold all chargèd,
And fifty wagons well-laden in a cart-train.
But now to France he urges my departure,
And to my palace at Aix he'll follow after,
There change his faith for one of more advantage,
Become a Christian and of me hold his marches.
But his true purpose – for that I cannot answer.'
The French all say: 'We'd best be very guarded.'

14

The Emperor Charles had finished all his speech.
The County Roland, who fiercely disagrees,
Swift to oppose springs up upon his feet:
He tells the King: 'Nevermore trust Marsile!
Seven years long in land of Spain we've been.
I won for you both Noples and Commibles,
I took Valterna, the land of Pine I seized,
And Balagate, and Seville and Tudele.
Then wrought Marsile a very treacherous deed:
He sent his Paynims by number of fifteen,
All of them bearing boughs of the olive tree,
And with like words he sued to you for peace.
Then did you ask the French lords for their rede[a];
Foolish advice they gave to you indeed.

a counsel.

You sent the Paynim two counts of your meinie:
Basan was one, the other was Basile.
He smote their heads off in hills beneath Haltile.
This war you've started wage on, and make no cease;
To Saragossa lead your host in the field,
Spend all your life, if need be, in the siege,
Revenge the men this villain made to bleed!'

15

The Emperor Charles sat still with his head bended;
He stroked his beard and his moustaches gently;
Nor good nor ill he answers to his nephew.
The French are silent, Guènes alone excepted;
But he leaps up, strides into Carlon's presence,
And full of pride begins thus to address him.
He tells the King: 'Trust not a brawling fellow,
Me nor another; seek only your own welfare.
If King Marsile informs you by this message
He'll set his hands in yours, and fealty pledge you,
And hold all Spain from you, at your good pleasure,
And to that faith we follow give acceptance,
The man who tells you this plea should be rejected
Cares nothing, Sire, to what death he condemns us.
Counsel of pride must not grow swollen-headed;
Let's hear wise men, turn deaf ears to the reckless.'

16

Naimon at this stood forth before them all:
No better vassal was ever seen in hall.
He tells the King: 'Well have you heard, my lord,
The arguments Count Ganelon sets forth.
There's weight in them, and you should give them thought.
The King Marsile is vanquished in the war,
You've taken from him his castles and his forts,
With catapults you've broken down his walls,
You've burned his cities and his armies outfought.
Now that he comes on your mercy to call
Foul sin it were to vex him any more.

Since he'll find sureties his good faith to support,
We should make haste to cut this great war short.'
The French all say: 'The Duke speaks as he ought.'

17

'Barons, my lords, whom shall we send anon
To Saragossa, to King Marsilion?'
'I, by your leave,' saith Naimon, 'will begone,
Therefore on me bestow the glove and wand.'
'You are my wisest', the King makes answer prompt:
'Now by the beard my cheek and chin upon,
You shall not go so far this twelvemonth long.
Hence! sit you down, for we summon you not!'

18

'Barons, my lords, whom shall we send of you
To Saragossa, the Sarsen king unto?'
'Myself', quoth Roland, 'may well this errand do.'
'That shall you not', Count Oliver let loose;
'You're high of heart and stubborn of your mood,
You'd land yourself, I warrant, in some feud.
By the King's leave this errand I will do.'
The King replies: 'Be silent there, you two!
Nor you nor he shall on that road set foot.
By this my beard that's silver to the view,
He that names any of the Twelve Peers shall rue!'
The French say nothing: they stand abashed and mute.

19

Then from their ranks arose Turpin of Rheims;
He tells the King: 'Leave your French lords at ease;
Full sev'n long years in this land have you been,
Much have they suffered of perils and fatigue;
Pray you then, Sire, give wand and glove to me;
The Saracen of Spain I'll seek and see,
And in his looks his purpose will I read.'
The Emperor answers with anger in his mien:

'On that white carpet sit down and hold your peace;
Be still, I say, until I bid you speak.'

20

The Emperor said: 'My free and knightly band,
Come choose me out some baron of my land
To bring my message to King Marsilion's hand.'
Quoth Roland: 'Guènes my step-sire is the man.'
The French all say: 'Indeed, he is most apt;
If he's passed over you will not find his match.'
Count Ganelon is furious out of hand;
His great furred gown of marten he flings back
And stands before them in his silk bliaut clad.
Bright are his eyes, haughty his countenance,
Handsome his body, and broad his bosom's span;
The peers all gaze, his bearing is so grand.
He says to Roland: 'Fool! what has made thee mad?
I am thy step-sire, and all these know I am,
And me thou namest to seek Marsilion's camp!
If God but grant I ever thence come back
I'll wreak on thee such ruin and such wrack
That thy life long my vengeance shall not slack.'
Roland replies: 'This is all boast and brag!
Threats cannot fright me, and all the world knows that
To bear this message we must have a good man;
I'll take your place if the King says I can.'

21

Quoth Ganelon: 'My place thou shalt not take;
Thou'rt not my vassal, nor I thy suzerain.
Charles for his service commands me to obey.
I'll seek Marsile in Saragossa's gates;
But rather there some deadly trick I'll play
Than not find vent for my unbounded rage.'
When Roland heard him, then he laughed in his face.

22

When Ganelon sees Roland laugh outright
He's fit to burst for anger and despite,
And very nearly goes clean out of his mind.
He tells the Count: 'I love you not; not I;
You've picked on me unfairly, out of spite.
Just Emperor, here I stand before your eyes,
Ready to do whatever you think right.

23

To Saragossa I see that I must shift me;
There's no return for him that journeys thither.
Bethink you well that my wife is your sister,
A son she bare me fairest of goodly children,
Baldwin (quoth he) and a champion he will be.
To him I leave all my lands and my living;
No more I'll see him; take care, Sir, of your kinsman.'
Quoth Charles: 'Your heart is too tender within you;
Go now you must, for even so I bid you.'

24

Then said the King: 'Stand forward, Ganelon,
Here at my hand receive the glove and wand;
You've heard the French – you are the man they want.'
'Messire,' said Guènes, 'Roland hath done this wrong!
I'll never love him the whole of my life long,
Nor Oliver his friend and fellow fond,
Nor the Twelve Peers by whom he's doted on;
Sire, in your presence I defy the whole lot.'
Then said the King: 'Your passion is too hot;
I bid you go and so you must begone.'

ROLAND SOUNDS HIS OLIFANT

128

When County Roland sees all his brave men down,
To Oliver his friend he cries aloud:
'For God's sake, comrade, fair sire, what think you now?
See what good knights lie here upon the ground!
Well may we pity this fair sweet France of ours,
Thus left so barren of all her knighthood's flower.
Why aren't you here, O friend and Emperour?
Oliver, brother, what way is to be found?
How send him news of what is come about?'
Oliver said: 'And how should I know how?
I'd rather die than we should lose renown.'

129

'I'll sound', quoth Roland, 'my Olifant straightway;
When Carlon hears, passing through Gate of Spain,
I pledge my word, the French will turn again.'
Quoth Oliver: 'It would be foul disdain,
And to your kindred the reproach would be great:
All their lives long they'd not live down the shame.
When I desired you, why then you said me nay;
If now you do it, of me you'll get no praise.
Blow if you will – such conduct is not brave.
Nay, but how deep in blood your arms are bathed!'
The Count replies: 'I've struck good blows this day.'

130

Said Roland then: 'Full grievous is this fight.
I'll sound my horn, and Charles will hear the cry.'
Quoth Oliver: ''Twould ill beseem a knight.
I asked you, comrade, and you refused, for pride.
Had Charles been here, then all would have gone right;
He's not to blame, nor the men at his side.
Now by my beard (quoth he) if e'er mine eyes
Again behold my sister Aude the bright,
Between her arms never you think to lie.'

131

Quoth Roland: 'Why so angry with me, friend?'
And he: 'Companion, you got us in this mess.
There is wise valour, and there is recklessness:
Prudence is worth more than foolhardiness.
Through your o'erweening you have destroyed the French;
Ne'er shall we do service to Charles again.
Had you but given some heed to what I said,
My lord had come, the battle had gone well,
And King Marsile had been captured or dead.
Your prowess, Roland, is a curse on our heads.
No more from us will Charlemayn have help,
Whose like till Doomsday shall not be seen of men.
Now you will die, and fair France will be shent[a];
Our loyal friendship is here brought to an end;
A bitter parting we'll have ere this sun set.'

132

When the Archbishop thus hears them in dispute,
With his gold spurs he pricks his steed anew,
Draws near to them and utters this rebuke:
'Lord Oliver, and you, Lord Roland, too,
Let's have no quarrel, o'God's name, 'twixt you two.
It will not save us to sound the horn, that's true;
Nevertheless, 'twere better so to do.
Let the King come; his vengeance will be rude;
None shall to Spain ride home with merry news.
After, our French will light them down on foot,
Seek out our bodies and limbs in sunder hewn,
Lay us on biers borne upon sumpter-mules,
And weep for us with grief right pitiful;
In the church-close we shall have burial due,
And not be food for dogs and swine and wolves.'
Quoth Roland, 'Sir, your words are right and good.'

a put to shame.

133

Roland has set Olifant to his lips,
Firmly he holds it and blows it with a will.
High are the mountains, the blast is long and shrill,
Thirty great leagues the sound went echoing.
King Carlon heard it and all who rode with him.
'Lo, now, our men are fighting', quoth the King.
Guènes retorts: 'If any man said this
Except yourself, it were a lie, methinks.'

134

The County Roland with pain and anguish winds
His Olifant, and blows with all his might.
Blood from his mouth comes spurting scarlet-bright
He's burst the veins of his temples outright.
From hand and horn the call goes shrilling high:
King Carlon hears it who through the passes rides,
Duke Naimon hears, and all the French beside.
Quoth Charles: 'I hear the horn of Roland cry!
He'd never sound it but in the thick of fight.'
'There is no battle', Count Ganelon replies;
'You're growing old, your hair is sere and white,
When you speak thus, you're talking like a child.
Full well you know Roland's o'erweening pride;
'Tis strange that God endures him so long time!
Took he not Noples against your orders quite?
The Paynims made a sally from inside,
And there gave battle to Roland the great knight;
So he swilled down the field – a brave device
To keep the bloodstains from coming to your eyes!
For one small hare he'll blow from morn till night;
Now to the Peers he's showing-off in style.
Who dare attack him? No man beneath the sky!
Ride on, ride on! Why loiter here the while?
Our Fathers' land lies distant many a mile.'

135

Count Roland's mouth with running blood is red;
He's burst asunder the temples of his head;
He sounds his horn in anguish and distress.
King Carlon hears, and so do all the French.
Then said the King: 'This horn is long of breath.'
''Tis blown', quoth Naimon, 'with all a brave man's strength;
Battle there is, and that I know full well.
He that would stay you is but a traitor fell.
To arms! let sound your battle-cry to heav'n!
Make haste to bring your gallant household help!
You hear how Roland makes desperate lament!'

136

The Emperor Charles lets sound his horns aloft.
The French light down and arm themselves anon
With helm and hauberk and gilded swords girt on;
Goodly their shields, their lances stiff and strong,
Scarlet and white and blue the gonfalons.
Straightway to horse the warrior lords have got;
Swift through the passes they spur and never stop.
Each unto other they speak and make response:
'Might we reach Roland ere he were dead and gone,
We'ld strike good strokes beside him in the throng.'
What use is that? They have delayed too long.

(*Trans.* DOROTHY L. SAYERS)

CHRÉTIEN DE TROYES
(*fl.c.*1170)

YVAIN, THE KNIGHT OF THE LION

PROLOGUE

(*ll 1–20*)

Artus, li buens rois de Bretaingne,
La cui proesce nos ansaingne,
Que nos soiiens preu et cortois,
Tint cort si riche come rois
A cele feste, qui tant coste,
Qu'an doit clamer la pantecoste.
Li rois fu a Carduel an Gales.
Aprés mangier parmi cez sales
Li chevalier s'atropelerent
La, ou dames les apelerent
Ou dameiseles ou pucèles.
Li un recontoient noveles,
Li autre parloient d'amors,
Des angoisses et des dolors
Et des granz biens, qu'an ont sovant
Li deciple de son covant,
Qui lors estoit riches et buens.
Mes ore i a mout po des suens;
Que a bien pres l'ont tuit leissiee,
S'an est amors mout abeissiee.

(Yvain, ed. W. FOERSTER and T. B. W. REID)

PROLOGUE

(*ll 1–41*)

Arthur, the worthy King of Britain, whose chivalry teaches us prowess and courtliness, held court with the magnificence befitting a king at that festival which is so costly that it is customarily known as Pentecost.★ The king was at the Welsh town of Carlisle.† After meat the knights assembled in the halls, wherever they were summoned by the ladies, the maidens or young girls. Some recited stories, while others conversed of love and of the trials and tribulations, and of the great boons, too, which are often the lot of those who have joined the order of love, which at that time was prosperous and highly regarded. Now its members are few indeed. Most have left the order and love has fallen on hard times. In the past those who loved earned the reputation of being courtly, valorous, generous and honourable. Today they make a mockery of love. Though entirely ignorant of it, they claim to love, but in so doing they lie. They make a mockery and travesty of love, who boast about it whilst lacking any right to it. But let us leave our contemporaries and speak of those who lived in former times, for it seems to me that a courtly man now dead is nobler than a boor who is still alive. And so I should like to relate something which deserves a hearing and which concerns the king whose reputation was such that he is still spoken of far and near. In this sense I agree with the Bretons that his name will live for ever. It is he who puts us in mind of those chosen knights who laboured in the cause of honour.

YVAIN IS TRAPPED IN THE CASTLE OF ESCLADOS THE RED

(ll 907–60)

(The most critical moment in Yvain's first chivalric adventure.)

The gateway was very high and wide, but the central way-in itself so narrow that two men or two horses could not have entered together without great difficulty and discomfort, nor could they have met and passed inside the gateway. The gate was actually contrived like a trap which awaits the arrival of the rat intent on mischief. Concealed above it is the blade which shoots out and strikes home the moment it is released by anything touching the trigger mechanism, however gently. Similarly, beneath the gate there were

---

★ It is possible that the French involves a pun which we might render as Plentycost.

† Several romance-writers used 'Gales' to cover that area of the old British kingdom which is closely connected with the origins of Arthurian literature, namely S. W. Scotland (Strathclyde) and N.W. England.

two pivoted levers (*trebuchets*) which supported the iron portcullis above with its finely ground cutting edge. If anything passed over this mechanism, the portcullis came rattling down and anything that was caught underneath was simply cut to ribbons. The way through in the very middle was as narrow as a beaten track. The knight wisely sped down the centre, whilst Sir Yvain comes hurtling wildly after him, so close, indeed, that he has hold of the other's saddlebow. It was lucky for him that he was leaning forward, for had it not been for this fortunate circumstance, he would have been split clean in two, for his horse stepped on the plank which was linked to the iron portcullis. Like a demon from Hell the portcullis dropped straight down on to the saddle and croup of the horse, severing them completely. But, thank God, it scarcely touched Yvain, merely grazing his back and cutting off the rear portion of both his spurs flush with his heels. He fell shocked to the ground, whilst the mortally wounded knight escaped in the following way: further on, there was a second portcullis, just like the first, and the fleeing knight made his escape through this portcullis, which then fell behind him.

YVAIN'S FIRST MEETING WITH LAUDINE

(*ll 1950–2014*)

(The unexpected outcome of Yvain's first adventure, typically treated with humour. The love-plot is ambiguous and the depth of natural feeling hard to assess.)

I can assure you, Sir Yvain was absolutely terrified as he entered the room and spied the lady, who addressed not a word to him, a fact which only intensified his fear, as with dismay he imagined that he had been betrayed. And there he remained, some distance from the lady, until the maiden spoke up and said, 'Five hundred curses on whoever thus admits to the presence of a beautiful lady a knight who neither approaches her nor has the tongue in his mouth or wit in his head to introduce himself!' And so saying she grabbed him by the arm and declared, 'Come over here, knight, and don't be afraid my lady will bite you; seek reconciliation with her instead and I will join with you in asking her to forgive you for killing her lord, Esclados the Red.'

Sir Yvain now clasps his hands together and falls to his knees and declares like a true lover, 'Lady, I shall not ask for your forgiveness, but rather I shall thank you for whatever you choose to do with me, for nothing you may do could be displeasing to me.'

'Really not? And what if I kill you?'

'May it please you, my lady, you shall never hear me say anything different.'

'I never heard of such a thing: you thus voluntarily place yourself entirely in my power, without any coercion on my part?'

'Lady, truly there is no other force so strong as the one which impels me to submit completely to your wishes. Nothing you might bid me do should I hesitate to carry out and if only I could make amends for the death – in which I played an entirely innocent part – then I would without more ado.'

'What's that?', she said, 'Tell me then, and I will absolve you from any need to make amends, did you really commit no offence when you killed my lord?'

'May it please you, my lady, but when I was attacked by your lord, what wrong did I do in defending myself? If someone wants to kill another man or capture him and that man defends himself and kills the first, then tell me, what wrong has he done?'

'Well, I suppose, strictly speaking, none; so it would have been pointless of me to kill you. But I'd very much like to know the origin of this force which impels you to submit entirely to my wishes. I absolve you from all wrong-doing. Now, come and sit down and tell me what has made you so docile.'

YVAIN IS DENOUNCED BY LAUDINE'S MESSENGER

(ll 2694–766)

(This explicit criticism of the hero, who fails to keep an agreement with his newly won wife, precipitates the central crisis of the romance, the hero's madness; after which Yvain must learn the slow route to recovery.)

King Arthur was sitting with them, when suddenly Yvain's thoughts took a turn which gave him a greater shock than anything that had occurred to him since he had taken leave of his lady. He suddenly realized that he had broken his promise to her and that the deadline for his return had passed. He had to struggle to keep back his tears; only shame held them back. And so he brooded, when into view came a maiden, hastening straight towards them on a piebald palfrey. She dismounts before the tent without anyone to help her down or to take her horse. Then the moment she saw the King, she cast off her cloak and thus uncovered went straight inside the tent to where the King was sitting and delivered the greetings which her lady sent to the King, to Sir Gawain and to everyone except Yvain, the faithless traitor and lying deceiver, who abandoned and betrayed her:

'She has seen through the guile of the man who cast himself in the role of perfect lover, who was all the time treacherous, deceitful and dishonest. This thief hoodwinked my lady, who did not suspect any trickery and who never imagined that he would later steal away her heart. Those who love do not steal hearts, but there are some who call them thieves and who themselves cheat in love without knowing anything about it. The true lover takes his lady's heart in such a way that he does not steal it, but rather takes care of it, so that it is not stolen by thieves made to resemble honest men. Those who scheme to steal hearts about which they do not care are dishonest rogues and hypocrites. The true lover, wherever he goes, holds dear the heart and returns it safely. But Yvain has become the death of my lady, for she believed that he would look after her heart and bring it back to her before the year went by. Yvain, you were very forgetful. You failed to remember that you were supposed to be back with my lady within a year. She gave you till Midsummer's Eve and you paid such little attention to her, that she has never entered your thoughts since. In her room my lady has drawn a list of the days and the seasons, for someone in love is in a state of great agitation, cannot sleep properly and spends the whole night counting and crossing off the days as they go past. Have you any idea of the way lovers behave? They keep a reckoning of the time and the season. My lady's complaint is neither unjust nor premature. I am not concerned with making a formal charge, but this much I will say: she who married you to my lady has betrayed us.'

YVAIN RESCUES THE LION

(ll 3341–415)

(The second adventure which Yvain undertakes after he has recovered from his madness and which gives him his new title 'The
Knight of the Lion'.)

Lost in thought, Yvain was riding along through a dense forest, when
he suddenly heard from the depths of the wood a very loud cry
of pain and at once made for the place from which he had heard
the cry come. And when he reached the place, he found a clearing
in which a lion was being held by its tail by a dragon which was
scorching its rear-quarters with fierce flames. Sir Yvain did not waste
time watching this extraordinary spectacle, but took thought for
which of the two beasts he should assist and he promptly declares
that he will go to the aid of the lion, for all that is venomous and
wicked deserves only harm and there is no doubt that the dragon
is venomous – it is breathing fire – and full of treachery. Sir Yvain
therefore decides that it shall be the first to be killed. He draws his
sword and advances, holding his shield in front of his face, so that
he is not harmed by the evil fire pouring out from the dragon's
mouth, which was wider than a pot. If the lion attacks him afterwards, then it, too, shall have battle, but, whatever may happen to
him later, he will help it for the present. The claims of pity impel
him to help the noble-hearted beast. With his keen-edged sword
he attacks the wicked dragon, cutting it right through to the ground,
cleaving it in two and raining down so many blows on it, that it
is cut to pieces. But he had to nick a piece off the lion's tail, because
the wicked dragon had hold of it with its teeth. He cut off the bare
minimum that was necessary. When he had freed the lion he
imagined that he would have to fight with it and that it would attack
him. But the lion had no such intention. Hear now, what it did!
It behaved nobly and generously, showing signs that it wished to
surrender to his power, and, standing on its two hind feet, it bowed
its head and held out its paws to him. Then it knelt down again,
its face moist with tears of humility. Sir Yvain clearly recognizes
that the lion is thanking him and humbling itself before him on
account of his killing of the dragon and saving the lion from death.

He is delighted by the turn of events. Taking his sword, he wipes away the poison and filth left by the dragon and replaces the sword in its scabbard. Then he continues on his way and the lion goes along beside him, never to part from him. It will henceforth be his constant companion and will serve and protect him.

YVAIN AT THE CASTLE OF EVIL ADVENTURE

(ll 5360–96)

(The passage marks a pause in the middle of Yvain's most difficult adventure. The remarks on love, which recall the prologue, are most likely ironical.)

Sir Yvain enters the garden followed by his whole retinue. There he sees, reclining on a silk cloth which has been spread out on the ground, a worthy knight in whose presence a young girl was reading from a romance – about whom I don't know. And in order to listen to the romance a lady had come and lain down too: she was the girl's mother and the knight her father and they took much pleasure in hearing her read, for they had no other children and the girl, though not yet seventeen years old, was so beautiful and graceful that, if he had seen her, the God of Love would have done everything he could to serve her and allowed her to love no one else but himself. To serve her he would have become man, abandoned his deity and smitten himself with the arrow whose wound never heals unless treated by a faithless doctor. No one should be healed until he meets with faithlessness and anyone who is healed otherwise cannot be a faithful lover. About this wound I could go on for ever, if you wanted to hear about it, but there would sure to be someone who would quickly say that I was wasting your time. For people today know little about love and do not love as they used to. They don't even want to hear about it.

YVAIN'S COMBAT WITH GAWAIN

(ll 5998–6105)

(The hero's final chivalric adventure, which invites us to compare the two major protagonists of the romance. The rhetorical elaboration points to the underlying significance of this comparison.)

Those who were about to engage in combat did not recognize each other, though they had hitherto been the closest of friends. Do they then no longer love each other? 'Yes and no' is my answer and I'll justify myself by demonstrating the truth of both propositions. It is certainly true that Sir Gawain loves Yvain and regards him as his companion and Yvain loves him, too, wherever he may be. Even here, if only he recognized him, he would make a great fuss of him, he would lay down his life for him and the other would do likewise, rather than allow any harm to come to him. Is this not true and perfect love? Yes, of course it is. But then, is their hatred not equally manifest? Yes, for there is no doubt that each intends to split the other's head open or else do him such injury that he would suffer from it. Well then, there's the paradox: Love and mortal Hate side by side in the same receptacle. Heavens! how can two such contraries be lodged together in the same dwelling? I do not see how they can share the same accommodation, for the one could not live with the other in the same building without giving rise to discord and squabbles, once the one knew of the other's presence. But then on one floor there are several rooms, for there are loggia and interior rooms and this is how it may be here. Suppose that Love has settled in an inner room and that Hate has proceeded to the loggia overlooking the road in order to be seen. Now Hate is on the offensive and, riding hard against Love, spurs forward. But Love does not stir. Ah, Love! where are you hiding? Emerge now and see the ally enlisted against you by the enemies of your friends. The enemies are these same men who love each other with the most sacred love, for love which is neither false nor feigned is a precious and sacred thing. But in this case Love is quite blind and Hate also is unseeing. For Love, if it had recognized them, would surely have been obliged to prevent them from harming or touching each other. And so it is that Love is blinded, immobilized and confused, for it sees, but fails to recognize, those who rightly belong to it. And Hate cannot explain why the one knight hates the other, yet it tries to embroil the two of them wrongfully, so that the one feels mortal hatred for the other; and you don't need to be told that a man is scarcely loved by one who would humiliate him and gladly see him dead. What then? does Yvain wish to kill Sir Gawain, his own friend? Yes, indeed, and vice versa. Would Gawain really kill Yvain with his own hands or do even worse than I said? No! I assure you, the one would not wish to harm or injure the other for all that God has performed for mankind nor for the whole of the Roman Empire. But I tell you a gross untruth, for it is obvious that the one is about to attack the other with his lance raised on the rest and that neither is half-hearted in his desire to wound the other to his severe injury and distress. Well then, when one has beaten the other, who can the one who gets the worst of it complain about? – for I'm very much afraid that once battle is joined, they will continue to engage in fighting until a decisive outcome is obtained. If he is the loser, will Yvain honestly be able to say that he has been wronged and humiliated by a man who counts him amongst his friends and who never knew him as anything but a friend and companion? Or, if it should chance that Yvain, for his part, wounds the other knight or defeats him in some way, will the latter have any grounds for complaint? No, because he will not know whom he is dealing with.

(*Trans*. TONY HUNT)

EREC AND THE 'JOY OF THE COURT'

(ll 6048–155)

(The culminating adventure of the romance. Mabonagrain's predicament is often viewed as an *exemplum* by which we may understand the dangers which Erec has overcome in respect of his relationship with Enide.)

'Now hear who is responsible for keeping me in this garden for so long. I shall comply with your request and tell you the truth, however painful it may be for me. The girl sitting over there loved me since childhood and I her. We took pleasure in each other's company and our love grew and developed to the point that she asked a favour of me, without being specific about it. Who would deny his loved one anything? He is scarcely in love who does not wholeheartedly pursue his loved one's interests unhesitatingly and sincerely to the best of his ability. I agreed to her request, but when I had done so she insisted that I gave a formal undertaking. I would have done more than that, if she had required it, but she was ready to take my word for it and so I gave her my word, without really noticing what I said. And the time came for me to be made a knight. King Evrain – I'm his nephew – knighted me in the presence of many worthy men in this same garden where we are now. And my sweetheart, who is sitting over there, promptly reminded me of my word, saying that I had sworn never to leave this place until a knight should come and defeat me. It was right to stay, rather than break my word, for otherwise I should never have given it. Knowing as I did the good she represented, I could not reveal to the one I loved above all others that I was unhappy about anything, for if she had noticed, she would have taken back her heart – and that I would not have wished for anything in the world. And so in this way my sweetheart imagined that she could keep me here for a long time, for she never supposed that a knight might one day enter this garden and defeat me. And so she thought that she could detain me at her pleasure for as long as I lived and it would have been wrong and ignoble of me if I had pretended not to have defeated all those whom I had the power to overcome. Indeed, I can assure you that there is no friend so dear to me as to have made me even for a moment merely go through the motions with him. Never did I tire of bearing arms or show any aversion to fighting. Indeed, you have seen the helmets of those whom I have defeated and killed. Anyone, on close investigation, will find that I am guilty of no wrong, for I could not avoid all this without being dishonest, breaking my promise and being disloyal. So now I have told you the truth and, rest assured, you have gained no small honour for yourself. You have brought great joy to the court of my uncle and my friends, for now I shall be released from here: and because all those at court will have great joy of it, those who were awaiting it called it Joy of the Court. They have waited so long and now they will receive it from you, who have won it in battle. You have disarmed and cast a spell over my prowess and chivalry. Now it is only right that I should tell you my name, if you would like to know it. I am called Mabonagrain, but I am not known by this name in any of the regions that I have been seen in except this one, for when still a squire I never spoke or revealed my name. Sir, you now know the truth concerning all that you asked me. But I should add that in this garden there is a horn, which you have no doubt already seen. I cannot get out of here until you have blown the horn. Then you will have freed me from my prison and that will be the beginning of the Joy. Nothing will prevent those who hear it being blown from coming at once to court. So arise, Sir, and set to. Take the horn with gladness, for there is no cause for delay, and carry out what you have to do.'

(*Trans.* TONY HUNT)

THE ROMANCE OF THE CART

LANCELOT AND THE CART

(ll 323–98)

(The first of a series of trials which test Lancelot's love for Guinevere, who at the beginning of the romance has been abducted by Kay. The celebrated episode establishes the imperious nature of love and reveals its problematic role in Lancelot's fortunes as a knight.)

At that time the cart served the same purpose as does the pillory today and in every sizeable town where you may now find more than three thousand of them, there was in those days no more than one and, just like the pillory, the cart was used equally for those who commit treason or murder, those defeated in judicial combat and for thieves who have stolen other people's property or taken it by force on the roads. Whoever was caught committing a crime was placed in the cart and dragged through the streets, being deprived from then on of all his legal rights and becoming persona non grata at any court. The carts were so barbaric in those days that the expression arose 'If you should see or come across a cart, make the sign of the cross and commend yourself to God, that no harm may befall you'.

The knight without any lance[a] who is following on foot behind the cart sees a dwarf perched on the shafts holding in his hand, as is the carter's custom, a long switch. The knight said to the dwarf, 'In God's name, dwarf, tell me if you have seen my lady, the Queen, pass by this way?'

The wicked, base-born dwarf refused to vouchsafe any information, saying instead, 'If you get into the cart I'm driving, you will know by tomorrow what has become of the Queen' and without more ado he made to continue on his way.

The knight hesitated only for a couple of seconds before jumping in, but it was a great mistake to fear the disgrace and not jump in straightaway. He will suffer for it. But Reason, which takes a quite

---

[a] Lancelot, who is being followed by Gawain.

different tack from Love, tells him to beware of jumping into the cart, warning him and instructing him to do or undertake nothing which may bring him shame or reproach. Reason, which dares to speak to him in this way, is the product of the mouth, not the heart. But Love, which bids and encourages him to get straight into the cart, is anchored in the heart. Love bids it and so in he jumps. The disgrace of this action does not worry him, since Love desires and dictates it.

And Sir Gawain goes spurring after the cart and is amazed to discover the knight sitting in it. Then he says to the dwarf, 'Tell me what you know about the Queen' and the latter replies, 'If you have such a low opinion of yourself as the knight sitting here, get in beside him, if you will, and I'll take you with him.'

When Sir Gawain heard what seemed to him such folly, he retorted that he will not get in, for to give up a horse for a cart would be a dishonourable exchange. 'Continue wherever you will and I shall follow wherever you go.'

(*Trans.* TONY HUNT)

PERCEVAL'S FIRST SIGHT OF THE GRAIL

(ll 3130–253)

(The most memorable episode in the part of the romance which deals with the young Perceval – much of the work is also concerned with the adventures of the contrasting protagonist, Gawain. At the castle of the Fisher King Perceval fails to ask those questions concerning the ceremony enacted before him which would have cured the King. The consequences of his failure are divulged to him by his cousin after he has left the castle the next day.)

As they sat there talking, a servitor came in through the door, bearing a sword round his neck which he handed to the distinguished host,[a] who, as soon as it was half-drawn, could see where it was made, for there was writing on the sword. And he could see, too, that it was of such fine steel that it would never break except under an exceptional strain, and no one knew what this was besides him who had forged and tempered it.

The servitor who had brought it said, 'My lord, the beautiful maiden with blonde hair, your niece, sent you this present. You have seen none lighter throughout its length and breadth. You may give it to whomever you please, but my lady would be very gratified if it were put to good use wherever it is given away. The person who made the sword produced only three and died before he could make another after this one.'

Then the lord girded him who was a stranger[b] there with the sword and the baldric, which were worth an enormous sum of money. The pommel of the sword was made of gold, the best from Arabia or Greece, and its scabbard of gold brocade from Venice. With its costly fittings the lord handed it over to the young man with the words, 'Sir, this sword was intended and destined for you and I sincerely wish you to have it. Fasten it on and draw it.'

a The Fisher King, *b* Perceval.

He thanks him for it and fastens it round him, not too tight, and then he draws the sword clean from its scabbard. And after holding it for a short while, he placed it back in the scabbard. You may be sure that it suited him, hanging by his side, and even more when held in his fist, and it was clear that in an emergency he would wield it like a warrior. Behind him he saw servants standing around the fire which was burning brightly. He saw amongst them the one who was looking after his arms and he handed over his sword to him and the servitor looked after it for him. Then he sat down next to the lord, who accorded him great honour. And the lighting there inside was as strong as the greatest that could be produced in a building by the use of candles.

And whilst they were discussing this and that, a servitor emerged from a room carrying a white lance, which he held in the middle, and passed between the fire and those who were sitting on the couch. And all inside saw the white lance and its white tip and from the topmost point of the lance came a drop of blood which ran, bright red, right the way down to the bearer's hand. The young man beheld the extraordinary sight which occurred that evening, but he refrained from asking how it came about, for he remembered the lesson he was given by the man who knighted him about not talking too much and he feared that, if he were to ask such a question, it might be held against him. And so he didn't ask. Then two other servitors entered, holding candelabra made of pure gold and inlaid with niello. The servitors bearing the candelabra made a fine sight. Each candelabrum took at least ten candles. And there was also a grail-dish[a] borne by a young woman who accompanied the servitors and who was beautiful, graceful and finely dressed. And when she came in bearing the dish there was given out a great light, so that the candles lost their radiance, just as the stars do at the rising of the sun or the moon, and then in turn came another young woman carrying a silver platter. The grail-dish, borne in front, was of the purest gold. There were

---

a The French has *un graal*, which in Chrétien's day denoted simply 'a dish', but which was quickly elaborated into a mysterious vessel which has defied definition. Wolfram von Eschenbach's grail was in fact a precious stone (*lapsit exillis*) of great luminosity.

all kinds of precious stones set in the dish, the most precious to be found on land or sea. Those in the dish easily surpassed all other stones. And, just like the lance before them, these objects were borne in front of the couch, passing from one room to the other.

And the young man watched them and did not dare to ask who was served from the dish, for he kept constantly in mind the words of his worthy mentor, but I fear that harm may come of it, for I have heard that one can say too little as well as, on occasion, too much. But whether good or harm shall befall him, he asks those present no questions.

(*Trans.* TONY HUNT)

ANONYMOUS

THE QUEST OF THE HOLY GRAIL
(*c.*1220)

GAWAIN UNDERTAKES THE QUEST OF THE HOLY GRAIL

(The first, miraculous appearance of the Grail, in response to which the knights at Arthur's court, following Gawain's initiative, vow to quest for the Grail in order to understand more fully its mysterious nature.)

The ladies then went down to hear vespers in honour of the day. And when the king returned from the minster and made his way to the upper hall of the palace he ordered that the tables should be set up. Every knight went to the place he had occupied that morning. When they were all seated and the noise was hushed, there came a clap of thunder so loud and terrible that they thought the palace must fall. Suddenly the hall was lit by a sunbeam which shed a radiance through the palace seven times brighter than had been before. In this moment they were all illumined as it might be by the grace of the Holy Ghost, and they began to look at one another, uncertain and perplexed. But not one of those present could utter a word, for all had been struck dumb, without respect of person.

When they had sat a long while thus, unable to speak and gazing at one another like dumb animals, the Holy Grail appeared, covered with a cloth of white samite; and yet no mortal hand was seen to bear it. It entered through the great door, and at once the palace was filled with fragrance as though all the spices of the earth had been spilled abroad. It circled the hall along the great tables and each place was furnished in its wake with the food its occupants desired. When all were served, the Holy Grail vanished, they knew not how nor whither. And those that had been mute regained the power of speech, and many gave thanks to Our Lord for the honour He had done them in filling them with the grace of the Holy Vessel. But greater than all was King Arthur's joy that Our Lord should have accorded him a favour never granted to any king before him.

This mark of Our Lord's goodwill was a source of joy to court and guests alike, who now felt sure that they were not forgotten. They talked of little else while the meal lasted. The king himself began to discuss it with those sitting closest to him, saying:

'In truth, my lords, our hearts should be lifted up for joy that Our Lord has shown us so great a sign of His love in deigning to feed us with His grace at this high feast of Pentecost.'

'Sire,' said Sir Gawain, 'you are not yet aware of the full extent of His favour: every man in this place was served with the food of his heart's desire. Such a thing was never seen at any court save that of the Maimed King. But we are so blinded and beguiled that we could not see it plain, rather was its true substance hidden from us. Wherefore I for my part make here and now this vow: in the morning I will set out on this Quest without more delay, and pursue it for a year and a day, or more if need be, nor will I return to court, come what may, until I have looked openly upon the mystery we have but glimpsed this day, provided that I am capable and worthy of such grace. And if it prove otherwise, I will return.'

THE NATURE OF THE HOLY GRAIL

(This final adventure of Perceval, Galaad and Bohort takes place at Corbenic. The nature of the Grail is only partially revealed, for complete knowledge will only come to Galaad in the holy city of Sarras, where, after another appearance of the Grail, he dies.)

Having discharged the functions of a priest as it might be at the office of the mass, Josephus went up to Galahad and kissed him, bidding him kiss his brethren likewise, which he did. Next he addressed them, saying:

'Servants of Jesus Christ, who have suffered and struggled and striven for some glimpse of the mysteries of the Holy Grail, be seated before this table and you shall be filled with the most sublime and glorious food that ever knights have tasted, and this at your Saviour's hand. You can justly claim to have laboured manfully, for you shall reap this day the highest recompense that ever knights received.'

When he had spoken thus, Josephus vanished from their midst, without their ever knowing what became of him. Fearfully they took their seats at the Table, their faces wet with tears of awe and love.

Then the companions, raising their eyes, saw the figure of a man appear from out of the Holy Vessel, unclothed, and bleeding from his hands and feet and side; and he said to them:

'My knights, my servants and my faithful sons who have attained to the spiritual life whilst in the flesh, you who have sought me so diligently that I can hide myself from you no longer, it is right you should see some part of my secrets and my mysteries, for your labours have won a place for you at my table, where no knight has eaten since the days of Joseph of Arimathea. As for the rest, they have had the servant's due: which means that the knights of this castle and many more beside have been filled with the grace of the Holy Vessel, but never face to face as you are now. Take now and eat of the precious food that you have craved so long and for which you have endured so many trials.'

Then he took the Holy Vessel in his hands, and going to Galahad, who knelt at his approach, he gave his Saviour to him. And Galahad, with both hands joined in homage, received with an overflowing heart. So too did the others, and to every one it seemed that the host placed on his tongue was made of bread. When they had all received the holy food, which they found so honeyed and delectable that it seemed as though the essence of all sweetness was housed within their bodies, he who had fed them said to Galahad:

'Son, who art as cleansed and free from stain as any may be in this life, knowst thou what I am holding?'

'No,' replied Galahad, 'unless thou tell it me.'

'It is,' he answered, 'the platter in which Jesus Christ partook of the paschal lamb with His disciples. It is the platter which has shown itself agreeable to those whom I have found my faithful servants, the same whose sight has ever been most hurtful to the faithless. And because it has shown itself agreeable to all my people it is called most properly the Holy Grail. Now hast thou seen the object of thy heart's most fervent longing; yet shalt thou see it plainer still one day. Knowst thou where this shall be? In the city of Sarras, in the spiritual palace; and to this end it is imperative thou leave this place and escort the sacred Vessel on its way, for it is to leave the kingdom of Logres this same night and neither it nor the adventures it gave rise to shall ever more be seen there. Knowst thou the reason for its leaving? The inhabitants of this country neither serve nor honour it as is its due. They have lapsed into dissolute and worldly ways, despite the fact that they have ever been sustained by the grace of the Holy Vessel. And forasmuch as they have made such poor return I strip them of the honour I had granted them. This is why I would have thee go tomorrow morning to the sea, where thou shalt find the ship whence thou didst take the Sword of the Strange Belt. And so that thou shouldst not ride alone, I wish thee to take Bors and Perceval to keep thee company. However, since I would not have thee leave this place without the Maimed King's being healed, thou shalt take first some blood of this lance and anoint his legs with it: for this and this alone can bring him back to health.'

'Ah, Lord,' said Galahad, 'why wilt thou not allow them all to come with me?'

'Such is not my wish,' he answered, 'rather are you to figure my apostles. For as they ate with me at the Last Supper, even so did you eat with me now at the table of the Holy Grail. And you are twelve, as they too numbered twelve, and I the thirteenth over and above you, to be your shepherd and your master. And even as I dispersed them and sent them throughout the world to preach the true law, so do I send you too, some one way, some another.'

With that he gave them his blessing and vanished in such a manner that they knew not what became of him, save that they saw him rising heavenwards.

Then Galahad went to the lance which lay across the table, and touching the blood with his fingers, he walked across to the Maimed King and anointed his legs with it where the steel had pierced him. And immediately the king put on a gown, and springing hale and sound from his bed, he offered thanks to Our Lord for looking so graciously upon him. He lived for a long time after, but not in the world, however, for he left at once to enter a monastery of white monks, where Our Lord for love of him performed in after days many notable miracles, which are not mentioned in this story since they are not essential to its purpose.

(*Trans.* P. M. MATARASSO)

POEM OF MY CID
(Late twelfth or early thirteenth century)

POEMA DE MIO CID

Cantar primero

LAISSE I

De los sos ojos   tan fuertemientre llorando,
tornava la cabeça   e estávalos catando;
vio puertas abiertas   e uços sin cañados,
alcándaras vazías,   sin pielles e sin mantos
e sin falcones   e sin adtores mudados.
Sospiró Mio Cid,   ca mucho avié grandes cuidados;
fabló Mio Cid   bien e tan mesurado:
'¡Grado a ti, Señor,   Padre que estás en alto!
Esto me an buelto   mios enemigos malos.'

2

Allí piensan de aguijar,   allí sueltan las rriendas;
a la exida de Bivar   ovieron la corneja diestra
e entrando a Burgos   oviéronla siniestra.
Meció Mio Cid los ombros   e engrameó la tiesta:
'¡Albricia, Álbar Fáñez,   ca echados somos de tierra!'

3

Mio Cid Rruy Díaz   por Burgos entrava,
en su conpaña   *sessaenta* pendones.
Exiénlo ver   mugieres e varones,
burgeses e burgesas   por las finiestras son,
plorando de los ojos,   tanto avién el dolor;
de las sus bocas   todos dizían una rrazón:
'¡Dios, qué buen vassallo,   si oviesse buen señor!'

First Cantar

THE CID IS EXILED FROM CASTILE

LAISSE I

Tears streamed from his eyes as he turned his head and stood
looking at them. He saw doors left open and gates unlocked, empty

pegs without fur tunics or cloaks, perches without falcons or moulted hawks. The Cid sighed, for he was weighed down with heavy cares. Then he said, with dignity and restraint: 'I give Thee thanks, O God, our Father in Heaven. My wicked enemies have contrived this plot against me.'

2

They made ready for the journey and slackened their reins. As they left Vivar a crow flew on the right, and as they entered Burgos they saw it on the left. The Cid shrugged his shoulders and nodded his head: 'Good cheer, Álvar Fáñez, for we are banished from this land.'

3

Ruy Díaz entered Burgos with his company of sixty knights. Men and women came out to see him pass, while the burghers and their wives stood at their windows, sorrowfully weeping. With one accord they all said, 'What a good vassal. If only he had a good lord!'

THE CID DEFENDS ALCOCER

35

The men clasped their shields to their hearts and lowered their lances, each with its pennon flying. With heads bent down over their saddle-bows, they dashed to the attack courageously. The Cid, sure of success, shouted his battle cry: 'Attack them, my knights, for the love of God! I am Ruy Díaz of Vivar, the Cid Campeador!' They assailed the Moorish ranks, where Pedro Bermúdez was already in the thick of the fight. There were three hundred knights with lance and pennon, and with every lance-thrust a Moor fell dead. On returning to the charge they killed as many more.

36

Who could say how many lances rose and fell, how many shields were pierced, coats of mail torn asunder and white pennons stained red with blood, how many riderless horses ranged the field? The Moors called on Muhammad and the Christians on St James. In a short time one thousand three hundred Moors fell dead upon the field.

37

How well the Cid Ruy Díaz, that great soldier, fought, bending down over his gilded saddle-bow! (Fighting there also were) Minaya Álvar Fáñez, lord of Zorita, Martín Antolínez, the worthy citizen of Burgos, Muño Gustioz, a member of the Cid's household, Martín Muñoz, governor of Montemayor, Álvar Álvarez and Álvar Salvadórez, Galín García, the worthy Aragonese, and Félez Muñoz, the Cid's nephew. From this moment onward the whole host rallied in support of the standard and of the Cid Campeador.

38

Minaya's horse was killed under him and the Christian troops dashed to his aid. His lance was broken, but he grasped his sword and fought manfully on foot. The Cid Ruy Díaz of Castile saw his plight; he approached a Moorish leader mounted on a fine horse and dealt him such a blow with his sword that he cut him through the waist and hurled the rest of him to the ground. Then he rode up to Minaya and gave him the horse, saying: 'Mount him, Minaya, my good right arm! I shall have your full support in the fight today. The Moors are making a firm stand and still hold the field.' Minaya rode, sword in hand, fighting hard to make his way through the Moorish troops, dispatching all those his sword could reach. The Cid Ruy Díaz had struck three blows at King Fáriz; two had missed but the third went home. With blood dripping down his coat of mail, Fáriz turned his horse to flee the field. The battle was decided by that blow.

39

Martín Antolínez struck one blow at Galve, hewed the garnets from his helmet and cut through it to the flesh. Galve dared not wait for another blow. The Moorish leaders, Fáriz and Galve, were defeated! What a great day it was for Christendom when the Moors fled from the place! The Cid's followers pursued the fleeing ranks. Fáriz took refuge in Terrer, but Galve fled farther and made at full speed for Calatayud. The Campeador and his men continued the pursuit as far as that town.

Second Cantar

THE CID CAPTURES VALENCIA

73

... 'Whoever wishes to go with me to besiege Valencia, let him come freely and of his own accord, for there is no compulsion. I shall wait three days for him at Cella.'

74

Those were the words of the Cid, the loyal Campeador, who then returned to Murviedro, which he had taken earlier. The proclamation was carried everywhere, and all who scented plunder came in haste. Crowds of good Christians flocked to join him, and the Cid's riches were steadily mounting. When Don Rodrigo saw these crowds assembled he was filled with joy. Without delay he marched against Valencia and began the siege. He encircled the city completely, allowing no one to go in or come out. The Cid's fame had spread through the lands. Great numbers came and few left. He set a certain time limit for them to surrender if no relief came. For nine whole months he besieged them, and when the tenth month came they were forced to surrender. There was great rejoicing in the whole region when the Cid took Valencia and entered the city. Those who had fought on foot were given horses, and as there were untold quantities of gold and silver, all who took part became rich. The Cid commanded his fifth share of the booty to be set apart, and in this there fell to him thirty thousand marks, while the value of the rest in kind was beyond reckoning. The Campeador and his men rejoiced to see his standard flying from the highest point of the citadel.

Third Cantar

THE INFANTES OUTRAGE THE CID'S DAUGHTERS

127

Abengalbón the Moor, who was a fine brave fellow, rode out with his two hundred horsemen displaying feats of arms. He halted in front of the Infantes and uttered these harsh words: 'Tell me, what have I done to you, Infantes of Carrión? I have kept faith with you and in return you have plotted my death. If I did not forbear for the sake of the Cid, Rodrigo of Vivar, I should exact such vengeance as would startle the world. Then I should escort his daughters to the loyal Campeador, and you would never return to Carrión.

128

Here I take leave of you as evildoers and traitors. With your permission, Doña Elvira and Doña Sol, I shall depart; I go with the poorest possible opinion of the Infantes of Carrión. God grant that the Campeador may not have cause to regret this marriage.' When he had finished speaking the Moor turned away, recrossed the river Jalón, displaying his skill in horsemanship and arms, and prudently returned to Molina. The Infantes moved on from Ansarera and travelled without stopping day or night. Leaving the mighty cliff of Atienza on the left, they crossed the Sierra de Miedes and spurred hastily through the Montes Claros. They passed to the right of Griza, founded by Álamos, and the caves where he imprisoned Elpha. They left on the right San Esteban, which lies further on. Then they entered the oak forest of Corpes, where the branches of the lofty trees seemed to stretch up to the clouds, and the wild beasts roamed at large. They found a grassy clearing with a fresh spring, and there the Infantes ordered a tent to be set up. On this spot they spent the night with all their company, and with their wives, to whom they showed signs of tender love. They proved that love in a strange way when the sun rose next morning. They gave orders that the pack animals should be loaded with all their valuables, that the tent in which they had spent the night should be folded and that all members of their household should go on ahead. No man or woman was to remain behind except their wives, Doña Elvira and Doña Sol, with whom they wished to disport themselves. When all the rest had gone on and only those four were left alone, the Infantes set about carrying out their wicked plan. (To their wives they said) 'Do you hear, Doña Elvira and Doña Sol? We are going to show our contempt and scorn for you here in this wild forest. Today we shall separate and you will be abandoned by us. You will then have no claim to any of our lands in Carrión. This is the news that will go to the Cid Campeador; this is our vengeance for the dishonour with the lion.'

There and then the young men took off their wives' cloaks and fur tunics and left them in nothing but their shifts and tunics of cloth of gold. These wicked traitors put on their spurs and took hold of their strong, hard straps. When the ladies saw them do this Doña Sol cried: 'We implore you, Don Diego and Don Fernando, in God's name! You have two sharp swords, Colada and Tizón. Cut off our heads and make martyrs of us. Everyone will condemn this action of yours, for we have done nothing to deserve it. Do not ill-treat us like this, for if we are beaten you will be disgraced and men will charge you with this crime in assemblies and courts of justice.' The ladies pleaded in vain. The Infantes began at once to beat them with their buckled straps and to hack their flesh cruelly with their sharp spurs. They tore through their shifts to the flesh and the clear red blood poured out over their golden tunics. They were pierced to the heart with shame. If only it had pleased God to send the Cid Campeador at this moment! The Infantes beat them so hard that they were benumbed with pain, their shifts and tunics all stained with blood. The two young men struck till they were weary, trying to see which of them could deal the hardest blows. Doña Elvira and Doña Sol could not utter a word, and were left for dead in the oak forest of Corpes.

THE CID AT THE COURT OF TOLEDO

136

The King made ready to return to Toledo, but the Cid decided not to cross the Tagus that night. 'I beg a favour in God's name. Do you, my liege lord, return to the city while I remain in San Servando, for I expect the rest of my company to arrive tonight. I shall keep vigil in this consecrated place, and tomorrow morning I shall enter the town and shall meet you at the palace before the mid-day meal.' The King replied: 'I give you free permission to do this.' King Alfonso then went back to Toledo, while the Cid Ruy Díaz retired to San Servando. He requested that candles be placed on the altar, for he desired to keep vigil in that holy place, praying to God and communing in secret. Minaya and the Cid's loyal men were ready when morning came. Towards dawn matins and prime were said.

415

137

Mass was over before the sun rose, and they all made fitting and generous offerings. The Cid then gave these instructions to his followers: 'You, Minaya Álvar Fáñez, my good right arm, will accompany me and so also will the bishop, Don Jerome, Pedro Bermúdez, Muño Gustioz, Martín Antolínez, worthy citizen of Burgos, Álvar Álvarez, the ever fortunate Martín Muñoz, and my nephew Félez Muñoz. Mal Anda, an expert in law, will also accompany me and Galindo Garcíaz, the worthy Aragonese. One hundred good men here present will make up your numbers. I wish you all to put on your padded tunics which help you to bear the armour, over them your coats of mail shining like the sun and, over these, ermine or other fur tunics with strings pulled tight to hide the coats of mail; under your cloaks carry your sharp, well tempered swords. That is how I wish to go to the court to demand justice and plead my case. If the Infantes of Carrión should commit any breach of the peace, I shall fear nothing with a hundred like you behind me.' They answered with one accord: 'We agree to do what you wish.' As they said this they all made ready. Thereupon the Cid covered his legs with good cloth hose, and over these he drew his finely worked shoes. He then put on a linen shirt, snow-white and fastened neatly at the wrist with gold and silver links according to his own instructions. Over this undergarment he wore an elegant silk gown beautifully worked in gold brocade. His fur-lined coat was red, with fringes of gold—the one he always wore. On his head he wore a cambric coif embroidered in gold, made on purpose so that no one might pluck his hair. The good Campeador wore his beard long but caught in with a circlet of cord to avoid any possibility of insult. He then covered everything with a cloak so rich that it would attract the attention of all beholders. Dressed like this for his appearance at court, he mounted quickly and left San Servando with those hundred knights whom he had ordered to get ready. At the main entrance to the palace the Cid alighted and entered with sober mien, surrounded by his hundred followers. On seeing the Cid enter, good King Alfonso and Counts Henry and Raymond of Burgundy rose, and after them all other members of the court, to give him an honourable welcome. Neither Count García Ordóñez nor any of the Carrión faction took the trouble to rise. The King took the Cid by the hand, saying: 'Come and sit near me, Campeador, on this bench which was a gift to me from you. Although many will begrudge it to you, I give you the place of greatest honour.' The conqueror of Valencia thanked the King warmly and said: 'Remain in the seat of honour as king and liege lord; I shall stay where I am with these followers of mine.' These words of the Cid pleased the King greatly. The Campeador then took his seat on a finely turned bench with his hundred men in attendance around him. All the court gazed at the Cid, with his long beard caught in with the cord, displaying his manly worth in all his accoutrements – all except the Infantes of Carrión, who dared not look at him for shame ...

(*Trans.* RITA HAMILTON and JANET PERRY)

THE PLAY OF ADAM

(c.1150)

LE MYSTÈRE D'ADAM (*Ordo representacionis Ade*)

Tunc tristis et vultu demisso recedet [Diabolus] ab Adam et ibit usque ad portas inferni, et colloquium habebit cum aliis demoniis. Post ea vero discursum faciet per populum. De hinc ex parte Eve accedet ad paradisum, et Evam leto vultu blandiens sic alloquitur:

DIABOLUS. Eva, ça sui venuz a toi!

EVA. Di moi, Sathan, or tu pur quoi?

DIABOLUS. Jo vois querant tun pru, tun honor!

EVA. Ço dunge Deu!

DIABOLUS.   N'aiez poür!
     Mult a grant tens que jo ai apris
     Toz les conseils de paraïs:
     Une partie t'en dirrai.

EVA. Ore le comence, e jo l'orrai.

DIABOLUS. Orras me tu?

EVA.   Si frai bien:
     Ne te curcerai de rien.

DIABOLUS. Celeras m'en?

EVA.   Oïl, par foi!

DIABOLUS. Iert descovert.

EVA.   Nenil par moi.

DIABOLUS. Or me mettrai en ta creance:
     Ne voil de toi altre fiance.

EVA. Bien te puez creire a ma parole!

DIABOLUS. Tu as esté en bone escole!
     Jo vi Adam: mais trop est fols.

EVA. Un poi est durs.

DIABOLUS.   Il serra mols.
     Il est plus dors que n'est emfers!

EVA. Il est mult francs.

DIABOLUS.   Ainz est mult serf!
     Cure nen voelt prendre de soi;
     Car la prenge sevals de toi!
     Tu es fieblette e tendre chose,
     E es plus fresche que n'est rose;

Then sadly and with downcast look SATAN *shall leave* ADAM *and go to the gates of hell, where he shall talk with the other devils. After that he shall run around among the spectators; and then he shall approach Paradise, on* EVE'S *side, and with a pleasant expression on his face suavely address her:*

(ll 205–334)

SATAN.	Eve, I've come to talk to you.
EVE.	Tell me, Satan, what on earth for?
SATAN.	I've come in your best interests.
EVE.	God's blessing on it!
SATAN.	Don't be afraid.
	I have known for quite a while
	All the secrets of Paradise.
	I'll pass on some of them to you.
EVE.	Go on, begin, I'm listening.
SATAN.	Will you hear me out?
EVE.	Why, certainly.
	I shan't put you in a temper.
SATAN.	You'll keep it quiet?
EVE.	Of course I will.
SATAN.	It'll get out.
EVE.	It won't through me.
SATAN.	I put myself into your hands;
	For me your word is good enough.
EVE.	You will be safe – I've promised you.
SATAN.	You have been very well brought up.
	I've seen Adam – but he's a fool.
EVE.	A bit severe.
SATAN.	He'll soften up.
	Harder than hell he is just now.
EVE.	He's a gentleman.
SATAN.	A menial, rather.
	Even if he neglects himself,
	At least he might look after you.
	You're delicate and sensitive,
	Sweeter to look at than a rose;

A crystal-clear complexion (like
Snow in an icebound valley falling).
You two! God made a bad match there:
You have feelings – *Adam* has none.
All the same, you are the one with sense,
Mature and wise to the finger-tips.
Obviously you're the one to deal with;
I'd like a word.

EVE.   You can trust me.

SATAN. No one must know.

EVE.   Why, who should know?

SATAN. Not even Adam.

EVE.   Not even him.

SATAN. All right, I'll tell you. Listen now.
There's no one here except us two.
And Adam over there – but he can't hear.

EVE.   Speak up, he'll never catch a word.

SATAN. You are the victims of a trick,
A trick – worked in this very spot.
The fruit which God has given you –
There's hardly any goodness in it;
The fruit you *aren't* allowed to eat
Has in it most amazing power –
The very gift of life itself,
Of strength, and of authority,
Of all knowledge, both good and evil.

EVE.   How does it taste?

SATAN.   It's heavenly.
With your figure and your face
You deserve a chance like this –
To be first lady in the world
Queen of heaven and of hell –
Knowing all that is to be,
And being mistress of it all.

EVE.   Is that the fruit?

SATAN.   Yes, that's the one.

Then shall EVE *look carefully at the forbidden fruit, and having looked for a long time she shall say:*

420

EVE.   It does me good simply to *see* it.

SATAN.   Well, just imagine *eating* it!

EVE.   I? How can I?

SATAN.   You won't believe me!
         Pick it first, give Adam some.
         At once you'll have the crown of heaven,
         Be on a par with Him who made you.
         He'll have no secrets from you then.
         As soon as you have eaten the fruit,
         You'll feel completely different;
         You'll be with God, I guarantee,
         In equal goodness, equal power.
         Taste it and see!

EVE.   I'm thinking of it.

SATAN.   Don't believe Adam.

EVE.   I will do it.

SATAN.   When will you do it?

EVE.   Let me be,
         I'll wait till Adam's having a rest.

SATAN.   Come on, eat it, don't be afraid.
         Only children put things off.

Then shall SATAN *leave* EVE *and go to hell.* ADAM, *however, shall
come to* EVE, *taking it badly that the Devil has been talking with her,
and he shall say to her*:

ADAM.   Tell me, Eve, what was he after,
         That devil Satan? What did he want?

EVE.   He spoke to me of our well-being.

ADAM.   Now – don't believe a word he says,
         He's a traitor, I know he is.

EVE.   How do you know?

ADAM.   I've tried him out.

EVE.   What does it matter if I see him?

ADAM.   He'll influence the way you think.

EVE.   He won't, you know. I shan't believe
         A thing he says until *I've* tried it.

ADAM.   Don't let him come near you again!
         He's not a person one can trust;
         He wanted to betray his master,
         And put himself in the high command.
         I shouldn't like that kind of blackguard
         To come crawling to you for help.

Then shall a serpent cunningly contrived climb up the trunk of the forbidden tree; EVE *shall put her ear up to it as if listening to its advice. Then* EVE *shall take the apple and offer it to* ADAM. ADAM, *however, shall not yet take it, and* EVE *shall say to him:*

EVE.   Eat it! You don't know what it's like.
         We mustn't lose our opportunity.
ADAM.   Is it so good?
EVE.   You'll see it is.
         You'll never know unless you taste.
ADAM.   I'm not so sure.
EVE.   Well, leave it!
ADAM.   I won't.
EVE.   You're a coward to put it off.
ADAM.   But I *will* take it.
EVE.   Come on, then! Bite!
         Full understanding's in your grasp, –
         Of good and evil. I'll eat it first.
ADAM.   And I will afterwards.
EVE.   That's right.

Then shall EVE *eat part of the apple, and say to* ADAM:

EVE.   I've tasted it. Oh, God! The flavour!
         I've never tasted such a sweetness.
         This apple has a taste like ... like ...
ADAM.   Like what?
EVE.   Like no one's ever tasted.
         At last my eyes are opened – wide;
         I feel like God – God, the almighty.
         All past and future circumstance

I have it all, all in my grasp.
Eat, Adam, eat – don't hesitate.
It's the best thing you'll ever do.

Then shall ADAM *take the apple from* EVE'S *hand, saying:*

ADAM.   I'll trust in you – you are my wife.
EVE.   Eat! there's nothing for you to fear.

Then shall ADAM *eat part of the apple; as soon as it is eaten he shall
realize his sin; and, bending down so that the onlookers cannot see him,
he shall take off his fine clothes and put on poor clothes sewn with figleaves.
Then simulating the greatest possible grief he shall begin his lament:*

ADAM.   Oh! What wickedness I've done!
No escape left, but death alone.
No hope of rescue – dead am I.
So evil is my destiny:
Evilly changed, good fortune gone;
I had bright hopes, now I've none.
I have betrayed the Lord of life
Through counsel of a wicked wife.
I know my guilt; what shall I do?
My Lord, I cannot look on you.
How can I gaze on holiness
Forsaken through my foolishness?
I never made a worse exchange;
Now I know truly what sin is.
O, death, why don't you seize on me?
Why cannot earth from guilt be free?
Why do I cumber up the world?
Into hell I must be hurled.
In hell shall be my dwelling-place
Till he shall come who shall me save.

(*Trans.* RICHARD AXTON and JOHN STEVENS)

JEAN BODEL
(d.*c.*1209)

THE PLAY OF SAINT NICHOLAS

(ll 115–314)

(In the opening lines of the play, the story of the king's lost treasure, miraculously restored by Saint Nicholas, is outlined by a 'preacher'.)

Enter the KING, SENESCHAL, CONNART, *attendants. Enter separately* AUBERON.

AUBERON.	O King, Mahomet who begot you
	Save and keep you and all your barons!
	And give you strength to defend yourself
	From those who are attacking you,
	Ravaging and ruining your land.
	Our gods they neither invoke nor honour
	For they are Christians, a stinking tribe.
KING.	Away from me, by great Apollo!
	Are Christians in my land, you say?
	And have they mounted an attack?
	Are they so impudent and bold?
AUBERON.	King, never, since Noah built the ark,
	Was such an army, such a force,
	As the one which has invaded us.
	Their foragers run all over the place –
	Whores, and bawds, and lecherous brutes
	Go burning your kingdom down to ashes.
	King, unless you plan defence,
	The land will go to rack and ruin.
KING.	[*to* TERVAGAN] Tervagan, son of a whore!
	Have you permitted this to happen?
	How I regret the gold with which
	I cover your filthy face and body!
	I swear, if my magic doesn't teach me
	How to destroy every single Christian,
	I'll have you burnt and melted down

And handed out around my people;
For you are worth far more than silver –
You're finest gold of Araby.

[*To* SENESCHAL]

Seneschal, I'm almost mad –
Spite and anger are killing me.

SENESCHAL. [*to* KING]

Ah King, you never should have uttered
Such blasphemous and senseless things.
It doesn't become a count or a king
To pour such scorn upon his gods;
In doing so, you're much to blame.
But since I'm bound to give you counsel,
Let's go to Tervagan together
On our bare elbows, and bare knees –
To pray that he will give us pardon,
To pray that through his holy power
The Christians may be overcome,
And, if we are to win the day,
That he will clearly let us have
Some utterance, some kind of sign
By which we may be reassured.
There's no deceit in this advice;
You'd better promise Tervagan
Ten pounds of gold to fatten his face.

KING. [*to* SENESCHAL]

Let's go then, since that's your advice.

[*The* KING *prostrates himself on the steps of* TERVAGAN'S *altar*]

Tervagan, in a wicked mood,
I said many stupid things today –
Better for me they'd been unsaid!
But I was drunker than a coot.
I pray you mercy, confessing my sin
On naked elbows and naked knees.
Lord, support and succour me;
This day recall to mind our Faith

Which Christians think to take away;
Already they're spread through my vast realm.
By oracle and by prophecy
Show me how they can be dislodged.
Lord, show it clearly to your friend
By oracle or by magic art –
Shall I succeed in my defence?
This is the way to let me know:
If victory is mine, then smile;
But if I am to lose, then weep.
Seneschal, what's your opinion?
Tervagan has both wept and smiled:
Here's some deep significance.

SENESCHAL. Your Majesty, you speak the truth;
From Tervagan's smile you can take
Great certainty and great confidence.

KING. Seneschal, in Mahomet's name
As you are my loyal servant,
Plainly expound me this oracle.

SENESCHAL. Your Highness, by my loyal bond,
If this prediction were declared,
I think it wouldn't please you at all.

KING. Seneschal, don't be afraid:
I swear to you by all my gods,
Just let it be a game, a joke!

SENESCHAL. Sir, I believe your godly oath;
But I'd believe you very much more,
If you'd tap your finger-nail on your tooth.

KING. Seneschal, you've no need to fear
Look! the sign of highest trust!
If you had killed my very father
You'd have no further call for fear.

SENESCHAL. Now I can let my tongue run freely;
The oracles shall be expounded: –
That Tervagan smiled first – it's good;
You'll be victorious over the Christians
At the moment you attack them.
And it was right that, next, he wept;

	For it's a matter for grief and pity,
	That in the end you'll give him up:
	And this is what the future holds.
KING.	A hundred times cursed be he
	Who uttered this, or even thought it!
	But, by the faith I owe my friends,
	If I hadn't placed finger on tooth,
	Mahomet himself could not have saved you.
	I would have had you done to death.
	But what's the use? Now to our business:
	Go now, and have the army summoned.
	All are to come upon my business
	From the Orient right to Catalonia.
SENESCHAL.	Connart, where are you? Cry this at once!

[CONNART *runs through the 'place'*]

CONNART.	Oyez, oyez, oyez, good men,
	Your honour and your interest!
	Summons from the King of Africa:
	That all men come, both poor and rich,
	Furnished with arms, as is required.
	Let no man dally, from the land
	Of Prester John to Caramania,
	Alexandrians, Babylonians,
	The Canaanites, the Achoparts,
	Let all come armed, in this direction
	And every other savage nation.
	If anyone remains behind
	Be sure the king will have him killed.
	That's all; now you can yell again.

[*Exit*]

KING.	[*to* AUBERON]
	Hallo, there, messenger! Are you around?
	[*Enter* AUBERON]
AUBERON.	Yes, here, your Highness! Always dutiful.

KING.   Auberon, give your whole mind to courier-work!
               Go all around, call Giants and Canaanites,
               Display my letters patent, show my seal,
               Tell how my Faith through Christians is destroyed.
               Those who remain at home can be quite sure
               They and their heirs will live as slaves for ever.
               Be off! You should be miles away by now.

AUBERON.   My Lord, take heart! The fastest camel could run
               A mile, and I would still have passed him by
               And left him well behind at the halfway mark.

[AUBERON *leaves the palace and crosses the 'place' by the tavern.* CLIQUET
sits inside the tavern, drinking. The TAVERNER *comes out of the tavern
to attract* AUBERON'S *attention*]

TAVERNER.   Dine well, inside! Dine well, inside!
               We've got hot bread! Hot herring, too,
               And wine of Auxerre by the barrel.

AUBERON.   Ah, holy Bene't, your ring-sign –

                   [*He points to the tavern sign*]

               I'd like to meet it every day.
               What are you selling?
TAVERNER.   What am I selling?
               My friend, a wine as thick as cream.
AUBERON.   How much do you charge?
TAVERNER.   The local rate.
               I'm never like to be in trouble
               For over-charging or short-measure.
               Take a seat in the bower here.
AUBERON.   Taverner, you can draw me a pint.
               And I'll despatch it standing up.
               I don't intend to stay here long.
               I have to see to my own affairs.
TAVERNER.   Who is your boss?
AUBERON.   I'm the King's man.
               I carry his seal and his authority.

TAVERNER.   Take this, you'll feel the effects of it.
             Drink up, the best is at the bottom.
AUBERON.   This tankard isn't very deep –
             Only adequate for a taster.
             But tell me, how much do I owe you?
             I'm a fool to hang about so long.
TAVERNER.   Pay me a penny, and then next time
             You'll have a pint for a halfpenny –
             It sells at a shilling, and no mistake.
             Pay me a penny, or have another!
AUBERON.   No, you shall have the halfpenny now –
             And the penny next time that I come.
TAVERNER.   Are you trying to pull a fast one?
             You owe me, at the least, three farthings.
             Before you slip away from here,
             I'm going to know just how I stand.
AUBERON.   But, Landlord, when I'm back again,
             You'll get a penny for the pint.
TAVERNER.   Yes, that'll be when the cows come home –
             You've nothing to gain by trying it on!
AUBERON.   I'll never be able to settle with you,
             Unless I cut a halfpenny in two.
CLIQUET.   Who wants to gamble on the cut,
             A little game, to keep us amused?
TAVERNER.   Did you hear, you courier?
             Come and settle your affair.
AUBERON.   Well, for one farthing, to keep the peace!
CLIQUET.   One farthing! No, for all you owe.
AUBERON.   You must consult the taverner first.
CLIQUET.   That wouldn't be a bad idea.
             Tell me, sir, will you settle at that?
TAVERNER.   Yes, before anyone makes off.
AUBERON.   Play 'Highest Points'! No cheating, now.

             [CLIQUET *throws three dice*]

CLIQUET.   There they go! I haven't touched them.
AUBERON.   Good heavens, you haven't a five or a six,

	Double-three, only, and a one.
CLIQUET.	That only makes seven, bad luck!
	The dice will never run right for me.
AUBERON.	At any rate, I'm still to throw – [*he throws*]
	Well, my good friend, whatever you've got,
	You're paying for what you never tasted!
	I've got two fours for my worst throw.
CLIQUET.	Damnation to all messengers,
	They're always slippery customers.
AUBERON.	Sir, this young gentleman pays the bill.
	He insulted me – but let that pass.
TAVERNER.	Get out! I wish we'd never seen you.

[AUBERON *leaves the tavern and runs to the far edge of the 'place', where he salutes the Emirs in turn*]

(*Trans.* RICHARD AXTON *and* JOHN STEVENS)

MARCABRU
(*fl.*1135–50)

A la fontana del vergier,
on l'erb' es vertz josta · l gravier,
a l'ombra d'un fust domesgier,
en aiziment de blancas flors
e de novelh chant costumier,
trobey sola, ses companhier,
selha que no vol mon solatz.

So fon donzelh' ab cors belh
filha d'un senhor de castelh;
e quant ieu cugey que l'auzelh
li fesson joy e la verdors,
e pel dous termini novelh,
e quez entendes mon favelh,
tost li fon sos afars camjatz.

Dels huelhs ploret josta la fon
e del cor sospiret preon.
'Ihesus,' dis elha, reys del mon,
per vos mi creys ma grans dolors,
quar vostra anta mi cofon,
quar li mellor de tot est mon
vos van servir, mas a vos platz.

By the fountain in the orchard

By the fountain in the orchard,
where the grass is green down to the sandy banks,
in the shade of a planted tree,
in a pleasant setting of white flowers
and the ancient song of the new season,
I found her alone, without a companion,
this girl who does not want my company.

431

She was a young girl, and beautiful,
the daughter of a castle lord.
And just as I reckoned the birds
must be filling her with joy, and the green things,
in this sweet new time,
and she would gladly hear my little speech,
suddenly her whole manner changed.

Her eyes welled up beside the fountain,
and she sighed from the depths of her heart,
'Jesus,' she said, 'King of the world,
because of You my grief increases,
I am undone by your humiliation,[a]
for the best men of this whole world
are going off to serve you, that is your pleasure.

'With you departs my so
handsome, gentle, valiant, noble friend;
here, with me, nothing of him remains but the great distress,
the frequent desiring, and the tears.
Ai! damn King Louis,
he gave the orders and the sermons,
and grief invaded my heart.'

When I heard how she was losing heart,
I came up to her beside the clear stream.
'Beautiful one,' I said, 'with too much weeping
your face grows pale, the colour fades;
you have no reason to despair, now,
for He who makes the woods burst into leaf
has the power to give you joy in great abundance.'

'Lord,' she said, 'I do believe
that God may pity me
in the next world, time without end,

---

[a] The capture of the Holy City in 1147, the occasion of the crusade led by Louis VII, King of France.

like many other sinners,
but here He wrests from me the one thing
that made my joy increase. Nothing matters now[a],
for he has gone so far away.'

(*Trans.* FREDERICK GOLDIN)

I say he's a wise man

I say he's a wise man, no doubt about it,
who makes out, word for word,
what my song signifies,
and how the theme unfolds:
for I myself take pains
to cast some light on the obscurity[b]

of those troubadours with childish minds
who worry honest men:
they scourge and improve
what Truth itself puts forth,
always taking pains to make their words
tangled up and meaningless.

And they put up that false love of theirs
against true love, as though it were as good.
And I say: whoever settles down with Lust[c]
wars against himself;
for afterwards, when his wallet is empty,
Lust shows such fools its cruelty.

It fills me with anger and grief
to hear that pack of perjurers telling us
that Love deceives and tortures
a man by cooling down his lust.

a Or 'He cares little for me',   b Literally 'on dark, obscure speech',   c literally
'bitterness'.

They are liars, for the happiness of lovers
is Joy, Patience, Restraint.

Such lovers, if they don't go off
in two directions, bear witness,
since good Love is their neighbour,
to the one single longing of two desires,
in trust that is firm,
white, precious, true, pure.

For Love has the meaning
of emerald and sard,[a]
it is the top and root of Joy,
it is a lord who rules with truth,
and its power overcomes
every creature.

By its word, its action, and its look,
it comes from a true heart
when it gives its promise and pledge –
if only it does not befoul its gifts;
and whoever does not hasten to it
bears the name of fool.

No sermon, no preaching
is worth a hen's egg
with this fool – they say foolishness
has to do vile things and[b] belts are made of leather;
for I know, when Lust is the mode of their desiring,
it is false to many men, and full of tricks.

The fool, since everything he hears he sings to others,
does not follow reason, he just makes noise,
for his love lives on what it grabs.

a The emerald was said to restrain lust, the sard to encourage humility, chastity and restraint,   b 'as surely as'.

Well, I'll agree: his love really loves,
and Costans is constancy,[a]
and cheating is justice.

The end of this *vers*
takes its stand and turns
on a vile people, dogs
whom an evil star keeps in the dark,
all pompous with their dumb ideas,
barren of the deeds that bring happiness.

May the ideas they're so proud of
make them miserable.

(*Trans.* FREDERICK GOLDIN)

a *Costans*, as a proper noun, stands for the talebearers and the false lovers in Marcabru's songs.

GUILHEM IX OF AQUITAINE
(1071–1127)

In the sweetness of new spring

In the sweetness of new spring
the woods grow leafy, little birds,
each in their own language, sing,
rehearse new stanzas with new words,
and it is good that man should find
the joy that most enchants his mind.

I see no messenger or note
from her, my first source of delight;
my heart can neither sleep nor laugh,
I dare not make a further move,
till I know what the end will be –
is she what I would have her be?

Our love together goes the way
of the branch on the hawthorn-tree,
trembling in the night, a prey
to the hoar-frost and the showers,
till next morning, when the sun
enfolds the green leaves and the boughs.

One morning I remember still
we put an end to skirmishing,
and she gave me so great a gift:
her loving body, and her ring.
May God keep me alive until
my hands again move in her mantle!

For I shun that strange talk which might pull
my Helpmeet and myself apart;
I know that words have their own life,
and swift discourses spread about –

let others vaunt love as they will,
we have love's food, we have the knife!

(*Trans.* PETER DRONKE)

JAUFRÉ RUDEL
(*fl.* mid twelfth century)

When days are long in May

When days are long in May,
I enjoy the sweet song of the birds far away,
and when I am parted from their song,
the parting reminds me of a love far away:
I go bent with desire, head bowed down;
then neither the song nor the hawthorn's flower
pleases me more than the winter's ice.

I shall consider him my lord, in truth, the man
who lets me see this love far away;
but for one good thing that falls to me,
I get two evils, for this love is far away.
Ai! I wish I were a pilgrim there,
my staff and my cloak
reflected in her beautiful eyes.

My joy will come forth, when I entreat her
for the love of God, the love far away,
and, if it pleases her, I shall lodge
close to her, though now I am far away.
Then what fine conferring will come forth,
when the lover come from afar will be so close
I shall know the comfort of her sweet words.

Sad and rejoicing I shall part from her,
when I have seen this love far away:
but when I shall see her I do not know,
our lands are very far away:

there are many ways and roads,
and I am no prophet . . .
but as it pleases God!

I shall have no pleasure in love
if it is not the pleasure of this love far away,
for I do not know a gentler or a better one
anywhere, not close by, not far away:
her worth is true, and perfect, so
that there, in the kingdom of the Saracens,
I wish I were a prisoner for her.

God, who made everything that comes and goes
and formed this love far away,
give me the power – for I have the heart –
to see this love far away
face to face, in such pleasant dwellings
that the chamber and the garden
would all the while be a palace to my eyes.

He speaks the truth who says I crave
and go desiring this love far away,
for no other joy pleases me more
than the rich enjoyment of this love far away.
But the path is blocked to my desire,
for my godfather gave me this fate:
I must love and not be loved.

But the path is blocked to my desire,
a great curse on this godfather
who doomed me to be unloved.

(*Trans.* FREDERICK GOLDIN)

BERNART DE VENTADORN
(*fl.* 1150–80)

When I see the lark moving

When I see the lark moving
its wings in joy against the light,
rising up into forgetfulness, letting go, and falling
for the sweetness that comes to its heart,
alas, what envy then comes over me
of everyone I see rejoicing,
it makes me wonder that my heart,
right then, does not melt with desire.

I, weary, how much I thought I knew
about love, and how little I know,
because I cannot keep myself from loving
one from whom I shall get no favour.
She has it all: she took my heart, and me,
and herself, and the whole world.
And when she took herself away from me, she left me nothing
but desire and a heart still wanting.

I have never had the power of myself,
I have not been my own man since that moment
when she let me look into her eyes,
into a mirror that gives great pleasure, even now.
Mirror, since I beheld myself in you,
the sighs from my depths have slain me,
and I have lost myself, as fair Narcissus
lost himself in the fountain.

I give up all hope in women.
I shall not put my faith in them again;
as much as I used to hold them up,
now I shall let them fall,
because I do not see one who is of any use to me
with her, who destroys me and brings me down.
I shall fear and distrust them all.
because they are all alike, I know it well.

This is how she shows herself a woman indeed,
my lady, and I reproach her for it:
she does not want what one ought to want,
and what she is forbidden to do, she does.
I have fallen in evil grace,
I have acted like the madman on the bridge,[a]
and how this came about I cannot say,
except that I climbed too high on the mountain.

In truth, kindness is lost from the world,
and I never knew it;
for she who ought to have the most of it
has none, and where shall I look?
Ah, you would never guess, when you look at her,
that she would let this man, miserable with desire,
who can never be well without her,
just die, just let him die and not help him.

Since these things do me no good with my lady,
prayer, pity, the rights I have,
and since it is no pleasure to her
that I love her, I shall not tell her again.
Thus I part from her, and I give it all up.
She has given me death, and I will answer her with death,
and I am going away, because she does not retain me,
a broken man, in exile, I know not where.

Tristan, you will have nothing more from me,
for I go away, a broken man, I know not where;
I shall withdraw from singing, I renounce it,
far from joy and love, I hide myself away.

(*Trans.* FREDERICK GOLDIN)

a A proverb says that a wise man never rides his horse across a bridge.

COMTESSA (BEATRIZ) DE DIA
(Late twelfth century)

I have been in great distress

I have been in great distress
for a knight for whom I longed;
I want all future times to know
how I loved him to excess.
   Now I see I am betrayed –
he claims I did not give him love –
such was the mistake I made,
   naked in bed, and dressed.

How I'd long to hold him pressed
naked in my arms one night –
if I could be his pillow once,
would he not know the height of bliss?
   Floris was all to Blanchefleur,
yet not so much as I am his:
I am giving my heart, my love,
   my mind, my life, my eyes.

Fair, gentle lover, gracious knight,
if once I held you as my prize
and lay with you a single night
and gave you a love-laden kiss –
   my greatest longing is for you
to lie there in my husband's place,
but only if you promise this:
   to do all I'd want to do.

(*Trans.* PETER DRONKE)

PEIRE VIDAL
(*fl.* 1180–1205)

With my breath

With my breath I draw toward me the air
that I feel coming from Provence;
everything that comes from there rejoices me,
so that when I hear good of it
I listen smiling,
and for every word demand a hundred:
so much it pleases me when I hear good of it.

For no one knows so sweet a country
as from the Rhône to Vence,
enclosed between the sea and the Durance,
and nowhere knows a joy so pure that shines.
And so among those noble people
I have left my rejoicing heart
with her who brings laughter back to the afflicted.

For a man cannot draw bad luck
the day he thinks of her,
for joy is born in her and comes forth to us.
And whoever praises her
and whatever he says, he tells no lie:
for there's no arguing: she's the best
and the gentlest beheld in this world.

And if I can do or say a thing or two,
let the thanks be hers, for she
gave me the understanding and the craft,
because of her I am courtly, and a poet.
And everything I do that is fitting
I infer from her beautiful body,
and even these words of longing, rising from my heart.

(*Trans.* FREDERICK GOLDIN)

ANONYMOUS

Deep in an orchard

Deep in an orchard, under hawthorn leaves,
the lady holds her lover in her arms,
until the watcher cries, he sees the dawn.
Dear God, the daybreak! oh how soon it comes!

'If only God let night stay without end,
and my beloved never left my side,
and never again the guard saw day or dawn –
dear God, the daybreak! oh how soon it comes!

'Let us kiss, sweet beloved, you and I,
down in the meadows where the birds now sing –
defy my jealous husband and do all!
Dear God, the daybreak! oh how soon it comes!

'Let us create new love-sports, sweet beloved,
down in the meadows where the birds now sing –
until the watcher plays his pipe again.
Dear God, the daybreak! oh how soon it comes!

'In the sweet wind that came to me from there
I drank a ray of my beloved's breath,
my fair and gay and gracious lover's breath –
dear God, the daybreak! oh how soon it comes!'

The lady is delightful, lovable,
admired by many for her beauty's sake,
and holds her heart most loyally in love.
Dear God, the daybreak! oh how soon it comes!

(*Trans.* PETER DRONKE)

MINNESANG

HEINRICH VON MORUNGEN
(?d.1222)

On the heath I heard

Ich hôrt ûf der heide
lûte stimme und süezen klanc.
dâ von wart ich beide
fröiden rîch und trûrens kranc.
nâch der mîn gedanc
   sêre ranc
     unde swanc,
die vant ich ze tanze dâ
  si sanc.
âne leide
   ich dô spranc.

Ich vant si verborgen
eine und ir wengel naz,
dô si an dem morgen
mînes tôdes sich vermaz.
der vil lieben haz
   tuot mir baz
     danne daz,
dô ich vor it kniete dâ si saz
und ir sorgen
    gar vergaz.

Ich vants an der zinnen,
eine, und ich was zir besant.
dâ moht ichs ir minnen
wol mit fuoge hân gepfant.
dô wând ich diu lant
   hân verbrant
    sâ zehant,

wan daz mich ir süezen minne
    bant
an den sinnen
        hât erblant.

On the heath I heard
clear voices and sweet sound;
through this I became
strong in joy, infirm in grief:
she towards whom my thoughts
        pressed on
            and swung,
at the dance I found her – she
    was singing.
Without pain
        I danced there too.

I found her hiding,
alone, and her cheeks wet,
for on that morning
she had surmised my death.
Even my loved one's hate
        is more welcome
            than that,
when I knelt before her as she sat
and quite forgot
        her cares.

I found her on the battlements,
alone, and was called to her.
There I might have well won
the forfeit of her love.
And I thought I had
        burnt up the world
            there and then,
but no, the bonds of her sweet
    love

had left my senses
    dazzled.

    (*Trans.* PETER DRONKE)

    Alas, shall her body never again

Alas, shall her body never again
stream its light through the night for me?
– body whiter than snow,
formed so perfectly,
it deceived my sight:
I thought that it must be
a ray of the moon's light;
then the day came.

'Alas, shall he never again
greet daybreak here with me?
If night could pass away,
so that we need not cry
"alas, now it is day",
as was his way
when last he lay at my side.
Then the day came.'

Alas, they were numberless,
her kisses as I slept.
Then to the ground would fall
the tears she wept;
and yet I solaced her,
that she, without a tear,
embraced me utterly.
Then the day came.

'Alas that so often, gazing,
he lost himself in me,
uncovering me to gaze on
me, poor in my nakedness,

without a sheet, without a dress.
It was a miracle that he
could never tire of this.
Then the day came.'

(*Trans.* PETER DRONKE)

ANONYMOUS

You are mine, I am yours,
of this you must be sure.
   You are locked
   within my heart,
the little key is lost:
there you must for ever rest!

(*Trans.* PETER DRONKE)

DER VON KÜRENBERC
(*fl.* mid twelfth century)

I nurtured a falcon

I nurtured a falcon   for more than a year.
When I had him tamed   exactly as I wished
and had gracefully decked   his feathers with gold,
he raised himself so high   and flew to other lands.

Since then I've seen that falcon   flying superbly:
he was wearing silken   fetters on his feet
and the whole of his plumage   was all red gold.
May God bring those together   who want each other's love!

(*Trans.* PETER DRONKE)

FRIEDRICH VON HAUSEN
(c.1150–90)

I think sometimes

I think sometimes about
what I would tell her
if I were near enough.
It makes the miles shorter
to call my sorrow out
to her, with thoughts.
Often the people here
see in me the figure
of a carefree man,
for so I let it seem.

Had I not taken on
such lofty love,
I might be saved.
I did it without thinking.
And every moment now I suffer
pain that presses deep.
Now my own constancy
has tied down my heart
and will not let it part
from her, as things are now.

It is a great wonder:
she whom I love with greatest torment
has always acted like my enemy.
Now may no man ever get to know
what such a burden is,
it weighs down hard.
I thought I knew what it was before,
now I know it better.
Over there, where home is, I was sad,
and here three times more.

However little good it does me,
still I have this pleasure:
no one can stop me
from thinking close to her,
wherever on earth I turn.
This comfort she must let me have.
If she takes it well,
that gives me joy forever,
for I, more than any other man,
was always hers.

(*Trans*. FREDERICK GOLDIN)

WALTHER VON DER VOGELWEIDE
(c.1170–c.1230)

Lady, accept this garland

'Lady, accept this garland' –
these were the words I spoke to a pretty girl:
'then you will grace the dance
with the lovely flowers crowning you.
If I had priceless stones,
they would be for your hair –
indeed you must believe me,
by my faith, I mean it truly!'

She took my offering
as a gently nurtured child would take it.
Her cheeks became as red
as the rose that stands besides the lilies.
Her shining eyes were lowered then in shame,
yet she curtsied graciously.
That was my reward –
if any more becomes mine, I'll hold it secret.

'You are so fair,
that I want to give you my chaplet now,
the very best I have.
I know of many flowers, white and red,
so far away, on the heath over there,
where they spring up beautiful,
and where the birds are singing –
let us pluck them together there.'

I thought that never yet
had I known such bliss as I knew then.
From the tree the flowers
rained on us endlessly as we lay in the grass.
Yes, I was filled with laughter in sheer joy.
Just then, when I was so gloriously

rich in my dreaming,
then day broke, and I was forced to wake.

She has stirred me so
that this summer, with every girl I meet,
I must gaze deep in her eyes:
perhaps one will be mine: then all my cares are gone.
What if she were dancing here?
Ladies, be so kind,
set your hats back a little.
Oh if only, under a garland, I could see that face!

(*Trans.* PETER DRONKE)

To be long silent

To be long silent was my thought:
now I shall sing once again as before.
Gentle people brought me back to it:
they have the right to command me.
I shall sing and make up words,
and do what they desire; then they must lament my grief.

Listen to this wonder, how I fared
for all my hard work:
a certain woman will not look at me –
and it was I that brought her up to that esteem
which makes her so high-minded now.
She does not know: when I leave off singing, her praise
    will die away.

Lord what curses she'd endure,
were I now to stop my song!
All those who praise her now, I know
they'll rebuke her then – against my will.
A thousand hearts were made happy
by her kindness to me; they will suffer for it if she lets me perish.

When it seemed that she was gentle,
who was more devoted then than I?
But that's all over: whatever she does to me,
she can expect the same –
if she frees me from this distress,
her life receives the glory of my life; if I perish, she is dead.

If I grow old in her service,
she won't get much younger in that time.
Maybe then my hair'll have such a look
she'll want a young man at her side.
So help you God, avenge me,
you young man, and have a go with switches on her ancient hide.

(*Trans.* FREDERICK GOLDIN)

NEIDHART VON REUENTAL
(*fl.*1210–40)

Young and old, rejoice

Young and old, rejoice.
May with its might
has pushed winter out,
the flowers have sprung up.
How sweetly the nightingale
sings on the branch
in varied notes
its echoing song.

The woods are in beautiful leaf.
'My mother can't believe it,'
said a joyous maid,
'but I swear if they tied
one foot with a cord,
I still have to go
with the kids
to the lime tree on the meadow.'

Her mother heard that –
'And I'll strew you your feed
with a stick on your back,
you little peewee,
where are you hopping to
out of the nest?
Sit down and sew me
my sleeve back on.'

'Mother, they should use that stick
to beat out the wrinkles
of the old, like a drum.
This year you're an even greater fool
than you were at the start.
It doesn't take much

to kill you
if you die from a torn-off sleeve.'

And up she sprang in a flash.
'May the Devil bark in your mouth,
I give up on you,
you'll come to a bad end.'
'Yes, Mother, but I am awake,
and you can only dream.
Where there ought to be a sleeve,
there's just a hole along the seam.'

(*Trans.* FREDERICK GOLDIN)

ALEXANDER, DER WILDE
(Late thirteenth century)

Long ago when we were children

Long ago, when we were children,
and time was moving in those years
that we ran across the meadows,
over from those, now back to these,
there, where we at times
found violets,
you now see cattle leap for flies.

I remember how we sat
deep in flowers, and decided
which girl was the prettiest.
Our young looks were radiant then
with the new garland
for the dance.
And so the time goes by.

Look, there we ran to find strawberries,
ran to the beech from the fir-tree,
over sticks and stones,
as long as the sun shone.
Then a forester called out
through the branches
'Come along, children, go home!'

All our hands were stained,
picking strawberries yesterday;
to us it was nothing but play.
Then, again and again, we heard
our shepherd calling
and moaning:
'Children, the forest is full of snakes!'

One child walked in the tall grass,
started, and cried aloud:

'Children, right here there was a snake!
He bit our playmate who held the stakes –
it will never heal;
it must always
remain poisoned and unwell.'

'Come along then, out of the forest!
If you do not now make haste
it will happen as I say:
if you are not sure to be gone
from the forest while there is day,
you will lose your way
and your joy will become a moan.'

Do you know that five young women
loitered in the meadow-lands
till the king locked up his hall?
Great were their moans and their distress –
for the bailiffs tore
their clothes away,
so that they stood naked, without a dress.

(*Trans.* PETER DRONKE)

WOLFRAM VON ESCHENBACH
(fl. early thirteenth century)

PARZIVAL

(794.1ff.)

(The arrival of Parzival and his brother Feirefiz, and how the sick
Anfortas found happiness.)

The newcomers found a great multitude of people there: fine old
knights in number, noble pages, many men-at-arms. The mournful
Household had good cause to rejoice at their coming! Feirefiz
Angevin and Parzival were well received on the flight of steps leading
up to the Palace, into which they then all went.

Here, according to custom, lay a hundred large round carpets,
each with a cushion of down on it and a long quilt of samite. If
the pair went about it tactfully they could find seats somewhere or
other till their armour was taken from them.

A chamberlain now went up to them bringing them robes of equal
splendour. All the knights present sat down, and many precious cups
of gold – *not* glass – were set before them. After drinking, Feirefiz
and Parzival went to the sorrowful Anfortas.

You have already heard all about his reclining instead of sitting,
and how richly his bed was adorned. Anfortas now received the pair
joyfully, yet with signs of anguish, too.

'I have suffered torments of expectation, wondering if you were
ever going to restore me to happiness. Now, the last time, you left
me in such a way that if yours is a kind and helpful nature you
will show remorse for it. If you are a man of reputation and honour,
ask the knights and maidens here to let me die, and so end my agony.
If you are Parzival, keep me from seeing the Gral for seven nights
and eight days – then all my sorrows will be over! I dare not prompt
you otherwise. Happy you, if people were to say you succoured
me! Your companion here is a stranger: I am not content that he
should stand in my presence. Why do you not let him go to take
his ease?'

alweinde Parzivâl dô sprach
   'saget mir wâ der grâl hie lige.
op diu gotes güete an mir gesige,
des wirt wol innen disiu schar.'
sîn venje er viel des endes dar
drîstunt zêrn der Trinitât:
er warp daz müese werden rât
des trûrgen mannes herzesêr.
er riht sich ûf und sprach dô mêr
'œheim, waz wirret dier?'
der durch sant Silvestern einen stier
Von tôde lebendec dan hiez gên,
unt der Lazarum bat ûf stên,
der selbe half daz Anfortas
wart gesunt unt wol genas.
swaz der Franzoys heizt flôrî,
der glast kom sînem velle bî.
Parzivâls schœn was nu ein wint,
und Absalôn Dâvîdes kint,
von Ascalûn Vergulaht,
und al den schœne was geslaht,
unt des man Gahmurete jach
dô mann în zogen sach
ze Kanvoleiz sô wünneclîch,
ir decheins schœn was der gelîch,
die Anfortas ûz siechheit truoc.
got noch künste kan genuoc.

Parzival wept. 'Tell me where the Gral is,' he said. 'If the goodness of God triumphs in me, this Company here shall witness it!' Thrice did he genuflect in its direction to the glory of the Trinity, praying that the affliction of this man of sorrows be taken from him. Then, rising to his full height, he added: 'Dear Uncle, what ails you?'

He Who for St Sylvester's sake bade a bull return from death to life and go, and Lazarus stand up, now helped Anfortas to become whole and well again. The lustre which the French call 'fleur' entered his complexion – Parzival's beauty was as nothing beside it, and that of Absalom son of David, and Vergulaht of Ascalun, and of all who were of handsome race, and the good looks conceded to Gahmuret when they saw the delightful sight of him marching into Kanvoleiz – the beauty of none of these was equal to that which Anfortas carried out from his illness. God's power to apply his artistry is undiminished today.

No other Election was made than of the man the Gral Inscription had named to be their lord. Parzival was recognized forthwith as King and Sovereign. If I am any judge of wealth, I imagine no one would find a pair of men as rich as Parzival and Feirefiz in any other place. The Lord and Master and his guest were served assiduously.

I do not know how many leagues Condwiramurs had ridden by then towards Munsalvæsche in happy mood. – She had learnt the truth earlier on, a message had come to her that her sad state of deprivation was over. Duke Kyot and many other worthy men had thereupon conducted her thence into the forest at Terre salvæsche, where Segramors had been felled by a lance-thrust and the snow and blood had so resembled her. There Parzival was to fetch her, an excursion he could well endure!

A Templar reported to him as follows. 'A group of courtly knights have brought the Queen with all ceremony.' Parzival decided to take some of the Gral Company and ride out to Trevrizent's, whose heart rejoiced at the news that Anfortas's fortunes now stood at the point where he was not to die of his lance-wound, and the Question had won him peace.

'God has many mysteries,' Trevrizent told Parzival. 'Whoever sat at His councils or who has fathomed His power? Not all the Host of Angels will ever get to the bottom of it. God is Man and His Father's Word, God is both Father and Son, His Spirit has power to bring great succour. A greater marvel never occurred, in that, after all, with your defiance you have wrung the concession from God that His everlasting Trinity has given you your wish. I lied as a means of distracting you from the Gral and how things stood concerning it. Let me atone for my error – I now owe you obedience, Nephew and my lord. You heard from me that the banished angels were at the Gral with God's full support till they should be received back into His Grace. But God is constant in such matters: He never ceases to war against those whom I named to you here as forgiven. Whoever desires to have reward from God must be in feud with those angels. For they are eternally damned and chose their own perdition. But I am very sorry you had such a hard time. It was never the custom that any should battle his way to the Gral: I wished to divert you from it. Yet your affairs have now taken another turn, and your prize is all the loftier! Now guide your thoughts towards humility.'

'I wish to see the woman I have not seen once in five years,' said Parzival to his uncle. 'When we were together she was dear to me, as she indeed still is. – Of course I wish to have your advice as long as we are both alive: you advised me well in the past, when I was in great need. Now I wish to ride and meet my wife who, as I have heard, has reached a place on the Plimizœl on her way to me.'

Parzival asked Trevrizent for leave to go, and the good man commended him to God.

Parzival rode through the night, for the Forest was well-known to his companions. When it dawned, he was approaching a place where many tents had been pitched, a find that pleased him greatly. Many pennants of the land of Brobarz had been planted there, with many shields that had marched behind them. They were the Princes of his own country who were encamped there. Parzival inquired where the Queen herself was quartered, and if she had her own separate ring, and they showed him where she lay surrounded by tents in a sumptuous ring.

Now Duke Kyot of Katelangen had risen early. Parzival and his men were riding up. The ray of dawn was still silver-grey, yet Kyot at once recognized the Gral escutcheon worn by the company, for they were displaying nothing but Turtle-doves. The old man fetched a sigh when he saw it, since his chaste Schoysiane had won him great happiness at Munsalvæsche and then died giving birth to Sigune.

Kyot went up to Parzival and received him and his people kindly. He sent a page to the Queen's Marshal to ask him to provide good lodgment for whatever knights he saw had reined in there. Parzival himself he led by the hand to where the Queen's wardrobe stood, a small tent of buckram. There they unarmed him completely.

Of this the Queen as yet knew nothing. In a tall and spacious pavilion in which numerous fair ladies were lying, here, there, and everywhere, Parzival found Loherangrin and Kardeiz beside her, and

– joy perforce overwhelmed him! – Kyot rapped on the coverlet
and told the Queen to wake up and laugh for sheer happiness. She
opened her eyes and saw her husband. She had nothing on her but
her shift, so she swung the coverlet round her and sprang from the
bed on to the carpet, radiant Condwiramurs! As to Parzival, he took
her into his arms, and I am told they kissed.

'Welcome! Fortune has sent you to me, my heart's joy,' she said.
'Now I ought to scold you, but I cannot. All honour to this day
and hour that have brought me this embrace, banishing all my sadness! I have my heart's desire. Care will get nothing from me!'

The boys Kardeiz and Loherangrin, who lay there naked in the
bed, now woke up. Parzival, nothing loth, kissed them affectionately.
Tactful Kyot then had the boys carried out. He also hinted to those
ladies that they should leave the pavilion, and this they did after
welcoming their lord back from his long journey. Kyot then
courteously commended the Queen's husband to her and led the
young ladies away. It was still very early. The chamberlains closed
the flaps.

If ever on a past occasion the company of his wits had been snatched
away from him by blood and snow (he had in fact seen them on
this very meadow!), Condwiramurs now made amends for such
torment: she had it there. He had never received Love's aid for Love's
distress elsewhere, though many fine women had offered him their
love. As far as I know, he disported himself there till towards mid-
morning. The men from Brobarz rode up from the whole encamp-
ment to gaze at the spectacle of the Templars, who were splendidly
arrayed, though their shields were well battered and holed by lance-
thrusts delivered at full tilt, as well as gashed by swords. Each was
wearing a surcoat either of brocade or samite. They were still wearing
their steel jambs, but their other armour had been removed from
them.

There can be no more sleeping.

The King and Queen rose, a priest sang Mass. There was much
jostling in the ring among the gallant knights who had once fought
Clamide. After the benediction all those valiant knights who were
Parzival's vassals received him loyally and with honour.

The flaps and side-walls of the pavilion were now removed.

'Which of the two boys is to rule over your country as its

Sovereign?' asked the King. 'By rights he shall hold Waleis and Norgals, Kanvoleiz and Kingrivals, Anjou and Bealzenan,' he announced to all those Princes. 'If he attains to manhood, accompany him there. My father's name was Gahmuret, and he left it to me by right of true inheritance. By happy dispensation I have inherited the Gral. Here and now, if I find you to be loyal, receive your fiefs from my son!'

This was done with good will. Many pennants were brought to the fore, and a tiny hand enfeoffed them with broad domains in many regions. Kardeiz was then crowned. Later, he ruled Kanvoleiz and much else that had been Gahmuret's.

Benches were taken and a spacious ring was formed on a meadow beside the Plimizœl, where they were to break bread. After a hasty breakfast, the army made ready for the homeward journey. The tents were all taken down, and they rode back with the young King.

Many young ladies-in-waiting and other members of the Queen's train took leave of her with an open expression of their sorrow. Then his lovely mother and the Templars took Loherangrin and rode away briskly towards Munsalvæsche.

'Once upon a time in this forest,' said Parzival, 'I saw a cell through which ran a swift, clear brook. If you know it, show me the way there.'

His companions told him they knew of one. 'A maiden dwells there, abandoned to lamentation over her lover's tomb. She is a treasure-chest of virtue. Our path takes us very close to her. One never sees her free of sorrow.'

'We shall visit her,' said the King, and for their part they complied.

They rode on straight ahead at a brisk pace and late that same evening found Sigune dead on her knees in prayer. There the Queen saw a harrowing sight. They broke through the wall to Sigune, and Parzival had them raise the stone slab of the tomb for his cousin's sake, revealing Schionatulander, lambent as one embalmed, untouched by decay. Close to his side they now laid her in, who, while she lived, had given him virginal love. They then closed the grave. I am told that Condwiramurs broke out into lamentation for her cousin, her great happiness all gone, since the dead maiden's mother Schoysiane (who was Parzival's maternal aunt) had reared her when she was a child – this is why her happiness left her.

If the Provençal spoke true, King Kardeiz's tutor Duke Kyot knew nothing of his daughter's death: this story goes straight and truthfully, not curved like a bow. They did what their journey required and rode by night towards Munsalvæsche, where Feirefiz had whiled away the hours pleasantly as he waited for them. They lit candles in such numbers you would have thought the whole forest was on fire. A Templar of Patrigalt in full armour was escorting the Queen. The courtyard was vast. On it many separate companies were drawn up. These all welcomed the Queen, their lord and his son. Then Loherangrin was taken to his uncle Feirefiz. Seeing him all black and white, the boy did not want to kiss him. Noble children are still said to be a prey to fears. The Infidel laughed at this. When the Queen had dismounted, those on the courtyard dispersed, enriched by the happiness her coming had brought. And now she was led to where there was a noble bevy of comely ladies. Beside them on the steps, Feirefiz and Anfortas stood most attentively. Repanse de Schoye, Garschiloye of Greenland and Florie of Lunel were bright of eye and fair of skin, with the added glory of maiden-hood. Also standing there, lithe as a wand, was the maiden Ampflise, Jernis of Ryl's daughter, who lacked neither beauty nor virtue. I am told that Clarischanze of Tenabroc was standing there, a sweet girl, her fair complexion quite perfect and with a waist drawn in like an ant's.

Feirefiz stepped towards his lady the Queen, who asked him to kiss her, and she kissed Anfortas too, and expressed her joy at his deliverance. Feirefiz led her by the hand to where she saw their lord's aunt Repanse de Schoye standing, with much kissing to be gone through. Moreover Condwiramurs' mouth was red enough already, yet it now had to endure a veritable ordeal of kisses, so that I am much put out that I cannot take on this labour for her, for she was already weary when she arrived among them. Young ladies now led their mistress away.

The knights remained in the Palace which was amply furnished with candles that burned with a brilliant light. And now solemn preparation was made for the Gral.

The Gral was not carried in at all times as a mere spectacle for the Household, but only for particular festivities. That evening, time past, when they were desolated over the Bloody Lance, the Gral had been brought in because they needed help and imagined consolation was at hand – only Parzival had soon left them to their sorrows. But now it will be carried in to them in jubilation, since their sorrows are now utterly vanquished.

When the Queen had removed her travelling clothes and donned her head-dress, she came in a style altogether queenly. Feirefiz received her at a door. Now when all is said, it is beyond dispute that no one ever heard or spoke at any time of a woman more lovely. Moreover, she wore on her person a cloth-of-gold woven by a skilful hand according to that weave devised by Sarant in Thasme so ingeniously. Shedding her radiance about her, she was escorted in by Feirefiz Angevin. Three great fires redolent of wood of aloes had been made along the middle of the Palace. There were forty carpets and more seats than on a certain occasion when Parzival had also seen the Gral brought out. One seat was magnificent beyond all others. On it, Feirefiz and Anfortas were to sit beside the lord of that Castle. Those who wished to give service when the Gral was to appear, behaved with discretion and understanding.

You heard enough before as to how they carried the Gral into the presence of Anfortas. They are now seen to do likewise before noble Gahmuret's son and Tampenteire's daughter. The maidens do not keep us waiting – for here they come in due order everywhere, to the number of five and twenty.

The appearance of the first-comers, with their hair falling in locks, struck the Infidel as comely; but those who came hard behind them he judged even lovelier, the gowns of all most costly. The faces of all those maidens were without exception sweet, charming, winsome. Following them all came fair Repanse de Schoye, a maiden most rare. By her alone, no other, I am told, did the Gral let itself be carried. Great purity dwelt in her heart. The flesh without was a blossoming of all brightness.

(Trans. A. T. HATTO)

GOTTFRIED VON STRASSBURG
(*fl.*1210)

TRISTAN

14. THE PROOF

sus kam diu küniginne Isot,
daz vroliche morgenrot,
und vuorte ir sunnen an ir hant,
daz wunder von Irlant,
die liehten maget Isote;
diu sleich ir morgenrote
lise unde stæteliche mite
in einem spor, in einem trite,
suoze gebildet über al,
lanc, uf gewollen unde smal,
gestellet in der wæte,
als si diu Minne dræte
ir selber zeinem vederspil,
dem wunsche zeinem endezil,
da vür er niemer komen kan.
si truoc von brunem samit an
roc unde mantel, in dem snite
von Franze, und was der roc da mite
da engegene, da die siten
sinkent uf ir liten,
gefranzet unde genget,
nahe an ir lip getwenget
mit einem borten, der lac wol,
da der borte ligen sol.
der roc der was ir heinlich,
er tet sich nahen zuo der lich:
ern truoc an keiner stat hin dan,
er suohte allenthalben an
al von obene hin ze tal;

(The Lord Steward of Ireland has claimed that he slew the dragon, having removed its head while Tristan was unconscious. But Tristan had previously removed the tongue and now at a splendid courtly gathering it is to be put to the test who has won Isolde.)

And so Queen Isolde, the glad Dawn, came leading by the hand her Sun, the wonder of Ireland, the resplendent maiden Isolde. The girl glided gently forward, keeping even pace with her Dawn, on the same path, with the same step, exquisitely formed in every part, tall, well-moulded, and slender, and shaped in her attire as if Love had formed her to be her own falcon, an ultimate unsurpassable perfection! She wore a robe and mantle of purple samite cut in the French fashion and accordingly, where the sides slope down to their curves, the robe was fringed and gathered into her body with a girdle of woven silk, which hung where girdles hang. Her robe fitted her intimately, it clung close to her body, it neither bulged nor sagged but sat smoothly everywhere all the way down, clinging between her knees as much as each of you pleases. Her mantle was set off by a lining of white ermine with the spots arranged diaper-fashion. For length it was just right, neither dragging nor lifting at the hem. At the front it was trimmed with fine sable cut to perfect measure, neither too broad nor too narrow, and mottled black and grey — black and grey were so blended there as to be indistinguishable. The sable beside the ermine curved all along its seam, where sable and ermine match so well! Where the clasps go, a tiny string of white pearls had been let in, into which the lovely girl had inserted her left thumb. She had brought her right hand farther down, you know, to where one closes the mantle, and held it decorously together with two of her fingers. From here it fell unhampered in a last fold revealing this and that — I mean the fur and its covering. One saw it inside and out, and — hidden away within — the image that Love had shaped so rarely in body and in spirit! These two things — lathe and needle — had never made a living image more perfect! Rapacious feathered glances flew thick as falling snow, ranging from side to side in search of prey. I know that Isolde robbed many a man of his very self! On her head she wore a circlet of gold, perfectly slender and ingeniously wrought. It was encrusted with gems, fabulous stones, emerald and jacinth, sapphire and chalcedony, which, despite their small size, were very dazzling and the best in all the land. These were so finely inlaid in their various places that no goldsmith's cunning ever set stones with greater artistry. Gold and gold, the circlet and Isolde, vied to outshine each other. There was no man so discerning who, had he not seen the stones already, would have said that there was a circlet there, so much did her hair resemble gold, and so utterly did it merge with it.

Thus Isolde went with Isolde, the daughter with her mother, happy and carefree. The swing of her steps was measured, they were neither short nor long, yet partook of the quality of either. Her figure was free and erect as a sparrow-hawk's, well-preened as a parakeet's. She sent her eyes roving like a falcon on its bough: they sought their quarry together, not too gently, nor yet too firmly; but softly they went hunting, and so smoothly and sweetly that there was scarce a pair of eyes to whom her two mirrors were not a marvel and delight. This joy-giving Sun shed its radiance everywhere, gladdening the hall and its people, as softly she paced beside her mother. Mother and daughter were pleasantly occupied with two different kinds of salutation – spoken greeting and silent bowing. The rôle of each was as fixed as it was clear. The one gave a greeting, the other inclined her head; the mother spoke, the daughter said nothing. The well-bred pair were engaged in this way, and such was their occupation.

15. THE LOVE-POTION

(Through an error Tristan and Isolde, on the way to Cornwall, drink the love-potion intended for Mark and Isolde.)

Now, apart from the Queen, there was nobody in the cabin but some very young ladies-in-waiting. 'Look,' said one of them, 'here is some wine in this little bottle.' No, it held no wine, much as it resembled it. It was their lasting sorrow, their never-ending anguish, of which at last they died! But the child was not to know that. She rose and went at once to where the draught had been hidden in its vial. She handed it to Tristan, their Captain, and he handed it to Isolde. She drank after long reluctance, then returned it to Tristan, and he drank, and they both of them thought it was wine. At that moment in came Brangane, recognized the flask, and saw only too

467

well what was afoot. She was so shocked and startled that it robbed her of her strength and she turned as pale as death. With a heart that had died within her she went and seized that cursed, fatal flask, bore it off and flung it into the wild and raging sea!

'Alas, poor me,' cried Brangane, 'alas that ever I was born! Wretch that I am, how I have ruined my honour and trust! May God show everlasting pity that I ever came on this journey and that death failed to snatch me, when I was sent on this ill-starred voyage with Isolde! Ah, Tristan and Isolde, this draught will be your death!'

Now when the maid and the man, Isolde and Tristan, had drunk the draught, in an instant that arch-disturber of tranquillity was there, Love, waylayer of all hearts, and she had stolen in! Before they were aware of it she had planted her victorious standard there and bowed them beneath her yoke. They who were two and divided now became one and united. No longer were they at variance: Isolde's hatred was gone. Love, the reconciler, had purged their hearts of enmity, and so joined them in affection that each was to the other as limpid as a mirror. They shared a single heart. Her anguish was his pain: his pain her anguish. The two were one both in joy and in sorrow, yet they hid their feelings from each other. This was from doubt and shame. She was ashamed, as he was. She went in doubt of him, as he of her. However blindly the craving in their hearts was centred on one desire, their anxiety was how to begin. This masked their desire from each other.

When Tristan felt the stirrings of love he at once remembered loyalty and honour, and strove to turn away. 'No, leave it, Tristan,' he was continually thinking to himself, 'pull yourself together, do not take any notice of it.' But his heart was impelled towards her. He was striving against his own wishes, desiring against his desire. He was drawn now in one direction, now in another. Captive that he was, he tried all that he knew in the snare, over and over again, and long maintained his efforts.

The loyal man was afflicted by a double pain: when he looked at her face and sweet Love began to wound his heart and soul with her, he bethought himself of Honour, and it retrieved him. But this in turn was the sign for Love, his liege lady, whom his father had served before him, to assail him anew, and once more he had to submit. Honour and Loyalty harassed him powerfully, but Love harassed him more. Love tormented him to an extreme, she made him suffer more than did Honour and Loyalty combined. His heart smiled upon Isolde, but he turned his eyes away: yet his greatest grief was when he failed to see her. As is the way of captives, he fixed his mind on escape and how he might elude her, and returned many times to this thought: 'Turn one way, or another! Change this desire! Love and like elsewhere!' But the noose was always there. He took his heart and soul and searched them for some change: but there was nothing there but Love – and Isolde.

And so it fared with her. Finding this life unbearable, she, too, made ceaseless efforts. When she recognized the lime that bewitching Love had spread and saw that she was deep in it, she endeavoured to reach dry ground, she strove to be out and away. But the lime kept clinging to her and drew her back and down. The lovely woman fought back with might and main, but stuck fast at every step. She was succumbing against her will. She made desperate attempts on many sides, she twisted and turned with hands and feet and immersed them ever deeper in the blind sweetness of Love, and of the man. Her limed senses failed to discover any path, bridge, or track that would advance them half a step, half a foot, without Love being there too. Whatever Isolde thought, whatever came uppermost in her mind, there was nothing there, of one sort or another, but Love, and Tristan.

This was all below the surface, for her heart and her eyes were at variance – Modesty chased her eyes away, Love drew her heart towards him. That warring company, a Maid and a Man, Love and Modesty, brought her into great confusion; for the Maid wanted the Man, yet she turned her eyes away: Modesty wanted Love, but told no one of her wishes. But what was the good of that? A Maid and her Modesty are by common consent so fleeting a thing, so short-lived a blossoming, they do not long resist. Thus Isolde gave up her struggle and accepted her situation. Without further delay the vanquished girl resigned herself body and soul to Love and to the man.

Isolde glanced at him now and again and watched him covertly, her bright eyes and her heart were now in full accord. Secretly and lovingly her heart and eyes darted at the man rapaciously, while the man gave back her looks with tender passion. Since Love would

not release him, he too began to give ground. Whenever there was
a suitable occasion the man and the maid came together to feast each
other's eyes. These lovers seemed to each other fairer than before –
such is Love's law, such is the way with affection. It is so this year,
it was so last year and it will remain so among all lovers as long
as Love endures, that while their affection is growing and bringing
forth blossom and increase of all lovable things, they please each
other more than ever they did when it first began to burgeon. Love
that bears increase makes lovers fairer than at first. This is the seed
of Love, from which it never dies.

16. THE AVOWAL

(For some time after drinking the potion the lovers dare not declare
their feelings for each other.)

   With this they both grew aware (as is inevitable in such matters)
that their thoughts for each other ran somewhat in the direction of
Love, and they began at once to behave in affectionate accord and
watch for time and opportunity for their whispered conversations.
Love's huntsmen as they were, again and again, with question and
answer, they laid their nets and their snares for one another, they set
up their coverts and lurking-places. They had much to say to each
other. The words with which Isolde began were very much those
of a maid: she approached her friend and lover in a roundabout way,
from afar. She reminded him of all that had happened: how he had
come floating in a skiff to Dublin, wounded and alone; how her
mother had taken charge of him and how she had duly healed him;
how, in all detail, she had learned the whole art of writing, under
his tuition, and Latin and stringed instruments. It was with much
beating about the bush that she recalled his valiant exploit, and the
dragon, too, and how she had twice recognized him – in the bog, and
in his bath. Their talk was now mutual; she addressed him and he her.
   'Alas,' said Isolde, 'when I had so good a chance and failed to kill
you in your bath, God in Heaven, why did I do as I did? Had I
known then what I know now, I swear you would have died!'
   'Why, lovely Isolde?' he asked, 'why are you so distressed, what
is it that you know?'

'All that I know distresses me, all that I see afflicts me. The sky and sea oppress me, my life has become a burden to me!'

She leant against him with her elbow – such was the beginning of their daring! The bright mirrors of her eyes filled with hidden tears. Her heart began to swell within her, her sweet lips to distend; her head drooped on her breast. As for her friend, he took her in his arms, neither too closely nor yet too distantly, but as was fitting in an acquaintance.

'Come now, sweet, lovely woman,' he whispered tenderly, 'tell me, what is vexing you, why do you complain so?'

'*Lameir* is what distresses me,' answered Love's falcon, Isolde, 'it is *lameir* that so oppresses me, *lameir* it is that pains me so.'

Hearing her say *lameir* so often he weighed and examined the meaning of the word most narrowly. He then recalled that *l'ameir* meant 'Love', *l'ameir* 'bitter', *la meir* the sea: it seemed to have a host of meanings. He disregarded the one, and asked about the two. Not a word did he say of Love, who was mistress of them both, their common hope and desire. All that he discussed was 'sea' and 'bitter'.

'Surely, fair Isolde, the sharp smack of sea is the cause of your distress? The tang of the sea is too strong for you? It is this you find so bitter?'

'No, my lord, no! What are you saying? Neither of them is troubling me, neither the sea nor its tang is too strong for me. It is *lameir* alone that pains me.'

When he got to the bottom of the word and discovered 'Love' inside it, 'Faith, lovely woman,' he whispered, 'so it is with me, *lameir* and you are what distress me. My dearest lady, sweet Isolde, you and you alone and the passion you inspire have turned my wits and robbed me of my reason! I have gone astray so utterly that I shall never find my way again! All that I see irks and oppresses me, it all grows trite and meaningless. Nothing in the wide world is dear to my heart but you.'

Isolde answered 'So you, sir, are to me.'

28. THE PARTING

(In despair at being unable to be together, the lovers take a final risk which proves their undoing.)

Now Tristan did just as Adam did; he took the fruit which his Eve offered him and with her ate his death! He came. And Brangane joined the ladies and sat down among them in fear and foreboding. She ordered the chamberlains to close all the doors and admit nobody, unless she herself allowed him in. The doors were shut, and when Brangane had sat down again she went over it all in her mind and deplored it that fear of watchers and spies should have failed to impress her lady.

Now while she was brooding thus, one of the chamberlains left by the main door and was scarcely outside when the King came in past him into the orchard and asked after the Queen in a manner that brooked no delay. 'I think she is sleeping, Sire!' the young ladies answered together. Lost in thought as she had been, Brangane was taken by surprise, and did not say a word. Her head dropped on her shoulder, her hands and heart dropped away from her. 'Tell me, where is the Queen sleeping?' asked the King. They motioned him towards the garden, Mark repaired there at once – and found his mortal pain there! He found his wife and his nephew tightly enlaced in each other's arms, her cheek against his cheek, her mouth on his mouth. All that the coverlet permitted him to see – all that emerged to view from the sheets at the upper end – their arms and hands, their shoulders and breasts – was so closely locked together that, had they been a piece cast in bronze or in gold, it could not have been joined more perfectly. Tristan and Isolde were sleeping very peacefully after some exertion or other.

Only now, when the King saw his woe so plainly, was his irrevocable affliction brought home to him. Once more he had found his way. His old overload of doubt and suspicion was gone – he no longer fancied, he *knew*. What he had always desired had now been given him in full. But truly, in my opinion, he would have been far better off with suspicion than with certainty. All his past efforts to rid himself of doubt had now ended in living death. He went away in silence. He drew his councillors and vassals aside. He made a beginning and said that he had been told for a fact that Tristan and the Queen were together, and that they were all to accompany him and take note of the pair, so that if they were found there as stated he should be given summary judgement against them in accordance with the law of the land.

472

Now Mark had scarce left the bedside and gone but a short way when Tristan awoke and saw him receding from the bed. 'Oh,' he said, 'what have you done Brangane, faithful woman! God in Heaven, Brangane, if you ask me, this sleeping will cost us our lives. Isolde, wake up, poor lady! Wake up, queen of my heart! I think we have been betrayed.'

'Betrayed!' exclaimed Isolde. 'How, sir?'

'My lord was just standing over us. He saw us, and I saw him. He is just going away and I know for a fact, as sure as I shall die, that he has gone to fetch help and witnesses – he means to have us killed! Dearest lady, lovely Isolde, we must part, and in such a way that, it seems, such chances of being happy together may never come our way again. Consider what perfect love we have cherished till now, and see that it endures. Keep me in your heart; for whatever happens to mine, you shall never leave it! Isolde must dwell in Tristan's heart for ever! See to it, dear mistress, that absence and distance do not harm me in your affections. Do not forget me, whatever befalls you! Fair Isolde, sweet friend, kiss me and give me leave to go!'

Isolde stepped back a pace and addressed him with a sigh. 'My lord, our hearts and souls have been engrossed with each other too long, too closely and too intimately, ever to know what forgetting could be between them. Whether you are near or far, there shall be no life in my heart nor any living thing, save Tristan, my life and being! It is a long time now, sir, since I surrendered my life to your keeping. See to it that no living woman ever comes between us to prevent us from remaining always fresh in our affection, in which we have been so perfect all this long time. Now accept this ring. Let it be a witness to our love and our devotion. If you should ever be moved to love any thing but me, let this remind you of how my heart now feels. Remember this farewell, and how deeply it affects us. Remember many an anxious time that I have gone through for your sake, and let none be nearer to your heart than your friend, Isolde! Do not forget me for anyone. We two have brought our joys and sorrows up to this hour in such companionship that we are bound to keep its memory till our dying day. My lord, there is no need for me to exhort you thus far. If Isolde was ever united with Tristan in one heart and bond, it will always remain fresh, it will endure for ever!

But I will ask one thing: to whichever corners of the earth you go, take care of yourself, my life! For when I am orphaned of you, then I, your life, will have perished. I will guard myself, your life, with jealous care, not for my sake but yours, knowing that our two lives are one. We are one life and flesh. Keep your thoughts on me, your very life, your Isolde. Let me see my life again, in you, as soon as ever possible; and may you see yours in me! The life we share is in your keeping. Now come here and kiss me. You and I, Tristan and Isolde, shall for ever remain one and undivided! Let this kiss be a seal upon it that I am yours, that you are mine, steadfast till death, but one Tristan and Isolde!'

When these words had been given their seal, Tristan went his way in great grief and anguish. His life, his other self, Isolde, remained there in deep sorrow. The two companions had never yet parted in such torment as here.

(*Trans.* A. T. HATTO)

GUILLAUME DE LORRIS
(*fl.c.*1240)

THE *ROMANCE OF THE ROSE*

LE ROMAN DE LA ROSE

Grant piece ai ilec demoré,
qu'em Bel Acueil grant amor é
et grant compaignie trovee;
et quant je voi qu'i ne me vee
ne son solaz ne son servise,
une chose li ai requise,
qui fet bien a amentevoir:
≪ Sire, fi ge, sachiez de voir
que durement sui envieus
d'avoir un baisier precieus
de la rose qui soëf flaire;
et s'il ne vos devoit desploire,
je le vos requerroie en dons.
Sire, por Dieu, dites moi dons
se il vos plest que je la bese,
car ce n'ert ja tant qu'il vos plaise.
   – Amis, fet il, se Dex m'aïst,
se Chasteé ne m'enhaïst,
ja ne vos fust par moi veé;
mes je n'osse por Chasteé
vers qui je ne veus pas mesprendre.

(ll 3361–480)

THE LOVER SEEKS A KISS FROM THE ROSE

Long time I lingered there when I had gained
Fair Welcome's love and good companionship;
And, when I found that he would not deny
His service or his solace, made request
For one thing that 'tis well to mention here.
'Fair sir,' said I, 'I have a great desire   THE LOVER

To gain a precious kiss from that sweet Rose;
And, if you're not displeased with my request,
I ask that boon. For God's sake, tell me now
If you'll permit the kiss; for certainly
Unless it please you I'll not think of it.'   FAIR WELCOME

   He made reply, 'So help me God, dear friend,
If Chastity did not so frown on me,
I'd not deny you; but I am afraid
Of her, and would not act against her will.
She always tells me not to grant a kiss
To any lover who may ask for it;
For whosoever may a kiss attain
Can hardly be content with nothing more.
You know that one who has a kiss been given
Has gained the better and more pleasing half –
An earnest of the prize that he expects.'

   When I had heard Fair Welcome thus reply,
I begged no more, fearing to anger him.
One ne'er should press his friend immoderately
Nor agonize too much. The earliest stroke
Ne'er cuts the oak in two. One drinks no wine
Until the mash is squeezed within the press.
Long time my suit to gain the wished-for kiss
Had been delayed if Venus, e'er at war
With Chastity, had not supplied her aid.
She is the mother of the God of Love,
Who many a lover helps. In her right hand
She held the ruddy brand that has enflamed
Full many a lady's heart. She was so quaint
And wore such bright attire that she did seem
Goddess or fairy; by her ornaments
Well could one guess she was not any nun.
I'll not take time her clothing to describe –
Her golden headdress and her coverchief,
Her brooch, her girdle – I must not delay;
You know that she most richly was attired,
Though quite devoid of pride. Her way she made
To where Fair Welcome stood, and thus she spoke:

'Why so disdainful do you make yourself   VENUS
To this man when he begs a savoury kiss?
It should not be denied him; for he serves
And loves, as you can see, in loyalty.
His beauty makes him worthy to be loved.
See how agreeable, fair, and genteel –
How sweet and frank he is to everyone;
And, what is better, he is young, not old.
There is no woman – not a high-born dame –
Whom I'd not call a fool him to refuse.
It will not cause his character to change
If you permit the kiss; 'twere good employ
For one who has so sweet a breath as he.
His mouth's not bad, but seems expressly made
For solace and delight; his lips are red;
His teeth are white and clean and undefiled.
It's my opinion that it would be right
To grant the kiss. Trust me, and give it him;
For to delay would be but to waste time.'

    Fair Welcome felt the heat of Venus' brand,
And, such its power and hers, immediately
He granted me the boon I asked – a kiss.
Nor did I linger, but at once did take
A sweet and savoury lipful from the Rose.
Let no man ask if then I felt delight!
My senses quickly were in perfume drowned
That purged my body from its pain, and soothed
The woes of love that had so bitter been.
Never before was I so much at ease.
Completely cured are all who kiss a flower
So pleasing and agreeable in smell.
The very memory of that caress
Henceforth will keep me from all sorrowing
And fill me with delight and joy, in spite
Of all I've suffered – all the woes I've had –
Since first I kissed the Rose. A little wind
Suffices to disturb the calmest sea;

So easily Love changes, never fixed –
One hour pours oil on waves, another raises storm.

(ll 3481–778)

JEALOUSY, FEAR AND SHAME ARE AROUSED AGAINST THE LOVER

Now rightly I should tell how Shame, by whom
I was much grieved, entered the strife, and how
The mighty walls and tower were raised, that long
The forces of the God of Love withstood.
No laziness shall make me interrupt
The full completion of this history
In hope that it may please a lady fair
(God bless her!) who may all my toil requite
Better than most, whenever she may wish.
　　Next Evil Tongue, who thinks or fancies wrong
In all affairs of lovers, and retails
All that he knows or weens, began to spy,
Between me and Fair Welcome, sweet accord.
Because he is old Scolding's son, and has
A dirty, bitter, biting gift of speech –
Her legacy – he could not hold his peace.
So Evil Tongue began to slander me,
Saying that ill relationship he'd seen
Betwixt me and Fair Welcome. Recklessly
The rascal talked of Courtesy's fair son
And me till he awakened Jealousy,
Who roused in fright when she the jangler heard.
Then to Fair Welcome did she run like mad
(In far Etampes or Meaux he'd better been!)
And thus assailed him: 'Good-for-nothing boy,　　JEALOUSY
Are you out of your wits to entertain
A youth of whom I have much ill report?
'Twould seem that all too lightly you believe
Palaver of a stranger. Don't expect
That I shall trust you more. You shall be bound

Or locked up in a tower, for certainly
I see no help for it. Shame's left you quite;
She's given you too much rope, nor taken pains
To guard you well. I've noted oftentimes
How she neglects her sister, Chastity,
And lets a lawless youth invade our realm
To bring disgrace on both myself and her.'

   Fair Welcome knew not how to make reply;
He would have hidden himself but that we two
Were caught together there, to prove his guilt;
Though when I heard the scold start her attack
I took to flight, for quarrels bother me.
Then Shame came forward, showing in her face
She feared much to be taken in a fault.
In place of maiden wimple, veil she wore;
Humble and plain was she, like abbey nun.
Now much abashed, she spoke in accents low:
'For God's sake, dame, believe not Evil Tongue;   SHAME
A scandalmonger he, who lightly lies,
Deceiving many a worthy man. If he
Now blames Fair Welcome, it is nothing new.
He is accustomed to recount false tales
Of squires and demoiselles. Though I admit
Fair Welcome gives himself too long a leash
In gathering friends with whom he should not deal,
I certainly do not believe that he
Had least desire for foolishness or sin.
Indeed, 'tis true his mother, Courtesy,
Has taught him no affection to pretend
And surely not to show a foolish love.
Fair Welcome has no other wish or thought
Than to be full of jollity and fun
And to converse with hosts of genial friends.
Undoubtedly too easy I have been
With him, neglecting reprimand and guard;
For this I pardon beg. Disconsolate
Am I if I'm too soft to do what's best.
But I repent my folly, and I'll watch

Fair Welcome with due care from this time forth.
I'll never from this duty ask release.'
'Ah, Shame,' said Jealousy, 'great fear have I
To be betrayed, for Lechery so reigns
That everyone's in danger of disgrace.
Nor groundless is my fear; Vice rules o'er all
And endlessly seems to increase his power.
Chastity no longer is secure
Even in cloister or in nunnery.
Hence I must with a stronger wall enclose
The roses and the rosary; no more
Shall they remain displayed to all men's sight,
For I can not depend upon your guard.
Now I perceive and know it for a fact:
'Best deputies deserve no confidence.'
If I'm not careful, scarce a year will pass
When I shall not be made to seem a fool.
Against that to provide is but good sense.
I'll close the road to those who come to spy
Upon my roses, making me their dupe.
I'll not be idle till a fortress's made
To enclose the rosary; and in the midst
A lofty tower shall be Fair Welcome's jail,
For fear of further treason. I will keep
So well his person that he'll have no power
To issue forth, companionship to have
With youths who flatter him with winning words,
Purposing but to bring him to disgrace.
Truant sots and fools too much have swarmed
About here in deceit; but, as I live,
Know this for truth: it was an evil hour
For him when first he granted them his smiles.'
    At that came Fear, trembling and dismayed
And daring not to say a single word.
Since she perceived what ire her talking showed,
She stood apart till Jealousy withdrew.
Then Shame and Fear were left together there,
Shivering to their very buttock bones,

Till Fear, abashed, addressed her cousin Shame:
'Heavy it weighs upon my soul that we
Must bear the blame for what we have not done.
Many a time have May and April passed,
And we've had no reproach till Jealousy
Suspiciously heaped insult on abuse.
Let us immediately Danger seek
And show him well, and carefully explain,
That he has wrought great mischief not to guard
More warily the garden; far too much
He has allowed Fair Welcome openly
To work his will. He must amend his ways
Or necessarily flee from the land,
Since he could never brave the war for which
Mad Jealousy has provocation great
If she should likewise take his deeds amiss.'

    At this agreement they arrived, and went
To Danger, who beneath a hawthorn lay.
The boor, in place of pillow for his head,
Was dozing on a biggish heap of hay
Till Shame awoke him, pitching into him
With chiding: 'How then! By what evil chance
Are you asleep at such a time as this?
A fool were he who held you of more use
For guarding roses than some mutton tail.
Too lax and negligent are you, who should
Be strict, and harshly deal with everyone.
You foolishly Fair Welcome did allow
To introduce a man who gets us blamed.
You doze while we get undeserved rebuke.
Do you still sleep? Get up and mend the hedge,
And no exception make for anyone.
To side-step trouble little suits your name.
Fair Welcome's free and frank, but you should be
Savage and rude and harsh and insolent.
A courteous churl is an anomaly;
And, as I've oft heard quoted in reproof,
'No man can of a buzzard make a hawk.'

Who finds you debonair should think you mad.
With help and favour do you try to please?
You will be charged with cowardice if you
Henceforth shall have the name of being lax,
So readily believing flatterers.'

Then Fear took up the word: 'I'm much surprised   FEAR
That you're not wide-awake to mind your charge.
You soon for this may suffer; Jealousy
May fan her wrath, for she is proud and fell
And prompt to chide. Today she Shame assailed
And by her menace chased Fair Welcome off,
Declaring that she'll never rest until
She's walled him up alive. All this occurred
By your neglect, because you rigour lack.
I fear your heart has failed you; you'll pay dear
With grief and pain if Jealousy learns the truth.'

The churl his shock head raised. He shook himself,
Wrinkled his nose, and rubbed and rolled his eyes.
Hearing himself thus blamed, he showed his ire,
And thus he spoke: 'If you think that I am licked,   DANGER
You give me cause for anger. If I've failed
To keep my charge, then I have lived too long;
Burn me alive if any man gets by.
The heart within my breast feels much chagrin
That any foot this place has ever trod.
I'd rather have two swords thrust through my breast.
That I have been a fool I plainly see;
But, for the sake of you two, I'll amend.
Never again will I be lax to guard
This place; if I catch anybody here,
He'll wish that he had stayed in Pavia.
I swear and vow, to the last day of my life
You ne'er again will think me recreant.'

Danger arose and fiercely looked about;
Seizing his club, he searched the rosary
For hole or gap or passageway to block.
Thenceforth the situation was reversed,
For Danger came to be more hard and fell

Than he was wont to be. I nearly died
Because I had aroused his anger so.
No longer could I feast my eyes upon
The sight for which I longed. My spirits drooped
At being from Fair Welcome so estranged.
You may believe my frame with shivers shook
When of the Rose I thought, which I at will
Had seen close by – when I recalled the kiss
Which through my being spread a balm so sweet
That I near fainted but still let me keep
Within my soul the savour of the Rose.
Know well that, when I realized that I
Must go away, I wished for death, not life.
Evil the hour when once I touched the bud
With eyes, with lips, with face, if ne'er again
The God of Love permit renewed caress!
My soul was fanned to flame with a desire
That was more great because I'd had a taste.
Then sighs and tears and sleeplessness returned –
Prickings and shivers, mournful thoughts, complaints.
My multitudinous pains put me in hell.
Accurst be Evil Tongue, whose lying lips
Purchased for me such store of bitter condiment!

(*Trans.* H. W. ROBBINS)

JEAN DE MEUNG
(c. 1240–1305)

THE *ROMANCE OF THE ROSE*

(ll 4263–310)

REASON REMONSTRATES WITH THE LOVER

'Love is a troubled peace, an amorous war –
A treasonous loyalty, disloyal faith –
A fear that's full of hope, a desperate trust –
A madman's logic, reasoned foolishness –
A pleasant peril in which one may drown –
A heavy burden that is light to bear –
Charybdis gracious, threatening overthrow –
A healthy sickness and most languorous health –
A famine swallowed up in gluttony –
A miserly sufficiency of gold –
A drunken thirst, a thirsty drunkenness –
A sadness gay, a frolicsomeness sad –
Contentment that is full of vain complaints –
A soft malignity, softness malign –
A bitter sweetness, a sweet-tasting gall –
A sinful pardon, and a pardoned sin –
A joyful pain – a pious felony –
A game of hazard, ne'er dependable –
A state at once too movable, too firm –
An infirm strength, a mighty feebleness
Which in its struggles moves the very world –
A foolish wisdom, a wise foolishness;
It is prosperity both glum and gay –
A laughter full of sighs and full of tears –
Laborious repose by day and night –
A happy Hell, a saddened Paradise –
A prison which delights its prisoners –
A springtime mantled yet with winter's snow –
A moth that feeds on frieze as well as silk,

For love lives just as well in coarsest clothes
As in a diaper material.
No man is found so highborn or so wise,
No man of such proved strength and hardiness,
No man of other qualities so good
That Love could never conquer him.

(ll 18917–19024)

NATURE ABSOLVES THE HEAVENS AND THE WHOLE NATURAL
WORLD WITH THE EXCEPTION OF MANKIND WHICH SHE
DENOUNCES

'In windy war the ocean waves are raised   NATURE
And foam-lipped breakers kiss the very clouds;
Then peace comes o'er the sea, which roars no more.
And stills its bounding billows, but for tides
Which ebb and flow, by influence of the moon
Compelled to motion; naught can hinder them.
If more profoundly one investigate
The miracles that heavenly bodies cause
Upon the earth, he'll find in them so much
That's marvelous that never he'll succeed
To put it all in writing in a book.
So I acquit the heavens of revolt
Against me, for by their beneficence
They do so much of good that I perceive
That duly all their duty they fulfil.
     'Nor do I of the elements complain;
For my commandments fully they obey,
Blending and resolving, each in turn.
All is corruptible beneath the moon;
Naught is so nourished that it cannot rot.
By their own composition and the intent
Of nature all must follow this fixed law
Which never fails: all whence it comes returns.
So general this rule, it cannot fail
To function in respect to elements.

'Nor do I of the vegetable world
Complain. The plants are never slow to heed
My will, but are attentive to my laws.
Long as they live they spread their roots and leaves –
Expand in trunk and branches, flower and fruit.
Each year each one produces what it can,
As herb or bush or tree, until it dies.

　　'Nor do I of the fish and fowl complain.
They are most fair to see, and well they know
And follow all my rules. Good scholars they!
All tug the traces fastened to my yoke.
They breed according to their several wonts,
And thus do honour to their lineage.
Great comfort 'tis to see how each of them
Strives to prevent his race from dying out.

　　'Nor do I of the animals complain,
Who bow their heads continually to earth
And never warfare wage against my rule.
All do my service as their fathers did.
Each male goes with his female, and they mate
Fairly and pleasingly, and in their joy
Their young engender, coupling just as oft
As may seem good to them. No bargaining
Delays their union when they're in accord.
With courtesy that is most debonair
It pleases each to do the other's will;
And all for what they do feel amply paid
By blessings that upon them I bestow.
So do my fairest insects: flies and ants
And butterflies. Even the worms that breed
In rottenness cease not to keep my laws.
Adders and snakes are studious to do my work.'

'Mankind alone, to whom I've freely given
All blessings that I know how to bestow –
Mankind alone, whom I have so devised
And made that he towards Heaven turns his face –
Mankind alone, whom I have brought to birth

Bearing the very likeness of his God –
Mankind alone, for whom I toil and moil,
Who is the very culmination of my work,
Who has no more, except what I have given,
As to his body, in his trunk and limbs,
Than what a ball of pomander would buy,
And, as to soul, but just one single thing:
For, as I may assert who am his dame,
He has from me in body and in soul
Three energies – existence, feeling, life –
Of great advantage to the wretch if he
Were wise and good, for he's provided well
With all the good things God has placed on earth –
Companion he to creatures everywhere
And sharer of the blessings they enjoy –
Being he owns in common with the stones;
Life he enjoys in common with the herbs;
Feeling he has in common with the beasts;
Thinking in common with the angel host
He has, excelling all the others thus
(What more need I enumerate of him?)
He has whatever humans can conceive;
He is a microcosm in himself –
Yet worse than any wolf cub uses me.'

(*Trans.* H. W. ROBBINS)

NJAL'S SAGA
(c.1280)

THE BURNING OF NJAL'S HOME
(from chs 125–32)

(These chapters describe the central event of *Njal's Saga*. Njal's household consists of himself and his wife Bergthora; his three sons, Skarp-Hedin, Helgi and Grim; his son-in-law Kari; two of his daughters, three daughters-in-law, and the child Thord, Kari's son. Most of the other people mentioned by name in this extract are the enemies of Njal's sons, led by Flosi; the exceptions are Hjalti Skeggjason, Hildiglum, and Geirmund, none of whom is involved in the feud. The account of the Burning is preceded and followed by supernatural events which provide a symbolical moral commentary upon the event.)

125

At Reykjum á Skeithum bjó Rúnólfr Thórsteinsson. Hildiglúmr hét sonr hans. Hann gekk út dróttinsdagsnótt, thá er tólf vikur váru til vetrar. Hann heyrthi brest mikinn, svá at hónum thótti skjálfa bæthi jörth ok himinn. Síthan leit hann í vestrættina. Hann thóttist sjá thangat hring ok eldslit á ok í hringinum mann á gráum hesti. Hann bar skjótt yfir, ok fór hann hart. Hann hafthi loganda brand í hendi. Hann reith svá nær honum, at hann mátti görla sjá hann. Hann var svartr sem bik. Hann kvath vísu thessa meth mikilli raust:

> Ek ríth hesti
> hélugbartha,
> úrigtoppa,
> ills valdanda.
> Eldr 's í endum,
> eitr í mithju.
> Svá 's of Flosa ráth
> sem fari kefli,
> svá 's of Flosa ráth
> sem fari kefli.

Thá thótti honum hann skjóta brandinum austr til fjallanna, ok thótti honum hlaupa upp eldr mikill í móti, svá at hann thóttist ekki sjá til fjallanna fyrir. Honum sýndist sjá mathr rítha austr undir eldinn, ok hvarf thar.

Síthan gekk hann inn ok til rúms síns ok fekk langt óvit ok rétti vith ór því. Hann munthi allt that, er fyrir hann hafthi borit, ok sagthi föthur sínum, en hann bath hann seggja Hjalta Skeggjasyni.

Hann fór ok sagthi honum. 'Thú hefir sét gandreith,' segir Hjalti, 'ok er that jafnan fyrir stórtíthindum.'

(For the convenience of English readers, 'th' has been substituted for the special letters representing this sound in Icelandic.)

125

At Reykir in Skeid lived a man called Runolf Thorsteinsson, who had a son called Hildiglum. On the Sunday night twelve weeks before winter, Hildiglum was outside the house; then he heard a tremendous crash, and the earth and sky seemed to quiver. He looked to the west, and thought he saw a ring of fire with a man on a grey horse inside the circle, riding furiously. He rushed past Hildiglum with a blazing firebrand held aloft, so close that Hildiglum could see him distinctly; he was as black as pitch, and Hildiglum could hear him roaring out:

> 'I ride a horse
> With icy mane,
> Forelock dripping,
> Evil-bringing.
> Fire at each end,
> And poison in the middle,
> Flosi's plans
> Are like this flying firebrand –
> Flosi's plans
> Are like this flying firebrand.'

Before Hildiglum's eyes, it seemed, the rider hurled the firebrand east towards the mountains; a vast fire erupted, blotting out the mountains from sight. The rider rode east towards the flames and vanished into them.

Hildiglum returned to the house and went to his bed, where he fainted and lay unconscious for a long time. When he recovered he could remember every detail of the apparition he had seen, and he told his father about it. His father asked him to tell it to Hjalti Skeggjason.

Hildiglum went to Hjalti and told him. Hjalti said, 'You have seen the witch-ride, and that is always a portent of disaster.'

126

Two months before the beginning of winter, Flosi made ready for his journey west, and summoned all those men who had promised to make it with him. They all came to Svinafell, each with two horses and good weapons, and stayed there overnight. Early on Sunday morning Flosi had matins said and then sat down to table. He told each member of the household what work was to be done during his absence, and then went to his horses.

Flosi and his company set off west towards Sand. He warned them not to ride too hard at first, saying they would have enough of that to do before the journey's end. He said that all should wait for anyone who had to drop back. They rode west to the Skogar District and reached Kirkby, where Flosi asked all his men to attend church and pray.

They did so. Then they remounted and rode up into the mountains, passing Fiskiwaters on the west side and then heading due west for Sand, keeping Eyjafells Glacier on their left. From there they descended to Godaland and on to Markar River, and reached Thrihyrning Ridges early in the afternoon of the second day. They waited there until mid-evening, by which time everyone had arrived except Ingjald of Keldur. The Sigfussons denounced him, but Flosi told them not to abuse him in his absence – 'we shall pay him back later, nonetheless.'

127

Meanwhile, over at Bergthorsknoll, [Njal's sons] Grim and Helgi were away on a visit to Holar, where their children were being fostered; they had told Njal that they would not be back that night. They spent the whole day at Holar.

Some beggarwomen came there, who claimed to have travelled a long way; the brothers asked them what news they had, and they replied that they had none to speak of, apart from one thing that had seemed unusual.

The Njalssons asked what that might be, and told them to keep nothing back. They agreed.

'We have just come down from Fljotshlid,' said the women, 'and there we saw all the Sigfussons riding fully-armed, making for Thrihyrning Ridges; they were in a group of fifteen. We also saw Grani Gunnarsson and Gunnar Lambason, in a group of five, all heading the same way. One might say that everyone is on the go these days.'

Helgi Njalsson said, 'In that case, Flosi must have arrived from the east, and they will all be going to join him. Grim and I ought now to be with Skarp-Hedin.'

Grim agreed, and they set off home.

At Bergthorsknoll, Bergthora was saying to the members of her household, 'You are all to choose your favourite food tonight, for this is the last evening on which I shall serve a meal for my household.'

Those who heard her denied this strenuously.

'It shall be so, nevertheless' she replied, 'and I could tell you much more if I wished to; but let this suffice as proof, that Grim and Helgi will be home tonight before this meal is over. If that comes true, the rest of what I have said will come true.'

After that, she brought food to the table.

Suddenly Njal said, 'How strange! I seem to see all four corners of the room before my eyes, and both the gable walls are down, and there is blood all over the table and the food.'

Everyone was greatly perturbed except Skarp-Hedin, who told them that they must not wail or do anything disgraceful that people would talk about afterwards – 'for our behaviour will be judged by stricter standards than that of others, and that is as it should be.'

Grim and Helgi arrived home before the tables were taken away, and everyone was greatly taken aback. Njal asked why they had been in such a hurry to return, and they told him what they had heard.

Njal told everyone not to go to bed that night.

128

Meanwhile, Flosi was saying to his men, 'We shall now ride to Bergthorsknoll, to reach there by nightfall.'

When they arrived, they rode into a hollow by the knoll, where they tethered their horses and waited until late into the night.

'Now we shall walk slowly up to the house,' said Flosi, 'keeping close together, and see what they do.'

Njal was standing outside with his sons and Kari and all the servants ranged in front of the house. They were nearly thirty in all.

Flosi halted and said, 'We shall note carefully what action they take, for I suspect that we shall never get the better of them if they stay out of doors.'

'This would turn out a sorry trip if we did not dare to make an attack on them,' said Grani.

'We shall certainly attack them,' said Flosi, 'even though they remain outside. But we would have to pay a heavy price, and not many would live to tell the tale, whichever side wins.'

Njal said to his men, 'How many do you think they are?'

'They are a tightly-knit force,' said Skarp-Hedin, 'and strong in numbers too; but they suspect that they will have a hard task to overcome us, and that is why they have halted.'

'I do not think so,' said Njal. 'I want everyone to go inside, for they found it hard to overcome Gunnar of Hlidarend, even though he was only one against many. This house is just as strongly built as his was, and they will never be able to overcome us.

'That is the wrong way to look at it,' said Skarp-Hedin. 'The men who attacked Gunnar were chieftains of such character that they would have preferred to turn back rather than burn him in his house. But these people will not hesitate to use fire if they cannot overcome us in any other way, for they will resort to any means to destroy us. They will assume, and rightly, that it will cost them their lives if we escape. And I for one am reluctant to be suffocated like a fox in his den.'

Njal said, 'Now you are going to override my advice and show me disrespect, my sons – and not for the first time. But when you were younger you did not do so, and things were better for you then.'

'Let us do as our father wishes,' said Helgi. 'That will be best for all of us.'

'I am not so sure of that,' said Skarp-Hedin, 'for he is a doomed man now. But still, I do not mind pleasing my father by burning in the house with him, for I am not afraid of dying.'

To Kari he said, 'Let us all keep close together, brother-in-law, so that we do not get separated.'

'That is what I had intended,' said Kari, 'but if fate wills it otherwise, then it will be so and nothing can be done about it.'

'Then you avenge us,' said Skarp-Hedin, 'and we shall avenge you if we survive.'

Kari agreed. Then they all went inside and stood guard at the doors.

Flosi said, 'Now they are doomed, for they have gone indoors. We shall advance on the house at once and form up in strength round the doors to make sure that not one of them escapes, neither Kari nor the Njalssons; for otherwise it will cost us our lives.'

Flosi and his men came up to the house and surrounded the whole building, in case there might be a secret door somewhere. Flosi himself and his own men went up to the front of the house. Hroald Ozurarson rushed at Skarp-Hedin and lunged at him with a spear; Skarp-Hedin hacked the spear-shaft in two and sprang at him, swinging his axe. The axe fell on Hroald's shield and dashed it against him; the upper horn of the axe caught him full in the face, and he fell back dead at once.

Kari said, 'There is no escaping you, Skarp-Hedin; you are the bravest of us all.'

'I don't know about that,' said Skarp-Hedin, and he was seen to draw back his lips in a grin.

Kari and Grim and Helgi lunged often with their spears and wounded many men, and Flosi and the attackers were kept at bay.

Flosi said, 'We have suffered heavy losses among our men, several wounded and one dead, the one we would least have wanted to lose. It is obvious that we cannot defeat them with weapons; and there are many here who are showing less fight than they said they would. Now we must resort to another plan. There are only two courses open to us, neither of them good: we must either abandon the attack, which would cost us our own lives, or we must set fire to the house and burn them to death, which is a grave responsibility before God, since we are Christian men ourselves. But that is what we must do.'

129

Then they kindled a fire and made a great blaze in front of the doors.

Skarp-Hedin said, 'So you're making a fire now, lads! Are you thinking of doing some cooking?'

'Yes,' said Grani, 'and you won't need it any hotter for roasting.'

'So this is your way,' said Skarp-Hedin, 'of repaying me for avenging your father, the only way you know; you value more highly the obligation that has less claim on you.'

The women threw whey on the flames and doused the fire.

Kol Thorsteinsson said to Flosi, 'I have an idea. I have noticed that there is a loft above the cross-beams of the main room. That is where we should start a fire, and we can use the heap of chickweed behind the house as kindling.'

They brought the chickweed up and set fire to it, and before those inside knew what was happening, the ceiling of the room was ablaze from end to end. Flosi's men also lit huge fires in front of all the doors. At this, the womenfolk began to panic.

Njal said to them, 'Be of good heart and speak no words of fear, for this is just a passing storm and it will be long before another like it comes. Put your faith in the mercy of God, for He will not let us burn both in this world and in the next.'

Such were the words of comfort he brought them, and others more rousing than these.

Now the whole house began to blaze. Njal went to the door and said, 'Is Flosi near enough to hear my words?'

Flosi said that he could hear him.

Njal said, 'Would you consider making an agreement with my sons, or letting anyone leave the house?'

'I will make no terms with your sons,' replied Flosi. 'We will settle matters now, once and for all, and we are not leaving until every one of them is dead. But I shall allow the women and children and servants to come out.'

Njal went back inside the house and said to his household, 'All those with permission to go out must do so now. Leave the house now, Thorhalla Asgrim's-daughter, and take with you all who are allowed to go.'

Thorhalla said, 'This is not the parting from [my husband] Helgi that I had ever expected; but I shall urge my father and my brothers to avenge the killings that are committed here.'

'You will do well,' said Njal, 'for you are a good woman.'

She went out, taking many people with her.

Astrid of Djupriverbank [the wife of Grim Njalsson,] said to Helgi,

494

'Come out with me. I will drape you in a woman's cloak and put a head-scarf over you.'

Helgi protested at first, but finally yielded to their entreaties. Astrid wrapped a scarf round his head, and [Skarp-Hedin's wife] Thorhild laid the cloak over his shoulders. Then he walked out between them, along with his sisters Thorgerd and Helga and several other people.

When Helgi came outside, Flosi said, 'That's a very tall and broad-shouldered woman – seize her.' When Helgi heard this, he threw off the cloak; he was carrying a sword under his arm, and now he struck out at one of the men, slicing off the bottom of his shield and severing his leg. Then Flosi came up and struck at Helgi's neck, cutting off his head with one blow.

Flosi went up to the door and called Njal and Bergthora over to speak with him; when they came, he said, 'I want to offer you leave to come out, for you do not deserve to burn.'

'I have no wish to go outside,' said Njal, 'for I am an old man now and ill-equipped to avenge my sons; and I do not want to live in shame.'

Flosi said to Bergthora, 'You come out, Bergthora, for under no circumstances do I want you to burn.'

Bergthora replied, 'I was given to Njal in marriage when young, and I have promised him that we would share the same fate.'

Then they both went back inside.

'What shall we do now?' asked Bergthora.

'Let us go to our bed,' said Njal, 'and lie down.'

Then Bergthora said to little Thord, Kari's son, 'You are to be taken out. You are not to burn.'

The boy replied, 'But that's not what you promised, grandmother. You said that we would never be parted; and so it shall be, for I would much prefer to die beside you both.'

She carried the boy to the bed. Njal said to his steward, 'Take note where we lay ourselves down and how we dispose ourselves, for I shall not move from here however much the smoke or flames distress me. Then you can know where to look for our remains.'

The steward said he would.

An ox had recently been slaughtered, and the hide was lying nearby. Njal told the steward to spread the hide over them, and he promised to do so.

Njal and Bergthora lay down on the bed and put the boy between them. Then they crossed themselves and the boy, and commended their souls to God. These were the last words they were heard to speak. The steward took the hide and spread it over them, and then left the house. Ketil of Mork seized his arm and dragged him clear, and questioned him closely about his father-in-law Njal; the steward told him everything that had happened.

Ketil said, 'Great sorrow has been allotted us, that we should all share such terrible ill-luck.'

Skarp-Hedin had seen his father go to lie down, and the preparations he had made. 'Father is going to bed early,' he said. 'And that is natural, for he is an old man.'

Skarp-Hedin and Kari and Grim snatched up the blazing brands as soon as they fell and hurled them at those outside. After a while the attackers threw spears at them, which they caught in flight and hurled back. Flosi told his men to stop – 'for we shall always come off worse in every exchange of blows with them. You would be wiser to wait until the fire conquers them.'

They did as he said.

Now the main beams fell down from the roof.

Skarp-Hedin said, 'My father must be dead now, and not a groan or a cough has been heard from him.'

They went over to the far end of the room. One end of the cross-beam had fallen there, and it was almost burned through in the middle. Kari said to Skarp-Hedin, 'Use that beam to jump out, and I shall give you a hand and come right behind you. That way we can both escape, for the smoke is all drifting in this direction.'

'You go first,' said Skarp-Hedin, 'and I shall follow you at once.'

'That is not wise,' said Kari, 'for I can go out some other way if this does not succeed.'

'No,' said Skarp-Hedin, 'you go out first, and I shall be right on your heels.'

Kari said, 'It is every man's instinct to try to save his own life, and I shall do so now. But this parting will mean that we shall never see each other again. Once I jump out of the flames, I shall not feel inclined to run back into the fire to you; and then each of us must go his own way.'

'I shall laugh, brother-in-law, if you escape,' said Skarp-Hedin, 'for you will avenge us all.'

Kari took hold of a blazing brand and ran up the sloping cross-beam; he hurled the brand down from the wall at those who were in his way outside, and they scattered. Kari's clothes and hair were on fire by now, as he threw himself down off the wall and dodged away in the thick of the smoke.

Someone said: 'Was that a man jumping down from the roof?'

'Far from it,' said someone else. 'It was Skarp-Hedin throwing another brand at us.'

After that, no one suspected anything.

Kari ran until he reached a small stream; he threw himself into it and extinguished his blazing clothes. From there he ran under cover of the smoke until he reached a hollow, where he rested. It has ever since been called Kari's Hollow.

130

Meanwhile, Skarp-Hedin had jumped on to the cross-beam directly behind Kari, but when he reached that part of the beam which was most severely burned, it broke beneath him. Skarp-Hedin managed to land on his feet and make a second attempt at once, by taking a run at the wall. But the roof-beam came down on him and he toppled back once more.

'It is clear now what is to be,' said Skarp-Hedin, and made his way along the wall.

Gunnar Lambason jumped up on to the wall and saw Skarp-Hedin. 'Are you crying now, Skarp-Hedin?' he asked.

'No,' said Skarp-Hedin, 'but it is true that my eyes are smarting. Am I right in thinking that you are laughing?'

'I certainly am,' said Gunnar, 'and for the first time since you killed [my uncle] Thrain.'

'Then here is something to remind you of it,' said Skarp-Hedin.

He took from his purse the jaw-tooth he had hacked out of Thrain, and hurled it straight at Gunnar's eye; the eye was gouged from its socket on to the cheek, and Gunnar toppled off the wall.

Skarp-Hedin went over to his brother Grim. They joined hands and stamped on the fire. But when they reached the middle of the room, Grim fell dead. Skarp-Hedin went to the gable-end of the house; then, with a great crash, the whole roof fell in. Skarp-Hedin was pinned between roof and gable, and could not move an inch.

Flosi and his men stayed by the blaze until broad daylight. Then a man came riding towards them. Flosi asked him his name, and he replied that he was Geirmund, a kinsman of the Sigfussons.

'You have taken drastic action here,' said Geirmund.

'People will call it a drastic action, and an evil one too,' said Flosi. 'But nothing can be done about it now.'

Geirmund asked, 'How many people of note have perished here?'

Flosi said, 'Among the dead here are Njal and Bergthora, their sons Helgi, Grim and Skarp-Hedin, Kari Solmundarson and his son Thord, and Thord Freedman. We are not sure about those others who are less well known to us.'

'You have listed among the dead a man who to my certain knowledge has escaped,' said Geirmund, 'for I talked to him only this morning.'

'Who is that?' asked Flosi.

'Kari Solmundarson,' said Geirmund. 'My neighbour Bard and I met him with his hair burned off and his clothes badly charred, and Bard lent him a horse.'

'Had he any weapons with him?' asked Flosi.

'He was carrying the sword "Life-Taker",' said Geirmund, 'and one of its edges was blue and discoloured. We said that the metal must have softened, but Kari replied that he would soon harden it again in the blood of the Sigfussons and the other Burners.'

'What did he tell you of Skarp-Hedin and Grim?' asked Flosi.

'He said that they were both alive when he left them,' replied Geirmund, 'but that they must be dead by now.'

'What you have told us,' said Flosi, 'gives us little hope of being left in peace, for the man who has escaped is the one who comes nearest to being the equal of Gunnar of Hlidarend in everything. You had better realize, you Sigfussons and all the rest of our men, that this Burning will have such consequences that many of us will lie lifeless and others will forfeit all their wealth.'

. . .

Flosi climbed on to the gable wall with Glum Hildisson and several others.

'Is Skarp-Hedin dead yet, do you think?' asked Glum.

The others said that he must have been dead for some time.

The fire still burned fitfully, flaring up and sinking again. Then they heard this verse being uttered somewhere down amongst the flames:

> 'The woman will find it hard
> To stop the cloudburst of her tears
> At this outcome
> Of the warrior's last battle.'

Grani Gunnarsson said, 'Was Skarp-Hedin alive or dead when he spoke that verse?'

'I shall not make any guesses about that,' replied Flosi.

Grani said, 'Let us look for Skarp-Hedin and the others who were burned to death in there.'

'No,' said Flosi, 'and only stupid men like you would make such a suggestion, at a time when forces must be gathering throughout the district; and he who lingers here will be so terrified that he will not know which way to run. It is my advice that we all ride away as quickly as possible.'

. . .

132

[Next day] Kari asked Hjalti [Skeggjason] to go with him to search for Njal's bones – 'for everyone will accept your account and your impressions.'

Hjalti readily agreed to go, and to bring Njal's remains to the church.

They set off, fifteen in all, and rode east over Thjors River, where they summoned others to accompany them until they numbered a hundred, including Njal's neighbours.

They reached Bergthorsknoll at noon. Hjalti asked Kari whereabouts under the ruins Njal's body would be lying, and Kari showed them. They dug through a deep layer of ashes, and underneath they found the ox-hide; the flames had shrivelled it. They lifted it up, and found Njal and Bergthora lying there, quite unmarked by the flames. They all gave praise to God for this, and thought it a great miracle. Then they lifted up the boy who had been lying between them; one finger, which he had stretched out from under the hide, had been burned off.

Njal and Bergthora were carried out, and everyone came up to see the bodies.

'How do these bodies impress you?' asked Hjalti.

'We would rather hear your verdict first,' they replied.

'I shall put it into plain words,' said Hjalti. 'I think that Bergthora's body is rather better preserved than could have been expected; but Njal's countenance and body appear to have a radiance which I have never seen on a dead man before.'

They all agreed.

Then they looked for Skarp-Hedin. The servants showed them the place where Flosi and his men had heard the verse uttered. The roof had collapsed there beside the gable wall, and that was where Hjalti told them to dig. They did so, and found the body of Skarp-Hedin. He had held himself upright against the wall; his legs were almost burnt off below the knees, but the rest of him was unburnt. He had bitten hard on his lip. His eyes were open but not swollen. He had driven his axe into the gable with such violence that half the full depth of the blade was buried in the wall, and the metal had not softened. His body was carried out, with the axe. Hjalti picked up the axe and said, 'This is a rare weapon. Few could wield it.'

'I know the man to wield it,' said Kari.

'Who is that?' asked Hjalti.

'Thorgeir Skorar-Geir,' replied Kari. 'He is the outstanding member of that family now.'

They stripped Skarp-Hedin's body, for the clothes had not been burnt off. He had crossed his arms, with the right one over the left. They found two marks on his body, one between the shoulders, the other on his chest, both of them burn-marks in the shape of a cross; they came to the conclusion that he had branded them on himself. They all agreed that they found it less uncomfortable to see Skarp-Hedin dead than they had expected; for no one felt any fear of him.

They searched for Grim, and found his remains in the middle of the main room. Opposite him, under the side wall, they found Thord Freedman, and in the weaving-room they found the old woman Sæunn and three other people. They found the remains of eleven people in all. They took all the bodies to church. Hjalti then rode home, and Kari went with him.

(*Trans.* MAGNUS MAGNUSSON and
HERMANN PÁLSSON)

THE SAGA OF THE GREENLANDERS

(The saga describes how the American mainland was accidentally sighted by Bjarni Herjolfsson in 985/6, and deliberately explored by Leif Eiriksson in 1001; Leif named the most southerly area he reached *Vinland*. The passage chosen here, from ch. 5, deals with an encounter between a later exploring party and American Indians, 'Skrælings'.)

Thorvald [Eiriksson] prepared his expedition with his brother Leif's guidance and engaged a crew of thirty. When the ship was ready they put out to sea and there are no reports of their voyage until they reached Leif's Houses in Vinland. There they laid up the ship and settled down for the winter, catching fish for their food.

In the spring Thorvald said they should get the ship ready, and that meanwhile a small party of men should take the ship's boat and sail west along the coast and explore that region during the summer.

They found the country there very attractive, with woods stretching almost down to the shore and white sandy beaches. There were numerous islands there, and extensive shallows. They found no traces of human habitation or animals, except on one westerly island, where they found a wooden stack-cover. That was the only man-made thing they found; and in the autumn they returned to Leif's Houses.

Next summer Thorvald sailed east with his ship and then north along the coast ... Soon they found themselves at the mouth of two fjords, and sailed up to the promontory that jutted out between them; it was heavily wooded. They moored the ship alongside and put out the gangway, and Thorvald went ashore with all his men.

'It is beautiful here,' he said. 'Here I should like to make my home.'

On their way back to the beach they noticed three humps on the sandy beach just in front of the headland. When they went closer they found that these were three skin-boats, with three men under each of them. Thorvald and his men divided forces and captured all of them except one, who escaped in his boat. They killed the other eight and returned to the headland, from which they scanned the surrounding country. They could make out a number of humps further up the fjord, and concluded that these were settlements.

Then they were overwhelmed by such a heavy drowsiness that they could not stay awake, and they all fell asleep – until they were awakened by a voice that shouted, 'Wake up, Thorvald, and all your men, if you want to stay alive! Get to your ship with all your company and get away as fast as you can!'

A great swarm of skin-boats was then heading towards them down the fjord. Thorvald said, 'We shall set up breastworks on the gunwales and defend ourselves as best we can, but fight back as little as possible.'

They did this. The Skrælings shot at them for a while, and then turned and fled as fast as they could. Thorvald asked his men if any of them were wounded; they all replied that they were unhurt.

'I have a wound in the armpit,' said Thorvald. 'An arrow flew up between the gunwale and my shield, under my arm – here it is. This will lead to my death. I advise you now to go back as soon as you can. But first I want you to take me to the headland I thought so suitable for a home. I seem to have hit on the truth when I said I would settle there for a while. Bury me there and put crosses at my head and feet, and let the place be called *Krossaness* for ever afterwards.'

With that Thorvald died, and his men did exactly as he had asked of them. Afterwards they sailed back and joined the rest of the expedition and exchanged all the news they had to tell.

They spent the winter there and gathered grapes and vines as cargo for the ship. In the spring they set off on the voyage back to Greenland; they made land at Eiriksfjord, and had plenty of news to tell Leif.

(*Trans.* MAGNUS MAGNUSSON and
HERMANN PÁLSSON)

DANTE ALIGHIERI
(1265–1321)

THE DIVINE COMEDY

INFERNO

Canto I

(It is the eve of Good Friday, 1300: Dante is thirty-one. He comes
to himself in the dark wood of Error. After attempting the Delectable
Mountain of virtue, he meets the spirit of Virgil, who will be his
guide till the last part of his journey.)

> Nel mezzo del cammin di nostra vita
>   mi ritrovai per una selva oscura,
>   che la diritta via era smarrita.
> Ah quanto a dir qual era è cosa dura
>   esta selva selvaggia e aspra e forte,
>   che nel pensier rinnova la paura!
> Tanto è amara che poco è più morte;
>   ma per trattar del ben ch'io vi trovai
>   dirò de l'altre cose ch'io v'ho scorte.
> Io non so ben ridir com'io v'entrai,
>   tant'era pieno di sonno a quel punto
>   che la verace via abbandonai.
> Ma poi ch'io fui al piè d'un colle giunto,
>   là dove terminava quella valle
>   che m'avea di paura il cor compunto,
> guardai in alto e vidi le sue spalle
>   vestite già dei raggi del pianeta
>   che mena dritto altrui per ogni calle.
> Allor fu la paura un poco queta
>   che nel lago del cor m'era durata
>   la notte ch'io passai con tanta pieta.

> At midpoint of the journey of our life
>   I woke to find me astray in a dark wood,
>   perplexed by paths with the straight way at strife.

Ah, had I words, if such there be, that could
   describe this forest wild and rough and dour,
   by which, in thought, my terror is renew'd!
So bitter it is that death is scarcely more;
   but of the good I found there I will treat
   by saying what else there I'd discerned before.
I cannot well recall how I entered it,
   so drowsy at that moment did I feel
   when first from the true way I turned my feet.
But after I had reached the base of a hill
   where to an end that valley came which had
   so pierced my heart with fear and pierced it still,
I looked on high and saw its shoulders clad
   already with the planet's beams whose light
   leadeth men straight, through all paths good or bad.
Then did the fear a little lose its might,
   which in my heart's lake had persisted there
   through the long hours of such a piteous night.
And as a man who, gasping still for air,
   'scaped from deep sea to shore and scarce alive,
   turns to the perilous wave, his eyes a-stare,
so did my spirit, still a fugitive,
   turn back to view the pass whose deadly power
   ne'er let a body held in it survive.
My tired limbs somewhat rested, I once more
   pursued my way across the lone hillside,
   so that the firm foot was always the lower.
And lo, just ere the steep began, there hied
   leopard, light and nimble in the extreme,
   covered with hair by spots diversified;
nor did it shun me, rather did it seem
   so much to block my road of set design,
   that, to retreat, my feet were oft in trim.
The hour was that when dawn begins to shine:
   the Sun was mounting with the stars whose ways
   marched with his own, when first by Love divine
were set in motion those fair presences;
   thus the sweet season and the time of day

alike conspired within my heart to raise
good hope of that wild beast with skin so gay;
    yet not such as to leave me undismay'd
    when there appeared a lion in the way;
which appeared coming against me, with his head
    held high and with a raging hunger, so
    that even the air appeared thereof afraid;
and a she-wolf, that looked as lean as though
    still burdened with all ravenings – yea, her might
    ere this had made much people live in woe;
which, for the fear that issued from the sight
    of her, o'erwhelmed me with a lassitude
    so heavy, that I lost hope of the height.
And even as he who joys in gaining, should
    the time arrive which makes him lose, will suit
    whate'er he thinks of to his saddened mood;
such was I rendered by the unresting brute,
    which, coming against me, pushed me pace by pace
    back to the region where the Sun is mute.
While I was ruining to that low place,
    before my eyes presented himself one
    who seemed enfeebled through long silentness.
To him, in that great waste where else was none,
    '*Miserere mei*,' I cried, 'whatso thou be,
    whether a shade or real man!' Whereon
'Not man – man once I *was*,' he answered me:
    'my parents, members of the Lombard State,
    were Mantuans by birth, both he and she.
Sub Julio was I born, albeit 'twas late,
    and lived at Rome when the good Augustus reign'd,
    what time false gods that lied were worshipped yet.
Poet I *was*, and sang of virtue's friend,
    that just Anchisiades who came from Troy,
    when flames had brought proud Ilion to an end.
But thou, to misery so fearful why
    turn'st back? Why climb'st thou not the blissful mount?
    which is the cause and principle of all joy?'
'And art thou, then, that Virgil, thou that fount

whence pours a stream of speech so broad and bright?'
    thus I replied to him with bashful front.
'O of all other poets honour and light,
    may the great love that long hath made me pore
    over thy volume stead me in this plight.
Thou art my master and my author; nor
    from any save from thee came I to take
    the style whose beauty I've been honoured for.
Behold the beast which turned me backward: make
    me safe from her, renownéd sage, for she
    causes each vein and pulse in me to quake.'
'Another course must needs be held by thee'
    he answered, when he marked my sobbing breath,
    'wilt thou from out this savage place win free:
for yonder beast which now occasioneth
    thy cries, lets no one pass along her way,
    but so impedes him as to cause his death;
and is so evil, so malign, no prey
    can ever glut her greedy appetite,
    which feeding does but aggravate, not stay.
Many are the animals she's paired with: quite
    as many more there will be, till the Hound
    comes, who with painful death shall quell her might.
Not lands nor pelf he'll feed on – nought beyond
    wisdom and love and valour; and between
    Feltro and Feltro his birthplace shall be found.
Safety for that poor Italy he'll win
    which Turnus, Nisus and Euryalus bled
    and died for, and Camilla the virgin.
'Tis he will hunt the wolf from stead to stead,
    till back in hell he puts her by duress,
    e'en there whence first by envy she was sped.
Therefore I judge this fittest for thy case –
    to follow me, and I will be thy guide
    and draw thee hence through an eternal place,
where thou shalt hear them crying whose hope hath died,
    shalt see the olden spirits in pain who attest
    by shrieks the second death wherein they abide;

and thou shalt see those who contented rest
    within the fire, as hoping in the end,
    come when it may, to arrive among the Blest.
To whom thereafter wouldst thou fain ascend,
    there'll be, for that, a worthier soul than I;
    she, when I leave thee, will thy steps befriend:
for that imperial Ruler, there on high,
    since I was alien to his ordering,
    will have none to his court through me draw nigh.
In all parts he is emperor, there he's king;
    there is his city and his lofty seat:
    oh blest whom thither he elects to bring!'
And I made answer: 'Poet, I entreat
    thee by that God thou knewest not, that so
    I may escape this evil and worse than it,
to bring me thither where thou saidst but now
    I may behold Saint Peter's gate and find
    those thou describest as so full of woe.'
Then he moved on, and I kept close behind.

Canto V

(ll 72 to end)

(The descent to the Second Circle of Hell; here are the souls of carnal sinners. Dante's Hell is a funnel-shaped cavity reaching from the earth's surface to the centre. The sides of the cavity form a series of diminishing circles on which the successive classes of ever worse offenders are punished. Virgil points out famous lovers.)

I began: 'Poet, much do I feel inclined
    to address yon two, together going by,
    who seem to float so lightly on the wind.'
And he to me: 'Watch till they come more nigh;
    and then by that same love which they obey,
    do thou entreat them, and they will comply.'
So when the wind had drifted them our way,
    I lifted up my voice: 'O souls toil-worn,
    come, speak with us, saith not Another nay.'

As doves, when longing summons them, return
    with open steady wings to their sweet nest,
    cleaving the air, by their volition borne;
so they, from out the troop where Dido's placed,
    at once through the malign air tow'rds us sped,
    such power had my compassionate request.
'O kind and gracious being, unafraid
    to venture through the perse air visiting
    us who in dying tinged the world blood-red,
had we for friend the universe's King,
    we would petition him to give thee peace
    who pitiest so our perverse suffering.
All that thou fain wouldst hear and speak of, this
    we will both hear, and speak with you thereo'er,
    while the wind, lulled as now, for us doth cease.
Throned is my native city on the shore
    where, to have peace, the Po comes flowing down
    together with the streams that swell his power.
Love, that of noble heart takes hold full soon,
    took *him* for the fair body, from me removed;
    and still I'm sore-bested by the way 'twas done.
Love, that from loving lets off none beloved,
    took *me* for the beauty of him so strongly, that
    it still hath, as thou seëst, my master proved.
Love led us to one death: predestinate
    to Cain is he by whom our blood was shed.'
    These words were borne to us from them; whereat,
when I had heard those souls, thus sore-bested,
    I bowed my face, and held it down so long,
    that 'On what musest thou?' the poet said.
'Ah me, sweet thoughts how many, and what strong
    desire brought these unto the woeful pass!'
    When first I spoke, these words from me were wrung.
Then, turning back to them, now I it was
    who spoke: 'Francesca,' I said, 'thine agonies
    move me to weep, such pity and grief they cause.
But tell me: in the season of sweet sighs
    what sign made Love that led you to confess

your vague desires? How opened he your eyes?'
And she to me: 'Nought brings one more distress,
    as well thy teacher knows, than to recall
    in time of misery former happiness.
But if to know the primal root of all
    our love thou hast so great a longing, I
    will do as one that weeps, yet tells withal.
Reading we were one day, entranced thereby,
    of Lancelot, how by love he was fast held:
    we were alone and deemed no danger nigh.
That reading oft and oft our eyes impell'd
    to meet, and blanched our faces' hue: but o'er
    us one point, and one point alone, prevail'd.
When read we of the smile, so thirsted for,
    being kissed by such a lover, he that may
    now from myself be parted nevermore,
all trembling, kissed my mouth: destined to play
    our Gallehault was the book and he, as well,
    who wrote it: further read we not that day.'
While the one spirit said this, throughout the tale
    so piteous were the tears the other shed,
    I swooned, as though in death: and down I fell
as a man's body drops, when dropping dead.

PURGATORIO

Canto VI

(ll 61–138)

(Dante and Virgil are seeking how to ascend the island-mountain of
Purgatory. Virgil sees a shade sitting alone and asks it the quickest
way.)

We came to it. O Lombard spirit, how
    haughty and scornful was thine attitude,
    the movement of thine eyes how grave and slow!
It said no word as we our way pursued,
    but let us still go on, not doing aught
    save watch us, as a couching lion would.

Yet Virgil, drawing close to it, besought
   that it would point us out what we desired,
   the best way up; to which it answered nought,
but of our country and of our life enquired;
   and the loved guide began, at this request:
   'Mantua . . .', and the shade, all self-retired,
rose tow'rds him from where it before was placed
   saying: 'O Mantuan, I'm Sordello of thy
   own city!', and the one the other embraced.
Ah, enslaved Italia, sorrow's mansionry,
   ship without pilot in a raging gale,
   not lady of provinces, but harlots' sty!
Thus did his zeal that noble soul impel,
   merely at the sweet sound of his city's name,
   to bid his fellow-townsman here all-hail;
and now in thee war ceases not to inflame
   thy living men, and one the other devours,
   though the same wall, same moat encloses them.
Search, wretch, thy seaboard, all around its shores,
   then look within thy breast, if any part
   in thee enjoy the boon of peaceful hours.
What boots it that for thee Justinian's art
   retrimmed the bit, if no one mounts the steed?
   The shame would, but for that, less keenly smart.
Ah, folk that should be given to prayer, and need
   but to let Caesar fill the saddle again,
   paid ye to God's direction proper heed,
look how this beast, for lack of spurs to train
   and curb its ardour, still more savage grows,
   ever since ye laid hand upon the rein.
O German Albert, who thine eyes dost close
   to her, grown wild and vicious, though by right
   'tis thou who shouldst bestride her saddle-bows,
may a just judgment from the stars alight
   upon thy blood: be't strange and manifest,
   that thy successor may thereat take fright.
For, like thy father, thou — held back, in quest
   of lands o'er there, by greed that nought abates —

hast let the empire's garden run to waste.
Come and see Montagues and Capulets,
 Monaldi and Filippeschi, O heedless man:
 these dreading ill which those e'en now besets!
Come, cruel! come and see how oppressive can
 thy nobles be, and the ills they've wrought make good;
 and thou'lt see Santafiór, how it needs thy ban!
Come, see thy Rome, in lonely widowhood
 weeping, and calling day and night: 'Oh, why,
 my Caesar, dost thou leave me in solitude?'
Come and see how they love each other, thy
 good folk, and if nought else thy pity move,
 come for thy own repute's sake, shamed thereby.
And, be't lawful for me, O highest Jove
 who wast on Earth for our sake crucified,
 I'll ask, do thy just eyes elsewhither rove?
Or art thou thus preparing, but dost hide
 in thy unfathomed counsel, some good end
 by our weak vision wholly undescried?
For all the lands of Italy now bend
 to tyrants, and no churl exists but he's
 a right Marcellus, be he faction's friend.
Thou, my own Florence, well may'st be at ease
 with this digression, withers quite unwrung,
 thanks to thy folk who are so prompt with pleas.
Many love justice, but their bows are strung
 with caution, and they shoot the word with care;
 but *thy* folk have it on the tip of the tongue.
Many refuse the common load to share:
 but *thy* folk eagerly respond, nor wait
 to be asked, but cry: 'For me 'tis light to bear.'
Count thyself – and with reason – fortunate:
 thou wealthy, thou at peace, and thou so wise!
 a truth I leave the facts to demonstrate.

Canto XVI

(ll 58–114)

(Dante and Virgil are now on the terrace of the Wrathful, who move
in a cloud of smoke and can be heard praying for mercy. Dante speaks
with one of these spirits.)

　　　　　　　　　　　　　　　　　　　　. . . curst
　　indeed the world is, as thy words make clear,
　　　bereft of every virtue, and big with all
　　　　that's evil, which o'erwhelms it everywhere.
　　Point me out, prithee, what makes this befall,
　　　that I may see and show it to others too;
　　　　for some deem heav'n, some earth, the criminal.'
　　A deep sigh, forced by grief into 'heigh-ho!',
　　　broke from him first: then 'Brother,' he began,
　　　　'the world is blind, and thence, 'tis clear, com'st thou.
　　All causes are referred by living man
　　　to the heav'ns alone, as did they everything
　　　　move with themselves on some predestined plan.
　　But this, if true, would to destruction bring
　　　free choice, nor were it justice to requite
　　　　good deeds with joy and ill with suffering.
　　The heav'ns *do* your first impulses incite;
　　　I say not all, but, grant it said, e'en then
　　　　to discern good from ill ye are given light
　　and free will; which, though subject to great strain
　　　in its first battles with the heav'ns, in the end
　　　　will, if well nourished, total victory gain.
　　You, free, are by a mightier force constrain'd,
　　　by a better nature; and through this holds sway
　　　　the mind in you, which the heav'ns lack power to bend.
　　Hence, if the world at present goes astray,
　　　in you is the cause, in you it should be sought,
　　　　to which I'll put thee now on the right way.
　　Forth from His hand, who yearns to her in thought
　　　ere she exists, comes, like a little maid
　　　　all tears and smiles, eager to play with aught,

the little simple soul, in life unread,
    save that, by her glad Maker moved, with zest
    she turns to that by which her joy is fed.
Of trivial good at first she tries the taste;
    thereby deceived, after it will she scour,
    if guide or curb do not divert her quest.
Whence need of law for curb; and need, moreo'er,
    of one who can, in regal state aloof,
    of the true city glimpse at least the tower.
Laws there *are*, but by what hand put to proof?
    No one's: because the leading shepherd, who
    can chew the cud, lacks the divided hoof;
Wherefore the people, seeing their guide pursue
    only that good whereof their greed is fain,
    pasture on that, and other foods eschew.
Your corrupt nature, then, is not your bane;
    ill-guidance – *that* is why the world hath trod
    the way of sin; see *there* the cause writ plain.
Rome, that once kept the world good by her rod,
    was wont to have two Suns, whose light made clear
    both roads, that of the world and that of God.
One hath the other quenched; to crozier
    hath now been joined the sword, and it must needs
    be ill going, when the two together fare;
for, when joined, neither power the other dreads:
    if still thou doubt, look to the ripened grain,
    since every plant is made known by its seeds.

PARADISO

Canto XXXIII

(In this final Canto of *The Divine Comedy*, St Bernard's prayer to
the Virgin Mary is granted. And Dante prays that a glimpse of the
divine mystery may be conveyed to man through his verse.)

'Maiden and mother, daughter of thy son,
    lowly and high, o'er creatures else, display'd,
    chosen of God, ere time had yet begun,

thine's the nobility which so array'd
    man's nature that its Maker thought no shame
    to make himself of that himself had made.
Within thy womb rekindled glowed the flame
    of love that fed the germ from which this flower
    in timeless peace to such perfection came.
Noon-torch of charity to us in our
    world here, thou art a well of hope on earth,
    whence mortal men draw draughts of quickening power.
Lady, so great thou art and such thy worth,
    that whoso longs for grace nor calls on thee,
    bids the wish fly, yet wingless speeds it forth.
Thy loving heart not only grants the plea
    of every suppliant, but ofttimes, ere yet
    'tis uttered, answers prayer spontaneously.
Merciful, mighty in deed, compassionate,
    all virtues that created being can boast,
    in thee, have all in thee, together met.
Behold this man, who from the nethermost
    sink of the whole world up to this high place
    hath seen the realm of spirits, coast by coast,
and now beseeches thee that of thy grace
    strength be vouchsafed unto his eyes yet higher
    to raise him tow'rds the final blessedness.
And I, who for myself was ne'er on fire
    more than for him, to see this vision, pray
    thee instantly – oh, spurn not my desire –
by means of thy own prayers to chase away
    all clouds of his mortality, that so
    he see the perfect joy in full display.
Further I pray thee, sovereign, who canst do
    whate'er thou wilt, after a sight so fair
    keep his affections healthy through and through.
Control his human springs with watchful care:
    behold how many saints with Beatrice
    pray thee with claspéd hands to grant my prayer!'
The eyes which God reveres and loves, at this
    gazed on the pleader, and thus proved it right

how dear to her all true devotion is;
then were directed to the eternal light,
    into whose essence we must deem no eye
    of creature pierces with such keen insight.
And I, who to the end was drawing nigh
    of all desires, the yearning deep instilled
    within me ended, of necessity.
With nod and smiling visage Bernard willed
    that I should upward gaze; but I foreknew
    and had already his behest fulfilled;
because my vision, as it clearer grew
    still more and more kept entering through the ray
    of the high Light, which in itself is true.
Thenceforth my seeing surpassed what we can say
    by means of words, which fail at sight so fair;
    and memory to such excess gives way.
As one who sees in dream, remains aware,
    when the dream's gone, of all it made him feel,
    while all he saw is lost beyond repair;
even such am I; my vision fades, until
    it all but ceases, yet my heart is awed
    by its sweet effluence which pervades me still.
Thus melts the imprinted snow by sunshine thawed;
    thus was the wisdom of the Sibyl, writ
    on frail leaves, to the breezes cast abroad.
O Light supreme, so far above the wit
    of man exalted, let my mind again
    with some pale semblance of thy beams be lit,
and make my tongue so eloquent that when
    it chants thy glory, a future age may find
    at least one spark of it inspire the strain;
for, by returning somewhat to my mind
    and sounding faintly in these verses, thou
    wilt make men to thy victory less blind.
Bewildered would mine eyes have been, I trow,
    by the keen living ray, whose utmost brunt
    they suffered, had they turned them from it now.
And I remember that on this account

I endured more boldly, till my look grew one
    with the infinite goodness at its central fount.
Oh abundant grace, whereby thus daring grown
    I fixed my vision through the eternal light
    so far, that sight I wholly spent thereon!
Within its depths I marked how by the might
    of love the leaves, through all creation strowed,
    bound in a single volume, there unite:
substance and accidents with each its mode,
    as 'twere conflated, in such wise that what
    I'm saying gives but a glimmer of how it showed.
The universal form that ties this knot
    I think I saw, because I feel, whene'er
    I speak of it, to ampler joy upcaught.
One moment more bedims what I saw there
    than five and twenty centuries the Quest
    which made Neptune at Argo's shadow stare.
Thus bode my mind, to gazing all-addressed,
    in rapt attention and, the more it tried
    to see, of keener vision was possess'd.
In presence of that light so satisfied
    the mind is, that it never could consent
    to turn therefrom to glance at aught beside;
because the good, on which the will is bent,
    is all there; and, outside it, incomplete
    are things which, in it, find their complement.
Henceforth my tongue, in struggling to repeat
    e'en what remembrance holds, will have less power
    than hath a babe's which still sucks at the teat.
Although there was one aspect, and no more,
    within the living light which met my view –
    for that is always what it was before –
yet as my vision, since it stronger grew
    the more I gazed, kept changing, so it found
    one sole appearance take on changes too.
In the sublime light's deep pellucid ground
    did, visibly to me, three circles show,
    of three hues and in one dimension bound;

the first by the second as rainbow by rainbow
　　reflected seemed; the third was like a flame
　　which equally from either seemed to flow.
How scant is language, all too weak to frame
　　my thoughts! And these are such, that, set beside
　　my vision, 'faint' is word too weak for them.
O Light that aye sole in thyself dost bide,
　　sole understand'st thyself, and being self-known,
　　self-knowing, lov'st thyself, self-gratified!
That circle which, begotten thus, was shown
　　in thee as light reflected, when I turned
　　mine eyes and let them somewhile dwell thereon,
of the same hue with which it inly burned,
　　seemed limned in the similitude of Man;
　　which made my sight wholly therewith concerned.
As geometrician, trying as best he can
　　to square the circle, but without the clue
　　he needs to guide him, ends where he began;
so I, before that marvel strange and new,
　　wished to discover how the image lay
　　within the circle, and how joined thereto –
flight too sublime for my own wings to essay,
　　had not a flash of insight countervailed,
　　and struck my blindness into sudden day.
To the high fantasy here vigour failed,
　　but now, as a wheel's turned that never jars,
　　were my desire and will by love impelled,
the Love that moves the Sun and th'other stars.

(*Trans.* GEOFFREY L. BICKERSTETH)

JUAN RUIZ
(*fl.* first half fourteenth century)

THE BOOK OF GOOD LOVE

44. Palabra es de sabio, e díxola Catón,
que omne a sus cuidados que tiene en el su coraçón
entreponga plazeres e alegre razón,
ca la mucha tristeza mucho pecado pon'.

45. E porque de buen seso non puede omne reír,
avré algunas burlas aquí a enxerir;
cada que las oyeres non quieras comedir
salvo en la manera del trobàr e dezir.

46. Entiende bien mis dichos e piensa la sentencia;
non acaesca contigo como al dotor de Grecia
con el ribald romano e su poca sabencia,
quando demandó Roma a Grecia la ciencia.

47. Assí fue que romanos las leyes non avían,
e fuéronlas demandar a griegos que las tenían;
respondieron los griegos que las non merecían
nin las podrían entender, pues tan poco sabían;

48. pero que si las querían para por ellas usar,
que ante les convenía con sus sabios desputar
por ver si las entendrían e las merecían levar:
esta respuesta fermosa davan por se escusar.

HOW THE BOOK SHOULD BE UNDERSTOOD

44. It is the saying of a wise man, and Cato said it, that among the cares man has in his heart he should intersperse pleasures and merry words, for much sadness brings much sin.

45. And since a person cannot laugh at sensible things, I will insert a few jokes here; whenever you hear them pay attention only to the way they are put into song and verse.

46. Understand my words correctly and ponder their meaning; don't let it happen to you as it happened to the wise man from Greece with the Roman hoodlum of very little knowledge, when Rome petitioned Greece for learning.

47. Once upon a time the Romans had no laws, and they went to ask for them from the Greeks who did have them; the Greeks answered that the Romans did not deserve them, nor would they be able to understand them because they had so little knowledge;

48. although, if the Romans did want laws in order to conduct themselves by them, it was first of all necessary for them to hold a debate with the wise men of Greece in order to determine whether the Romans could understand laws and deserved to have them: this was the gracious answer they gave in order to get out of it.

49. The Romans answered that this suited them [and they would do it] gladly; they drew up a signed agreement for the debate; but since they would not be able to understand the language which they themselves did not speak, they asked to debate by means of gestures and the sign-language used by learned men.

50. Both parties agreed on a specified day for the contest; the Romans were in distress; they did not know what to do because they were not educated and would not be able to understand the Greek doctors nor their great wisdom.

51. While they were in this difficulty, a certain citizen told them to select a hoodlum, a Roman roughneck, and [tell him that] whatever gestures God might inspire him to make with his hand, these he should make; and it was good advice for them.

52. They approached a hoodlum, who was very big and pugnacious; they told him: 'We have an appointment with the Greeks to debate by gestures; ask for anything you want and we will give it to you: only spare us from this contest.'

53. They put on him rich robes of great price, as though he were a doctor of philosophy; he climbed up on to the lecture seat and said boastfully: 'Now let those Greeks come, challenge and all.'

54. A Greek stepped forth, a very polished doctor, selected from among the Greeks and highly renowned among all; he mounted the other high seat, with all the people assembled; they began their gestures, as had been agreed upon.

55. The Greek rose, calmly, slowly, and held out one finger, the one next to the thumb; then he sat down in his place. The hoodlum rose, savage and in a bad temper;

56. he held out three fingers towards the Greek, the thumb and

the two fingers next to it, like a trident, with the last two fingers folded in; quickly he sat down, gazing at his robes.

57. The Greek stood up and held out his open palm, and then he sat down, he with his fine mind; the hoodlum got up, he with his vacuous fancies, and stuck out his clenched fist: he wanted to get into a brawl.

58. The Greek sage said to all the Greeks: 'The Romans deserve laws, I will not deny them to them.' All the people arose in peace and with calm; Rome gained great honor through a worthless tramp.

59. They asked the Greek what he had said to the Roman by his gestures, and what he had answered him. He said: 'I said that there is one God; the Roman said He was One in Three Persons, and made a sign to that effect.

60. Next I said that all was by the will of God; he answered that God held everything in his power, and he spoke truly. When I saw that they understood and believed in the Trinity, I understood that they deserved assurance of [receiving] laws.'

61. They asked the hoodlum what his notion was; he replied: 'He said that with his finger he would smash my eye; I was mighty unhappy about this and I got mighty angry, and I answered him with rage, with anger, and with fury,

62. that, right in front of everybody, I would smash his eyes with my two fingers and his teeth with my thumb; right after that he told me to watch him because he would give me a big slap on my ears [that would leave them] ringing.

63. I answered him that I would give him such a punch that in all his life he would never get even for it. As soon as he saw that he had the quarrel in bad shape, he quit making threats in a spot where they thought nothing of him.'

64. This is why the proverb of the shrewd old woman says: 'No word is bad if you don't take it badly.' You will see that my word is well said if it is well understood: understand my book well and you will have a lovely lady.

65. Whatever joke you may hear, don't despise it; the nature of the book must be understood by you as subtle, an art [knowledge] of praising and vilifying, cryptic and graceful; you won't find here just one of a thousand troubadours.

66. You will find many herons, you won't find a single egg; not

every new tailor can do a good job of mending; don't imagine that I am impelled to compose poems as a fool does: what good love says, I will prove to you with good reasoning.

67. The text speaks to everyone in general; people of good sense will discern its wisdom; as for frivolous young people, let them refrain from folly: let him who is fortunate select the better side.

68. The utterances of good love are veiled: strive to find their true meanings; if you understand the meaning of what is said or hit upon the sense, you will not speak ill of the book which you now censure.

69. Where you think it is telling lies, it is speaking the greatest truth; in the bright-colored stanzas is where great ugliness lies; judge a statement to be complimentary or derogatory, point by point [with hairsplitting reasoning]; praise or condemn the stanzas for their points [musical notes].

70. I, this book, am akin to all instruments of music: according as you point [play music] well or badly, so, most assuredly, will I speak; in whatever way you choose to speak, make a point [stop] there and hold fast; if you know how to point me [pluck my strings], you will always hold me in mind.

REFLECTIONS ON LOVE, AND A BURLESQUE SONG

105. As Solomon says, and he speaks the truth, the things of this world are vanity; they are all fleeting, they pass away with time: save for the love of God, they are all frivolity.

106. And I, when I saw that the lady had withdrawn and changed, said: 'Loving when I am not loved would be doing a thing worth nothing; answering when I am not being called is clearly futile.' I abandoned my suit since she had withdrawn from me.

107. God knows that I always tried to give protection to this lady and all the ladies I have ever seen, and I have always served them; if I could not serve them, I never did them a disservice; I always wrote good things about any well-mannered lady.

108. I would be very churlish and a boorish bumpkin if I should say a vile thing about a noble lady, for in a lively, lovely, and courtly woman is all the good in the world and all pleasure.

109. If God, when he formed man, had considered that woman was a bad thing, He would not have given her to man for a com-

panion, nor would He have made her out of man; if she had not been for good, she would not have turned out so noble.

110. If man did not love woman well, Love would not have as many captives as he does; no matter how saintly a man or a woman may be, I know none who does not long for a consort if he is living alone.

111. It is said in a proverb, which I will tell now, that 'a solitary bird neither sings nor sobs well'; the mast cannot stand forever without its sail, nor are cabbages grown so well without the water-wheel.

112. And since I was alone, without companionship, I craved to have what someone else had for himself; I laid eyes on another woman, not saintly but foolish: I suffered the torments of crucifixion for her, and somebody else got her at no cost.

113. Since I could not speak to her as things were, I picked as my messenger a comrade of mine, believing that I would have success; but he knew how to drive the spike into me [trick me]: he ate the fodder and made me chew the cud.

114. Out of my great grief I wrote this burlesque song; if any lady hears it, let her not disdain me because of it, for I should call myself stupid and more than an ass if I did not compose a mocking song [or 'find a joke'] from such a big joke on me.

> 115. My eyes will not behold the light,
> for I have lost [my] Cross.
> 116. Crisscrossed Cross, baker girl,
> I took her for my paramour;
> I mistook a footpath for a highway,
> as the Andalusian does.
> 117. Expecting that I would get her,
> I told Ferrand García
> to deliver my plea
> and be persuasive and sweet-spoken.
> 118. He told me that this suited him;
> he made himself intimate with Cross;
> to me he gave husks to chew on,
> he ate the tastiest bread.
> 119. He promised her at my request
> some year-old wheat that I had;

and he himself presented her with a rabbit,
the false, deceitful traitor.
   120. May God confound a messenger
so prompt and so speedy!
may God not prosper a rabbit-hound
that retrieves game that way!

121. Whenever I beheld the Cross, I always knelt down; I crossed myself before her whenever I encountered her; my comrade did his worshipping right alongside the Cross; against crusade trouble I was not on guard.

THE ART OF LOVE

429. If you will read Ovid, who was my disciple, in him you will find statements that were taught to him by me, and many useful ways for a lover: Pamphilus and Ovid were instructed by me.

430. If you want to have a lady to love or any other woman, you must first learn a great many things in order to make her willing to accept you in love: first of all learn how to select the woman.

431. Look for a woman who is pretty and witty and full of spirit, who is not very tall nor yet dwarfish; if possible, try not to fall in love with a low-born woman, for that kind knows nothing of love: she is like a straw scarecrow.

432. Look for a woman with a good figure and with a small head; hair that is blonde but not from henna; whose eyebrows are spaced apart, long and arched in a peak; who is nice and plump in the buttocks: this is the figure of a lady;

433. whose eyes are large, prominent, colorful, shining; and with long lashes that show good and clearly; with small, delicate ears; mark well if she has a long throat: that is the kind men want;

434. with a finely chiseled nose; and nice small teeth that are even and good and white, a trifle separated; with red gums, good sharp teeth; her lips red and nicely fine-drawn;

435. her mouth nice and small, just so, in a pleasing way; her face white, hairless, bright, and smooth. Try to get hold of some woman who can see her without her blouse on, who will tell you about the form of her body: arrange this.

436. Be sure that the woman you send to carry messages is a

relative of yours who will be truly faithful to you; don't let her be your loved one's servant; don't let the lady discover your intentions because the messenger refuses to tell lies. It cannot be that a woman who has married unhappily will fail to repent it.

437. Make sure, as best you can, that your go-between is well-spoken, subtle, and familiar with her job; that she knows how to tell beautiful lies and stay on the trail, for the pot boils hardest when the lid is on.

438. If you have no such relative, choose one of those old women who prowl around the churches and are familiar with every alley, who wear lumpy rosaries around their necks and know a number of sayings, and with what are called Moses' Tears bewitch the hearer's ears.

439. These old pea-hens are great experts; they roam everywhere, through public squares and enclosed lands; they raise up their rosary beads to God and bewail their hardships: O how much wickedness these old gadabouts know!

440. Take one of those old crones who pretend to be herb-healers; they go from house to house proclaiming themselves as midwives; with powders and cosmetics and with vials of eye makeup they cast their spells on girls and blind them indeed.

441. And seek out your messenger from among those black she-devils whom friars, nuns, and pious women consort with so much; they are great ones for walking and really earn the price of their shoes; these convent-trotters arrange many deals.

442. Where these women resort there is always much merriment; few women can be displeased with them; so that they won't lie to you, you must learn how to flatter them, for they practice such magic that they can easily blind one.

443. Of all those old women, this one is the best; beg her not to lie to you, display good love towards her, for a good broker is able to sell plenty of poor cattle, and lots of poor clothes can be covered by a good cloak.

444. If she tells you that your chosen lady does not have long limbs, nor thin arms, ask her next if she has small breasts; and if she says 'Yes,' inquire about her whole figure, so that you can be more sure.

445. If your messenger tells you that your beloved's underarms

are just a little damp, and that she has small legs and long flanks, is nice and wide in the hips, with small, arched feet, this is the kind of woman that is not found in every marketplace.

446. In bed really wild, around the house very sensible, don't lose track of such a woman, but keep her constantly in mind. What I am counselling you is in agreement with Ovid; and she is the kind that a good procuress looks for.

447. There are three things that I dare not reveal to you now, they are hidden defects, very rude to mention; there are very few women who can avoid them; if I were to mention them, the women would burst out laughing.

448. Take great care that your lady is not hairy or bearded; may Hell rid us of such a half-devil as that! If her hand is small, her voice delicate and high, you should, if you possibly can, try to change her from her prudent ways.

LADY SLOE APPEARS

653. O God! how beautiful Lady Sloe is, coming across the town square! What a figure! What grace! What a long, slender throat, like a heron's! What hair! What a darling mouth! What color! What a graceful walk! She wounds with love's arrows when she raises her eyes.

654. Yet this was no place to speak of love; I was beset right away by great fear and trembling; my feet and my hands were not masters of themselves; I lost my wits, I lost my strength, all my color faded away.

655. I had a few words all thought out to say to her; the fear of the people around us made me say something else; I hardly knew myself, and I didn't know where to turn; my speech could not keep pace with my desires.

656. Talking to a woman in the town square is a very public affair; sometimes a vicious dog is tied behind an open [i.e. welcoming] door; it is a good thing to play a pretty game, to set up a blind; when a place is safe it is well to speak in earnest.

657. 'Lady, my niece, who lives in Toledo, commends herself warmly to you and sends you a thousand greetings; if she could find the right time and place, from all she has heard about you, she would

like very much to see you, and she would like to make your acquaintance.

658. There my family wanted, at this time, to marry me off to a very rich young lady, the daughter of Sir Halfpenny; my answer to everybody was that I did not love her at all, that my person would belong only to the one who [now] possesses my heart.'

659. I lowered my voice and told her that I was speaking in jest because all the people in the square were looking at us; when I saw that they were gone, that none remained there, I began to utter my complaint about the love that was besetting me.

MUSIC'S SALUTE TO EASTER AND SPRING

1225. It was the most holy day of Easter Sunday: the sun came up all bright and of splendorous color; men and birds and every precious flower all went forth singing to welcome Love.

1226. The birds welcomed him, jays and nightingales, larks and parrots, large and small; they sang joyful songs full of sweet delights; the ones that were the best singers did the most rejoicing.

1227. The trees welcomed him with branches and flowers of diverse kinds and lovely colors; men and ladies in love welcomed him; the drums came forth accompanied by many instruments of music.

1228. The Moorish guitar came forth singing, sharp of voice and harsh of note; the paunchy lute, which accompanies the rustic trisca dance; the Spanish guitar joined in their flock.

1229. The singing rebec [small, two-stringed guitar], with its shrill note; beside it went the rote [small harp] playing *el alborayn*; the psaltery with them, higher than the peak of La Mota; the quill-played viol danced with them.

1230. The Moorish psaltery and the harp, with the Moorish rebec; in their midst, merriment – the Frenchified garible [a shrill, gay song]; the flute sounded in concert with them, higher than a crag; with it the timbrel, since without one the flute is not worth a sour peach.

1231. The viol that is played with a bow made sweet cadences, dreamily at times, loud at others, sweet, pleasing, clear, and well-played melodies; it gladdens people and keeps them all contented.

1232. The sweet full-psaltery came forth with the tambourine [which] with its brass jingles made a sweet sound; there the portable organ sang Provençal *chançonetas* and motets; the clownish mandora [a lute-like instrument] intruded among them.

1233. The bagpipe and the Moorish flute and the swollen *albogón* [seven-holed, cone-shaped wind instrument], the hurdy-gurdy and the baldosa [multi-stringed instrument] joined in this festival; the little French bagpipe harmonized with them; the oafish bandore [three stringed lute] put its sound in here.

1234. Trumpets and Moorish horns stepped forth with the kettle-drums. Not for a long time had there been such rejoicing, revelry so great and so widespread; the slopes and open fields were filled with minstrels.

ON NUNS

1332. She said to me: 'My friend, listen to me a little: take some nun as a sweetheart, trust my advice; she won't get married right away, nor display herself in public; you will have a love affair of extraordinary duration.

1333. I worked for nuns once and stayed there a good ten years; they keep their lovers in comfort and free from embarrassments. Who could name all their fine dishes and their very generous presents, their endless sweet confections, rich and so rare?

1334. They give their lovers many sweet confections time and again: candied citron, quince jelly and sweet nut-paste; other sweets in larger quantities, made of cheap carrots, they send to each other daily, taking turns;

1335. confection of cumin seed from Alexandria, with good gum-tragacanth candy, abbot's candied citron, with fine ginger, rose-flavored honey, cumin syrup, dianthus syrup[?] goes ahead of it; and the new-fashioned rose confection which I should have mentioned previously;

1336. tiny candies and sugar-almond paste, with aromatic stomatichon, and clove candy, with electuary of powdered pearls, very fine sandalwood paste, with satyrion trifolium paste which is a valued and splendid gift for courtship.

1337. You should know that every kind of sugar is poured out by the handfuls there: powdered, lump, and rock-sugar, and quantities of the rose-flavored kind, sugar for confections and violet-flavored sugar, and of many other kinds that I have forgotten now.

1338. Montpelier, Alexandria, and famed Valencia do not have so many sweets nor so many spices; the nun who considers herself best offers the finest ones; they all put their efforts into refinements of love.

1339. I will tell you something more of what I learned there: since they have Toro wine, they don't drink the common stuff; after I left there I was deprived of this luxury. A man who doesn't make love to a nun is not worth a penny.

1340. Apart from all these fine things, they have very nice ways; they are very discreet, generous, pleasing; their kitchen maids know more and are better for worldly love than ladies who have trappings on their saddles.

1341. Like painted statues, of great beauty, gentlewomen most bountiful and generous by nature, much given to speaking loving words, their love is everlasting; they are thoughtful, accomplished, and have every sort of courtesy.

1342. Every pleasure in the world and every nice love-word, most sweet enjoyment and affectionate fondling: all this is to be found in nuns, more than anywhere else; try it this time and make up your mind now to be at peace.'

THE LOVE OF THE NUN

1499. In the name of God I went to morning Mass; I saw the nun at prayer, full of life, a long throat like a heron's, fresh rosy color: whoever ordered her to dress in coarse wool did wrong.

1500. Help me, Holy Mary! I clasp my hands! Who gave to a white rose a nun's habit and black veil? It would be better for this lovely thing to have children and a grandchild than a black veil like that, or a hundred nun's habits.

1501. Although sinning with a nun is for the wooer an offence against God, O God, how I wish I were that sinner, to do penance for this sin after it was consummated!

1502. She gazed at me with eyes that looked like flame; I sighed for them; my heart said: 'Behold her!' I went to the lady, she spoke to me and I to her; the nun captured my heart and I captured hers.

1503. The lady accepted me as her true paramour; I was ever her obedient and loyal lover; many a good thing did she do for me, with God's help, in unsullied love; as long as she lived God was my guide.

1504. With many a supplication she prayed to God for me; by her abstinence she aided me greatly; her immaculate life found delight in God; she never busied herself with the mad sensuality of this world.

1505. Nuns are [made] for love like this, for praying to God while doing pious works, since they are very risky for earthly, sensual love, and they are very furtive, laggard and untruthful.

1506. My fate was such that, after two months had passed the sweet lady died, and I was again heavy with cares; all men that are alive, or are yet to be born, must die: God forgive her soul and our sins.

(*Trans.* R. S. WILLIS)

GIOVANNI BOCCACCIO
(1313–75)

THE *DECAMERON*

FROM DAY ONE: INTRODUCTION

Dico adunque che già erano gli anni della fruttifera Incarnazione' del Figliuolo di Dio al numero pervenuti di milletrecentoquarantotto, quando nella egregia città di Fiorenza, oltre ad ogni altra italica nobilissima, pervenne la mortifera pestilenza, la quale o per operazione de' corpi superiori' o per le nostre inique opere da giusta ira di Dio a nostra correzione mandata sopra i mortali, alquanti anni davanti nelle parti orientali incominciata, quelle d'innumerabile quantità di viventi avendo private, senza ristare, d'un luogo in uno altro continuandosi, verso l'Occidente miserabilmente s'era ampliata. E in quella non valendo alcuno senno né umano provvedimento, per lo quale fu da molte immondizie purgata la città da oficiali sopra ciò ordinati e vietato l'entrarvi dentro a ciascuno infermo e molti consigli dati a conservazion della sanità, né ancora umili supplicazioni non una volta ma molte e in processioni ordinate e in altre guise a Dio fatte dalle divote persone, quasi nel principio della primavera dell'anno predetto orribilmente cominciò i suoi dolorosi effetti, e in miracolosa maniera, a dimostrare.

I say, then, that the sum of thirteen hundred and forty-eight years had elapsed since the fruitful Incarnation of the Son of God, when the noble city of Florence, which for its great beauty excels all others in Italy, was visited by the deadly pestilence. Some say that it descended upon the human race through the influence of the heavenly bodies, others that it was a punishment signifying God's righteous anger at our iniquitous way of life. But whatever its cause, it had originated some years earlier in the East, where it had claimed countless lives before it unhappily spread westward, growing in strength as it swept relentlessly on from one place to the next.

In the face of its onrush, all the wisdom and ingenuity of man were unavailing. Large quantities of refuse were cleared out of the city by officials specially appointed for the purpose, all sick persons were forbidden entry, and numerous instructions were issued for safeguarding the people's health, but all to no avail. Nor were the countless petitions humbly directed to God by the pious, whether by means of formal processions or in any other guise, any less ineffectual. For in the early spring of the year we have mentioned, the plague began, in a terrifying and extraordinary manner, to make its disastrous effects apparent.

FROM DAY SIX TALE SEVEN

(Madonna Filippa defends herself ingeniously before the magistrate.)

'Sir, it is true that Rinaldo is my husband, and that he found me last night in Lazzarino's arms, wherein, on account of the deep and perfect love I bear towards him, I have lain many times before; nor shall I ever deny it. However, as I am sure you will know, every man and woman should be equal before the law, and laws must have the consent of those who are affected by them. These conditions are not fulfilled in the present instance, because this law only applies to us poor women, who are much better able than men to bestow our favours liberally. Moreover, when this law was made, no woman gave her consent to it, nor was any woman even so much as consulted. It can therefore justly be described as a very bad law.

'If, however, to the detriment of my body and your soul, you wish to give effect to this law, that is your own affair. But before you proceed to pass any judgement, I beseech you to grant me a small favour, this being that you should ask my husband whether or not I have refused to concede my entire body to him, whenever and as often as he pleased.'

Without waiting for the *podestà* to put the question, Rinaldo promptly replied that beyond any doubt she had granted him whatever he required in the way of bodily gratification.

'Well then,' the lady promptly continued, 'if he has always taken as much of me as he needed and as much as he chose to take, I ask you, Messer Podestà, what am I to do with the surplus? Throw it to the dogs? Is it not far better that I should present it to a gentleman who loves me more dearly than himself, rather than allow it to turn bad or go to waste?'

The nature of the charge against the lady, coupled with the fact that she was such a well-known figure in society, had brought almost all the citizens of Prato flocking to the court, and when they heard the charming speech she made in her defence, they rocked with mirth and, as with a single voice, they all exclaimed that the lady was right and that it was well spoken. And at the *podestà*'s suggestion, before they left the court, they amended the harsh statute so that in future it would apply only to those wives who took payment for being unfaithful to their husbands.

After making such a fool of himself, Rinaldo departed from the scene feeling quite mortified; and his wife, now a free and contented woman, having, so to speak, been resurrected from the flames, returned to her house in triumph.

FROM DAY SIX TALE TEN

(Friar Cipolla, having promised the crowd that he will show them a feather of the Angel Gabriel finds some coal has been put in its place.)

When the entire populace was assembled in front of the church, Friar Cipolla began to preach his sermon, never suspecting for a moment that any of his things had been tampered with. He harangued his audience at great length, carefully stressing what was required of them, and on reaching the point where he was to display the Angel Gabriel's feather, he first recited the *Confiteor* and caused two torches to be lit; then, throwing back the cowl from his head, he carefully unwound the taffeta and drew forth the casket, which, after a few words in praise and commendation of the Angel Gabriel and his relic, he proceeded to open. When he saw that it was full of coal, Guccio Balena was the last person he suspected of playing him such a trick, for he knew him to be incapable of rising to such heights of ingenuity. Nor did he even blame the man for being so careless as to allow others to do it, but inwardly cursed his own stupidity in entrusting his things to Guccio's care, knowing full well, as he did, that he was negligent, disobedient, careless and witless. Without changing colour in the slightest, however, he raised his eyes and hands to Heaven, and in a voice that could be heard by all the people present, he exclaimed:

'Almighty God, may Thy power be forever praised!'

Then, closing the casket and turning to the people, he said:

'Ladies and gentlemen, I must explain to you that when I was still very young, I was sent by my superior into those parts where the sun appears, with express instructions to seek out the privileges of the Porcellana,ᵃ which, though they cost nothing to seal and deliver, bring far more profit to others than to ourselves.

'So away I went, and after setting out from Venison, I visited the Greek Calends, then rode at a brisk pace through the Kingdom of Algebra and through Bordello, eventually reaching Bedlam, and not long afterwards, almost dying of thirst, I arrived in Sardintinia. But why bother to mention every single country to which I was directed by my questing spirit? After crossing the Straits of Penury, I found myself passing through Funland and Laughland, both of which countries are thickly populated, besides containing a lot of people. Then I went on to Liarland, where I found a large number of friars belonging to various religious orders including my own, all of whom were forsaking a life of discomfort for the love of God, and paying little heed to the exertions of others so long as they led to their own profit. In all these countries I coined a great many phrases, which turned out to be the only currency I needed.

'Next I came to the land of Abruzzi, where all the men and women go climbing the hills in clogs, and clothe pigs in their own entrails; and a little further on I found people carrying bread on staves, and wine in pouches, after which I arrived at the mountains of the Basques, where all the waters flow downwards.

'In short, my travels took me so far afield that I even went to Parsnipindia, where I swear by this habit I am wearing that I saw the feathers flying – an incredible spectacle for anyone who has never witnessed it. And if any of you should doubt my words, Maso del Saggio will bear me out on this point, for he has set up a thriving business in that part of the world, cracking nuts and selling the shells retail.

'But being unable to find what I was seeking, or to proceed any

---

a Like many of the other mystifying phrases in Cipolla's sermon, the 'privileges of the Porcellana' probably connote the practice of sodomy, a vice to which monks and friars were traditionally susceptible.

further except by water, I retraced my steps and came at length to the Holy Land, where in summertime the cold bread costs fourpence a loaf, and the hot is to be had for nothing. There I met the Reverend Father Besokindas Tocursemenot, the most worshipful Patriarch of Jerusalem, who, out of deference to the habit of the Lord Saint Anthony, which I have always worn, desired that I should see all the holy relics he had about him. These were so numerous, that if I were to give you a complete list, I would go on for miles without reaching the end of it. But so as not to disappoint the ladies, I shall mention just a few of them.

'First of all he showed me the finger of the Holy Ghost, as straight and firm as it ever was; then the forelock of the Seraph that appeared to Saint Francis; and a cherub's fingernail; and one of the side-bits of the Word-made-flash-in-the-pan; and an article or two of the Holy Catholic faith; and a few of the rays from the star that appeared to the three Magi in the East; and a phial of Saint Michael's sweat when he fought with the Devil; and the jawbone of Death visiting Saint Lazarus; and countless other things.

'And because I was able to place freely at his disposal certain sections of the Rumpiad in the vernacular, together with several extracts from Capretius, which he had long been anxious to acquire, he gave me a part-share in his holy relics, presenting me with one of the holes from the Holy Cross, and a small phial containing some of the sound from the bells of Solomon's temple, and the feather of the Angel Gabriel that I was telling you about, and one of Saint Gherardo da Villamagna's sandals, which not long ago in Florence I handed on to Gherardo di Bonsi, who holds him in the deepest veneration; and finally, he gave me some of the coals over which the blessed martyr Saint Lawrence was roasted. All these things I devoutly brought away with me, and I have them to this day.

'True, my superior has never previously allowed me to exhibit them, until such time as their authenticity was established. However, by virtue of certain miracles they have wrought, and on account of some letters he has received from the Patriarch, he has now become convinced that they are genuine, and has granted me permission to display them in public. But I am afraid to entrust them to others, and I always take them with me wherever I go.

'Now, the fact is that I keep the feather of the Angel Gabriel in a casket to prevent it being damaged, and in another casket I keep the coals over which Saint Lawrence was roasted. But the two caskets are so alike that I often pick up the wrong one, which is what has happened today; for whereas I intended to bring along the one containing the feather, I have brought the one with the coals. Nor do I consider this a pure accident; on the contrary I am convinced that it was the will of God, and that it was He who put the casket of coals into my hands, for I have just remembered that the day after tomorrow is the Feast of Saint Lawrence. And since it was God's intention that I should show you the coals over which he was roasted, and thus rekindle the devotion which you should all feel towards Saint Lawrence in your hearts, He arranged that I should take up, not the feather which I had meant to show you, but the blessed coals that were extinguished by the humours of that most sacred body. You will therefore bare your heads, my blessed children, and step up here in order to gaze devoutly upon them.'

FROM DAY EIGHT TALE SEVEN

(The scholar and the lady.)

'Madam,' replied the scholar, who was only too delighted to converse with her, 'it was not because you loved me that you took me into your confidence, but to recover the love that you had lost, and hence you deserve to be treated even more harshly. Moreover you are out of your mind if you suppose that this was the only way I had of obtaining the revenge that I coveted. I had a thousand others, and I had placed a thousand snares around your feet whilst pretending to love you, so that even if this one had failed, you would inevitably have stumbled into another before very long. True, you could not have chosen to fall into a trap which would bring you greater shame and suffering than this, but then I laid it in this way, not in order to spare your pain, but to enhance my pleasure. And even supposing that all my little schemes had failed, I should still have had my pen, with which I should have lampooned you so mercilessly, and with so much eloquence, that when my writings came to your notice (as they certainly would), you would have wished, a thousand times a day, that you had never been born.

'The power of the pen is far greater than those people suppose who have not proved it by experience. I swear to God (and may He grant that my revenge will continue to be as sweet from now until its end as it has been in its beginning), that you yourself, to say nothing of others, would have been so mortified by the things I had written that you would have put out your eyes rather than look upon yourself ever again. It's no use reproaching the sea for having grown from a tiny stream.'

FROM DAY NINE TALE TEN

(Father Gianni's spell is ruined.)

Some years ago, in Barletta, there was a priest called Father Gianni di Barolo, who, because he had a poor living and wished to supplement his income, took to carrying goods, with his mare, round the various fairs of Apulia, and to buying and selling. In the course of his travels, he became very friendly with a man called Pietro da Tresanti, who practised the same trade as his own, but with a donkey, and in token of his friendship and affection he always addressed him, in the Apulian fashion, as Neighbour Pietro. And whenever Pietro came to Barletta, Father Gianni always invited him to his church, where he shared his quarters with him and entertained him to the best of his ability.

For his own part, Neighbour Pietro was exceedingly poor and had a tiny little house in Tresanti, hardly big enough to accommodate himself, his donkey, and his beautiful young wife. But whenever Father Gianni turned up in Tresanti, he took him to his house and entertained him there as best he could, in appreciation of the latter's hospitality in Barletta. However, when it came to putting him up for the night, Pietro was unable to do as much for him as he would have liked, because he only had one little bed, in which he and his beautiful wife used to sleep. Father Gianni was therefore obliged to bed down on a heap of straw in the stable, alongside his mare and Pietro's donkey.

Pietro's wife, knowing of the hospitality which the priest accorded to her husband in Barletta, had offered on several occasions, when the priest came to stay with them, to go and sleep with a neighbour of hers called Zita Carapresa di Giudice Leo, so that the priest could sleep in the bed with her husband. But the priest wouldn't hear of it, and on one occasion he said to her:

'My dear Gemmata, don't trouble your head over me. I am quite all right, because whenever I choose I can transform this mare of mine into a fair young maid and turn in with her. Then when it suits me I turn her back into a mare. And that is why I'd never be without her.'

The young woman was astonished, believed every word of it, and told her husband, adding:

'If he's as good a friend as you say, why don't you get him to teach you the spell, so that you can turn me into a mare and run your business with the mare as well as the donkey? We should earn twice as much money, and when we got home you could turn me back into a woman, as I am now.'

Being more of a simpleton than a sage, Neighbour Pietro believed all this and took her advice to heart; and he began pestering Father Gianni for all he was worth to teach him the secret. Father Gianni did all he could to talk him out of his folly, but without success, and so he said to him:

'Very well, since you insist, tomorrow we shall rise, as usual, before dawn, and I shall demonstrate how it's done. To tell the truth, as you'll see for yourself, the most difficult part of the operation is to fasten on the tail.'

That night, Pietro and Gemmata were looking forward so eagerly to this business that they hardly slept a wink, and as soon as the dawn was approaching, they scrambled out of bed and called Father Gianni, who, having risen in his nightshirt, came to Pietro's tiny little bedroom and said:

'I know of no other person in the world, apart from yourself, for whom I would perform this favour, but as you continue to press me, I shall do it. However, if you want it to work, you must do exactly as I tell you.'

They assured him that they would do as he said. So Father Gianni picked up a lantern, handed it to Neighbour Pietro, and said:

'Watch me closely, and memorize carefully what I say. Unless you want to ruin everything, be sure not to utter a word, no matter what you may see or hear. And pray to God that the tail sticks firmly in place.'

Neighbour Pietro took the lantern and assured him he would do as he had said. Then Father Gianni got Gemmata to remove all her clothes and to stand on all fours like a mare, likewise instructing her not to utter a word whatever happened, after which he began to fondle her face and her head with his hands, saying:

'This be a fine mare's head.'

Then he stroked her hair, saying:

'This be a fine mare's mane.'

And stroking her arms, he said:

'These be fine mare's legs and fine mare's hooves.'

Then he stroked her breasts, which were so round and firm that a certain uninvited guest was roused and stood erect. And he said:

'This be a fine mare's breast.'

He then did the same to her back, her belly, her rump, her thighs and her legs: and finally, having nothing left to attend to except the tail, he lifted his shirt, took hold of the dibber that he did his planting with, and stuck it straight in the appropriate furrow, saying:

'And this be a fine mare's tail.'

Until this happened, Neighbour Pietro had been closely observing it all in silence, but he took a poor view of this last bit of business, and exclaimed:

'Oh, Father Gianni, no tail! I don't want a tail!'

The vital sap which all plants need to make them grow had already arrived, when Father Gianni, standing back, said:

'Alas! Neighbour Pietro, what have you done? Didn't I tell you not to say a word no matter what you saw? The mare was just about to materialize, but now you've ruined everything by opening your mouth, and there's no way of ever making another.'

'That suits me,' said Neighbour Pietro. 'I didn't want the tail. Why didn't you ask me to do it? Besides, you stuck it on too low.'

To which Father Gianni replied:

'I didn't ask you because you wouldn't have known how to fasten it on, the first time, as deftly as I.'

The young woman, hearing these words, stood up and said to her husband, in all seriousness:

'Pah! what an idiot you are! Why did you have to ruin everything for the pair of us? Did you ever see a mare without a tail? So help me God, you're as poor as a church mouse already, but you deserve to be a lot poorer.'

Now that it was no longer possible to turn the young woman into a mare because of the words that Neighbour Pietro had uttered, she put on her clothes again, feeling all sad and forlorn. Meanwhile her husband prepared to return to his old trade, with no more than a donkey as usual: then he and Father Gianni went off to the fair at Bitonto together, and he never asked the same favour of him again.

FROM THE CONCLUSION

'Graceful ladies, the wisdom of mortals consists, as I think you know, not only in remembering the past and apprehending the present, but in being able, through a knowledge of each, to anticipate the future, which grave men regard as the acme of human intelligence.

'Tomorrow, as you know, a fortnight will have elapsed since the day we departed from Florence to provide for our relaxation, preserve our health and our lives, and escape from the sadness, the suffering and the anguish continuously to be found in our city since this plague first descended upon it. These aims we have achieved, in my judgement, without any loss of decorum. For as far as I have been able to observe, albeit the tales related here have been amusing, perhaps of a sort to stimulate carnal desire, and we have continually partaken of excellent food and drink, played music, and sung many songs, all of which things may encourage unseemly behaviour among those who are feeble of mind, neither in word nor in deed nor in any other respect have I known either you or ourselves to be worthy of censure. On the contrary, from what I have seen and heard, it seems to me that our proceedings have been marked by a constant sense of propriety, an unfailing spirit of harmony, and a continual feeling of brotherly and sisterly amity. All of which pleases me greatly, as it surely redounds to our communal honour and credit.

'Accordingly, lest aught conducive to tedium should arise from a custom too long established, and lest, by protracting our stay, we should cause evil tongues to start wagging, I now think it proper, since we have all in turn had our share of the honour still invested in me, that with your consent we should return from whence we came. If, moreover, you consider the matter carefully, our company being known to various others hereabouts, our numbers could increase in such a way as to destroy all our pleasure. And so, if my advice should command your approval, I shall retain the crown that was given me until our departure, which I propose should take effect tomorrow morning. But if you decide otherwise, I already have someone in mind upon whom to bestow the crown for the next day to follow.'

(*Trans*. G. H. McWILLIAM)

DAFYDD AP GWILYM
(Mid fourteenth century)

MAY

God knew how fitting
the tender start of the growth of May would be.
Unfailing green shoots put forth
on the first of the gentle pure month of May.
Untrembling tree-tops detained me;
great God gave May yesterday.
The poets' treasure did not deceive me;
May's coming was a blessing for me.
   A fine handsome youth rewarded me;
May is a generous, open-handed prince.
He sent me true coins:
clean green leaves of May's gentle hazels.
Twigs' florins don't disappoint me,
May's fleur-de-lis wealth.
He kept me safe from treachery
under the wings of leaves of the cloaks of May.
   I'm brimming with anger that May would not
stay for ever. What is it to me? —
I tamed a girl who greeted me,
a tender lady, under May's chancel.
May, who honoured me, is the foster father
of fine poets and gentle lovers.
Great is the dignity of bright green May,
godson of the Immaculate Lord.
From heaven came he who fitted me
for the world; May is my life.
     Green was the hillside, happy was the love-messenger,
long was the day in the green woods of May.
Greenish, unhidden, were
the spurs and twigs of May's brushwood.
Short was the night, a journey no burden,
handsome were the hawks and blackbirds of May.
Happy was the nightingale where she dwelt,

voluble were May's little birds.
Quick was the vigour that he taught me;
there is no great glory save May.
Which of a thousand green-winged town-house peacocks
is better than May? May is the best.
Who would build one out of leaves
in a month but May?
A green wall would rear it up,
May's bright, little-leaved green hazels.

      Winter is puddle-pitted, best
when done with; May is kindest.
When Spring ended, I cared not;
May's golden wealth is purest gold.
The beginning of full Summer scattered him,
whom tears had nourished; May is faultless.

      Green barked hazels' leaves clothed me;
the coming of May is a blessing for me.
God and Mary decided wisely and steadfastly
to uphold May.

SUMMER

Alas for us, Adam's frail race,
for the shortness of summer – a flash-flood of blessings.
By God, in truth, because it must end,
the coming of summer is painful,
though its gentle sky is so clear
with a joyful sun colouring it in summer,
and the air is still and calm,
and the world is lovely in summer.

      A very good crop, unblemished flesh,
comes from the old earth in summer;
summer was given to grow leaves on trees
and turn them the fairest green.
I laugh, seeing such lovely
hair on a sprightly summer birch;
who does not laugh when it's summer,

the paradise to which I sing?
I praise it very diligently
in fitting style – ah, what a gift summer is!
     Under branches I love one twice as fair
as foam; and her rashness is summer.
The amorous cuckoo sings, if I ask,
at the beginning of the summer sun,
the fine grey bird I licence
as vesper bell for midsummer.
The pretty nightingale's fluent voice
is robust and proud beneath summer's penthouse.
The cock-thrush with its merry summer chatter's here
– while I flee from strife.
Ovid's man, on the loveliest long day,
pays court to summer with proud speech;
but old Jealous, Adam's bastard,
does not care if summer has come.
Winter was given for people of his age;
summer is the lovers' share.
     Under birches in the copse's houses
I only want summer's cloaks –
to don a fine web,
a gleaming surcoat of summer's fair hair.
I unravel ivy leaves;
summer's long day is never cold.
If I greet a gentle girl,
I protect her cheerfully on a summer slope!
     Song is no use – coldest omen –
summer's bard is banned;
wind does not leave; I put on clothes;
the trees are full blown. Summer has gone!
There's a shameless longing
in my breast for summer's weather.
When autumn comes, with snow and ice,
to drive out summer, winter's here.
'Alas, Christ,' I ask,
'if it makes off so soon, where is summer?'

THE MIST

Yesterday, Thursday, a drinking day,
a gift befell me. I was glad to receive
auspicious instruction – for which I am famished –
in the whole art of love; I got
a bright-branched walk under green woods
with a girl; she granted me a meeting.

There wasn't, thanks to her,
a person below God the Father who knew
if it was to be Thursday at day break.
I was so full of happiness
going, to see the fair form,
to the land where the tall slim maiden was,
when, in truth, there came onto the long moor
mist like night;
a great scroll enveloping the rain,
grey battalions to hinder me;
a rusting tin sieve,
a snare for the birds of the black earth;
a vague fence in narrow paths,
endless blanket in the sky;
grey cowl greying the earth,
covert over every deep hollow valley:
high hurdles are visible,
a great streak above the hill, vapour of the land,
a thick-grey, white-grey straggling fleece
the colour of smoke, the field's cowl,
rain's enclosure to thwart prosperity,
coat-of-arms of shower's tyranny.

Men it deceived, dark-faced,
rough cloak of the country.
Towers progressing on high,
Gwyn's folk[a], the wind's crown,
its dour cheeks cover the ground,
like torches smoking out the planets;

a Fairies, people of Annwfn (the other-world).

a thick, ugly darkness
blinding the world to delude a poet.
Broad web of de luxe cambric
coiled abroad like rope,
a spider's web, French booth's produce;
moor-headland of Gwyn and his folk;
speckled smoke, exhalation
that is often around May woods;
hideous vapour where dogs stand at bay,
bath of the witches of Annwfn,
sinisterly, like dew, it moistens
the habergeon of the heavy wet earth.

    It's easier to walk on moors by night
than in mist by day.
The stars appear in the sky
like wax candles' flames,
but in the mist – ah, foolish hope! –
neither the moon nor God's stars appear.
The mist made me, so dark was it, into
a swarthy, boorish bondman.
Every road under heaven was barred to me;
a dark grey veil hinders the messenger of love
and I am prevented from a swift attempt at
reaching my thin-browed girl.

DISILLUSIONMENT

Ill luck is mine and affliction of anger.
Shame on him who ruined me!
That is (though fear does not defy him)
the thief Eiddig[a], that boorish Jew.
He left no wealth with me,
no aid was near; God judged against me.
    Sociable, well-descended, free-born,
rich and wealthy I used to be.

---

[a] Eiddig (literally 'Jealous') is Dafydd's name for Morfudd Llwyd's husband.

I gaily took leave of high spirits,
passion in my heart, and now I am poor.
Generosity, worthless love's custom,
has reduced me to nothing, through no fault of mine.
        Let no lord, head held high, ever give
his heart to the treacherous world.
Feckless lad, if he gives it truly
he'll be deceived, losing the world.
Wealth is an illusion and an enemy,
a bitter battle and man's betrayer.
At times it comes yonder in its pride,
at times it goes for sure,
like ebbing on the edges of a shore
after a tide of praise and fortune.
    The wise, unembittered blackbird chortles
in the green grove, a house of polished song.
No marled soil is ploughed for her
(but the seed is fertile), nor does she plough,
and there's none more wanton with chatter
than that little short-legged bird.
By the Lord, she's happy
shaping song in the wooded copse.
Happiest and freest of thought
are the minstrels with their staves;
but I lament with saddest passion,
scourged with tears, calling for a fair woman,
and ever-praised Mary knows
that I do not shed tears for riches,
for there is not (good old custom)
a Welsh-speaking region of Wales
where I cannot find (may I be eloquent,
passionate lad!) riches for my work.
But of her generation another like her
could not be found under the sun's rim.
I have been cheated of Morfudd Llwyd,
my candle bright as day.

(*Trans.* PATRICK SIMS-WILLIAMS)

FRANCESCO PETRARCH
(1304–74)

CANZONE CXXVI

Chiare, fresche e dolci acque,
ove le belle membra
pose colei che sola a me par donna;
    gentil ramo, ove piacque
(con sospir mi rimembra)
a lei di fare al bel fianco colonna;
    erba e fior, che la gonna
leggiadra ricoverse
co l'angelico seno;
aere sacro sereno,
ove Amor co' begli occhi il cor m'aperse:
date udienzia insieme
a le dolenti mie parole estreme.

S'egli è pur mio destino,
e 'l cielo in ciò s'adopra,
ch'Amor quest'occhi lagrimando chiuda,
    qualche grazia il meschino
corpo fra voi ricopra,
e torni l'alma al proprio albergo ignuda;
    la morte fia men cruda
se questa spene porto
a quel dubbioso passo;
ché lo spirito lasso
non poria mai in piú riposato porto
né in piú tranquilla fossa
fuggir la carne travagliata e l'ossa.

CANZONE CXXVI

Clear, fresh, and sweet waters, where she who alone to me seems
woman rested her lovely limbs; gentle trunk, of which she liked (as
I remember with sighs) to make a column for her lovely side; grass
and flower, which the gay dress covered as well as the heavenly

bosom; holy calm air, where Love opened my heart with those lovely eyes: give hearing all together to my last grieving words.

If it is my destiny (and heaven works for this) that Love should close these eyes even while they weep, may some kindness inter my miserable body in your midst, and may my soul return naked to its own abode. Death will be less cruel if I can go forward with this hope to that uncertain pass; as my weary spirit could never fly from my troubled flesh and bones to a more restful haven or a quieter grave.

Perhaps a time will come again when this mild and lovely fierce one may come back to her accustomed haunt; and there, where she noticed me upon that blessed day, may turn her happy eager face to look for me; and, o pity! seeing me already earth among the stones, Love may inspire her to sigh so softly that she will obtain mercy for me, and have her way with Heaven, drying those eyes with that lovely veil.

From the lovely branches there came down (sweet in memory) a rain of flowers into her lap, and she sat modest amid so great glory, covered now by the loving shower. A flower fell upon her hem, another on her fair hair which seemed polished gold and pearl that day; one rested on the ground, and another upon the wave; one, in charmed flight, turning as it fell, seemed to say: here Love reigns.

How many times did I say then full of fear: she was born, for certain, in Paradise! Her divine bearing and face and words had so weighted me with forgetfulness and cut me off from the true image of things that I said sighing: how did I come here, or when? believing myself in Heaven, not where I really was. From that time forth this grass has so pleased me that I find peace in no other place.

[Song], if you had as much ornament as you have desire, you could leave the wood boldly and go among people.

SONNET I

You who hear in my scattered rhymes the sound of those sighs on which I fed my heart in my first youthful mistake, when I was in part another man from the one I am now; for the varied manner in which I weep and reflect there, amid vain hopes and vain grief,

I hope to have pity, not only pardon, from whosoever by experience knows love.

But I see clearly today how I was the talk of everyone for a long time, and for this often, within me, I grow ashamed of myself: and I see how shame is the fruit of my having strayed, and repentance, and the clear knowledge that whatever the world loves is a brief dream.

SONNET XXXV

Alone and thoughtful, I go pacing the most deserted fields with slow hesitant steps, and I am watchful so as to flee from any place where human traces mark the sand. I find no other defence that protects me from the open awareness of people; because they can see from without, in my actions bereft of joy, how I inwardly flame:

so that now I believe that mountains and banks, and rivers and woods know what the tenour of my life is, which is hidden from others. And yet I cannot find any paths so harsh or wild that Love will not always come, talking with me the while, and I with him.

CANZONE CXXIX

From thought to thought, from mountain to mountain Love leads me; since I find every marked path hostile to the life of quiet. If there is a stream or fountain on a lonely slope, if, between two hills, lies a shady vale, there the frightened soul calms itself: and, as Love bids, now laughs, now weeps, now fears, now is assured: and my face which follows the soul, wherever it leads, is disturbed and clears, and stays little time in the one state; so that a man learned in such a life would say on seeing me: This one burns, and is uncertain of his fortune.

In high mountains and in wild woods I find some rest; each inhabited place is the mortal enemy of my eyes. With each pace some new thought of my mistress is born, which often turns the torment I bear for her to joy; and as soon as I would change my sweet and bitter life, then I say: perhaps Love is still preserving you for a better time; perhaps, though hateful to yourself, you are dear to another:

and, sighing the while, I go on: But could this be true? but how? but when?

Where a tall pine tree or a hill offers shade, sometimes I stop, and on the nearest stone trace mentally her lovely face. When I come to myself again, I find my breast wet from tenderness; and then I say: Alas, what have you come to, and what have you left behind? But as long as I can keep my mind steadily upon that first thought, and gaze on her and forget myself, I feel Love so closely that my mind is ravished by its own delusion. I see her in so many places and her so lovely, that were the deception to last, I ask nothing more.

I have many times (now who will believe me?) seen her vividly in clear water or on green grass, and in the trunk of a beech tree and on a white cloud, so fashioned that Leda would have surely said that her daughter is eclipsed, like a star that the Sun obscures with its rays: and the wilder the place, the lonelier the strand where I happen to be, so much the lovelier does my thought shadow her forth. Then when the truth clears away that sweet deception, still I sit there the same, sit cold, dead stone on living stone, like a man who thinks and weeps and writes.

An intense desire continually draws me to the loftiest, most advantageous crest which the shadow of other mountains does not touch. From there I begin to judge my sufferings with my eyes, and weep then, and ease the heart, oppressed by a sorrowful mist, when I see and think what a space separates me from that lovely face, which is always so near to me and so far. Then softly to myself: What are you doing, wretch? Perhaps over there she sighs for your being far away: and in this thought the soul breathes.

My song, beyond that mount, where the sky is clearer and more glad, you will see me again by a running stream where the breeze smells of a fresh and fragrant laurel grove. There is my heart, and she who steals it from me: here you can see only my effigy.

SONNET CLXIV

Now that the heavens and the earth and the wind is silent, and the wild beasts and the birds are bridled by sleep, night leads its starry car upon its round, and, without one wave, the sea lies in its bed;

I see, think, burn, and weep; and she who is my undoing is always before me to my sweet pain: my state is one of war, full of rage and grief; and only in thinking of her do I have some peace.

So from one clear and living fountain the sweet and the bitter move upon which I feed; one single hand heals and pierces me. And so that my suffering may not come to shore, I die a thousand times each day, a thousand I am born; so far am I from my salvation.

SONNET CCXCII

The eyes of which I so warmly spoke, and the arms and the hands and the feet and the face which had so separated me from myself, and marked me out from other people; the waving hair of pure and shining gold, and the flashing of the angelic smile which used to make a paradise on earth, are now a little dust which feels no mortal thing.

And yet I live; at which I grieve and despise myself, left as I am without the light I so loved, in a great storm, in a disabled ship. Now let there be here an end to my loving song: dry is the vein of accustomed skill, and my lyre all turned to weeping.

SONNET CCCXI

That nightingale that is so softly weeping perhaps for its children or its dear mate, fills the heavens and the fields with the sweetness of so many pitiful and brilliant notes, and all night, it seems, accompanies me, and reminds me of my hard fate: for I have none for whom to grieve but myself; because I did not believe that Death could reign in Goddesses.

O how easy it is, the deceiving of one who feels secure! Who would ever have thought to see two lovely lights, clearer far than the sun, become dark earth? Now I know that my savage fate is to make me learn, living and weeping, that nothing here below delights and lasts.

SONNET CCCLXV

I keep weeping over my past which I spent in loving a mortal thing, without lifting myself to flight, although I had wings to give perhaps no mean proof of myself. You, who see my unworthy and wicked ills, king of heaven, unseen, everlasting, help this soul, lost and frail, and make good its infirmity with your grace:

so that, if I have lived in war and tempest, I may die in peace and in port; and, if my sojourn was vain, my leave taking at least may be just. May your hand deign to be near in that little of life which is left to me and in my death. You know full well that I place no hope in any other being.

(*Trans.* GEORGE KAY)

CANZONE CCLXIV

I go thinking and in thought pity for myself assails me, so strong that it often leads me to a weeping different from my accustomed one: for, seeing every day the end coming near, a thousand times I have asked God for those wings with which our intellect raises itself from this mortal prison to Heaven.

But until now no prayer or sigh or weeping of mine has helped me; and that is just, for he who, able to stand, has fallen along the way deserves to lie on the ground against his will. Those merciful arms in which I trust I see still open; but fear grasps my heart at the examples of others, and I tremble for my state; another spurs me and I am perhaps at the end.

One thought speaks to my mind and says: 'What are you yearning for still? whence do you expect help? Wretch, do you not understand with how much dishonor for you time is passing? Decide wisely, decide, and from your heart pluck up every root of the pleasure that can never make one happy and does not let one breathe.

'If you have already long been tired and disgusted by that false fleeting sweetness which the treacherous world gives, why do you place your hopes in it any longer? for it lacks any peace or stability. As long as your body is alive, you have in your own keeping the rein of your thoughts. Ah, grasp it now while you can, for delay is perilous, as you know, and to begin now will not be early.

'You know very well how much sweetness your eyes have taken from the sight of her who I wish were still to be born so we might have peace. You remember well, and you must remember, her

552

image, when it ran to your heart, where perhaps a flame from any other torch could not have entered.

'She set it afire, and if the deceiving flame has lasted many years, awaiting a day that, luckily for our salvation, will never come, now raise yourself to a more blessed hope by gazing at the heavens that revolve about you, immortal and adorned; for if down here your desire, so happy in its ills, is satisfied by a glance, a talk, a song, what will that pleasure be, if this is so great?'

On the other side a sweet sharp thought, enthroned within my soul in difficult and delightful weight, oppresses my heart with desire and feeds it with hope; for the sake of kindly glorious fame, it does not feel when I freeze or when I flame, or if I am pale or thin; and if I kill it, it is reborn stronger than before.

This thought has been growing with me day by day since I slept in swaddling clothes, and I fear that one tomb will enclose us both; for when my soul is naked of my members, this desire will not be able to come with it. But if the Latins and the Greeks talk of me after my death, that is a wind; therefore, since I fear to be always gathering what one hour will scatter, I wish to embrace the truth, to abandon shadows.

But that other desire of which I am full seems to overshadow all others born beside it, and time flies while I write of another, not caring about myself; and the light of those lovely eyes, which gently melts me with its clear heat, holds me in with a rein against which no wit or force avails me.

What does it profit me therefore to oil my little bark, since it is held among the rocks by two such knots? You who entirely free me from all the other knots which in different ways bind the world, my Lord, why do you not finally take from my brow this shame? For like a dreamer I seem to have Death before my eyes, and I wish to defend myself but have no weapons.

I see what I am doing, and I am not deceived by an imperfect knowledge of the truth; rather Love forces me, who never lets anyone who too much believes him follow the path of honour; and from time to time I feel in my heart a noble disdain, harsh and severe, which brings all my hidden thoughts to my brow, where others can see them.

For the more one desires honour, the more one is forbidden to love a mortal thing with the faith that belongs to God alone. And this with a loud voice calls back my reason, which wanders after my senses; but although it hears and thinks to come back, its bad habit drives it further and depicts for my eyes her who was born to make me die, since she pleased me and herself too much.

Nor do I know what space was ordained for me by the heavens when I came newly down to earth to suffer the bitter war that I have managed to combine against myself; nor, because of my bodily veil, can I foresee the day that closes life; but I see my hair changing and every desire within.

Now that I believe I am near or not very far from the time of my departure, like one whom losing has made wary and wise, I go thinking back where I left the journey to the right, which reaches a good port: and on one side I am pierced by shame and sorrow, which turn me back; on the other I am not freed from a pleasure so strong in me by habit that it dares to bargain with Death.

Song, here I am, and my heart is much colder with fear than frozen snow, since I feel myself perishing beyond all doubt, for still deliberating I have wound on the spool a great part now of my short thread; nor was weight ever so heavy as what I now sustain in this state, for with Death at my side I seek new counsel for my life, and I see the better but I lay hold on the worse.

(*Trans.* ROBERT M. DURLING)

GIACOMO DA LENTINI*
(First half of thirteenth century)

SONNET

I have set my heart to serving God so that I may go to Paradise, to the holy place where, as I have heard, there is always entertainment, play, and laughter: without my lady I would not want to go there, she who has the fair hair and clear brow, as without her I could not rejoice, being separated from my lady.

But I do not say this with the intention of committing a sin, if I do not see her graceful mien, her lovely face, and soft gaze: for it would keep me in great contentment to see my lady standing there in glory.

GIACOMINO PUGLIESE
(First half of thirteenth century)

BALLAD

Her sweet and pleasant face and her loving expression delight my heart and mind when she comes before me; so readily I look on her whom I have loved; I still desire and long for the mouth I kissed.

I sought her fragrant mouth and both her breasts, I held her in my arms; kissing, she asked me: 'Sir, if you call in passing, do not stay, for it is not mannerly to leave love and depart.'

Then when I separated from her and said, 'I commend you to God', that fair one looked towards me, sighing and weeping; so frequent were her sighs that she hardly answered me: that sweet fair of mine did not let me leave.

I was not so far away that my love had left me, and I do not think that Tristan loved Iseult as much. When I see that fragrant one appear among the women, my heart leads me from sufferings and my mind rejoices.

GUIDO GUINIZZELLI
(c. 1240–76)

SONNET

I have seen the shining star of morning which shows before day yields its first light, and which has taken the shape of a human being, I think she gives more brightness than any other. Face like snow tinged with red, shining eyes that are gay and full of love; I do not believe that in the world there is a Christian girl so full of beauty and worth.

And I am beset by love of her with so fierce a battle of sighs that I would not dare say anything in her presence. Then, would that she knew my desires, so that, without speaking, I should be requited by the pity she would take upon my torments.

SONNET

I wish to praise my lady most truly and compare her to the rose and the lily: she appears, outshining the morning star, and I liken her to what is lovely on high. I compare green banks and the air to her, all colours of flowers, yellow and crimson, gold and blue and rich jewels to be offered, love itself is made purer through her.

She goes by, comely and so kind, that she humbles the pride of whom she greets and makes him of our faith if he does not already believe it; and no man who is base can approach; and more, I tell you she has greater power: no man can think evil from the time he has seen her.

GUIDO CAVALCANTI
(c. 1260–1300)

SONNET

Who is this who comes, that every man looks on her, who makes the air tremble with brightness, and brings Love with her, so that no man can speak, but each one sighs? O, just how she looks when she glances round, let love say, for I could never describe it: she seems so much a woman of modesty, that every other one beside her is to be called a thing of wrath.

Her pleasantness could not be described, since every gentle virtue bends to her, and beauty shows her for its goddess. Our minds have never been so exalted, nor have we in ourselves so much grace, that we can ever rightly have knowledge of this.

SONNET

O my lady, did you not see him who held his hand upon my heart when I answered you, feeble and low for fear of his blows? He was Love who, on discovering us, stayed with me since he came from afar, in the form of a swift Syrian archer, girded only to kill people.

And he drew sighs from your eyes then, which he shot so violently into my heart that I fled terrified. Then suddenly Death appeared to me accompanied by those agonies that are wont to consume us in weeping.

CINO DA PISTOIA
(c. 1270–1336/7)

SONNET

I was upon the high and blessed mountain, which I worshipped, kissing the holy stone; and fell upon that headstone, weary, where Honesty laid her forehead, and which shut off the fountainhead of every virtue that day when the woman of my heart went through death's bitter pass, alas! she who was once full of every brighter charm.

There I called on Love in this manner: 'My sweet god, let death take me here, since my heart lies here.' But when my Lord did not hear me, I left, still calling on Selvaggia: I passed over the mountain with the voice of grief.

(*Trans.* GEORGE KAY)

FRANÇOIS RABELAIS
(?1494–?1553)

GARGANTUA AND PANTAGRUEL

COMMENT PANTAGRUEL RENCONTRA UN LIMOSIN QUI
CONTREFAISOIT LE LANGAIGE FRANÇOIS

Quelque jour, je ne sçay quand, Pantagruel se pourmenoit après soupper avecques ses compaignons par la porte dont l'on va à Paris. Là recontra un escholier tout jolliet qui venoit par icelluy chemin; et, après qu'ilz se furent saluéz, luy demanda: 'Mon amy, dont viens-tu à ceste heure?'

L'escholier luy respondit:
'De l'alme, inclyte et célèbre académie que l'on vocite Lutèce.
— Qu'est-ce à dire? dist Pantagruel à un de ses gens.
— C'est (respondit-il) de Paris.
— Tu viens doncques de Paris? (dist-il). Et à quoy passez-vous le temps, vous aultres messieurs estudiens audict Paris?'

Respondit l'escholier:
'Nous transfretons la Sequane au dilicule et crépuscule; nous déambulons par les compites et quadrivies de l'urbe; nous despumons la verbocination latiale, et, comme verisimiles amorabonds, captons la bénévolence de l'omnijuge, omniforme et omnigène sexe féminin. Certaines diecules, nous invisons les lupanares, et en ecstase vénéréique, inculcons nos veretres ès penitissimes recesses des pudendes de ces meretricules amicabilissimes; puis cauponizons ès tabernes méritoires de la Pomme de pin, du Castel, de la Magdaleine et de la Mulle, belles spatules vervecines, perforaminées de petrosil.

(from Book 2, ch. 6)

HOW PANTAGRUEL MET A LIMOUSIN WHO MURDERED THE
FRENCH LANGUAGE

One day, I do not know when, Pantagruel was walking with his friends after supper near the gate on to the Paris road, when he met a pretty spruce young scholar coming along the way, of whom, after they had exchanged greetings, he asked: 'Where are you coming from at this hour, my friend?'

'From the alme, inclite, and celebrated academy that is vocitated Lutetia,' replied the scholar.

'What does that mean?' Pantagruel asked one of his people.

'It means from Paris,' he answered.

'So you come from Paris,' said Pantagruel. 'And how do you spend your time, you gentlemen students at this same Paris?'

'We transfretate the Sequana at the dilucule and crepuscule; we deambulate through the compites and quadrives of the urb; we despumate the Latin verbocination and, as verisimile amorabunds, we captate the benevolence of the omnijugal, omniform, and omnigenous feminine sex. At certain intervals we invisitate the lupanars, and in venerean ecstasy we inculcate our veretres into the penitissim recesses of the pudenda of these amicabilissime meretricules. Then we cauponizate, in the meritory taverns of the Pineapple, the Castle, the Magdalen, and the Slipper, goodly vervecine spatules, perforaminated with petrosil. And if by fort fortune there is rarity or penury of pecune in our marsupies, and they are exhausted of ferruginous metal, for the scot we dimit our codices and vestments oppingnerated, prestolating the tabellaries to come from the penates and patriotic lares.'

At which Pantagruel exclaimed: 'What devilish language is this? By God, you must be a heretic.'

'No, signor,' answered the scholar. 'For libentissimily, as soon as there illucesces any minutule slither of day, I demigrate into one of these excellently architected minsters; and there irrorating myself in fine lustral water, mumble a snatch of some missic precation of our sacrificules and, submirmillating my horary precules, I illave and absterge my anima from its nocturnal inquinaments. I revere the Olimpicoles. I latrially venerate the supernal astripotent. I dilect and redame my proximes. I observe the decalogical precepts, and according to the facultatule of my vires, do not discede from it by the latitude of an unguicule. It is veriform, nevertheless, since Mammon does not supergurgitate a drop in my locules, that I am a little rare and neglectful in supererogating the eleemosynes to those indigents who hostially solicit their stipe.'

'A turd, a turd!' exclaimed Pantagruel. 'What does this fool mean? I believe he is coining some new devilish language for us here, and throwing an enchanter's spell on us.'

'My lord, there's no doubt about it,' replied one of his followers. 'This fellow's trying to imitate the Parisians' language. But all he is doing is murdering Latin. He thinks he is pindarizing, and imagines he's a great orator in French because he disdains the common use of speech.'

'Is that true?' asked Pantagruel.

'My lord, sir,' answered the scholar, 'My genius is not aptly nate, as this flatigious nebulon asserts, to excoriate the cuticle of our vernacular Gallic, but vice-versally I gnave opere, and by sail and oar I enite to locuplete it from the latinicome redundance.'

'By God,' cried Pantagruel, 'I'll teach you to speak. But before I do so, tell me one thing. Where do you come from?'

To which the scholar replied: 'The primaeval origin of my aves and ataves was indigenous to the Lemovic regions, where requiesces the corpus of the hagiotate Saint Martial.'

'I understand you all right,' said Pantagruel. 'What it comes to is that you're a Limousin, and here you want to play the Parisian. Well, come on then, and I'll give you a combing.' Then he took him by the throat and continued: 'You murder Latin, by Saint John, I'll make you skin the fox. I'll skin you alive.'

Then the poor Limousin began to plead: 'Haw, guid master! Haw, lordie! Help me, St Marshaw. Ho, let me alane, for Gaud's sake, and dinna hairm me!'

Whereupon Pantagruel replied: 'Now you're speaking naturally,' and released him. But the poor Limousin beshat all his breeches, which were cut codtail fashion and not full-bottomed.

At which Pantagruel exclaimed: 'By St Alipentine, what a sweet scent! Devil take this turnip-eater, how he stinks!' And he let him go.

But this gave the Limousin such a lifelong terror and such a thirst that he would often swear Pantagruel held him by the throat; and after some years he died a Roland's death, this being a divine vengeance and proving the truth of the Philosopher Aulus Gellius's observation, that we ought to speak the language in common use, and of Octavian Augustus's maxim, that we should shun obsolete words as carefully as ships' pilots avoid the rocks at sea.

(Book 3, ch. 3)

PANURGE'S PRAISE OF DEBTORS AND BORROWERS

'But', asked Pantagruel, 'when will you be out of debt?'

'At the Greek Kalends,' replied Panurge, 'when all the world will be content, and you will be your own heir. God forbid that I should be debt-free . . . I give myself to the good saint, St Babolin, if I haven't all my life looked upon debts as the connecting link between Earth and Heaven, the unique mainstay of the human race . . . A world without debts! There among the planets there will be no regular tracks; all will be in disorder. Not recognizing his debt to Saturn, Jupiter will dispossess him of his sphere, and with his Homeric chain hold all Intelligences, Gods, Heavens, Demons, Geniuses, Heroes, Devils, Earth, Sea, and all the elements in suspense. Saturn will ally himself to Mars, and they will put this whole world into confusion. Mercury will refuse to subject himself to the others; he will cease to be their Camillus, as he was called in the Etruscan tongue. For he will be in no way their debtor. Venus will not be venerated, for she will have lent nothing. The moon will remain bloody and dark. For why should the Sun impart his light to her? He will be in no way bound to. The Sun will not throw light on the Earth. The Stars will not send down their good influences. For the Earth will have given up lending them nourishment in the form of those vapours and exhalations, by which – as Heraclitus said, the Stoics proved, and Cicero maintained – the Stars are fed. Amongst the Elements there will be no combinations, alternations, or transmutations of any kind. For one will not feel obliged by another, which has lent it nothing. Earth then will not be made into Water; Water will not be transmuted into Air; from Air no Fire will be made; Fire will not warm Earth. Earth will produce nothing but monsters, Titans, Aloids, and Giants; rain will not rain on it; light will not light it; the wind will not blow on it, and it will have no summer or autumn. Lucifer will break his bonds and, issuing from the depths of hell with the Furies, fiends, and horned devils, will try to dislodge the gods of all nations, major and minor alike, from the heavens.

'This world in which nothing is lent will be no better than a dog-fight, a more disorderly wrangle than the election of a Rector in Paris, an interlude more confused than the devils' play at the

Mysteries of Doué. Among men, one will not save the other; it will be lost labour to cry, "Help!" "Fire!" "Water!" "Murder!" No one will go to help. Why? Because he has lent nothing; no one owes him anything. No one has any interest in his fire, his shipwreck, in his ruin, in his death. Not only has he not lent anything till then, but he would not have lent anything afterwards . . .

'And if on the model of this peevish and perverse world which lends nothing, you imagine the other little world, which is man, there you will find a terrible confusion. The head will refuse to lend the sight of his eyes to guide the feet and hands; the feet will not agree to carry it, and the hands will cease to work for it. The heart will grow tired of continually beating for the benefit of the pulses in the limbs, and will lend them no more help. The lungs will not oblige it with their bellows. The liver will not send it blood for its nourishment. The bladder will not care to be in debt to the kidneys – and the urine will be stopped. When the brain considers this unnatural state of things, it will fall into a daze, and give no feeling to the nerves, no movement to the muscles. In brief, in this disorganised world, which will owe nothing, lend nothing, and borrow nothing, you will see a more pernicious conspiracy than Aesop imagined in his *Apology*. The man will perish, no doubt; and not only perish but perish soon, even if he be Aesculapius himself. The body will rot immediately; and the soul in indignation will take its flight to all the devils, following my money.'

(Book 4, ch. 19)

THE BEHAVIOUR OF PANURGE AND FRIAR JOHN DURING THE STORM

First Pantagruel implored the help of the great God, our Protector, and offered up a public prayer of fervent devotion. Then, on the captain's advice, he clung tight and firmly to the mast. Friar John had stripped to his doublet to help the seamen, and so had Epistemon, Ponocrates, and the others. But Panurge remained squatting on the deck, weeping and moaning. Friar John noticed him as he was passing along the middle deck, and called to him: 'For God's sake, Panurge you calf, Panurge you blubberer, Panurge you coward, come and help us! That would be far better than moaning away there like a cow, squatting on your ballocks like a baboon.'

'Be, be, be, bous, bous, bous,' wailed Panurge, 'Oh Brother John, oh my dear friend, oh my dear father, I'm drowning, I'm drowning, my friend, I'm drowning. It's all up with me, my ghostly father, my friend, I'm done for. Your cutlass couldn't save me from this. Alas, alas, now we're higher than the top-note, right out of the scale. Be be be, bous, bous! Alas, and now we're below the bottom C. I'm drowning. Oh my father, my uncle, my all! The water has got into my shoes by way of my shirt collar. Bous, bous, bous, paisch, hu, hu, hu, hu, ho, ho, ho, ho, ho. I'm drowning! Alas, alas, hu, hu, hu, hu, hu, hu! Bebe, bous, bous, bobous, bobous, ho, ho, ho, ho, ho! Alas, alas! Now I'm just like a forked tree, with my legs in the air, and my head down. Would to God I were at this moment in that ship with the good and blessed council-bound fathers whom we saw this morning. Such fat and devout and jolly fellows they were, so sleek and so gracious. Heigh-ho, heigh-ho, heigh-ho, alas, alas, that devilish wave – *mea culpa Deus* – I mean God's blessed wave will drive our ship to the bottom. Alas, Father John, my father, my friend, take my confession! Here you see me on my knees. *Confiteor*, your holy benediction.'

'Come, you hangdog devil,' cried Friar John. 'Come, in the name of the thirty legions of hell, come and help us! . . . But will he come?'

'Let's not swear at this moment, my friend and father,' said Panurge. 'Tomorrow we'll swear as much as you like. Heigh-ho, heigh-ho, alas, our ship's letting water, I'm drowning. Alas, alas! Be be be be be bous bous, bous, bous! Now we're on the bottom. Alas, alas! I'll give eighteen hundred thousand crowns in rents to anyone who'll put me ashore, all stinking and shitten as I am, if ever a man was in my shitten country. *Confiteor*. Alas, listen to just one word of a will, or a little codicil at least.'

'May a thousand devils leap on this cuckold's body,' cried Friar John. 'In God's name, why talk about wills at this moment? We're in extreme peril, and we must bestir ourselves now or never. Here, will you come, you devil? Bo'sun, my hearty! That was neat work, mate. Here, Gymnaste, up on the bridge! That wave fairly did for us. Look, our light's put out. We're rushing headlong to meet those million devils.'

'Alas, alas,' cried Panurge, 'alas! Bou, bou, bou, bou, bous. Alas, alas! was it here that we were fated to perish? Ho, ho, good people, I'm drowning, I'm a dead man. *Consummatum est*. I'm done for.'

'Magna, gna, gna,' exclaimed Friar John. 'Isn't he a sight, the shitten blubberer? Here, boy, in all the devils' names, look to the pump. Are you hurt? For God's sake, cling on to one of the stanchions. Here, on this side, in the devil's name! Ho, like this, my boy.'

'Oh, brother John, my spiritual father, my friend, let's not swear. It's a sin. Alas, alas! Be, be, be, bous, bous, bous. I'm drowning, I'm a dead man, my friends. I pardon everyone. Goodbye. *Into Thy hands*. Bous, bous, bououououous! St Michael of Aure, St Nicholas, help me now or never! Here I make a solemn vow to you and to Our Lord, that if you come to my help now – I mean if you save me from this danger and put me ashore – I'll build you a great lovely little chapel or two,

> Between Candes and Montsoreau,
> Where cow or calf shall never graze.

Alas, alas, more than eighteen bucketsful or more have poured into my mouth. Bous, bous, bous. It's very salty and bitter.'

'By the virtue of the blood, flesh, belly, and head of God,' cried Friar John, 'If I hear you moaning again, you devil's cuckold, I'll maul you like a sea-wolf. By God, why don't we throw the man to the bottom of the sea? That's neat work, you at the oars! Like that, my friend! Hold on tight, up there! I think all the devils are unchained today, or else Proserpine's in labour. All the devils are dancing a morris.'

(Book 5, ch. 3)

HOW THERE IS ONLY ONE POPINJAY IN THE RINGING ISLAND

We then asked Master Aeditus why, since every other species of these venerable birds multiplied, there was only one popinjay. He answered that this had been so since the beginning and that it was so ordained by the stars; that from the clerijays were born the priestjays and monajays without physical copulation, as in the case of the bees. From the priestjays came the bishojays; from them the great cardinjays, and each cardinjay, if death did not intervene, ended up as popinjay; but of these there is only one, as there is only one king in a hive of bees, and only one sun in the sky.

When the popinjay dies, another is produced in his place out of the whole brood of cardinjays; also, be it understood, without physical copulation. Therefore it is that this species consists of but one individual with a perpetuity of succession exactly like that of the phoenix of Arabia. True it is that about two thousand seven hundred and sixty months ago Nature produced two popinjays. But this was the greatest calamity that the island had ever known. 'For,' said Aeditus, 'all these birds so pecked and clawed one another that the island was in danger of losing all its inhabitants. One faction of them adhered to one and supported him, another faction stuck to the other and defended him, while part of them remained dumb as fish and did not sing, and some of the bells seemed to be under an interdict, for they did not sound at all. During these disorderly times they called for the aid of all the Emperors, Kings, Dukes, Marquises, Counts, Barons, and all the world's republics lying on the mainland and on *terra firma*; and this mutinous schism did not come to an end till one of the popinjays departed this life and the plurality was reduced to unity.'

Then we asked what caused these birds to sing so continuously. Aeditus answered that it was the bells hanging above their cages, and went on to say: 'Would you like me to make these monajays whom you see swathed in hoods like mulled-wine strainers, sing like so many larks in the air?'

'If you please,' we replied. Upon which he sounded just six strokes on the bell. Then the monajays rushed up, and the monajays started singing.

'And if I were to ring this bell, should I make these ones sing too?' asked Panurge – 'the ones with plumage the colour of a red herring, I mean.'

'Yes, just the same,' said Aeditus.

Panurge rang, and immediately these smoked birds rushed up, and sang all together. But they had hoarse and unpleasant voices, and Aeditus explained to us that they lived on fish alone, like the herons and cormorants of this world, and that they were a fifth species – the cowljays, newly minted. He added, furthermore, that he had received notice from Robert Valbringue, who had passed by recently on his way back from Africa, that a sixth species would shortly fly in, which he called Capucinjays, a more woe-begone, sterile, and loathsome species than any in the whole island.

'Africa,' said Pantagruel, 'is always producing things both new and monstrous.'

(*Trans.* J. M. COHEN)

PART V

APPENDIX

COMPILED BY ROSEMARY MORRIS

FOR FURTHER READING AND REFERENCE

LIST OF ABBREVIATIONS

B.H.S.	Bulletin of Hispanic Studies
C.F.M.A.	Classiques Français du Moyen Age
M.L.N.	Modern Language Notes
M.L.R.	Modern Language Review
P.M.L.A.	Publications of the Modern Language Association of America
S.A.T.F.	Société des Anciens Textes Français
T.L.F.	Textes Littéraires Français
Fr.	French
Eng.	English
Ger.	German
Lat.	Latin
Sp.	Spanish
ed.	edited, editor
edn	edition
mod.	modern
refs	references
rev.	revised
vol.(s)	volume(s)
trans.	translated/translation
c.	circa
b.	born
d.	died
fl.	floruit

The field of medieval studies is very unevenly covered, and this is inevitably reflected in the bibliography. In dealing with individual authors and works, the aim has been to list a bibliography; one or more good editions; one or more good translations; and a selection of critical works. The aim throughout is to guide the interested reader to a point from which he will be able to make his own way. Whilst every effort has been made to list works written in, or which have been translated into, English, it should be borne in mind that serious study of any medieval literature ideally requires a good knowledge of the corresponding modern language.

FOR FURTHER READING AND REFERENCE

General Background

I. GENERAL HISTORY

Artz, F. B. *The Mind of the Middle Ages* (Chicago and London, 1953; 1980)

Bishop, M. G. *The Penguin Book of the Middle Ages* (Penguin, 1971)

Brooke, C. *Europe in the Central Middle Ages, 962–1154* (London, 1964)

Davis, R. H. C. *A History of Medieval Europe* (London, 1970)

Dawson, C. *The Making of Europe* (London, 1932)

Evans, J. (ed.) *The Flowering of the Middle Ages* (London, 1966)

Fowler, K. A. *The Age of Plantagenet and Valois* (London, 1967)

Green, V. H. H. *Medieval Civilization in Western Europe* (London, 1971)

Hale, J. R., Highfield, J. R. L. and Smalley, B. *Europe in the Late Middle Ages* (London, 1965)

Hay, D. *The Medieval Centuries* (London, 1964)

Heer, F. *The Medieval World* (London, 1962)

Hollister, C. W. *Medieval Europe: A Short History* (New York, 1964; 4th edn, 1976)

Huizinga, J. *The Waning of the Middle Ages* (London, 1924; Penguin, 1965)

Keen, M. *The Pelican History of Medieval Europe* (Penguin, 1969)

Ker, W. P. *The Dark Ages* (London, 1904)

Matthew, D. *The Medieval European Community* (London, 1977)

McEvedy, C. *The Penguin Atlas of Medieval History* (Penguin, 1969)

Munby, J. H. *Europe in the High Middle Ages* (London, 1973)

Pullan, B. S. *Sources for the History of Medieval Europe* (Oxford, 1966)

Southern, R. W. *The Making of the Middle Ages* (London, 1953; latest edn, 1968)

Talbot Rice, D. (ed.) *The Dark Ages* (London, 1965)

Trevor-Roper, H. *The Rise of Christian Europe* (London, 1965; 1966)

Tuchman, B. W. *A Distant Mirror: The Calamitous Fourteenth Century* (London, 1979; Penguin, 1981)

von Gierke, O. *Political Theories of the Middle Ages* (Cambridge, 1900)

Waley, D. *Later Medieval Europe* (London, 1964)

Wallace-Hadrill, J. M. *Early Medieval History* (Oxford, 1975)

Wright, E. *The Medieval and Renaissance World* (London, 1979)

II. POLITICAL THOUGHT

Foltz, R. *The Concept of Empire in Western Europe from the Fifth to the Fourteenth Century* (London, 1969)

Ganshof, F. L. *The Middle Ages: A History of International Relations* (New York, 1971)

Kantorowicz, E. M. *The King's Two Bodies* (Princeton, N.J., 1957)

Kern, F. *Kingship and Law in the Middle Ages* (Oxford, 1939)

Skinner, Q. *The Foundations of Modern Political Thought* (Cambridge, 1978)

Smalley, B. (ed.) *Trends in Medieval Political Thought* (Oxford, 1965)

Tierney, B. *The Crisis of Church and State, 1050–1500* (Englewood Cliffs, N.J., 1964)

Ullmann, W. *Principles of Government and Politics in the Middle Ages* (London, 1961; 4th edn, 1978)

Ullmann, W. *Medieval Political Thought* (Penguin, 1979)

III. SOCIAL AND ECONOMIC HISTORY

Baker, D. (ed.) *Medieval Women* (Oxford, 1978)

Barber, R. *The Knight and Chivalry* (Boydell Press, 1970)

Bautier, R. H. *The Economic Development of Medieval Europe* (London, 1971)

Bloch, M. *Feudal Society* (2 vols, London, 1961)

Brooke, C. *The Structure of Medieval Society* (London, 1971)

Chenu, M.-D. *Nature, Man and Society in the Twelfth Century* (Chicago, 1968)

Dales, R. C. *The Scientific Achievement of the Middle Ages* (Philadelphia, 1973)

Doehaerd, R. *Le haut moyen âge occidental: économies et sociétés* (Paris, 1971)

Duby, G. *Medieval Marriage* (Baltimore, 1977)

Duby, G. *The Chivalrous Society* (London, 1977)

Duby, G. *Medieval Agriculture, 900–1500* (London, 1969)

Duby, G. *Rural Economy and Country Life in the Medieval West* (London, 1968)

Ganshof, F. L. *Feudalism* (London, 1952; 3rd edn, 1964)

Gilchrist, J. T. I. *The Church and Economic Activity in the Middle Ages* (London, 1969)

Gimpel, J. *The Medieval Machine* (London, 1977)

Havighurst, A. F. (ed.) *The Pirenne Thesis* (Boston, 1958)

Latouche, R. *The Birth of Western Economy* (London, 1961; 1967)

Le Roy Ladurie, E. *Montaillou: Cathars and Catholics in a French Village 1294–1324* (London, 1978; Penguin, 1981)

Lindberg, D. C. (ed.) *Science in the Middle Ages* (Chicago and London, 1978)

Lopez, R. S. *The Commercial Revolution of the Middle Ages, 950–1300* (New Jersey, 1971)

Lopez, R. S. and Raymond, I. W. (eds) *Medieval Trade in the Mediterranean World* (London, 1955)

Murray, A. *Reason and Society in the Middle Ages* (Oxford, 1978)

Pirenne, H. *Economic and Social History of Medieval Europe* (London, 1937)

Pirenne, H. *Mahomet and Charlemagne* (London, 1940)

Pirenne, H. *Medieval Cities* (Princeton, 1925)

Pounds, N. J. G. *An Historical Geography of Europe 450 B.C. – A.D. 1300* (Cambridge, 1973)

Power, E. (ed. M. M. Postan) *Medieval Women* (Cambridge, 1975)

Reuter, T. (ed.) *The Medieval Nobility* (Amsterdam, 1978)

Ullmann, W. *The Individual and Society in the Middle Ages* (Baltimore, 1966; London, 1967)

Ziegler, P. *The Black Death* (London, 1967)

IV. THE CHURCH

Brooke, R. *The Coming of the Friars* (London, 1975)

Deansely, M. *A History of the Medieval Church, 500–1500* (London, 1969)

Hamilton, B. *The Medieval Inquisition* (London, 1981)

Hughes, P. *A History of the Church, 2: Augustine to Aquinas* (London, 1938; 3rd edn, 1979)

Knowles, D. and Obolensky, D. *The Christian Centuries*, Vol. 2: *The Middle Ages* (London, 1969)

Lambert, M. D. *Medieval Heresy* (London, 1977)

Latourette, K. S. (rev. R. D. Winter) *A History of Christianity, 1: Beginnings to 1500* (New York, Hagerstown, San Francisco, London, 1953; 1975)

Mollat, G. *The Popes at Avignon, 1305–78* (London, 1963)

Peters, E. *Heresy and Authority in Medieval Europe* (Philadelphia, 1980)

Southern, R. W. *Western Society and the Church in the Middle Ages* (Pelican History of the Church, II) (Penguin, 1970; 2nd edn, 1971)

Ullmann, W. *The Growth of Papal Government in the Middle Ages* (London, 1955; 3rd edn, 1970)

Ullmann, W. *A Short History of the Papacy in the Middle Ages* (London, 1972; 1974)

Watt, J. A. *The Theory of Papal Monarchy in the Thirteenth Century* (London and New York, 1965)

V. THE ARTS

The New Oxford History of Music, Vol. 2 (London, 1954)

Apel, W. *Gregorian Chant* (London, 1958)

Backhouse, J. *The Illuminated Manuscript* (Oxford and New York, 1979)

Beckwith, J. *Early Christian and Byzantine Art* (Penguin, 1979)

Beckwith, J. *Early Medieval Art: Carolingian, Ottonian, Romanesque* (London, 1964)

Caldwell, J. *Medieval Music* (London, 1978)

Conant, K. J. *Carolingian and Romanesque Architecture, 800–1200* (Penguin, 1959; 3rd edn, 1973)

Dodwell, C. R. *Painting in Europe 800–1200* (Penguin, 1971)

Duby, G. *The Europe of the Cathedrals* (Geneva, 1966)

Focillon, H. (ed. J. Bony) *The Art of the West in the Middle Ages* (2 vols, London, 1969)

Frankl, P. *Gothic Architecture* (Penguin, 1962)

Friedländer, M. J. *From Van Eyck to Breughel* (Oxford, 1956)

Gérold, T. *La Musique au moyen âge* (CFMA, 1932)

Grodecki, L., Prache, A. and Recht, R. *Gothic Architecture* (New York, 1977)

Harthen, J. *Books of Hours* (London, 1977)

Hearn, M. F. *Romanesque Sculpture* (Oxford, 1981)

Henderson, G. *Early Medieval Art* (Penguin, 1972)

Henderson, G. *Gothic Art* (Penguin, 1967)

Henderson, G. *Chartres* (Penguin, 1968)

Krautheimer, R. *Early Christian and Byzantine Architecture* (Penguin, 1965; 3rd edn, 1980)

Lasko, P. *Ars Sacra 800–1200* (Penguin, 1972)

Martindale, A. *Gothic Art* (London, 1967)

Morrocco, W. T. and Sandon, N. *The Oxford Anthology of Medieval Music* (Oxford, 1977)

Mütherich, F. and Gaehde, J. E. *Carolingian Painting* (London, 1977)

Nordenfalk, C. *Celtic and Anglo-Saxon Painting* (London, 1977)

Pächt, O. *The Rise of Pictorial Narrative in Twelfth-Century England* (Oxford, 1962)

Robertson, A. *Ancient Forms of Polyphony* (Pelican History of Music, ed. A. Robertson and D. Stevenson, Vol. i) (Penguin, 1962)

Salter, E. and Pearsall, D. *Landscapes and Seasons of the Medieval World* (London, 1973)

Shaver-Crandell, A. *The Middle Ages* (Cambridge Introduction to the History of Art) (Cambridge, 1981)

Stenton, F. et al., *The Bayeux Tapestry* (2nd edn, London, 1965)

Weizmann, K. *Late Antique and Early Christian Book Illumination* (London, 1977)

Wilkins, N. *Music in the Age of Chaucer* (Cambridge, Brewer, 1979)

VI. EDUCATION, THOUGHT AND LEARNING

The Cambridge History of Later Greek and Early Medieval Philosophy (1967)

The Cambridge History of Later Medieval Philosophy (1981)

Brooke, C. *The Twelfth-Century Renaissance* (London, 1969)

Bowen, J. *A History of Western Education, 2: Civilization of Europe, Sixth to Sixteenth Century* (London, 1975)

Crombie, A. C. *Augustine to Galileo: The History of Science A.D. 400–1650* (London, 1952)

Gilson, E. *Christian Philosophy in the Middle Ages* (new edn, London, 1980)

Knowles, D. *The Evolution of Medieval Thought* (London, 1962)

Laistner, M. L. W. *Thought and Letters in Western Europe, A.D. 500–900* (London, 1931; 1957)

Leff, G. *Medieval Thought: St Augustine to Ockham* (London, 1959)

Morris, C. *The Discovery of the Individual 1050–1200* (London, 1972)

Murphy, J. (ed.) *Medieval Eloquence: Studies in the Theory and Practice of Medieval Rhetoric* (Berkeley and London, 1978)

Piltz, A. *The World of Medieval Learning* (Oxford, 1981)

Poole, R. L. *Illustrations of the History of Medieval Thought and Learning* (London, 1884; 1920)

Rasdall, H. (eds F. M. Powicke and A. B. Emden) *The Universities of Europe in the Middle Ages* (3 vols, Oxford, 1895; 1936)

Riché, P. *Écoles et enseignement dans le haut moyen âge* (Paris, 1979)

Smalley, B. *The Study of the Bible in the Middle Ages* (Oxford, 1941; 1952)

Southern, R. W. *Medieval Humanism and Other Studies* (Oxford, 1970)

Wolff, P. *The Awakening of Europe* (Pelican History of European Thought, 1) (Penguin, 1968)

VII. WARS AND WARFARE

Beeler, J. *Warfare in Medieval Europe 730–1200* (Ithaca and London, 1971)

Burne, A. H. *The Agincourt War* (London, 1956; reprint, Westport, Connecticut, 1976)

Keen, M. *The Laws of War in the Late Middle Ages* (London, 1965)

Oman, C. *A History of the Art of War in the Middle Ages* (2 vols, London, 1898; 1978)

Perroy, E. *La Guerre de cent ans* (Paris, 1945)

Riley-Smith, J. *What were the Crusades?* (London, 1977)

Runciman, J. C. S. *The History of the Crusades* (3 vols, Cambridge, 1951–4)

Russell, F. H. *The Just War in the Middle Ages* (Cambridge, 1975)

Setton, K. M. (ed.) *The Crusades* (6 vols, 2nd edn, University of Wisconsin Press, 1967–79)

Historical Background: Individual Countries

ANGLO–SAXON ENGLAND

Blair, P. H. *An Introduction to Anglo-Saxon England* (Cambridge, 1956; 1977)

Blair, P. H. *Northumbria in the Days of Bede* (London, 1976)

Douglas, D. C. (ed.) *English Historical Documents 1042–1189* (primary sources in trans.) (London, 1953; 1981)

Fisher, D. J. V. *The Anglo-Saxon Age c. 400–1042* (London, 1973)

Hinton, D. A. *Alfred's Kingdom: Wessex and the South 800–1500* (London, 1973)

Laing, Ll. and Laing, J. *A Guide to the Dark Age Remains in Britain* (London, 1979)

Loyn, H. R. *Anglo-Saxon England and the Norman Conquest* (London, 1962)

Sherley-Price, L. (trans.) *Bede: A History of the English Church and People* (Penguin, 1955)

Stenton, F. M. *Anglo-Saxon England* (The Oxford History of England, 1) (fundamental textbook) (Oxford, 1943; 3rd edn, 1971; new edn imminent)

Whitelock, D. (ed.) *English Historical Documents c. 500–1042* (primary sources in trans.) (London, 1955; 1979)

Wilson, D. M. *The Anglo-Saxons* (archaeology) (Penguin, 1971)

Crossley-Holland, K. *The Anglo-Saxon World* (anthology of texts in trans., arranged by topic) (The Boydell Press, Woodbridge, 1982)

Page, R. I. *Life in Anglo-Saxon England* (London, 1970)

Whitelock, D. *The Beginnings of English Society* (Pelican History of England, 2) (Penguin, 1952)

Godfrey, J. *The Church in Anglo-Saxon England* (Cambridge, 1962)

Stanley, E. G. *The Search for Anglo-Saxon Paganism* (Ipswich and Totowa, N.J., 1975)

Alexander, J. J. G. *Insular Manuscripts, 6th–9th Century* (London, 1978)

Dolley, R. H. M. (ed.) *Anglo-Saxon Coins* (London, 1961)

Dodwell, C. R. *Anglo-Saxon Art* (Manchester University Press, 1982)

Kendrick, T. D. *Anglo-Saxon Art to A.D. 900* (London, 1938)

Taylor, H. M. and Taylor, J. *Anglo-Saxon Architecture* (complete survey) (3 vols to date; Cambridge, 1965, 1978, 1981)

Temple, E. *Anglo-Saxon Manuscripts 900–1066* (London, 1976)

BYZANTIUM

Arnott, P. *The Byzantines and Their World* (London, 1973)

Baynes, N. H. and Moss, H. St L. B. (eds) *Byzantium* (Oxford, 1948)

Brand, C. M. *Byzantium Confronts the West* (Cambridge, Mass., 1968)

Bréhier, L. *Le Monde byzantin* (Paris, 1950)

Diehl, Ch. *History of the Byzantine Empire* (New York, 1969)

Geanakopolos, D. J. *Byzantine East and Latin West* (Oxford and New York, 1966; reprint, Hamden, Connecticut, 1976)

Hussey, J. M. *The Byzantine World* (London, 1957; 1967)

Obolensky, D. *The Byzantine Commonwealth* (on the eastern and Slav regions of the empire) (London, 1971)

Ostrogorsky, G. *History of the Byzantine State* (Oxford, 1957; 1968)

Whiting, P. (ed.) *Byzantium: An Introduction* (Oxford, 1971; 1981)

Ahrweiler, H. *L'Idéologie politique de l'empire byzantin* (Paris, 1975)

Alexander, P. J. *Religious and Political History and Thought in the Byzantine Empire* (collection of studies) (Variorum Reprints, London, 1978)

Every, G. *The Byzantine Patriarchate 451–1204* (London, 1942; 1962)

Runciman, J. C. S. *The Eastern Schism* (London, 1955)

Runciman, J. C. S. *Byzantine Style and Civilization* (with useful bibliography on Byzantine art) (Penguin, 1975)

Talbot Rice, D. *Art of the Byzantine Era* (London, 1973)

CELTIC-SPEAKING COUNTRIES

Anderson, M. O. *Kings and Kingship in Early Scotland* (Edinburgh, 1973)

Barrow, G. W. S. *The Kingdom of the Scots* (London, 1973)

Byrne, F. J. *Irish Kings and High Kings* (London, 1973)

Chadwick, N. K. (ed.) *Celt and Saxon* (collection of essays) (Cambridge, 1963)

Chadwick, N. K. and Dillon, M. *The Celtic Realms* (London, 1967; 1972)

Hughes, K. *Celtic Britain in the Early Middle Ages* (collection of articles) (Ipswich and Totawa, N.J., 1980)

Jack, R. I. *Medieval Wales* (Cambridge, 1972)

Jackson, K. H. *Language and History in Early Britain* (Edinburgh, 1953)

Jenkins, D. and Owen, M. E. (eds) *The Welsh Law of Women* (Cardiff, 1980)

Lloyd, J. E. *History of Wales from the Earliest Times to the Edwardian Conquest* (2 vols, London, 1911; 3rd edn, 1939)

Lydon, J. *Ireland in the Later Middle Ages* (Dublin, 1973)

Mac Niocaill, G. *Ireland before the Vikings* (Dublin, 1972)

Ó Corráin, D. *Ireland before the Normans* (Dublin, 1972)

Otway-Ruthven, A. J. *A History of Medieval Ireland* (London, 1968)

de Paor, M. and de Paor, L. *Early Christian Ireland* (London, 1958)

Powell, T. G. E. *The Celts* (London, 1958)

Raftery, J. (ed.) *The Celts* (scripts from radio talks) (Dublin, 1964)

Roderick, A. J. (ed.) *Wales through the Ages, Vol. 1: From the Earliest Times to 1485* (Llandybie, 1959)

Ross, A. A. *Pagan Celtic Britain* (London and New York, 1967)

Thomas, C. *Britain and Ireland in Early Christian Times* (London, 1971)

Thorpe, L. (trans.) *Gerald of Wales: The Journey through Wales and The Description of Wales* (two fascinating twelfth-century source-books) (Penguin, 1978)

Chadwick, N. K. *et al. Studies in the Early British Church* (Cambridge, 1958)

Hughes, K. *The Church in Early Irish Society* (London, 1966)

Hughes, K. *Early Christian Ireland: Introduction to the Sources* (Cambridge, 1972)

Kenney, J. F. *The Sources for the Early History of Ireland: Ecclesiastical* (Columbia, 1929; 1966; reprint, Dublin, 1979)

Victory, S. *The Celtic Church in Wales* (London, 1977)

Watt, J. *The Church in Medieval Ireland* (Dublin, 1972)

Williams, G. *The Welsh Church from Conquest to Reformation* (Cardiff, 1962)

Norman, E. R. and St Joseph, J. K. S. *The Early Development of Irish Society: The Evidence of Aerial Photography* (Cambridge, 1969)

Finlay, I. *Celtic Art: An Introduction* (London, 1973)

Henry, F. *Irish Art in the Early Christian Period* (London, 1940; 1965)

Henry, F. *Irish Art during the Viking Invasions* (London, 1967)

Henry, F. *Irish Art in the Romanesque Period* (London, 1970)

Mitchell, G. F. *et al. Treasures of Irish Art* (New York, 1977)

FRANCE

There is no good up-to-date history of medieval France. The following books are useful:

Fawtier, R. *The Capetian Kings of France* (London, 1960)

Funck-Brentano, Fr. *Le Moyen Âge* (Paris, 1923)

Hallam, E. M. *Capetian France 987–1328* (London and New York, 1980)

Lewis, P. S. *Later Medieval France* (London, 1968)

Petit-Dutaillis, C. E. *The Feudal Monarchy in France and England* (London, 1936)

Evans, J. *Life in Medieval France* (Oxford, 1925; 1957)

Luchaire, A. *Social France at the Time of Philip Augustus* (New York, 1967)

Avril, F. *Manuscript Painting at the Court of France, 1310–1380* (London, 1978)

Mâle, E. *L'Art religieux du 12ᵉ siècle en France* (Paris, 1922; 1924)

Mâle, E. *The Gothic Image: Religious Art in France of the Thirteenth Century* (New York, Evanston, San Francisco, London, 1958; 1972)

Sauerländer, W. *Gothic Sculpture in France 1140–1270* (London, 1972)

Stoddard, W.S. *Art and Architecture in Medieval France* (Lion Editions, New York, 1972)

Thomas, M. *The Golden Age: Manuscript Painting at the Time of Jean, duc de Berry* (London, 1980)

GERMANY

Barraclough, G. *The Origins of Modern Germany* (Oxford, 1946; 1947)

Barraclough, G. (ed.) *Medieval Germany 911–1250* (2 vols, Oxford, 1967)

Bleckenstein, J. *Early Medieval Germany* (Amsterdam, New York, Oxford, 1978)

Cavillier, J.-P. *L'Allemagne mediévale* (Paris, 1979)

Folz, R. *La Naissance du Saint-Empire* (anthology of texts) (Paris, 1967)

Hampe, K. *Germany under the Salians and Hohenstaufen Emperors* (Totawa, N.J., 1973)

Hill, B. H. *Medieval Monarchy in Action: The German Empire from Henry I to Henry IV* (London, New York, 1972)

Leuschner, J. *Germany in the Later Middle Ages* (Amsterdam, New York, Oxford, 1980)

Dollinger, P. *The German Hansa* (London, 1970)

Busch, H. *Deutsche Gotik* (Vienna and Munich, 1969)

Deusch, W. R. *Deutsche Malerei des dreizehnten und vierzehnten Jahrhunderts* (Berlin, 1940)

Deusch, W. R. *Deutsche Malerei des fünfzehnten Jahrhunderts* (Berlin, 1934)

Lubke, W. *Ecclesiastical Art in Germany during the Middle Ages* (Longwood Press, 1978)

Picton, H. W. *Early German Art and its Origins from the Beginnings to about 1050* (London, 1939)

ITALY

Luzzatto, G. (ed. R. Palmarocchi) *Cronisti del trecento* (Milan, 1935)

Runciman, J. H. S. *The Sicilian Vespers* (Cambridge, 1958)

Salvatorelli, L. *L'Italia communale* (Milan, 1948)

Schevill, F. *History of Florence from the Founding of the City through the Renaissance* (London, 1932; republished New York, 1961)

Sestan, E. *Italia medievale* (Naples, 1968)

Waley, D. *The Italian City Republics* (London, 1969)

Wickham, C. *Early Medieval Italy* (London, 1981)

Hyde, J. K. *Society and Politics in Medieval Italy* (London, 1973)

Larner, J. *Culture and Society in Italy, 1290–1420* (London, 1971)

Larner, J. *Italy in the Age of Dante and Petrarch 1216–1380* (London, 1980)

Luzzato, G. *Economic History of Italy* (London, 1961)

Cummings, C. A. *A History of Architecture in Italy from the Time of Constantine to the Dawn of the Renaissance* (2 vols, Boston, 1927)

Decker, H. *Romanesque Art in Italy* (New York, 1959)

Dewald, E. T. *Italian Painting 1200–1600* (New York, 1961)

Lavignino, E. *Storia dell'arte medioevale italiana* (Turin, 1936)

Smart, A. *The Dawn of Italian Painting 1250–1400* (Oxford, 1978)

SCANDINAVIA

Brondsted, J. *The Vikings* (Penguin, 1965)

Ellis Davidson, H. R. *Pagan Scandinavia* (London, 1967)

Foote, P. G. and Wilson, D. M. *The Viking Achievement* (London, 1970)

Graham-Campbell, J. *The Viking World* (London, 1980)

Graham-Campbell, J. and Kidd, D. *The Vikings* (London, 1980)

Jones, G. *The Norse Atlantic Saga* (London, 1964)

Klindt-Jensen, O. *Denmark before the Vikings* (London, 1957)

Krogh, K. J. *Viking Greenland* (with a supplement of saga texts trans. by G. Jones) (Copenhagen, 1967)

Musset, L. *Les Peuples scandinaves au moyen âge* (Paris, 1951)

Wilson, D. M. *The Vikings and their Origins* (London, 1970; 1980)

Wilson, D. M. (ed.) *The Northern World* (London, 1980)

Ellis Davidson, H. R. *Gods and Myths of Northern Europe* (Penguin, 1964)

Wilson, D. M. and Klindt-Jensen, O. *Viking Art* (London, 1966)

SPAIN

Castro, A. *The Structure of Spanish History* (use with caution) (Princeton, 1954)

Hillgarth, J. N. *The Spanish Kingdoms, 1250–1516* (2 vols, Oxford, 1976, 1978)

Jackson, G. *The Making of Medieval Spain* (London, 1972)

Lévi-Provençal, E. *Histoire de l'Espagne musulmane* (Cairo, 1944; 2nd edn, Paris, 1950)

Lomax, D. W. *The Reconquest of Spain* (London, 1978)

Mackay, A. *Spain in the Middle Ages* (London, 1977)
Merlino, M. *El medioevo cristiano* (Historia informal de España) (Madrid, 1978)
Thompson, E. A. *The Goths in Spain* (Oxford, 1969)
Watt, W. M. *A History of Islamic Spain* (Edinburgh, 1975)

Burckhardt, T. *Moorish Culture in Spain* (London, 1972)
Vicens Vives, T. *An Economic History of Spain* (Princeton, 1960)
Linehan, P. *The Spanish Church and the Papacy in the Thirteenth Century* (Cambridge, 1971)

Durliat, M. *L'Art roman en Espagne* (Paris, 1962)
Lambert, W. *Art gothique en Espagne aux douzième et treizième siècles* (Paris, 1931; reprint, New York, 1971)
Pita-Andrade, J. M. *Treasures of Spain from Altamira to the Catholic Kings* (Geneva, 1967)
Porter, A. K. *Spanish Romanesque Sculpture* (2 vols, Florence, 1968)
Smith, V. C. *Spanish Medieval Art* (Interbook Inc., 1975)
Wehli, T. *Painting in Medieval Spain* (Budapest, 1980)
Williams, J. *Early Spanish Manuscript Illumination* (London, 1977)
Yarza, J. *Arte y arquitectura en España 500–1250* (Madrid, 1979)

Literary Background

VIII. GENERAL

Bibliography: appears annually in *The Year's Work in Modern Language Studies* (1930–)
Guide to recent work: Fisher, J. H. *The Medieval Literature of Western Europe: a Review of Research 1930–1960* (New York and London, 1966)
Anthologies: Bishop, M. G. (ed.) *A Medieval Storybook* (anthology of trans. from various languages; lightweight but enjoyable) (Ithaca, New York, 1970)
Reinhard, J. H. *Medieval Pageant* (a wider-ranging anthology of texts in trans.) (London, 1939)
Rickard, P. *et al. Medieval Comic Tales* (Brewer, Cambridge, 1972)
Ross, R. B. and McLaughlin, M. M. *Portable Medieval Reader* (wide-ranging, rather heavy anthology) (Penguin, 1977)
Studies: Auerbach, E. *Literary Language and its Public in Late Latin Antiquity and in the Middle Ages* (Princeton, 1965)
Auerbach, E. *Mimesis* (studies the representation of reality in a selection of important texts) (New York, 1957)
Boase, R. *The Origin and Meaning of Courtly Love* (Manchester, 1977)
Chaytor, H. J. *From Script to Print* (excellent short introduction to medieval studies) (Heffers, Cambridge, 1945)
Curtius, E. R. *European Literature and the Latin Middle Ages* (London, 1953)
Daiches, D. and Thorlby, A. (eds) *The Mediaeval World* (Literature and

Western Civilization, II) (gives much interesting background information) (London, 1973)

Haskins, C. H. *The Renaissance of the Twelfth Century* (Cambridge, Mass., 1928; 6th edn, 1976)

Jackson, W. T. *The Literature of the Middle Ages* (New York, 1960)

Jackson, W. T. *Medieval Literature: a History and a Guide* (New York, 1966)

Ker, W. P. *Epic and Romance* (old, but still very useful introductory study) (London, 1896; reprint, New York, 1957)

Lewis, C. S. *The Discarded Image* (Cambridge, 1964)

Pickering, F. D. *Literature and Art in the Middle Ages* (Coral Gables, Florida, 1970)

Tuve, R. *Allegorical Imagery* (Princeton, 1966)

IX. EPIC

Bibliography: appears annually in the *Bulletin bibliographique de la société Rencesvals* (Paris, 1958–   )

Studies: there is no general history of medieval epic. The following works are useful:

Bowra, C. M. *Heroic Poetry* (London, 1952)

Chadwick, H. M. and Chadwick, N. K. *The Growth of Literature*, Vol. 1: *The Heroic Age* (Cambridge, 1912)

Hatto, A. T. (ed.) *Transitions of Heroic and Epic Poetry*, Vol. I (London, 1980)

Lord, A. B. *The Singer of Tales* (Cambridge, Mass., 1960)

Merchant, P. *The Epic* (The Critical Idiom) (London, 1971)

de Vries, J. *Heroic Song and Heroic Legend* (London, 1963)

X. ROMANCE

Bibliography: bibliography on the Arthurian Romance appears annually in the *Bulletin bibliographique de la société internationale arthurienne* (Paris, 1949–   ). Pickford, C. E. and Last, R. W. *The Arthurian Bibliography*, Vol. I: *Author Listing*; Vol. II: *Index* (D. S. Brewer, Woodbridge, 1981–2; supplements will appear at five-year intervals)

Anthology: Barber, R. *The Arthurian Legends* (medieval and later texts in trans.; beautifully illustrated) (Boydell Press, Woodbridge, 1979)

Loomis, R. S. and Loomis, L. H. *Medieval Romances* (New York, 1957)

Studies: Bezzola, R. R. *Les Origines et la formation de la littérature courtoise en occident, 500–1200* (5 vols, Paris, 1958–67)

Green, D. H. *Irony in the Medieval Romance* (Cambridge, 1979)

Hanning, R. W. *The Individual in Twelfth-Century Romance* (London, 1977)

Lewis, C. S. *The Allegory of Love* (Oxford, 1936)

Loomis, R. S. (ed.) *The Arthurian Legend in the Middle Ages* (a collaborative history; of uneven quality and somewhat dated, but an invaluable reference-book) (Oxford, 1959)

Owen, D. D. R. (ed.) *Arthurian Romance: Seven Essays* (Edinburgh, 1970)

Patch, H. R. *The Other World, according to Descriptions in Medieval Literature* (Cambridge, Mass., 1939)

Stevens, J. *The Medieval Romance* (excellent introductory work) (London, 1973)

Vinaver, E. *The Rise of Romance* (less comprehensive than the title suggests, but of great interest) (Oxford, 1971)

XI. LYRIC

Anthologies: Goldin, F. (trans.) *German and Italian Lyrics of the Middle Ages* (New York, 1973)

Goldin, F. (trans.) *Lyrics of the Troubadours and Trouvères* (New York, 1973)

Dronke, P. *Medieval Latin and the Rise of European Love-Lyric* (rather bewildering) (2 vols, London, 1965, 1966)

Dronke, P. *The Medieval Lyric* (Cambridge, 1968; 2nd edn, London, 1977)

Dronke, P. *Poetic Individuality in the Middle Ages* (studies of selected works) (Oxford, 1970)

Kelly, D. *Medieval Imagination: Rhetoric and the Poetry of Courtly Love* (Madison, Wisconsin, 1977)

Jackson, W. T. *The Interpretation of Medieval Lyric Poetry* (Columbia U.P., New York, 1980)

O'Donoghue, B. *The Courtly Love Tradition* (selected texts with trans. on facing page, and commentary) (Manchester U.P., 1982)

XII. DRAMA

Bibliography: Stratman, C. J. *Bibliography of Medieval Drama* (2 vols, Berkeley, Cal., 1954; 1966)

Anthology: Bevington, D. (ed.) *Medieval Drama* (includes Lat. and Anglo-Norman plays with facing trans.) (Boston, 1975)

Studies: Axton, R. *European Drama of the Early Middle Ages* (London, 1974)

Chambers, E. K. *The Medieval Stage* (Oxford, 1903)

Cohen, G. *Histoire de la mise-en-scène dans le théâtre religieux français du moyen-âge* (Paris, 1908; 2nd edn, Brussels, 1926)

Collins, F., Jr (ed.) *Medieval Church Music-Dramas* (Charlottesville, 1976)

Hardison, O. B., Jr *Christian Rite and Christian Drama in the Middle Ages* (Baltimore, 1965)

Kinghorn, A. M. *Medieval Drama* (London, 1968)

Marshall, M. H. 'Aesthetic values in the liturgical drama' in *Medieval English Drama*, eds J. Taylor and A. H. Nelson (Chicago, 1972)

Nagler, A. M. *The Medieval Religious Stage: Shapes and Phantoms* (New Haven, 1976)

Nicoll, A. *Masks, Mimes and Miracles* (New York, 1931)

Rey-Flaud, H. *Pour une dramaturgie du moyen âge* (Paris, 1980)

Schmidt, L. *Le Théâtre populaire européen* (Paris, 1965)

Stevens, J. 'Medieval drama' in *The New Grove Dictionary of Music and Musicians*, ed. S. Sadie (excellent survey of kinds of drama from a musical point of view) (London, 1980), Vol. 12, 21–58

Sticca, S. (ed.) *The Medieval Drama* (New York, 1972)

Tydemann, W. *The Theatre in the Middle Ages* (Cambridge, 1978)

Wickham, G. *The Medieval Stage* (London, 1974)

Young, K. *The Drama of the Medieval Church* (the indispensable study) (2 vols, London, 1933)

Literary Background: Individual Countries

THE LATIN BACKGROUND

McGuire, M. R. P. *Introduction to Medieval Latin Studies: a Syllabus and Bibliographical Guide* (Washington, 1964; 1977)

Anthologies: Beeson, C. H. *A Primer of Medieval Latin* (excellent anthology of short excerpts, with helpful notes but no trans.; best introduction for the intending student) (Glenview, Illinois, 1953; reprint, Folkestone, 1973)

Harrington, K. P. *Medieval Latin* (anthology; no trans.) (London and Chicago, 1962)

Raby, F. J. E. *The Oxford Book of Medieval Latin Verse* (no trans.) (Oxford, 1969)

Waddell, H. *Beasts and Saints* (anthology in trans.) (London, 1934)

Waddell, H. *Mediaeval Latin Lyrics* (texts, with trans. on facing page) (London, 1929; 4th edn, 1933)

Some important texts in trans.: James, M. R. *De Nugis Curialium* (A Courtier's Trifles, by Walter Map: fascinating collection of anecdotes by twelfth-century English scholar) (London, 1923; rev. edn, C. N. L. Brooke and R. A. B. Mynors, Oxford, 1983)

McGarry, D. D. *John of Salisbury: The Metalogicon* (literary treatise of the twelfth-century renaissance) (Berkeley, Cal., 1955)

Nims, M. F. *The 'Poetria Nova' of Geoffrey of Vinsauf* (literary theory) (Toronto, 1967)

Parry, J. J. *Andreas Capellanus: The Art of Courtly Love* (essential reading for the student of courtly love; possibly written tongue-in-cheek) (New York, 1959)

Pike, J. B. *Frivolities of Courtiers and Footprints of Philosophers: Selections from the 'Policraticus' of John of Salisbury* (Minneapolis, 1938)

Radice, B. *The Letters of Abelard and Heloise* (one of the most famous human documents of the Middle Ages) (Penguin, 1974)

Ryan, G. and Ripperger, H. *The Golden Legend* (universal source-book of medieval story) (New York, 1948)

Sheridan, J. J. *Alan of Lille: Anticlaudianus* (scholarly twelfth-century hexameter poem; ideas in common with *Roman de la Rose*) (Toronto, 1973)

Stahl, W. H., Johnson, R. and Burge, E. L. *Martianus Capella: The Marriage of Philology and Mercury* in *Martianus Capella and the Seven Liberal Arts*, Vol. 2 (New York, 1977) (possible source for Chrétien and others)

Thorpe, L. *Geoffrey of Monmouth: The History of the Kings of Britain* (hugely successful pseudo-history; fountainhead of Arthurian romance) (Penguin, 1966)

Watts, V. E. *Boethius: the Consolation of Philosophy* (favourite philosophical work of the Middle Ages) (Penguin, 1969)

Studies: Manitius, M. *Geschichte der lateinischen Literatur des Mittelalters* (the definitive work; heavy reading) (3 vols, Munich, 1911–13; reprinted, 1965–73)

Raby, F. J. E. *Secular Latin Poetry* (2 vols, Oxford, 1934; 1957)

Raby, F. J. E. *Christian Latin Poetry* (Oxford, 1927; 1953)

Reynolds, L. D. and Wilson, N. G. *Scribes and Scholars* (on the survival and transmission of classical literature) (2nd edn, Oxford, 1974)

Waddell, H. *The Wandering Scholars* (very enjoyable study) (London, 1927; 7th edn, 1945)

ANGLO-SAXON

Bibliography: appears annually in *Anglo-Saxon England* (Cambridge, 1972–). Select bibliography (rather capricious) in Robinson, F. C. *Old English Literature: A Select Bibliography* (Toronto, 1970). A full bibliography by S. B. Greenfield is imminent.

Anthologies: Fowler, R. *Old English Prose and Verse* (short selections; no trans.) (London, 1966; 1973)

Gordon, R. K. *Anglo-Saxon Poetry* (in trans.) (London and New York, 1926; 1974)

Swanton, M. *Anglo-Saxon Prose* (in trans.) (London and New York, 1975)

Whitelock, D. (ed.) *Sweet's Anglo-Saxon Reader* (a perennial introductory student's book) (London, 1967)

Studies: *The Cambridge History of English Literature*, Vol. 1 (Cambridge, 1920)

Bessinger, J. B., Jr and Kahrl, S. J. (eds) *Essential Articles for the Study of Old English Poetry* (Hamden, Connecticut, 1968)

Greenfield, S. B. *A Critical History of Old English Literature* (New York, 1965)

Greenfield, S. B. *The Interpretation of Old English Poems* (London and Boston, 1972)

Nicholson, L. E. and Freese, D. W. (eds) *Old English Poetry: Essays in Appreciation* (Notre Dame and London, 1975)

Niles, J. D. (ed.) *Old English Literature in Context* (Cambridge, Brewer and Totawa, N.J., 1980)

Pearsall, D. *Old English and Middle English Poetry* (London, 1977)

Quirk, R., Adams, V. and Davy, D. *Old English Literature: A Practical Introduction* (London, 1975)

Raw, B. C. *The Art and Background of Old English Poetry* (London, 1978)

Shippey, T. A. *Old English Verse* (London, 1972)

Stanley, E. G. (ed.) *Continuations and Beginnings* (assorted studies) (London, 1966)

Wrenn, C. L. *A Study of Old English Literature* (London, 1967)

BYZANTIUM

Byzantine literature is extremely difficult of access for English-speaking readers. The best starting-point is Browning, R. 'Byzantine Literature' in *The Penguin Companion to Literature*, 4: *Classical and Byzantine, Oriental and African* (Penguin, 1969), 179–216. (Useful outline notes on each work and/or author, with references, including trans. – often Fr. or Ger. – and bibliography)

The following may also be consulted:

Beck, H.-G. *Geschichte der byzantinischen Volksliteratur* (Munich, 1971)

Beck, H.-G. *Kirche und theologische Literatur im byzantinischen Reich* (Munich, 1959)

Cantarella, P. *Poeti byzantini* (anthology) (2 vols, Milan, 1948)

Hunger, H. *Die hochsprachliche profane Literatur der Byzantiner* (2 vols, Munich, 1968)

Knös, B. *L'Histoire de la littérature néo-grecque* (Stockholm, 1962)

Krumbacher, K. *Geschichte der byzantinischen Literatur* (dated but indispensable) (Munich, 1891; 1897, reprint, New York, 1970)

Montelatici, G. *Storia della letteratura bizantina* (Milan, 1916)

Trypanis, C. (ed.) *Medieval and Modern Greek Poetry: an Anthology* (Oxford, 1951)

CELTIC–SPEAKING COUNTRIES

Bibliography: Bromwich, R. W. *Medieval Celtic Literature: A Select Bibliography* (excellent guide for the beginner) (Toronto, 1974)

Anthologies and important works in trans.: Clancy, J. P. *Medieval Welsh Lyrics* (in trans.) (London and New York, 1965)

Clancy, J. P. *The Earliest Welsh Poetry* (in trans.) (London and New York, 1970)

Conran, A. *The Penguin Book of Welsh Verse* (in trans.), 13–187 (Penguin, 1967)

Cross, T. P. and Slover, C. H. *Ancient Irish Tales* (in trans.) (New York, 1936)

Gantz, J. *Early Irish Myths and Sagas* (Penguin, 1981)

Gantz, J. *The Mabinogion* (Penguin, 1976)

Greene, D. and O'Connor, F. *A Golden Treasury of Irish Poetry, A.D. 600 to 1200* (texts and trans.) (London, 1967)

Jackson, K. H. *The Gododdin* (Edinburgh, 1969)

Jackson, K. H. *A Celtic Miscellany* (attractive anthology of short extracts) (London, 1951; Penguin, 1971)

Jones, G. and Jones, T. *The Mabinogion* (the best trans.; interesting introductory essay) (London and New York, 1949)

Jones, G. (ed.) *The Oxford Book of Welsh Verse in English* (London, 1977)

Kinsella, T. *The Táin* (i.e. The Cattle-Raid of Cooley) (Dublin and London, 1969; 1970)

Murphy, G. *Early Irish Lyrics, Eighth to Twelfth Century* (texts and trans.) (Oxford, 1956)

Williams, G. *The Burning Tree* (Welsh poetry, texts and trans.; trans. revised and reprinted as *Welsh Poems, Sixth Century to 1600*, London, 1973) (London, 1956)

Studies: Bromwich, R. S. *Trioedd Ynys Prydein: the Welsh Triads* (contains valuable annotated list of characters in medieval Welsh sources, 263–523) (Cardiff, 1961; 1978)

Dillon, M. *Early Irish Literature* (London, 1966)

Flower, R. *The Irish Tradition* (Oxford, 1947)

Jackson, K. H. *Early Celtic Nature Poetry* (Cambridge, 1935)

Jackson, K. H. *The International Popular Tale and Early Welsh Tradition* (Cardiff, 1961)

Jarman, A. O. H. and Rees Hughes, G. (eds) *A Guide to Welsh Literature*, Vols 1 and 2 (Swansea, 1976, 1979)

Knott, T. and Murphy, G. *Early Irish Literature* (London, 1966)

Mac Cana, P. *Celtic Mythology* (many refs to the literature; fine illustrations) (London, New York, Sydney, Toronto, 1970)

Mac Cana, P. *The Mabinogi* (Cardiff, 1977)

Parry, T. (trans. H. I. Bell) *A History of Welsh Literature*, 1–149 (Oxford, 1955)

Williams, G. *An Introduction to Welsh Poetry* (London, 1954; reprint, Freeport, New York, 1970)

Williams, I. (ed. R. S. Bromwich) *The Beginnings of Welsh Poetry* (collected essays by the doyen of medieval Welsh scholarship) (Cardiff, 1972)

Williams, I. *Lectures on Early Welsh Poetry* (Dublin, 1944; reprint, 1970)

Williams, J. E. C. *The Poets of the Welsh Princes* (Cardiff, 1978)

See also articles of general interest appearing in *Cambridge Medieval Celtic Studies* (Leamington Spa, 1981–)

FRANCE

Bibliography: Bossuat, R. *Manuel bibliographique de la littérature française du moyen âge* (Paris, 1955; occasional supplements by J. Monfrin)

Woledge, B. and Clive, H. P. *Répertoire des plus anciens textes en prose française depuis 842 jusqu'aux premières années du XIII siècle* (Geneva, 1964)

Woledge, B. *Bibliographie des romans et nouvelles en prose française antérieurs à 1500* (Lille, 1954; supplement, Geneva, 1975)

Anthologies: Aspland, C. W. *A Medieval French Reader* (student's anthology; no trans.) (Oxford, 1979)

Lagarde et Michard: *Moyen Age* (Collection littéraire) (anthology and intensive study aids; mostly in trans.) (Paris, 1963)

Bec, P. *La Lyrique française au moyen âge: études et textes* (2 vols, Paris, 1977, 1978)

Mary, A. *Anthologie poétique française: moyen âge* (wide-ranging anthology; trans. into mod. Fr. on facing page) (2 vols, Paris, 1967)

Pauphilet, A.: three Pléiade anthologies. Complete texts or long extracts.

Spelling regularized; explanatory notes, glossary and excellent short introductions to each selection. Highly recommended:

 Historiens et chroniqueurs du moyen âge (Paris, 1958)
 Jeux et sapience du moyen âge (Paris, 1960)
 Poètes et romanciers du moyen âge (Paris, 1958)

Studer, P. and Waters, E. E. R. *Historical French Reader: Medieval Period* (no-nonsense student anthology) (London, 1924)

Wilkins, N. *One Hundred Ballades, Rondeaux and Virelais from the Late Middle Ages* (no trans.) (Cambridge, 1969)

Woledge, B. *The Penguin Book of French Verse*, Vol. 1 (with prose trans. at foot of page) (Penguin, 1961)

Studies: Bloch, R. H. *Medieval French Literature and Law* (Berkeley and London, 1977)

Bossuat, R. *Le Moyen Âge* (Paris, 1955)

Champion, P. *Histoire poétique du xve siècle* (2 vols, Paris, 1923)

Cohen, G. *La Vie littéraire en France au moyen âge* (Paris, 1949)

Cohen, G. *Littérature française du moyen âge* (Brussels, 1951)

Crosland, J. *Medieval French Literature* (Oxford, Blackwell, 1956)

Ferrier, J. *French Prose Writers of the Fourteenth and Fifteenth Centuries* (Oxford, 1966)

Fourrier, A. *Le Courant réaliste dans le roman courtois* (Paris, 1960)

Fox, J. *The Middle Ages* (A Literary History of France, Vol. 1; useful introduction to the field) (London, 1974)

Pauphilet, A. *Le Legs du moyen âge* (collection of excellent studies on individual texts) (Melun, 1950)

Payen, J. C. *Littérature française: le moyen âge I* (Paris, 1970)

Poirion, D. *Littérature française: le moyen âge II* (Paris, 1971)

Rasmussen, J. *La Prose narrative française du xve siècle* (Paris, 1912)

Zumthor, P. *Histoire littéraire de la France médiévale* (Paris, 1954)

Zumthor, P. *Essai de poétique médiévale* (Paris, 1972)

GERMANY

Anthologies: de Boor, H. *Die deutsche Literatur. Texte und Zeugnisse*, Vols 1/1 and 1/2 (recommended anthology, with some trans. into modern German) (Munich, 1965)

Schlosser, H. D. *Althochdeutsche Literatur* (anthology with trans. into mod. Ger.) (Frankfurt am Main, 1970)

Walshe, M. O'C. *A Middle High German Reader* (no trans.) (London, 1974)

Höer, W. and Kiepe, E. *Epochen der deutschen Lyrik*, 1: *Von den Anfangen bis 1300* (with trans. into mod. Ger.) (Munich, 1978)

Studies: de Boor, H. and Newald, R. *Geschichte der deutschen Literatur von den Anfängen bis zur Gegenwart*, Vol. 2 (Munich, 1953; 10th edn, 1979)

Bostock, J. K. *A Handbook on Old High German Literature* (Oxford, 1955; 2nd edn, rev. K. C. King and D. R. McLintock, London, 1976)

Ehrismann, G. *Geschichte der deutschen Literatur bis zum Ausgang des Mittelalters* (2 vols, Munich, 1918; 1935)

Ruh, K. *et al.* (eds) *Die deutsche Literatur des Mittelalters: Verfasserlexikon* (Vol. I, Berlin and New York, 1978; other vols in preparation)

Ruh, K. *Höfische Epik des deutschen Mittelalters* (2 vols, Berlin, 1967; 1980)

Schwietering, J. *Die deutsche Dichtung des Mittelalters* (Darmstadt, 1957)

Walshe, M. O'C. *Medieval German Literature* (good starting-point) (Cambridge, Mass., 1962)

Wapnewski, P. *Deutsche Literatur des Mittelalters* (brief history) (Göttingen, 1975)

ITALY

Anthologies: Contini, G. *Letteratura italiana delle origini* (Florence, 1970)

Contini, G. *Poeti del Duecento* (2 vols, Milan, 1960)

Contini, G. *Letteratura italiana del Quattrocento* (Florence, 1976)

Marti, M. *Poeti del Dolce Stil Nuovo* (Florence, 1969)

Sapegno, N. *Poeti minori del Trecento* (Milan, 1952)

Segre, G. and Marti, M. *La prosa del Duecento* (Milan, 1959)

Studies: Cecchi, E. and Sapegno, N. (eds) *Storia della letteratura italiana*, Vols 1 and 2 (Milan, 1965)

Donadoni, E. *A History of Italian Literature*, Vol. 1, 1–164 (New York and London, 1969)

Sapegno, N. *Storia letteraria del Trecento* (Milan, 1963)

Schiaffini, A. *Tradizione e poesia dalla latinità medievale al Boccaccio* (Geneva, 1934; Rome, 1943)

Toffanin, G. *Storia dell'Umanismo dal XIII al XVI secolo* (2 vols, Naples, 1933; Bologna, 1964)

Wilkins, E. H. *A History of Italian Literature*, 1–131 (good starting-point) (London, 1954; 2nd edn, rev. T. G. Bergin, Cambridge, Mass., 1974)

SCANDINAVIA

Anthologies: Hollander, L. M. *The Skalds* (anthology in trans.) (New York, 1947)

Hollander, L. M. *Old Norse Poems* (in trans.) (New York, 1936)

Studies: Einarsson, S. *A History of Icelandic Literature* (New York, 1957)

Frank, F. *Old Norse Court Poetry* (Ithaca and London, 1978)

Munch, P. A. (rev. M. Olsen) *Norse Mythology* (London, 1926)

Phillpotts, B. S. *The Elder Edda and Ancient Scandinavian Drama* (Cambridge, 1920)

Polomé, E. C. (ed.) *Old Norse Literature and Mythology: A Symposium* (Austin and London, 1969)

Schlauch, M. *Romance in Iceland* (London, 1934)

Turville-Petre, E. O. G. *Myth and Religion of the North* (Westport, Connecticut, 1964)

Turville-Petre, E. O. G. *The Heroic Age of Scandinavia* (London, 1951; reprint, Westport, Connecticut, 1976)

Turville-Petre, E. O. G. *Origins of Icelandic Literature* (Oxford, 1953)

SPAIN

Anthologies: Alonso, D. *Poesía de la edad media* (no trans.) (Buenos Aires, 1942)

Peers, E. A. *A Critical Anthology of Spanish Verse*, 1–98 (no trans.) (Berkeley and London, 1949; reprint, New York, 1968)

Studies: Alborg, J. G. *Historia de la literatura española*, Vol. 1 (Madrid, 1966)

Brenan, G. *The Literature of the Spanish People*, 17–117 (Cambridge, 1951)

Deyermond, A. D. *The Middle Ages* (A Literary History of Spain, 1) (London, 1971)

Diaz-Plaja, G. (ed. H. A. Harter) *A History of Spanish Literature*, 1–81 (New York, 1971)

Green, O. H. *Spain and the Western Tradition*, Vol. 1 (Madison, Wisconsin, 1963)

AUTHORS AND WORKS

BEOWULF: Anglo-Saxon epic poem in alliterative verse, written in the eighth century, probably in East Anglia; narrates exploits of pagan Geatish warrior chief, Beowulf, against the monster Grendel and a great fire-drake; Christian overtones.

Bibliography: Fry, D. K. *'Beowulf' and the Fight at Finnsburh: A Bibliography* (Charlottesville, 1969)

Editions: Klaeber, Fr. *Beowulf* (London, 1923; 3rd edn, Lexington, Mass., 1950)

Swanton, M. *Beowulf* (with introduction, notes, and prose trans. on facing page) (Manchester and New York, 1978)

Translations: Alexander, M. *Beowulf* (verse) (Penguin, 1973)

Garmonsway, G. N., Simpson, J. and Ellis Davidson, H. R. *'Beowulf' and its Analogues* (prose) (London and New York, 1968; 1980)

Studies: Bessinger, J. D., Jr *A Concordance to 'Beowulf'* (Ithaca, 1969)

Bliss, A. J. *The Metre of 'Beowulf'* (Oxford, 1963)

Brodeur, A. G. *The Art of 'Beowulf'* (Berkeley and Los Angeles, 1959)

Chambers, R. W. *'Beowulf': An Introduction* (Cambridge, 1921; 3rd edn, rev. C. L. Wrenn, 1959)

Clemoes, P. 'Action in *Beowulf* and our perception of it' in D. G. Calder: *Old English Poetry: Essays on Style* (Berkeley and London, 1979), 147–68

Girvan, R. *'Beowulf' and the Seventh Century* (London, 1935; reissue, 1971)

Goldsmith, M. E. *The Mode and Meaning of 'Beowulf'* (London, 1970)

Irving, E. B., Jr *A Reading of 'Beowulf'* (New Haven and London, 1968)

Irving, E. B., Jr *Introduction to 'Beowulf'* (Englewood Cliffs, N.J., 1969)

Lawrence, W. W. *'Beowulf' and Epic Tradition* (New York, 1961)

Nicholson, L. E. (ed.) *An Anthology of 'Beowulf' Criticism* (Notre Dame, 1963)

Shippey, T. A. *Beowulf* (London, 1978)

Tolkien, J. R. R. *'Beowulf*: the Monsters and the Critics', *Proc. British Academy*, XII (1936), 3–53

Whitelock, D. *The Audience of 'Beowulf'* (Oxford, 1951)

GIOVANNI BOCCACCIO (1313–75): Italian writer, poet, and humanist. Born in Paris, grew up in Florence. Worked for Bardi banking concern in Naples, where also studied canon law, and frequented court of Angevin king of the Two Sicilies, Robert of Anjou. Fell in love with 'Fiametta', who features in many of his works. After meeting Petrarch (1350) turned his attention to Latin and to humanist scholarship. Held various municipal and diplomatic offices in Florence, 1350–67, but never achieved the success and recognition which he desired. Passed latter part of his life at Certaldo, where he died. Principal works: *Filicolo* (*c.*1336): prose romance based on the Fr. tale of Floris and Blanchefleur. *Filostrato* (?1335): poem in *ottava rima*, based on story of Troilus and Cressida. *Teseida* (?1339–41): epic in *ottava rima*. *Il ninfale d'Ameto* (c.1342): prose and *terza rima*; tells how a shepherd is ennobled by love. *L'amorosa visione* (1342): allegorical poem. *Il Decameron* (1349–51): his master-piece. Succession of prose tales, supposed to have been told by various noble Florentines who had fled from the city to escape the Black Death; witty, satiric, sophisticated; wide range of sources.

Bibliography: Esposito, E. *Boccacciana: bibliografia delle edizioni e delle scritti critici 1939–1974* (Ravenna, 1976)

Editions: Complete works: Branca, V. *Giovanni Boccaccio: Tutte le opere* (10 vols, Milan, 1964–7)

Branca, V. *Il Decameron* (Florence, 1960)

Marti, M. *Il Decameron* (Milan, 1958)

Translations: McWilliam, G. H. *The Decameron* (Penguin, 1972)

Rigg, J. M. *The Decameron* (with an introduction by E. Hutton) (London, 1930, in 2 vols; 1978, in 1 vol.)

Cohen, M. (ed.) *Tales from the Decameron* (London, 1969)

Studies: Almansi, G. *The Writer as Liar: Narrative Technique in 'The Decameron'* (London, 1975)

Baratto, M. *Realtà e Stile nel Decameron* (Vicenza, 1970)

Billanovich, G. (ed.) *Restauri boccacceschi* (Rome, 1946)

Bosco, V. *Il Decameron* (Rieti, 1929)

Branca, V. *Boccaccio: the Man and his Works* (Hassocks, 1976)

Chiari, A. 'Polemico sul Boccaccio', in *Indagani e letture* (Città di Castello, 1946)

Dombroski, R. S. (ed.) *Critical Perspectives on the 'Decameron'* (London, 1976)

Getto, G. *Vita di forme e forme di vita nel Decameron* (Turin, 1957; 1966)

MacManus, F. *Boccaccio* (London, 1947)

Petronio, G. *Il Decameron* (Bari, 1935)

di Pinio, G. *La polemica del Boccaccio* (Florence, 1953)

Scaglione, A. D. *Nature and Love in the Late Middle Ages: An Essay on the Cultural Context of Boccaccio's 'Decameron'* (Berkeley, 1963)

CHRÉTIEN DE TROYES (*fl. c.*1170): Northern French *trouvère* and romancer. Nothing certain known of life, but certainly worked under the patronage of Marie, Countess of Champagne, *c.*1160–80, and then for Philip of Alsace, Count of Flanders, *c.*1180–90. Chiefly known for his five great Arthurian romances, the first surviving works in this field: octosyllabic rhyming verse, stories probably drawn from Celtic and folkloric materials; sophisticated analysis of love and adventure.

Bibliography: Kelly, D. *Chrétien de Troyes: An Analytic Bibliography* (London, 1976)

Editions: *Erec et Enide: c.*1170, possibly decade later: stylistically less sophisti-cated than some of later works. Major themes are marital love and kingship: ed. W. Förster (Halle, 1896), from many MSS; ed. M. Roques (C.F.M.A., 1953), from Guiot MS.

*Cligés: c.*1176 or a decade later; based on Byzantine material, is generally interpreted as a critique of the passionate love exemplified in the relationship of Tristan and Yseult: ed. W. Förster (Halle, 1888); ed. A. Micha (C.F.M.A., 1939)

Yvain or *Le Chevalier au lion:* c.1177 or possibly later; his most successful work. Major theme is public-spirited chivalry: ed. W. Förster (Halle, 1891; 1902); ed. M. Roques (C.F.M.A., 1960); ed. T. Reid (Manchester, 1942), student edn

Lancelot or *Le Chevalier de la charette:* a romance of the adulterous love of Lancelot and Guinevere: ed. W. Förster (Halle, 1899); ed. M. Roques (C.F.M.A., 1958)

Perceval or *Le Conte du graal:* unfinished, perhaps because of Chrétien's death (?1191). His most religious romance: ed. A. Hilka (Halle, 1932); ed. F. Lecoy, 2 vols (C.F.M.A., 1972; 1975); ed. W. Roach (T.L.F., 1959)

Translations: Cline, R. H. *Yvain or the Knight with the Lion* (verse) (University of Georgia Press, Athens, 1975)

Comfort, W. W. *Chrétien de Troyes: Arthurian Romances* (not including *Perceval*. Very dreary trans., but useful crib. Second edn has useful introduction by D. D. R. Owen) (London, reprint 1967; 1975)

Linker, R. W. *The Story of the Grail* (prose trans. of *Perceval*.) (Chapel Hill, N. C., 1952; 1960)

Studies: Bezzola, R. R. *Le Sens de l'aventure et de l'amour* (detailed study of *Erec*) (Paris, 1947)

Frappier, J. *Étude sur 'Yvain' ou 'Le Chevalier au lion' de Chrétien de Troyes* (Paris, 1969)

Frappier, J. *Chrétien de Troyes: l'homme et l'œuvre* (good introductory study; perhaps slightly dated) (Paris, 1957)

Frappier, J. *Chrétien de Troyes et le mythe du Graal* (Paris, 1972)

Haidu, P. *Aesthetic Distance in Chrétien de Troyes. Irony and Comedy in 'Cligés' and 'Perceval'* (Geneva, 1968)

Hofer, S. *Chrétien de Troyes* (good introductory study; in Ger.) (Graz, 1954)

Holmes, U. T. *Chrétien de Troyes* (New York, 1970)

Kelly, D. F. *Sens and Coinjointure in the 'Chevalier de la charrette'* (The Hague, 1966)

Laurie, H. C. R. *Two Studies in Chrétien de Troyes* (Geneva, 1972)

Loomis, R. S. *Arthurian Tradition and Chrétien de Troyes* (on sources; interesting, but use with caution) (New York, 1949)

Luttrell, C. *The Creation of the First Arthurian Romance* (study of *Erec*. Takes opposite line to Loomis's) (London, 1974)

Micha, A. *La Tradition manuscrite de Chrétien de Troyes* (invaluable guide to a complex subject, and to the whole problem of editing medieval texts) (Paris, 1939; 1966)

Topsfield, L. *Chrétien de Troyes: A Study of the Arthurian Romances* (Cambridge, 1981)

Zaddy, Z. P. *Chrétien Studies* (second vol. imminent) (Glasgow, 1973)

CID: THE POEMA DE MIO CID: Anonymous epic poem in assonanced verse;

earliest and best of the Spanish epics, and the only one to survive in its original form. Written late twelfth or early thirteenth century. Recounts exploits of semi-legendary eleventh-century Spanish hero, Ruy or Rodrigo Diaz de Vivar, known by Arabic title of 'sayyidī' ('my lord') or 'Mio Cid'. Sophisticated and humane masterpiece, sounding many areas of human experience.

Bibliography: Magnotta, M. *Historia y bibliografía de la crítica sobre el 'Poema de mio Cid', 1750–1971* (Chapel Hill, 1976)

Deyermond, A. D. 'Tendencies in *Mio Cid* scholarship, 1943–1973' in *'Mio Cid' Studies* (London, 1977), 13–47

Editions: Michael, I. *The Poem of the Cid* (with prose trans. by R. Hamilton and J. Perry) (Manchester, 1975)

Michael, I. *Poema de Mío Cid* (Madrid, 1976; 1978)

Smith, C. C. *The 'Poema de mio Cid'* (Oxford, 1972)

Smith, C. C. *Poema de mio Cid* (Sp. version of the Eng. edn; the latter is now out of print) (Madrid, 1976)

Translations: Merwin, W. S. *The Poem of the Cid* (verse) (London, 1959)

Simpson, L. S. *The Poem of the Cid* (prose) (Berkeley, Cal., 1957)

Studies: de Chasca, E. V. *El arte juglaresco en el 'Poema de mio Cid'* (Madrid, 1967; 1972)

Clissold, J. S. H. *In Search of the Cid* (useful but derivative work on the historical background to the poem) (London, 1965)

Deyermond, A. D. (ed.) *'Mio Cid' Studies* (London, 1977)

Dunn, P. N. 'Theme and myth in the Poema de mio Cid', *Romania*, 83 (1962), 348–69

Dunn, P. N. 'Levels of meaning in the Poema de mio Cid', M.L.N., 85 (1970), 104–9

Menéndez Pidal, R. *The Cid and his Spain* (fundamental background study, but self-indulgent at times) (London, 1934)

Menéndez Pidal, R. *En torno al 'Poema de mio Cid'* (collected articles) (Barcelona, 1963)

Montgomery, T. 'The Cid and the Count of Barcelona', *Hispanic Review*, 30 (1962), 1–11

Russell, P. E. *Temas de 'La Celestina' y otros estudios del 'Cid' al 'Quijote'* (collected articles, containing much new and important material) (Barcelona, 1978)

Smith, C. C. *Estudios cidianos* (collected articles) (Madrid, 1977)

Smith, C. C. *The Making of the 'Poema de mio Cid'* (Cambridge, 1983)

DAFYDD AP GWILYM (b. *c*.1325): The greatest Welsh poet. Born, probably near Aberystwyth, into a family of *uchelwyr* (Welsh nobility living under English domination after the 1282 conquest by Edward III). Probably educated in culture and bardic art by his uncle, Llywelyn ap Gwilym, constable of Newcastle Emlyn. Learned and developed traditional Welsh metres, especially the *cywydd*, which he employed with dazzling virtuosity. Wrote praise-poetry, especially for lord Ifor ap Llywelyn 'the generous'; satire; verse-contests with another poet, Gruffudd Gryg; love poems to various ladies, especially Morfudd and Dyddgu. Said to be buried in Ystrad Fflur (Strata Florida), near Aberystwyth.

Edition: Parry, T. *Gwaith Dafydd ap Gwilym* (entirely in Welsh) (Cardiff, 1952; 2nd edn, 1973)

Translations: Bell, H. I. and Bell, D. *Dafydd ap Gwilyn: Fifty Poems* (free trans.) (London, 1942)

Bromwich, R. S. *Dafydd ap Gwilym: A Selection of Poems* (Llandysul, 1981)

Heseltine, N. *Twenty-five Poems by Dafydd ap Gwilym* (free trans., prose) (Banbury, Oxon, 1968)

Selections in Conran, *Welsh Verse*, 137–50; Jones, *Welsh Verse in English*, 34–41

Clancy, *Medieval Welsh Lyrics*, 23–106; Williams, *Burning Tree*, 88–98 (text and facing trans.)

Studies: Bromwich, R. S. 'Dafydd ap Gwilym' in *Guide to Welsh Literature*, 2, 112–43 (good introductory study, with bibliography including studies in Welsh)

Bromwich, R. S. *Dafydd ap Gwilym* (Cardiff, 1974)

Bromwich, R. S. *Tradition and Innovation in the Poetry of Dafydd ap Gwilym* (Cardiff, 1967)

Stephens, M. (ed.) *Poetry Wales*: special Dafydd ap Gwilym number, Spring 1973 (collection of studies)

DANTE ALIGHIERI (1265–1321): Italian philosopher, poet and national idol. Born in Florence of an old business family wedded to the cause of the Guelphs. Married Gemma Donati *c.*1285. Inspired throughout his life by ideal love for Beatrice Portinari (wife of Simone de' Bardi; d.1290), whom he first saw when he was nine years old. Studied classics under Franciscan and Dominican masters. Took part in battle of Campaldino against Ghibellines of Arezzo, 1289. Involved in Florentine politics from 1295. Exiled from Florence after takeover by Charles of Valois, 1300, and never returned. Lived at various times in Bologna, Verona and Ravenna, where he died and was buried. Principal works: *La vita nuova* (*c.*1293): prose and verse narrative tracing course of his love for Beatrice. *Il convivio* (1304–7): a 'banquet of knowledge' in form of allegorical and ethical *canzoni* with commentaries (unfinished). *De vulgari eloquentia* (*c.*1304–7): Lat. prose treatise on problems of literary style, and on the choice of a vernacular language to use for literary purposes (unfinished). *De monarchia* (*c.*1310): Latin political treatise. *La divina commedia* (*c.*1307–21): the supreme achievement of Italian, and perhaps of medieval, literature. Allegorical poem in *terza rima* describing Dante's imagined journey through Hell, Purgatory and Paradise, summarizing on the way the poet's knowledge and beliefs about every aspect of human experience, and written in incomparable poetry.

Bibliography: appears annually in *L'Alighieri: rassegna bibliografica dantesca* (Rome, 1960–)

Editions: Società Dantesca Italiana (ed.): *Le opere di Dante* (Florence, 1920; reprint, 1960)

Blasucci, L. *Dante Alighieri: Tutte le opere* (Florence, 1965)

La divina commedia: innumerable editions exist. The beginner may use Sinclair, J. N. *The Divine Comedy* (3 vols, London, 1971) (with good plain prose trans. on facing page) and then go on to one of the critical editions, e.g. Sapegno, N. *La divina commedia* (3 vols, Milan, 1957)

Translations: Milano, P. *The Portable Dante* (substantial selections from the complete works, in trans. with short bibliography: good introductory vol.) (New York, 1969; Penguin, 1978)

Bickersteth, G. L. *The Divine Comedy* (faithful rendering, in successful *terza rima*) (rev. edn, Oxford 1981)

Sinclair, J. D. *The Divine Comedy* (prose, lucid and dignified) (3 vols, Oxford, 1939; 1946)

Singleton, C. D. *The Divine Comedy* (prose) (3 vols, Princeton, 1971; 1972; 1975)

Sisson, C. H. *The Divine Comedy* (introduction, commentary and notes by D. H. Higgins) (Manchester, 1980)

For analysis and comparison of many trans., see Cunningham, G. F. *The Divine Comedy in Translation 1901–1966* (London, 1966)

Studies: (there is a terrifyingly large literature on Dante. The following recommendations are merely a few leaves from the forest)

Anderson, W. *Dante the Maker* (London, 1980)

Auerbach, E. *Dante, Poet of the Secular World* (Chicago, 1961)

Auerbach, E. *Mimesis* (New York, 1957)

Boyde, P. *Dante: Philomythes and Philosopher* (Cambridge, 1981)

Eliot, T. S. *Dante* (London, 1929)

Foster, K. *The Two Dantes* (London, 1977)

Freccero J. (ed.) *Dante: A Collection of Critical Essays* (Englewood Cliffs, N.J., 1965)

Gilson, E. *Dante the Philosopher* (London, 1949)

Grayson, C. (ed.) *The World of Dante* (Oxford, 1980)

Hollander, R. *Allegory in Dante's 'Commedia'* (Princeton, N.J., 1969)

Holmes, G. *Dante* (Oxford, 1980)

Lewis, C. S. 'Dante's Similes', in *Studies in Mediaeval and Renaissance Literature* (Cambridge, 1966) 67–77

Lewis, C. S. *The Discarded Image* (Cambridge, 1964)

Limentani, U. (ed.) *The Mind of Dante* (Cambridge, 1965)

Mazzeo, J. A. *Structure and Thought in the 'Paradiso'* (Ithaca, N.Y., 1958)

Mazzeo, J. A. *Medieval Cultural Tradition in Dante's 'Comedy'* (Ithaca, N.Y., 1960)

Moore, E. *Studies in Dante* (4 vols, Oxford, 1896–1917, reprinted 1968–1969)

Singleton, C. S. *Dante Studies* (2 vols, Cambridge, Mass., 1954, 1958)

Toynbee, P. (rev. C. S. Singleton) *A Dictionary of Proper Names and Notable Matters in the Works of Dante* (Oxford, 1968)

For Dante's use of imagery, the reader may begin with the analysis by Scaglione, A. 'Imagery and Thematic Patterns in *Paradiso* XXIII', in Bergin, T. G. *From Time to Eternity* (ed.) (New Haven and London, 1967) 137–172.

GOTTFRIED VON STRASSBURG (*fl. c.*1210): German romancer. No details of life known, but obviously a man of culture and learning. Sole surviving work is the romance of *Tristan*, adapted from the French version of 'Thomas of England'. Rhyming couplets; incomplete. Story re-told with a high moral purpose, presenting the tragic course of an ideal love-relationship between two paragons of courtly nobility.

Bibliography: Steinhoff, H.-H. *Bibliographie zu Gottfried von Strassburg* (Berlin, 1971)

Editions: Ganz, P. *Tristan* (good edn with helpful introduction and notes; in Ger.) (Wiesbaden, 1978)

Ranke, F. *Tristan und Isold* (14th edn, Berlin, 1969)

Translations: Hatto, A. T. *Gottfried von Strassburg: Tristan* (excellent prose version) (Penguin, 1960)

Studies: Batts, M. S. *Gottfried von Strassburg* (excellent all-round introduction) (New York, 1971)

Bayer, H. *Gralsburg und Minegrotte: die religiös-ethische Heilslehre Wolframs von Eschenbach und Gottfrieds von Strassburg* (Berlin, 1978)

Eisner, S. *The Tristan Legend: a Study in Sources* (Evanston, Illinois, 1969)

Ferrante, J. M. *The Conflict of Love and Honour: the Medieval Tristan Legend in France, Germany and Italy* (The Hague, 1973)

Jackson, W. T. H. *The Anatomy of Love: the 'Tristan' of Gottfried von Strassburg* (New York, Columbia U.P., 1971)

Newstead, H. 'The Origin and Growth of the Tristan Legend', and Whitehead, F. 'The Early Tristan Poems', in Loomis, R. S. (ed.) *Arthurian Literature in the Middle Ages* (Oxford, 1959)

Picozzi, R. *A History of Tristan Scholarship* (Berne, 1971)

Wolf, A. (ed.) *Gottfried von Strassburg* (assorted studies; varying quality) (Darmstadt, 1973). See especially Ranke, F. 'Die Allegorie der Minnegrotte in Gottfrieds "Tristan" '.

THE ICELANDIC SAGAS: NJAL'S SAGA: written in Iceland *c.*1280. Epic prose narrative, tracing the grim consequences of the burning alive of Njal and his household by their enemies. Perhaps the greatest of the 'family sagas'.

Edition: Sveinsson, E. O. *Brennu-Njáls saga* (Reykjavik, 1954)

Translations: Dasent, D. W. *The Story of Burnt Njal* (Olde Englishe trans.) (London, 1861; reprinted, with an introduction by E. O. G. Turville-Petre, 1957)

Fell, E. and Lucas, J. *Egil's Saga* (London, 1975)

Magnusson, M. and Pálsson, H. *Njál's Saga* (Penguin, 1960)
Studies: Allen, R. F. *Fire and Iron: Critical Approaches to Njál's Saga* (Pittsburgh, 1971)
 Fox, D. 'Njálssaga and Western Literary Tradition', *Comparative Literature*, xv (1963), 289–310.
 Lönnroth, L. *Njáls Saga: A Critical Introduction* (Berkeley, Los Angeles, London, 1976)
 Sweinsson, E. O. *Njáls Saga: A Literary Masterpiece* (Lincoln, Nebraska, 1971)
Other sagas in translation: Finch, R. G. *The Saga of the Volsungs* (London, 1960)
 Foote, P. G. and Quirk, R. *The Saga of Gunnlang Serpent-Tongue* (London, 1957)
 Hight, G. A. *The Saga of Grettir the Strong* (London, 1965)
 Johnston, G. *The Saga of Gisli* (with an introductory essay by P. G. Foote) (London, 1963)
 Jones, G. *Erik the Red and other Icelandic Sagas* (London, 1961)
 Laing, S. *Sagas of the Norse Kings* (London, 1961)
 Laing, S. *The Olaf Sagas* (London, 1964) (the two together make up the *Heimskringla*)
 Magnusson, M. and Pálsson, H. *The Vinland Sagas* (Penguin, 1965)
 Magnusson, M. and Pálsson, H. *Laxdaela Saga* (Penguin, 1969)
 Pálsson, H. *Hrafnkel's Saga and Other Stories* (Penguin, 1971)
 Pálsson, H. and Edwards, P. *Egil's Saga* (Penguin, 1976)
 Press, M. A. C. *The Laxdale Saga* (London, 1964)
 Taylor, P. B., Auden, W. H. and Salus, P. H. *The Elder Edda: A Selection* (London, 1969)
Studies: Andersson, T. M. *The Icelandic Family Saga* (Cambridge, Mass., 1967)
 Andersson, T. M. *The Problem of Icelandic Saga Origins* (New Haven and London, 1964)
 Hallberg, P. *The Icelandic Saga* (Lincoln, Nebraska, 1962)
 Koht, H. *The Old Norse Sagas* (New York, 1931; reprint, New York, 1971)
 Liestøl, K. *The Origin of the Icelandic Family Sagas* (Cambridge, Mass., 1930; reprint, Westport, Connecticut, 1974
 Nordal, S. *The Historical Element in Icelandic Family Sagas* (Glasgow, 1957)
 Steblin-Kamemeskij, M. I. *The Saga Mind* (Odense, 1973)
 Sveinsson, E. O. *The Age of the Sturlungs* (Ithaca, 1953)
 Sveinsson, E. O. *Dating the Icelandic Sagas* (London, 1958)

JEU D'ADAM and JEU DE SAINT NICHOLAS
Medieval French theatre: Frank, G. *The Medieval French Drama* (Oxford, 1954)
 Konigson, E. *L'Espace théâtral médiéval* (Paris, 1975) (on staging)
Anthology: Axton, R. and Stevens, J. *Medieval French Plays* (Oxford, 1971) (verse trans. for acting)

JEU D'ADAM: Mystery play on the Fall and its consequences, intended to be

played in conjunction with Lat. church service. Stage directions in Lat.; text
in Fr. rhyming couplets. Written in England, c.1140.

Editions: Aebischer, P. *Le Mystère d'Adam* (Geneva, 1963)
Noomen, W. *Le Jeu d'Adam* (C.F.M.A., 1971)
Odenkirchen, C. J. *The Play of Adam* (with introduction, notes and trans.)
(Brookline, Mass., 1976)
Also in Bevington, *Medieval Drama* (with facing trans.)
Translation: Axton and Stevens, 1–36 (acting text in verse trans., with music;
omits the 'procession of prophets' with which the original text ends)

Studies: Accarie, M. 'Théologie et morale dans le *Jeu d'Adam*', *Revue de
Linguistique Romane*, 83 (1978), 123–47
Atkinson, J. C. 'Theme, structure and motif in the *Mystère d'Adam*',
Philological Quarterly, 56 (1977), 27–42
Auerbach, *Mimesis*, ch. 7
Calin, W. C. 'Cain and Abel in the *Mystère d'Adam*', M.L.R., 58 (1963),
172–6
Legge, M. D. *Anglo-Norman Literature and Its Background* (Oxford, 1963),
312–21
Muir, L. M. *Liturgy and Drama in the Anglo-Norman 'Adam'* (Oxford, 1973)
Noomen, W. 'Le *Jeu d'Adam*: étude descriptive et analytique', *Romania*,
89 (1968), 172–93

JEU DE SAINT NICHOLAS, by Jean Bodel (d. c.1209): French poet, native
of the town of Arras, which nourished a strong literary, and especially
dramatic, tradition in the thirteenth century. Public servant and member of
the 'Confrérie des jongleurs et des bourgeois d'Arras'. Intended to go on
crusade, but caught leprosy and was forced to dwell in isolation, as he laments
in his famous *Congés* (poems of farewell). Other works: collection of
Pastourelles; La chanson des Saisnes (epic poem attached to Charlemagne
cycle).

Editions: Henry, A. *Le 'Jeu de Saint Nicholas' de Jean Bodel*. (T.L.F., 1980)
Jeanroy, A. *Le Jeu de saint Nicholas* (C.F.M.A., 1925)
Warne, F. J. *Le Jeu de saint Nicholas* (Oxford, 1951)
Translation: Axton and Stevens, 71–136

Studies: Foulon, C. 'La représentation et les sources du *Jeu de Saint Nicholas*'
in *Mélanges d'histoire du théâtre du Moyen Age et de la Renaissance offerts
à Gustave Cohen* (Paris, 1950), 55–66
Payen, J.-C. 'Les Éléments idéologiques dans le *Jeu de Saint Nicholas*',
Romania, 94 (1973), 181–504
Rey-Flaud, H. 'Le Sentiment religieux dans le *Jeu de Saint Nicholas*', in
*Mélanges de langue et de littérature françaises du moyen âge offerts à Pierre
Jonin* (Aix-en-Provence, 1977), 567–77
Vincent, P. R. *The 'Jeu de Saint Nicholas' of Jean Bodel: A Literary Analysis*
(Baltimore, 1954)
Zink, M. 'Le *Jeu de Saint Nicholas* de Jean Bodel: drame spirituel', *Romania*,
99 (1978), 31–46

AUTHORS AND WORKS

MINNESANG:

Edition: the great repertoire of *Minnesang* is: Lachmann, K., Haupt, M., Vogt, F. and von Kraus, C. *Des Minnesangs Frühling* (36th edn, 2 vols, Stuttgart, 1977)

Bibliography: Tervooren, H. *Bibliographie zum Minnesang und zu den Dichtern aus 'Des Minnesangs Frühling'* (Berlin, 1969)

Anthologies: Goldin, F. *German and Italian Lyrics of the Middle Ages: An Anthology and a History* (New York, 1973) (in trans.)

  von Kraus, C. *Deutsche Liederdichter des 13. Jahrhunderts* (2 vols, Tübingen, 1952; 1958; 1978)

  Sayce, O. *Poets of the Minnesang* (no trans.) (Oxford, 1967)

  Taylor, R. J. *The Art of the Minnesinger* (anthology: with music) (2 vols, Cardiff, 1968)

  Wehrli, M. *Deutsche Lyrik des Mittelalters* (Zürich, 2nd edn, 1962)

General studies: Fromm, H. (ed.) *Der deutsche Minnesang* (Bad Homburg, 1961, Darmstadt, 1966)

  Frank, I. *Trouvères et Minnesänger* (Saarbrücken, 1952)

  Grimmiger, R. *Poetik des frühen Minnesangs* (Munich, 1969)

  Sayce, O. *The Medieval German Lyric 1150–1300* (London, 1981)

Music (Ger.): Taylor, R. *Die Melodien der weltlichen Lieder des Mittelalters* (2 vols, Stuttgart, 1964).

  Jammers, E., *Ausgewählte Melodien des Minnesangs* (Tübingen, 1963)

Record: Minnesang und Spruchdichtung um 1200–1320: Walther von der Vogelweide, Neidhart, Wizlaw, Frauenlob u.a. Telefunken SAWT 9487-A.

Individual Minnesänger:

WALTHER VON DER VOGELWEIDE (*c.*1170–1230): Birthplace unknown, but certainly lived for a time in Austria. Patronized by duke Leopold V of Austria, but lost favour at that court upon the succession of Leopold VI. In 1198 espoused cause of the Hohenstaufen, Philip of Swabia, against the Guelph, Otto of Brunswick. Wrote political and anti-papal polemical poetry. Served various other patrons including Hermann of Thuringia. In 1212 supported Guelph emperor Otto IV against Pope Innocent III; when Frederick II became emperor in 1215 Walther received a small fief in Wurzburg. About 200 poems extant: Spruche (political, moral, religious); Tone (melodic); love-lyrics; long poem in praise of the Virgin.

Bibliography: Scholz, M. G. *Bibliographie zu Walther von der Vogelweide* (Berlin, 1969)

Editions: Lachmann, C., von Kraus, C. and Kuhn, H. *Die Gedichte Walthers von der Vogelweide* (13th edn, Berlin, 1965)

  Schaefer, J. *Walter von der Vogelweide: Werke* (Darmstadt, 1972)

Studies: Halbach, K. H. *Walter von der Vogelweide* (Stuttgart, 1965; 1968)

  Jones, G. F. *Walther von der Vogelweide* (New York, 1968)

KURENBERG, DER VON (*fl.* mid twelfth century): the earliest named German lyric poet.

Edition: M.F., vol. I, 24–7

Study: Grimmiger, R. *Poetik des frühen Minnesangs* (Munich, 1969)

VON HAUSEN, FRIEDRICH (*c.*1150–90)

Edition: M.F., vol. I, 73–96

Study: Brinkmann, H. *Friedrich von Hausen* (Bad Oeynhausen, 1948)

VON MORUNGEN, HEINRICH (d.1222)

Edition: M.F., vol. I, 236–84

Study: Brandes, K. Heinrich von Morungen, *Zyklische Liedgruppen* (Göppingen, 1974)

VON REUENTAL, NEIDHART (*fl.* 1210–40)

Editions: Wiessner, E. *Die Lieder Neidharts* (3rd edn, Tübingen, 1968)

Beyschlag, S. *Die Lieder Neidharts* (Darmstadt, 1975)

Studies: Simon, E. *Neidhart von Reuental, Geschichte der Forschung und Bibliographie* (Cambridge, Mass., 1968)

Simon, E. *Neidhart von Reuental* (Boston, 1975)

ALEXANDER 'DER WILDE' (*fl.* late thirteenth century)

Edition: von Kraus, C. Deutsche Liederdichter des 13. Jahrhunderts (2nd edn, 2 vols, Tübingen, 1978), Vol. I, 1–19

FRANCESCO PETRARCH (1304–74): Italian humanist and poet. Born in Arezzo, where his father was living as an exile from Florence. Studied law at Montpellier and Bologna, 1316–26. Took minor orders at Avignon, but also frequented the (to some extent secularized) papal court, and for a time led a dissolute life; though later repented, always had to fight an urge towards worldliness and dissipation. First saw 'Laura', his ideal love, 1327. Journeyed widely in the service of Cardinal Giovanni Colonna, 1330–47. Spiritually transformed by the famous ascent of Mount Ventoux, and by a visit to Rome, 1336–7. For a time lived in solitude at Vaucluse, near Avignon, to which retreat he returned periodically in later life. Crowned with laurel at Rome, 1341. Supported popular government of Cola di Rienzi in Rome, 1347–50. Lived in Milan 1353–61 and undertook diplomatic missions for the Visconti; enjoyed a considerable reputation as a diplomat. In Venice 1362–7; Padua 1367–74; had a retreat at Arqua, near Padua, where he died. Principal works: *Africa* (1338–9): Lat. epihexameter poem. *Epistolae metrici* (1350–63) collected letters in verse. Diverse subject-matter. *De viris illustribus* (1338–43): biographies of famous men, from Adam onwards. *Secretum meum* (1342–3): revealing autobiographical treatise, not intended for publication. *De vita solitaria* (1346); *De otio religioso* (1347): together trace theme of Man's spiritual development in solitary communion with Nature and with God. *De remediis utriusque fortunae* (1354–66): vast book of treatises on human life. *Rerum vulgarium fragmenta* (1358–74): Petrarch's own selection of his vernacular poetry. Very influential; virtually created modern genre of lyric poetry.

Trionfi: (1351): poem in *terza rima*; traces Man's progress from earthly passions to knowledge of God; unfinished.

Editions: Bigi, E. and Ponti, G. (eds) Fr. Petrarca: *Opere* (Milan, 1964) (with Italian trans. of the Latin works)

    Carrara, E. *Lettere autobiografiche* (Milan, 1928)

    Carrara, E. *Il mio segreto* (Florence, 1943)

    Carducci, G. and Ferraril, S. *Le rime di Francesco Petrarca* (Florence, 1899)

    Chioborli, E. *Le rime sparsi e i Trionfi* (Bari, 1930)

    Griffith, T. G. and Hainsworth, P. R. J. *Petrarch: Selected Poems* (useful starting-point) (Manchester, 1971)

    Neri, F., Martelotti, G., Bianchi, E. and Sapegno, N. *Rime, Trionfi e poesie latine* (Milan, 1951)

    Synge, J. M. and Skelton, R. *Some Sonnets from 'Laura in death'* (with trans. on facing page) (Dublin, 1971)

Translations: Bishop, M. G. *Letters from Petrarch* (Bloomington, Indiana, 1966)

    Durling, R. M. *Petrarch's Lyric Poems* (Cambridge, Mass., 1976) (recommended)

    Mortimer, H. *Selected Poems of Petrarch* (University of Alabama Press, 1977)

    Thompson, D. *Petrarch: a Humanist among Princes* (selections in trans.) (New York, 1971)

    Wilkins, E. H. *The Triumphs of Petrarch* (verse) (Chicago, 1962)

Studies: Bergin, T. G. *Petrarch* (New York, 1970)

    Bernardo, A. S. *Petrarch, Laura and the 'Triumphs'* (Albany, New York, 1974)

    Billanovich, G. *Petrarca letterata* (Rome, 1947)

    Bishop, M. G. *Petrarch and his World* (London, 1964; reissue, Washington, 1973)

    Bosco, U. *Petrarca* (Turin, 1946)

    Dotti, U. *Petrarca e la scoperta della coscienza moderna* (Milan, 1978)

    Forster, L. *The Icy Fire: Five Studies in European Petrarchism* (Cambridge, 1969)

    Foster, K. 'Beatrice or Medusa?', in *Italian Studies presented to E. R. Vincent* (Cambridge, 1962), 41–56

    Jerrold, M. F. *Francesco Petrarca, Poet and Humanist* (Port Washington, N.Y., 1970)

    Montanari, F. *Studi sul Canzoniere del Petrarca* (Rome, 1958)

    de Nolhac, P. *Pétrarque et l'humanisme* (2 vols, Paris, 1892; 1907)

    Quaglio, A. E. *Francesco Petrarca* (Milan, 1967)

    Trinkaus, C. *The Poet as Philosopher: Petrarch and the Formation of Renaissance Consciousness* (New Haven and London, 1979)

    Whitfield, J. H. *Petrarch and the Renascence* (Oxford, 1943)

    Wilkins, E. H. *Life of Petrarch* (Chicago, 1961)

    Wilkins, E. H. *The Making of the 'Canzoniere' and other Petrarchan Studies* (Rome, 1951)

    Wilkins, E. H. *Studies in the Life and Work of Petrarch* (Cambridge, Mass., 1955)

RABELAIS, FRANÇOIS (c.1494–1553): French satirist and humanist. Born near Chinon, the son of a lawyer. Details of early life uncertain. Entered Franciscan friary of Fontenay-le-Comte, 1520. Transferred to Benedictine order, 1524–5. Secretary to the Bishop of Maillezais, 1525–7; in this capacity, travelled widely in rural France. Went to Paris 1528; 1530 renounced monastic life and went to study medicine at Montpellier. Physician in Lyons, 1532–5. Dismissed for absenteeism, 1535, and went to Rome. Returned to Benedictines; led a restless, wandering life, constantly under threat of religious persecution. Journeyed intermittently in service of Cardinal Jean du Bellay. 1551 acquired livings of Meudon and Saint-Christophe du Jambet, but probably never resided there. Died in Paris. Principal work the *Life of Gargantua and Pantagruel*, in 5 vols: *Pantagruel* (1532); *Gargantua* (prologue to *Pantagruel*) (1534); *Le Tiers Livre* (1546); *Le Quart Livre* (1552); *Le Quint Livre* (1564) (published posthumously). Story rambles, but centres on a fantastic voyage of discovery. Figures of the giants, Gargantua and Pantagruel, probably derive from Fr. folklore. Seriousness and buffoonery intermingled throughout. Varied, rich, uneven.

There is a large literature on Rabelais, but it tends to skirt the basic necessities. There is no bibliography except J. Plattard: *État présent des études rabelaisiennes* (Paris, 1927), and no good critical edition. The best one available is:

Edition: Boulenger, J. (rev. L. Scheler): *Rabelais: Œuvres complètes* (Paris, Pléiade, 1959)

Translations: Putnam, S. *The Portable Rabelais* (substantial selections) (Penguin, 1977)

Urquhat, T. and Motteux, P. A. *Gargantua and Pantagruel* (reissue of a famous seventeenth-century translation) (London, 1970)

Studies: Bakhtin, M. *Rabelais and His World* (Eng. trans. Cambridge, Mass., 1968)

Beaujour, G. *Le Jeu de Rabelais* (Paris, 1969)

Coleman, D. *Rabelais: A Study in Prose Fiction* (Cambridge, 1971)

de Diéguez, M. *Rabelais* (Paris, 1978)

Febvre, L. *Le Problème de l'incroyance au 16ᵉ siècle: la religion de Rabelais* (Paris, 1942)

Krailsheimer, A. J. *Rabelais and the Franciscans* (Oxford, 1963)

Larmat, J. *Rabelais* (Paris, 1963)

Masters, B. *A Student's Guide to Rabelais* (London, 1971)

Screech, M. *Rabelais* (London, 1979)

Tilley, A. *François Rabelais* (New York, 1970)

LE ROMAN DE LA ROSE: Allegorical Fr. narrative poem in octosyllabic couplets. Begun by Guillaume de Lorris (*fl. c.*1240), and completed by Jean Clopinel (Jean de Meung) (c.1240–1305) scholar, translator, satirist. Guillaume's part is a charming account of the Lover's quest for the Rose (his lady-love), assisted and opposed by various allegorized characters such

as Friend, Fair Welcome, Danger, Shame, etc. Jean de Meung's much longer
contribution is full of forceful digressions on innumerable aspects of contemporary opinion and philosophy, and provoked a lively literary *querelle*,
especially as it was taken to be anti-feminist. Immensely influential; allegorical
method widely adopted by lyric poets. Trans. by Chaucer among others;
adapted in the sixteenth century by Clement Marot.

Editions: Langlois, E. *Le Roman de la Rose* (5 vols, S.A.T.F., 1914–25) (definitive
critical edn)

Lecoy, F. *Le Roman de la Rose* (useful working edn with study aids and
an outline summary of the poem – almost essential when reading Jean
de Meung's part) (3 vols, C.F.M.A. 1965, 1966, 1970)

Meon, D. M. (ed.) *Le Roman de la Rose* (4 vols, Paris, 1814)

Baridan, S. F. (ed.) and Viscardi, A. (introd.) *'Le Roman de la Rose' dans
la version attribuée à Clément Marot* (2 vols, Milan, 1954, 1957)

Translations: Robbins, H. W. (ed. C. W. Dunn) *The Romance of the Rose*
(verse; more of a paraphrase than a trans. but useful) (New York, 1962)

Dahlberg, C. *The 'Romance of the Rose' by Guillaume de Lorris and Jean de
Meun* (prose) (Princeton, N.J., 1971)

Ellis, F. S. *The Romance of the Rose* (prose) (London, 1900)

Studies: Badel, P. Y. *Le 'Roman de la Rose' au XIVᵉ siècle. Etude de la réception
de l'œuvre* (Geneva, 1980)

Bruning, D. *Clement Marots Bearbeitung des Rosenromans, Studien zur
Rezeption des Rosenromans im frühen sechszehnten Jahrhundert* (Berlin, 1972)

Fleming, J. V. *The 'Roman de la Rose': A Study in Allegory and Iconography*
(Princeton, N.J., 1969)

Gunn, A. M. F. *The Mirror of Love* (Lubbock, Texas, 1952)

Hicks, E. *Le Débat sur le Roman de la Rose* (texts by notable contemporaries
of Jean de Meung) (Paris, 1977)

Kelly, D. '"Li chastiaus ... Qu'Amors prist puis par ses esforz": the conclusion of Guillaume de Lorris' *Rose*', in N.J. Lacy (ed.) *A Medieval
Miscellany* (Lawrence, Kansas, 1972), 61–78

Langlois, E. 'Origines et sources du Roman de la Rose', in *Romania*, 89
(1968), 554–5

Lejeune, R. 'A propos de la structure du Roman de la Rose de Guillaume
de Lorris', in *Études de langue et de littérature du moyen âge offertes à Felix
Lecoy* (Paris, 1973), 315–48

Paré, G. *Les Idées et les lettres au XIIIᵉ siècle. Le 'Roman de la Rose'*
(Montreal, 1947)

Payen, J. C. 'Genèse et finalité de la poésie allégorique au Moyen Age',
in *Revue de metaphysique et de morale*, 78 (1973), 466–79

Payen, J. C. *La Rose et l'Utopie. Révolution sexuelle et communisme nostalgique
chez Jean de Meung* (Paris, 1976)

Thuasne, L. *Le 'Roman de la Rose'* (Paris, 1929)

Topsfield, L. 'The *Roman de la Rose* of Guillaume de Lorris and the love-
lyric of the early troubadours', in *Reading Medieval Studies*, 1 (1975),
30–54

JUAN RUIZ (c.1295–after 1353): archpriest of Hita. Spanish poet. Nothing known of his life, except what he tells us in his surviving masterpiece, the *Libro de buen amor* (Book of good love). Apparently was born in Alcalá de Henares and was active in New Castile. The *Libro de buen amor* was probably composed in c.1343. Written in rhyming quatrains (*cuaderna vía*); rich and cheerfully ambivalent work, purporting to inculcate a hatred of vice and a desire for 'good' love (of God?), but actually including a variety of amusing and even scabrous tales. Wide range of sources, including French and Latin.

Editions: Corominas, J. *El libro de buen amor* (Madrid, 1967)

Criado de Val, M. and Naylor, E. W. *El libro de buen amor* (Madrid, 1965; glossary, Barcelona, 1973)

Joset, J. *El libro de buen amor* (2 vols, Madrid, 1975)

Willis, R. S. *Libro de buen Amor* (critical edn, with Eng. paraphrase on facing page) (Princeton, N.J., 1972)

Studies: Beltrán, L. *Razones de buen amor* (Madrid, 1977)

Dutton, B. ' "Con Dios en buen amor": a semantic analysis of the title of the *Libro de buen amor*', B.H.S., 43 (1966), 161–76

de Ferraresi, A. G. *De amor y poesía en la España medieval: prólogo a Juan Ruiz* (Mexico City, 1976)

Gariano, C. *El mundo poético de Juan Ruiz* (Madrid, 1968)

Gybbon–Monypenny, G. B. ' "Lo que buen amor dize con razón te lo pruevo" ' B.H.S., 38 (1961), 13–24

Gybbon–Monypenny, G. B. (ed.) *'Libro de buen amor' Studies* (London, 1970)

Lecoy, F. *Recherches sur le 'Libro de buen amor'* (Paris, 1938; reproduced, with a prologue and modernized bibliography, by A. D. Deyermond, Westmead, 1974)

Lida de Malkiel, M. R. *Two Spanish masterpieces: the Book of Good Love and the Celestina* (Urbana, Illinois, 1961)

Lida de Malkiel, M. R. *Juan Ruiz: selección del 'Libro de buen amor' y estudios críticos* (Buenos Aires, 1973)

Richardson, H. B. *An Etymological Vocabulary to the 'Libro de buen amor'* (very useful study aid) (New Haven, 1930)

Walker, R. M. 'Towards an interpretation of the *Libro de buen amor*' B.H.S., 43 (1966), 1–10

Zahareas, A. *The Art of Juan Ruiz* (Madrid, 1965)

THE SONG OF ROLAND AND FRENCH EPIC: CHANSON DE ROLAND: first and greatest of the medieval French epics, dating from c.1100 in its present form; manuscript, written in England, c.1130–40. *Laisses* of assonanced lines. Tells of the heroic defeat of Charlemagne's rearguard at the pass of Roncevaux in the Pyrenees, and of Charlemagne's revenge.

Bibliography: Duggan, J. J. *A Guide to Studies on the 'Chanson de Roland'* (London, 1976)

Editions: Bédier, J. *La Chanson de Roland* (with trans. into mod. Fr.) (Paris, 1924)

Brault, G. J. *The Song of Roland: An Analytical Edition* (with trans.) (2 vols, University Park, Pennsylvania, 1978)

Whitehead, F. *La Chanson de Roland* (student edn with introduction, notes, vocabulary and short bibliography) (Oxford, 1942)

Translations: Owen, D. D. R. *The Song of Roland* (verse) (London, 1972)

Robertson, H. S. *The Song of Roland* (verse) (London, 1972)

Sayers, D. L. *The Song of Roland* (verse) (Penguin, 1957)

Studies: Auerbach, E. 'Roland against Ganelon', in *Mimesis*, ch. 5

Bédier, J. *Les Légendes épiques: recherches sur la formation des chansons de geste* (great but controversial work by an outstanding scholar) (4 vols, Paris, 1908–13)

Burger, A. *Turold: poète de la fidélité* (Geneva, 1977)

Crosland, J. *The Old French Epic* (Oxford, 1951)

Dodwell, C. R. 'The Bayeux Tapestry and the French Secular Epic', *The Burlington Magazine*, CVIII (1966), 549–60

Faral, E. *La Chanson de Roland* (Paris, 1934) (good, sound introduction)

Le Gentil, P. *The Chanson de Roland* (Cambridge, Mass., 1969)

Lejeune, R. and Stiennon, J. *The Legend of Roland in the Middle Ages* (trans. C. Trollope, New York and London, 1971)

Jones, G. F. *The Ethos of the Song of Roland* (Baltimore, 1963)

Menéndez Pidal, R. *La Chanson de Roland* (Fr. trans. of Sp. original) (Paris, 1960)

Mireaux, E. *La Chanson de Roland et l'histoire de France* (Paris, 1943)

de Riquer, M. *Les chansons de geste françaises* (Fr. trans of Sp. original) (Paris, 1957)

Rychner, J. *La Chanson de geste: Essai sur l'art épique des jongleurs* (*Publications Romanes et Francaises*, LIII, Geneva and Lille, 1955, reprint 1968)

Vance, E. *Reading the Song of Roland* (Englewood Cliffs, N.J., 1970)

THE TROUBADOURS

Bibliography: in R. Baehr: *Der provenzalische Minnesang* (Darmstadt, 1967)

Anthologies: Bec, P. *Anthologie des troubadours* (with trans. into mod. Fr.) (Paris, 1979)

Berry, A. *Florilège des troubadours* (Paris, 1930)

Blackburn, P. *Proensa: An Anthology of Troubadour Poetry* (in trans.) (Berkeley, Los Angeles, London, 1978)

Bonner, A. *Songs of the Troubadours* (in trans.) (New York, 1972)

Frank, I. *Répertoire métrique de la poésie des troubadours* (2 vols, Paris, 1953; 1957)

Goldin, F. *Lyrics of the Troubadours and Trouvères: An Anthology and a History* (in trans.) (New York, 1973)

Hill, R. and Bergins, T. *Anthology of the Provençal Troubadours* (2nd edn, 2 vols, New Haven and London, 1973)

Studies: Hoepffner, E. *Les Troubadours* (Paris, 1955)

Jeanroy, A. *La Poésie lyrique des troubadours* (2 vols, Paris, 1934)

Topsfield, L. *Troubadours and Love* (Cambridge, 1975)

Wilhelm, J. *Seven Troubadours: The Creators of Modern Verse* (University Park, Pennsylvania, and London, 1970)

Music: Gennrich, F. *Der Musikalische Nachlass der Troubadours* (3 vols, Darmstadt, 1958–65)

van der Werf, Hendrik, *The Chansons of the Troubadours and Trouvères: A Study of the Melodies and Their Relation to the Poems* (Utrecht, 1972)

Record: Chansons der Troubadours: Lieder und Spielmusik aus dem 12. Jahrhundert. Telefunken S A W T 6.41126 A S

INDIVIDUAL TROUBADOURS

WILLIAM IX, DUKE OF AQUITAINE (1071–1127): a relation of Eleanor of Aquitaine. Seized the Toulouse region while its ruler was on the First Crusade, and ruled it from 1086 until his death. Was often at odds with the Church and was twice excommunicated, but later went on crusade himself. Considered to be the first of the troubadours; also a patron of the arts.

Edition: Jeanroy, A. *Les Chansons de Guillaume IX* (C.F.M.A., 1913; 1927)

Study: William IX is discussed in every work on the troubadours, and in Dronke, *Medieval Latin and the Rise of the European Love-Lyric and The Medieval Lyric.*

MARCABRU (*fl.* c.1130–60): perhaps the greatest of the troubadours. Probably a Gascon. Worked under patronage of the Count of Poitou until 1137; then travelled through Aquitaine and Spain in search of patronage.

Edition: Lucien, J.-M. *Poésies complètes du troubadour Marcabru* (Toulouse, 1909; reprint, New York, 1971)

Studies: Vossler, K. *Der Trobador Marcabru und die Anfänge des gekünstelten Stiles* (Munich, 1913)

Errante, G. *Marcabru e le fonti sacre dell'antica lirica romana* (Florence, 1948)

RUDEL, JAUFRÉ (*fl.* mid twelfth century): Count of Blaye, near Angoulême. Supposed to have fallen in love ('amor de lonh') with the Countess of Tripoli, without ever having met her; eventually set sail for Tripoli, but fell ill on the voyage and expired in the Countess's arms. In his poetry, aspirations to profane love mingle with Christian idealism.

Edition: Jeanroy, A. *Les chansons de Jaufré Rudel* (C.F.M.A., 1915; 1924)

Studies: Spitzer, L. *L'amour lointain de Jaufré Rudel et le sens de la poésie des troubadours* (Chapel Hill, 1944)

Casella, M. *Jaufré Rudel: Liriche* (Florence, 1948)

DE VENTADORN, BERNART (1150–80): probably a native of Limousin. Addressed love-songs to Eleanor of Aquitaine and was patronized by Count Raimon V of Toulouse. Writes with apparent naïveté, but with sharp and sensitive observation.

Edition: Appel, C. *Bernart von Ventadorn* (Halle, 1915)
  Lazar, M. *Bernart de Ventadour, troubadour du IIIᵉ siècle: Chansons d'amour* (Paris, 1966)
  Nichols, S. *et al.* *The Songs of Bernart de Ventadorn* (with trans.) (Chapel Hill, 1962)
Study: Ghezzi, D. *La personalità e la poesia di Bernart de Ventadorn* (Genoa, 1948)

DE DIA, COUNTESS BEATRIZ (*fl.* late twelfth century)
Edition: Kussler-Ratye, G. 'Les chansons de la comtesse Beatrix de Dia', in *Archivum Romanum*, I (1917), 161–82
Studies: Santy, S. *La Comtesse de Die* (Paris, 1893)
  Wilhelm, J. *Seven Troubadours*, 131–41

VIDAL, PEIRE (*fl.* 1180–1205): from Toulouse. Called by his biographer 'the maddest man in all the world'. Supposed to have pursued amorous adventures throughout France and Spain, and to have dressed himself in a wolf-skin and had himself pursued by hounds in order to compliment a lady named Loba ('she-wolf'). Nevertheless a successful courtly poet.
Edition: d'Arco, S.A. *Peire Vidal: Poesie* (2 vols, Milan and Naples, 1960)
Study: Hoe pffner, E. *Le troubadour Peire Vidal, sa vie et son œuvre* (Paris, 1961)

ANONYMOUS, 'EN UN VERGIER SOTZ FUELLA D'ALBESPI'
Edition: Berry, A. *Florilège des troubadours* (Paris, 1930)

WOLFRAM VON ESCHENBACH: PARZIVAL: (*fl.* early thirteenth century): German poet and romancer. Belonged to Bavarian lower nobility. Served various Franconian lords and frequented famous court, centre of literary patronage, of Hermann of Thuringia at Wartburg. Works: eight lyric poems; *Willehalm* (religious epic based on French *Bataille d'Aliscans*); *Parzival* (great poem of the Grail, derived partly from Chrétien; traces ideal of Christian spiritual development, triumphing in chivalry); *Titurel* (develops an incident in *Parzival*).
Bibliography: Bumke, J. *Die Wolfram von Eschenbach Forschung seit 1945: Bericht und Bibliographie* (Munich, 1970)
  Pretzel, U., Bachofer, W. *et al.* *Bibliographie zu Wolfram von Eschenbach* (Berlin, 1968)
Editions: Bartsch, K. *Parzival und Titurel* (helpful linguistic notes; all in Ger.) (Leipzig, 1870–71; 4th edn, rev. M. Marti, 3 vols, Leipzig, 1929–35)
  Lachmann, K. *Wolfram von Eschenbach* (Berlin, 1833; 6th edn, 1926)
  Martin, E. *Parzival und Titurel* (invaluable commentary in second vol.) (2 vols, Halle, 1900; 1903)
  Weber, G. and Hoffmann, W. *Parzival* (Darmstadt, 1963)

Translations: Mustard, H. M. and Passage, C. E. *Parzifal* (dubious prose trans.; useful supplementary material) (New York, 1961)

Hatto, A. T. *Parzival* (prose; very sound) (Penguin, 1980)

Studies: Blamires, D. *Characterization and Individuality in Wolfram's 'Parzifal'* (Cambridge, 1966). See also the review article by P. Johnson in M.L.R., 64 (1969), 68–83.

Bumke, J. *Wolfram von Eschenbach* (excellent introductory study) (Stuttgart, 1964; 4th edn, 1976)

Deinert, W. *Ritter und Kosmos im 'Parzifal'* (Munich, 1960)

Green, D. H. and Johnson, L. P. *Approaches to Wolfram von Eschenbach* (Bern, 1978)

Johnson, L. P. 'Löhelin and the Grail Horses', M.L.R. 63 (1968), 612–17

Mohr, W. *Wolfram von Eschenbach Aufsätze* (excellent essays) (Göppingen, 1979)

Parshall, L. B. *The Art of Narration in Wolfram's 'Parzival' and Albrecht's 'Jüngerer Titurel'* (Cambridge, 1980)

Rupp, H. (ed.) *Wolfram von Eschenbach* (assorted studies; see especially those by Mohr, Wehrli and Ranke) (Darmstadt, 1966)

Sacker, H. D. *An Introduction to Wolfram's 'Parzival'* (Cambridge, 1963)

Weigand, H. J. *Wolfram's 'Parzival': Five Essays* (very illuminating) (Ithaca, New York, 1969)

Wynn, M. 'Geography of fact and fiction in Wolfram's "Parzival" ', M.L.R. 56 (1961), 28–43

ACKNOWLEDGEMENTS

Thanks are due to the copyright holders and publishers of the following works for permission to quote from them in this volume:

Beowulf, trans. Michael Alexander. Copyright © Michael Alexander, 1973. Excerpts reprinted by permission of Penguin Books Ltd.

The Penguin Book of Greek Verse, trans. C. A. Trypanis. Copyright © C. A. Trypanis, 1971. Excerpts reprinted by permission of Penguin Books Ltd.

Fourteen Byzantine Rulers, by Michael Psellus, trans. E. R. A. Sewter and published by Penguin Books Ltd. Copyright © the Estate of E. R. A. Sewter, 1966. Excerpt reprinted by permission of Mrs E. R. A. Sewter.

Digenes Akrites, trans. J. Mavrogordato. Copyright © Oxford University Press, 1956. Excerpt reprinted by permission of Oxford University Press.

The Song of Roland, trans. Dorothy L. Sayers and published by Penguin Books Ltd. Copyright © the Executors of Dorothy L. Sayers, 1957. Excerpts reprinted by permission of David Higham Associates Ltd.

The Quest of the Holy Grail, trans. P. M. Matarasso. Copyright © P. M. Matarasso, 1969. Excerpts reprinted by permission of Penguin Books Ltd.

The Poem of the Cid, ed. Ian Michael and trans. Rita Hamilton and Janet Perry. Ed. of Spanish text, introd., notes and map, copyright © Ian Michael, 1975. Trans. copyright © Rita Hamilton, 1975. Excerpts reprinted by permission of Manchester University Press.

Medieval French Plays, ed. R. Axton and J. Stevens. Copyright © Basil Blackwell, 1971. Excerpts reprinted by permission of Basil Blackwell, Publisher, Ltd.

'By the fountain in the orchard', 'I say he's a wise man', 'When days are long in May', 'When I see the lark moving' and 'With my breath', from *Lyrics of the Troubadours and the Trouvères*, trans. Frederick Goldin. Copyright © 1973 by Frederick Goldin. Reprinted by permission of Doubleday & Company, Inc.

'I think sometimes about', 'To be long silent' and 'Young and old, rejoice', from *German and Italian Lyrics of the Middle Ages*, trans. Frederick Goldin. Copyright © 1973 by Frederick Goldin. Reprinted by permission of Doubleday & Company, Inc.

'In the sweetness of new spring', 'I have been in great distress' 'Deep in an orchard', 'You are mine, I am yours', 'I nurtured a falcon', 'On the heath I heard', 'Alas, shall her body never again', 'Lady, accept this garland'

ACKNOWLEDGEMENTS

and 'Long ago, when we were children', from *The Medieval Lyric*, by Peter Dronke. Copyright © Peter Dronke, 1968 and 1978. Excerpts reprinted by permission of Hutchinson & Co. (Publishers) Ltd.

Parzival, by Wolfram von Eschenbach, trans. A. T. Hatto. Copyright © A. T. Hatto, 1980. Excerpt reprinted by permission of Penguin Books Ltd.

Tristan, by Gottfried von Strassburg, trans. A. T. Hatto. (Revised edn, 1967.) Copyright © A. T. Hatto, 1960. Excerpts reprinted by permission of Penguin Books Ltd.

The Romance of the Rose, by Guillaume de Lorris and Jean de Meung, trans. Harry W. Robbins. English Translation Copyright © 1962 by Florence L. Robbins. Reprinted by permission of the publisher, E. P. Dutton, Inc.

Njal's Saga, trans. Magnus Magnusson and Hermann Pálsson. Copyright © Magnus Magnusson and Hermann Pálsson, 1960. Excerpts reprinted by permission of Penguin Books Ltd.

The Divine Comedy, by Dante Alighieri, trans. G. L. Bickersteth. Copyright © Ursula Bickersteth, 1982. Excerpts reprinted by permission of Basil Blackwell, Publisher, Ltd.

Juan Ruiz: Libro de Buen Amor, Raymond S. Willis, ed., Copyright © 1972 by Princeton University Press. Excerpts reprinted by permission of Princeton University Press.

The *Decameron*, by Giovanni Boccaccio, introd., trans. and notes by G. H. McWilliam. Copyright © G. H. McWilliam, 1972. Excerpts reprinted by permission of Penguin Books Ltd.

The Penguin Book of Italian Verse, trans. George Kay. (Revised edn, 1965.) Copyright © George Kay, 1958 and 1965. Excerpts reprinted by permission of Penguin Books Ltd.

'I go thinking', from *Petrarch's Lyric Poems*, ed. R. M. Durling, 1976. Excerpt (in trans. only) reprinted by permission of Harvard University Press.

Gargantua and Pantagruel, by François Rabelais, trans. J. M. Cohen. Copyright © J. M. Cohen, 1955. Excerpts reprinted by permission of Penguin Books Ltd.

Every effort has been made to trace copyright holders. The publishers would be interested to hear from any copyright holders not here acknowledged.

NOTES ON CONTRIBUTORS

RICHARD AXTON Fellow of Christ's College and Lecturer in English in the University of Cambridge. A director of The Medieval Players, Ltd. Author of *European Drama of the Early Middle Ages* (1974), translator (with John Stevens) of *Medieval French Plays* (1974), editor of *Three Rastell Plays* (1979) and General Editor (with Marie Axton) of a new *Tudor Interludes* series of play texts.

DEREK BREWER Master of Emmanuel College and Professor of English Literature at the University of Cambridge. Author of *Chaucer* (3rd edn, 1974), *Chaucer and his World* (1978), *Symbolic Stories* (1980), etc.

ROBERT BROWNING Professor of Classics, Birkbeck College, University of London, until his retirement in 1981. Vice-President of the Association Internationale d'Etudes Byzantines (1981). Publications include *Medieval and Modern Greek* (1969), *Justinian and Theodora* (1971), *The Emperor Julian* (1976), *Byzantium and Bulgaria* (1975), *Studies in Byzantine History, Literature and Education* (1978), *The Byzantine Empire* (1980).

PETER BURKE Fellow of Emmanuel College, and Lecturer in History in the University of Cambridge. His publications include *The Renaissance Sense of the Past* (1969), *Culture and Society in Renaissance Italy* (1972), and *Popular Culture in Early Modern Europe* (1978).

INGEBORG GLIER Professor of Germanic Languages and Literatures, Yale University. She is the author of *Artes amandi: Untersuchungen zu Geschichte, Überleiferung und Typologie der deutschen Minnereden* (1971), and co-editor of *Deutsche Dichtung des Mittelalters*, 3 vols (1981).

JIM HOLT Master of Fitzwilliam College and Professor of Medieval History, University of Cambridge. His publications include *The Northerners* (1961), *Magna Carta* (1965) and *Robin Hood* (1982).

TONY HUNT Reader in French Literature at the University of St Andrews, Scotland. He is author of numerous articles on medieval language and literature.

L. PETER JOHNSON Fellow and Tutor of Pembroke College, and Lecturer in German in the University of Cambridge. With D. H. Green, author of *Approaches to Wolfram von Eschenbach* (1978), 'The German Language' *Germany: A Comparison to German Studies*, ed. Malcolm Pasley (1972), editor (with others) of *Studien zur Fruhmittelhoch – deutzchen Literatur* (1974).

ROBIN KIRKPATRICK Fellow of Robinson College and Lecturer in Italian in the University of Cambridge. His publications include *Dante's Paradiso* (1978), *The Limitations of Modern Criticism* and articles on Chaucer, Boccaccio, Spenser and Shakespeare.

PHILIP MCNAIR Serena Professor and Head of the Department of Italian in the University of Birmingham. He has published on Dante, Poliziano, Ochino, Peter Martyr, Juan de Valdès and aspects of church history.

IAN MICHAEL King Alfonso XIII Professor of Spanish Studies in the University of Oxford and Fellow of Exeter College since 1982. His publications include medieval Spanish texts, a literary interpretation of the medieval Spanish Alexander-book and a critical edition of the *Poem of my Cid* (1975).

ROSEMARY MORRIS Research Fellow of Emmanuel College, 1977–80. Her Doctorate was in medieval Arthurian literature. She is now working as a freelance linguist and researcher.

JOHN SCOTT Professor of Italian, University of Western Australia. He is the author of *Dante magnanimo* (1977) and of various studies on Petrarch, Ronsard and Baudelaire, and co-author of *The Continental Renaissance* (1971).

GEOFFREY SHEPHERD Professor of Medieval Language and Literature in the University of Birmingham. He is the author of *Acrene Wisse* (1959) and *Apology for Poetry* (1965).

JACQUELINE SIMPSON Author of *The Northmen Talk: A Choice of Tales from Iceland* (1965), *Icelandic Folktales and Legends* (1972), and *The Viking World* (1980).

PATRICK-SIMS WILLIAMS Fellow of St John's College, and Lecturer in the Department of Anglo-Saxon, Norse and Celtic in the University of Cambridge. He writes on aspects of the language, literature and history of early medieval Ireland, Wales and England, and edits *Cambridge Medieval Celtic Studies*, a journal which makes new research accessible to a wide range of medievalists.

COLIN SMITH Fellow of St Catharine's College, and Professor and Head of the Department of Spanish in the University of Cambridge. He is author of

Collins' Spanish Dictionary (1971; 10th reprint, 1981), an edition of *Poema de mio Cid* (1972; Spanish version, 1976), *Estudios cidianos* (1977) (jointly with A. L. F. Rivet), *Place-names of Roman Britain* (1979). He was also General Editor of *Modern Language Review*, 1977–81.

LESLIE TOPSFIELD Died 1981. Was a Fellow of St Catharine's College, and Lecturer in French and Provençal in the University of Cambridge until his death. He was the author of *Les Poésie du troubadour – Raimonde Miraval* (1971), *Troubadours and Love* (1975) and *Chrétien de Troyes: A Study of the Arthurian Romances* (1981).

INDEX